Family in Transition

TWELFTH EDITION

Arlene S. Skolnick

New York University

Jerome H. Skolnick

New York University

Boston   New York   San Francisco
Mexico City   Montreal   Toronto   London   Madrid   Munich   Paris
Hong Kong   Singapore   Tokyo   Cape Town   Sydney

Editor in Chief: *Karen Hanson*
Series Editor: *Jeff Lasser*
Editorial Assistant: *Andrea Christie*
Marketing Manager: *Judeth Hall*
Editorial-Production Service: *Omegatype Typography, Inc.*
Manufacturing Buyer: *JoAnne Sweeney*
Composition Buyer: *Linda Cox*
Cover Administrator: *Linda Knowles*
Electronic Composition: *Omegatype Typography, Inc.*

For related titles and support materials, visit our online catalog at www.ablongman.com.

Copyright © 2003, 2001, 1999, 1997, 1994, 1992, 1989 Pearson Education, Inc.

Library of Congress Cataloging-in-Publication Data

Family in transition / [edited by] Arlene S. Skolnick, Jerome H. Skolnick.—12th ed.
        p.   cm.
    Includes bibliographical references.
    ISBN 0-205-35104-2
    1. Family.   I. Skolnick, Arlene S.   II. Skolnick, Jerome H.

    HQ518 .F336   2003
    306.85—dc21

                                                                2002066688

Printed in the United States of America

10   9   8   7   6   5   4   3   2   RRD-VA   07   06   05   04   03   02

Contents

PART FOUR • *Families in Society*   299

9 *Work and Family*   303

10 *Dimensions of Diversity*   365

Preface

In this edition as in the past, we have had three aims. First, we looked for articles that make sense of current trends in family life. Second, we tried to balance excellent older articles with newer ones that are at the cutting edge of family scholarship. Third, we tried to select articles that are scholarly and yet understandable to an audience of undergraduates.

Among the new readings are the following:

- An analysis of how changes in family life over the past thirty years have led to a revolution in family law, by Mary Ann Mason, Mark A. Fine, and Sarah Carnochan
- A study of the striking differences between U.S. and Dutch parents in their attitudes toward teenaged sexuality, by Amy T. Schalet
- A study of how a revolution in adoption is transforming the meaning of family, by Mary L. Shanley
- A critique of the way in which public debates about the family typically pit one extreme position against the opposite extreme, by Andrew J. Cherlin
- A study of how adult children of Korean and Vietnamese immigrants apply the idea of the "normal U.S. family" to their own lives, by Karen Pyke
- An analysis of how the longevity revolution and other changes are making family relationships between generations increasingly important, by Vern L. Bengtson

We would like to thank all those who over the years have helped us with suggestions for this book. Thanks again to Rifat Salam of the New York University sociology department, whose knowledge of both family literature and the publishing process were of enormous help.

Last but not least, thanks to the reviewers who offered many good suggestions for this edition: Preston A. Britner, Ph.D., University of Connecticut; Elizabeth B. Farnsworth, Lynchburg College; Amy A. Holzgang, Cerritos College; Mary E. Kelly, Central Missouri State University; and Margaret Walsh, Keene State College.

Introduction: Family in Transition

Even before the attacks on September 11, 2001, it was clear that we had entered a period of profound and unsettling transformations. "Every once in a great while," states the introduction to a *Business Week* issue on the twenty-first century, "the established order is overthrown. Within a span of decades, technological advances, organizational innovations, and new ways of thinking transform economies" (Farrell, 1994, p. 16).

Whether we call the collection of changes *globalization, the information age,* or *postindustrial society*, they are affecting every area of the globe and every aspect of life, including the family. Although the state of the U.S. family has been the subject of great public attention in recent years, the discussion of family has been strangely disconnected from talk of the other transformations we are living through. Instead, family talk is suffused with nostalgia, confusion, and anxiety—what happened, we wonder, to the fifties family of Ozzie and Harriet?

The readings in this book show why this backward-looking approach to understanding the U.S. family is seriously flawed. Of course family life has changed massively in recent decades, and too many children and families are beset by serious stresses and troubles. But we can't understand these changes and problems without understanding the impact of large-scale changes in society on the small worlds of everyday family life. All the industrialized nations, and many of the emerging ones, have experienced the same changes the United States has—a transformation in women's roles, rising divorce rates, lower marriage and birth rates, and an increase in single-parent families. In no other country, however, has family change been so traumatic and divisive as in the United States.

For example, the two-earner family has replaced the breadwinner/housewife family as the norm in the United States, even when there are young children in the home. In the mid-nineties, more than 60 percent of married women with children under six were in the paid labor force (Han and Moen, 1999). Yet the question of whether mothers "should" work or stay home is still a hotly debated issue (except if the mother is on welfare).

A range of other, once-"deviant" lifestyles—from living with a partner while unmarried, to remaining single or childless, or even having a child while single (à la Murphy Brown)—has become both acceptable and controversial. It was once unthinkable that gay and lesbian families could be recognized or even tolerated, but despite persisting stigma and the threat of violence, they have been. Local governments and some leading corporations have granted these families increasing recognition as domestic partnerships entitled to spousal benefits.

The changes of recent decades have affected more than the forms of family life; they have been psychological as well. A major study of U.S. attitudes over two decades revealed a profound shift in how people think about family life, work, and themselves (Veroff, Douvan, and Kulka, 1981). In 1957 four-fifths of respondents thought that a man or woman who did not want to marry was sick, immoral, and selfish. By 1976 only one-fourth of respondents thought that choice was bad. Summing up many complex findings, the authors conclude that the United States underwent a "psychological revolution" in the two decades between surveys.

Ever since the 1970s, the mass media have been serving up stories and statistics that seemingly show the family is disintegrating, falling apart, or on the verge of disappearing. In the 1990s, public discussion of family issues turned into a polarized, often angry political debate. In the 1992 election, then–Vice President Dan Quayle set off a firestorm by attacking the fictional television character Murphy Brown for having a child without being married. The attack backfired. The public sided with Murphy Brown, who defended families no matter what their form.

Yet less than a year after the election, "Dan Quayle was right" became the new national consensus. A sudden blizzard of newspaper columns, magazine articles, and talk show "experts" warned that divorce and single parenthood are inflicting serious damage on children and on society in general. This family structure, they argued, is the single biggest problem facing the country, because it is the root cause of all the rest—poverty, crime, drugs, school failure, youth violence, and other social ills.

The proposed solution? Restore the "traditional" family. Make divorce and single parenthood socially unacceptable once again. Do away with welfare and make divorces more difficult to obtain. These arguments flooded the media as welfare reform was being debated in Congress: both sides of the debate cited social science evidence to bolster their case. But putting social science into the middle of the "argument culture" (Tannen, 1998) that dominates our media and politics these days is not an effective way to deal with the complexities of either the research or family life itself.

Popular political talk shows such as *Crossfire* and *Hardball*, which often amount to little more than shouting matches, are the most extreme examples. Such shows typically feature the most assertive advocates from each side. None of the media is immune, including newspapers and magazines. Howard Kurtz, a media critic, observes that "the middle ground, the sensible center, is dismissed as too squishy, too dull, too likely to send the audience channel-surfing" (1996, p. 4).

It's not surprising then that public debate about the family often sinks to the level of a "food fight" as it lurches from one hot topic to another—single mothers, divorce, gay marriage, nannies, and working mothers. Each issue has only two sides: Are you for or against the two-parent family? Is divorce bad or good for children? Should mothers of young children work or not? Is the family "in decline" or not?

As Andrew Cherlin points out in his article on p. 284, when one extreme position debates the opposite extreme position, it becomes difficult to realistically discuss the issues and problems facing the country. It doesn't describe the range of views among family scholars, and it doesn't fit the research evidence. For example, if someone takes the position that "divorce is damaging to children," the argument culture leads us to assume that there are people on the other "side" who will argue just the opposite—in other words, that divorce is "good," or at least not harmful. But as researcher Paul Amato suggests, the right question to ask is "Under what circumstances is divorce harmful or beneficial to children?" (1994). In most public debates about divorce, however, that question is never asked, and the public never hears the useful information they should.

Still another problem with popular discourse about the family is that it exaggerates the extent of change. For example, we sometimes hear that the traditional nuclear family no longer exists, or has shrunk to a tiny percentage of the population. But that statement depends on a very narrow definition of family—two biological parents, in their first marriage, with a full-time breadwinner husband and a full-time homemaker wife, and two or three children under the age of 18. Of course that kind of family has declined—for the simple reason that most wives and mothers now work outside the home. It has also declined because there are more married couples with grown children than there used to be.

Similarly, we hear that divorce rates have shot up since the 1950s, but we are not told that the trend toward higher divorce rates started in the nineteenth century, with more marital breakups in each succeeding generation. Nor do we hear that despite the current high divorce rates (actually down from 1979), the United States has the highest marriage rates in the industrial world. About 90 percent of Americans marry at some point in their lives, and virtually all who do either have, or want to have, children. Further, surveys repeatedly show that family is central to the lives of most Americans. They find family ties their deepest source of satisfaction and meaning, as well as the source of their greatest worries (Mellman, Lazarus, and Rivlin, 1990). In sum, family life in the United States is a complex mixture of both continuity and change.

While the transformations of the past three decades do not mean the end of family life, they have brought a number of new difficulties. For example, most families now depend on the earnings of wives and mothers, but the rest of society has not caught up to the new realities. There is still an earnings gap between men and women. Employed wives and mothers still bear most of the workload in the home. For both men and women, the demands of the job are often at odds with family needs.

UNDERSTANDING THE CHANGING FAMILY

During the same years in which the family was becoming the object of public anxiety and political debate, a torrent of new research on the family was pouring forth. The study of the family had come to excite the interest of scholars in a range of disciplines—history, demography, economics, law, psychology. As a result of this research, we now have much more information available about the family than ever before. Ironically, much of the new scholarship is at odds with the widespread assumption that the family had a long, stable history until hit by the social "earthquake" of the 1960s and 1970s. We have learned from historians that the "lost" golden age of family happiness and stability we yearn for never actually existed.

Because of the continuing stream of new family scholarship, as well as shifts in public attitudes toward the family, each edition of *Family in Transition* has been different from the one before it. When we put together the first edition of this book in the early 1970s, the first rumblings of change were beginning to be felt. The youth movements of the 1960s and the emerging women's movement were challenging many of the assumptions on which conventional marriage and family patterns had been based. The mass media were regularly presenting stories that also challenged in one way or another traditional views on sex, marriage, and family. Many people were defying conventional standards of behavior: College girls were beginning to live openly with young men, unwed movie actresses were publicizing rather than hiding their pregnancies, and homosexuals were beginning openly to protest persecution and discrimination.

It seemed as if something was happening to family life in the United States, even if there were no sharp changes in the major statistical indicators. People seemed to be looking at sex, marriage, parenthood, and family life in new ways, even if behavior on a mass scale was not changing very noticeably.

In putting together the readings for that first edition of *Family in Transition*, we found that the professional literature of the time seemed to deny that change was possible. An extreme version of this view was the statement by an anthropologist that the nuclear family (mother, father, and children) "is a biological phenomenon . . . as rooted in organs and physiological structures as insect societies" (LaBarre, 1954, p. 104). Any changes in the basic structure of family roles or in child rearing were assumed to be unworkable, if not unthinkable.

The family in modern society was portrayed as a streamlined, more highly evolved version of a universal family. According to the sociological theorist Talcott Parsons and his followers (1951, 1954), the modern family, with sharply contrasting male and female roles, had become more specialized. It transferred work and educational roles to other agencies and specialized in child rearing and emotional support. No less important for having relinquished certain tasks, the modern family was now the only part of society to carry out such functions.

The family theories of the postwar era were descriptively correct insofar as they portrayed the ideal middle-class family patterns of a particular society at a particular historical period. But they went astray in elevating the status quo to the level of a timeless necessity. In addition, the theories did not acknowledge the great diversity among families that has always existed in the United States.

Still another flaw in the dominant view was its neglect of internal strains within the family, even when it was presumably functioning as it was supposed to. Paradoxically, these strains were vividly described by the very theorists who idealized the role of the family in modern society. Parsons, for example, observed that when home no longer functioned as an economic unit, women, children, and old people were placed in an ambiguous position. They became dependent on the male breadwinner and were cut off from society's major source of achievement and status.

Women's roles were particularly difficult: even at the height of the June Cleaver era, being a housewife was not seen as a real occupation; it was vaguely defined, highly demanding, yet not considered real work in a society that measures achievement by the size of one's paycheck. The combination of existing strains and the demystifying effects of the challenges to the family status quo seems to have provided, as Judith Blake (1978, p. 11) pointed out, a classic set of conditions for social change.

Part of the confusion surrounding the current status of the family arises from the fact that the family is a surprisingly problematic area of study; there are few if any self-evident facts, even statistical ones. Researchers have found, for example, that when the statistics of family life are plotted for the entire twentieth century, or back into the nineteenth century, a surprising finding emerges: Today's young people—with their low marriage, high divorce, and low fertility rates—appear to be behaving in ways consistent with long-term historical trends (Cherlin, 1981; Masnick and Bane, 1980). The recent changes in family life only appear deviant when compared to what people were doing in the 1940s and 1950s. But it was the postwar generation that married young, moved to the suburbs, and had three, four, or more children that departed from twentieth-century trends. As one study put it, "Had the 1940s and 1950s not happened, today's young adults would appear to be behaving normally" (Masnick and Bane, 1980, p. 2).

Thus, the meaning of change as a particular indicator of family life depends on the time frame in which it is placed. If we look at trends over too short a period of time—say ten or twenty years—we may think we are seeing a marked change, when, in fact, an older pattern may be reemerging. For some issues, even discerning what the trends are can be a problem.

For example, whether we conclude that there is an "epidemic" of teenage pregnancy depends on how we define adolescence and what measure of illegitimacy we use. Contrary to the popular notion of skyrocketing teenage pregnancy, teenaged childbearing has actually been on the decline during the past two decades (Luker, this volume, Reading 33). It is possible for the *ratio* of illegitimate births to all births to go up at the same time as there are declines in the *absolute number* of births and in the likelihood that an individual will bear an illegitimate child. This is not to say that concern about teenage pregnancy is unwarranted; but the reality is much more complex than the simple and scary notion an "epidemic" implies. Given the complexities of interpreting data on the family, it is little wonder that, as Joseph Featherstone observes (1979), the family is a "great intellectual Rorschach blot. (p. 37)"

1. *The Myth of Universality*

To say that the family is the same everywhere is in some sense true. Yet families vary in organization, membership, life cycles, emotional environments, ideologies, social and kinship networks, and economic and other functions. Although anthropologists have tried to come up with a single definition of family that would hold across time and place, they generally have concluded that doing so is not useful (Geertz, 1965; Stephens, 1963).

Biologically, of course, a woman and a man must unite sexually to produce a child—even if only sperm and egg meet in a test tube. But no social kinship ties or living arrangements flow inevitably from biological union. Indeed, the definition of marriage is not the same across cultures. Although some cultures have weddings and notions of monogamy and permanence, many cultures lack one or more of these attributes. In some cultures, the majority of people mate and have children without legal marriage and often without living together. In other societies, husbands, wives, and children do not live together under the same roof.

In our own society, the assumption of universality has usually defined what is normal and natural both for research and therapy and has subtly influenced our thinking to regard deviations from the nuclear family as sick or perverse or immoral. As Suzanne Keller (1971) once observed:

> The fallacy of universality has done students of behavior a great disservice. By leading us to seek and hence to find a single pattern, it has blinded us to historical precedents for multiple legitimate family arrangements.

2. *The Myth of Family Harmony*

To question the idea of the happy family is not to say that love and joy are not found in family life or that many people do not find their deepest satisfactions in their families. Rather, the happy-family assumption omits important, if unpleasant, aspects of family life. Intimate relations inevitably involve antagonism as well as love. This mixture of strong positive and negative feelings sets close relationships apart from less intimate ones.

Western society has not always assumed such an idealized model of the family. From the Bible to the fairy tale, from Sophocles to Shakespeare, from Eugene O'Neill to the soap opera, there is a tragic tradition of portraying the family as a high-voltage emotional setting, charged with love and hate, tenderness and spite, even incest and murder.

There is also a low-comedy tradition. George Orwell once pointed out that the world of henpecked husbands and tyrannical mothers-in-law is as much a part of the Western cultural heritage as is Greek drama. Although the comic tradition tends to portray men's discontents rather than women's, it scarcely views the family as a setting for ideal happiness.

In recent years, family scholars have been studying family violence such as child abuse and wife beating to better understand the normal strains of family life. Long-known facts about family violence have recently been incorporated into a general analysis of the family. More police officers are killed and injured dealing with family fights than in dealing with any other kind of situation; of all the relationships between murderers and their victims, the family relationship is most common. Studies of family violence reveal that it is much more widespread than had been assumed, cannot easily be attributed to mental illness, and is not confined to the lower classes. Family violence seems to be a product of psychological tensions and external stresses that can affect all families at all social levels.

The study of family interaction has also undermined the traditional image of the happy, harmonious family. About three decades ago, researchers and therapists began to bring mental patients and their families together to watch how they behaved with one another. Oddly, whole family groups had not been systematically studied before.

At first the family interactions were interpreted as pathogenic: a parent expressing affection in words but showing nonverbal hostility; alliances being made between different family members; families having secrets; one family member being singled out as a scapegoat to be blamed for the family's troubles. As more and more families were studied, such patterns were found in many families, not just in those families with a schizophrenic child. Although this line of research did not uncover the cause of schizophrenia, it made an important discovery about family life: So-called normal families can often seem dysfunctional, or, in the words of one study, "difficult environments for interaction."

3. *The Myth of Parental Determinism*

The kind of family a child grows up in leaves a profound, lifelong impact. But a growing body of studies shows that early family experience is not the all-powerful, irreversible influence it has sometimes been thought to be. An unfortunate childhood does not doom a person to an unhappy adulthood. Nor does a happy childhood guarantee a similarly blessed future (Emde and Harmon, 1984; Macfarlane, 1964; Rubin, 1996).

First, children come into this world with their own temperamental and other individual characteristics. As parents have long known, child rearing is not like molding clay or writing on a blank slate. Rather, it's a two-way process in which both parent and child shape each other. Further, children are active perceivers and interpreters of the world. Finally, parents and children do not live in a social vacuum; children are also influenced by the world around them and the people in it—the kin group, the neighborhood, other children, the school, and the media.

Recently, the traditional view of parental determinism has been challenged by the extreme opposite view. Psychologist Judith Rich Harris asserts that parents have very little impact on their childrne's development. In her book, *The Nurture Assumption: Why Children Turn Out the Way They Do* (1998), Harris argues that genes and peer groups, not parents, determine a child's future. As Andrew Cherlin argues in his article (p. 284), both extremes oversimplify the complex realities of growing up.

4. *The Myth of a Stable, Harmonious Past*

Laments about the current state of decay of the family imply some earlier era when the family was more stable and harmonious. But unless we can agree what earlier time should be chosen as a baseline and what characteristics of the family should be specified, it makes little sense to speak of family decline. Historians have not, in fact, located a golden age of the family.

Indeed, they have found that premarital sexuality, illegitimacy, generational conflict, and even infanticide can best be studied as a part of family life itself rather than as separate categories of deviation. For example, William Kessen (1965), in his history of the field of child study, observes:

> Perhaps the most persistent single note in the history of the child is the reluctance of mothers to suckle their babies. The running war between the mother, who does not want to nurse, and the philosopher–psychologists, who insist she must, stretches over two thousand years. (pp. 1–2)

The most shocking finding of recent years is the prevalence of infanticide throughout European history. Infanticide has long been attributed to primitive peoples or assumed to be the desperate act of an unwed mother. It now appears that infanticide provided a major means of population control in all societies lacking reliable contraception, Europe included, and that it was practiced by families on legitimate children (Hrdy, 1999).

Rather than being a simple instinctive trait, having tender feelings toward infants— regarding a baby as a precious individual—seems to emerge only when infants have a decent chance of surviving and adults experience enough security to avoid feeling that children are competing with them in a struggle for survival. Throughout many centuries of European history, both of these conditions were lacking.

Another myth about the family is that of changelessness—the belief that the family has been essentially the same over the centuries, until recently, when it began to come apart. Family life has always been in flux; when the world around them changes, families change in response. At periods when a whole society undergoes some major transformation, family change may be especially rapid and dislocating.

In many ways, the era we are living through today resembles two earlier periods of family crisis and transformation in U.S. history (see Skolnick, 1991). The first occurred in the early nineteenth century, when the growth of industry and commerce moved work out of the home. Briefly, the separation of home and work disrupted existing patterns of daily family life, opening a gap between the way people actually lived and the cultural blueprints for proper gender and generational roles (Ryan, 1981). In the older pattern, when most people worked on farms, a father was not just the head of the household, but also boss of the family enterprise. Mother and children and hired hands worked under his supervision. But when work moved out, father—along with older sons and daughters—went with it, leaving behind mother and the younger children. These dislocations in the functions and meaning of family life unleashed an era of personal stress and cultural confusion.

Eventually, a new model of family emerged that not only reflected the new separation of work and family, but also glorified it. No longer a workplace, the household now became idealized as "home sweet home," an emotional and spiritual shelter from the heartless world outside. Although father remained the head of the family, mother was now the central figure in the home. The new model celebrated the "true woman's" purity, virtue, and selflessness. Many of our culture's most basic ideas about the family in U.S. culture, such as "a woman's place is in the home," were formed at this time. In short, the family pattern we now think of as traditional was in fact the first version of the modern family.

Historians label this model of the family "Victorian" because it became influential in England and Western Europe as well as in the United States during the reign of Queen Victoria. It reflected, in idealized form, the nineteenth-century middle-class family. However, the Victorian model became the prevailing cultural definition of family. Few families could live up to the ideal in all its particulars; working-class, black, and ethnic families, for example, could not get by without the economic contributions of wives, mothers, and daughters. And even for middle-class families, the Victorian ideal prescribed a standard of perfection that was virtually impossible to fulfill (Demos, 1986).

Eventually, however, social change overtook the Victorian model. Beginning around the 1880s, another period of rapid economic, social, and cultural change unsettled Victorian family patterns, especially their gender arrangements. Several generations of so-called new women challenged Victorian notions of femininity. They became educated, pursued careers, became involved in political causes—including their own—and created the first wave of feminism. This ferment culminated in the victory of the women's suffrage movement. It was followed by the 1920s' jazz-age era of flappers and flaming youth—the first, and probably the major, sexual revolution of the twentieth century.

To many observers at the time, it appeared that the family and morality had broken down. Another cultural crisis ensued, until a new cultural blueprint emerged—the companionate model of marriage and the family. The new model was a revised, more relaxed version of the Victorian family; companionship and sexual intimacy were now defined as central to marriage.

This highly abbreviated history of family and cultural change forms the necessary backdrop for understanding the family upheavals of the late twentieth and early twenty-first centuries. As in earlier times, major changes in the economy and society have destabilized an existing model of family life and the everyday patterns and practices that have sustained it.

We have experienced a triple revolution: first, the move toward a postindustrial service and information economy; second, a life course revolution brought about by the reductions in mortality and fertility; and third, a psychological transformation rooted mainly in rising educational levels.

Although these shifts have profound implications for everyone in contemporary society, women have been the pacesetters of change. Most women's lives and expectations over the past three decades, inside and outside the family, have departed drastically from those of their own mothers. Men's lives today also are different from their fathers' generation, but to a much lesser extent.

THE TRIPLE REVOLUTION

The Postindustrial Family

The most obvious way the new economy affects the family is in its drawing women, especially married women, into the workplace. A service and information economy produces large numbers of jobs that, unlike factory work, seem suitable for women. Yet as Jessie Bernard (1982) once observed, the transformation of a housewife into a paid worker outside the home sends tremors through every family relationship. It creates a more "symmetrical" family, undoing the sharp contrast between men's and women's roles that marks the breadwinner/housewife pattern. It also reduces women's economic dependence on men, thereby making it easier for women to leave unhappy marriages.

Beyond drawing women into the workplace, shifts in the nature of work and a rapidly changing globalized economy have unsettled the lives of individuals and families at all class levels. The well-paying industrial jobs that once enabled a blue-collar worker to own a home and support a family are no longer available. The once secure jobs that sustained the "organization men" and their families in the 1950s and 1960s have been made shaky by downsizing, an unstable economy, corporate takeovers, and a rapid pace of technological change.

The new economic climate has also made the transition to adulthood increasingly problematic. The uncertainties of work is in part responsible for young adults' lower fertility rates and for women flooding the workplace. Further, the family formation patterns of the 1950s are out of step with the increased educational demands of today's postindustrial society. In the postwar years, particularly in the United States, young people entered adulthood in one giant step—going to work, marrying young and moving to a separate household from their parents, and having children quickly. Today, few young adults can afford to marry and have children in their late teens or early twenties. In an economy where a college degree is necessary to earn a living wage, early marriage impedes education for both men and women.

Those who do not go on to college have little access to jobs that can sustain a family. Particularly in the inner cities of the United States, growing numbers of young people have come to see no future for themselves at all in the ordinary world of work. In middle-class families, a narrowing opportunity structure has increased anxieties about downward mobility for offspring, and parents as well. The "incompletely launched young adult syndrome" has become common: Many young adults deviate from their parents' expectations by failing to launch careers and become successfully independent adults, and many even come home to crowd their parents' empty nest (Schnaiberg and Goldenberg, 1989).

The Life Course Revolution

The demographic transformations of the twentieth century were no less significant than the economic ones. We cannot hope to understand current predicaments of family life without understanding how radically the demographic and social circumstances of U.S. culture have changed. In earlier times, mortality rates were highest among infants, and the possibility of death from tuberculosis, pneumonia, or other infectious diseases was an ever-present threat to young and middle-aged adults. Before the turn of the twentieth century, only 40 percent of women lived through all the stages of a normal life course—growing up, marrying, having children, and surviving with a spouse to the age of 50 (Uhlenberg, 1980).

Demographic and economic change has had a profound effect on women's lives. Women today are living longer and having fewer children. When infant and child mortality rates fall, women no longer have to have five or seven or nine children to make sure that two or three will survive to adulthood. After rearing children, the average woman can look forward to three or four decades without maternal responsibilities. Because traditional assumptions about women are based on the notion that they are constantly involved with pregnancy, child rearing, and related domestic concerns, the current ferment about women's roles may be seen as a way of bringing cultural attitudes in line with existing social realities.

As people live longer, they can stay married longer. Actually, the biggest change in contemporary marriage is not the proportion of marriages disrupted through divorce, but the potential length of marriage and the number of years spent without children in the home. By the 1970s the statistically average couple spent only 18 percent of their married lives raising young children, compared with 54 percent a century ago (Bane, 1976). As a result, marriage is becoming defined less as a union between parents raising a brood of children and more as a personal relationship between two individuals.

A Psychological Revolution

The third major transformation is a set of psychocultural changes that might be described as "psychological gentrification" (Skolnick, 1991). That is, cultural advantages once enjoyed only by the upper classes—in particular, education—have been extended to those lower down on the socioeconomic scale. Psychological gentrification also involves greater leisure time, travel, and exposure to information, as well as a general rise in the standard of living. Despite the persistence of poverty, unemployment, and economic insecurity in the industrialized world, far less of the population than in the historical past is living at the level of sheer subsistence.

Throughout Western society, rising levels of education and related changes have been linked to a complex set of shifts in personal and political attitudes. One of these is a more psychological approach to life—greater introspectiveness and a yearning for warmth and intimacy in family and other relationships (Veroff, Douvan, and Kulka, 1981). There is also evidence of an increasing preference on the part of both men and women for a more companionate ideal of marriage and a more democratic family. More broadly, these changes in attitude have been described as a shift to "postmaterialist values," emphasizing self-expression, tolerance, equality, and a concern for the quality of life (Inglehart, 1990).

The multiple social transformations of our era have brought both costs and benefits: Family relations have become both more fragile and more emotionally rich; mass longevity has brought us a host of problems as well as the gift of extended life. Although change has brought greater opportunities for women, persisting gender inequality means women have borne a large share of the costs of these gains. But we cannot turn the clock back to the family models of the past.

Paradoxically, after all the upheavals of recent decades, the emotional and cultural significance of the family persists. Family remains the center of most people's lives and, as numerous surveys show, a cherished value. Although marriage has become more fragile, the parent–child relationship—especially the mother–child relationship—remains a core attachment across the life course (Rossi and Rossi, 1990). The family, however, can be both "here to stay" and beset with difficulties. There is widespread recognition that the massive social and economic changes we have lived through call for public and private-sector policies in support of families. Most European countries have recognized for some time that governments must play a role in supplying an array of supports to families—health care, children's allowances, housing subsidies, support for working parents and children (such as child care, parental leave, and shorter work days for parents), as well as an array of services for the elderly.

Each country's response to these changes, as we've noted earlier, has been shaped by its own political and cultural traditions. The United States remains embroiled in a cultural war over the family; many social commentators and political leaders have promised to reverse the recent trends and restore the "traditional" family. In contrast, other Western nations, including Canada and the other English-speaking countries, have responded to family change by establishing policies aimed at mitigating the problems brought about by economic and social transformations. As a result of these policies, these countries have been spared much of the poverty and other social ills that have plagued the United States in recent decades.

Looking Ahead

The world at the beginning of the twenty-first century is vastly different from what it was at the beginning, or even the middle, of the twentieth century. Families are struggling to adapt to new realities. The countries that have been at the leading edge of family change still find themselves caught between yesterday's norms, today's new realities, and an uncertain future. As we have seen, changes in women's lives have been a pivotal factor in recent family trends. In many countries there is a considerable difference between men's and women's attitudes and expectations of one another. Even where both partners accept a more equal division of labor in the home, there is often a gap between beliefs and behavior. In no country have employers, the government, or men fully caught up to the changes in women's lives.

But a knowledge of family history reveals that the solution to contemporary problems will not be found in some lost golden age. Families have always struggled with outside circumstances and inner conflict. Our current troubles inside and outside the family are genuine, but we should never forget that many of the most vexing issues confronting us derive from benefits of modernization few of us would be willing to give up—for example, longer, healthier lives, and the ability to choose how many children to have and when to have them. There was no problem of the aged in the past, because most people never aged; they died before they got old. Nor was adolescence a difficult stage of the life cycle when children worked, education was a privilege of the rich, and a person's place in society was determined by heredity rather than choice. And when most people were hungry illiterates, only aristocrats could worry about sexual satisfaction and self-fulfillment.

In short, there is no point in giving in to the lure of nostalgia. There is no golden age of the family to long for, nor even some past pattern of behavior and belief that would guarantee us harmony and stability if only we had the will to return to it. Family life is bound up with the social, economic, and ideological circumstances of particular times and places. We are no longer peasants, Puritans, pioneers, or even suburbanites circa 1955. We face conditions unknown to our ancestors, and we must find new ways to cope with them.

A Note on "the Family"

Some family scholars have suggested that we drop the term *the family* and replace it with *families* or *family life*. The problem with *the family* is that it calls to mind the stereotyped image of the Ozzie and Harriet kind of family—two parents and their two or three minor children. But those other terms don't always work. In our own writing we use the term *the family* in much the same way we use *the economy*—a set of institutional arrangements through which particular tasks are carried out in a society.

An economy deals with goods and service; the family deals with reproduction and child rearing, care and support for adults, and so on.

References

Amato, P. R. 1994. Life span adjustment of children to their parents' divorce. *The Future of Children* 4, no 1. (Spring).

Bane, M. J. 1976. *Here to Stay*. New York: Basic Books.

Bernard, J. 1982. *The Future of Marriage*. New York: Bantam.

Blake, J. 1978. Structural differentiation and the family: A quiet revolution. Presented at American Sociology Association, San Francisco.

Cherlin, A. J. 1981. *Marriage, Divorce, Remarriage*. Cambridge, Mass.: Harvard University Press.

Demos, John. 1986. *Past, Present, and Personal*. New York: Oxford University Press.

Emde, R. N., and R. J. Harmon, eds. 1984. *Continuities and Discontinuities in Development*. New York: Plenum Press.

Farrell, Christopher. 1994. Twenty-first century capitalism: The triple revolution. *Business Week* (November 18): 16–25.

Featherstone, J. 1979. Family matters. *Harvard Educational Review* 49, no. 1: 20–52.

Geertz, G. 1965. The impact of the concept of culture on the concept of man. In *New Views of the Nature of Man*, edited by J. R. Platt. Chicago: University of Chicago Press.

Han, S.-K., and P. Moen. 1999. Work and family over time: A life course approach. *The Annals of the American Academy of Political and Social Sciences* 562: 98–110.

Harris, J. R. 1998. *The Nurture Assumption: Why Children Turn Out the Way They Do*. New York: Free Press.

Hrdy, Sarah B. 1999. *Mother Nature*. New York: Pantheon Books.

Inglehart, Ronald. 1990. *Culture Shift*. New Jersey: Princeton University Press.

Keller, S. 1971. Does the family have a future? *Journal of Comparative Studies*, Spring.

Kessen, W. 1965. *The Child*. New York: John Wiley.

Kurtz, H. 1996. *Hot Air: All Talk All the Time*. New York: Times Books.

LaBarre, W. 1954. *The Human Animal*. Chicago: University of Chicago Press.

Macfarlane, J. W. 1964. Perspectives on personality consistency and change from the guidance study. *Vita Humana* 7: 115–126.

Masnick, G., and M. J. Bane. 1980. *The Nation's Families: 1960–1990*. Boston: Auburn House.

Mellman, A., E. Lazarus, and A. Rivlin. 1990. Family time, family values. In *Rebuilding the Nest*, edited by D. Blankenhorn, S. Bayme, and J. Elshtain. Milwaukee: Family Service America.

Parsons, T. 1951. *The Social System*. Glencoe, Ill.: Free Press.

Parsons, T. 1954. The kinship system of the contemporary United States. In *Essays in Sociological Theory*. Glencoe, Ill.: Free Press.

Rossi, A. S., and P. H. Rossi. 1990. *Of Human Bonding: Parent-Child Relations Across the Life Course*. Hawthorne, New York: Aldine de Gruyter.

Rubin, L. 1996. *The Transcendent Child*. New York: Basic Books.

Ryan, M. 1981. *The Cradle of the Middle Class*. New York: Cambridge University Press.

Schnaiberg, A., and S. Goldenberg. 1989. From empty nest to crowded nest: The dynamics of incompletely launched young adults. *Social Problems* 36, no. 3 (June): 251–269.

Skolnick, A. 1991. *Embattled Paradise: The American Family in an Age of Uncertainty*. New York: Basic Books.

Stephens, W. N. 1963. *The Family in Cross-Cultural Perspective*. New York: World.

Tannen, D. 1998. *The Argument Culture*.

Uhlenberg, P. 1980. Death and the family. *Journal of Family History* 5, no. 3: 313–320.

Veroff, J., E. Douvan, and R. A. Kulka. 1981. *The Inner American: A Self-Portrait from 1957 to 1976*. New York: Basic Books.

I   *The Changing Family*

The study of the family does not belong to any single scholarly field; genetics, physiology, archaeology, history, anthropology, sociology, psychology, and economics all touch on it. Religious and ethical authorities claim a stake in the family, and troubled individuals and families generate therapeutic demands on family scholarship. In short, the study of the family is interdisciplinary, controversial, and necessary for the formulation of social policy and practices.

Interdisciplinary subjects present characteristic problems. Each discipline has its own assumptions and views of the world, which may not directly transfer into another field. Some biologists and physically oriented anthropologists, for example, analyze human affairs in terms of individual motives and instincts; for them, society is a shadowy presence, serving mainly as the setting for biologically motivated individual action. Many sociologists and cultural anthropologists, in contrast, perceive the individual as an actor playing a role written by culture and society. One important school of psychology sees people neither as passive recipients of social pressures nor as creatures driven by powerful lusts, but as information processors trying to make sense of their environment. There is no easy way to reconcile such perspectives. Scientific paradigms—characteristic ways of looking at the world—determine not only what answers will be found, but also what questions will be asked. This fact has perhaps created special confusion in the study of the family.

"We speak of families," R. D. Laing has observed, "as though we know what families are. We identify, as families, networks of people who live together over time, who have ties of marriage or kinship to one another" (Laing, 1971, p. 3).

There is the assumption that family life, so familiar a part of everyday experience, is easily understood. But familiarity may breed a sense of destiny—what we experience is transformed into the "natural":

> One difficulty in the psychological sciences lies in the familiarity of the phenomena with which they deal. A certain intellectual effort is required to see how such phenomena can pose serious problems or call for intricate explanatory theories. One is inclined to take them for granted as necessary or somehow "natural." (Chomsky, 1968, p. 21)

Another obstacle to understanding family life is that it is hard to see the links between the larger world outside the home and the individuals and families inside. The selections in Part One aim to show us these links. For example, Anthony Giddens argues that there is a global revolution going on in sexuality, in marriage and the family, and in

15

how people think of themselves and their relationships. He argues that we are living through another wave of technological and economic modernization that is having a profound impact on personal life. Further, he sees a strong parallel between the ideals of a democratic society and the emerging new ideals of family relationships. For example, a good marriage is coming to be seen as a relationship between equals. Giddens recognizes that many of the changes in family life are worrisome, but we can't go back to the family patterns of an earlier time. Nor would most of us really want to. Nostalgic images of the family in earlier times typically omit the high mortality rates that prevailed before the twentieth century. Death could strike at any age, and was a constant threat to family stability. Arlene Skolnick's article reveals the profound impact of high mortality on family relationships, and how new problems arose from the lengthening of the life span over the course of the twentieth century.

Stephanie Coontz points to flaws in our nostalgic assumptions about the families of a more recent era—the 1950s—the era that Americans are most likely to think of as a golden age of family. People living at the time did not see it that way. Yet, Coontz argues, in many ways, because of a strong economy and governmental policies such as the GI Bill of Rights, the country really was a better place for families than it is today.

The readings in Chapter 2 are concerned with the meaning of family in modern society. As women increasingly participate in the paid workforce, argues Sharon Hays, they find themselves caught up in a web of cultural contradictions that remain unresolved and indeed have deepened. There is no way, she further maintains, for contemporary women to get it "just right." Both stay-at-home and working mothers maintain an intensive commitment to motherhood, although they work it out in different ways. Women who stay at home no longer feel comfortable and fulfilled being defined by themselves and others as "mere housewives." Correspondingly, working women are frequently anxious about the time away from children and the complexities of balancing parental duties with the demands of serious employment.

The cultural contradictions that trouble motherhood can be seen as a part of the larger "cultural war" over the family. But there are more than two sides in the family wars. Janet Z. Giele carefully diagrams *three* positions on the family: the conservative, the liberal, and the feminist. The latter, for Giele, is the most promising for developing public policies that would combine conservative and liberal perspectives. The feminist vision, she argues, appreciates the both the "premodern nature of the family" with the inevitable interdependence of family with a modern, fast-changing economy.

The dramatic changes in family life over the past three decades have led to a revolution in family law, according to Mary Ann Mason, Mark A. Fine, and Sarah Carnochan. They review the shifts in many aspects of the law, including marriage, divorce, child custody, unwed fathers, adoption, and so on. Noting that the law generally lags behind social reality, they predict that we are likely to see still further changes in the legal system.

References

Chomsky, N. 1968. *Language and Mind*. New York: Harcourt, Brace and World.
Laing, R. D. 1971. *The Politics of the Family*. New York: Random House.

1 Families Past and Present

■ READING 1

The Global Revolution in Family and Personal Life

Anthony Giddens

Among all the changes going on today, none are more important than those happening in our personal lives—in sexuality, emotional life, marriage and the family. There is a global revolution going on in how we think of ourselves and how we form ties and connections with others. It is a revolution advancing unevenly in different regions and cultures, with many resistances.

As with other aspects of the runaway world, we don't know what the ratio of advantages and anxieties will turn out to be. In some ways, these are the most difficult and disturbing transformations of all. Most of us can tune out from larger problems for much of the time. We can't opt out, however, from the swirl of change reaching right into the heart of our emotional lives.

There are few countries in the world where there isn't intense discussion about sexual equality, the regulation of sexuality and the future of the family. And where there isn't open debate, this is mostly because it is actively repressed by authoritarian governments or fundamentalist groups. In many cases, these controversies are national or local—as are the social and political reactions to them. Politicians and pressure groups will suggest that if only family policy were modified, if only divorce were made harder or easier to get in their particular country, solutions to our problems could readily be found.

But the changes affecting the personal and emotional spheres go far beyond the borders of any particular country, even one as large as the United States. We find the same issues almost everywhere, differing only in degree and according to the cultural context in which they take place.

In China, for example, the state is considering making divorce more difficult. In the aftermath of the Cultural Revolution, very liberal marriage laws were passed. Marriage is a working contract, that can be dissolved, I quote: "when husband and wife both desire it."

Even if one partner objects, divorce can be granted when "mutual affection" has gone from the marriage. Only a two week wait is required, after which the two pay $4 and are henceforth independent. The Chinese divorce rate is still low as compared with Western countries, but it is rising rapidly—as is true in the other developing Asian societies. In Chinese cities, not only divorce, but cohabitation is becoming more frequent.

In the vast Chinese countryside, by contrast, everything is different. Marriage and the family are much more traditional—in spite of the official policy of limiting childbirth through a mixture of incentives and punishment. Marriage is an arrangement between two families, fixed by the parents rather than the individuals concerned.

A recent study in the province of Gansu, which has only a low level of economic development, found that 60% of marriages are still arranged by parents. As a Chinese saying has it: "meet once, nod your head and marry." There is a twist in the tail in modernising China. Many of those currently divorcing in the urban centres were married in the traditional manner in the country.

In China there is much talk of protecting the family. In many Western countries the debate is even more shrill. The family is a site for the struggles between tradition and modernity, but also a metaphor for them. There is perhaps more nostalgia surrounding the lost haven of the family than for any other institution with its roots in the past. Politicians and activists routinely diagnose the breakdown of family life and call for a return to the traditional family.

Now the "traditional family" is very much a catch-all category. There have been many different types of family and kinship systems in different societies and cultures. The Chinese family, for instance, was always distinct from family forms in the West. Arranged marriage was never as common in most European countries, as in China, or India. Yet the family in non-modern cultures did, and does, have some features found more or less everywhere.

The traditional family was above all an economic unit. Agricultural production normally involved the whole family group, while among the gentry and aristocracy, transmission of property was the main basis of marriage. In mediaeval Europe, marriage was not contracted on the basis of sexual love, nor was it regarded as a place where such love should flourish. As the French historian, Georges Duby, puts it, marriage in the middle ages was not to involve "frivolity, passion, or fantasy."

The inequality of men and women was intrinsic to the traditional family. I don't think one could overstate the importance of this. In Europe, women were the property of their husbands or fathers—chattels as defined in law.

In the traditional family, it wasn't only women who lacked rights—children did too. The idea of enshrining children's rights in law is in historical terms relatively recent. In premodern periods, as in traditional cultures today, children weren't reared for their own sake, or for the satisfaction of the parents. One could almost say that children weren't recognised as individuals.

It wasn't that parents didn't love their children, but they cared about them more for the contribution they made to the common economic task than for themselves. Moreover, the death rate of children was frightening. In Colonial America nearly one in four infants died in their first year. Almost 50% didn't live to age 10.

Except for certain courtly or elite groups, in the traditional family sexuality was always dominated by reproduction. This was a matter of tradition and nature combined.

The absence of effective contraception meant that for most women sexuality was inevitably closely connected with childbirth. In many traditional cultures, including in Western Europe up to the threshold of the 20th Century, a woman might have 10 or more pregnancies during the course of her life.

Sexuality was regulated by the idea of female virtue. The sexual double standard is often thought of as a creation of the Victorian period. In fact, in one version or another it was central to almost all non-modern societies. It involved a dualistic view of female sexuality—a clear cut division between the virtuous woman on the one hand and the libertine on the other.

Sexual promiscuity in many cultures has been taken as a positive defining feature of masculinity. James Bond is, or was, admired for his sexual as well as his physical heroism. Sexually adventurous women, by contrast, have nearly always been beyond the pale, no matter how much influence the mistresses of some prominent figures might have achieved.

Attitudes towards homosexuality were also governed by a mix of tradition and nature. Anthropological surveys show that homosexuality—or male homosexuality at any rate—has been tolerated, or openly approved of, in more cultures than it has been outlawed.

Those societies that have been hostile to homosexuality have usually condemned it as specifically unnatural. Western attitudes have been more extreme than most; less than half a century ago homosexuality was still widely regarded as a perversion and written up as such in manuals of psychiatry.

Antagonism towards homosexuality is still widespread and the dualistic view of women continues to be held by many—of both sexes. But over the past few decades the main elements of people's sexual lives in the West have changed in an absolutely basic way. The separation of sexuality from reproduction is in principle complete. Sexuality is for the first time something to be discovered, moulded, altered. Sexuality, which used to be defined so strictly in relation to marriage and legitimacy, now has little connection to them at all. We should see the increasing acceptance of homosexuality not just as a tribute to liberal tolerance. It is a logical outcome of the severance of sexuality from reproduction. Sexuality which has no content is by definition no longer dominated by heterosexuality.

What most of its defenders in Western countries call the traditional family was in fact a late, transitional phase in family development in the 1950's. This was a time at which the proportion of women out at work was still relatively low and when it was still difficult, especially for women, to obtain divorce without stigma. On the other hand, men and women by this time were more equal than they had been previously, both in fact and in law. The family had ceased to be an economic entity and the idea of romantic love as basis for marriage had replaced marriage as an economic contract.

Since then, the family has changed much further. The details vary from society to society, but the same trends are visible almost everywhere in the industrialised world. Only a minority of people now live in what might be called the standard 1950's family—both parents living together with their children of the marriage, where the mother is a full time housewife, and the father the breadwinner. In some countries, more than a third of all births happen outside wedlock, while the proportion of people living alone has gone up steeply and looks likely to rise even more.

In most societies, like the U.S., marriage remains popular—the U.S. has aptly been called a high divorce, high marriage society. In Scandinavia, on the other hand, a large proportion of people living together, including where children are involved, remain unmarried. Moreover, up to a quarter of women aged between 18 and 35 in the U.S. and Europe say they do not intend to have children—and they appear to mean it.

Of course in all countries older family forms continue to exist. In the U.S., many people, recent immigrants particularly, still live according to traditional values. Most family life, however, has been transformed by the rise of the couple and coupledom. Marriage and the family have become what I termed in an earlier lecture shell institutions. They are still called the same, but inside their basic character has changed.

In the traditional family, the married couple was only one part, and often not the main part, of the family system. Ties with children and other relatives tended to be equally or even more important in the day to day conduct of social life. Today the couple, married or unmarried, is at the core of what the family is. The couple came to be at the centre of family life as the economic role of the family dwindled and love, or love plus sexual attraction, became the basis of forming marriage ties.

A couple once constituted has its own exclusive history, its own biography. It is a unit based upon emotional communication or intimacy. The idea of intimacy, like so many other familiar notions I've discussed in these lectures, sounds old but in fact is very new. Marriage was never in the past based upon intimacy—emotional communication. No doubt this was important to a good marriage but it was not the foundation of it. For the couple, it is. Communication is the means of establishing the tie in the first place and it is the chief rationale for its continuation.

We should recognise what a major transition this is. "Coupling" and "uncoupling" provide a more accurate description of the arena of personal life now than do "marriage and the family." A more important question for us than "are you married?" is "how good is your relationship?"

The idea of a relationship is also surprisingly recent. Only 30 or so years ago, no one spoke of "relationships." They didn't need to, nor did they need to speak in terms of intimacy and commitment. Marriage at that time was the commitment, as the existence of shotgun marriages bore witness. While statistically marriage is still the normal condition, for most people its meaning has more or less completely changed. Marriage signifies that a couple is in a stable relationship, and may indeed promote that stability, since it makes a public declaration of commitment. However, marriage is no longer the chief defining basis of coupledom.

The position of children in all this is interesting and somewhat paradoxical. Our attitudes towards children and their protection have altered radically over the past several generations. We prize children so much partly because they have become so much rarer, and partly because the decision to have a child is very different from what it was for previous generations. In the traditional family, children were an economic benefit. Today in Western countries a child, on the contrary, puts a large financial burden on the parents. Having a child is more of a distinct and specific decision than it used to be, and it is a decision guided by psychological and emotional needs. The worries we have about the effects of divorce upon children, and the existence of many fatherless families, have to be understood against the background of our much higher expectations about how children should be cared for and protected.

There are three main areas in which emotional communication, and therefore intimacy, are replacing the old ties that used to bind together people's personal lives—in sexual and love relations, parent-child relations and in friendship.

To analyse these, I want to use the idea of what I call the "pure relationship." I mean by this a relationship based upon emotional communication, where the rewards derived from such communication are the main basis for the relationship to continue.

I don't mean a sexually pure relationship. Also I don't mean anything that exists in reality. I'm talking of an abstract idea that helps us understand changes going on in the world. Each of the three areas just mentioned—sexual relationships, parent-child relations and friendship—is tending to approximate to this model. Emotional communication or intimacy, in other words, are becoming the key to what they are all about.

The pure relationship has quite different dynamics from more traditional social ties. It depends upon processes of active trust—opening oneself up to the other. Self-disclosure is the basic condition of intimacy.

The pure relationship is also implicitly democratic. When I was originally working on the study of intimate relationships, I read a great deal of therapeutic and self-help literature on the subject. I was struck by something I don't believe has been widely noticed or remarked upon. If one looks at how a therapist sees a good relationship—in any of the three spheres just mentioned—it is striking how direct a parallel there is with public democracy.

A good relationship, of course, is an ideal—most ordinary relationships don't come even close. I'm not suggesting that our relations with spouses, lovers, children or friends aren't often messy, conflictual and unsatisfying. But the principles of public democracy are ideals too, that also often stand at some large distance from reality.

A good relationship is a relationship of equals, where each party has equal rights and obligations. In such a relationship, each person has respect, and wants the best, for the other. The pure relationship is based upon communication, so that understanding the other person's point of view is essential.

Talk, or dialogue, are the basis of making the relationship work. Relationships function best if people don't hide too much from each other—there has to be mutual trust. And trust has to be worked at, it can't just be taken for granted.

Finally, a good relationship is one free from arbitrary power, coercion or violence.

Every one of these qualities conforms to the values of democratic politics. In a democracy, all are in principle equal, and with equality of rights and responsibilities comes mutual respect. Open dialogue is a core property of democracy. Democratic systems substitute open discussion of issues—a public space of dialogue—for authoritarian power, or for the sedimented power of tradition. No democracy can work without trust. And democracy is undermined if it gives way to authoritarianism or violence.

When we apply these principles—as ideals, I would stress again—to relationships, we are talking of something very important—the possible emergence of what I shall call, a democracy of the emotions in everyday life. A democracy of the emotions, it seems to me, is as important as public democracy in improving the quality of our lives.

This holds as much in parent-child relations as in other areas. These can't, and shouldn't, be materially equal. Parents must have authority over children, in everyone's interests. Yet they should presume an in-principle equality. In a democratic family, the authority of parents should be based upon an implicit contract. The parent in effect says to the child: "If you were an adult, and knew what I know, you would agree that what I ask you to do is legitimate."

Children in traditional families were—and are—supposed to be seen and not heard. Many parents, perhaps despairing of their children's rebelliousness, would dearly like to resurrect that rule. But there isn't any going back to it, nor should there be. In a democracy of the emotions, children can and should be able to answer back.

An emotional democracy doesn't imply lack of discipline, or absence of authority. It simply seeks to put them on a different footing.

Something very similar happened in the public sphere, when democracy began to replace arbitrary government and the rule of force. And like public democracy the democratic family must be anchored in a stable, yet open, civil society. If I may coin a phrase—"It takes a village."

A democracy of the emotions would draw no distinctions of principle between heterosexual and same-sex relationships. Gays, rather than heterosexuals, have actually been pioneers in discovering the new world of relationships and exploring its possibilities. They have had to be, because when homosexuality came out of the closet, gays weren't able to depend upon the normal supports of traditional marriage. They have had to be innovators, often in a hostile environment.

To speak of fostering an emotional democracy doesn't mean being weak about family duties, or about public policy towards the family. Democracy, after all, means the acceptance of obligations, as well as rights sanctioned in law. The protection of children has to be the primary feature of legislation and public policy. Parents should be legally obliged to provide for their children until adulthood, no matter what living arrangements they enter into. Marriage is no longer an economic institution, yet as a ritual commitment it can help stabilise otherwise fragile relationships. If this applies to heterosexual relationships, I don't see why it shouldn't apply to homosexual ones too.

There are many questions to be asked of all this—too many to answer in a short lecture. I have concentrated mainly upon trends affecting the family in Western countries. What about areas where the traditional family remains largely intact, as in the example of China with which I began? Will the changes observed in the West become more and more global?

I think they will—indeed that they are. It isn't a question of whether existing forms of the traditional family will become modified, but when and how. I would venture even further. What I have described as an emerging democracy of the emotions is on the front line in the struggle between cosmopolitanism and fundamentalism that I described in the last lecture. Equality of the sexes, and the sexual freedom of women, which are incompatible with the traditional family, are anathema to fundamentalist groups. Opposition to them, indeed, is one of the defining features of religious fundamentalism across the world.

There is plenty to be worried about in the state of the family, in Western countries and elsewhere. It is just as mistaken to say that every family form is as good as any other, as to argue that the decline of the traditional family is a disaster.

I would turn the argument of the political and fundamentalist right on its head. The persistence of the traditional family—or aspects of it—in many parts of the world is more worrisome than its decline. For what are the most important forces promoting democracy and economic development in poorer countries? Well, they are the equality and education of women. And what must be changed to make these possible? Most importantly, what must be changed is the traditional family.

In conclusion, I should emphasise that sexual equality is not just a core principle of democracy. It is also relevant to happiness and fulfilment.

Many of the changes happening to the family are problematic and difficult. But surveys in the U.S. and Europe show that few want to go back to traditional male and female roles, much less to legally defined inequality.

If ever I were tempted to think that the traditional family might be best after all, I remember what my great aunt said. She must have had one of the longest marriages of anyone. She married young, and was with her husband for over 60 years. She once confided to me that she had been deeply unhappy with him the whole of that time. In her day there was no escape.

■ READING 2

The Life Course Revolution

Arlene Skolnick

Many of us, in moments of nostalgia, imagine the past as a kind of Disneyland—a quaint setting we might step back into with our sense of ourselves intact, yet free of the stresses of modern life. But in yearning for the golden past we imagine we have lost, we are unaware of what we have escaped.

In our time, for example, dying before reaching old age has become a rare event; about three-quarters of all people die after their sixty-fifth birthday. It is hard for us to appreciate what a novelty this is in human experience. In 1850, only 2 percent of the population lived past sixty-five. "We place dying in what we take to be its logical position," observes the social historian Ronald Blythe, "which is at the close of a long life, whereas our ancestors accepted the futility of placing it in any position at all. In the midst of life we are in death, they said, and they meant it. To them it was a fact; to us it is a metaphor."

This longevity revolution is largely a twentieth-century phenomenon. Astonishingly, two-thirds of the total increase in human longevity since prehistoric times has taken place since 1900—and a good deal of that increase has occurred in recent decades. Mortality rates in previous centuries were several times higher than today, and death commonly struck at any age. Infancy was particularly hazardous; "it took two babies to make one adult," as one demographer put it. A white baby girl today has a greater chance of living to be sixty than her counterpart born in 1870 would have had of reaching her first birthday. And after infancy, death still hovered as an ever-present possibility. It was not unusual for young and middle-aged adults to die of tuberculosis, pneumonia, or other infectious diseases. (Keats died at twenty-five, Schubert at thirty-one, Mozart at thirty-five.)

These simple changes in mortality have had profound, yet little-appreciated effects on family life; they have encouraged stronger emotional bonds between parents and children, lengthened the duration of marriage and parent-child relationships, made grandparenthood an expectable stage of the life course, and increased the number of grandparents whom children actually know. More and more families have four or even five generations alive at the same time. And for the first time in history, the average couple has more parents living than it has children. It is also the first era when most of the parent-child relationship takes place after the child becomes an adult.

In a paper entitled "Death and the Family," the demographer Peter Uhlenberg has examined some of these repercussions by contrasting conditions in 1900 with those in 1976. In 1900, for example, half of all parents would have experienced the death of a child; by 1976 only 6 percent would. And more than half of all children who lived to the age of fifteen in 1900 would have experienced the death of a parent or sibling, compared with less than 9 percent in 1976. Another outcome of the lower death rates was a decline in the number of orphans and orphanages. Current discussions of divorce rarely take into account the almost constant family disruption children experienced in "the good old days." In 1900, 1 out of 4 children under the age of fifteen lost a parent; 1 out of 62 lost both. The corresponding figures for 1976 are, respectively, 1 out of 20 and 1 out of 1,800.

Because being orphaned used to be so common, the chances of a child's not living with either parent was much greater at the turn of the century than it is now. Indeed, some of the current growth in single-parent families is offset by a decline in the number of children raised in institutions, in foster homes, or by relatives. This fact does not diminish the stresses of divorce and other serious family problems of today, but it does help correct the tendency to contrast the terrible Present with an idealized Past.

Today's children rarely experience the death of a close relative, except for elderly grandparents. And it is possible to grow into adulthood without experiencing even that loss. "We never had any deaths in my family," a friend recently told me, explaining that none of her relatives had died until she was in her twenties. In earlier times, children were made aware of the constant possibility of death, attended deathbed scenes, and were even encouraged to examine the decaying corpses of family members.

One psychological result of our escape from the daily presence of death is that we are ill prepared for it when it comes. For most of us, the first time we feel a heightened concern with our own mortality is in our thirties and forties when we realize that the years we have already lived outnumber those we have left.

Another result is that the death of a child is no longer a sad but normal hazard of parenthood. Rather, it has become a devastating, life-shattering loss from which a parent may never fully recover. The intense emotional bonding between parents and infants that we see as a sociobiological given did not become the norm until the eighteenth and nineteenth centuries. The privileged classes created the concept of the "emotionally priceless" child, a powerful ideal that gradually filtered down through the rest of society.

The high infant mortality rates of premodern times were partly due to neglect, and often to lethal child-rearing practices such as sending infants off to a wet nurse* or, worse, infanticide. It now appears that in all societies lacking reliable contraception, the careless treatment and neglect of unwanted children acted as a major form of birth control. This does not necessarily imply that parents were uncaring toward all their children; rather, they seem to have practiced "selective neglect" of sickly infants in favor of sturdy ones, or of later children in favor of earlier ones.† In 1801 a writer observed of Bavarian peasants:

> The peasant has joy when his wife brings forth the first fruit of their love, he has joy with the second and third as well, but not with the fourth. . . . He sees all children coming thereafter as hostile creatures, which take the bread from his mouth and the mouths of his family. Even the heart of the most gentle mother becomes cold with the birth of the fifth child, and the sixth, she unashamedly wishes death, that the child should pass to heaven.

Declining fertility rates are another major result of falling death rates. Until the baby boom of the 1940s and 1950s, fertility rates had been dropping continuously since the eighteenth century. By taking away parents' fear that some of their children would not survive to adulthood, lowered early-childhood mortality rates encouraged careful planning of births and smaller families. The combination of longer lives and fewer, more closely spaced children created a still-lengthening empty-nest stage in the family. This in turn has encouraged the companionate style of marriage, since husband and wife can expect to live together for many years after their children have moved out.

Many demographers have suggested that falling mortality rates are directly linked to rising divorce rates. In 1891 W. F. Willcox of Cornell University made one of the most accurate social science predictions ever. Looking at the high and steadily rising divorce rates of the time, along with falling mortality rates, he predicted that around 1980, the two curves would cross and the number of marriages ended by divorce would equal those ended by death. In the late 1970s, it all happened as Willcox had predicted. Then divorce rates continued to increase before leveling off in the 1980s, while mortality rates continued to decline. As a result, a couple marrying today is more likely to celebrate a fortieth wedding anniversary than were couples around the turn of the century.

In statistical terms, then, it looks as if divorce has restored a level of instability to marriage that had existed earlier due to the high mortality rate. But as Lawrence Stone

---

*Wet-nursing—the breastfeeding of an infant by a woman other than the mother—was widely practiced in premodern Europe and colonial America. Writing of a two-thousand-year-old "war of the breast," the developmental psychologist William Kessen notes that the most persistent theme in the history of childhood is the reluctance of mothers to suckle their babies, and the urgings of philosophers and physicians that they do so. Infants were typically sent away from home for a year and a half or two years to be raised by poor country women, in squalid conditions. When they took in more babies than they had milk enough to suckle, the babies would die of malnutrition.

The reluctance to breast-feed may not have reflected maternal indifference so much as other demands in premodern, precontraceptive times—the need to take part in the family economy, the unwillingness of husbands to abstain from sex for a year and a half or two. (Her milk would dry up if a mother became pregnant.) Although in France and elsewhere the custom persisted into the twentieth century, large-scale wet-nursing symbolizes the gulf between modern and premodern sensibilities about infants and their care.

†The anthropologist Nancy Scheper-Hughes describes how impoverished mothers in northeastern Brazil select which infants to nurture.

observes, "it would be rash to claim that the psychological effects of the termination of marriage by divorce, that is by an act of will, bear a close resemblance to its termination by the inexorable accident of death."

THE NEW STAGES OF LIFE

In recent years it has become clear that the stages of life we usually think of as built into human development are, to a large degree, social and cultural inventions. Although people everywhere may pass through infancy, childhood, adulthood, and old age, the facts of nature are "doctored," as Ruth Benedict once put it, in different ways by different cultures.

The Favorite Age

In 1962 Phillipe Ariès made the startling claim that "in medieval society, the idea of childhood did not exist." Ariès argued not that parents then neglected their children, but that they did not think of children as having a special nature that required special treatment; after the age of around five to seven, children simply joined the adult world of work and play. This "small adult" conception of childhood has been observed by many anthropologists in preindustrial societies. In Europe, according to Ariès and others, childhood was discovered, or invented, in the seventeenth and nineteenth centuries, with the emergence of the private, domestic, companionate family and formal schooling. These institutions created distinct roles for children, enabling childhood to emerge as a distinct stage of life.

Despite challenges to Ariès's work, the bulk of historical and cross-cultural evidence supports the contention that childhood as we know it today is a relatively recent cultural invention; our ideas about children, child-rearing practices, and the conditions of children's lives are dramatically different from those of earlier centuries. The same is true of adolescence. Teenagers, such a conspicuous and noisy presence in modern life, and their stage of life, known for its turmoil and soul searching, are not universal features of life in other times and places.

Of course, the physical changes of puberty—sexual maturation and spurt in growth—happen to everyone everywhere. Yet, even here, there is cultural and historical variation. In the past hundred years, the age of first menstruation has declined from the mid-teens to twelve, and the age young men reach their full height has declined from twenty-five to under twenty. Both changes are believed to be due to improvements in nutrition and health care, and these average ages are not expected to continue dropping.

Some societies have puberty rites, but they bring about a transition from childhood not to adolescence but to adulthood. Other societies take no note at all of the changes, and the transition from childhood to adulthood takes place simply and without social recognition. Adolescence as we know it today appears to have evolved late in the nineteenth century; there is virtual consensus among social scientists that it is "a creature of the industrial revolution and it continues to be shaped by the forces which defined that revolution: industrialization, specialization, urbanization . . . and bureaucratization of human organizations and institutions, and continuing technological development."

In America before the second half of the nineteenth century, youth was an ill-defined category. Puberty did not mark any new status or life experience. For the majority of young people who lived on farms, work life began early, at seven or eight years old or even younger. As they grew older, their responsibility would increase, and they would gradually move toward maturity. Adults were not ignorant of the differences between children and adults, but distinctions of age meant relatively little. As had been the practice in Europe, young people could be sent away to become apprentices or servants in other households. As late as the early years of this century, working-class children went to work at the age of ten or twelve.

A second condition leading to a distinct stage of adolescence was the founding of mass education systems, particularly the large public high school. Compulsory education helped define adolescence by setting a precise age for it; high schools brought large numbers of teenagers together to create their own society for a good part of their daily lives. So the complete set of conditions for adolescence on a mass scale did not exist until the end of the nineteenth century.

The changed family situations of late-nineteenth- and early-twentieth-century youth also helped make this life stage more psychologically problematic. Along with the increasing array of options to choose from, rapid social change was making one generation's experience increasingly different from that of the next. Among the immigrants who were flooding into the country at around the time adolescence was emerging, the generation gap was particularly acute. But no parents were immune to the rapid shifts in society and culture that were transforming America in the decades around the turn of the century.

Further, the structure and emotional atmosphere of middle-class family life was changing also, creating a more intimate and emotionally intense family life. Contrary to the view that industrialization had weakened parent-child relations, the evidence is that family ties between parents and adolescents intensified at this time: adolescents lived at home until they married, and depended more completely, and for a longer time, on their parents than in the past. Demographic change had cut family size in half over the course of the century. Mothers were encouraged to devote themselves to the careful nurturing of fewer children.

This more intensive family life seems likely to have increased the emotional strain of adolescence. Smaller households and a more nurturing style of child rearing, combined with the increased contact between parents, especially mothers, and adolescent children, may have created a kind of " 'Oedipal family' in middle class America."

The young person's awakening sexuality, particularly the young male's, is likely to have been more disturbing to both himself and his parents than during the era when young men commonly lived away from home. . . . There is evidence that during the Victorian era, fears of adolescent male sexuality, and of masturbation in particular, were remarkably intense and widespread.

Family conflict in general may have been intensified by the peculiar combination of teenagers' increased dependence on parents and increased autonomy in making their own life choices. Despite its tensions, the new emotionally intense middle-class home made it more difficult than ever for adolescents to leave home for the heartless, indifferent world outside.

By the end of the nineteenth century, conceptions of adolescence took on modern form, and by the first decades of the twentieth century, *adolescence* had become a household word. As articulated forcefully by the psychologist G. Stanley Hall in his 1904 treatise, adolescence was a biological process—not simply the onset of sexual maturity but a turbulent, transitional stage in the evolution of the human species: "some ancient period of storm and stress when old moorings were broken and a higher level attained."

Hall seemed to provide the answers to questions people were asking about the troublesome young. His public influence eventually faded, but his conception of adolescence as a time of storm and stress lived on. Adolescence continued to be seen as a period of both great promise and great peril: "every step of the upward way is strewn with the wreckage of body, mind and morals." The youth problem—whether the lower-class problem of delinquency, or the identity crises and other psychological problems of middle-class youth—has continued to haunt America, and other modern societies, ever since.

Ironically, then, the institutions that had developed to organize and control a problematic age ended by heightening adolescent self-awareness, isolating youth from the rest of society, and creating a youth culture, making the transition to adulthood still more problematic and risky. Institutional recognition in turn made adolescents a more distinct part of the population, and being adolescent a more distinct and self-conscious experience. As it became part of the social structure of modern society, adolescence also became an important stage of the individual's biography—an indeterminate period of being neither child nor adult that created its own problems. Any society that excludes youth from adult work, and offers them what Erikson calls a "moratorium"—time and space to try out identities and lifestyles—and at the same time demands extended schooling as the route to success is likely to turn adolescence into a "struggle for self." It is also likely to run the risk of increasing numbers of mixed-up, rebellious youth.

But, in fact, the classic picture of adolescent storm and stress is not universal. Studies of adolescents in America and other industrialized societies suggest that extreme rebellion and rejection of parents, flamboyant behavior, and psychological turmoil do not describe most adolescents, even today. Media images of the youth of the 1980s and 1990s as a deeply troubled, lost generation beset by crime, drug abuse, and teenage pregnancy are also largely mistaken.

Although sexual activity and experimenting with drugs and alcohol have become common among middle-class young people, drug use has actually declined in recent years. Disturbing as these practices are for parents and other adults, they apparently do not interfere with normal development for most adolescents. Nevertheless, for a significant minority, sex and drugs add complications to a period of development during which a young person's life can easily go awry—temporarily or for good.

More typically, for most young people, the teen years are marked by mild rebelliousness and moodiness—enough to make it a difficult period for parents but not one of a profound parent-child generation gap or of deep alienation from conventional values. These ordinary tensions of family living through adolescence are exacerbated in times of rapid social change, when the world adolescents confront is vastly different from the one in which their parents came of age. Always at the forefront of social change, adolescents in industrial societies inevitably bring discomfort to their elders, who "wish to see their children's adolescence as an enactment of the retrospectively distorted memory of their own. . . . But such intergenerational continuity can occur only in the rapidly disappearing isolation of the desert or the rain forest."

If adolescence is a creation of modern culture, that culture has also been shaped by adolescence. Adolescents, with their music, fads, fashions, and conflicts, not only are conspicuous, but reflect a state of mind that often extends beyond the years designated for them. The adolescent mode of experience—accessible to people of any age—is marked by "exploration, becoming, growth, and pain."

Since the nineteenth century, for example, the coming-of-age novel has become a familiar literary genre. Patricia Spacks observes that while Victorian authors looked back at adolescence from the perspective of adulthood, twentieth-century novelists since James Joyce and D. H. Lawrence have become more intensely identified with their young heroes, writing not from a distance but from "deep inside the adolescence experience." The novelist's use of the adolescent to symbolize the artist as romantic outsider mirrors a more general cultural tendency. As Phillipe Ariès observes, "Our society has passed from a period which was ignorant of adolescence to a period in which adolescence is the favorite age. We now want to come to it early and linger in it as long as possible."

The Discovery of Adulthood

Middle age is the latest life stage to be discovered, and the notion of mid-life crisis recapitulates the storm-and-stress conception of adolescence. Over the course of the twentieth century, especially during the years after World War II, a developmental conception of childhood became institutionalized in public thought. Parents took it for granted that children passed through ages, stages, and phases: the terrible twos, the teenage rebel. In recent years the idea of development has been increasingly applied to adults, as new stages of adult life are discovered. Indeed much of the psychological revolution of recent years—the tendency to look at life through psychological lenses—can be understood in part as the extension of the developmental approach to adulthood.

In 1976 Gail Sheehy's best-selling *Passages* popularized the concept of mid-life crisis. Sheehy argued that every individual must pass through such a watershed, a time when we reevaluate our sense of self, undergo a crisis, and emerge with a new identity. Failure to do so, she warned, can have dire consequences. The book was the most influential popular attempt to apply to adults the ages-and-stages approach to development that had long been applied to children. Ironically, this came about just as historians were raising questions about the universality of those stages.

Despite its popularity, Sheehy's book, and the research she reported in it, have come under increasing criticism. "Is the mid-life crisis, if it exists, more than a warmed-over identity crisis?" asked one review of the research literature on mid-life. In fact, there is little or no evidence for the notion that adults pass through a series of sharply defined stages, or a series of crises that must be resolved before passing from one stage to the next.

Nevertheless, the notion of a mid-life crisis caught on because it reflected shifts in adult experience across the life course. Most people's decisions about marriage and work are no longer irrevocably made at one fateful turning point on the brink of adulthood. The choices made at twenty-one may no longer fit at forty or fifty—the world has changed; parents, children, and spouses have changed; working life has changed. The kind of issue that makes adolescence problematic—the array of choices and the need to fashion a coherent, continuous sense of self in the midst of all this change—recurs throughout adulthood. As a Jules Feiffer cartoon concludes, "Maturity is a phase, but adolescence is forever."

Like the identity crisis of adolescence, the concept of mid-life crisis appears to reflect the experience of the more educated and advantaged. Those with more options in life are more likely to engage in the kind of introspection and reappraisal of previous choices that make up the core of the mid-life crisis. Such people realize that they will never fulfill their earlier dreams, or that they have gotten what they wanted and find they are still not happy. But as the Berkeley longitudinal data show, even in that segment of the population, mid-life crisis is far from the norm. People who have experienced fewer choices in the past, and have fewer options for charting new directions in the future, are less likely to encounter a mid-life crisis. Among middle Americans, life is dominated by making ends meet, coping with everyday events, and managing unexpected crises.

While there may be no fixed series of stages or crises adults must pass through, middle age or mid-life in our time does have some unique features that make it an unsettled time, different from other periods in the life course as well as from mid-life in earlier eras. First, as we saw earlier, middle age is the first period in which most people today confront death, illness, and physical decline. It is also an uneasy age because of the increased importance of sexuality in modern life. Sexuality has come to be seen as the core of our sense of self, and sexual fulfillment as the center of the couple relationship. In mid-life, people confront the decline of their physical attractiveness, if not of their sexuality.

There is more than a passing resemblance between the identity problems of adolescence and the issues that fall under the rubric of "mid-life crisis." In a list of themes recurring in the literature on the experience of identity crisis, particularly in adolescence, the psychologist Roy Baumeister includes: feelings of emptiness, feelings of vagueness, generalized malaise, anxiety, self-consciousness. These symptoms describe not only adolescent and mid-life crises but what Erikson has labeled identity problems—or what has, of late, been considered narcissism.

Consider, for example, Heinz Kohut's description of patients suffering from what he calls narcissistic personality disorders. They come to the analyst with vague symptoms, but eventually focus on feelings about the self—emptiness, vague depression, being drained of energy, having no "zest" for work or anything else, shifts in self-esteem, heightened sensitivity to the opinions and reactions of others, feeling unfulfilled, a sense of uncertainty and purposelessness. "It seems on the face of it," observes the literary critic Steven Marcus, "as if these people are actually suffering from what was once called unhappiness."

The New Aging

Because of the extraordinary revolution in longevity, the proportion of elderly people in modern industrial societies is higher than it has ever been. This little-noticed but profound transformation affects not just the old but families, an individual's life course, and society as a whole. We have no cultural precedents for the mass of the population reaching old age. Further, the meaning of *old age* has changed—indeed, it is a life stage still in process, its boundaries unclear. When he came into office at the age of sixty-four, George Bush did not seem like an old man. Yet when Franklin Roosevelt died at the same age, he did seem to be "old."

President Bush illustrates why gerontologists in recent years have had to revise the meaning of "old." He is a good example of what they have termed the "young old" or the "new elders"; the social historian Peter Laslett uses the term "the third age." Whatever it is called, it represents a new stage of life created by the extension of the life course in industrialized countries. Recent decades have witnessed the first generations of people who live past sixty-five and remain healthy, vigorous, alert, and, mostly due to retirement plans, financially independent. These people are "pioneers on the frontier of age," observed the journalist Frances Fitzgerald, in her study of Sun City, a retirement community near Tampa, Florida, "people for whom society had as yet no set of expectations and no vision."

The meaning of the later stages of life remains unsettled. Just after gerontologists had marked off the "young old"—people who seemed more middle-aged than old—they had to devise a third category, the "oldest old," to describe the fastest-growing group in the population, people over eighty-five. Many if not most of these people are like Tithonus, the mythical figure who asked the gods for eternal life but forgot to ask for eternal youth as well. For them, the gift of long life has come at the cost of chronic disease and disability.

The psychological impact of this unheralded longevity revolution has largely been ignored, except when misconstrued. The fear of age, according to Christopher Lasch, is one of the chief symptoms of this culture's alleged narcissism. But when people expected to die in their forties or fifties, they didn't have to face the problem of aging. Alzheimer's disease, for example, now approaching epidemic proportions, is an ironic by-product of the extension of the average life span. When living to seventy or eighty is a realistic prospect, it makes sense to diet and exercise, to eat healthy foods, and to make other "narcissistic" investments in the self.

Further, "the gift of mass longevity," the anthropologist David Plath argues, has been so recent, dramatic, and rapid that it has become profoundly unsettling in all post-industrial societies: "If the essential cultural nightmare of the nineteenth century was to be in poverty, perhaps ours is to be old and alone or afflicted with terminal disease."

Many people thus find themselves in life stages for which cultural scripts have not yet been written; family members face one another in relationships for which tradition provides little guidance. "We are stuck with awkward-sounding terms like 'adult children' and . . . 'grandson-in-law.' " And when cultural rules are ambiguous, emotional relationships can become tense or at least ambivalent.

A study of five-generation families in Germany reveals the confusion and strain that result when children and parents are both in advanced old age—for example, a great-great-grandmother and her daughter, who is herself a great-grandmother. Who has the right to be old? Who should take care of whom? Similarly, Plath, who has studied the problems of mass longevity in Japan, finds that even in that familistic society the traditional meaning of family roles has been put into question by the stretching out of the life span. In the United States, some observers note that people moving into retirement communities sometimes bring their parents to live with them. Said one disappointed retiree: "I want to enjoy my grandchildren; I never expected that when I was a grandparent I'd have to look after my parents."

■ READING 3

What We Really Miss about the 1950s

Stephanie Coontz

In a 1996 poll by the Knight-Ridder news agency, more Americans chose the 1950s than any other single decade as the best time for children to grow up. And despite the research I've done on the underside of 1950s families, I don't think it's crazy for people to feel nostalgic about the period. For one thing, it's easy to see why people might look back fondly to a decade when real wages grew more in any single year than in the entire ten years of the 1980s combined, a time when the average 30-year-old man could buy a median-priced home on only 15–18 percent of his salary.

But it's more than just a financial issue. When I talk with modern parents, even ones who grew up in unhappy families, they associate the 1950s with a yearning they feel for a time when there were fewer complicated choices for kids or parents to grapple with, when there was more predictability in how people formed and maintained families, and when there was a coherent "moral order" in their community to serve as a reference point for family norms. Even people who found that moral order grossly unfair or repressive often say that its presence provided them with something concrete to push against.

I can sympathize entirely. One of my most empowering moments occurred the summer I turned 12, when my mother marched down to the library with me to confront a librarian who'd curtly refused to let me check out a book that was "not appropriate" for my age. "Don't you *ever* tell my daughter what she can and can't read," fumed my mom. "She's a mature young lady and she can make her own choices." In recent years I've often thought back to the gratitude I felt toward my mother for that act of trust in me. I wish I had some way of earning similar points from my own son. But much as I've always respected his values, I certainly wouldn't have walked into my local video store when he was 12 and demanded that he be allowed to check out absolutely anything he wanted!

Still, I have no illusions that I'd actually like to go back to the 1950s, and neither do most people who express such occasional nostalgia. For example, although the 1950s got more votes than any other decade in the Knight-Ridder poll, it did not win an outright majority: 38 percent of respondents picked the 1950s; 27 percent picked the 1960s or the 1970s. Voters between the ages of 50 and 64 were most likely to choose the 1950s, the decade in which they themselves came of age, as the best time for kids; voters under 30 were more likely to choose the 1970s. African Americans differed over whether the 1960s, 1970s, or 1980s were best, but all age groups of blacks agreed that later decades were definitely preferable to the 1950s.

Nostalgia for the 1950s is real and deserves to be taken seriously, but it usually shouldn't be taken literally. Even people who *do* pick the 1950s as the best decade generally end up saying, once they start discussing their feelings in depth, that it's not the family arrangements in and of themselves that they want to revive. They don't miss the way women used to be treated, they sure wouldn't want to live with most of the fathers they knew in their neighborhoods, and "come to think of it"—I don't know how many times I've recorded these exact words—"I communicate with my kids *much* better than my parents or grandparents did." When Judith Wallerstein recently interviewed 100 spouses in "happy" marriages, she found that only five "wanted a marriage like their parents'." The husbands "consciously rejected the role models provided by their fathers. The women said they could never be happy living as their mothers did."

People today understandably feel that their lives are out of balance, but they yearn for something totally *new*—a more equal distribution of work, family, and community time for both men and women, children and adults. If the 1990s are lopsided in one direction, the 1950s were equally lopsided in the opposite direction.

What most people really feel nostalgic about has little to do with the internal structure of 1950s families. It is the belief that the 1950s provided a more family-friendly economic and social environment, an easier climate in which to keep kids on the straight and narrow, and above all, a greater feeling of hope for a family's long-term future, especially for its young. The contrast between the perceived hopefulness of the fifties and our own misgivings about the future is key to contemporary nostalgia for the period. Greater optimism *did* exist then, even among many individuals and groups who were in terrible circumstances. But if we are to take people's sense of loss seriously, rather than merely to capitalize on it for a hidden political agenda, we need to develop a historical perspective on where that hope came from.

Part of it came from families comparing their prospects in the 1950s to their unstable, often grindingly uncomfortable pasts, especially the two horrible decades just before. In the 1920s after two centuries of child labor and income insecurity, and for the first time in American history, a bare majority of children had come to live in a family with a male breadwinner, a female homemaker, and a chance at a high school education. Yet no sooner did the ideals associated with such a family begin to blossom than they were buried by the stock market crash of 1929 and the Great Depression of the 1930s. During the 1930s domestic violence soared; divorce rates fell, but informal separations jumped; fertility plummeted. Murder rates were higher in 1933 than they were in the 1980s. Families were uprooted or torn apart. Thousands of young people left home to seek work, often riding the rails across the country.

World War II brought the beginning of economic recovery, and people's renewed interest in forming families resulted in a marriage and childbearing boom, but stability was still beyond most people's grasp. Postwar communities were rocked by racial tensions, labor strife, and a right-wing backlash against the radical union movement of the 1930s. Many women resented being fired from wartime jobs they had grown to enjoy. Veterans often came home to find that they had to elbow their way back into their families, with wives and children resisting their attempts to reassert domestic authority. In one recent study of fathers who returned from the war, four times as many reported painful, even traumatic, reunions as remembered happy ones.

By 1946 one in every three marriages was ending in divorce. Even couples who stayed together went through rough times, as an acute housing shortage forced families to double up with relatives or friends. Tempers frayed and generational relations grew strained. "No home is big enough to house two families, particularly two of different generations, with opposite theories on child training," warned a 1948 film on the problems of modern marriage.

So after the widespread domestic strife, family disruptions, and violence of the 1930s and the instability of the World War II period, people were ready to try something new. The postwar economic boom gave them the chance.

The 1950s was the first time that a majority of Americans could even *dream* of creating a secure oasis in their immediate nuclear families. There they could focus their emotional and financial investments, reduce obligations to others that might keep them from seizing their own chance at a new start, and escape the interference of an older generation of neighbors or relatives who tried to tell them how to run their lives and raise their kids. Oral histories of the postwar period resound with the theme of escaping from in-laws, maiden aunts, older parents, even needy siblings.

The private family also provided a refuge from the anxieties of the new nuclear age and the cold war, as well as a place to get away from the political witch-hunts led by

Senator Joe McCarthy and his allies. When having the wrong friends at the wrong time or belonging to any "suspicious" organization could ruin your career and reputation, it was safer to pull out of groups you might have joined earlier and to focus on your family. On a more positive note, the nuclear family was where people could try to satisfy their long-pent-up desires for a more stable marriage, a decent home, and the chance to really enjoy their children.

THE 1950s FAMILY EXPERIMENT

The key to understanding the successes, failures, and comparatively short life of 1950s family forms and values is to understand the period as one of *experimentation* with the possibilities of a new kind of family, not as the expression of some longstanding tradition. At the end of the 1940s, the divorce rate, which had been rising steadily since the 1890s, dropped sharply; the age of marriage fell to a 100-year low; and the birth rate soared. Women who had worked during the depression or World War II quit their jobs as soon as they became pregnant, which meant quite a few women were specializing in child raising; fewer women remained childless during the 1950s than in any decade since the late nineteenth century. The timing and spacing of childbearing became far more compressed, so that young mothers were likely to have two or more children in diapers at once, with no older sibling to help in their care. At the same time, again for the first time in 100 years, the educational gap between young middle-class women and men increased, while job segregation for working men and women seems to have peaked. These demographic changes increased the dependence of women on marriage, in contrast to gradual trends in the opposite direction since the early twentieth century.

The result was that family life and gender roles became much more predictable, orderly, and settled in the 1950s than they were either twenty years earlier or would be twenty years later. Only slightly more than one in four marriages ended in divorce during the 1950s. Very few young people spent any extended period of time in a nonfamily setting: They moved from their parent's family into their own family, after just a brief experience with independent living, and they started having children soon after marriage. Whereas two-thirds of women aged 20–24 were not yet married in 1990, only 28 percent of women this age were still single in 1960.

Ninety percent of all the households in the country were families in the 1950s, in comparison with only 71 percent by 1990. Eighty-six percent of all children lived in two-parent homes in 1950, as opposed to just 72 percent in 1990. And the percentage living with both biological parents—rather than, say, a parent and stepparent—was dramatically higher than it had been at the turn of the century or is today: 70 percent in 1950, compared with only 50 percent in 1990. Nearly 60 percent of kids—an all-time high—were born into male breadwinner-female homemaker families; only a minority of the rest had mothers who worked in the paid labor force.

If the organization and uniformity of family life in the 1950s were new, so were the values, especially the emphasis on putting all one's emotional and financial eggs in the small basket of the immediate nuclear family. Right up through the 1940s, ties of work, friendship, neighborhood, ethnicity, extended kin, and voluntary organizations were as important a source of identity for most Americans, and sometimes a *more* important source of obligation, than marriage and the nuclear family. All this changed in the post-war era. The spread of suburbs and automobiles, combined with the destruction of older ethnic neighborhoods in many cities, led to the decline of the neighborhood social club. Young couples moved away from parents and kin, cutting ties with traditional extra-familial networks that might compete for their attention. A critical factor in this trend was the emergence of a group of family sociologists and marriage counselors who followed Talcott Parsons in claiming that the nuclear family, built on a sharp division of labor between husband and wife, was the cornerstone of modern society.

The new family experts tended to advocate views such as those first raised in a 1946 book, *Their Mothers' Sons*, by psychiatrist Edward Strecker. Strecker and his followers argued that American boys were infantalized and emasculated by women who were old-fashioned "moms" instead of modern "mothers." One sign that might be that dreaded "mom," Strecker warned women, was if you felt you should take your aging parents into your own home, rather than putting them in "a good institution . . . where they will receive adequate care and comfort." Modern "mothers" placed their parents in nursing homes and poured all their energies into their nuclear family. They were discouraged from diluting their wifely and maternal commitments by maintaining "competing" interests in friends, jobs, or extended family networks, yet they were also supposed to cheerfully grant early independence to their (male) children—an emotional double bind that may explain why so many women who took this advice to heart ended up abusing alcohol or tranquilizers over the course of the decade.

The call for young couples to break from their parents and youthful friends was a consistent theme in 1950s popular culture. In *Marty*, one of the most highly praised TV plays and movies of the 1950s, the hero almost loses his chance at love by listening to the carping of his mother and aunt and letting himself be influenced by old friends who resent the time he spends with his new girlfriend. In the end, he turns his back on mother, aunt, and friends to get his new marriage and a little business of his own off to a good start. Other movies, novels, and popular psychology tracts portrayed the dreadful things that happened when women became more interested in careers than marriage or men resisted domestic conformity.

Yet many people felt guilty about moving away from older parents and relatives; "modern mothers" worried that fostering independence in their kids could lead to defiance or even juvenile delinquency (the recurring nightmare of the age); there was considerable confusion about how men and women could maintain clear breadwinner-homemaker distinctions in a period of expanding education, job openings, and consumer aspirations. People clamored for advice. They got it from the new family education specialists and marriage counselors, from columns in women's magazines, from government pamphlets, and above all from television. While 1950s TV melodramas warned against letting anything dilute the commitment to getting married and having kids, the new family sitcoms gave people nightly lessons on how to make their marriage or rapidly expanding family work—or, in the case of *I Love Lucy*, probably the most popular show of the era, how *not* to make their marriage and family work. Lucy and Ricky gave weekly comic reminders of how much trouble a woman could get into by wanting a career or hatching some hare-brained scheme behind her husband's back.

At the time, everyone knew that shows such as *Donna Reed, Ozzie and Harriet, Leave It to Beaver,* and *Father Knows Best* were not the way families really were. People didn't watch those shows to see their own lives reflected back at them. They watched them to see how families were *supposed* to live—and also to get a little reassurance that they were headed in the right direction. The sitcoms were simultaneously advertisements, etiquette manuals, and how-to lessons for a new way of organizing marriage and child raising. I have studied the scripts of these shows for years, since I often use them in my classes on family history, but it wasn't until I became a parent that I felt their extraordinary pull. The secret of their appeal, I suddenly realized, was that they offered 1950s viewers, wracked with the same feelings of parental inadequacy as was I, the promise that there were easy answers and surefire techniques for raising kids.

Ever since, I have found it useful to think of the sitcoms as the 1950s equivalent of today's beer ads. As most people know, beer ads are consciously aimed at men who *aren't* as strong and sexy as the models in the commercials, guys who are uneasily aware of the gap between the ideal masculine pursuits and their own achievements. The promise is that if the viewers on the couch will just drink brand X, they too will be able to run 10 miles without gasping for breath. Their bodies will firm up, their complexions will clear up, and maybe the Swedish bikini team will come over and hang out at their place.

Similarly, the 1950s sitcoms were aimed at young couples who had married in haste, women who had tasted new freedoms during World War II and given up their jobs with regret, veterans whose children resented their attempts to reassert paternal authority, and individuals disturbed by the changing racial and ethnic mix of postwar America. The message was clear: Buy these ranch houses, Hotpoint appliances, and child-raising ideals; relate to your spouse like this; get a new car to wash with your kids on Sunday afternoons; organize your dinners like that—and you too can escape from the conflicts of race, class, and political witch-hunts into harmonious families where father knows best, mothers are never bored or irritated, and teenagers rush to the dinner table each night, eager to get their latest dose of parental wisdom.

Many families found it possible to put together a good imitation of this way of living during the 1950s and 1960s. Couples were often able to construct marriages that were much more harmonious than those in which they had grown up, and to devote far more time to their children. Even when marriages were deeply unhappy, as many were, the new stability, economic security, and educational advantages parents were able to offer their kids counted for a lot in people's assessment of their life satisfaction. And in some matters, ignorance could be bliss: The lack of media coverage of problems such as abuse or incest was terribly hard on the casualties, but it protected more fortunate families from knowledge and fear of many social ills.

There was tremendous hostility to people who could be defined as "others": Jews, African Americans, Puerto Ricans, the poor, gays or lesbians, and "the red menace." Yet on a day-to-day basis, the civility that prevailed in homogeneous neighborhoods allowed people to ignore larger patterns of racial and political repression. Racial clashes were ever-present in the 1950s, sometimes escalating into full-scale antiblack riots, but individual homicide rates fell to almost half the levels of the 1930s. As nuclear families moved into the suburbs, they retreated from social activism but entered voluntary relationships with people who had children the same age; they became involved in PTAs together, joined bridge clubs, went bowling. There does seem to have been a stronger sense of neighborly commonalities than many of us feel today. Even though this local community was often the product of exclusion or repression, it sometimes looks attractive to modern Americans whose commutes are getting longer and whose family or work patterns give them little in common with their neighbors.

The optimism that allowed many families to rise above their internal difficulties and to put limits on their individualistic values during the 1950s came from the sense that America was on a dramatically different trajectory than it had been in the past, an upward and expansionary path that had already taken people to better places than they had ever seen before and would certainly take their children even farther. This confidence that almost everyone could look forward to a better future stands in sharp contrast to how most contemporary Americans feel, and it explains why a period in which many people were much worse off than today sometimes still looks like a better period for families than our own.

Throughout the 1950s, poverty was higher than it is today, but it was less concentrated in pockets of blight existing side-by-side with extremes of wealth, and, unlike today, it was falling rather than rising. At the end of the 1930s, almost two-thirds of the population had incomes below the poverty standards of the day, while only one in eight had a middle-class income (defined as two to five times the poverty line). By 1960, a majority of the population had climbed into the middle-income range.

Unmarried people were hardly sexually abstinent in the 1950s, but the age of first intercourse was somewhat higher than it is now, and despite a tripling of nonmarital birth rates between 1940 and 1958, more than 70 percent of nonmarital pregnancies led to weddings before the child was born. Teenage birth rates were almost twice as high in 1957 as in the 1990s, but most teen births were to married couples, and the effect of teen pregnancy in reducing further schooling for young people did not hurt their life prospects the way it does today. High school graduation rates were lower in the 1950s than they are today, and minority students had far worse test scores, but there were jobs for people who dropped out of high school or graduated without good reading skills— jobs that actually had a future. People entering the job market in the 1950s had no way of knowing that they would be the last generation to have a good shot at reaching middle-class status without the benefit of postsecondary schooling.

Millions of men from impoverished, rural, unemployed, or poorly educated family backgrounds found steady jobs in the steel, auto, appliance, construction, and shipping industries. Lower middle-class men went further on in college during the 1950s than they would have been able to expect in earlier decades, enabling them to make the transition to secure white-collar work. The experience of shared sacrifices in the depression and war, reinforced by a New Deal–inspired belief in the ability of government to make life better, gave people a sense of hope for the future. Confidence in government, business, education, and other institutions was on the rise. This general optimism affected people's experience and assessment of family life. It is no wonder modern Americans yearn for a similar sense of hope.

But before we sign on to any attempts to turn the family clock back to the 1950s, we should note that the family successes and community solidarities of the 1950s rested on a totally different set of political and economic conditions than we have today. Contrary to widespread belief, the 1950s was not an age of laissez-faire government and free market competition. A major cause of the social mobility of young families in the 1950s was that federal assistance programs were much more generous and widespread than they are today.

In the most ambitious and successful affirmative action program ever adopted in America, 40 percent of young men were eligible for veterans' benefits, and these benefits were far more extensive than those available to Vietnam-era vets. Financed in part by a federal income tax on the rich that went up to 87 percent and a corporate tax rate of 52 percent, such benefits provided quite a jump start for a generation of young families. The GI bill paid most tuition costs for vets who attended college, doubling the percentage of college students from prewar levels. At the other end of the life span, Social Security began to build up a significant safety net for the elderly, formerly the poorest segment of the population. Starting in 1950, the federal government regularly mandated raises in the minimum wage to keep pace with inflation. The minimum wage may have been only $1.40 as late as 1968, but a person who worked for that amount full-time, year-round, earned 118 percent of the poverty figure for a family of three. By 1995, a full-time minimum-wage worker could earn only 72 percent of the poverty level.

An important source of the economic expansion of the 1950s was that public works spending at all levels of government comprised nearly 20 percent of total expenditures in 1950s as compared to less than 7 percent in 1984. Between 1950 and 1960, nonmilitary, nonresidential public construction rose by 58 percent. Construction expenditures for new schools (in dollar amounts adjusted for inflation) rose by 72 percent; funding on sewers and waterworks rose by 46 percent. Government paid 90 percent of the costs of building the new Interstate Highway system. These programs opened up suburbia to growing numbers of middle-class Americans and created secure, well-paying jobs for blue-collar workers.

Government also reorganized home financing, underwriting low down payments and long-term mortgages that had been rejected as bad business by private industry. To do this, government put public assets behind housing lending programs, created two new national financial institutions to facilitate home loans, allowed veterans to put down payments as low as a dollar on a house, and offered tax breaks to people who bought homes. The National Education Defense Act funded the socioeconomic mobility of thousands of young men who trained themselves for well-paying jobs in such fields as engineering.

Unlike contemporary welfare programs, government investment in 1950s families was not just for immediate subsistence but encouraged long-term asset development, rewarding people for increasing their investment in homes and education. Thus it was far less likely that such families or individuals would ever fall back to where they started, even after a string of bad luck. Subsidies for higher education were greater the longer people stayed in school and the more expensive the school they selected. Mortgage deductions got bigger as people traded up to better houses.

These social and political support systems magnified the impact of the postwar economic boom. "In the years between 1947 and 1973," reports economist Robert Kuttner, "the median paycheck more than doubled, and the bottom 20 percent enjoyed the greatest gains." High rates of unionization meant that blue-collar workers were making much more financial progress than most of their counterparts today. In 1952, when eager home buyers flocked to the opening of Levittown, Pennsylvania, the largest planned community yet constructed, "it took a factory worker one day to earn enough money to pay the closing costs on a new Levittown house, then selling for $10,000." By 1991, such a home was selling for $100,000 or more, and it took a factory worker *eighteen weeks* to earn enough money for just the closing costs.

The legacy of the union struggle of the 1930s and 1950s, combined with government support for raising people's living standards, set limits on corporations that have disappeared in recent decades. Corporations paid 23 percent of federal income taxes in the 1950s as compared to just 9.2 percent in 1991. Big companies earned higher profit margins than smaller firms, partly due to their dominance of the market, partly to America's postwar economic advantage. They chose (or were forced) to share these extra earnings, which economists call "rents," with employees. Economists at the Brookings Institution and Harvard University estimate that 70 percent of such corporate rents were passed on to workers at all levels of the firm, benefiting secretaries and janitors as well as CEOs. Corporations routinely retained workers even in slack periods, as a way of ensuring workplace stability. Although they often received more generous tax breaks from communities than they gave back in investment, at least they kept their plants and employment offices in the same place. AT&T, for example, received much of the technology it used to finance its postwar expansion from publicly funded communications research conducted as part of the war effort, and, as current AT&T chairman Robert Allen puts it, there "used to be a lifelong commitment on the employee's part and on our part." Today, however, he admits, "the contract doesn't exist anymore."

Television trivia experts still argue over exactly what the fathers in many 1950s sitcoms did for a living. Whatever it was, though, they obviously didn't have to worry about downsizing. If most married people stayed in long-term relationships during the 1950s, so did most corporations, sticking with the communities they grew up in and the employees they originally hired. Corporations were not constantly relocating in search of cheap labor during the 1950s; unlike today, increases in worker productivity usually led to increases in wages. The number of workers covered by corporate pension plans and health benefits increased steadily. So did limits on the work week. There is good reason that people look back to the 1950s as a less hurried age: The average American was working a shorter workday in the 1950s than his or her counterpart today, when a quarter of the work-force puts in 49 or more hours a week.

So politicians are practicing quite a double standard when they tell us to return to the family forms of the 1950s, while they do nothing to resolve the job programs and family subsidies of that era, the limits on corporate relocation and financial wheeling-dealing, the much higher share of taxes paid by corporations then, the availability of union jobs for noncollege youth, and the subsidies for higher education such as the National Defense Education Act loans. Furthermore, they're not telling the whole story when they claim that the 1950s was the most prosperous time for families and the most secure decade for children. Instead, playing to our understandable nostalgia for a time when things seemed to be getting better, not worse, they engage in a tricky chronological shell game with their figures, diverting our attention from two important points. First, many individuals, families, and groups were excluded from the economic prosperity, family optimism, and social civility of the 1950s. Second, the all-time high point of child well-being and family economic security came not during the 1950s but *at the end of the 1960s*.

2 Public Debates and Private Lives

The Mommy Wars: Ambivalence, Ideological Work, and the Cultural Contradictions of Motherhood

Sharon Hays

I have argued that all mothers ultimately share a recognition of the ideology of intensive mothering. At the same time, all mothers live in a society where child rearing is generally devalued and the primary emphasis is placed on profit, efficiency, and "getting ahead." If you are a mother, both logics operate in your daily life.

But the story is even more complicated. Over half of American mothers participate directly in the labor market on a regular basis; the rest remain at least somewhat distant from that world as they spend most of their days in the home. One might therefore expect paid working mothers to be more committed to the ideology of competitively maximizing personal profit and stay-at-home mothers to be more committed to the ideology of intensive mothering. As it turns out, however, this is not precisely the way it works.

Modern-day mothers are facing two socially constructed cultural images of what a good mother looks like. Neither, however, includes the vision of a cold, calculating businesswoman—that title is reserved for childless career women. If you are a good mother, you *must* be an intensive one. The only "choice" involved is whether you *add* the role of paid working woman. The options, then, are as follows. On the one side there is the portrait of the "traditional mother" who stays at home with the kids and dedicates her energy to the happiness of her family. This mother cheerfully studies the latest issue of *Family Circle*, places flowers in every room, and has dinner waiting when her husband comes home. This mother, when she's not cleaning, cooking, sewing, shopping, doing the laundry, or comforting her mate, is focused on attending to the children and ensuring their proper development. On the other side is the image of the successful "supermom." Effortlessly juggling home and work, this mother can push a stroller with one hand and carry a briefcase in the other. She is always properly coiffed, her nylons have no runs, her suits are freshly pressed, and her home has seen the white tornado. Her children are immaculate and well mannered but not passive, with a strong spirit and high self-esteem.

Although both the traditional mom and the supermom are generally considered socially acceptable, their coexistence represents a serious cultural ambivalence about how mothers should behave. This ambivalence comes out in the widely available indictments of the failings of both groups of women. Note, for instance, the way Mecca, a welfare mother, describes these two choices and their culturally provided critiques:

> The way my family was brought up was, like, you marry a man, he's the head of the house, he's the provider, and you're the wife, you're the provider in the house. Now these days it's not that way. Now the people that stay home are classified, quote, "lazy people," we don't "like" to work.
>
> I've seen a lot of things on TV about working mothers and nonworking mothers. People who stay home attack the other mothers 'cause they're, like, bad mothers because they left the kids behind and go to work. And, the other ones aren't working because we're lazy. But it's not lazy. It's the lifestyle in the 1990s it's, like, too much. It's a demanding world for mothers with kids.

The picture Mecca has seen on television, a picture of these two images attacking each other with ideological swords, is not an uncommon one.

It is this cultural ambivalence and the so-called choice between these paths that is the basis for what Darnton (1990) has dubbed the "mommy wars." Both stay-at-home and paid working mothers, it is argued, are angry and defensive; neither group respects the other. Both make use of available cultural indictments to condemn the opposing group. Supermoms, according to this portrait, regularly describe stay-at-home mothers as lazy and boring, while traditional moms regularly accuse employed mothers of selfishly neglecting their children.

My interviews suggest, however, that this portrait of the mommy wars is both exaggerated and superficial. In fact, the majority of mothers I spoke with expressed respect for one another's need or right to choose whether to go out to work or stay at home with the kids. And, as I have argued, they also share a whole set of similar concerns regarding appropriate child rearing. These mothers have not formally enlisted in this war. Yet the rhetoric of the mommy wars draws them in as it persists in mainstream American culture, a culture that is unwilling, for various significant reasons, to unequivocally embrace either vision of motherhood, just as it remains unwilling to embrace wholeheartedly the childless career woman. Thus, the charges of being lazy and bored, on the one hand, or selfish and money-grubbing, on the other, are made available for use by individual mothers and others should the need arise.

What this creates is a no-win situation for women of child-bearing years. If a woman voluntarily remains childless, some will say that she is cold, heartless, and unfulfilled as a woman. If she is a mother who works too hard at her job or career, some will accuse her of neglecting the kids. If she does not work hard enough, some will surely place her on the "mommy track" and her career advancement will be permanently slowed by the claim that her commitment to her children interferes with her workplace efficiency (Schwartz 1989). And if she stays at home with her children, some will call her unproductive and useless. A woman, in other words, can never fully do it right.

At the same time that these cultural images portray all women as somehow less than adequate, they also lead many mothers to feel somehow less than adequate in their daily lives. The stay-at-home mother is supposed to be happy and fulfilled, but how can she be when she hears so often that she is mindless and bored? The supermom is supposed to be able to juggle her two roles without missing a beat, but how can she do either job as well as she is expected if she is told she must dedicate her all in both directions? In these circumstances, it is not surprising that many supermoms feel guilty about their inability to carry out both roles to their fullest, while many traditional moms feel isolated and invisible to the larger world.

Given this scenario, both stay-at-home and employed mothers end up spending a good deal of time attempting to make sense of their current positions. Paid working mothers, for instance, are likely to argue that there are lots of good reasons for mothers to work in the paid labor force; stay-at-home mothers are likely to argue that there are lots of good reasons for mothers to stay at home with their children. These arguments are best understood not as (mere) rationalizations or (absolute) truths but rather as socially necessary "ideological work." Berger (1981a) uses this notion to describe the way that all people make use of available ideologies in their "attempt to cope with the relationship between the ideas they bring to a social context and the practical pressures of day-to-day living in it" (15). People, in other words, select among the cultural logics at their disposal in order to develop some correspondence between what they believe and what they actually do. For mothers, just like others, ideological work is simply a means of maintaining their sanity.

The ideological work of mothers, as I will show, follows neither a simple nor a straightforward course. First, as I have pointed out, both groups face two contradictory cultural images of appropriate mothering. Their ideological work, then, includes a recognition and response to both portraits. This duality is evident in the fact that the logic the traditional mother uses to affirm her position matches the logic that the supermom uses to express ambivalence about her situation, and the logic that the employed mother uses to affirm her position is the same logic that the stay-at-home mother uses to express ambivalence about hers. Their strategies, in other words, are mirror images, but they are also incomplete—both groups are left with some ambivalence. Thus, although the two culturally provided images of mothering help mothers to make sense of their own positions, they simultaneously sap the strength of mothers by making them feel inadequate in one way or the other. It is in coping with these feelings of inadequacy that their respective ideological strategies take an interesting turn. Rather than taking divergent paths, as one might expect, both groups attempt to resolve their feelings of inadequacy by returning to the logic of the ideology of intensive mothering.

THE FRUMPY HOUSEWIFE AND THE PUSH TOWARD THE OUTSIDE WORLD

Some employed mothers say that they go out to work for pay because they need the income. But the overwhelming majority also say that they *want* to work outside the home. First, there's the problem of staying inside all day: "I decided once I started working that I need that. I need to work. Because I'll become like this big huge hermit frumpy person if I stay home." Turning into a "big huge hermit frumpy person" is connected to the feeling of being confined to the home. Many women have had that experience at one time or another and do not want to repeat it:

> When I did stay home with him, up until the time when he was ten months old, I wouldn't go out of the house for three days at a time. Ya know, I get to where I don't want to get dressed, I don't care if I take a shower. It's like, what for? I'm not going anywhere.

Not getting dressed and not going anywhere are also tied to the problem of not having a chance to interact with other adults:

> I remember thinking, "I don't even get out of my robe. And I've gotta stay home and breast-feed and the only adult I hear is on *Good Morning America*—and he's not even live!" And that was just for a couple of months. I don't even know what it would be like for a couple of years. I think it would be really difficult.

Interacting with adults, for many paid working mothers, means getting a break from the world of children and having an opportunity to use their minds:

> When I first started looking for a job, I thought we needed a second income. But then when I started working it was like, this is great! I do have a mind that's not *Sesame Street!* And I just love talking with people. It's just fun, and it's a break. It's tough, but I enjoyed it; it was a break from being with the kids.

If you don't get a break from the kids, if you don't get out of the house, if you don't interact with adults, and if you don't have a chance to use your mind beyond the *Sesame Street* level, you might end up lacking the motivation to do much at all. This argument is implied by many mothers:

> If I was stuck at home all day, and I did do that 'cause I was waiting for day care, I stayed home for four months, and I went crazy, I couldn't stand it. I mean not because I didn't want to spend any time with her, but because we'd just sit here and she'd just cry all day and I couldn't get anything done. I was at the end of the day exhausted, and feeling like shit.

Of course, it is exhausting to spend the day meeting the demands of children. But there's also a not too deeply buried sense in all these arguments that getting outside the home and using one's mind fulfill a longing to be part of the larger world and to be recognized by it. One mother made this point explicitly:

> [When you're working outside the home] you're doing something. You're using your mind a little bit differently than just trying to figure out how to make your day work with your kid. It's just challenging in a different way. So there's part of me that wants to be, like, *recognized*. I think maybe that's what work does, it gives you a little bit of a sense of recognition, that you don't feel like you get [when you stay home].

Most employed mothers, then, say that if they stay at home they'll go stir-crazy, they'll get bored, the demands of the kids will drive them nuts, they won't have an opportunity to use their brains or interact with other adults, they'll feel like they're going nowhere, and they'll lose their sense of identity in the larger world. And, for many of these mothers, all these points are connected:

> Well, I think [working outside is] positive, because I feel good about being able to do the things that I went to school for, and keep up with that, and use my brain. As they grow older, [the children are] going to get into things that they want to get into, they're going to be out with their friends and stuff, and I don't want to be in a situation where my whole life has been wrapped around the kids. That's it. Just some outside interests so that I'm not so wrapped up in how shiny my floor is. [She laughs.] Just to kind of be out and be stimulated. Gosh, I don't want this to get taken wrong, but I think I'd be a little bit bored. And the other thing I think of is, I kind of need a break, and when you're staying at home it's constant. It's a lot harder when you don't have family close by, [because] you don't get a break.

In short, paid working mothers feel a strong pull toward the outside world. They hear the world accusing stay-at-home moms of being mindless and unproductive and of lacking an identity apart from their kids, and they experience this as at least partially true.

Stay-at-home mothers also worry that the world will perceive them as lazy and bored and watching television all day as children scream in their ears and tug at their sleeves. And sometimes this is the way they feel about themselves. In other words, the same image that provides working mothers with the reasons they should go out to work accounts for the ambivalence that stay-at-home mothers feel about staying at home.

A few stay-at-home mothers seem to feel absolutely secure in their position, but most do not. Many believe that they will seek paid work at some point, and almost all are made uncomfortable by the sense that the outside world does not value what they do. In all cases, their expressions of ambivalence about staying at home mimic the concerns of employed mothers. For instance, some women who stay at home also worry about becoming frumpy: "I'm not this heavy. I'm, like, twenty-seven pounds overweight. It sounds very vain of me, in my situation. It's like, I'm not used to being home all the time, I'm home twenty-four hours. I don't have that balance in my life anymore." And some stay-at-home mothers feel as if they are physically confined inside the home. This mother, for example, seems tired of meeting the children's demands and feels that she is losing her sense of self:

> There's a hard thing of being at home all the time. You have a lot of stress, because you're constantly in the house. I think having a job can relieve some of that stress and to make it a lot more enjoyable, to want to come home all the time. . . . My outings are [limited]. I'm excited when I have to go grocery shopping. Everything I pick is what they eat, everything they like, or what they should eat. Me, I'm just *there*. I'm there for them. I feel that I'm here for them.

Both of these stay-at-home mothers, like over one-third of the stay-at-home mothers in my sample, plan to go out to work as soon as they can find paid employment that offers sufficient rewards to compensate (both financially and ideologically) for sending the kids to day care. Most of the remaining mothers are committed to staying at home with the children through what they understand as formative years. The following mother shares that commitment, while also echoing many paid working mothers in her hopes that one day she will have a chance to be around adults and further her own growth:

Well, we could do more, we'd have more money, but that's really not the biggest reason I'd go back to work. I want to do things for myself, too. I want to go back and get my master's [degree] or something. I need to grow, and be around adults, too. I don't know when, but I think in the next two years I'll go back to work. The formative years—their personality is going to develop until they're about five. It's pretty much set by then. So I think it's pretty critical that you're around them during those times.

One mother stated explicitly that she can hardly wait until the kids are through their formative years:

At least talking to grown-ups is a little more fulfilling than ordering the kids around all day. My life right now is just all theirs. Sometimes it's a depressing thought because I think, "Where am I? I want my life back." . . . I mean, they are totally selfish. It's like an ice cream. They just gobble that down and say, "Let me have the cinnamon roll now."
. . . [But] I had them, and I want them to be good people. So I've dedicated myself to them right now. Later on I get my life back. They won't always be these little sponges. I don't want any deficiency—well, nobody can cover all the loopholes—but I want to be comfortable in myself to know that I did everything that I could. It's the least I can do to do the best I can by them.

Mothers, she seems to be saying, are like confections that the kids just gobble down—and then they ask for more.

Thus, many stay-at-home moms experience the exhaustion of meeting the demands of children all day long, just as employed mothers fear they might. And many stay-at-home mothers also experience a loss of self. Part of the reason they feel like they are losing their identity is that they know the outside world does not recognize a mother's work as valuable. This woman, committed to staying at home until her youngest is at least three years old, explains:

You go through a period where you feel like you've lost all your marbles. Boy, you're not as smart as you used to be, and as sharp as you used to be, and not as respected as you used to be. And those things are really hard to swallow. But that's something I've discussed with other mothers who are willing to stay home with their kids, and we've formed a support group where we've said, "Boy, those people just don't know what they're talking about." We're like a support group for each other, which you have to have if you've decided to stay at home, because you have so many people almost pushing you to work, or asking "Why don't you work?" You're not somehow as good as anybody else 'cause you're staying at home; what you're doing isn't important. We have a lot of that in this society.

Another mother, this one determined to stay at home with her kids over the long haul, provides a concrete example of the subtle and not-so-subtle ways in which society pushes mothers to participate in the paid labor force, and of the discomfort such mothers experience as a result:

As a matter of fact, somebody said to me (I guess it was a principal from one of the schools) . . . "Well, what do you *do*? Do you have a *job*?" And it was just very funny to me that he was so uncomfortable trying to ask me what it was in our society that I did. I guess that they just assume that if you're a mom at home that it means nothing. I don't know, I just don't consider it that way. But it's kind of funny, worrying about what you're gonna say at a dinner party about what you do.

And it's not just that these mothers worry about being able to impress school principals and people at cocktail parties, of course. The following mother worries about being "interesting" to other women who do not have children:

> I find myself, now that I'm not working, not to have as much in common [with other women who don't have children]. We don't talk that much because I don't have that much to talk about. Like I feel I'm not an interesting person anymore.

In short, the world presents, and mothers experience, the image of the lazy mindless, dull housewife—and no mother wants to be included in that image.

THE TIME-CRUNCHED CAREER WOMAN AND THE PULL TOWARD HOME

Stay-at-home mothers use a number of strategies to support their position and combat the image of the frumpy housewife. Many moms who are committed to staying at home with their kids often become part of formal or informal support groups, providing them an opportunity to interact with other mothers who have made the same commitment. Others, if they can afford the cost of transportation and child care, engage in a variety of outside activities—as volunteers for churches, temples, and community groups, for instance, or in regular leisure activities and exercise programs. They then have a chance to communicate with other adults and to experience themselves as part of a larger social world (though one in which children generally occupy a central role).

But the primary way that stay-at-home mothers cope with their ambivalence is through ideological work. Like paid working mothers, they make a list of all the good reasons they do what they do. In this case, that list includes confirming their commitment to good mothering, emphasizing the importance of putting their children's needs ahead of their own, and telling stories about the problems that families, and especially children, experience when mothers go out to work for pay.

Many stay-at-home mothers argue that kids require guidance and should have those cookies cooling on the kitchen counter when they come home from school:

> The kids are the ones that suffer. The kids need guidance and stuff. And with two parents working, sometimes there isn't even a parent home when they come home from school. And that's one thing that got me too. I want to be home and I want to have cookies on the stove when they come home from school. Now we eat meals together all the time. It's more of a homey atmosphere. It's more of a *home* atmosphere.

Providing this homey atmosphere is difficult to do if one works elsewhere all day. And providing some period of so-called quality time in the evening, these mothers tell me, is not an adequate substitute. One mother elaborates on this point in response to a question about how she would feel if she was working outside the home:

> Oh, guilty as anything. I know what I'm like after dinner, and I'm not at my best. And nei-
> ther are my kids. And if that's all the time I had with them, it wouldn't be, quote, "qual-
> ity time." I think it's a bunch of b.s. about quality time.

And quality time, even if it *is* of high quality, cannot make up for children's lack of a quantity of time with their mothers. This argument is often voiced in connection with the
problem of paid caregiver arrangements. Most mothers, whether they work for pay or
not, are concerned about the quality of day care, but stay-at-home mothers often use this
concern to explain their commitment to staying at home. This mother, for example, argues that children who are shuffled off to a series of day-care providers simply will not
get the love they need:

> I mean, if I'm going to have children I want to *raise* them. I feel really strongly about that.
> Really strongly. I wish more people did that. Myself, I think it's very underestimated the
> role the mother plays with the child. I really do. From zero to three [years], it's like their
> whole self-image. [Yet, working mothers will say,] "Well, okay, I've got a caretaker now,"
> "Well, that nanny didn't work out." So by the time the children are three years old they've
> had four or five people who have supposedly said "I'll love you forever," and they're gone.
> I think that's really tough on the kids.

Since paid caregivers lack that deep and long-lasting love, I'm told, they won't ever be as
committed to ministering to the child's needs as a mom will:

> I don't think anybody can give to children what a mother can give to her own children. I
> think there's a level of willingness to put up with hard days, crying days, cranky days, whin-
> ing days, that most mothers are going to be able to tolerate just a little bit more than a
> caretaker would. I think there's more of a commitment of what a mother wants to give her
> children in terms of love, support, values, etcetera. A caretaker isn't going to feel quite the
> same way.

Stay-at-home mothers imply that all these problems of kids who lack guidance,
love, and support are connected to the problem of mothers who put their own interests
ahead of the interests of their children. A few stay-at-home mothers will explicitly argue,
as this one does, that employed mothers are allowing material and power interests to take
priority over the well-being of their kids:

> People are too interested in power, they just aren't interested in what happens to their
> kids. You know, "Fine, put them in day care." And I just feel sad. If you're so interested in
> money or a career or whatever, then why have kids? Why bring them into it?

Putting such interests ahead of one's children is not only somehow immoral; it also produces children with real problems. The following mother, echoing many stories about
"bad mothers" that we have heard before, had this to say about her sister:

> My sister works full-time—she's a lawyer. And her kids are the most obnoxious, whiny
> kids. I can't stand it. They just hang on her. She thinks she's doing okay by them because
> they're in an expensive private school and they have expensive music lessons and they have

expensive clothes and expensive toys and expensive cars and an expensive house. I don't know. Time will tell, I guess. But I can't believe they're not going to have some insecurities. The thing that gets me is, they don't need it. I mean, he's a lawyer too. Basically, it's like, "Well, I like you guys, but I don't really want to be there all day with you, and I don't want to have to do the dirty work."

These are serious indictments indeed.

It is just these sorts of concerns that leave paid working mothers feeling inadequate and ambivalent about *their* position. Many of them wonder at times if their lives or the lives of their children might actually be better if they stayed at home with the kids. Above all, many of them feel guilty and wonder, "Am I doing it right?" or "Have I done all I can do?" These are the mothers who, we're told, have it all. It is impossible to have it all, however, when "all" includes two contradictory sets of requirements. To begin to get a deeper sense of how these supermoms do not always feel so super, two examples might be helpful.

Angela is a working-class mother who had expected to stay home with her son through his formative years. But after nine months she found herself bored, lonely, and eager to interact with other adults. She therefore went out and got a full-time job as a cashier. She begins by expressing her concern that she is not living up to the homemaking suggestions she reads in *Parenting* magazine, worrying that she may not be doing it right:

> I get *Parenting* magazine and I read it. I do what is comfortable for me and what I can do. I'm not very creative. Where they have all these cooking ideas, and who has time to do that, except for a mother who stays home all day? Most of this is for a mother who has five, six hours to spend with her child doing this kind of thing. I don't have time for that.
>
> So then that's when I go back to day care. And I know that she's doing this kind of stuff with him, teaching him things. You know, a lot of the stuff that they have is on schooling kinds of things, flash cards, that kind of thing. Just things that I don't do. That makes me feel bad. Then I think, "I should be doing this" and "Am I doing the right thing?" I know I have a lot of love for him.

Although she loves her son and believes that this is probably "the most important thing," she also feels guilty that she may not be spending a sufficient amount of time with him, simply because she gets so tired:

> I think sometimes that I feel like I don't spend enough time with him and that's my biggest [concern]. And when I am with him, sometimes I'm not really up to being with him. Even though I am with him, sometimes I want him to go away because I've been working all day and I'm exhausted. And I feel sometimes I'll stick him in bed early because I just don't want to deal with him that day. And I feel really guilty because I don't spend enough time with him as it is. When I do have the chance to spend time with him, I don't want to spend time with him, because I'm so tired and I just want to be with myself and by myself.

Even though Angela likes her paid work and does not want to give it up, the problems of providing both a quantity of time and the idealized image of quality time with her child, just like the challenge of applying the creative cooking and child-rearing ideas she finds in *Parenting* magazine, haunt her and leave her feeling both inadequate and guilty.

Linda is a professional-class mother with a well-paying and challenging job that gives her a lot of satisfaction. She spent months searching for the right preschool for her son and is relieved that he is now in a place where the caregivers share her values. Still, she worries and wonders if life might be better if she had made different choices:

> I have a friend. She's a very good mom. She seems very patient, and I never heard her raise her voice. And she's also not working. She gets to stay home with her children, which is another thing I admire. I guess I sort of envy that too. There never seems to be a time where we can just spend, like, playing a lot. I think that's what really bothers me, that I don't feel like I have the time to just sit down and, in a relaxing way, play with him. I can do it, but then I'm thinking "Okay, well I can do this for five minutes." So that's always in the back of my mind. Time, time, time. So I guess that's the biggest thing.
>
> And just like your question, "How many hours a day is he at preschool and how many hours do you spend per day as the primary caregiver?" just made me think, "Oh my gosh!" I mean they're watching him grow up more than I am. They're with him more than I am. And that makes me feel guilty in a way, and it makes me feel sad in a way. I mean I can just see him, slipping, just growing up before me. Maybe it's that quality-time stuff. I don't spend a lot of time, and I don't know if the time I do spend with him is quality.
>
> [But] if I just stay at home, I'll kind of lose, I don't know if I want to say my sense of identity, but I guess I'll lose my career identity. I'm afraid of that I guess. . . . My friend who stays at home, she had a career before she had her children, but I forget what it was. So that whole part of her, I can't even identify it now.

On the one hand, Linda envies and admires stay-at-home moms and worries about not spending enough quality time with her son, or enough play time. She is also upset that her day-care provider spends more hours with her son each day than she can. On the other hand, Linda worries that if she did stay at home she'd lose her identity as a professional and a member of the larger society. "Time, time, time," she says, there's never enough time to do it all—or at least to do it all "right."

The issue of time is a primary source of paid working mothers' ambivalence about their double shift. Attempting to juggle two commitments at once is, of course, very difficult and stressful. This mother's sense of how time pressures make her feel that she is always moving too fast would be recognizable to the majority of paid working mothers:

> I can see when I get together with my sister [who doesn't have a paid job] . . . that she's so easygoing with the kids, and she takes her time, and when I'm with her, I realize how stressed out I am sometimes trying to get things done.
>
> And I notice how much faster I move when I shop. . . . She's so relaxed, and I think I kind of envy that.

The problem of moving too fast when shopping is connected to the problem of moving too fast when raising children. Many paid working mothers envy those who can do such things at a more relaxed pace.

For a few employed mothers (two out of twenty in my sample) the problems of quality and quantity time outweigh the rewards of paid work, and they intend to leave their jobs as soon as they can afford to do so. This woman is one example:

> I believe there's a more cohesive family unit with maybe the mother staying at home. Because a woman tends to be a buffer, mediator, you name it. She pulls the family together.

But if she's working outside the home, sometimes there's not that opportunity anymore for her to pull everyone together. She's just as tired as the husband would be and, I don't know, maybe the children are feeling like they've been not necessarily abandoned but, well, I'm sure they accept it, especially if that's the only life they've seen. But my daughter has seen a change, even when I was only on maternity leave. I've seen a change in her and she seemed to just enjoy it and appreciate us as a family more than when I was working. So now she keeps telling me, "Mom, I miss you."

When this mother hears her daughter say "I miss you," she feels a tremendous pull toward staying at home. And when she talks about the way a family needs a mother to bring its members together, she is pointing to an idealized image of the family that, like quality and quantity time, weighs heavily in the minds of many mothers.

The following paid working mother also wishes she could stay at home with the kids and wishes she could be just like the television mom of the 1950s who bakes cookies every afternoon. But she knows she has to continue working for financial seasons:

> Yes. I want to be Donna Reed, definitely. Or maybe Beaver Cleaver's mother, Jane Wyatt. Anybody in an apron and a pretty hairdo and a beautiful house. Yes. Getting out of the television set and making the most of reality is really what I have to do. Because I'll always have to work.

But the majority of paid working mothers, as I have stated, not only feel they need to work for financial reasons but also *want* to work, as Angela and Linda do. Nonetheless, their concerns about the effects of the double shift on their children match the concerns of those employed moms who wish they could stay at home as well as mimicking those of mothers who actually do stay at home. This mother, for instance, loves her paid work and does not want to give it up, but she does feel guilty, wondering if she's depriving her kids of the love and stimulation they need, particularly since she does not earn enough to justify the time she spends away:

> Honestly, I don't make that much money. So that in itself brings a little bit of guilt, 'cause I know I work even though we don't have to. So there's some guilt associated. If kids are coming home to an empty house every day, they're not getting the intellectual stimulation [and] they're not getting the love and nurturing that other mothers are able to give their kids. So I think in the long run they're missing out on a lot of the love and the nurturing and the caring.

And this mother does not want it to seem that she is putting her child second, but she feels pressure to live up to the image of a supermom:

> I felt really torn between what I wanted to do. Like a gut-wrenching decision. Like, what's more important? Of course your kids are important, but you know, there's so many outside pressures for women to work. Every ad you see in magazines or on television shows this working woman who's coming home with a briefcase and the kids are all dressed and clean. It's such a lie. I don't know of anybody who lives like that.
>
> There's just a lot of pressure that you're not a fulfilled woman if you're not working outside of the home. But yet, it's just a real hard choice.

This feeling of being torn by a gut-wrenching decision comes up frequently:

> I'm constantly torn between what I feel I should be doing in my work and spending more time with them. . . . I think I would spend more time with them if I could. Sometimes I think it would be great not to work and be a mom and do that, and then I think, "well?"
>
> I think it's hard. Because I think you do need to have contact with your kid. You can't just see him in the morning and put him to bed at night because you work all day long. I think that's a real problem. You need to give your child guidance. You can't leave it to the schools. You can't leave it to churches. You need to be there. So, in some ways I'm really torn.

The overriding issue for this mother is guidance; seeing the children in the morning and putting them to bed at night is just not enough.

This problem, of course, is related to the problem of leaving kids with a paid caregiver all day. Paid working mothers do not like the idea of hearing their children cry when they leave them at day care any more than any other mother does. They are, as we have seen, just as concerned that their children will not get enough love, enough nurturing, enough of the right values, enough of the proper education, and enough of the right kind of discipline if they spend most of their time with a paid caregiver. To this list of concerns, paid working mothers add their feeling that when the kids are with a paid caregiver all day, it feels as if someone else is being the mother. One woman (who stayed at home until her son was two years old) elaborates:

> Well, I think it's really sad that kids have to be at day care forty hours a week. Because basically the person who's taking care of them is your day-care person. They're pretty much being the mother. It's really sad that this other person is raising your child, and it's basically like having this other person *adopting* your child. It's *awful* that we have to do that. I just think it's a crime basically. I wish we didn't have to do it. I wish everybody could stay home with their kids and have some kind of outlet. . . .
>
> And I think having a career is really important, but I think when it comes time to have children, you can take that time off and spend it with your kid. Because you can't go backwards, and time does fly with them. It's so sad . . . I hear people say, "Oh, my day-care lady said that so-and-so walked today or used a spoon or something." I mean it's just so devastating to hear that you didn't get to see that.

Leaving one's child with a paid caregiver for hours on end is therefore a potential problem not only because that "other mother" may not be a good mother but also because the real mother misses out on the joys that come from just being with the child and having a chance to watch him or her grow. This is a heart rending issue for many mothers who work outside the home.

Once again, the arguments used by stay-at-home mothers to affirm their commitment to staying home are mimicked by the arguments paid working mothers use to express their ambivalence about the time they spend away from their children. And again, though the reasoning of these women is grounded in their experiences, it is also drawn from a widely available cultural rhetoric regarding the proper behavior of mothers.

THE CURIOUS COINCIDENCE OF PAID WORK AND THE IDEOLOGY OF INTENSIVE MOTHERING

Both paid working moms and stay-at-home moms, then, do the ideological work of making their respective lists of the reasons they should work for pay and the reasons they should stay at home. Yet both groups also continue to experience and express some ambivalence about their current positions, feeling pushed and pulled in two directions. One would assume that they would cope with their ambivalence by simply returning to their list of good reasons for doing what they do. And stay-at-home mothers do just that: they respond to the push toward work in the paid labor force by arguing that their kids need them to be at home. But, as I will demonstrate, working mothers do not use the mirror strategy. The vast majority of these women do not respond to the pull toward staying at home by arguing that kids are a pain in the neck and that paid work is more enjoyable. Instead, they respond by creating a new list of all the reasons that they are good mothers even though they work outside the home. In other words, the ideological work meant to resolve mothers' ambivalence generally points in the direction of intensive mothering.

Most paid working mothers cope with the ambivalence by arguing that their participation in the labor force is ultimately good for their kids. They make this point in a number of ways. For instance, one mother thinks that the example she provides may help to teach her kids the work ethic. Another says that with the "outside constraints" imposed by her work schedule, she's "more organized and effective" as a mom. Yet another mother suggests that her second child takes just as much time and energy away from her first child as her career does:

> I think the only negative effect [of my employment] is just [that] generally when I'm over-stressed I don't do as well as a mother. But work is only one of the things that gets me overstressed. In fact it probably stresses me less than some other things. I think I do feel guilty about working 'cause it takes time away from [my oldest daughter]. But it struck me that it's acceptable to have a second child that takes just as much time away from the other child. *That* I'm not supposed to feel guilty about. But in some ways this [pointing to the infant she is holding] takes my time away from her more than my work does. Because this is constant.

More often, however, paid working mothers share a set of more standard explanations for why their labor-force participation is actually what's best for their kids. First, just as Rachel feels that her income provides for her daughter's toys, clothing, outings, and education, and just as Jacqueline argues, "I have weeks when I don't spend enough time with them and they suffer, but those are also the weeks I bring home the biggest paychecks," many mothers point out that their paid work provides the financial resources necessary for the well-being of their children:

> How am I supposed to send her to college without saving up? And also the money that I make from working helps pay for her toys, things that she needs, clothes. I never have to say, "Oh, I'm on a budget, I can't go buy this pair of shoes." I want the best for her.

Some mothers express a related concern—namely, what would happen to the family if they did not have paying jobs and their husbands should die or divorce them? One women expressed it this way:

> Well, my dad was a fireman, so I guess there was a little bit of fear, well, if anything happened to him, how are we gonna go on? And I always kind of wished that [my mother] had something to fall back on. I think that has a lot to do with why I continue to work after the kids. I've always just felt the need to have something to hold on to.

The second standard argument given by employed mothers is that paid caregiver arrangements can help to further children's development. With respect to other people's kids, I'm told, these arrangements can keep them from being smothered by their mothers or can temporarily remove them from bad family situations. With reference to their own children, mothers emphasize that good day care provides kids with the opportunity to interact with adults, gives them access to "new experiences" and "different activities," "encourages their independence," and allows them to play with other kids—which is very important, especially now that neighborhoods no longer provide the sort of community life they once did:

> They do say that kids in preschool these days are growing up a little more neurotic, but I don't think that my daughter would have had a better life. In fact I think her life would have been a thousand times worse if I was a low-income mother who stayed home and she only got to play with the kids at the park. Because I think that preschool is really good for them. Maybe not a holding tank, but a nice preschool where they play nice games with them and they have the opportunity to play with the same kids over and over again. I think that's really good for them. Back in the 1950s, everybody stayed home and there were kids all over the block to play with. It's not that way now. The neighborhoods are deserted during the week.

Third, several mothers tell me that the quality of the time they spend with their kids actually seems to increase when they have a chance to be away from them for a part of the day. Listen to these mothers:

> When I'm with them too long I tend to lose my patience and start yelling at them. This way we both get out. And we're glad to see each other when we come home.

> If women were only allowed to work maybe ten to fifteen hours a week, they would appreciate their kids more and they'd have more quality time with them, rather than having to always just scold them.

> I think I have even less patience [when I stay home with the children], because it's like, "Oh, is this all there is?" . . . Whereas when I go to work and come home, I'm glad to see him. You know, you hear people say that they're better parents when they work because they spend more quality time, all those clichés, or whatever. For me that happens to be true.

> And now when I come home from work (although I wish I could get off earlier from work), I think I'm a better mom. There you go! Because when I come home from work, I don't

have *all* day, just being with the kids. It's just that when I'm working I feel like I'm competent, I'm a person!

Getting this break from the kids, a break that reinforces your feeling of competence and therefore results in more rewarding time with your children is closely connected to the final way paid working mothers commonly attempt to resolve their ambivalence. Their children's happiness, they explain, is dependent upon their *own* happiness as mothers. One hears this again and again: "Happy moms make happy children"; "If I'm happy in my work then I think I can be a better mom"; and "I have to be happy with myself in order to make the children happy." One mother explains it this way:

> In some ways working is good. It's definitely got its positive side, because I get a break. I mean, now what I'm doing [working part-time] is perfect. I go to work. I have time to myself. I get to go to the bathroom when I need to go to the bathroom. I come home and I'm very happy to see my kids again. What's good for the mother and makes the mother happy is definitely good for the kids.

In all these explanations for why their participation in the paid labor force is actually good for their kids, these mothers want to make it clear that they still consider children their primary interest. They are definitely not placing a higher value on material success or power, they say. Nor are they putting their own interests above the interests of their children. They want the children to get all they need. But part of what children need, they argue, is financial security, the material goods required for proper development, some time away from their mothers, more quality time when they are with their mothers, and mothers who are happy in what they do. In all of these statements, paid working mothers clearly recognize the ideology of intensive mothering and testify that they are committed to fulfilling its requirements.

To underline the significance of this point, let me remind the reader that these paid working mothers use methods of child rearing that are just as child-centered, expert-guided, emotionally absorbing, labor-intensive, and financially expensive as their stay-at-home counterparts; they hold the child just as sacred, and they are just as likely to consider themselves as primarily responsible for the present and future well-being of their children. These are also the very same mothers who put a tremendous amount of time and energy into finding appropriate paid caregiver arrangements. Yet for all that they do to meet the needs of their children, they still express some ambivalence about working outside the home. And they still resolve this ambivalence by returning to the logic of intensive mothering and reminding the observer that ultimately they are most interested in what is best for their kids. This is striking.

CONTINUING CONTRADICTIONS

All this ideological work is a measure of the power of the pushes and pulls experienced by American mothers today. A woman can be a stay-at-home mother and claim to follow tradition, but not without paying the price of being treated as an outsider in the larger public world of the market. Or a woman can be a paid worker who participates in that larger world, but she must then pay the price of an impossible double shift. In both cases, women are enjoined to maintain the logic of intensive mothering. These contradictory pressures mimic the contradictory logics operating in this society, and almost all mothers experience them. The complex strategies mothers use to cope with these contradictory logics highlight the emotional, cognitive, and physical toll they take on contemporary mothers.

As I have argued, these strategies also highlight something more. The ways mothers explain their decisions to stay at home or work in the paid labor force, like the pushes and pulls they feel, run in opposite directions. Yet the ways they attempt to resolve the ambivalence they experience as a result of those decisions run in the *same* direction. Stay-at-home mothers, as I have shown, reaffirm their commitment to good mothering, and employed mothers maintain that they are good mothers even though they work. Paid working mothers do not, for instance, claim that child rearing is a relatively meaningless task, that personal profit is their primary goal, and that children are more efficiently raised in child-care centers. If you are a mother, in other words, although both the logic of the workplace and the logic of mothering operate in your life, the logic of intensive mothering has a *stronger* claim.

This phenomenon is particularly curious. The fact that there is no way for either type of mother to get it right would seem all the more reason to give up the logic of intensive mothering, especially since both groups of mothers recognize that paid employment confers more status than motherhood in the larger world. Yet images of freshly baked cookies and *Leave It to Beaver* seem to haunt mothers more often than the housewives' "problem that has no name" (Friedan 1963), and far more often than the image of a corporate manager with a big office, a large staff, and lots of perks. Although these mothers do not want to be defined as "mere" housewives and do want to achieve recognition in the outside world, most would also like to be there when the kids come home from school. Mothers surely try to balance their own desires against the requirements of appropriate child rearing, but in the world of mothering, it is socially unacceptable for them (in word if not in deed) to place their own needs above the needs of their children. A good mother certainly would never simply put her child aside for her own convenience. And placing material wealth or power on a higher plane than the well-being of children is strictly forbidden. It is clear that the two groups come together in holding these values as primary, despite the social devaluation of mothering and despite the glorification of wealth and power.

The portrait of the mommy wars, then, is overdrawn. Although the ideological strategies these groups use to explain their choice of home or paid work include an implicit critique of those "on the other side," this is almost always qualified, and both groups, at least at times, discuss their envy or admiration for the others. More important, as should now be abundantly clear, both groups ultimately share the same set of beliefs and the same set of concerns. Over half the women in my sample explicitly state that the choice between home and paid work depends on the individual woman, her interests, desires, and circumstances. Nearly all the rest argue that home is more important than paid work because children are simply more important than careers or the pursuit of financial gain. The paid working women in my sample were actually twice as likely as their stay-at-home counterparts to respond that home and children are more important and rewarding than paid work. Ideologically speaking, at least, home and children actually seem to become more important to a mother the more time she spends away from them.

There *are* significant differences among mothers—ranging from individual differences to more systematic differences of class, race, and employment. But in the present context, what is most significant is the commitment to the ideology of intensive mothering that women share in spite of their differences. In this, the cultural contradictions of motherhood persist.

The case of paid working mothers is particularly important in this regard, since these are the very mothers who, arguably, have the most to gain from redefining motherhood in such a way as to lighten their load on the second shift. As we have seen, however, this is not exactly what they do. It is true, as Gerson (1985) argues, that there are ways in which paid working mothers do redefine motherhood and lighten their load—for instance, by sending their kids to day care, spending less time with them than their stay-at-home counterparts, legitimating their paid labor-force participation, and engaging in any number of practical strategies to make child-rearing tasks less energy- and time-consuming. But, as I have argued, this does not mean that these mothers have given up the ideology of intensive mothering. Rather, it means that, whether or not they actually do, they feel they should spend a good deal of time looking for appropriate paid caregivers, trying to make up for the lack of quantity time by focusing their energy on providing quality time, and remaining attentive to the central tenets of the ideology of intensive child rearing. It also means that many are left feeling pressed for time, a little guilty, a bit inadequate, and somewhat ambivalent about their position. These stresses and the strain toward compensatory strategies should actually be taken as a measure of the persistent strength of the ideology of intensive mothering.

To deepen the sense of paradox further, one final point should be repeated. There are reasons to expect middle-class mothers to be in the vanguard of transforming ideas about child rearing away from an intensive model. First, middle-class women were historically in the vanguard of transforming child-rearing ideologies. Second, while many poor and working-class women have had to carry a double shift of wage labor and domestic chores for generations, middle-class mothers have had little practice, historically speaking, in juggling paid work and home and therefore might be eager to avoid it. Finally, one could argue that employed mothers in the middle class have more to gain from reconstructing ideas about appropriate child rearing than any other group—not only because their higher salaries mean that more money is at stake, but also because intensive mothering potentially interferes with their career trajectories in a more damaging way than is true of less high-status occupations. But, as I have suggested, middle-class women are, in some respects, those who go about the task of child rearing with the greatest intensity.

When women's increasing participation in the labor force, the cultural ambivalence regarding paid working and stay-at-home mothers, the particular intensity of middle-class mothering, and the demanding character of the cultural model of appropriate child rearing are taken together, it becomes clear that the cultural contradictions of motherhood have been deepened rather than resolved. The history of child-rearing ideas demonstrates that the more powerful the logic of the rationalized market became, so too did its ideological opposition in the logic of intensive mothering. The words of contemporary mothers demonstrate that this trend persists in the day-to-day lives of women.

Editors' Note: *References for this reading can be found in the original source.*

▪READING 5

Decline of the Family: Conservative, Liberal, and Feminist Views

Janet Z. Giele

In the 1990s the state of American families and children became a new and urgent topic. Everyone recognized that families had changed. Divorce rates had risen dramatically. More women were in the labor force. Evidence on rising teenage suicides, high rates of teen births, and disturbing levels of addiction and violence had put children at risk.

Conservatives have held that these problems can be traced to a culture of toleration and an expanding welfare state that undercut self-reliance and community standards. They focus on the family as a caregiving institution and try to restore its strengths by changing the culture of marriage and parenthood. Liberals center on the disappearance of manual jobs that throws less educated men out of work and undercuts their status in the family as well as rising hours of work among the middle class that makes stable two-parent families more difficult to maintain. Liberals argue that structural changes are needed outside the family in the public world of employment and schools.

The feminist vision combines both the reality of human interdependence in the family and individualism of the workplace. Feminists want to protect diverse family forms that allow realization of freedom and equality while at the same time nurturing the children of the next generation.

THE CONSERVATIVE EXPLANATION: SELFISHNESS AND MORAL DECLINE

The new family advocates turn their spotlight on the breakdown in the two-parent family, saying that rising divorce, illegitimacy, and father absence have put children at greater risk of school failure, unemployment, and antisocial behavior. The remedy is to restore religious faith and family commitment as well as to cut welfare payments to unwed mothers and mother-headed families.

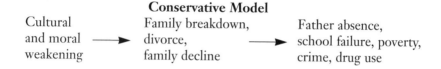

Conservative Model

Cultural and moral weakening ⟶ Family breakdown, divorce, family decline ⟶ Father absence, school failure, poverty, crime, drug use

Cultural and Moral Weakening

To many conservatives, the modern secularization of religious practice and the decline of religious affiliation have undermined the norms of sexual abstinence before marriage and the prohibitions of adultery or divorce thereafter. Sanctions against illegitimacy or divorce have been made to seem narrow-minded and prejudiced. In addition, daytime television and the infamous example of Murphy Brown, a single mother having a child out of wedlock, helped to obscure simple notions of right and wrong. Barbara Dafoe Whitehead's controversial article in the *Atlantic* entitled "Dan Quayle Was Right" is an example of this argument.[1]

Gradual changes in marriage law have also diminished the hold of tradition. Restrictions against waiting periods, race dissimilarity, and varying degrees of consanguinity were gradually disappearing all over the United States and Europe.[2] While Mary Ann Glendon viewed the change cautiously but relativistically—as a process that waxed and waned across the centuries—others have interpreted these changes as a movement from status to contract (i.e., from attention to the particular individual's characteristics to reliance on the impersonal considerations of the market place).[3] The resulting transformation lessened the family's distinctive capacity to serve as a bastion of private freedom against the leveling effect and impersonality of public bureaucracy.

Erosion of the Two-Parent Family

To conservatives, one of the most visible causes of family erosion was government welfare payments, which made fatherless families a viable option. In *Losing Ground*, Charles Murray used the rise in teenage illegitimate births as proof that government-sponsored welfare programs had actually contributed to the breakdown of marriage.[4] Statistics on rising divorce and mother-headed families appeared to provide ample proof that the two-parent family was under siege. The proportion of all households headed by married couples fell from 77 percent in 1950 to 61 percent in 1980 and 55 percent in 1993.[5] Rising cohabitation, divorce rates, and births out of wedlock all contributed to the trend. The rise in single-person households was also significant, from only 12 percent of all households in 1950 to 27 percent in 1980, a trend fed by rising affluence and the undoubling of living arrangements that occurred with the expansion of the housing supply after World War II.[6]

The growth of single-parent households, however, was the most worrisome to policymakers because of their strong links to child poverty. In 1988, 50 percent of all children were found in mother-only families compared with 20 percent in 1950. The parental situation of children in poverty changed accordingly. Of all poor children in 1959, 73 percent had two parents present and 20 percent had a mother only. By 1988, only 35 percent of children in poverty lived with two parents and 57 percent lived with a mother only. These developments were fed by rising rates of divorce and out-of-wedlock births. Between 1940 and 1990, the divorce rate rose from 8.8 to 21 per thousand married women. Out-of-wedlock births exploded from 5 percent in 1960 to 26 percent in 1990.[7]

To explain these changes, conservatives emphasize the breakdown of individual and cultural commitment to marriage and the loss of stigma for divorce and illegitimacy. They understand both trends to be the result of greater emphasis on short-term gratification and on adults' personal desires rather than on what is good for children. A young woman brings a child into the world without thinking about who will support it. A husband divorces his wife and forms another household, possibly with other children, and leaves children of the earlier family behind without necessarily feeling obliged to be present in their upbringing or to provide them with financial support.

Negative Consequences for Children

To cultural conservatives there appears to be a strong connection between erosion of the two-parent family and the rise of health and social problems in children. Parental investment in children has declined—especially in the time available for supervision and companionship. Parents had roughly 10 fewer hours per week for their children in 1986 than in 1960, largely because more married women were employed (up from 24 percent in 1940 to 52 percent in 1983) and more mothers of young children (under age six) were working (up from 12 percent in 1940 to 50 percent in 1983). By the late 1980s just over half of mothers of children under a year old were in the labor force for at least part of the year.[8] At the same time fathers were increasingly absent from the family because of desertion, divorce, or failure to marry. In 1980, 15 percent of white children, 50 percent of black children, and 27 percent of children of Hispanic origin had no father present. Today 36 percent of children are living apart from their biological fathers compared with only 17 percent in 1960.[9]

Without a parent to supervise children after school, keep them from watching television all day, or prevent them from playing in dangerous neighborhoods, many more children appear to be falling by the wayside, victims of drugs, obesity, violence, suicide, or failure in school. During the 1960s and 1970s the suicide rate for persons aged fifteen to nineteen more than doubled. The proportion of obese children between the ages of six and eleven rose from 18 to 27 percent. Average SAT scores fell, and 25 percent of all high school students failed to graduate.[10] In 1995 the Council on Families in America reported, "Recent surveys have found that children from broken homes, when they become teenagers, have 2 to 3 times more behavioral and psychological problems than do children from intact homes."[11] Father absence is blamed by the fatherhood movement for the rise in violence among young males. David Blankenhorn and others reason that the lack of a positive and productive male role model has contributed to an uncertain masculine identity which then uses violence and aggression to prove itself. Every child deserves a father and "in a good society, men prove their masculinity not by killing other people, impregnating lots of women, or amassing large fortunes, but rather by being committed fathers and loving husbands."[12]

Psychologist David Elkind, in *The Hurried Child*, suggests that parents' work and time constraints have pushed down the developmental timetable to younger ages so that small children are being expected to take care of themselves and perform at levels which are robbing them of their childhood. The consequences are depression, discouragement, and a loss of joy at learning and growing into maturity.[13]

Reinvention of Marriage

According to the conservative analysis, the solution to a breakdown in family values is to revitalize and reinstitutionalize marriage. The culture should change to give higher priority to marriage and parenting. The legal code should favor marriage and encourage parental responsibility on the part of fathers as well as mothers. Government should cut back welfare programs which have supported alternate family forms.

The cultural approach to revitalizing marriage is to raise the overall priority given to family activities relative to work, material consumption, or leisure. Marriage is seen as the basic building block of civil society, which helps to hold together the fabric of volunteer activity and mutual support that underpins any democratic society.[14] Some advocates are unapologetically judgmental toward families who fall outside the two-parent mold. According to a 1995 *Newsweek* article on "The Return of Shame," David Blankenhorn believes "a stronger sense of shame about illegitimacy and divorce would do more than any tax cut or any new governmental program to maximize the life circumstances of children." But he also adds that the ultimate goal is "to move beyond stigmatizing only teenage mothers toward an understanding of the terrible message sent by all of us when we minimize the importance of fathers or contribute to the breakup of families."[15]

Another means to marriage and family revitalization is some form of taking a "pledge." Prevention programs for teenage pregnancy affirm the ideal of chastity before marriage. Athletes for Abstinence, an organization founded by a professional basketball player, preaches that young people should "save sex for marriage." A Baptist-led national program called True Love Waits has gathered an abstinence pledge from hundreds of thousands of teenagers since it was begun in the spring of 1993. More than 2,000 school districts now offer an abstinence-based sex education curriculum entitled "Sex Respect." Parents who are desperate about their children's sexual behavior are at last seeing ways that society can resist the continued sexualization of childhood.[16]

The new fatherhood movement encourages fathers to promise that they will spend more time with their children. The National Fatherhood Initiative argues that men's roles as fathers should not simply duplicate women's roles as mothers but should teach those essential qualities which are perhaps uniquely conveyed by fathers—the ability to take risks, contain emotions, and be decisive. In addition, fathers fulfill a time-honored role of providing for children as well as teaching them.[17]

Full-time mothers have likewise formed support groups to reassure themselves that not having a job and being at home full-time for their children is an honorable choice, although it is typically undervalued and perhaps even scorned by dual-earner couples and women with careers. A 1994 *Barron's* article claimed that young people in their twenties ("generation X,") were turning away from the two-paycheck family and scaling down their consumption so that young mothers could stay at home. Although Labor Department statistics show no such trend but only a flattening of the upward rise of women's employment, a variety of poll data does suggest that Americans would rather spend less time at work and more time with their families.[18] Such groups as Mothers at Home (with 15,000 members) and Mothers' Home Business Network (with 6,000 members) are trying to create a sea change that reverses the priority given to paid work outside the home relative to unpaid caregiving work inside the family.[19]

Conservatives see government cutbacks as one of the major strategies for strengthening marriage and restoring family values. In the words of Lawrence Mead, we have "taxed Peter to pay Paula."[20] According to a *Wall Street Journal* editorial, the "relinquishment of personal responsibility" among people who bring children into the world without any visible means of support is at the root of educational, health, and emotional problems of children from one-parent families, their higher accident and mortality rates, and rising crime.[21]

The new congressional solution is to cut back on the benefits to young men and women who "violate social convention by having children they cannot support."[22] Sociologist Brigitte Berger notes that the increase in children and women on welfare coincided with the explosion of federal child welfare programs—family planning, prenatal and postnatal care, child nutrition, child abuse prevention and treatment, child health and guidance, day care, Head Start, and Aid to Families with Dependent Children (AFDC), Medicaid, and Food Stamps. The solution is to turn back the debilitating culture of welfare dependency by decentralizing the power of the federal government and restoring the role of intermediary community institutions such as the neighborhood and the church. The mechanism for change would be block grants to the states which would change the welfare culture from the ground up.[23] Robert Rector of the American Heritage Foundation explains that the states would use these funds for a wide variety of alternative programs to discourage illegitimate births and to care for children born out of wedlock, such as promoting adoption, closely supervised group homes for unmarried mothers and their children, and pregnancy prevention programs (except abortion).[24]

Government programs, however, are only one way to bring about cultural change. The Council on Families in America puts its hope in grassroots social movements to change the hearts and minds of religious and civil leaders, employers, human service professionals, courts, and the media and entertainment industry. The Council enunciates four ideals: marital permanence, childbearing confined to marriage, every child's right to have a father, and limitation of parents' total work time (60 hours per week) to permit adequate time with their families.[25] To restore the cultural ideal of the two-parent family, they would make all other types of family life less attractive and more difficult.

ECONOMIC RESTRUCTURING: LIBERAL ANALYSIS OF FAMILY CHANGE

Liberals agree that there are serious problems in America's social health and the condition of its children. But they pinpoint economic and structural changes that have placed new demands on the family without providing countervailing social supports. The economy has become ever more specialized with rapid technological change undercutting established occupations. More women have entered the labor force as their child-free years have increased due to a shorter childbearing period and longer lifespan. The family has lost economic functions to the urban workplace and socialization functions to the school. What is left is the intimate relationship between the marital couple, which, unbuffered by the traditional economic division of labor between men and women, is subject to even higher demands for emotional fulfillment and is thus more vulnerable to breakdown when it falls short of those demands.

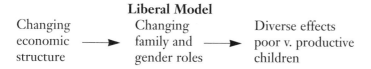

Liberal Model

Changing economic structure → Changing family and gender roles → Diverse effects poor v. productive children

The current family crisis thus stems from structural more than cultural change—changes in the economy, a paired-down nuclear family, and less parental time at home. Market forces have led to a new ethic of individual flexibility and autonomy. More dual-earner couples and single-parent families have broadened the variety of family forms. More single-parent families and more working mothers have decreased the time available for parenting. Loss of the father's income through separation and divorce has forced many women and children into poverty with inadequate health care, poor education, and inability to save for future economic needs. The solution that most liberals espouse is a government-sponsored safety net which will facilitate women's employment, mute the effects of poverty, and help women and children to become economically secure.

Recent Changes in the Labor Market

Liberals attribute the dramatic changes in the family to the intrusion of the money economy rather than cultural and moral decline. In a capitalist society individual behavior follows the market. Adam Smith's "invisible hand" brings together buyers and sellers who maximize their satisfaction through an exchange of resources in the marketplace. Jobs are now with an employer, not with the family business or family farm as in preindustrial times. The cash economy has, in the words of Robert Bellah, "invaded" the diffuse personal relationships of trust between family and community members and transformed them into specific impersonal transactions. In an agricultural economy husbands and wives and parents and children were bound together in relationships of exchange that served each others' mutual interests. But modern society erodes this social capital of organization, trust among individuals, and mutual obligation that enhances both productivity and parenting.[26]

The market has also eroded community by encouraging maximum mobility of goods and services. Cheaper labor in the South, lower fuel prices, and deeper tax breaks attracted first textile factories, then the shoe industry, and later automobile assembly plants which had begun in the North. Eventually, many of these jobs left the country. Loss of manufacturing jobs has had dramatic consequences for employment of young men without a college education and their capacity to support a family. In the 1970s, 68 percent of male high school graduates had a full-time, year-round job compared with only 51 percent in the 1980s. Many new jobs are located in clerical work, sales, or other service occupations traditionally associated with women. The upshot is a deteriorating employment picture for less well educated male workers at the same time that there are rising opportunities for women. Not surprisingly, even more middle income men and women combine forces to construct a two-paycheck family wage.[27]

Changing Family Forms

Whereas the farm economy dictated a two-parent family and several children as the most efficient work group, the market economy gives rise to a much wider variety of family forms. A woman on the frontier in the 1800s had few other options even if she were married to a drunken, violent, or improvident husband. In today's economy this woman may have enough education to get a clerical job that will support her and her children in a small apartment where the family will be able to use public schools and other public amenities.[28]

Despite its corrosive effect on family relations, the modern economy has also been a liberating force. Women could escape patriarchal domination; the young could seek their fortune without waiting for an inheritance from their elders—all a process that a century ago was aligned with a cultural shift that Fred Weinstein and Gerald Platt termed "the wish to be free."[29] Dramatic improvements took place in the status of women as they gained the right to higher education, entry into the professions, and the elective franchise.[30] Similarly, children were released from sometimes cruel and exploitive labor and became the object of deliberate parental investment and consumption.[31] Elders gained pensions for maintenance and care that made them economically independent of their adult children. All these developments could be understood as part of what William J. Goode has referred to as the "world revolution in family patterns" which resulted in liberation and equality of formerly oppressed groups.[32]

The current assessment of change in family forms is, however, mostly negative because of the consequences for children. More parental investment in work outside the family has meant less time for children. According to liberals, parents separate or divorce or have children outside of marriage because of the economic structure, not because they have become less moral or more selfish. Young women have children out of wedlock when the young men whom they might marry have few economic prospects and when the women themselves have little hope for their own education or employment.[33] Change in the family thus begins with jobs. Advocates of current government programs therefore challenge the conservatives' assertion that welfare caused the breakup of two-parent families by supporting mothers with dependent children. According to William Julius Wilson, it is partly the lack of manual labor jobs for the would-be male breadwinner in inner-city Chicago—the scarcity of "marriageable males"—which drives up the illegitimacy rate.[34]

Among educated women, it is well known that the opportunity costs of foregone income from staying home became so high during the 1950s and 1960s that ever increasing numbers of women deserted full-time homemaking to take paid employment.[35] In the 1990s several social scientists have further noted that Richard Easterlin's prediction that women will return to the home during the 1980s never happened. Instead, women continued in the labor force because of irreversible normative changes surrounding women's equality and the need for women's income to finance children's expensive college education.[36] Moreover, in light of globalization of the economy and increasing job insecurity in the face of corporate downsizing, economists and sociologists are questioning Gary Becker's thesis that the lower waged worker in a household (typically the woman) will tend to become a full-time homemaker while the higher waged partner becomes the primary breadwinner. Data from Germany and the United States on the trend toward women's multiple roles suggests that uncertainty about the future has made women invest more strongly than ever in their own careers. They know that if they drop out for very long they will have difficulty reentering if they have to tide over the family when the main breadwinner loses his job.[37]

Consequences for Children

The ideal family in the liberal economic model, according to political philosopher Iris Young, is one which has sufficient income to support the parents and the children and "to foster in those children the emotional and intellectual capacities to acquire such well-paid, secure jobs themselves, and also sufficient to finance a retirement."[38] Dependent families do not have self-sufficient income but must rely on friends, relatives, charity, or the state to carry out their contribution to bringing up children and being good citizens.

Among liberals there is an emerging consensus that the current economic structure leads to two kinds of underinvestment in children that are implicated in their later dependency—material poverty, characteristic of the poor, and "time" poverty, characteristic of the middle class.

Thirty years ago Daniel Patrick Moynihan perceived that material poverty and job loss for a man put strain on the marriage, sometimes to the point that he would leave. His children also did less well in school.[39] Rand Conger, in his studies of Iowa families who lost their farms during the 1980s, found that economic hardship not only puts strain on the marriage but leads to harsh parenting practices and poorer outcomes for children.[40] Thus it appears possible that poverty may not just be the result of family separation, divorce, and ineffective childrearing practices; it may also be the *cause* of the irritability, quarrels, and violence which lead to marital breakdown. Material underinvestment in children is visible not just with the poor but in the changing ratio of per capita income of children and adults in U.S. society as a whole. As the proportion of households without children has doubled over the last century (from 30 to 65 percent), per capita income of children has fallen from 71 percent of adult income in 1870 to 63 percent in 1930 and 51 percent in 1983.[41]

The problem of "time" poverty used to be almost exclusively associated with mothers' employment. Numerous studies explored whether younger children did better if their mother was a full-time homemaker rather than employed outside the home but found no clear results.[42] Lately the lack of parental time for children has become much more acute because parents are working a total of twenty-one hours more per week than in 1970 and because there are more single-parent families. In 1965 the average child spent about thirty hours a week interacting with a parent, compared with seventeen hours in the 1980s.[43] Moreover, parents are less dependent on their children to provide support for them during old age, and children feel less obligated to do so. As skilled craftsmanship, the trades, and the family farms have disappeared, children's upbringing can no longer be easily or cheaply combined with what parents are already doing. So adults are no longer so invested in children's futures. The result is that where the social capital of group affiliations and mutual obligations is the lowest (in the form of continuity of neighborhoods, a two-parent family, or a parent's interest in higher education for her children), children are 20 percent more likely to drop out of high school.[44]

It is not that parents prefer their current feelings of being rushed, working too many hours, and having too little time with their families. Economist Juliet Schor reports that at least two-thirds of persons she surveyed about their desires for more family time versus more salary would take a cut in salary if it could mean more time with their families. Since this option is not realistically open to many, what parents appear to do is spend more money on their children as a substitute for spending more time with them.[45]

Fixing the Safety Net

Since liberals believe in a market economy with sufficient government regulation to assure justice and equality of opportunity, they support those measures which will eradicate the worst poverty and assure the healthy reproduction of the next generation.[46] What particularly worries them, however, is Charles Murray's observation that since

1970 the growth of government welfare programs has been associated with a *rise* in poverty among children. Payments to poor families with children, while not generous, have nevertheless enabled adults to be supported by attachment to their children.[47] Society is faced with a dilemma between addressing material poverty through further government subsidy and time poverty through policies on parental leave and working hours. It turns out that the United States is trying to do both.

Measures for addressing material poverty would stimulate various kinds of training and job opportunities. The Family Support Act of 1988 would move AFDC mothers off the welfare rolls by giving them job training and requiring them to join the labor force. Such action would bring their economic responsibility for supporting their children into line with their parental authority. A whole program of integrated supports for health insurance, job training, earned income tax credits for the working poor, child support by the noncustodial parent, and supported work is put forward by economist David Ellwood in *Poor Support*.[48] An opposite strategy is to consolidate authority over children with the state's economic responsibility for their care by encouraging group homes and adoption for children whose parents cannot support them economically.[49]

Means for addressing time poverty are evident in such legislative initiatives as the Family and Medical Leave Act of 1993. By encouraging employers to grant parental leave or other forms of flexible work time, government policy is recognizing the value of parents having more time with their children, but the beneficiaries of such change are largely middle-class families who can afford an unpaid parental leave.[50] Another tactic is to reform the tax law to discourage marital splitting. In a couple with two children in which the father earns $16,000 annually and the mother $9,000, joint tax filing gives them no special consideration. But if they file separately, each taking one child as a dependent, the woman will receive about $5,000 in Earned Income Tax Credit and an extra $2,000 in food stamps.[51] Changing the tax law to remove the incentives for splitting, establishing paternity of children born out of wedlock, and intensifying child support enforcement to recover economic support from fathers are all examples of state efforts to strengthen the kinship unit.

INTERDEPENDENCE: THE FEMINIST VISION OF WORK AND CAREGIVING

A feminist perspective has elements in common with both conservatives and liberals: a respect for the family as an institution (shared with the conservatives) and an appreciation of modernity (valued by the liberals). In addition, a feminist perspective grapples with the problem of women's traditionally subordinate status and how to improve it through both a "relational" and an "individualist" strategy while also sustaining family life and the healthy rearing of children.[52] At the same time feminists are skeptical of both conservative and liberal solutions. Traditionalists have so often relied on women as the exploited and underpaid caregivers in the family to enable men's activities in the public realm. Liberals are sometimes guilty of a "male" bias in focusing on the independent individual actor in the marketplace who does not realize that his so-called "independence," is possible only because he is actually *dependent* on all kinds of relationships that made possible his education and life in a stable social order.[53]

By articulating the value of caregiving along with the ideal of women's autonomy, feminists are in a position to examine modern capitalism critically for its effects on families and to offer alternative policies that place greater value on the quality of life and human relationships. They judge family strength not by their *form* (whether they have two-parents) but by their functioning (whether they promote human satisfaction and development) and whether both women and men are able to be family caregivers as well as productive workers. They attribute difficulties of children less to the absence of the two-parent family than to low-wage work of single mothers, inadequate child care, and inhospitable housing and neighborhoods.

Feminist Model

Lack of cooperation among community, family, and work $\longrightarrow$ Families where adults are stressed and overburdened $\longrightarrow$ Children lack sufficient care and attention from parents

Accordingly, feminists would work for reforms that build and maintain the social capital of volunteer groups, neighborhoods, and communities because a healthy civil society promotes the well-being of families and individuals as well as economic prosperity and a democratic state. They would also recognize greater role flexibility across the life cycle so that both men and women could engage in caregiving, and they would encourage education and employment among women as well as among men.

Disappearance of Community

From a feminist perspective, family values have become an issue because individualism has driven out the sense of collective responsibility in our national culture. American institutions and social policies have not properly implemented a concern for all citizens. Comparative research on family structure, teenage pregnancy, poverty, and child outcomes in other countries demonstrates that where support is generous to help *all* families and children, there are higher levels of health and general education and lower levels of violence and child deviance than in the United States.[54]

Liberal thinking and the focus on the free market have made it seem that citizens make their greatest contribution when they are self-sufficient, thereby keeping themselves off the public dole. But feminist theorist Iris Young argues that many of the activities that are basic to a healthy democratic society (such as cultural production, caretaking, political organizing, and charitable activities) will never be profitable in a private market. Yet many of the recipients of welfare and Social Security such as homemakers, single mothers, and retirees are doing important volunteer work caring for children and helping others in their communities. Thus the social worth of a person's contribution is not just in earning a paycheck that allows economic independence but also in making a social contribution. Such caretaking of other dependent citizens and of the body politic should be regarded as honorable, not inferior, and worthy of society's support and subsidy.[55]

In fact it appears that married women's rising labor force participation from 41 percent in 1970 to 58 percent in 1990 may have been associated with their withdrawal from unpaid work in the home and community.[56] Volunteer membership in everything from the PTA to bowling leagues declined by over 25 percent between 1969 and 1993. There is now considerable concern that the very basis that Alexis de Tocqueville thought necessary to democracy is under siege.[57] To reverse this trend, social observers suggest that it will be necessary to guard time for families and leisure that is currently being sucked into the maw of paid employment. What is needed is a reorientation of priorities to give greater value to unpaid family and community work by both men and women.

National policies should also be reoriented to give universal support to children at every economic level of society, but especially to poor children. In a comparison of countries in the Organization for Economic Cooperation and Development, the United States ranks at the top in average male wages but near the bottom in its provision for disposable income for children. In comparison with the $700 per month available to children in Norway, France, or the Netherlands in 1992, U.S. children of a single nonemployed mother received only slightly under $200.[58] The discrepancy is explained by very unequal distribution of U.S. income, with the top quintile, the "fortunate fifth," gaining 47 percent of the national income while the bottom fifth receives only 3.6 percent.[59] This sharp inequality is, in turn, explained by an ideology of individualism that justifies the disproportionate gains of the few for their innovation and productivity and the meager income of the poor for their low initiative or competence. Lack of access to jobs and the low pay accruing to many contingent service occupations simply worsen the picture.

Feminists are skeptical of explanations that ascribe higher productivity to the higher paid and more successful leading actors while ignoring the efforts and contribution of the supporting cast. They know that being an invisible helper is the situation of many women. This insight is congruent with new ideas about the importance "social capital" to the health of a society that have been put forward recently by a number of social scientists.[60] Corporations cannot be solely responsible for maintaining the web of community, although they are already being asked to serve as extended family, neighborhood support group, and national health service.

Diversity of Family Forms

Those who are concerned for strengthening the civil society immediately turn to the changing nature of the family as being a key building block. Feminists worry that seemingly sensible efforts to reverse the trend of rising divorce and single parenthood will privilege the two-parent family to the detriment of women; they propose instead that family values be understood in a broader sense as valuing the family's unique capacity for giving emotional and material support rather than implying simply a two–parent form.

The debate between conservatives, liberals, and feminists on the issue of the two-parent family has been most starkly stated by sociologist Judith Stacey and political philosopher Iris Young.[61] They regard the requirement that all women stay in a marriage as an invitation to coercion and subordination and an assault on the principles of freedom and self-determination that are at the foundation of democracy. Moreover, as Christopher Jencks and Kathryn Edin conclude from their study of several hundred welfare families, the current welfare reform rhetoric that no couple should have a child unless they can support it, does not take into account the uncertainty of life in which people who start out married or with adequate income not always remain so. In the face of the worldwide dethronement of the two-parent family (approximately one-quarter to one-third of all families around the globe are headed by women), marriage should not be seen as the cure for child poverty. Mothers should not be seen as less than full citizens if they are not married or not employed (in 1989 there were only 16 million males between the ages of 25 and 34 who made over $12,000 compared with 20 million females of the same age who either had a child or wanted one).[62] National family policy should instead begin with a value on women's autonomy and self-determination that includes the right to bear children. Mother-citizens are helping to reproduce the next generation for the whole society, and in that responsibility they deserve at least partial support.

From a feminist perspective the goal of the family is not only to bring up a healthy and productive new generation; families also provide the intimate and supportive group of kin or fictive kin that foster the health and well-being of every person—young or old, male or female, heterosexual, homosexual, or celibate. Recognition as "family" should therefore not be confined to the traditional two-parent unit connected by blood, marriage, or adoption, but should be extended to include kin of a divorced spouse (as Stacey documented in her study of Silicon Valley families), same-sex partnerships, congregate households of retired persons, group living arrangements, and so on.[63] Twenty years ago economist Nancy Barrett noted that such diversity in family and household form was already present. Among all U.S. households in 1976, no one of the six major types constituted more than 15–20 percent: couples with and without children under eighteen with the wife in the labor force (15.4 and 13.3 percent respectively); couples with or without children under 18 with the wife not in the labor force (19.1 and 17.1 percent); female- or male-headed households (14.4 percent); and single persons living alone (20.6 percent).[64]

Such diversity both describes and informs contemporary "family values" in the United States. Each family type is numerous enough to have a legitimacy of its own, yet no single form is the dominant one. As a result the larger value system has evolved to encompass beliefs and rules that legitimate each type on the spectrum. The regressive alternative is "fundamentalism" that treats the two-parent family with children as the only legitimate form, single-parent families as unworthy of support, and the nontraditional forms as illegitimate. In 1995 the general population appears to have accepted diversity of family forms as normal. A Harris poll of 1,502 women and 460 men found that only 2 percent of women and 1 percent of men defined family as "being about the traditional nuclear family," One out of ten women defined family values as loving, taking care of, and supporting each other, knowing right from wrong or having good values, and nine out of ten said society should value all types of families.[65] It appears most Americans believe that an Aunt Polly single-parent type of family for a Huck Finn that provides economic support, shelter, meals, a place to sleep and to withdraw, is better than no family at all.

Amidst gradual acceptance of greater diversity in family form, the gender-role revolution is also loosening the sex-role expectations traditionally associated with breadwinning and homemaking. Feminists believe that men and women can each do both.[66] In addition, women in advanced industrial nations have by and large converged upon a new life pattern of multiple roles by which they combine work and family life. The negative outcome is an almost universal "double burden" for working women in which they spend eighty-four hours per week on paid and family work, married men spend seventy-two hours, and single persons without children spend fifty hours.[67] The positive consequence, however, appears to be improved physical and mental health for those women who, though stressed, combine work and family roles.[68] In addition, where a woman's husband helps her more with the housework, she is less likely to think of getting a divorce.[69]

The Precarious Situation of Children

The principal remedy that conservatives and liberals would apply to the problems of children is to restore the two-parent family by reducing out-of-wedlock births, increasing the presence of fathers, and encouraging couples who are having marital difficulties to avoid divorce for the sake of their children. Feminists, on the other hand, are skeptical that illegitimacy, father absence, or divorce are the principal culprits they are made out to be. Leon Eisenberg reports that over half of all births in Sweden and one-quarter of births in France are to unmarried women, but without the disastrous correlated effects observed in the United States. Arlene Skolnick and Stacey Rosencrantz cite longitudinal studies showing that most children recover from the immediate negative effects of divorce.[70]

How then, while supporting the principle that some fraction of women should be able to head families as single parents, do feminists analyze the problem of ill health, antisocial behavior, and poverty among children? Their answer focuses on the *lack of institutional supports* for the new type of dual-earner and single-parent families that are more prevalent today. Rather than attempt to force families back into the traditional mold, feminists note that divorce, lone-mother families, and women's employment are on the rise in every industrialized nation. But other countries have not seen the same devastating decline in child well-being, teen pregnancy, suicides and violent death, school failure, and a rising population of children in poverty. These other countries have four key elements of social and family policy which protect all children and their mothers: (1) work guarantees and other economic supports; (2) child care; (3) health care; and (4) housing subsidies. In the United States these benefits are scattered and uneven; those who can pay their way do so; only those who are poor or disabled receive AFDC for economic support, some help with child care, Medicaid for health care, and government-subsidized housing.

A first line of defense is to raise women's wages through raising the minimum wage, then provide them greater access to male-dominated occupations with higher wages. One-half of working women do not earn a wage adequate to support a family of four above the poverty line. Moreover, women in low-wage occupations are subject to frequent lay-offs and lack of benefits. Training to improve their human capital, provision of child care, and broadening of benefits would help raise women's capacity to support a family. Eisenberg reports that the Human Development Index of the United Nations (HDI), which ranks countries by such indicators as life expectancy, educational levels, and per capita income, places the United States fifth and Sweden sixth in the world. But when the HDI is recalculated to take into account equity of treatment of women, Sweden rises to first place and the United States falls to ninth. Therefore, one of the obvious places to begin raising children's status is to "raise the economic status and earning power of their mothers."[71]

A second major benefit which is not assured to working mothers is child care. Among school-age children up to thirteen years of age, one-eighth lack any kind of after-school child care. Children come to the factories where their mothers work and wait on the lawn or in the lobby until their mothers are finished working. If a child is sick, some mothers risk losing a job if they stay home. Others are latchkey kids or in unknown circumstances such as sleeping in their parents' cars or loitering on the streets. Although 60 percent of mothers of the 22 million preschool children are working, there are only 10 million child care places available, a shortfall of one to three million slots.[72] Lack of good quality care for her children not only distracts a mother, adds to her absences from work, and make her less productive, it also exposes the child to a lack of attention and care that leads to violent and antisocial behavior and poor performance in school.

Lack of medical benefits is a third gaping hole for poor children and lone-parent families. Jencks and Edin analyze what happens to a Chicago-area working woman's income if she goes off welfare. Her total income in 1993 dollars on AFDC (with food stamps, unreported earnings, help from family and friends) adds up to $12,355, in addition to which she receives Medicaid and child care. At a $6 per hour full-time job, however, without AFDC, with less than half as much from food stamps, with an Earned Income Tax Credit, and help from relatives, her total income would add to $20,853. But she would have to pay for her own medical care, bringing her effective income down to $14,745 if she found free child care, and $9,801 if she had to pay for child care herself.[73]

Some housing subsidies or low-income housing are available to low-income families. But the neighborhoods and schools are frequently of poor quality and plagued by violence. To bring up children in a setting where they cannot safely play with others introduces important risk factors that cannot simply be attributed to divorce and single parenthood. Rather than being protected and being allowed to be innocent, children must learn to be competent at a very early age. The family, rather than being child-centered, must be adult-centered, not because parents are selfish or self-centered but because the institutions of the society have changed the context of family life.[74] These demands may be too much for children, and depression, violence, teen suicide, teen pregnancy, and school failure may result. But it would be myopic to think that simply restoring the two-parent family would be enough to solve all these problems.

Constructing Institutions for the Good Society

What is to be done? Rather than try to restore the two-parent family as the conservatives suggest or change the economy to provide more jobs as recommended by the liberals, the feminists focus on the need to revise and construct institutions to accommodate the new realities of work and family life. Such an undertaking requires, however, a broader interpretation of family values, a recognition that families benefit not only their members but the public interest, and fresh thinking about how to schedule work and family demands of everyday life as well as the entire life cycle of men and women.

The understanding of family values has to be extended in two ways. First, American values should be stretched to embrace all citizens, their children and families, whether they are poor, white, or people of color, or living in a one-parent family. In 1977, Kenneth Keniston titled the report of the Carnegie Commission on Children *All Our Children*. Today many Americans still speak and act politically in ways suggesting that they *disown* other people's children as the next generation who will inherit the land and support the economy. Yet in the view of most feminists and other progressive reformers, all these children should be embraced for the long-term good of the nation.[75] By a commitment to "family values" feminists secondly intend to valorize the family as a distinctive intimate group of many forms that is needed by persons of all ages but especially children. To serve the needs of children and other dependent persons, the family must be given support and encouragement by the state to carry out its unique functions. Iris Young contends that marriage should not be used to reduce the ultimate need for the state to serve as a means to distribute needed supports to the families of those less fortunate.[76] Compare the example of the GI Bill of Rights after World War II, which provided educational benefits to those who had served their country in the military. Why should there not be a similar approach to the contribution that a parent makes in raising a healthy and productive youngster?[77]

At the community level families should be embraced by all the institutions of the civil society—schools, hospitals, churches, and employers—as the hidden but necessary complement to the bureaucratic and impersonal workings of these formal organizations. Schools rely on parents for the child's "school readiness." Hospitals send home patients who need considerable home care before becoming completely well. The work of the church is carried out and reinforced in the family; and when families fail, it is the unconditional love and intimacy of family that the church tries to replicate. Employers depend on families to give the rest, shelter, emotional support, and other maintenance of human capital that will motivate workers and make them productive. Increasingly, the professionals and managers in these formal organizations are realizing that they need to work more closely with parents and family members if they are to succeed.

Feminists would especially like to see the reintegration of work and family life that was torn apart at the time of the industrial revolution when productive work moved out of the home and into the factory. Several proposals appear repeatedly: parental leave (which now is possible through the Family and Medical Leave Act of 1993); flexible hours and part-time work shared by working parents but without loss of benefits and promotion opportunities; home-based work; child care for sick children and after-school supervision. Although some progress has been made, acceptance of these reforms has been very slow. Parental leave is still *unpaid*. The culture of the workplace discourages many persons from taking advantage of the more flexible options which do exist because they fear they will be seen as less serious and dedicated workers. In addition, most programs are aimed at mothers and at managers, although there is growing feeling that fathers and hourly workers should be included as well.[78]

Ultimately these trends may alter the shape of women's and men's life cycles. Increasingly, a new ideal for the life course is being held up as the model that society should work toward. Lotte Bailyn proposes reorganization of careers in which young couples trade off periods of intense work commitment with each other while they establish their families so that either or both can spend more time at home.[79] Right now both women and men feel they must work so intensely to establish their careers that they have too little time for their children.[80] For the poor and untrained, the problem is the opposite: childbearing and childrearing are far more satisfying and validating than a low-paying, dead-end job. The question is how to reorient educators or employers to factor in time with family as an important obligation to society (much as one would factor in military service, for example). Such institutional reorganization is necessary to give families and childrearing their proper place in the modern postindustrial society.

CONCLUSION

A review of the conservative, liberal, and feminist perspectives on the changing nature of the American family suggests that future policy should combine the distinctive contributions of all three. From the conservatives comes a critique of modernity that recognizes the important role of the family in maintaining child health and preventing child failure. Although their understanding of "family values" is too narrow, they deserve credit for raising the issue of family function and form to public debate. Liberals see clearly the overwhelming power of the economy to deny employment, make demands on parents as workers, and drive a wedge between employers' needs for competitiveness and families' needs for connection and community.

Surprising although it may seem, since feminists are often imagined to be "way out," the most comprehensive plan for restoring family to its rightful place is put forward by the feminists who appreciate both the inherently premodern nature of the family and at the same time its inevitable interdependence with a fast-changing world economy. Feminists will not turn back to the past because they know that the traditional family was often a straightjacket for women. But they also know that family cannot be turned into a formal organization or have its functions performed by government or other public institutions that are incapable of giving needed succor to children, adults, and old people which only the family can give.

The feminist synthesis accepts both the inherent particularism and emotional nature of the family and the inevitable specialization and impersonality of the modern economy. Feminists are different from conservatives in accepting diversity of the family to respond to the needs of the modern economy. They are different from the liberals in recognizing that intimate nurturing relationships such as parenting cannot all be turned into a safety net of formal care. The most promising social policies for families and children take their direction from inclusive values that confirm the good life and the well-being of every individual as the ultimate goal of the nation. The policy challenge is to adjust the partnership between the family and its surrounding institutions so that together they combine the best of private initiative with public concern.

Notes

1. Barbara Dafoe Whitehead, "Dan Qayle Was Right," *Atlantic Monthly* (April 1993): 47. Her chapter in [*Promises to Keep: Decline and Renewal of Marriage in America*, edited by D. Popenoe, J. B. Elshtain, and D. Blankenhorn] on the "Story of Marriage" continues the theme of an erosion of values for cultural diversity.

2. Mary Ann Glendon, "Marriage and the State: The Withering Away of Marriage," *Virginia Law Review* 62 (May 1976): 663–729.

3. See chapters by Milton Regan and Carl Schneider in [*Promises to Keep: Decline and Renewal of Marriage in America*, edited by D. Popenoe, J. B. Elshtain, and D. Blankenhorn].

4. Charles A. Murray, *Losing Ground: American Social Policy: 1950–1980* (New York: Basic Books, 1984). Critics point out that the rise in out-of-wedlock births continues, even though welfare payments have declined in size over the last several decades, thereby casting doubt on the perverse incentive theory of rising illegitimacy.

5. U.S. Bureau of the Census. *Statistical Abstract of the United States: 1994*, 114th ed. (Washington, DC: 1994), 59.

6. Suzanne M. Bianchi and Daphne Spain, *American Women in Transition* (New York: Russell Sage Foundation, 1986), 88.

7. Donald J. Hernandez, *America's Children: Resources from Family, Government, and the Economy* (New York: Russell Sage Foundation, 1993), 284, 70. Janet Zollinger Giele, "Woman's Role Change and Adaptation: 1920–1990," in *Women's Lives through Time: Educated American Women of the Twentieth Century*, ed. K. Hulbert and D. Schuster (San Francisco: Jossey-Bass. 1993), 40.

8. Victor Fuchs, "Are Americas Underinvesting in Children?" in *Rebuilding the Nest*, ed. David Blankenhorn, Stephen Bayme, and Jean Bethke Elshtain (Milwaukee: Family Service America, 1990), 66. Bianchi and Spain, *American Women in Transition*, 141, 201, 226. Janet Zollinger Giele, "Gender and Sex Roles," in *Handbook of Sociology*, ed. N. J. Smelser (Beverly Hills, CA: Sage Publications, 1988), 300.

9. Hernandez, *America's Children*, 130. Council on Families in America, *Marriage in America* (New York: Institute for American Values. 1995), 7.

10. Fuchs, "Are Americans Underinvesting in Children?" 61. Some would say, however, that the decline was due in part to a larger and more heterogeneous group taking the tests.

11. Council on Families in America, *Marriage in America*, 6. The report cites research by Nicholas Zill and Charlotte A. Schoenborn, "Developmental, Learning and Emotional Problems: Health of Our Nation's Children, United States, 1988." *Advance Data*, National Center for Health Statistics, Publication #120, November 1990. See also, Sara McLanahan and Gary Sandefur, *Growing Up with a Single Parent* (Cambridge, MA: Harvard University Press, 1994).

12. Edward Gilbreath, "Manhood's Great Awakening," *Christianity Today* (February 6, 1995): 27.

13. David Elkind, *The Hurried Child: Growing Up Too Fast Too Soon* (Reading, MA: Addison-Wesley, 1981).

14. Jean Bethke Elshtain, *Democracy on Trial* (New York: Basic Books, 1995).

15. Jonathan Alter and Pat Wingert, "The Return of Shame," *Newsweek* (February 6, 1995): 25.

16. Tom McNichol, "The New Sex Vow: 'I won't' until 'I do'," USA Weekend, March 25–27, 1994, 4 ff. Lee Smith. "The New Wave of Illegitimacy," *Fortune* (April 18, 1994): 81 ff.

17. Susan Chira, "War over Role of American Fathers," *New York Times*, June 19, 1994, 22.

18. Juliet Schor, "Consumerism and the Decline of Family and Community: Preliminary Statistics from a Survey on Time, Money, and Values." Harvard Divinity School, Seminar on Families and Family Policy, April 4, 1995.

19. Karen S. Peterson, "In Balancing Act, Scale Tips toward Family," *USA Today*, January 25, 1995.

20. Lawrence Mead, "Taxing Peter to Pay Paula," *Wall Street Journal*, November 2, 1994.

21. Tom G. Palmer, "English Lessons: Britain Rethinks the Welfare State," *Wall Street Journal*, November 2, 1994.

22. Robert Pear, "G.O.P. Affirms Plan to Stop Money for Unwed Mothers," *New York Times*, January 21, 1995, 9.

23. Brigitte Berger. "Block Grants: Changing the Welfare Culture from the Ground Up," *Dialogue* (Boston: Pioneer Institute for Public Policy Research), no. 3, March 1995.

24. Robert Rector, "Welfare," *Issues '94: The Candidate's Briefing Book* (Washington, DC: American Heritage Foundation, 1994), chap. 13.

25. Council on Families in America, *Marriage in America*, 13–16.

26. Robert Bellah, "Invasion of the Money World," in *Rebuilding the Nest*, ed. David Blankenhorn, Steven Bayme, and Jean Bethke Elshtain (Milwaukee: Family Service America, 1990), 227–36. James Coleman, *Foundations of Social Theory* (Cambridge, MA: Harvard University Press, 1990).

27. Sylvia Nasar, "More Men in Prime of Life Spend Less Time Working," *New York Times*, December 1, 1994, Al.

28. John Scanzoni, *Power Politics in the American Marriage* (Englewood Cliffs, NJ: Prentice-Hall, 1972). Ruth A. Wallace and Alison Wolf, *Contemporary Sociological Theory* (Englewood Cliffs, NJ: Prentice-Hall, 1991), 176.

29. Fred Weinstein and Gerald M. Platt, *The Wish to Be Free: Society, Psyche, and Value Change* (Berkeley, CA: University of California Press, 1969).

30. Kingsley Davis, "Wives and Work: A Theory of the Sex-Role Revolution and Its Consequenecs," in *Feminism, Children, and the New Families*, ed. S. M. Dornbusch and M. H. Strober (New York: Guilford Press. 1988), 67–86. Janet Zollinger Giele, *Two Paths to Women's Equality: Temperance, Suffrage, and the Origins of American Feminism* (New York: Twayne Publishers, Macmillan, 1995).

31. Vivianna A. Zelizer, *Pricing the Priceless Child: The Changing Social Value of Children* (New York: Basic Books, 1985).

32. William J. Goode, *World Revolution in Family Patterns* (New York: The Free Press, 1963).

33. Constance Willard Williams, *Black Teenage Mothers: Pregnancy and Child Rearing from Their Perspective* (Lexington, MA: Lexington Books, 1990).

34. William Julius Wilson, *The Truly Disadvantaged: The Inner City, the Underclass, and Public Policy* (Chicago: University of Chicago Press, 1987).

35. Jacob Mincer, "Labor-Force Participation of Married Women: A Study of Labor Supply," in *Aspects of Labor Economics*, Report of the National Bureau of Economic Research (Princeton, NJ: Universities-National Bureau Committee of Economic Research, 1962). Glen G. Cain. *Married Women in the Labor Force: An Economic Analysis* (Chicago: University of Chicago Press, 1966).

36. Richard A. Easterlin, *Birth and Fortune: The Impact of Numbers on Personal Welfare* (New York: Basic Books, 1980). Valerie K. Oppenheimer, "Structural Sources of Economic Pressure for Wives to Work—Analytic Framework," *Journal of Family History* 4, no. 2 (1979): 177–99. Valerie K. Oppenheimer, *Work and the Family: A Study in Social Demography* (New York: Academic Press, 1982).

37. Janet Z. Giele and Rainer Pischner, "The Emergence of Multiple Role Patterns Among Women: A Comparison of Germany and the United States," *Vierteljahrshefte zur Wirtschaftsforschung* (Applied Economics Quarterly) (Heft 1–2, 1994). Alice S. Rossi, "The Future in the Making," *American Journal of Orthopsychiatry* 63, no. 2 (1993): 166–76. Notburga Ott, *Intrafamily Bargaining and Household Decisions* (Berlin: Springer-Verlag, 1992).

38. Iris Young, "Mothers, Citizenship and Independence: A Critique of Pure Family Values," *Ethics* 105, no. 3 (1995): 535–56. Young critiques the liberal stance of William Galston, *Liberal Purposes* (New York: Cambridge University Press, 1991).

39. Lee Rainwater and William L. Yancey, *The Moynihan Report and the Politics of Controversy* (Cambridge, MA: MIT Press, 1967).

40. Glen H. Elder, Jr., *Children of the Great Depression* (Chicago: University of Chicago Press, 1974). Rand D. Conger, Xiao-Jia Ge, and Frederick O. Lorenz, "Economic Stress and Marital Relations," in *Families in Troubled Times: Adapting to Change in Rural America*, ed. R. D. Conger and G. H. Elder, Jr. (New York: Aldine de Gruyter, 1994), 187–203.

41. Coleman, *Foundations of Social Theory*, 590.

42. Elizabeth G. Menaghan and Toby L. Parcel, "Employed Mothers and Children's Home Environments," *Journal of Marriage and the Family* 53, no. 2 (1991): 417–31. Lois Hoffman, "The Effects on Children of Maternal and Paternal Employment," in *Families and Work*, ed. Naomi Gerstel and Harriet Engel Gross (Philadelphia: Temple University Press, 1987), 362–95.

43. Juliet Schor, *The Overworked American: The Unexpected Decline of Leisure* (New York: Basic Books, 1991). Robert Haveman and Barbara Wolfe, *Succeeding Generations: On the Effects of Investments in Children* (New York: Russell Sage Foundation, 1994), 239.

44. Coleman, *Foundations of Social Theory*, 596–97.

45. Schor, "Consumerism and Decline of Family."

46. Iris Young, "Mothers, Citizenship and Independence," puts Elshtain, Etzioni, Galston, and Whitehead in this category.

47. Coleman, *Foundations of Social Theory*, 597–609.

48. Sherry Wexler, "To Work and To Mother: A Comparison of the Family Support Act and the Family and Medical Leave Act" (Ph.D. diss. draft, Brandeis University, 1995). David T. Ellwood, *Poor Support: Poverty in the American Family* (New York: Basic Books, 1988).

49. Coleman, *Foundations of Social Theory*, 300–21. Coleman, known for rational choice theory in sociology, put forward these theoretical possibilities in 1990, fully four years ahead of what in 1994 was voiced in the Republican Contract with America.

50. Wexler, "To Work and To Mother."

51. Robert Lerman, "Marketplace," National Public Radio, April 18, 1995.

52. Karen Offen, "Defining Feminism: A Comparative Historical Approach," *Signs* 14, no. 1 (1988): 119–51.

53. Young, "Mothers, Citizenship and Independence."

54. Robert N. Bellah et al., *Habits of the Heart* (Berkeley, CA: University of California Press, 1985), 250–71. Gosta Esping-Andersen, *The Three Worlds of Welfare Capitalism* (Princeton, NJ: Princeton University Press, 1990). Susan Pedersen, *Family, Dependence, and the Origins of the Welfare State: Britain and France, 1914–1945* (New York: Cambridge University Press, 1993).

55. Young, "Mothers, Citizenship and Independence."

56. Giele, "Woman's Role Change and Adaptation" presents these historical statistics.

57. Elshtain, *Democracy on Trial*. Robert N. Bellah et al., *The Good Society* (New York: Knopf, 1991), 210. Robert D. Putnam, "Bowling Alone: America's Declining Social Capital," *Journal of Democracy* 4, no. 1 (1995): 65–78.

58. Heather McCallum, "Mind the Gap" (paper presented to the Family and Children's Policy Center colloquium, Waltham, MA, Brandeis University, March 23, 1995). The sum was markedly better for children of employed single mothers, around $700 per mother in the United States. But this figure corresponded with over $1,000 in eleven other countries, with only Greece and Portugal lower than the U.S. Concerning the high U.S. rates of teen pregnancy, see Planned Parenthood advertisement, "Let's Get Serious About Ending Teen Childbearing," *New York Times*, April 4, 1995, A25.

59. Ruth Walker, "Secretary Reich and the Disintegrating Middle Class," *Christian Science Monitor*, November 2, 1994, 19.

60. For reference to "social capital," see Coleman, *Foundations of Social Theory*; Elshtain, *Democracy on Trial*; and Putnam, "Bowling Alone." For "emotional capital," see Arlie Russell Hochschild, *The Managed Heart: The Commercialization of Human Feeling* (Berkeley, CA: University of California Press, 1983). For "cultural capital," see work by Pierre Bourdieu and Jurgen Habermas.

61. Judith Stacey, "Dan Quayle's Revenge: The New Family Values Crusaders," *The Nation*, July 25/August 1, 1994, 119–22. Iris Marion Young, "Making Single Motherhood Normal," *Dissent* (Winter 1994): 88–93.

62. Christopher Jencks and Kathryn Edin, "Do Poor Women Have a Right to Bear Children," *The American Prospect* (Winter 1995): 43–52.

63. Stacey, "Dan Quayle's Revenge." Arlene Skolnick and Stacey Rosencrantz, "The New Crusade for the Old Family," *The American Prospect* (Summer 1994): 59–65.

64. Nancy Smith Barrett, "Data Needs for Evaluating the Labor Market Status of Women," in *Census Bureau Conference on Federal Statistical Needs Relating to Women*, ed. Barbara B. Reagan (U.S. Bureau of the Census, 1979), Current Population Reports, Special Studies, Series P-23, no. 83, pp. 10–19. These figures belie the familiar but misleading statement that "only 7 percent" of all American families are of the traditional nuclear type because "traditional" is defined so narrowly—as husband and wife with two children under 18 where the wife is not employed outside the home. For more recent figures and a similar argument for more universal family ethic, see Christine Winquist Nord and Nicholas Zill, "American Households in Demographic Perspective," working paper no. 5, Institute for American Values, New York, 1991.

65. Tamar Levin, "Women Are Becoming Equal Providers," *New York Times*, May 11, 1995, A27.

66. Marianne A. Ferber and Julie A. Nelson, *Beyond Economic Man: Feminist Theory and Economics* (Chicago: University of Chicago Press, 1993).

67. Fran Sussner Rodgers and Charles Rodgers, "Business and the Facts of Family Life," *Harvard Business Review*, no. 6 (1989): 199–213, especially 206.

68. Ravenna Helson and S. Picano, "Is the Traditional Role Bad for Women?" *Journal of Personality and Social Psychology* 59 (1990): 311–20. Rosalind C. Barnett, "Home-to-Work Spillover Revisited: A Study of Full-Time Employed Women in Dual-Earner Couples," *Journal of Marriage and the Family* 56 (August 1994): 647–56.

69. Arlie Hochschild, "The Fractured Family," *The American Prospect* (Summer 1991): 106–15.

70. Leon Eisenberg, "Is the Family Obsolete?" *The Key Reporter* 60, no. 3 (1995): 1–5. Arlene Skolnick and Stacey Rosencrantz, "The New Crusade for the Old Family," *The American Prospect* (Summer 1994): 59–65.

71. Roberta M. Spalter-Roth, Heidi I. Hartmann, and Linda M. Andrews, "Mothers, Children, and Low-Wage Work: The Ability to Earn a Family Wage," in *Sociology and the Public Agenda*, ed. W. J. Wilson (Newbury Park, CA: Sage Publications, 1993), 316–38.

72. Louis Uchitelle, "Lacking Child Care, Parents Take Their Children to Work," *New York Times*, December 23, 1994, 1.

73. Jencks and Edin, "Do Poor Women Have a Right," 50.

74. David Elkind, *Ties That Stress: The New Family in Balance* (Boston: Harvard University Press, 1994).

75. It is frequently noted that the U.S. is a much more racially diverse nation than, say, Sweden, which has a concerted family and children's policy. Symptomatic of the potential for race and class division that

impedes recognition of all children as the nation's children is the book by Richard J. Herrnstein and Charles A. Murray, *The Bell Curve: Intelligence and Class Structure in American Life* (New York: The Free Press, 1994).

76. Young, "Making Single Motherhood Normal," 93.

77. If the objection is that the wrong people will have children, as Herrnstein and Murray suggest in *The Bell Curve*, then the challenge is to find ways for poor women to make money or have some other more exciting career that will offset the rewards of having children, "such as becoming the bride of Christ or the head of a Fortune 500 corporation," to quote Jencks and Edin, "Do Poor Women Have a Right," 48.

78. Beth M. Miller, "Private Welfare: The Distributive Equity of Family Benefits in America" (Ph.D. thesis, Brandeis University, 1992). Sue Shellenbarger, "Family-Friendly Firms Often Leave Fathers Out of the Picture," *Wall Street Journal*, November 2, 1994. Richard T. Gill and T. Grandon Gill, *Of Families, Children, and a Parental Bill of Rights* (New York: Institute for American Values, 1993). For gathering information on these new work-family policies, I wish to acknowledge help of students in my 1994–95 Family Policy Seminar at Brandeis University, particularly Cathleen O'Brien, Deborah Gurewich, Alissa Starr, and Pamela Swain, as well as the insights of two Ph.D students, Mindy Fried and Sherry Wexler.

79. Lotte Bailyn, *Breaking the Mold: Women, Men and Time in the New Corporate World* (New York: The Free Press, 1994).

80. Penelope Leach, *Children First: What Our Society Must Do and Is Doing* (New York: Random House, 1994).

■READING 6

Family Law in the New Millennium: For Whose Families?

Mary Ann Mason, Mark A. Fine, and Sarah Carnochan

Marriage and family have historically played an important role in U.S. society. According to one judge in a 1939 divorce case,

> one of the foundation pillars of our government is the sanctity of the marriage relation and the influences of the home life, where the holy bond of wedlock is looked upon with profound reverence and respect, and where the marriage vows are sedulously observed. (*Fania v. Fania*, 1939, p. 373)[1]

Marriage remains a cherished institution; 93% of Americans rate a happy marriage as one of their most important life goals (Gallagher & Waite, 2000). However, Americans are marrying less often and for shorter periods (Nagourney, 2000). In the last part of the 20th century, family law has focused on redefining the legal institution of marriage and, at the same time, recognizing other family and childrearing forms.

Although there is not a consensual definition, for the purposes of this article, *family law* is defined as the branch of law that addresses issues pertaining to romantically

Author's Note: *We acknowledge the assistance of Nicole Zayac with this article.*

involved partners (e.g., marriage, divorce, and domestic partnerships) and children (e.g., child custody following divorce, assisted reproduction, and adoption). Changes in family law have typically lagged behind societal changes; the law struggles to come to terms with new social realities (e.g., domestic partnerships, unwed fathers, and alternative reproduction) by either incorporating or reacting against those changes. However, in some instances, such as no-fault divorce statutes, changes in the law have served to facilitate social change. Finally, some family issues of great social importance are virtually neglected in family law, most strikingly, the role of stepparents.

Most issues in family law are decided state by state. Therefore, wide variations exist among states in fundamental issues, such as the division of property following divorce. Nonetheless, it is possible to recognize trends that cross all or most state lines. Although several federal laws have had substantial effects, family law remains solidly within states' jurisdiction.

Another part of the revolution in family law is the role played by the social sciences. Both legal rhetoric and judicial reasoning have been greatly influenced in some parts of family law by professionals in mental health and related social science disciplines. Judges often refer to research in their opinions regarding the best interests of the child, and mental health experts are routinely called on in familial disputes. Still, the application of the social sciences is uneven and uncertain, and there are many areas in which research is routinely ignored or manipulated.

TRENDS IN FAMILY LAW

Marriage

Although marriage remains a central cultural paradigm, substantial changes have occurred in marriage as a legal institution over the past 30 years. During most of U.S. history, a married couple was regarded as having a single legal identity. Although married women made significant progress in the 19th century in obtaining the right to own and manage their own property through the passage of property legislation, women were still largely considered dependents of their husbands. Husbands were responsible for the families' financial well-being, and women who worked were eligible for lesser benefits than their male counterparts based on the assumption that they were not the household's primary wage earner. Prenuptial agreements were not honored by the courts, and the obligations at divorce differed for men and women—only women could receive alimony. Debts incurred by women were their husbands' responsibility, but women had no corresponding responsibility for their husbands' debts (Regan, 1999). Moreover, there was no tort liability between spouses, spouses could not testify against one another in court, and police were hesitant to intervene in cases of domestic violence. For example, in *Ennis v. Donovan* (1960), a Maryland court held that "a married woman had no common-law right to sue her husband for injuries suffered by her as the result of his negligence, and, the Legislature has not yet seen fit to grant her such a right" (p. 543). Despite changes in women's position throughout the past century, the rhetoric of a unitary spousal identity—"husband and wife as 'a single person, represented by the husband' "—remained in judicial discourse into the 1970s (*Lewis v. Lewis*, 1976).

In the last three decades of the 20th century, this paradigm of dependence shifted toward a partnership model in which marriage is more like a contractual relationship between two individuals. Under the new model, a husband and wife are considered equal partners contracting in a marriage, and both retain an independent legal existence. The current law relating to marriage views "the marital relationship as one constituted by personal choice, the natural character of which is rooted in the desire of individuals to seek happiness through intimate association with another" (Regan, 1999, p. 652). With this shift, the nature of marriage has undergone a fundamental alteration. Spouses now hold mutual rights and responsibilities with respect to one another (*Queen's Medical Center v. Kagawa*, 1998). The presumption of the husband as breadwinner and the wife the homemaker has been replaced with the partnership concept. Spouses are now perceived as creating their own marital roles. This perception led courts to uphold and enforce the validity of prenuptial agreements upon divorce (*McHugh v. McHugh*, 1980). Under the partnership model, these agreements presumably do not weaken marriage by making divorce more desirable; they secure the rights of the individuals entering marriage against future disputes. Support obligations and responsibility for a spouse's debts are now placed equally on men and women, and contributions that women outside of the workforce make to the family are gaining recognition.

The push for equal treatment between men and women in marriage, and ultimately in divorce and child custody, was driven primarily by the movement to obtain equal rights for women (Mason, 1988). In addition to the recognition of the contributions that women make to a marriage, this feminist attentiveness has resulted in an increasing awareness that women often suffer when there are marital problems. As a result, law enforcement and the courts are now more likely to intervene when there are problems within a marriage. Domestic violence and marital rape are given more attention, and men and women now have the right to decide whether they will testify against their spouses in federal court (*Trammel v. United States*, 1980). Moreover, tort liability between spouses now exists in most states, albeit at a higher standard than between legal strangers (*Lewis v. Lewis*, 1976). These changes reflect recognition that legal institutions have a role to play in enforcing the rights and responsibilities created by marriage while also respecting the independent identity of each spouse.

Changes in reproductive laws also have affected the spousal relationship. U.S. Supreme Court decisions such as *Roe v. Wade* (1973) have given women more reproductive choices, and they have empowered them to make those choices independent of their husbands. Although married women could take few actions independent of husbands under the dependent marriage model, under the partnership model, women can make important reproductive decisions (e.g., to have an abortion) independently, even against their husbands' objections. This change reflects the increasing recognition of each spouse's independent identity and rights within marriage.

Divorce

The shift to a partnership model of marriage was accompanied by a change in how the partnership could be dissolved. The past 30 years ushered in what has been termed a *divorce revolution*. Drastic changes in divorce law rendered divorce a unilateral decision not based on fault. This made divorce far easier to obtain and in most states created a fundamentally different framework for the distribution of property and the allocation of support following divorce. Following the lead of California's revolutionary Family Law Act of 1969, all states by 1985 offered some form of no-fault divorce (Krause, 1986). In some states, one party had only to. complain that the marriage had reached a point of "irretrievable breakdown" with no requirement of proof; in other states, "incompatibility" or "irreconcilable differences" had to be demonstrated if one party objected, but if one partner chose to live separately for a period of time, that was also seen as proof of marital breakdown. There are debates about how much changes in divorce law contributed to rising divorce rates; some claim the rise was an extension of earlier increases that were temporarily reversed in the 1950s. Regardless of the reasons for the increase, demographic trends clearly reveal that the divorce rate doubled between 1966 and 1976. By the 1980s, it was predicted that half of all marriages would end in divorce (Cherlin, 1992).

The basic assumption underlying the changes in divorce and custody law was that men and women should be treated equally before the law. This was a sharp departure from the beliefs in the era of dependent marriage and fault-based divorce. Family law had then perhaps favored women (and children) by making divorce hard to obtain and by allowing extended support for wives and children after divorce, in the belief that wives were less able to take care of themselves economically than were husbands. A maternal presumption in custody, established by the early 20th century, also favored mothers, reflecting beliefs that they were more nurturing than fathers.

The assumption that men and women should be treated equally had serious consequences for the distribution of property and on alimony. Unless the woman was at fault, alimony or spousal support was routinely granted for life in most states, but collection and enforcement rates were low. As divorce law changed to reflect the equality of partners, the concept of alimony came under negative scrutiny. The Uniform Marriage and Divorce Act (UMDA) moved that alimony only be used when the spouse could not take care of herself and that fault in the divorce should not be a consideration. Fault also was deemed an inappropriate consideration in determining property division. UMDA did, however, pursue a substantial change, allowing women to have a claim to the equitable distribution of property in common law states where the person who held title, typically the husband, was usually granted the property.

The shift toward easy-to-obtain divorce has not gone unchallenged. One aspect of this backlash is the recent passage of "covenant marriage" statutes (Louisiana Act 1380, 1977; Ariz. Rev. Stat. Ann. § 25-901-906, 1998). These laws allow couples to enter into a marriage that can be ended only on statutorily specified grounds. Proponents argue that covenant marriage increases respect for marriage as an institution and will reduce the divorce rate. Supporters of covenant marriage also believe "that no-fault divorce is responsible for the high divorce rate and for other societal problems that are correlated with divorce and single-parent homes" (Pearson, 1999, p. 633). Opponents claim these statutes are both too restrictive (they may trap an individual in a bad marriage) and not restrictive enough (they are voluntarily entered and may be invalidated with the consent of both spouses). At their strongest, statutory covenant marriages eliminate only one aspect of the no-fault divorce statutes—absent wrong-doing, one spouse in a covenant marriage cannot unilaterally demand and be granted a divorce (Wardle, 1999).

Child Custody

Unlike previous eras where child custody issues ordinarily involved orphans or children of parents who could not care for them, the majority of child custody matters in the modern era are the product of divorce. Although under the jurisdiction of courts, most child custody determinations are made by the parties rather than by a judge at trial (Mason, 1994). In addition to increased volume, the substantive rules that the courts used to determine custody shifted drastically. This shift followed in the wake of radical divorce reforms and reflected the new emphasis on egalitarian marriage.

The simple fact of being a mother does not by itself indicate a capacity or willingness to render a quality of care different from that which the father can provide (*State ex rel. Watts v. Watts*, 1973). With this statement, a New York court challenged nearly a century of a judicial presumption in favor of mothers. Not all courts were as outspoken in reducing the importance of mothers; nevertheless, the presumption that the interest of a child of tender years is best served in the custody of the mother was legally abolished or demoted to a "factor to be considered" in nearly all states between 1960 and 1990. By 1982, only seven states gave mothers a custody preference over fathers for children of tender years (Atkinson, 1984). Rather, most states mandate that custody decisions be based on a consideration of the "best interests of the child," a standard that is far less clear and specific than the maternal preference standard. In an attempt to address this ambiguity, state legislatures drafted statutes to direct judges left with the task of applying the elusive best interests standard. Most legislatures also suggested joint custody as an alternative to awarding custody to one parent, giving fathers as much time with children as mothers, and thereby avoiding the problem of having to choose between legally equal parents. Some states adopted a primary caretaker preference, providing custody to the parent who spent the most time with the child (Mason, 1994).

California led the way in custody initiatives, as it had in no-fault divorce, by introducing a preference for joint legal custody in 1980. By 1988, 36 states had followed California's lead. Legislatures, and sometimes courts, produced several variations on the joint custody theme. Joint physical custody dictated that parents should share their time with the child as equally as possible. Joint legal custody, on the other hand, allowed a more traditional sole custody arrangement with visitation for the noncustodial parent. Both parents retained equal input into decisions affecting the child, such as choosing medical treatment and schools. By the end of the century, joint legal and physical custody was the preference in most states (Mason, 2000).

Remarriage and Stepfamilies

Because most partners who divorce eventually remarry, the dramatic increase in divorce resulted in a steep rise in the number of stepfamilies (Seltzer, 1994). Although changes in law and practice relating to marriage and divorce have led to more stepfamilies, little has changed with respect to the legal status of stepparents. Stepparents who do not adopt their stepchildren remain in an ambiguous role with no legal identity (Mahoney, 1994). Their rights and duties toward their stepchildren are largely undefined, and when they are defined, a consistent understanding of their role in the family is not reflected (Mason, 1998). The American Law Institute (2000) addressed some of the legal issues surrounding stepfamilies by defining de facto parents and parents by estoppel (i.e., individuals who are considered parents because they have presented themselves as parents and because it would be inequitable for them to later deny that role) and allowing them to petition for custody of children at divorce. Many stepparents would meet the requirements of these rules. However, even this measure is limited in its applicability because it only indirectly defines stepparent rights and responsibilities to stepchildren during marriage. For example, stepparents are often unable to consent to medical treatment or sign a school permission slip for their stepchildren (*State v. Miranda*, 1997). Generally, stepparents do not have a legal obligation to support their stepchildren, and those who take on such an obligation by acting in loco parentis (i.e., in the place of the parent) do so voluntarily and may end their obligation unilaterally at any time (*Niesen v. Niesen*, 1968). Nonetheless, some federal and state welfare programs take a stepparent's income into account when determining a child's eligibility, whereas others do not.

Stepchildren face legal obstacles in most states that prevent them from filing wrongful death suits on behalf of their stepparents or inheriting when a stepparent dies intestate (i.e., without a will) (*Champagne v. Mcdermott, Inc.*, 1992). Despite the confusion this ambiguity may cause for families, courts and legislatures have been hesitant to address the problem and define a legal role for stepparents. Thus, the changes that are occurring in the law relating to stepparent relationships come slowly and indirectly through changes designed to benefit others. For example, some stepparents are having success in obtaining visitation with their stepchildren following divorce. To a large extent, this success results from states' general third-party visitation statutes, which allow stepparents (and others) to petition for visitation when there is disruption in the family but do not create for stepparents the presumptive right to visitation that exists for biological parents.

Unwed Fathers

Through much of the 20th century, unwed fathers were largely invisible in family law. In the past 25 to 30 years, however, as the number of children born to unmarried parents has risen (McLanahan & Sandefur, 1994), substantial changes have occurred with regard to the legal consequences of "illegitimacy" and the paternity, custody, and child support rights and obligations of unwed fathers. It is difficult to determine the precise number of unwed fathers; they are frequently not listed on birth certificates, and when not involved in the child's life, they do not come into contact with the agencies that maintain data on families (Blank, 1997). However, the increase in unwed mothers over the past 30 years has clearly been accompanied by an increase in the number of unwed fathers. A number of high-profile cases has involved unmarried fathers seeking custody of their children, but these fathers as a group do not play a consistent parenting role for their children. Lerman (1993) estimated the number of unwed fathers who were not supporting their children at 1.6 million. Still, the rights and obligations of unwed fathers are increasingly recognized and enforced.

Beginning in the late 1960s, courts and state legislatures began offering rights and protections to "illegitimate" children comparable to those of nonillegitimate children (Sugarman, 1998). As the rights of illegitimate children began to be recognized, so did the rights and obligations of their fathers. Under the Uniform Parentage Act, based on common law tradition and adopted in numerous states, the husband of the child's mother is presumed to be the father. Historically, this presumption has barred an unwed father from claiming paternity to preserve intact families, protect the child, and ensure child support. The U.S. Supreme Court affirmed this presumption as recently as 1989, ruling that the biological unwed father's interest did not outweigh the state's interest in preserving an intact family (*Michael H. v. Gerald D.*, 1989). However, numerous state courts and legislatures have overridden the presumption, granting unwed fathers the right to claim paternity even when the mother is married to another. For example, the California Supreme Court granted an unwed father the right to establish paternity, arguing that the child was conceived before the mother married (Mason, 2000).

With the increasing recognition of an unwed father's right to claim paternity, courts and legislatures have begun to recognize rights in custody disputes and cases in which the mother has decided to relinquish the child for adoption. In *Stanley v. Illinois* (1971), the U.S. Supreme Court first recognized the custodial rights of an unwed father, ruling that an unwed father who had acted as a parent was entitled to a fitness hearing after the mother's death before the children were made wards of the court. However, the custody rights of an unwed father are not automatic. In subsequent decisions, the U.S. Supreme Court ruled that the biological link of an unwed father may be insufficient to confer rights and required that he acts as a father and participates in childrearing (*Caban v. Mohammed*, 1979; *Lehr v. Robertson*, 1983). State courts, however, have granted unmarried fathers rights comparable to those of married fathers (Mason, 2000).

Finally, as the number of children living in single-parent households has increased, policy initiatives in the past quarter century have focused on enforcing child support obligations. In 1985, only about 13% of never-married mothers reported receiving support from the fathers of their children (Lerman, 1993). In 1975, the Federal Office of Child Support Enforcement was created, with state agency counterparts, to increase child support collection. Subsequently, the Family Support Act of 1988 set stricter standards for state child support enforcement, resulting in increased enforcement among the Aid to Families with Dependent Children population. Despite enforcement efforts, the frequency and amount of child support awards and payments remain low (Mason, 2000). However, welfare reform, with time-limited benefits for parents to receive aid, has made the enforcement of child support a critical issue. As pressure grows to collect child support from both unmarried and formerly married fathers, remaining legal distinctions between them are likely to disappear.

Third-Party Visitation

Unwed fathers are not the only group that has won increased protection of their interests in maintaining a relationship with a child. As a result of the loosening hold of marriage, any number of adults, related and unrelated, are raising children with little or no legal backing. State legislatures and a number of courts have begun to recognize the roles of these multiple parties by expanding visitation rights to individuals other than parents. Third-party visitation statutes have been enacted in all states, granting a right to petition for visitation to certain categories of petitioners that may include stepparents, grandparents (upon the death or divorce of their child), unmarried parents, or in the broadest conception, any interested party (Elrod, Spector, & Atkinson, 1999). These statutes usually grant such rights because of family disruption, although some statutes are broadly worded to allow third-party visitation petitions any time.

Third-party visitation statutes have been challenged on constitutional grounds in a number of states with varied results. The state of Washington enacted one of the broadest statutes, allowing any person to petition for visitation at any time and authorizing courts to grant visitation on a showing of best interest. In *Troxel v. Granville* (2000), one of the few examples of U.S. Supreme Court intervention in a visitation dispute, the mother and unmarried father had two children before the father died. The paternal grandparents sought more extensive visitation than the mother desired and prevailed in the trial court. The state supreme court overruled the lower court, holding that the statute unconstitutionally infringed on parents' fundamental right to raise their children. The U.S. Supreme Court upheld this decision on the grounds that the statute was too broad and gave no weight to the parent's judgment regarding the children's best interest. The court refrained from deciding whether all third-party statutes require a showing of harm or potential harm if visitation were not awarded as a condition of granting visitation. The court's ruling displayed an explicit recognition of the important role played by third parties in children's lives, particularly when the traditional family model is not involved.

In contrast, a number of state courts have upheld third-party visitation statutes against constitutional challenges. For example, in *West v. West* (1998), the appellate court ruled that the Illinois statute did not violate the "long-recognized constitutionally protected interest of parents to raise their children without undue State influence" and affirmed the state's interest in maintaining relationships found to be in the child's best interest. In *Williams v. Williams* (1998), the court upheld Virginia's law, interpreting it to require a finding of harm if visitation were not granted. In a contrary holding, the Georgia Supreme Court found the state's grandparent visitation statute to be unconstitutional on the grounds that it did not clearly promote the welfare of the child and did not require a showing of harm (*Brooks v. Parkerson*, 1995). It is likely that the decisions affirming third-party visitation statutes will stand (*Troxel v. Granville*, 2000).

Nontraditional Partnerships

While the rise of single-parent households has been well documented and has received attention from policy makers and researchers, there has been a simultaneous increase in nontraditional or nonmarital partnerships, including cohabitation, same-sex marriage, and domestic partnerships. These nontraditional relationship forms raise legal issues relating to property division and support obligations following termination of the relationship, access to the legal benefits conferred on spouses, and parental rights issues such as custody, visitation, and second-parent adoption (i.e., the partner who is the nonbiological parent adopts the child).

Perhaps the most well-known case dealing with the rights of cohabiting partners is *Marvin v. Marvin* (1976), in which the California Supreme Court allowed the woman to sue her male partner for compensation following termination of the relationship on contractual grounds. The court held that when there is an explicit or implied contract between mutually assenting individuals in a nonmarital relationship, a court may use principles of equity to divide property at the termination of the relationship. Such a reading of a cohabitation relationship reflects a partnership rather than a dependency model. Subsequent decisions in other states have been more restrictive, however, requiring proof of a contract of cohabitation and refusing to enforce agreements based on sexual obligations or promises.

Recently, a Massachusetts court upheld the validity of a written cohabitation agreement (*Wilcox v. Trautz*, 1998). However, although a contractually based right to compensation may be recognized by the courts, cohabitation does not entitle participants to other benefits of marriage, such as social security benefits (Katz, 1999).

The issue of same-sex marriage has been far more controversial than the rights of cohabiting heterosexual couples. In the early 1970s, several cases challenging state marriage laws were rejected (Chambers & Polikoff, 1999). In the early 1990s, the issue gained national prominence when the Hawaiian Supreme Court set forth a presumption that the legislative ban on same-sex marriage violated the state's constitutional provision granting equal protection and barring sex-based discrimination (*Baehr v. Lewin*, 1993). Legislative responses to the decision have been almost uniformly negative. Hawaii passed a constitutional amendment limiting marriage to heterosexual couples, 29 states had enacted laws barring recognition of same-sex marriage by mid-1999, and the U.S. Congress enacted the Defense of Marriage Act, declaring that states have the right to refuse recognition to same-sex marriages from other states and defining marriage as heterosexual unions for federal law purposes (Chambers & Polikoff, 1999).

Most recently, Vermont passed a civil union statute, taking effect in July 2000, that grants to partners in civil unions, including same-sex partners, the benefits and responsibilities afforded to married couples under state laws. The legislature acted in response to the Vermont Supreme Court's decision in *Baker v. State of Vermont* (1999), holding that the state is constitutionally required to extend to same-sex couples the benefits and protections afforded to married couples, either through inclusion in the marriage laws or in an equivalent statutory alternative. It remains to be seen how these unions are treated by other states or by federal law (Bonauto, 2000). The Vermont civil union statute provides more benefits than the domestic partnership laws, which permit unmarried partners to register their relationships and/or provide benefits to partners of employees of the city, county, or state enacting the law. Numerous cities and counties have enacted such laws, and by 1999, Hawaii, New York, Oregon, and Vermont provided partner benefits to employees.

In contrast to the flurry of legislative activity relating to same-sex marriage and domestic partnership, states have for the most part declined to enact statutes regulating the rights of gay and lesbian parents in custody and visitation disputes, leaving the courts to develop the law in this area. Since the first cases arose in the 1970s, courts have ruled both for and against gay and lesbian parents in determining the best interests of the child but have more frequently denied gay and lesbian parents custody of their children. As recently as the late 1990s, state supreme court decisions in the South and Midwest have restricted visitation rights or transferred custody away from a gay or lesbian parent (*Marlow v. Marlow*, 1998; *Pulliam v. Smith*, 1998). Some states have acted on adoption or foster parenting by gay men or lesbians. The first was Florida, where a law prohibiting adoption by lesbians and gay men was enacted in 1977. However, in many other states, gay men and lesbians have been allowed to adopt in second-parent adoptions (Chambers & Polikoff, 1999).

Assisted Reproduction

The National Center for Health Statistics (NCHS) reported in 1995 that 6.1 million women between the ages of 15 and 44 experienced an impaired ability to have children; the number of infertile married couples was estimated at 2.1 million. NCHS (1995) further estimated that 9 million women had used infertility services by 1995. The development of medical technologies enabling infertile women and couples to bear children has presented legal and ethical challenges. Perhaps because of the rapidity of the developments, or perhaps due to the complexity of the relationships established by these new techniques, adequate legal and ethical structures or systems to guide participants in assisted reproduction have not been developed. As use of these technologies becomes more prevalent, courts and legislatures will be increasingly pressured to respond. This is already beginning; the National Conference of Commissioners on Uniform State Laws' 1998 Draft Revision of the Uniform Parentage Act includes provisions relating to assisted reproduction. These revisions are in discussion, and it may be years before the project is complete and states can consider adopting it.

Infertility treatment may include relatively uncontroversial procedures such as artificial insemination with a husband's sperm or ovarian stimulation to enhance the chances of conception. Other methods (e.g., in vitro fertilization and ovum donation) raise complex legal issues by introducing additional parties contributing genetic material or biological support to the reproductive process or by creating unprecedented decision-making options at each stage of the process. The involvement of a third party in a couple's efforts to create a family is not itself a new event. Donor sperm conception has long been available, as it does not require advanced medical intervention. Similarly, traditional surrogacy, in which a woman agrees to conceive and bear a child for a couple using the man's sperm, has also been historically available. The increasing range of treatment options, however, creates pressure for the law to respond.

Although the law is underdeveloped in the area of assisted reproduction, we can identify several issues that may require legal resolution. First, the standard in vitro fertilization process using the sperm and eggs of a couple seeking to conceive creates preembryos that exist outside of the uterus and can be frozen for an undetermined period. Consequently, disputes over the custody and control of the preembryos may arise between the partners, as in *Davis v. Davis* (1992), where the Tennessee Supreme Court ruled that both spouses had a right regarding procreation, but the father's desire not to procreate outweighed the mother's interest in donating the embryos. Second, with ovum donation, the donor may also claim an interest in decisions about the pregnancy, the embryos, or a child born of the process. Finally, with gestational and traditional surrogacy, disputes over decisions regarding pregnancy, embryos, or children may develop among the individuals intending to act as parents, the donors of genetic material, and the surrogate carrying the fetus. In the case of Baby M. (*In the Matter of Baby M.*, 1988), the court held that the surrogacy contract was void because it was contrary to public policy. Treating the case as a custody dispute between the biological surrogate mother and the biological father, the court granted custody to the father with limited visits for the surrogate mother. Claims by donors and surrogates challenge the law to address the interests of parties outside the marital or partnership relationship.

Federal and state legislation governing disputes between participants in assisted reproduction is rare, so the courts are playing the most significant role. Judges are relying on varying legal concepts and doctrines in resolving disputes, including property law, contract law, child custody law, and constitutional law (Triber, 1998). The more novel concept of intent to parent was articulated in a California Court of Appeals case where the court ruled that individuals who intend to and act to create a child through assisted reproduction technology become legally responsible for the resulting child, even where there is no genetic relationship to the child (*In re Marriage of Buzzanca*, 1998).

Adoption

Adoption is not a new phenomenon in family law. However, the following three trends merit attention: transracial, intercountry, and open adoptions. Intercountry and transracial adoptions are criticized on the grounds that parents whose racial, ethnic, or cultural identity differs from that of their children cannot provide an essential element of parenting in a society where racial and ethnic discrimination exists. Open adoption gives rise to a different controversy—the potential conflict between adopted children who seek information about and possible contact with birth parents and birth parents who may want to maintain anonymity.

The issue of transracial adoption arises primarily in the adoption of children in the foster care system whose parents' rights have been terminated by the state. In 1999, the U.S. Department of Health and Human Services estimated there were 117,000 children in the foster care system seeking adoption. Of these, 51% were African American, 32% were White, and 11% were Hispanic. The groups most likely to adopt include childless women, women with fecundity impairments, White women, and women with higher levels of income and education (Mosher & Bachrach, 1996). The number of transracial adoptions is unknown, but estimates range from 1% to 11% of all children in foster care (Avery & Mont, 1994). With the majority of foster children ready for adoption being African American and with White women seeking to adopt more frequently, the benefits and problems of transracial adoption deserve attention.

The federal government has enacted legislation to facilitate transracial adoption in the foster care system. The Howard Metzenbaum Multiethnic Placement Adoption Act of 1994 had the stated purpose of preventing discrimination in placement decisions on the basis of race, color, or national origin. In 1996, another federal law repealed and replaced the Multiethnic Placement Act with stronger provisions barring the use of race as a criterion in decisions about foster care,or adoption placements (1996b). For those who question "whether white, adoptive parents can raise Black children to be well-adjusted productive adults with a positive sense of racial identity" (Perry, 1999, p. 470), the federal government's promotion of transracial adoption is problematic. Others may view the federal government's response to the increasing number of African American children awaiting placement as consistent with a broader trend toward interracial marriage and partnerships, resulting in an increase in interracial parenting without adoption (Census Bureau, 1999).

Intercountry adoption also raises the question of parental competency when the parents' and the child's race, ethnicity, or culture differ. Over the past 10 years or so, the number of children adopted in the United States from other countries has more than doubled, from 8,102 in 1989 to 16,396 in 1999 (U.S. Department of State, 2000). On October 6, 2000, President Clinton signed the Inter-Country Adoption Act, ratifying the Hague Adoption Convention, which is designed to encourage intercountry adoption.

Open adoption, in which adopted children are provided with information about and in some cases the choice to contact birth parents, are another example of society's recognition that families can include more parties than two spouses and their biological children. Although adopted children may desire information about or a relationship with their birth parents, birth parents may want anonymity. Adoption laws changed from relatively open records to sealed records by the mid-1960s (Cahn & Singer, 1999). In the 1970s, adoptees began challenging sealed adoption records, seeking access to birth certificates through the courts. Rejected by the courts, adoptees pursued legislative remedies with success. Most states now provide nonidentifying information about birth parents and have established procedures for contact when there is mutual consent. The first state laws making original birth records fully accessible passed in 1999, with efforts underway in other states. The Oregon statute was challenged, but the U.S. Supreme Court denied a motion to not allow it to go into effect (Roseman, 2000).

LOOKING TO THE FUTURE

It is possible to develop optimistic hypotheses about family law in the new millennium. In regard to marriage, divorce, and nontraditional relationship forms, it seems clear that the partnership model will continue to prevail over the earlier dependence model. The underlying economic and social changes relating to the role of women in society are not likely to be reversed. Alternative relationships, such as those between same-sex couples, will slowly receive recognition as society strives to create structures that support stable relationships in which children can thrive. However, resistance to nontraditional families and relationships will continue to generate legislative responses such as the Defense of Marriage Act and covenant marriage statutes. Child custody laws and laws relating to unwed fathers will continue to promote fathers' parenting role, motivated in part by a desire to impose financial responsibility for child support. Similarly, nonparents will continue to gain access to children with whom they have close relationships; laws will still struggle to mediate varying interests in stepfamilies.

The legal ambivalence toward gay or lesbian parents should gradually fade if evidence of their children's well-being continues to accumulate. For families created through assisted reproduction technology and for stepfamilies, the courts and legislatures will continue to struggle with the interests of multiple parties. Recent reforms favoring transracial adoption may not endure—the pendulum could swing back in favor of same-race placements as Americans continue to struggle with race relations and racism. However, intercountry adoption seems unlikely to disappear. Individual countries may limit adoptions or make the adoption process more difficult, but economic pressures are likely to prevail.

Future Involvement of Social Science in the Law

As in the past century, shifts in family law are likely to be driven by demographic and social changes. Nevertheless, it is likely that social scientists will continue to influence legal processes. The factors that contributed to the increasing role of social science—more judicial flexibility, greater legitimacy of social science research, greater likelihood of courts requiring intervention programs, more need for expert testimony, and others—are likely to continue to expand social scientists' roles in legal proceedings. We support the use of social science research to inform and guide the development of the law. To maximize the extent to which research influences the process of legal reform, social scientists need to appropriately qualify and explain their findings so that professionals not trained in research methods can understand their work. Social scientists may need to educate legal professionals regarding the limits of research and the difficulties inherent in drawing generalizations that apply across contexts. However, it is unlikely that the role of social science will dramatically increase in the next century.

In which areas of family law are social scientists likely to make their greatest contributions? Divorce, remarriage, adoption, and in general, issues surrounding parenting and parent-child relationships will be in the forefront of social science contributions. For example, issues such as how children's time will be allocated among divorced parents and the effect of parenting plans will be of great interest. In addition, as technologies change how families are formed (e.g., surrogate childbearing), social science research may be helpful in working through the delicate issues related to the roles, rights, and responsibilities of the multiple parties involved in these family processes. Overall, in the future, we can expect a continuing revolution in family law as the ways in which families are formed and maintained continue to evolve. We can also expect that both law and social science will be seriously challenged to keep up with the changes.

Note

1. References for all cases and legal statutes may he obtained from the second author; e-mail: finem@missouri.edu.

References

American Law Institute. (2000). *Principles of the law of family dissolution: Analysis and recommendations* (Tentative Draft No. 4). Philadelphia: Author.

Atkinson, J. (1984). Criteria for deciding custody in the trial and appellate courts. *Family Law Quarterly, 18,* 11–32.

Avery, R. J., & Mont, D. M. (1994). *Special needs adoption in New York State: Final report on adoptive parent survey* (DHHS Contract No. 90CW1012). Washington, DC: Department of Health and Human Services.

Blaisure, K., & Geasler, M. (1999, July). *Divorce education across the U.S.* Paper presented at the Coalition for Marriage, Family and Couples Education Conference, Washington, DC.

Blank, R. M. (1997). *It takes a nation.* New York: Russell Sage.

Bogenschneider, K. (2000). Has family policy come of age? A decade review of the state of U.S. family policy in the 1990s. *Journal of Marriage and the Family, 62,* 1136–1159.

Bonauto, M. (2000). *Civil action update* [Online]. Available: www.glad.org

Cahn, N., & Singer, J. (1999). Adoption, identity, and the constitution: The case for opening closed records. *University of Pennsylvania Journal of Constitutional Law, 2,* 150–194.

Census Bureau. (1999). *Interracial married couples: 1960 to present* [Online]. Available: www.census.gov/population/socdemo/ms-la/tabms-3.txt

Chambers, D. L., & Polikoff, N. D. (1999). Family law and gay and lesbian family issues in the twentieth century. *Family Law Quarterly, 33,* 523–542.

Cherlin, A. (1992). *Marriage, divorce, remarriage.* Cambridge, MA: Harvard University Press.

Elrod, L. D., Spector, R. G., & Atkinson, J. (1999). A review of the year in family law: Children's issues dominate. *Family Law Quarterly, 32,* 661–717.

Emery, R. E. (1995). Divorce mediation: Negotiating agreements and renegotiating relationships. *Family Relations, 44,* 377–383.

Fine, M. A., & Demo, D. (2000). Divorce: Societal ill or normative transition? In R. Milardo & S. Duck (Eds.), *Families as relationships* (pp. 135–156). Chichester, UK: Wiley.

Fine, M. A., & Fine, D. (1994). An examination and evaluation of recent changes in divorce laws in five Western countries: The critical role of values. *Journal of Marriage and the Family, 56,* 249–263.

Gallagher, M., & Waite, L. (2000). *The case for marriage.* New York: Doubleday.

Goldstein, J., Freud, A., & Solnit, A. (1973). *Beyond the best interests of the child.* New York: Free Press.

Johnston, J., Kline, M., & Tschann, J. (1989). Ongoing postdivorce conflict: Effects on children of joint custody and frequent access. *American Journal of Orthopsychiatry, 59,* 576–592.

Katz, S. N. (1999). Establishing the family and family-like relationships: Emerging models for alternatives to marriage. *Family Law Quarterly, 33,* 663–675.

Krause, H. (1986). *Family law* (2nd ed.). St. Paul, MN: West.

Lerman, R. L.(1993). A national profile of young unwed fathers. In R. L. Lerman & T. J. Ooms (Eds.), *Young unwed fathers* (pp. 35–39). Philadelphia: Temple University Press.

Mahoney, M. (1994). *Stepfamilies and the law.* Ann Arbor: University of Michigan.

Mason, M. A. (1988). *The equality trap.* New York: Simon & Schuster.

Mason, M. A. (1994). *From father's property to children's rights.* New York: Columbia.

Mason, M. A. (1998).The modern American stepfamily: Problems and possibilities. In M. A. Mason, A. Skolnick, & S. D. Sugarman (Eds.), *All our families* (pp. 95–116). New York: Oxford University Press.

Mason, M. A. (2000). *The custody wars.* New York: Basic Books,

McLanahan, S., & Sandefur. G. (1994). *Growing up with a single parent.* Cambridge, MA: Harvard University Press.

Mosher, W. D., & Bachrach, C. A. (1996). Understanding U.S. fertility: Continuity and change in the National Survey of Family Growth, 1988–1995 [13 pages]. *Family Planning Perspectives* [Online serial], *28*(1). Available FTP: Hostname: agi-usa.org Directory: pubs/journals/2800496.html

Nagourney, E. (2000, February 15). Study finds families bypassing marriage. *The New York Times,* p. F8.

National Center for Health Statistics. (1995). Fertility/infertility [Online]. Available FTP: Hostname: cdc.gov Directory: nchs/fastats/fertile.htm

Patterson, C. J. (2000). Family relationships of lesbians and gay men. *Journal of Marriage and the Family, 62,* 1052–1069.

Pearson, J. (1999). Domestic and international legal framework of family law: Court services: Meeting the needs of twenty-first century families. *Family Law Quarterly, 33,* 617–635.

Perry, T. L. (1999). Race matters: Change, choice, and family law at the millennium. *Family Law Quarterly, 33,* 461–474.

Regan, M. C., Jr. (1999). Establishing the family and family-like relationships: Marriage at the millennium. *Family Law Quarterly, 33,* 647–662.

Roseman, E. (2000, Fall). OPEN 2000: Are you ready for open records? *Resolve of Northern California Quarterly Newsletter,* 6.

Seltzer, J. (1994). Intergenerational ties in adulthood and childhood experience. In A. Booth & J. Dunn (Eds.), *Stepfamilies* (pp. 89–96). Hillsdale. NJ: Lawrence Erlbaum.

Siegel, A. J. (2000). Note: Setting limits on judicial scientific, technical, and other specialized fact-finding in the new millennium. *Cornell Law Review, 86,* 167.

Sugarman, S. (1998). Single-parent families. In M. A. Mason, A. Skolnick, & S. Sugarman (Eds.), *All our families* (pp, 13–38). New York: Oxford University Press.

Triber, G. A. (1998). Growing pains: Disputes surrounding human reproductive interests stretch the boundaries of traditional legal concepts. *Seton Hall Legislative Journal, 23,* 103–140.

U.S. Department of State. (2000). *Hague convention on intercountry adoptions* [Online]. Available: www.travel.state.gov/adoption_info_sheet.html

Wardle, L. D. (1999). Reorganizing the family: Divorce reform at the turn of the millennium: Certainties and possibilities. *Family Law Quarterly, 33,* 783–800.

Warshak, R. A. (2000). Remarriage as a trigger of parental alienation syndrome. *American Journal of Family Therapy, 28,* 229–241.

Weithorn, L. A., & Grisso, T. (1987). Psychological evaluations in divorce custody: Problems, principles, and procedures. In L. Weithorn (Ed.), *Psychology and child custody determinations: Knowledge, roles, and expertise* (pp. 157–181). Lincoln: University of Nebraska Press.

II The Sexes

U.S. society has experienced both a sexual revolution and a gender revolution. The first has liberalized attitudes toward erotic behavior and expression; the second has changed the roles and status of women and men in the direction of greater equality. Both revolutions have been brought about by the rapid social changes in recent years, and both revolutions have challenged traditional conceptions of marriage.

The traditional idea of sexuality defines sex as a powerful biological drive continually struggling for gratification against restraints imposed by civilization. The notion of sexual instincts also implies a kind of innate knowledge: A person intuitively knows his or her own identity as male or female, he or she knows how to act accordingly, and he or she is attracted to the "proper" sex object—a person of the opposite gender. In other words, the view of sex as biological drive pure and simple implies "that sexuality has a magical ability, possessed by no other capacity, that allows biological drives to be expressed directly in psychological and social behaviors" (Gagnon and Simon, 1970, p. 24).

The whole issue of the relative importance of biological versus psychological and social factors in sexuality and sex differences has been obscured by polemics. On the one hand, there are the strict biological determinists who declare that anatomy is destiny. On the other hand, there are those who argue that all aspects of sexuality and sex-role differences are matters of learning and social construction.

There are two essential points to be made about the nature-versus-nurture argument. First, modern genetic theory views biology and environment as interacting, not opposing forces. Second, both biological determinists and their opponents assume that if a biological force exists, it must be overwhelmingly strong. But the most sophisticated evidence concerning both gender development *and* erotic arousal suggests that physiological forces are gentle rather than powerful. Despite all the media stories about a "gay gene" or "a gene for lung cancer," the scientific reality is more complicated. As one researcher wrote recently, "the scientists have identified a number of genes that may, under certain circumstances, make an individual more or less susceptible to the action of a variety of environmental agents" (cited in Berwick, 1998, p. 4).

In terms of scholarship, the main effect of the sex-role and sexual revolutions has been on awareness and consciousness. Many sociologists and psychologists used to take it for granted that women's roles and functions in society reflect universal physiological and temperamental traits. Since in practically every society women were subordinate to men, inequality was interpreted as an inescapable necessity of organized social life. Such analysis suffered from the same intellectual flaw as the idea that discrimination against nonwhites implies their innate inferiority. All such explanations failed to analyze the social institutions and forces producing and supporting the observed differences.

But as Robert M. Jackson points out, modern economic and political institutions have been moving toward gender equality. For example, both the modern workplace and the state have increasingly come to treat people as workers or voters without regard for their gender or their family status. Educational institutions from nursery school to graduate school are open to both sexes. Whether or not men who have traditionally run these institutions were in favor of gender inequality, their actions eventually improved women's status in society. Women have not yet attained full quality, but in Jackson's view, the trend in that direction is irreversible.

One reason the trend toward greater gender equality will persist is that young people born since the 1970s have grown up in a more equal society than their parents' generation. Kathleen Gerson reports on a number of findings from her study of 18- to 30-year-old "children of the gender revolution." First, she finds that whether a mother works or the number of parents in the home is not the major determinant of children's experience in the home. What seems to matter is, first, family process—how family members interact with one another. Second, life changes such as a major illness, alcoholism, job loss, or family move can have a major impact on a child, but can occur in any family structure. She finds that young adults of both sexes have similar high aspirations for themselves in work and family, valuing both commitment and autonomy. They understand that these are difficult goals, and that there is a lack of social and community resources, such as child care, in support of working families. But Gerson finds a loss of political vision in this generation; they see only private solutions to work and family issues.

In their article, Scott Coltrane and Michele Adams examine some reasons why the home lags behind other institutions in the shift toward greater symmetry in male–female roles. Although men are doing more housework than they did twenty years ago, they are still doing much less than women. Partly, the answer is that men retain a good deal of power in marriage because of their greater earning capacity. But there is also a culture lag; most people in the United States are ambivalent about women's equality in marriage and family life. And many feel uncomfortable about a man who works fewer hours to devote more time to his home and children.

For many Americans, the most worrisome aspect of the sexual revolution is the increase in teenage sexual activity. But in her study comparing Dutch and U.S. parents, Amy Schalet finds strikingly different attitudes toward teenage sexuality. "Would you permit your 16-year-old child to have a boy- or girlfriend sleep over at home?," she asks, among other questions.

For U.S. parents, the answer is clearly "no." Teenage sex is so obviously wrong and dangerous that they feel their opposition to it needs no explanation. In contrast, Dutch parents tend to "normalize" teen sexuality; they don't view it as dangerous in itself, as long as the adolescents have a close relationship and behave responsibly. Schalet argues that Dutch parents are not simply more "permissive" than their U.S. counterparts; rather, these attitudes are part of a larger set of cultural differences.

Attitudes toward sexuality have also been changing in the United States. Julia Ericksen and Sally A. Steffen show that attitudes toward premarital sex were changing even before the sexual revolution of the 1960s. They describe the difficulties that confronted those who had to advise college students about sex during those times of shifting manners and morals.

Although some aspects of sex and gender have changed, others have been remarkably persistent. In their article on contemporary dating, Mary Laner and Nicole Ventrone find that traditional attitudes and practices are alive and well. Female college students are somewhat more egalitarian than male college students, but both genders display a mixture of semi-egalitarian and semi-traditional perspectives. Moreover, best-selling advice manuals reinforce the old cultural scripts for dating and tend to exaggerate the differences between the sexes and ignore the similarities. This lingering traditionalism, the authors suggest, may not bode well for later success in marriage.

However, the meaning of marriage itself has changed. As Paula Kamen explains in her article, the current ideal for marriage is that the partners be best friends. Surveys reveal that both men and women rate "respect for each other" as the most important quality in a good marriage, followed by love, sexual fidelity, and communication about feelings. Financial security is still important, but it is not enough without the emotional qualities people seek. In her interviews with young women, Kamen finds that they enter marriage with far different expectations and on a different footing than in the past. They don't expect men to be the sole providers in the family, but they have greater demands for intimacy. They also want to share the housework and the child care, and young men express a willingness to share these tasks as well.

Elaborating on the theme that society should provide secure jobs and better child-care options, Kathryn Edin examines various theories about why poor women find it hard to find men who might make good husbands, no matter how much they would like to be married.

Despite all the changes, marriage remains a cherished U.S. institution; the Census Bureau estimates that 90 percent of Americans will marry at some point in their lives. Yet, the supposed decline of marriage has become a political issue. And public anxiety about the future of marriage, as Frank F. Furstenberg Jr. points out in his article, sometimes approaches hysterical levels. He argues that recent changes are not signs that marriage is disappearing or in a severe state of crisis, but that there *is* cause for concern. The traditional marriage bargain, he explains, in which women exchanged their domestic services for financial support, is no longer valid. Now that women work outside the home, they are no longer as dependent on men as they used to be. Further, most men no longer have jobs that pay enough to support a family. Both men and women say they believe in greater equality in marriage, but in practice, most women still do the lion's share of housework and child care.

Although people in all walks of life are grappling with new expectations of gender equality, for many young adults with low incomes, marriage has become a luxury item. Furstenberg finds that people still value marriage, but that living together or single parenthood has become "the budget way to start a family."

What does it mean for married couples to be living in a time when divorce has become a commonplace, no longer shameful, event? Do high divorce rates signify a decline in such family values as commitment and responsibility? Karla B. Hackstaff explores these questions through in-depth interviews contrasting couples who married in the 1950s and those who married in the 1970s. She finds that the issue of divorce is inseparably intertwined with the issue of gender equality. Historically, marriage has been a male-dominated institution. The 50s wives accepted this, yet they tended to think about divorce far more than their husbands did. The 70s couples try to work out more egalitarian arrangements, and have developed a "marital work ethic" to counter the threat of divorce. Hackstaff concludes that today's "divorce culture" may be a temporary phenomenon, part of the transition toward greater equality in all aspects of marriage.

The sharp increase in divorce rates since the 1960s has given rise to public alarm about the future of the family, and even proposals to make divorces harder to get. But, as the article by Paul Amato shows, divorce is not a single event, but a long process. It is a complex chain of events and life experiences that begins long before the divorce itself and continues long after. Amato applies insights from the research on stress to the divorce process. He argues that the process of "uncoupling"—the breakdown of a marriage—can involve a string of stressful events, such as economic decline, loss of emotional support, and so on. The outcomes for adults and children depend on the number of these stressors and their severity. Outcomes also depend on other factors that can act as shock absorbers and protect people against stress—their economic resources and their social skills. Although divorce is an emotionally wrenching process for all concerned, it's difficult to make blanket statements about its long-term effects. Divorce tends to be a different experience for men, women, and children; and individual reactions to it vary enormously.

Despite all its difficulties, marriage is not likely to go out of style in the near future. Ultimately we agree with Jessie Bernard (1982), who, after a devastating critique of traditional marriage from the point of view of a sociologist who is also a feminist, said this:

> The future of marriage is as assured as any social form can be. . . . For men and women will continue to want intimacy, they will continue to want to celebrate their mutuality, to experience the mystic unity which once led the church to consider marriage a sacrament. . . . There is hardly any probability such commitments will disappear or that all relationships between them will become merely casual or transient. (p. 301)

References

Bernard, Jessie. 1982. *The Future of Marriage*. New York: World.
Berwick, Robert C. 1998. The doors of perception. *The Los Angeles Times Book Review*. March 15.
Gagnon, J. H., and W. Simon. 1970. *The Sexual Scene*. Chicago: Aldine/Transaction.

3 *Changing Gender Roles*

■ **READING 7**

Destined for Equality

Robert M. Jackson

Over the past two centuries, women's long, conspicuous struggle for better treatment has masked a surprising condition. Men's social dominance was doomed from the beginning. Gender inequality could not adapt successfully to modern economic and political institutions. No one planned this. Indeed, for a long time, the impending extinction of gender inequality was hidden from all.

In the middle of the nineteenth century, few said that equality between women and men was possible or desirable. The new forms of business, government, schools, and the family seemed to fit nicely with the existing division between women's roles and men's roles. Men controlled them all, and they showed no signs of losing belief in their natural superiority. If anything, women's subordination seemed likely to grow worse as they remained attached to the household while business and politics became a separate, distinctively masculine, realm.

Nonetheless, 150 years later, seemingly against all odds, women are well on the way to becoming men's equals. Now, few say that gender equality is impossible or undesirable. Somehow our expectations have been turned upside down.

Women's rising status is an enigmatic paradox. For millennia women were subordinate to men under the most diverse economic, political, and cultural conditions. Although the specific content of gender-based roles and the degree of inequality between the sexes varied considerably across time and place, men everywhere held power and status over women. Moreover, people believed that men's dominance was a natural and unchangeable part of life. Yet over the past two centuries, gender inequality has declined across the world.

The driving force behind this transformation has been the migration of economic and political power outside households and its reorganization around business and political interests detached from gender. Women (and their male supporters) have fought against prejudice and discrimination throughout American history, but social conditions governed the intensity and effectiveness of their efforts. Behind the very visible conflicts between women and male-dominated institutions, fundamental processes concerning economic and political organization have been paving the way for women's success. Throughout these years, while many women struggled to improve their status and many men resisted those efforts, institutional changes haltingly, often imperceptibly, but persistently undermined gender inequality. Responding to the emergent imperatives of large-scale, bureaucratic organizations, men with economic or political power intermittently adopted policies that favored greater equality, often without anticipating the implications of their actions. Gradually responding to the changing demands and possibilities of households without economic activity, men acting as individuals reduced their resistance to wives and daughters extending their roles, although men rarely recognized they were doing something different from their fathers' generation.

Social theorists have long taught us that institutions have unanticipated consequences, particularly when the combined effect of many people's actions diverges from their individual aims. Adam Smith, the renowned theorist of early capitalism, proposed that capitalist markets shared a remarkable characteristic. Many people pursuing only selfish, private interests could further the good of all. Subsequently, Karl Marx, considering the capitalist economy, proposed an equally remarkable but contradictory assessment. Systems of inequality fueled by rational self-interest, he argued, inevitably produce irrational crises that threaten to destroy the social order. Both ideas have suffered many critical blows, but they still capture our imaginations by their extraordinary insight. They teach us how unanticipated effects often ensue when disparate people and organizations each follow their own short-sighted interests.

Through a similar unanticipated and uncontrolled process, the changing actions of men, women, and powerful institutions have gradually but irresistibly reduced gender inequality. Women had always resisted their constraints and inferior status. Over the past 150 years, however, their individual strivings and organized resistance became increasingly effective. Men long continued to oppose the loss of their privileged status. Nonetheless, although men and male-controlled institutions did not adopt egalitarian values, their actions changed because their interests changed. Men's resistance to women's aspirations diminished, and they found new advantages in strategies that also benefited women.

Modern economic and political organization propelled this transformation by slowly dissociating social power from its allegiance to gender inequality. The power over economic resources, legal rights, the allocation of positions, legitimating values, and setting priorities once present in families shifted into businesses and government organizations. In these organizations, profit, efficiency, political legitimacy, organizational stability, competitiveness, and similar considerations mattered more than male privileges vis-à-vis females. Men who had power because of their positions in these organizations gradually adopted policies ruled more by institutional interests than by personal prejudices. Over the long run, institutional needs and opportunities produced policies that worked against gender inequality. Simultaneously, ordinary men (those without economic or political power) resisted women's advancements less. They had fewer resources to use against the women in their lives, and less to gain from keeping women subordinate. Male politicians seeking more power, businessmen pursuing wealth and success, and ordinary men pursuing their self-interest all contributed to the gradual decline of gender inequality.

Structural developments produced ever more inconsistencies with the requirements for continued gender inequality. Both the economy and the state increasingly treated people as potential workers or voters without reference to their family status. To the disinterested, and often rationalized, authority within these institutions, sex inequality was just one more consideration with calculating strategies for profit and political advantage. For these institutions, men and women embodied similar problems of control, exploitation, and legitimation.

Seeking to further their own interests, powerful men launched institutional changes that eventually reduced the discrimination against women. Politicians passed laws giving married women property rights. Employers hired women in ever-increasing numbers. Educators opened their doors to women. These examples and many others show powerful men pursuing their interests in preserving and expanding their economic and political power, yet also improving women's social standing.

The economy and state did not systematically oppose inequality. On the contrary, each institution needed and aggressively supported some forms of inequality, such as income differentials and the legal authority of state officials, that gave them strength. Other forms of inequality received neither automatic support nor automatic opposition. Over time, the responses to other kinds of inequality depended on how well they met institutional interests and how contested they became.

When men adopted organizational policies that eventually improved women's status, they consciously sought to increase profits, end labor shortages, get more votes, and increase social order. They imposed concrete solutions to short-term economic and political problems and to conflicts associated with them. These men usually did not envision, and probably did not care, that the cumulative effect of these policies would be to curtail male dominance.

Only when they were responding to explicitly egalitarian demands from women such as suffrage did men with power consistently examine the implications of their actions for gender inequality. Even then, as when responding to women's explicit demands for legal changes, most legislators were concerned more about their political interests than the fate of gender inequality. When legislatures did pass laws responding to public pressure about women's rights, few male legislators expected the laws could dramatically alter gender inequality.

Powerful men adopted various policies that ultimately would undermine gender inequality because such policies seemed to further their private interests and to address inescapable economic, political, and organizational problems. The structure and integral logic of development within modern political and economic institutions shaped the problems, interests, and apparent solutions. Without regard to what either women or men wanted, industrial capitalism and rational legal government eroded gender inequality.

MAPPING GENDER INEQUALITY'S DECLINE

When a band of men committed to revolutionary change self-consciously designed the American institutional framework, they did not imagine or desire that it would lead toward gender equality. In 1776 a small group of men claimed equality for themselves and similar men by signing the Declaration of Independence. In throwing off British sovereignty, they inaugurated the American ideal of equality. Yet after the success of their revolution, its leaders and like-minded property-owning white men created a nation that subjugated women, enslaved blacks, and withheld suffrage from men without property.

These men understood the egalitarian ideals they espoused through the culture and experiences dictated by their own historical circumstances. Everyone then accepted that women and men were absolutely and inalterably different. Although Abigail Adams admonished her husband that they should "remember the ladies," when these "fathers" of the American nation established its most basic rights and laws, the prospect of fuller citizenship for women was not even credible enough to warrant the effort of rejection. These nation builders could not foresee that their political and economic institutions would eventually erode some forms of inequality much more emphatically than had their revolutionary vision. They could not know that the social structure would eventually extend egalitarian social relations much further than they might ever have thought desirable or possible.

By the 1830s, a half-century after the American Revolution, little had changed. In the era of Jacksonian democracy, women still could not vote or hold political office. They had to cede legal control of their inherited property and their income to their husbands. With few exceptions, they could not make legal contracts or escape a marriage through divorce. They could not enter college. Dependence on men was perpetual and inescapable. Household toil and family welfare monopolized women's time and energies. Civil society recognized women not as individuals but as adjuncts to men. Like the democracy of ancient Athens, the American democracy limited political equality to men.

Today women enjoy independent citizenship; they have the same liberty as men to control their person and property. If they choose or need to do so, women can live without a husband. They can discard an unwanted husband to seek a better alternative. Women vote and occupy political offices. They hold jobs almost as often as men do. Ever more women have managerial and professional positions. Our culture has adopted more affirmative images for women, particularly as models of such values as independence, public advocacy, economic success, and thoughtfulness. Although these changes have not removed all inequities, women now have greater resources, more choices in life, and a higher social status than in the past.

In terms of the varied events and processes that have so dramatically changed women's place in society, the past 150 years of American history can be divided into three half-century periods. The *era of separate spheres* covers roughly 1840–1890, from the era of Jacksonian democracy to the Gilded Age. The *era of egalitarian illusions*, roughly 1890–1940, extends from the Progressive Era to the beginning of World War II. The third period, the *era of assimilation*, covers the time from World War II to the present (see Table 1).

Over the three periods, notable changes altered women's legal, political, and economic status, women's access to higher education and to divorce, women's sexuality, and the cultural images of women and men. Most analysts agree that people's legal, political, and economic status largely define their social status, and we will focus on the changes in these. Of course, like gender, other personal characteristics such as race and age also define an individual's status, because they similarly influence legal, political, and economic rights and resources. Under most circumstances, however, women and men are

TABLE 1   *The Decline of Gender Inequality in American Society*

	1840–1890 The Era of Separate Spheres	1890–1940 The Era of Egalitarian Illusions	1940–1990 The Era of Assimilation	1990–? Residual Inequities
Legal and political status	Formal legal equality instituted	Formal political equality instituted	Formal economic equality instituted	Women rare in high political offices
Economic opportunity	Working-class jobs for single women only	Some jobs for married women and educated women	All kinds of jobs available to all kinds of women	"Glass ceiling" and domestic duties hold women back
Higher education	A few women admitted to public universities and new women's colleges	Increasing college; little graduate or professional education	Full access at all levels	Some prestigious fields remain largely male domains
Divorce	Almost none, but available for dire circumstances	Increasingly available, but difficult	Freely available and accepted	Women typically suffer greater costs
Sexuality and reproductive control	Repressive sexuality; little reproductive control	Positive sexuality but double standard; increasing reproductive control	High sexual freedom; full reproductive control	Sexual harassment and fear of rape still widespread
Cultural image	Virtuous domesticity and subordination	Educated motherhood, capable for employment & public service	Careers, marital equality	Sexes still perceived as inherently different

not systematically differentiated by other kinds of inequality based on personal characteristics, because these other differences, such as race and age, cut across gender lines. Educational institutions have played an ever-larger role in regulating people's access to opportunities over the last century. Changes in access to divorce, women's sexuality, and cultural images of gender will not play a central role in this study. They are important indicators of women's status, but they are derivative rather than formative. They reveal inequality's burden.

The creation of separate spheres for women and men dominated the history of gender inequality during the first period, 1840–1890. The cultural doctrine of separate spheres emerged in the mid-nineteenth century. It declared emphatically that women and men belonged to different worlds. Women were identified with the household and maintenance of family life. Men were associated with income-generating employment and public life. Popular ideas attributed greater religious virtue to women but greater civic virtue to men. Women were hailed as guardians of private morality while men were regarded as the protectors of the public good. These cultural and ideological inventions were responses to a fundamental institutional transition, the movement of economic activity out of households into independent enterprises. The concept of separate spheres legitimated women's exclusion from the public realm, although it gave them some autonomy and authority within their homes.

Women's status was not stagnant in this period. The cultural wedge driven between women's and men's worlds obscured diverse and significant changes that did erode inequality. The state gave married women the right to control their property and income. Jobs became available for some, mainly single, women, giving them some economic independence and an identity apart from the household. Secondary education similar to that offered to men became available to women, and colleges began to admit some women for higher learning. Divorce became a possible, though still difficult, strategy for the first time and led social commentators to bemoan the increasing rate of marital dissolution. In short, women's opportunities moved slowly forward in diverse ways.

From 1890 to 1940 women's opportunities continued to improve, and many claimed that women had won equality. Still, the opportunities were never enough to enable women to transcend their subordinate position. The passage of the Woman Suffrage Amendment stands out as the high point of changes during this period, yet women could make little headway in government while husbands and male politicians belittled and rejected their political aspirations. Women entered the labor market in ever-increasing numbers, educated women could get white-collar positions for the first time, and employers extended hiring to married women. Still, employers rarely considered women for high-status jobs, and explicit discrimination was an accepted practice. Although women's college opportunities became more like men's, professional and advanced degree programs still excluded women. Married women gained widespread access to effective contraception. Although popular opinion expected women to pursue and enjoy sex within marriage, social mores still denied them sex outside it. While divorce became more socially acceptable and practically available, laws still restricted divorce by demanding that one spouse prove that the other was morally repugnant. Movies portrayed glamorous women as smart, sexually provocative, professionally talented, and ambitious, but even they, if they were good women, were driven by an overwhelming desire to marry, bear children, and dedicate themselves to their homes.

Writing at the end of this period, the sociologist Mirra Komarovsky captured its implications splendidly. After studying affluent college students during World War II, Komarovsky concluded that young women were beset by "serious contradictions between two roles." The first was the feminine role, with its expectations of deference to men and a future focused on familial activities. The second was the "modern" role that "partly obliterates the differentiation in sex," presumably because the emphasis on education made the universal qualities of ability and accomplishment seem the only reasonable limitations on future activities. Women who absorbed the egalitarian implications of modern education felt confused, burdened, and irritated by the contrary expectations that they display a subordinate femininity. The intrinsic contradictions between these two role expectations could only end, Komarovsky declared, when women's real adult role was redefined to make it "consistent with the socioeconomic and ideological modern society."[1]

Since 1940, many of these contradictions have been resolved. At an accelerating pace, women have continually gained greater access to the activities, positions, and statuses formerly reserved to men.

Despite the tremendous gains women have experienced, they have not achieved complete equality, nor is it imminent. The improvement of women's status has been uneven, seesawing between setbacks and advances. Women still bear the major responsibility for raising children. They suffer from lingering harassment, intimidation, and disguised discrimination. Women in the United States still get poorer jobs and lower income. They have less access to economic or political power. The higher echelons of previously male social hierarchies have assimilated women slowest and least completely. For example, in blue-collar hierarchies they find it hard to get skilled jobs or join craft unions; in white-collar hierarchies they rarely reach top management; and in politics the barriers to women's entry seem to rise with the power of the office they seek. Yet when we compare the status of American women today with their status in the past, the movement toward greater equality is striking.

While women have not gained full equality, the formal structural barriers holding them back have largely collapsed and those left are crumbling. New government policies have discouraged sex discrimination by most organizations and in most areas of life outside the family. The political and economic systems have accepted ever more women and have promoted them to positions with more influence and higher status. Education at all levels has become equally available to women. Women have gained great control over their reproductive processes, and their sexual freedom has come to resemble that of men. It has become easy and socially acceptable to end unsatisfactory marriages with divorce. Popular culture has come close to portraying women as men's legitimate equal. Television, our most dynamic communication media, regularly portrays discrimination as wrong and male abuse or male dominance as nasty. The prevailing theme of this recent period has been women's assimilation into all the activities and positions once denied them.

This book [this reading was taken from] focuses on the dominant patterns and the groups that had the most decisive and most public roles in the processes that changed women's status: middle-class whites and, secondarily, the white working class. The histories of gender inequality among racial and ethnic minorities are too diverse to address adequately here.[2] Similarly, this analysis neglects other distinctive groups, especially lesbians and heterosexual women who avoided marriage, whose changing circumstances also deserve extended study.

While these minorities all have distinctive histories, the major trends considered here have influenced all groups. Every group had to respond to the same changing political and economic structures that defined the opportunities and constraints for all people in the society. Also, whatever their particular history, the members of each group understood their gender relations against the backdrop of the white, middle-class family's cultural preeminence. Even when people in higher or lower-class positions or people in ethnic communities expressed contempt for these values, they were familiar with the middle-class ideals and thought of them as leading ideas in the society. The focus on the white middle classes is simply an analytical and practical strategy. The history of dominant groups has no greater inherent or moral worth. Still, except in cases of open, successful rebellion, the ideas and actions of dominant groups usually affect history much more than the ideas and actions of subordinate groups. This fact is an inevitable effect of inequality.

THE MEANING OF INEQUALITY AND ITS DECLINE

We will think differently about women's status under two theoretical agendas. Either we can try to evaluate how short from equality women now fall, or we can try to understand how far they have come from past deprivations.

Looking at women's place in society today from these two vantage points yields remarkably different perspectives. They accentuate different aspects of women's status by altering the background against which we compare it. Temporal and analytical differences separate these two vantage points, not distinctive moral positions, although people sometimes confuse these differences with competing moral positions.

If we want to assess and criticize women's disadvantages today, we usually compare their existing status with an imagined future when complete equality reigns. Using this ideal standard of complete equality, we would find varied shortcomings in women's status today. These shortcomings include women's absence from positions of political or economic power, men's preponderance in the better-paid and higher-status occupations, women's lower average income, women's greater family responsibilities, the higher status commonly attached to male activities, and the dearth of institutions or policies supporting dual-earner couples.

Alternatively, if we want to evaluate how women's social status has improved, we must turn in the other direction and face the past. We look back to a time when women were legal and political outcasts, working only in a few low-status jobs, and always deferring to male authority. From this perspective, women's status today seems much brighter. Compared with the nineteenth century, women now have a nearly equal legal and political status, far more women hold jobs, women can succeed at almost any occupation, women usually get paid as much as men in the same position (in the same firm), women have as much educational opportunity as men, and both sexes normally expect women to pursue jobs and careers.

As we seek to understand the decline of gender inequality, we will necessarily stress the improvements in women's status. We will always want to remember, however, that gender inequality today stands somewhere between extreme inequality and complete equality. To analyze the modern history of gender inequality fully, we must be able to look at this middle ground from both sides. It is seriously deficient when measured against full equality. It is a remarkable improvement when measured against past inequality.

Editors' Note: *Notes for this reading can be found in the original source.*

■READING 8

Children of the Gender Revolution: Some Theoretical Questions and Findings from the Field

Kathleen Gerson

As a new century commences, it is clear that fundamental changes in family, work, and gender arrangements have transformed the experience of growing up in American society. Only several decades ago, an American child was likely to grow to adulthood in a two-parent home with a mother who worked outside the home either intermittently or not at all. No such common situation unites children today. With less than fourteen percent of American households containing a married couple with a breadwinning husband and homemaking wife, children living in a "traditional family" now form a distinct minority (Ahlburg and De Vita, 1992; Gerson, 1993). Regardless of race, ethnicity, or class, most younger Americans have lived, or will live, in a family situation that departs significantly from a pattern once thought to be enduring. Many have grown up in a two-parent home in which both parents have pursued strong and sustained ties to work outside the home. Others have lived through marital disruptions and perhaps the remarriage of one or both parents. Still others have been raised by a single mother who never married the father of her children. Most of these children have experienced shifting circumstances, in which some substantial change occurred in their family situation before they left their parents' home.

This revolution in the experience of childhood has provided an unprecedented opportunity to unravel the processes of human development and better understand the consequences of growing up in diverse family situations. We are living through a natural social experiment that makes it possible to assess the effects of family arrangements as well as other social and cultural institutions on the lives of children. As the recipients of widespread gender and family change, this generation is ideally positioned to shed light on a number of important theoretical questions.

First, what is the relationship between family composition and children's welfare? Is family structure, as measured by the household's composition and gender division of labor, the most consequential aspect of a child's developmental environment, as has been generally assumed, or is family form mediated by other factors, such as interactional processes within the home and contextual factors outside it? Second, what are the links between parental choices and children's reactions? How do children make sense of their family situations and their parents' circumstances, and what strategies do they develop to cope with their situations? Are children inclined to adopt their parents' choices and beliefs, and when and under what circumstances are they more likely to reject or modify them?

Third, what part do institutions outside the family, and especially community, educational, and labor market structures, play in shaping a child's outlook and developmental trajectory? And, finally, as new generations of women and men respond to widespread cultural changes outside the home and shifting dynamics within it, what personal, social, and political strategies are they developing to cope with the new contingencies wrought by the family and gender revolutions? What do the experiences of this pivotal generation portend for the future of gender—as a cultural belief and a lived experience?

The "children of the gender revolution" have grown to adulthood in a wide range of circumstances, and their experiences offer a window through which to glimpse both general processes of human development and historically embedded social shifts. By taking a careful look at the developmental paths and personal conflicts of this generation, we can untangle the role that family structure plays in children's lives and discover the other processes and factors that either mitigate or explain its effects. And since members of this generation are now negotiating the transition to adulthood and thus poised to craft their own work and family strategies, they offer important clues to the future course of the transformation in family, work, and gender patterns begun by their parents.

CHANGES IN CHILDREN'S LIVES: CONTENDING WITH THEORETICAL APPROACHES AND THE "FAMILY VALUES" DEBATE

The diversification of family forms has produced disputes among American social scientists (as well as among politicians and ordinary citizens) about the effects of family and gender transformations on the welfare of children. These debates have been framed in "either/or" terms, in which those who decry the decline of the homemaker–breadwinner family have clashed with those who defend and, to some extent, celebrate the rise of alternative family forms.

Analysts concerned that family and gender transformations threaten children's welfare and undermine the larger social fabric have developed a perspective that emphasizes "family decline." (See, for example, Blankenhorn, 1994; Popenoe, 1989 and 1996; Whitehead, 1997.) This approach tends to view the "traditional family," characterized by permanent heterosexual commitment and a clear sexual division of labor between stay-at-home mothers and breadwinning fathers, as the ideal family form. The rise in divorce, out-of-wedlock parenthood, and employment among mothers thus represent a serious family breakdown that is putting new generations of younger Americans at risk. From this perspective, "nontraditional families," such as dual-earner and single-parent households, are part of a wider moral breakdown, in which the spread of an individualistic ethos has encouraged adults to pursue their own self-interest at the expense of children.

While compelling, the "family decline" contains both logical and empirical deficiencies. First, it treats family change as if it were a cause rather than an effect. Yet new family forms are inescapable reactions to basic economic and social shifts that have propelled women into the workplace and expanded the options for personal development in adulthood. By idealizing the mid-twentieth century homemaker–breadwinner household, this perspective also tends to downplay the positive aspects of change and especially the expansion of options for women. We now know, however, that family life in the past rarely conformed to our nostalgic images and that many homemaker–breadwinner families were rife with unhappiness and abuse (Coontz, 1992).

In response to the critique of family change, less pessimistic analysts have responded that family life is not declining but rather adapting, as it has always done in response to new social and economic exigencies. These analysts point out that a return to family forms marked by significant gender inequality is neither possible nor desirable and would not solve the predicaments parents and children now face. (See, for example, Skolnick, 1991; Stacey, 1990 and 1996; Coontz, 1997.) The roots of the family and gender revolution extend deep into the foundations of the economy, the society, and the culture. Single parents and employed mothers have thus become scapegoats for social ills with deeper economic and political roots.

Despite the polarized nature of the American "family values" debate, both perspectives have tended to focus on family structure as the crucial arena of contention. Yet research suggests that family structure, taken alone, cannot explain or predict outcomes for children. While children living with both biological parents appear on average to fare better than children in one-parent homes, most of the difference can be traced to the lower economic and social resources available to single parents as well as to factors such as high family conflict that promote parental break-up in the first place (Cherlin et al., 1991; McLanahan and Gary Sandefur, 1994).

In the case of employed mothers, circumstantial factors also appear to trump family structure. Despite the persisting concern that children are harmed when their mothers work outside the home, decades of research have yielded virtually no support for this claim. Instead, the critical ingredients in providing for children's welfare are such factors as a mother's satisfaction with her situation, the quality of care a child receives, and the involvement of fathers and other supportive caretakers (Barnett and Rivers, 1996; Hoffman, 1987). Even comparisons between oft-labeled "traditional" and "nontraditional" families show that diversity within family types is generally as large as differences between them (Acock and Demo, 1994).

The focus on family structure has thus obscured a number of more basic questions about the short- and long-run consequences of these complicated and deeply rooted social changes. While it is clear that a return to a world marked by a clear sexual division of labor, an unquestioned acceptance of gender inequality, and the predominance of patriarchal families, is neither desirable nor possible, it is less clear what new social forms will or should emerge. To understand this process, we need to delve beneath the polarized controversy over family values to clarify the consequences of diversifying family forms, increasing female autonomy, and shifting adult commitments to those who are the most direct recipients of change. How has the generation born during this period of rapid and tumultuous change experienced, interpreted, and responded to the gender revolution forged by their parents?

UNDERSTANDING THE CHILDREN OF THE GENDER REVOLUTION

To answer these questions, I have interviewed a group that can be considered the "children of the gender revolution." These late adolescents and young adults, between the ages of 18 and 30, are members of the generation that is young enough to have experienced the dynamics of family change at close hand, yet old enough to have a perspective on their childhood circumstances and to be formulating their own plans for the future. Since family change may have been experienced differently in different economic and social contexts, the group has been drawn from a range of racial and ethnic backgrounds and a variety of poor, working-class, and middle-class communities. Of the 120 people interviewed, approximately 56% are non-Hispanic white, 20% are African-American, 18% are Hispanic, and 6% are Asian. They were randomly selected from a range of urban and suburban neighborhoods in the New York metropolitan area. (Most respondents were selected by a random sampling procedure as part of a larger study of the children of immigrants and native-born Americans. To ensure that the parents of my respondents had been born and grown up amid the changing family circumstances of American society, my sample was drawn entirely from the native-born group. (See Mollenkopf et al. for a description of the study and sampling techniques.)

To illuminate how these "children of the gender revolution" have made sense of their childhoods and are formulating strategies for adulthood, in-depth, life-history interviews elicited information on their experiences growing up, their strategies for coping with past and present difficulties, and their outlooks on the future. Most lived in some form of "nontraditional" family arrangement before reaching eighteen. About a third lived in a single-parent home at some point in their childhood, and an additional 40% grew up in homes in which both parents held full-time jobs for a sustained period of time. Even the remaining group, who described their families as generally "traditional," were likely to grow up in homes that underwent some form of notable change as mothers went to work or marriages faced crises. As a whole, this diverse group experienced the full range of changes now emerging in U.S. family and gender arrangements.

The experiences of these strategically placed young women and men call into question a number of long-held assumptions about the primacy of family structure in human development. Their life paths and outlooks point, instead, to the importance of processes of family change, the shape of opportunities outside the family, and children's active strategies to cope with their circumstances amid inescapable but uncertain social shifts.

FAMILY STRUCTURE OR FAMILY TRAJECTORIES?

Despite the theoretical focus on "family structure," which generally refers to the composition and division of labor in the household, these young women and men offer a different view of how they formed their sense of self and their outlook on the future. From their perspective, what matters instead are more subtle family processes and pathways. Indeed, simple family typologies, based on differences among homemaker–breadwinner, dual-earner, and single-parent homes, mask important variations within such family forms. Indeed, regardless of the apparent "structure" of the household, most children experience some form of change in their family life over time. While a minority can point to stable, supportive family environments marked by few noticeable changes, the more common experience involves transitions, sometimes abrupt and always consequential, from one "family environment" to another. Surprisingly, this experience of change applies to many whose parents remained married and not just to those whose households underwent a break-up. More important than household structure at one point in time are the "trajectories" that families follow as they develop throughout the life of a child.

From the time a child is born to the time she or he leaves home, the family environment can develop in different ways. From the point of view of the child, these family experiences assume the form of family trajectories, or pathways, that can either remain stable or move in different directions over time. A "stable" trajectory may remain relatively harmonious, supportive, and secure, or it may remain chronically conflictual and unsupportive. A "changing" trajectory may become more stable and supportive as family conditions improve over the span of childhood and adolescence, or it may become more conflictual and insecure as family conditions deteriorate.

These trajectories are important, but they are not closely linked to prevailing notions of "traditional" and "nontraditional" family structures. While classical theories might predict that traditional households would be more stable and harmonious than nontraditional ones, the experiences of these young women and men reveal no such clear relationship. For example, a number of apparently stable "traditional" households are actually marked by chronic conflict or some kind of less readily noticeable change. In one case, a family's outward stability masked chronic parental addictions and abuse that never improved, despite their status as a two-parent home. In another case, a drug-addicted, distant father moved out of the family home in response to his wife's demand that he break his addiction or leave. Several years later, after a successful recovery, he returned to become a supportive, involved parent. This outwardly stable but internally riven "traditional" family thus became more harmonious and secure over time.

A comparable diversity of processes and practices can be found in nontraditional households. While all children undergo some kind of change if their parents separate or divorce, the transition can bring improvement or deterioration. One young woman, for example, felt relieved when her father divorced her neglectful, emotionally abusive mother, and she found stability and support when he remarried a nurturing, economically successful woman.

Static categories of "family type" thus offer limited clues about the dynamics between parents and children or the unfolding nature of family life. Children rarely perceive their families as fixed arrangements, but rather as a range of situations in flux, which either offer or deny them support over time. These processes are important in providing for a child's welfare, but they are not simple reflections of family structure. A breadwinner–homemaker arrangement does not guarantee a stable or supportive home, and those with dual-earning, single, or stepparents are clearly able to provide support and care.

EMPLOYED MOTHERS AND OTHER PARENTS

If family process is more important than family structure, then a mother's well-being is also more important than whether or not she works outside the home. While most of these young women and men grew up in homes in which their mothers were strongly involved in earning a living, the fact of working or not working mattered less than whether or not mothers (and fathers) appeared satisfied with their lives as workers and parents.

Young women and men reared by work-committed mothers generally agreed that the ensuing benefits outweighed any hypothetical losses. In many cases, a mother's job kept the family from falling into poverty, and in some, it helped propel the household up the class ladder. A mother's employment also gave both parents increased autonomy and appeared to enhance parental equality. While some worried that their mothers and fathers had to toil at difficult, demanding, and low-paying jobs, no one felt neglected. To the contrary, they were appreciative of their mothers' efforts to provide for their own and their family's welfare. Working outside the home thus provided a way for mothers as well as fathers to become "good" parents.

Those whose mothers did not pursue independent avenues outside the domestic sphere expressed more ambivalence. While some were pleased to have their mothers' attention focused exclusively on home and family, others were concerned that the choice had been an unnecessary sacrifice. In these cases, when a homemaking mother seemed frustrated or unhappy, the child's reaction was more likely to center on guilt and minor resentment than on gratitude.

More important than the choice to work or stay home, however, is the child's perception about why the choice was made. When a parent, whether mother or father, appeared to work for the family's welfare as well as his or her own needs, the child accepted these choices as unproblematic. If, in contrast, a mother's choice appeared to contradict her family's needs or her own desires, the child responded with concern and doubt. Children felt supported when parents made choices that provided for everyone's needs and did not pit the wishes of mothers against the needs of children. They fared better, however, when contextual supports helped working parents resolve the conflicts between family and work. Most important were reliable, neighborhood-based child care resources, involvement from committed fathers, and satisfying and flexible jobs for both parents.

BEYOND FAMILY STRUCTURE: FAMILY PROCESSES AND OPPORTUNITY CONTEXTS

How did children from these diverse family situations fare as they negotiated the challenges and dangers of childhood and adolescence? Their diverse fates ranged from successful young adults who were able to launch promising college and work careers to those who became entangled in less felicitous patterns, such as school failure, involvement in crime, and early parenthood. Why were some able to negotiate the risks of adolescence while others were propelled down perilous paths? While it may be tempting to attribute these disparate outcomes to family structure, that does not appear to be the explanation. Not only were people from all types of families, including traditional ones, socially and emotionally sidetracked, but many from "nontraditional" households were able to avoid or overcome the dangers they faced.

Several important, interacting factors influence individual trajectories. First, processes within the family either provided or denied emotional and social support to the child. Second, social and economic resources outside the family, including neighborhood-based resources such as peer groups and schools and class-based resources such as economic support, provided or denied financial and "social capital" to either avoid or escape dangerous situations. Structural and cultural contexts outside the family thus influenced children's outlooks and trajectories, regardless of the kinds of families in which they lived.

School experiences, for example, ranged from academic involvement and success to minor alienation to school failure. Those who fared poorly were likely to have parents who lacked either the will, the skills, or the money to make a special effort to hold the child to reasonable standards, to fight for a child in the face of an indifferent bureaucracy, or to make financial sacrifices (such as choosing a parochial or private school). Those who succeeded, on the other hand, were fortunate in a variety of ways. Most possessed either class-related resources that provided access to good schools and the social pressures and expectations of school success. In the absence of class resources, the support of only one person who believed in and would fight for the child could made a crucial difference.

Yet single mothers, many of whom were poor, and dual-income parents with time-consuming jobs were just as likely as traditional families to provide these pressures and supports. For example, one young man attributed his college and graduate degrees to his struggling but feisty single mother, who fought against a school bureaucracy determined to consign him to the category of "learning disabled."

Experiences outside of school also ranged from engagement in constructive activities, such as organized sports and social service, to involvement in dangerous pursuits, such as crime, drugs, and sexual risk-taking. While opportunities to experiment in risky ways were more prevalent in poor and minority communities, there were inducements in all types of neighborhoods. Those who fell prey to more dangerous lifestyles were not more likely to live in nontraditional homes, but they were more likely to become integrated into peer groups that countered a family's influence. Indeed, avoiding risky behavior often required resisting local temptations, such as a street culture centered around illicit activities. Neighborhoods matter and can thwart the efforts of parents to protect their children from the influences of a burgeoning youth culture outside the home.

Class resources, however, offer a consequential buffer. Middle-class children were more likely to be shielded by their parents and their communities while they passed through a stage of adolescent experimentation, whether it involved drugs, sex, or petty crimes. Poor and minority children were more likely to "get caught," to become ensnared in a punitive system, and to pay a higher long-term price for youthful indiscretions. In all of these ways, class resources and family processes (especially in the form of parental support) provide the context for family life and tend to supercede family structure as crucial shapers of children's life chances and developmental trajectories.

CHILDREN'S INTERPRETIVE FRAMEWORKS AND COPING STRATEGIES

Family processes and class resources form the context for children's experiences, but these contexts are always sifted through a child's interpretive framework and personal coping strategies. These strategies and frameworks represent active efforts on the part of children to give meaning to the actions of others and to craft their own choices amid the uncertainties of changing circumstances.

As this strategic generation has confronted the ideas, opportunities, and models of work and family institutions in flux, most people have had to cope with a world in which high hopes and aspirations are colliding with subtle fears and constricted realities. Regardless of race or class position, most women and men strongly support those aspects of change that have opened up opportunities for women and created new possibilities for redefining gender. Yet these hopes co-exist with concerns about the difficulty of combining work and family, the dangers of economic insecurity, and the lack of institutionalized supports for nontraditional choices. Whether the issue is work, family, or how to combine the two, the men and women emerging from the gender revolution perceive both new opportunities and a new set of dilemmas with few clear resolutions. While most hold egalitarian and pluralist ideals, at least in the abstract, they are less sanguine about whether or how these ideals can be achieved. (In a study of children living in gender-equal families, Risman, 1998, also finds a gap between children's egalitarian ideals and their identities.)

Work

Among women and men of all classes, almost everyone aspires to better jobs than their parents secured or they have yet been able to find. However, if the desire for a good, well-paying, white-collar job or career is nearly universal, the expectation of achieving it is not. Rather, these young women and men are divided in their optimism about the future. These divisions reveal blurring gender boundaries even as class boundaries persist. Women and men alike thus hold high aspirations for work careers, although those with constricted opportunities are less confident about reaching them. Optimism seems well-founded for some (e.g., college-educated whites) and ill-founded for others (e.g., young, single mothers and high school drop-outs). Most are hoping to find "satisfying jobs," willing to settle for "economic security," and not confident that they will be able to achieve either.

The skepticism about long-term economic prospects is reflected in men's and women's expectations of each other. Both groups view their economic prospects in "individualist" terms. Since men generally do not expect to earn enough to support wives and families alone, and women do not expect to be able to rely on male breadwinners, both groups believe their economic fate depends on their own job market achievements rather than on forging a lasting commitment with one partner. Women are thus as likely as men to express high job aspirations, and men are as likely as women to long for respite from the demands of earning a living. Despite these shared aspirations, women remain aware that their opportunities are more constricted than men's. A common refrain is thus that, "Women have it better today than in the past, but men still have it better and probably always will."

Marriage

If economic security and job options remain a concern, most nevertheless believe it is easier to shape their own labor market fate than to control the fate of their personal relationships. The vast majority of women *and* men view egalitarian marriage as the ideal, not only because dual-earner marriages appear to provide the best economic alternative but also because they offer the best hope for balancing personal autonomy with mutual commitment. These are high standards for defining a "good marriage," and many are skeptical that they will be able to achieve it.

Gender provides a lens through which similar expectations are experienced differently. While women and men are equally skeptical of creating lasting commitments, women are more aware of the consequences for work and family. They are more likely to see the possibility of raising children alone and more likely to link this possibility to the need for economic autonomy. Yet women agree with men that it is better to go it alone than to become enmeshed in an unhappy or narrowly confining commitment. Even those few—mostly men—who view traditional marriage as the ideal are more wishful than certain. In the face of these ideals, however, women remain skeptical that men can be counted on to shoulder their fair share, and men doubt they will have the job flexibility to do so.

Parenthood

Changing views of marriage provide the context for shifting orientations toward parenthood. For most women and men, the best parenting appears to be equal parenting. The rise of employed mothers and dual-earning couples thus appears to be good for children—bringing in more family income, fostering happier marriages, and providing better examples of women's autonomy and gender justice. Most (though not all) have concluded that "ideal mothers" and "ideal fathers" are fundamentally indistinguishable, and, across races and classes, the majority are skeptical of family arrangements based on rigid or insurmountable gender differences.

Regardless of their own family experience, moreover, everyone agrees that a committed partnership and happy marriage provide the best context for raising a child. The problem, however, is that a happy marriage is difficult to achieve. Most also agree, therefore, in the context of a deteriorating or chronically conflictual marriage, a child cannot thrive. The key for this generation is that both parents remain involved and supportive even if they find they cannot sustain a commitment to each other.

Views of Gender

Larger cultural shifts, and especially the rising acceptance of and need for women's economic independence, have permeated everywhere, leaving children from all classes and family situations exposed to changing definitions of gender and new work and family options. Most support these changes, arguing that while women have gained considerable opportunities, they have not done so at men's expense.

Women as well as men place a high value on autonomy, and men are equally likely to espouse egalitarian ideals at home and at work. These ideals clash, however, with institutional options that put many of them out of reach. If egalitarian ideologies, support for diversity, and a desire for personal choice predominate, behavioral strategies may stray far from these ideals.

Despite the desire to span the perceived gap between goals and opportunities, few can envision effective social, institutional, or political resolutions to these intractable dilemmas. When asked whether employers or the government can or should help families, most reply that individuals in American society are on their own. The protracted political battle over "family values" has left this generation with little faith that political action can make a difference or that "personal" problems can have social causes and institutional solutions.

Self and Society Amid the Gender Revolution

A diverse and shifting set of experiences are sending these children of the gender revolution in a variety of new and unclear directions. Most hold high aspirations for the future but are also skeptical about the possibilities for achieving their fondest dreams. And because they do not generally see the link between their own seemingly intractable dilemmas and the larger social–structural forces that are shaping the contours of change, they lack a vision of the possibilities for social solutions to what are experienced as very personal problems.

Prepared to face a gap between ideals and options, they are determined to exercise some choice over which trade-offs to make—between work and family, parenthood and career, marriage and going it alone. If their work and family ideals prove to be false promises, they reserve the right to change their circumstances. Despite the uncertainty ahead, however, most agree that the future will not and should not bring a return to the idealized past of separate spheres for men and women. From their perspective, the era when most marriages were permanent, women stayed home with children, and men wielded unquestioned power is irretrievable and undesirable.

BEYOND THE "FAMILY VALUES" DEBATE

The emergence of diverse family arrangements in the United States offers a unique opportunity to develop a better theoretical grasp of the link between the institutions of child rearing, the experiences of growing up, and the long-term trajectories of children. While debate has focused on the importance of family structure, the developmental trajectories of those who have grown up amid these changes reveals a more complicated picture. The lessons gleaned from these lives suggest expansions to and reformulations of prevailing theoretical frameworks.

First, family processes and trajectories matter more than family structure. Not only can conflict and neglect be found in all types of families, including those that may appear outwardly stable and secure, but processes of nurturance and support also emerge in a range of family contexts. More important than a family's structure at one point in time are processes of family change over time. Does a child's family context involve increasing support and declining conflict or, in contrast, declining support and continuing or rising conflict? From the child's perspective, what matters in the long run are emotional and economic sustenance, mutually respectful dynamics within the home, and caring bonds with their parents and other caretakers. Traditional families cannot guarantee these conditions, and nontraditional ones are often able to provide them.

Similarly, the employment status of mothers matters less than the overall context in which mothers—and fathers—create their lives. Across classes and gender groups, children are less concerned about whether their mothers work outside the home than about why their mothers work (or do not work), how their mothers feel about working (or not working), and what kind of caretaking arrangements their mothers and fathers can rely on. On balance, children see their mothers' employment as a benefit on many levels. Mothers' jobs offer families greater economic security and increased resources, enhance mothers' satisfaction and autonomy, and provide an example worthy of emulation. Children do worry, however, about their mothers' and fathers' abilities to obtain jobs with good economic prospects, supportive working conditions, and enough flexibility for combining work with family life.

Given the varied and ambiguous influence of family structure, it is time to focus theoretical attention on the institutional arrangements and social processes that matter for children, regardless of the family form in which they happen to live. Community and economic resources are crucial, providing the context for family life and either opening opportunities or posing risks and dangers. Resources such as educational and work opportunities, child care services, and personal networks of adults and peers help shape parents' strategies for rearing their children and children's abilities to cope with difficult circumstances.

Finally, children are not passive recipients of parental and social influences. They actively interpret and respond to their social worlds, often in unexpected ways. As social actors facing unforeseen contingencies, they must make new sense out of received messages and develop a variety of innovative coping strategies. They are crafting these strategies in a changing cultural context, where new views of gender and shifting work and family opportunities are as likely to influence their outlooks as are immediate family experiences.

The trajectories and experiences of these "children of the gender revolution" suggest that a search for one "best" family form provides neither a fruitful theoretical avenue nor a useful practical agenda. Instead, the challenge is to understand how children experience and respond to family conditions that are usually in flux and always embedded in wider institutions. Regardless of a child's family circumstance, contextual supports are essential for enabling parents and children to cope with change in a satisfying way.

For those who have grown to adulthood during this era of fluid personal paths and family arrangements, the fundamental aspects of change appear irreversible and, on balance, desirable. The dismantling of the homemaker–breadwinner ideal has widened options that few are prepared to surrender. These changes in family life and women's options have not, however, been met with comparable changes in the workplace and community life. And although most have adopted nontraditional, egalitarian ideals, few can envision support from employers or the government for achieving their goals. Lacking faith in work or political institutions, they are resolved to seek individual solutions to unprecedented social dilemmas and to develop new ways of negotiating adulthood. The experiences and responses of this new generation are especially important in this era of irrevocable but incomplete transformation. They may be the inheritors of change, but their strategies for responding to their parents' choices and their own dilemmas will shape their future course.

References

Acock, Alan C., and David H. Demo. 1994. *Family Diversity and Well-Being.* Thousand Oaks, CA: Sage Publications.

Ahlburg, Dennis A., and Carol J. De Vita. 1992. "New Realities of the American Family." *Population Bulletin* 47 (2) (August): 1–44.

Barnett, Rosalind, and Caryl Rivers. 1996. *She Works/He Works: How Two-Income Families Are Happier, Healthier, and Better Off.* San Francisco, CA: HarperSanFrancisco.

Blankenhorn, David. 1994. *Fatherless America: Confronting Our Most Urgent Social Problem.* New York: Basic Books.

Cherlin, Andrew, et al. 1991. "Longitudinal Studies of Effects of Divorce on Children in Great Britain and the United States." *Science* 252 (June): 1386–1389.

Coontz, Stephanie. 1992. *The Way We Never Were: American Families and the Nostalgia Trap.* New York: Basic Books.

———. 1997. *The Way We Really Are: Coming to Terms with America's Changing Families.* New York: Basic Books.

Crosby, Faye J., ed. 1987. *Spouse, Parent, Worker: On Gender and Multiple Roles.* New Haven: Yale University Press.

Gerson, Kathleen. 1993. *No Man's Land: Men's Changing Commitments to Family and Work.* New York: Basic Books.

Hoffman, Lois. 1987. "The Effects on Children of Maternal and Paternal Employment." Pp. 362–395 in *Families and Work*, edited by Naomi Gerstel and Harriet Engel Gross. Philadelphia: Temple University Press.

McLanahan, Sara, and Gary Sandefur. 1994. *Growing Up with a Single Parent: What Hurts, What Helps.* Cambridge, MA: Harvard University Press.

Mollenkopf, John, Philip Kasinitz, and Mary Waters. 1997. "The School to Work Transition of Second Generation Immigrants in Metropolitan New York: Some Preliminary Findings." Paper presented at Levy Institute Conference on the Second Generation (October). New York: Bard College.

Popenoe, David. 1989. *Disturbing the Nest: Family Change and Decline in Modern Societies.* New York: Aldine de Gruyter.

———. 1996. *Life without Father: Compelling New Evidence that Fatherhood and Marriage Are Indispensable for the Good of Children and Society.* New York: Free Press.

Risman, Barbara J. 1998. *Gender Vertigo: American Families in Transition.* New Haven and London: Yale University Press.

Skolnick, Arlene. 1991. *Embattled Paradise: The American Family in an Age of Uncertainty.* New York: Basic Books.

Stacey, Judith. 1990. *Brave New Families: Stories of Domestic Upheaval in Late 20th Century America.* New York: Basic Books.

———. 1996. *In the Name of the Family: Rethinking Family Values in a Postmodern Age.* Boston: Beacon Press.

Whitehead, Barbara D. 1997. *The Divorce Culture.* New York: Alfred A. Knopf.

■ R E A D I N G   9

Men's Family Work: Child-Centered Fathering and the Sharing of Domestic Labor

Scott Coltrane and Michele Adams

According to popular wisdom, housework is so trivial that it is not worthy of serious discussion. According to recent scholarship from sociology and women's studies, however, examining the allocation of housework may tell us more about marital power and gender relations than almost any other subject. Families cannot function unless someone does the routine shopping, cooking, and cleaning that it takes to run a household. Identifying who avoids doing these household tasks is often an excellent indicator of who has the highest status in the couple or family. Who feels entitled to household services, who is obligated to perform them, and how couples evaluate the fairness of divisions of labor can tell us something important about the subtle exercise of power in intimate relationships. And such seemingly trivial household matters can also help us understand how and why gender inequity is perpetuated in the society-at-large.

Modern history shows that it has been women who have done most of the routine family housework, including shopping, cooking, meal cleanup, house cleaning, and laundry. In this chapter, we will see that the cultural ideal of separate spheres, which suggests that women belong in the private/home sphere and men belong in the public/work sphere, has encouraged this unbalanced distribution of household labor. More recently, however, as wives have moved into the paid labor force and started to share the bread-winning role with their husbands, social scientists have generally expected men to begin to share in housework responsibilities. Unfortunately for working women, this has not been the case, as most women have instead been expected to shoulder the burden of a "second shift" of housework on top of their employment responsibilities (Hochschild with Machung 1989).

In recent years, there have been some shifts in who is doing the housework in American families. Generally speaking, the amount of time per week that men spend doing housework has increased slightly. At the same time, women are now doing less housework than they used to, and, therefore, the percent of total housework which is being performed by men has increased. Nevertheless, the overall changes in men's contributions have been small. Thus, today, housework continues to be unequally distributed, with women spending roughly twice as much time on routine household tasks as men. In this chapter, we will look at the unbalanced distribution of housework, how it got to be that way, how it is changing, and how we think these changes will affect the balance of power between men and women in the future.

A BRIEF HISTORY OF SEPARATE SPHERES

In preindustrial America, which was largely rural and agricultural, husbands and wives (and children) generally worked on the family farm, producing most of the food, goods, and services needed for the family's survival. Through bartering and trading with other nearby farmers or in the village at small artisans' shops, families were able to obtain the goods and services that couldn't be produced at home. With the spread of the industrial revolution in the 1800s, however, items which had been produced at home and in village artisans' shops began to be replaced by goods and services produced in urban factories. Family farms and businesses found they could no longer compete with factory production. Farmers and artisans, finding themselves without a means of livelihood, began to monopolize factory jobs. When men later found their control over jobs threatened by women's entry into waged labor, the cult of domesticity (also known as the cult of true womanhood) developed to bolster the notion of separate spheres for men and women. According to these emergent cultural ideals, frail but morally pure women were expected to find true happiness and fulfillment in their domestic roles as wives and mothers, while rugged "manly" men left home each day to earn a family wage. The ideal middle-class woman was supposed to take care of the home (with help from servants), tend to her children, and humanize her husband, giving him respite from the cruel and competitive world beyond the family.

The boundary between home and work was never as distinct as these ideals implied, especially for poor and working-class families, but the romantic image of separate spheres gained widespread popularity. Moreover, belief in separate spheres for men and women functioned to structure access to the labor market; while women were expected to stay at home in the "private" sphere, men (especially middle-class white men) could have relatively unconstrained access to high-paying jobs in the public realm. Throughout modern history, separate spheres ideology has been revived periodically to encourage women to focus on domestic responsibilities, particularly in times of high unemployment when men are especially fearful of competing with women for jobs (Jackson 1992; Kimmel 1996).

Separate spheres ideology and the cult of domesticity were firmly embedded in the public consciousness by the beginning of the twentieth century. At the same time, a steadily increasing number of women were entering the paid labor force, with this increase becoming particularly steep after the onset of World War II. The rapid influx of women into paid labor served as a countervailing force to separate spheres thinking, although "modernized" versions of the cult of domesticity have continued to be invoked at certain periods throughout the century. Even today, remnants of separate spheres ideology affect how men and women view women's roles both in the home and in the workplace, with the result that women often question their own dedication to housework and hesitate to ask men to do more.

Nevertheless, married women continue to enter the paid labor force in record numbers, with the biggest increases seen for mothers of young children. Between 1960 and 1997, the percent of married women over 16 participating in the United States labor force nearly doubled, from 31.9 to 61.6 percent (*Statistical Abstract of the United States: 1998*, tables 652, 653). By 1997, nearly 78 percent of married women with school-aged children and 65 percent of those with preschool children were employed (*Statistical Abstract of the United States: 1998*, tables 654, 655).

CONTEMPORARY DIVISIONS OF HOUSEWORK

Most women enter the paid labor force because they need the money, but employment also provides personal satisfaction and fulfillment (Coontz 1997:58). Additionally, national and global economic restructuring has resulted in a substantial growth in service sector jobs and a decreased need for workers in agriculture and manufacturing (Coltrane 1998:72). Moreover, according to the U.S. Bureau of the Census, women's real wages increased between 1995 and 1996, while men's decreased slightly (U.S. Bureau of the Census 1997, Current Population Reports: Consumer Income P60-197). For these reasons, it is generally agreed that two incomes are necessary to maintain a middle-class standard of living, and dual-earner families are now the norm in the United States. In fact, in 1996, nearly 64 percent of families with children under 18 years old included both an employed father and an employed mother (*Statistical Abstract of the United States: 1998*, table 656). Working women, wives, and mothers, therefore, have less time available to perform household tasks which they routinely performed in the past.

Neither are working wives inclined to leave their paid employment. A recent national survey found that less than a third of working women would prefer to stay home even if money were no object (Coontz 1997:58). Other polls have found that over two-thirds of both men and women disagree that women should return to the role of stay-at-home housewife (Skolnick 1991:189; see also Coltrane 1998:74). Research on housework over the last several decades, therefore, has focused on how much of the housework slack men have taken up as women have moved into waged employment. In response to the rapid increase in women's labor force participation, and with opinion polls showing more people endorsing equality for women, many observers predicted that the division of household labor would rapidly become more gender-neutral. Contrary to this expectation, housework studies performed in the 1970s, 1980s, and 1990s offered little evidence that major changes were occurring (Coltrane 1999; Miller and Garrison 1982; Thompson and Walker 1989). Most studies find that women continue to do roughly two-thirds of the family's routine housework, generally taking responsibility for monitoring and supervising the work as well, even when they pay for domestic services or assign tasks to other family members. Moreover, married women, and those who have children, tend to perform an even greater proportion of housework than single women and those without children.

To get a sense of how housework is divided by gender across the country, researchers have examined the amount of time spent doing specific household tasks (see Blair and Lichter 1991). Studies have found that wives perform over 96 percent of the cooking, 92 percent of the dishwashing, 90 percent of the vacuuming, and 94 percent of bed making (Blair and Lichter 1991; see also Berk and Berk 1979; and Berk 1985). Men, in contrast, do over 86 percent of household repairs, 75 percent of lawn mowing, and 77 percent of snow shoveling (Blair and Lichter 1991; see also Schooler, Miller, Miller, and Richtand 1984).

The exasperation experienced by working women whose husbands contribute little to the more routine housework is captured in books such as Francine M. Deutsch's *Halving It All* (1999). One woman she interviewed, employed fifty-two hours a week, still did virtually all of the housework:

> Although tired and stressed, working a double day, Carol doesn't expect [her husband] to
> do much: "I just want him to pick up after himself. I don't particularly expect that he is
> going to vacuum . . . My husband doesn't even know how dishes go in the dish-
> washer . . . All I would really like him to do is pick up behind himself." (Deutsch 1999:67)

Another woman employed full-time singled out laundry as a particularly troublesome
task: "I get so sick of doing laundry. I do laundry constantly . . . he won't . . . lay a finger
on laundry" (Deutsch 1999:67). Vacuuming, washing dishes, and doing laundry, which
these women's husbands refused to do, are household chores that women are typically expected to perform. Auto repairs and lawn maintenance, on the other hand, are chores
which men are expected to do (Blair and Lichter 1991). How are these gendered expectations related? One husband explained to Deutsch that he "rides" on taking care of the
cars when his wife is insistent that he clean up the house: "If the cars have needed a lot
of work lately, I can ride on that for a bit because then I can have something quantifiable
I point to that I have been doing" (Deutsch 1999:71). At the microlevel, this segregation
of household tasks reinforces power differences between men and women by associating
women's tasks with the most routine, least enjoyable family chores. At the macrolevel, a
similar segregation of tasks is reflected in the gendered nature of particular occupations,
with service and support jobs labeled "women's work." Similar to women's household
tasks, "women's work" in the paid labor force is generally less prestigious and paid less
than men's work (Coltrane 1998).

   In fact, some household chores are more likely to be considered "housework" than
others. Household labor includes a number of different tasks, some occurring inside the
home and others taking place outside of it. There are five "indoor" chores that have repeatedly been shown to be the most time-consuming, and which we refer to as "housework" or "routine housework." These tasks involve meal preparation or cooking, house
cleaning, shopping for groceries and household goods, washing dishes or cleaning up
after meals, and laundry (including washing, ironing, and mending clothes) (Blair and
Lichter 1991; Robinson and Godbey 1997). These chores are more time-consuming, less
optional, and less able to be put off than other household tasks such as lawn care or house
repairs. Although some people do see this routine work (particularly the cooking) as
pleasant, most men and women report that they do not like doing housework (Devault
1991; Robinson and Milkie 1997, 1998). On the other hand, most people find other tasks
such as household repairs and yard care to be more flexible, more discretionary, and more
enjoyable than everyday routine housework tasks (Coltrane 1998; Larson, Richards, and
Perry-Jenkins 1994).

   These patterns of household labor allocation tend to generate feelings of entitlement among men. When Deutsch asked Carol's husband how he responds to his more-
than-full-time-employed wife's pleas for help around the house, he said, "I just chuckle"
(Deutsch 1999:67). And the husband in Deutsch's study who refused to do laundry said
he felt entitled to relax after work and on the weekends:

> She probably won't sit still on a Sunday . . . Sundays I usually relax . . . She's not happy un-
> less she's doing something. That's the difference between her and I. She's not happy un-
> less she's making a cake, making supper, doing laundry. She very rarely can sit down and

watch television, take a break . . . She's not happy unless she's doing something. I'm different. I can relax. (Deutsch 1999:68)

Not surprisingly, some people, mostly men, consider housework to be trivial. In a now classic article that was one of the first to consider the political significance of housework, Pat Mainardi (1970) noted that men resort to a number of verbal ploys to avoid it. Mainardi's husband insisted, for example, "I don't mind sharing the housework, but I don't do it very well. We should each do the things we're best at." And, "I don't mind sharing the housework, but you'll have to show me how to do it." Or, "I *hate* it more than you. You don't mind it so much." Then, finally, "Housework is too trivial to even talk about" (Mainardi 1970:449–450). Although men have used their superior bargaining position to trivialize and avoid housework, it remains essential to human well-being. The routine activities that provide food, clothing, shelter, and care for both children and adults are vital for survival. In fact, domestic work is just as important to maintaining society as is the productive work occurring in the formal market economy. Recent studies suggest that the total amount of time spent in family work (including child care, housework, and other household labor) is about equal to the time spent in paid labor (Robinson and Godbey 1997).

MEN'S PARTICIPATION IN HOUSEWORK

Relatively few cultural images exist which suggest that men could possibly be "as good" at housework as women are. With few exceptions, comic strips, television shows, and movies show us how inept men are when they attempt to perform "women's work." From Dagwood Bumstead in *Blondie* to Tim Allen on *Home Improvement*, men are shown as comic buffoons when it comes to doing the housework. Even films that celebrate fathers' efforts to care for their children, like Michael Keaton in *Mr. Mom*, Dustin Hoffman in *Kramer vs. Kramer*, and Robin Williams in *Mrs. Doubtfire* illustrate how ill-prepared men are for performing mundane domestic work. Thus, there are few cultural role models for boys or men to follow in assuming greater responsibility for household tasks. Scholars argue about whether media images mimic everyday life and promote or inhibit social change, but in the area of housework, it is clear that popular culture is not pushing most men to do more (Coltrane and Adams 1997; Coltrane and Allan 1994).

In real life, men's self-proclaimed ineptitude at doing housework often becomes an excuse for them to avoid it. One wife's exasperation at her husband's (feigned) incompetence is expressed by Deutsch:

He plays, you know, "How do you do this kind of thing?" and asks me fifteen questions so it would almost be easier for me to do it myself than to sit there and answer all his questions. That makes me angry because I feel like he's just playing stupid because he doesn't want to do it. (Deutsch 1999:77)

And, Deutsch notes, there are men who use praise of their wife as the "flip side" of their self-professed incompetence, as does the following father:

> She's wonderful (as a mother) . . . Some women, like I say, are geared to be business-
> women; Florence is geared to be a mother. She loves it. She's good at it. I feel real lucky
> to have her as a partner because it takes a lot of the burden off me. (Deutsch 1999:77)

By extolling Florence's virtues as a mother, her husband symbolically removes her from
the public realm of business while at the same time praising her for allowing him unfet-
tered access to it. Separate spheres ideology and the cult of domesticity never had it so
good.

Why does men's participation in housework remain so far behind their wives' in
spite of women's paid employment? A number of reasons have been suggested for men's
"housework lag." Some researchers believe that women may act as "gatekeepers" to
men's involvement in family work, using their traditional role as household managers to
restrict men's opportunities to learn how to do housework. By setting rigid standards for
housecleaning which men are unable (or unwilling) to maintain, it is argued, women
may be able to sustain their (conceptual) dominance in the private sphere (see Allen and
Hawkins 1999; Coltrane 1996, 1989; Feree 1991; Greenstein 1996). For example,
Deutsch notes the benefits of "doing it all" for a school psychologist who works forty-
five hours a week: "Embarrassed, Peg [said]: 'Another thing I can't ignore is I'm in control. That sounds terrible. That's not how I mean it, but I mean I'm able to structure
things . . . I feel like I want to be in control' " (Deutsch 1999:55). While Peg's admis-
sion that she wants to be in control may represent an example of maternal gatekeeping,
it is also likely a response to her husband's refusal to participate in family work in the
first place (see Allen and Hawkins 1999). Ethan, Peg's husband, observes:

> It's hard for me to do anything during the week. If I come home at six-thirty, seven, I'm
> tired, basically fatigued . . . so when 6 A.M. rolls around and the kids are getting up, the
> last thing I think I really want to volunteer for is extra duties. I shouldn't say extra duties,
> but [I'm] certainly not going out of my way. (Deutsch 1999:53)

Most theories examining why men's housework continues to lag behind women's
involve the issue of power in families and focus on the relative resources of husband and
wife, time availability, economic dependency, and gender ideology (Coltrane 1999;
Greenstein 1996; Vannoy-Hiller 1982). Theories using relative resource models suggest
that the person with more income (generally the husband) will do less housework, while
time availability theories imply that when people spend more time in paid work they will
spend less time doing housework. The economic dependency model of housework suggests that women make a contract with their husbands to exchange household labor in
return for economic support from a main breadwinner (Brines 1994). Finally, theories
drawing on gender ideology suggest that people brought up to believe in the gender-
segregation of work will conform to those beliefs when they later marry.

The difference in power between men and women in families has important implications for each of these theories, and suggests that the partner with the most power in
the relationship will be the one who can tacitly set the terms of the division of labor in
the family. Because most people (men and women alike) do not find housework to be particularly enjoyable and most men have relatively higher earnings and social power, it is
usually men who "opt out" of doing routine domestic chores. Moreover, power in mar-

riage is not just about conflict or other overt behavior, but also includes "invisible" or "hidden" power that relies on what Gramsci (1971) called "ideological hegemony." This notion suggests that both men and women tend to accept the idea that what is in the husband's best interest, is in the wife's best interest as well. The invisible power that promotes an acceptance of men's interests as primary also encourages both husbands and wives to "buy into" men's reduced participation in housework (Komter 1989) and their excuses for doing little (Pyke and Coltrane 1996). Wives are, therefore, often inadvertently complicit in permitting their husbands to avoid housework, protecting men from tasks that they find onerous. In this sense, it is not unusual for a woman to intentionally avoid asking her husband to do chores that she anticipates he will hate (Braverman 1991).

On the other hand, men are doing more housework now than they were twenty years ago, although they still do much less than their wives. Since the 1970s, men's contribution to cooking, cleaning, and washing has increased from about 2 to 3 hours per week to about 5 to 8 hours per week (different estimates result from different ways of collecting household labor data). While men's participation has increased, women have decreased the amount of time they spend in these tasks. In addition, employed women have shifted considerable housework to the weekends and now do about one-third less family work than other women (Robinson and Godbey 1997). Combining women's reductions with men's increases, we can say that men's percentage of contribution to housework in the average American household has more than doubled in two decades (Coltrane 1999).

What chores are men performing? Men have begun to take on at least a portion of the responsibility for some of the routine tasks normally identified with women, such as grocery shopping, cooking, and meal clean-up. On the other hand, there have been only modest increases in men's share of housecleaning, laundry, and other repetitive indoor housekeeping tasks. Studies show that men are still reluctant to take full responsibility for housework tasks, but are sometimes more willing to do them if they can act as "helpers" to their wives. With the increased attention paid to studying housework in the past two decades, we now know that men perform more housework and child care when they are employed fewer hours, when their wives work longer hours or earn more money, and when both spouses believe in gender equity (Coltrane 1999).

Studies also show us that sharing housework is usually a practical response to work and childcare demands. In general, substantial sharing between husbands and wives occurs only after wives actively bargain for it. If couples deliberately divide tasks early in the relationship, a pattern of sharing develops and becomes self-perpetuating. If, however, couples make the assumption that sharing will happen on its own, the tendency is for women to end up doing virtually everything (Coltrane 1996).

FAIRNESS AND ENTITLEMENT IN HOUSEWORK

A recent public opinion poll showed that fully 88 percent of women and 78 percent of men believe that women do more of the household chores in their family (To the Contrary Poll 1997). Interestingly, however, 60 percent of the women and 71 percent of the men answered "yes" to the question, "Is the way that you and your spouse share household chores fair to both of you?" This poll confirms what previous studies have suggested: In spite of the fact that the burden of housework falls disproportionately on women, a majority of both men and women consider it to be fair.

Fairness in household labor does not automatically mean sharing tasks equally or putting in the same amount of time. To evaluate just how much housework is considered to be fair, sociologists Mary Clare Lennon and Sarah Rosenfield (1994) examined the amount of household labor that men and women are willing to do before they see the task division as unfair to themselves. According to Lennon and Rosenfield, women are willing to do roughly two-thirds of the household labor (about 66 percent) before they start to see it as unfair to themselves. Men, on the other hand, will do approximately 36 percent of the household labor before they begin to see it as unfair to themselves. Thus, there appears to be general acceptance of highly unbalanced divisions of household labor, with both sexes expecting women to put in many more hours than men on domestic tasks. The relevant question then becomes: Why are women willing to accept such an unequal division of housework?

Social theories suggest that wives label unbalanced divisions of household labor as fair because they have less power (including invisible power) in the marriage. One reason wives continue to perceive lopsided housework distribution as fair is because of differences in their sense of entitlement relative to that of their spouse (see Ferree 1990; Hochschild 1989; Major 1987, 1993; and Thompson 1991). As noted above, men often see themselves as entitled to household services, a fact which sometimes makes women hesitant to ask for the help they need.

Sociologist Arlie Hochschild has described a "marital economy of gratitude" whereby husbands' and wives' images of themselves as masculine or feminine encourage them to see some actions in their marriage as gifts and others as burdens; for example, a man may see his wife's employment as either a gift or a burden, depending on how he views himself as a man (Hochschild with Machung 1989:18). This "emotional economy of marriage" includes feelings about entitlements, as well (Pyke and Coltrane 1996). While marital economies of gratitude are constantly negotiated in all couples, the more powerful spouse usually sets the terms for such negotiations. Thus, when one spouse is grateful for the actions of the other, he or she feels indebted and obligated to reciprocate. When, however, that spouse is displeased with the others' actions, he or she expects a spouse to compensate for the displeasing acts by doing more.

As suggested previously, it is generally the husband who is the more powerful spouse, due in large part to his greater financial and social leverage in the relationship. Therefore, the husband's pleasure or displeasure usually drives feelings of entitlement. These feelings of entitlement then reflect "invisible power" that leads both women and men to see fairness where fairness does not objectively exist. Men's culturally and economically driven feelings of entitlement to women's domestic services, therefore, may be important sources of women's acceptance of unbalanced distributions of housework.

Other factors may contribute to a perception of fairness in the distribution of housework, as well, such as the outcomes that are desired (more time, certain standards of cleanliness, care, or "keeping the peace," for example) (Major 1993; Thompson 1991). Also, whether an individual compares their household contributions to their partner's (cross-gender comparison), or to other women's or men's (within-gender comparison), may significantly impact their fairness evaluations (Thompson 1991; Coltrane 1990). Commenting on a father's boast that "Very few men on the face of this earth ever diapered as many bottoms as I have," Deutsch observes that it is easy to see these fathers as "extraordinary if you compare them to other men, but once the standard shifts to a comparison with their wives, their pride and the applause seem misplaced" (1999:103). Fathers who help out with child care are often praised and described in glowing terms for performing tasks that go unnoticed if performed by mothers. In an interview study of role-sharing parents, one woman said that she "appreciated her husband's willingness to help, [but] friends who called him perfect were a little out of touch" (Coltrane 1996:138). Men's contributions to housework, likewise, tend to be noticed and applauded, whereas women's are generally taken for granted (Robinson and Spitze 1992). Finally, whether the procedures that created the existing unbalanced distribution of housework are considered appropriate also contributes to perceptions of fairness, including, for example, forgiving a partner's lack of housework because of supposed ineptitude or because a prior joint decision was made about who should do the work.

The more hours women work in the paid labor force, the less fair they see the division of labor in the home (see Greenstein 1996; Sanchez 1994; Sanchez and Kane 1996). A number of studies also show that both men and women with more egalitarian gender attitudes tend to see the existing division of household labor as more unfair to the wife (Blair and Johnson 1992; DeMaris and Longmore 1996; Sanchez and Kane 1996). Interestingly, when measuring gender ideology by asking if employed spouses should share housework, egalitarian men rate the existing division of household labor as more fair to their wives, but egalitarian wives rate the existing division of labor as less fair to themselves (DeMaris and Longmore 1996). Apparently, egalitarian husbands are hesitant to admit to an unbalanced distribution of housework which contradicts their belief in equality. For egalitarian wives, on the other hand, an unequal division of tasks is likely to be particularly salient because of their belief in sharing, and their attitudes, therefore, are more likely to generate criticism of the present situation.

Women (and sometimes men) often see both their own and their spouse's housework as carrying emotional messages, such as love, caring, or appreciation. Symbolically equating housework with care can lead to demands for more task performance on the one hand, but it can also encourage women to consider men's expressions of affection or intent to do housework as sufficient (without actually *doing* the work), thereby encouraging these women to assess current unbalanced labor arrangements as fair. One woman who gave up a promising career to stay home with her children, asked only that her husband show some appreciation for her sacrifice and recognition of her domestic contributions: "You are at work with all these bigwigs and I'm home with children playing blocks. I've had a hard day too" (Deutsch 1999:69).

Perceptions of fairness may also intervene between the division of household labor and personal or marital well-being. When housework is believed to be fair, wives display fewer symptoms of depression, but when it is perceived as unfair, women are more depressed (Glass and Fujimoto 1994; Lennon and Rosenfield 1994). Being satisfied with one's husband's contribution to housework is also related to better marital interaction and more marital closeness, less marital conflict, and fewer thoughts of divorce (Piña and Bengtson 1993). Moreover, while perceived unfairness predicts both unhappiness and distress for women, it predicts neither for men (Robinson and Spitze 1992).

Men are almost universally satisfied with the division of housework, whereas women, particularly egalitarian women who are content with their paid work, are typically less satisfied (Baxter and Western 1998). In the end, the single most important predictor of how fair a wife sees the distribution of housework to be is what portion of the routine housework (cooking, cleaning, and laundry) her husband contributes. And, while husbands are making some limited progress in these areas, these also seem to be the areas where they are most resistant to change.

LINKING PAID WORK AND HOUSEWORK

Economist Heidi Hartmann once said that the family is "a primary arena where men exercise their patriarchal power over women's labor" (1981:377). That power is played out in the family at least partly through the unbalanced distribution of housework. In spite of recent endorsement of women's equality as shown in opinion polls, the division of labor in the home continues to disadvantage women.

The Victorian ideal of separate spheres for men and women relegated women to the "private sphere," where they were expected to care for their husband, their children, and their house. Men, on the other hand, were sent to the "public sphere" to earn wages outside of the home. In recent decades, women have moved into the paid labor force in record numbers, but their jobs have not relieved them of obligation to maintain the home. Many experience a "double day" because they work in paid employment during the day and, during the evening, perform the housework and "caring" work that is expected of them as wives, mothers, and daughters. Although women have reduced the number of hours they spend performing housework, men have not been as willing to take up the slack in domestic responsibilities.

On the other hand, men are doing more housework these days than they did in the past and, when coupled with women's reduction in household labor, they are actually doing a larger percentage of the housework as well. However, the changes in men's housework contributions have been small. Women continue to perform roughly two-thirds of the housework that is being done in America's families. Moreover, men and women both tend to see this imbalance as fair; the "tipping point" for women's sense of fairness is at about 66 percent of the household labor. Men, on the other hand, feel the housework division to be unfair to them when they do more than 36 percent of the total household labor. This general acceptance of the unequal nature of housework attests to a hidden power imbalance in families. Men feel entitled to benefit from women's labor in the home and women feel a corresponding sense of obligation to perform this labor in gratitude for the economic support which men (at least conceptually) provide. The power of housework lies in its ability to create a "Catch 22" for women: The more housework they do, the less able they are to participate in the waged workforce and provide their own economic support; relatedly, the less they participate in the waged workforce, the more housework they must perform in gratitude for economic support from their husbands. Not surprisingly, economists find that lower wages for women are directly related to women's greater responsibility for housework (Hersch and Stratton 1994, 1997).

Although most men feel that housework is a trivial concern, most women do not. As Hartmann (1981) and others suggest, housework links men's control of women in the private sphere to their control of women in the public sphere. Sharing housework equally would begin to break this link and reduce men's control over women. Men, however, are rarely motivated to break this link because they gain leisure time and other benefits from assuming that housework is women's work (Goode 1992).

Americans now accept the idea that women should work to (help) support the family, but most still assume that only certain jobs or public activities are appropriate for women. Few Americans admit that job discrimination against women is acceptable, yet most feel uncomfortable with a woman as a combat soldier, an auto mechanic, or an airline pilot. More women have been elected to public office than ever before, but most of them still sit on local school boards and city councils, rather than in state legislatures or in Congress. Most Americans say they would vote for a woman for president, but no woman has ever been nominated for that office by a major party. And Americans tend to be even more ambivalent about women's equality when it comes to marriage and family life. Although young women are now encouraged to be independent and professional, they are still expected to be generous and self-sacrificing within their marriages. Most Americans want to have it both ways.

Even though more women are going to college, taking jobs, and pursuing careers, they are still held accountable for what was once called "women's work." If their houses are a mess, their children are left alone, or worse, if they forego marriage altogether, they are subject to blame (Schur 1984). Similar equivocal feelings emerge about fathers and paid work. Although eight out of ten Americans now believe it is OK for women to hold jobs, half still think that men should be the *real* breadwinners (Wilkie 1993). By definition, men's jobs are supposed to be more important than women's jobs, and most people get uncomfortable if a wife makes more money than her husband (Gerson 1993). Americans want men to be more involved in family life, but most still feel uncomfortable if a father takes time off work "just" to be with his kids, or if a husband does most of the cooking and housekeeping (Coltrane 1996). Employers, too, are ambivalent about men's desires to be home instead of on the job. When men take advantage of parental leaves or part-time work, they are often considered unreliable or not serious and most "work-family" programs in the United States are tacitly designed to be used only by working mothers (Pleck 1993). It seems that the ideal of separate work spheres for men and women is still with us, even though the economic and social factors underylying it are in the midst of change.

Job segregation and unequal pay, along with women's lower employment levels, are associated with marriage bargains that include wives' obligation to perform domestic labor and husbands' sense of entitlement to receive unpaid domestic services. Nevertheless, we are beginning to see changes in both the private and public arenas. Not only are men doing a little more housework and women somewhat less, but the underlying factors associated with more equal power in marriages are becoming more common. For example, the gender wage gap is narrowing. Women's wages in the United States have shown steady increases since the 1970s, at the same time that men's wages have remained stagnant or declined. As of 1997, women who worked full-time, year-round were making 74 percent of what full-time, year-round men workers were making (U.S. Bureau of the Census, Women's Bureau 1998). This is far from equal, but women's relative earnings are significantly higher than in the 1970s, when they were earning just 59 percent of what men made.

With a further narrowing of the gender gap in employment levels and pay scales, we should see a movement toward more sharing of housework between husbands and wives. Cross-cultural studies show that societies with significant public participation by women also have significant domestic participation by men (Coltrane 1996). We suggest that the link between the two goes in both directions: when women have more money and public power, they can encourage more domestic participation from men; and when men cooperate with women in doing housework and child care, it encourages their acceptance of women as powerful public figures. If American men began doing substantially more of the housework and child care, we would see a further weakening of the separate spheres assumption that women should be paid less on the job, or be tracked into "women's" occupations. Such a movement would challenge the idea that it is "natural" for women to care for homes and "unnatural" for men to do this work. In this sense, housework is far from trivial.

References

Allen, Sarah M. and Alan J. Hawkins. 1999. "Maternal Gatekeeping: Mothers' Beliefs and Behaviors That Inhibit Greater Father Involvement in Family Work." *Journal of Marriage and the Family* 61:199–212.

Baxter, Janeen and Mark Western. 1998. "Satisfaction with Housework: Examining the Paradox." *Sociology* 32:101–120.

Berk, Richard A. and Sarah Fenstermaker Berk. 1979. *Labor and Leisure at Home: Content and Organization of the Household Day.* Beverly Hills, CA: Sage.

Berk, Sarah Fenstermaker. 1985. *The Gender Factory: The Apportionment of Work in American Households.* New York: Plenum.

Blair, Sampson Lee and Michael P. Johnson. 1992. "Wives' Perceptions of the Fairness of the Division of Household Labor: The Intersection of Housework and Ideology." *Journal of Marriage and the Family* 54:570–581.

Blair, Sampson Lee and Daniel T. Lichter. 1991. "Measuring the Division of Household labor: Gender Segregation of Housework Among American Couples." *Journal of Family Issues* 2(1):91–113.

Braverman, Lois. 1991. "The Dilemma of Housework: A Feminist Response to Gottman, Napier, and Pittman." *Journal of Marital and Family Therapy* 17(1):25–28.

Brines, Julie. 1994. "Economic Dependency, Gender, and the Division of Labor at Home." *American Journal of Sociology* 100:652–688.

Coltrane, Scott. 1999. "Research on Household Labor: Modeling and Measuring the Social Embeddedness of Routine Family Work." *Journal of Marriage and the Family.* In press.

Coltrane, Scott. 1998. *Gender and Families.* Thousand Oaks, CA: Pine Forge Press.

Coltrane, Scott. 1996. *Family Man: Fatherhood, Housework, and Gender Equity.* New York: Oxford University Press.

Coltrane, Scott. 1990. "Birth Timing and the Division of Labor in Dual-Earner Families: Exploratory Findings and Suggestions for Future Research." *Journal of Family Issues* 11:157–181.

Coltrane, Scott. 1989. "Household Labor and the Routine Production of Gender." *Social Problems* 36:473–490.

Coltrane, Scott and Michele Adams. 1997. "Work-Family Imagery and Gender Stereotypes: Television and the Reproduction of Difference." *Journal of Vocational Behavior* 50(2):323–347.

Coltrane, Scott and Kenneth Allan. 1994. " 'New' Fathers and Old Stereotypes: Representations of Masculinity in 1980s Television Advertising." *masculinities* 2(4):43–66.

Coontz, Stephanie. 1997. *The Way We Really Are: Coming to Terms with America's Changing Families.* New York: Basic Books.

DeMaris, Alfred and Monica A. Longmore. 1996. "Ideology, Power, and Equity: Testing Competing Explanations for the Perception of Fairness in Household Labor." *Social Forces* 74:1043–1071.

Deutsch, Francine M. 1999. *Halving It All*. Cambridge, MA: Harvard University Press.

DeVault, Marjorie. 1991. *Feeding the Family: The Social Organization of Caring and Gendered Work*. Chicago, IL: University of Chicago Press.

Ferree, Myra Marx. 1991. "The Gender Division of Labor in Two-Earner Marriages: Dimensions of Variability and Change." *Journal of Family Issues* 12:158–180.

Ferree, Myra Marx. 1990. "Beyond Separate Spheres: Feminism and Family Research." *Journal of Marriage and Family* 52:866–884.

Gerson, Kathleen. 1993. *No Man's Land: Men's Changing Committments to Family and Work*. New York: Basic Books.

Glass, Jennifer and Fujimoto, Tetsushi. (1994). "Housework, Paid Work, and Depression among Husbands and Wives." *Journal of Health and Social Behavior* 35:179–191.

Goode, William J. 1992. "Why Men Resist." In B. Thorne with M. Yalom (Eds.), *Rethinking the Family: Some Feminist Questions* (pp. 287–310). Boston, MA: Northeastern University Press.

Gramsci, Antonio. 1971. *Selections from the Prison Notebooks*, edited and translated by Q. Hoare and G. Nowell-Smith. London: Lawrence and Wishart.

Greenstein, Theodore N. 1996. "Gender Ideology and Perceptions of the Fairness of the Division of Household Labor: Effects on Marital Quality." *Social Forces* 74:1029–1042.

Hartmann, Heidi I. 1981. "The Family as the Locus of Gender, Class, and Political Struggle: The Example of Housework." *Signs: Journal of Women in Culture and Society* 6(3):366–394.

Hersch, Joni and Leslie S. Stratton. 1997. "Housework, Fixed Effects, and Wages of Married Workers." *Journal of Human Resources* 32:285–307.

Hersch, Joni and Leslie S. Stratton. 1994. "Housework, Wages, and the Division of Housework Time for Employed Spouses." *American Economic Review* 84:120–125.

Hochschild, Arlie with Anne Machung. 1989. *The Second Shift*. New York: Avon Books.

Jackson, Stevi. 1992. "Towards a Historical Sociology of Housework: A Materialist Feminist Analysis." *Women's Studies International Forum* 15(2):153–172.

Kimmel, Michael S. 1996. *Manhood in America: A Cultural History*. New York: Free Press.

Komter, Aafke. 1989. "Hidden Power in Marriage." *Gender and Society* 3(2):187–216.

Larson, Reed W., Maryse H. Richards, and Maureen Perry-Jenkins. 1994. "Divergent Worlds: The Daily Emotional Experience of Mothers and Fathers in the Domestic and Public Spheres." *Journal of Personality and Social Psychology* 67:1034–1046.

Lennon, Mary Clare and Sarah Rosenfield. 1994. "Relative Fairness and the Division of Housework: The Importance of Opinions." *American Journal of Sociology* 100:506–531.

Mainardi, Pat. 1970. "The Politics of Housework." In R. Morgan (Ed.), *Sisterhood Is Powerful: An Anthology of Writings from the Women's Liberation Movement* (pp. 447–453). New York: Random House.

Major, Brenda. 1993. "Gender, Entitlement, and the Distribution of Family Labor." *Journal of Social Issues* 49:141–159.

Major, Brenda. 1987. "Gender, Justice, and the Psychology of Entitlement." In P. Shaver and C. Hendricks (Eds.), *Review of Personality and Social Psychology* (pp. 124–140). Newbury Park, CA: Sage.

Miller, Joanne and Howard H. Garrison. 1982. "Sex Roles: The Division of Labor at Home and in the Workplace." *Annual Review of Sociology* 8:237–262.

Piña, Darlene L. and Vern L. Bengtson. 1993. "The Division of Household Labor and Wive's Happiness—Ideology, Employment, and Perceptions of Support." *Journal of Marriage and the Family* 55:901–912.

Pleck, Joseph. 1993. "Are 'Family-Supportive' Employer Policies Relevant to Men?" In J. C. Hood (Ed.), *Men, Work, and Family* (pp. 251–333). Newbury Park, CA: Sage.

Pyke, Karen and Scott Coltrane. 1996. "Entitlement, Obligation, and Gratitude in Family Work." *Journal of Family Issues* 17(1):60–82.

Robinson, John and Geoffrey Godbey. 1997. *Time for Life*. University Park: Pennsylvania State University Press.

Robinson, John and Glenna Spitze. 1992. "Whistle While You Work? The Effect of Household Task Performance on Women's and Men's Well-Being." *Social Science Quarterly* 73:844–861.

Robinson, John P. and Melissa Milkie. 1997. "Dances with Dust Bunnies: Housecleaning in America." *American Demographics* 37–40, 59.

Robinson, John P. and Melissa A. Milkie. 1998. "Back to the Basics: Trends in and Role Determinants of Women's Attitudes Toward Housework." *Journal of Marriage and the Family* 60:205–218.

Sanchez, Laura. 1994. "Gender, Labor Allocations, and the Psychology of Entitlement Within the Home." *Social Forces* 73:533–553.

Sanchez, Laura and Emily W. Kane. 1996. "Women's and Men's Constructions of Perceptions of Housework Fairness." *Journal of Family Issues* 17:358–387.

Schooler, Carmi, Joanne Miller, Karen A. Miller, and Carol N. Richtand. 1984. "Work for the Household: Its Nature and Consequences for Husbands and Wives." *American Journal of Sociology* 90:97–124.

Schur, Edwin M. 1984. *Labeling Women Deviant: Gender, Stigma, and Social Control.* Philadelphia, PA: Temple University Press.

Skolnick, Arlene. 1991. *Embattled Paradise: The American Family in an Age of Uncertainty.* New York: Basic Books.

Thompson, Linda. 1991. "Family Work: Women's Sense of Fairness." *Journal of Family Issues* 12:181–196.

Thompson, Linda and Alexis J. Walker. 1989. "Gender in Families: Women and Men in Marriage, Work, and Parenthood." *Journal of Marriage and the Family* 51:845–871.

To the Contrary Poll. 1997. <http://www.pbs.org/ttc/speakup/pollresults.html> 5 March 1999.

U.S. Bureau of the Census. 1997. *Money Income in the United States: 1996* (Current Population Reports: Household Economic Studies, Series P-60). Washington DC: Government Printing Office.

U.S. Bureau of the Census. 1998. *Statistical Abstract of the United States, 1998.* Washington, DC: Government Printing Office.

U.S. Bureau of the Census, Women's Bureau. 1998. "Women's Earnings as Percent of Men's, 1979–1996." (Current Population Reports, Series P-60, selected issues). Washington, DC: Government Printing Office. <www.dol.gov/dol/wb/> 5 May 1999.

Vannoy-Hiller, Dana. 1982. "Power Dependence and Division of Family Work." *Sex Roles* 10(11/12): 1003–1019.

Wilkie, Jane Riblett. 1993. "Changes in U.S. Men's Attitudes Toward the Family Provider Role, 1972–1989." *Gender and Society* 7(2):261–279.

4 Sexuality and Society

Raging Hormones, Regulated Love: Adolescent Sexuality in the United States and the Netherlands

Amy T. Schalet

Researchers have noted large differences among advanced industrial societies in public attitudes towards adolescent sexuality (Ester et al., 1993; Halman, 1991; Jones et al., 1986; Rademakers,1997). Public attitudes towards adolescent sexuality in the US have been characterized as "restrictive" and "non-accepting," and those in the Netherlands as occupying a midway position between the permissiveness of Scandinavian countries and the restrictiveness of southern Europe and the US (Rademakers, 1997). The clearest indicator of a sharp difference between the US and Netherlands comes from the European Value Systems Study Group. In 1981 this survey group found that 65 percent of the American public believed sex between people under the age of 18 was never justified while only 25 percent of the Dutch public agreed with this statement (Halman, 1991). The sexual practices, particularly the contraceptive behavior, of Dutch and American adolescents display an equally striking contrast. Although they become sexually active at roughly the same age, American teenage girls are nine times more likely to become pregnant than their Dutch counterparts. While teenage pregnancy is a rare occurrence in the Netherlands, 20 percent of American girls who are sexually active become pregnant each year (Brugman et al., 1995; Delft and Ketting, 1992; *Facts in Brief*, 1998).

THE STUDY

Between September 1991 and February 1992, I interviewed 14 American and 17 Dutch parents of teenagers. In each country I contacted half of the interviewees via a high-school parent organization and the other half through referrals from personal networks. The parents I interviewed all lived near or in a middle-sized university city in a metropolitan area. In both countries the parents differed from the national average since almost all were married, more than half were Catholic (although many Dutch interviewees describe themselves as non-religious), all were white, and most were well educated. Nine Dutch and ten American parents, had at least an MA degree. Two parents in each country had degrees from junior colleges. Six Dutch and two American parents had high-school degrees or less. Most of my interviews were with mothers but in each country some fathers participated. Their children were all around 16 years old and were as often boys as they were girls.

The interviews I conducted were semi-structured and centered around topics that concern parents of adolescents: school, work, friends, alcohol, sexuality, family and transitions into adulthood. My initial goal was to explore general differences and similarities in the way these Dutch and American parents constructed adolescence as a phase of life. Only in the course of these interviews did sexuality emerge as the most significant and clear point of divergence between the two sets of parents. Taking this divergence as a point of departure, I systematically compared the interview transcripts of the Dutch and American parents by topic. By counting the quantifiable answers and tracing the words, expressions and forms of reasoning parents used, I was able to reconstruct their different cultural logics. The presentation that follows combines description with interpretation to illuminate these logics. First, I discuss how the American and Dutch parents conceptualize adolescent sexuality. Then I turn to their strategies for managing it within the parental home.

THE DRAMATIZATION
OF ADOLESCENT SEXUALITY

Even before the interview turns to the subject of sexuality, 11 out of 14 American parents mention sex as something that characterizes and complicates the period of adolescence. They often refer to the sexual desire of an adolescent as "drives" or "urges" which they attribute to the physical processes of puberty. Puberty confuses the child, burdening him with a load of hormonally produced sexual feelings. One mother thinks the physical transition adolescents experience is

> . . . difficult for them, very difficult. Their bodies are changing, and they are experiencing feelings that they have never had before, and they are getting interested in the opposite sex per se and having feelings to deal with that they never had.

Expressions such as "raging hormones" and "hormones that are acting up" suggest that adolescent sexuality emerges from a biological source within the individual and possesses a disruptive power.

While many parents say it is normal for a teenager to experience sexual feelings, all of them also say that at 16 their child is not ready for a relationship involving sex. When parents talk about teenage sex, they usually refer to *other* teenagers, not to their own children. Parents describe teenage sexual involvement as an individual condition or activity; teenagers are "sexually active" or engaged in "sexual activity." American parents do not usually refer to a relational or emotional context when talking about the sexual activity of teenagers. One reason they do not associate teenage sexuality with love or an emotionally meaningful relationship is the widespread belief that 16-year-olds are unable to form deep or steady romantic attachments. One American mother says point-blank, "They're not mature enough to handle a serious relationship." Another doesn't think "a 16-year-old is going to be committed to that extent. I mean maybe this month, but next month it could be someone else." Even when long-term romantic attachments do exist between adolescents, parents do not believe sex is warranted. A mother whose daughter had dated the same boy throughout high school does not think "someone who is 16 is mature enough to really have a relationship that would be a meaningful relationship, one that would involve sex."

This dissociation of teenage sexuality from contexts of love and commitment explains why American parents often refer to teenage sexual activity as experimental, promiscuous, immoral or exclusively pleasure-driven. It is not uncommon, in fact, for parents to mention teenage sex in the same breath as drugs, excessive drinking or vandalism. However, parents do not attribute such negative qualities to sexuality in general. Adult sexuality is different from the sexual activity of "kids." "I very strongly feel that sex is not a child—shouldn't be an activity for children," says one mother. "I just think sex is another thing that's for adults and not for kids." The developmental maturity, economic independence or marital status of "adults" distinguishes them from "kids" and sanctions their "adult" sexual activity. Because teenagers lack these attributes, their motivations for engaging in sex and their sexual desires, motivations and experiences are thought to have a different, lesser value. "It's not that we don't approve of sex," says one mother. "It's that we don't approve of sex at a certain time in life."

Some religious parents believe that sexual intercourse, regardless of its consequences, poses a threat to the individual because pre-marital sex is wrong. Most parents, however, do not refer to sin but rather emphasize the negative consequences that sex can entail. One mother says that "sex is not good for a kid" and that with the spread of AIDS "it's terribly, terribly dangerous." Another father would disapprove of his son's becoming sexually involved because "tied in with that is this whole horror show of AIDS and related diseases." One mother feels her daughter is "at risk": "And [you worry] that their lives can get messed up more. If a girl gets pregnant, she has to deal with an abortion or a baby." Another mother says that her son could risk his future by getting sexually involved. Her advice to him: "You're really blessed. Don't blow it. You know. Don't throw it out the window on some cheap thrill because what's it going to get you?" Another father believes one should tell teenagers, "Don't do it. You're crazy. You're playing with a loaded gun. There's no other way that I can put it. You're going to ruin your life."

American parents assume that teenagers cannot guard against unwanted consequences of sexual involvement—for instance, by using contraceptives. They suggest that teenagers are unable to regulate their sexual impulses, making any sexual involvement tantamount to irresponsibility. The parents express similar notions about the inability of teenagers to exercise self-restraint when they discuss alcohol consumption. Eleven parents believe 16-year-olds should not be allowed to drink alcohol without parental supervision because they "would not know their limitations," "do not have any idea of their capacity" or "are not mature enough to be able to control something like that." Parents suggest that if teenagers are given free access to alcohol they will consume excessively rather than in moderation because they "don't know how to make those distinctions."

The notion that a teenager cannot restrain herself is related to the belief that she lacks a fully solidified internal reference point or a reliable moral compass. Like the biological process of puberty, the period of adolescence is thought to disrupt and confuse a person and to make one extremely susceptible to influences outside oneself. This "inner unreliability" renders teenagers unaccountable for their actions. Thus, many American parents explain the drinking and sexual behavior of teenagers not as a consequence of free will but as a result of "being pushed" or "forced" by others. "Too often a kid ends up having sex because it's a peer thing rather than something he's honestly ready for," one mother says. A father believes, "These kids get wrapped up in it. It's a trap. It's peer pressure." The *dramatization* of teenage sexuality thus involves the interplay of internal urges, external pressures and a self unable yet to direct or protect itself.

THE NORMALIZATION OF ADOLESCENT SEXUALITY

While the American parents emphasize how teenage sexuality is disruptive, the Dutch parents describe teenage sexuality as something that does not and should not present many problems. They often speak jokingly about the relationships and sexuality of teenage children. One mother tells of her amusement when her son said to her one day, "Now I want a girlfriend, the time is ripe for that." Another father describes how, as a joke for Christmas, he and his wife gave their children gold-colored condoms, which they had bought in Berkeley, California. Such jokes indicate the *normality* with which the Dutch parents approach the issue of adolescent sexuality. Dutch parents believe that sexuality should be talked about and dealt with in a "normal" way, meaning that it should not be made taboo or the cause of unnecessary difficulty. "We have always talked openly, normally about [reproduction and contraception]," says one mother. Another mother favors sex education at school because that way "it becomes very normal to talk about it."

The onset of sexual desire in teenagers is usually discussed in relation to a boyfriend or girlfriend, or in terms of being *verliefd* (in love or infatuated) with another person. In other words, Dutch parents think about the sexuality of teenagers in the context of a relationship and their emotional involvement with another person. Adolescents are not said to be "sexually active"; rather they "go to bed with each other" or have "sexual contact." "Yes, I do think that is a result of having a boyfriend or a girlfriend for a long time, that you surely have a sexual, thus an intimate, relationship," one mother says. Another mother explains why a young person would want to be sexual with a partner: "If you love each other, then you want to be together, don't you, to have that warmth."

This relationship-based conception of adolescent sexuality is not only descriptive, it is prescriptive. Dutch parents say that teenagers *should* view sexuality in the context of their emotions for and relationships with other people. One mother approves of sex education in school "as long as it is indeed about relationships, and not just sex, pure sex." When sex education is about "dealing with each other, having understanding for each other," then she finds it "extremely good." Another mother reiterates that sex education should include talking about "feelings, clearly taking the other person into account, for boys as well as for girls." It is the presence of a "relationship" which determines whether Dutch parents approve of teenagers having sex. A number of them indicate that the depth and stability of the relationship, rather than age or any other condition, are the criteria that make sex acceptable. One mother approves of sex at 16 "as long as they have a steady relationship, not every week with another person." Another mother says that young people should not have sex based on a momentary attraction but

> . . . if you are sixteen, and there comes a period of four or five months of going out really steadily, and you don't do any crazy things, then I would think it all right. . . . Yes. . . . As long as they have a steady girlfriend, or a steady boyfriend, then I think it is all right.

Parents stress that a person should be *er aan toe*. *Er aan toe zijn* means "to be ready for" or "at the right moment." Such readiness is the result of a gradual mental and physical process of development. What distinguishes the Dutch parents from the American parents is their belief that teenagers are capable of being *er aan toe*, or ready for a sexual relationship. Although most Dutch parents do not think their own 16-year-old is ready, eight think it is possible for a person to be *er aan toe* at 16. Another six think this can be the case at 17 or 18. Relative to their American counterparts, Dutch parents have little anxiety about their child becoming sexually involved prematurely. It is generally thought that if a person is not *er aan toe*, he or she will not want to have sex. The assumption behind the concept *er aan toe zijn* is that when a person feels ready and wants to have sex, he is indeed ready.

Unlike their American counterparts, Dutch parents do not envision a battle between bodily drives and rational control. Sexual desire and the personal development which makes it possible to experience sex in a good way are thought to go together. For that reason, parents trust that "the right moment" will best be recognized by a teenager herself. "You should ask him that," one mother responds when asked whether she thinks her son is ready for a relationship involving sex. "That is something he should decide for himself, whether he is ready or not." One father says his daughter was ready for sex at 16 "because she herself indicated she was ready." He had always told his daughters:

> I will never have any objection [to a sexual relationship] when they—really out of their own free will, and never because they have to do it or because of coercion or because they feel that they have to belong, or because otherwise the boyfriend won't like them anymore—but only when they themselves feel the need for that, and when they are themselves ready for it. And when that is, I don't know.

Dutch parents do not view adolescent sexuality as being dangerous in and of itself. They stress that teenagers should use contraceptives, and frequently mention their own role in urging their children to do so. "Without a condom, I will not allow them to make love," says one mother. One father would object if his daughter wanted to become sexually involved at 16. He says nonetheless, "When she has a boyfriend for a while, [her mother] says, 'Shall we go to the doctor to get the pill?'" One mother continually points out the necessity of contraceptives to her son because "it must become an automatism." If her daughter had continued to go steady with her boyfriend, one other mother says, she would have told her, "You must go on the pill." The Dutch parents do not regard sex as inherently risky because they expect their children will use contraceptives to protect themselves against unwanted consequences of sex. Asked whether he is worried about his daughter's sexual behavior, one father responds, "I do have that trust that if she were to do it, she would use contraceptives, she has a good enough head on her shoulders."

When they discuss drinking Dutch parents express a similar trust that their child will use common sense. Asked if their 16-year-old is old enough to drink, parents usually respond "yes, in moderation," implying that a 16-year-old is capable of self-imposed moderation. One mother says her son had "become acquainted with alcohol" on a school trip to Rome, where he had gotten "good and drunk." As a consequence he decided "out of himself" not to drink to excess in the future. In a similar way, the mechanism that moderates sexual desire and prevents pregnancy and disease is thought to be internal, within an adolescent. The notion that teenagers possess the ability to restrain themselves and to commit to others enables Dutch parents to normalize adolescent sexuality, to treat it, in other words, as something that neither is nor should be a problem.

Editor's Note: References and Notes for this reading can be found in the original source.

■READING 11

Premarital Sex before the "Sexual Revolution"

Julia Ericksen, with Sally A. Steffen

Two basic criticisms of research on premarital sex were that it lacked data on the all-important areas of attitudes toward sex in addition to the actual behavior and that the research utilized poor samples. I sought to meet these criticisms in my own work on premarital sex.

—Ira Reiss, 1972

In 1960 the family sociologist Lester Kirkendall proposed a solution to an issue troubling teachers of family courses: what to tell students who came for advice about whether to have sexual intercourse before marriage. Addressing his colleagues in the journal *Marriage and Family Living*, Kirkendall recommended that, in deciding what to do, couples should consider the consequences for their particular relationship. This meant examining their moral values and the strength of their feelings for each other. Lest his audience conclude that he was abandoning his own moral standards, he added that if the young followed his advice it would eliminate most premarital intercourse, since "the great bulk of it appears to be exploitive and advantage-taking."[1]

By this time "functional" family courses, that is, courses preparing students for marriage and family life, were a mainstay of sociology departments everywhere. One year earlier a report in the same journal had said that 82 percent of colleges and universities offered such courses, in which about 100,000 students enrolled annually.[2] The majority of students in the courses were women. Most students came to the courses to learn how to have a good marriage, and many wanted to know what their professors recommended about the troubling issue of premarital sex.

The journal published a symposium of reactions to Kirkendall's recommendations, and these reveal the turmoil professors felt about the issue.[3] If professors told students to wait for marriage, they risked seeming outmoded and irrelevant, but if they told students premarital sex was acceptable, they could be accused of encouraging the young to flout social rules. How could they retain the paternal authority so necessary to gain students' respect, yet not offend parents, state legislators, and others? Some of the symposium writers noted that if professors followed Kirkendall's recommendations students would realize their teachers were avoiding the issue and would lose faith. Others took the position that schools must uphold societal mores and forbid sex before marriage. Yet others answered that premarital sex was part of a changing society that professors should encourage, for it would help students achieve sexually satisfying marriages. This professorial debate occurred against a background of growing parental fears that children lived in an "adolescent society" whose values were at odds with those of the adult world.[4]

It seemed clear to all the professors that before they could recommend any behavior to students they needed to know what kinds of sexual activities their young charges were engaging in. In the late 1930s, when data from the marital adjustment surveys indicated increases in premarital sex, researchers had slowly begun interviewing the unmarried. By 1960 they had already completed about twenty such surveys. But in the permissive 1960s this mushroomed, and by 1975 over eighty surveys of the sexual behavior of unmarried young people appeared, almost all focusing on college students. The use of students was partly a matter of convenience but also resulted from a continued concern about the middle class.

Most of those writing before 1960 took it for granted that students should avoid premarital sex. Yet many were sympathetic to the strain this caused college students, whose lives away from home were filled with temptation and opportunity. And, while they believed both men and women would experience strain, researchers assumed that these would affect the genders differently. Men's desires were strong and innate, and arguments that they could withstand their hormonal urges had all but disappeared by World War II. College "girls," in contrast, experienced temptation after they fell in love and, even then, they were rightfully cautious about "going all the way."

The first survey of college students' sexual behavior was undertaken not by male professors but by two female journalists. In 1938 Dorothy Dunbar Bromley and Florence Haxton Britten promised readers the unvarnished truth in their report on interviews with students at a variety of colleges. For Bromley and Britten most of the consequences of sex before marriage were personal, not social. They considered college a serious place where young people should devote themselves to getting an education. Particularly anxious that young women not be distracted, they gave practical advice. Sex was problematic because "an intense love relationship tends to be more disturbing than tranquilizing" and "may interfere seriously with class work." Even so, it was not always to be discouraged, since "the chances for ultimate happiness seem to be about as good for deeply committed couples who adjust themselves to a complete physical relationship as for those who endure great strain, grow irritable and perhaps against their preferences turn to other mates whom their tricked and disappointed bodies have chosen instinctively as more likely sexual prospects."[5] Giving in to desire was wrong only in the pragmatic sense that love and work might not be compatible. This was particularly true for women, since for them premarital sex carried a heavy burden of secrecy.

While Bromley and Britten were unusual in depicting strong female sexual desire, they accepted contemporary beliefs about differences in male and female arousal. They took it for granted that women were aroused by love, while noting that, given the availability of attractive men in college, love was hard to resist. In these tempting surroundings, they reported, only 12 percent of their female respondents easily contained their desires. These had been raised in "the Victorian mode" by parents whose emphasis on chastity delayed arousal of their daughters' sex instincts. In contrast, most young women who remained virgins were "fully aware that the tempting fruit hangs heavy, heavy over their heads."[6] Bromley and Britten saw different pressures facing college men. Most lived in a state of great arousal and had happily given in to temptation. The few who had not had unusually low sex drives. These young men felt social pressure to test and prove their virility and even apologized for their lack of experience.

Other authors shared Bromley and Britten's beliefs about gender differences in sex drive, but not their ideas about the importance of women's careers. A decade later Winston Ehrmann interviewed almost 12,000 students at the University of Florida and, in a much-cited report on his survey, justified a double standard of sexual behavior.[7] Ehrmann posited that women's sexual interest resulted not only from love but also from a man's emotional commitment, and in the postwar world of the 1950s his message was unmistakable. Bromley and Britten had argued that early marriage was a poor solution to sexual urges because it interrupted women's education. Now marriage was the main goal of college women and that idea seemed an outdated vestige of early-twentieth-century feminism. Furthermore, if successful marriages rested on a strong erotic component, then for women love, not education, was the goal.

By now writers took a benign view of young men's uncontrollable urges. Where surveyors had once described young men's sexual incontinence as a threat to the family, they now reported that young unmarried men would inevitably acquire sexual experience. In 1950 Kirkendall undertook his first survey of young men. He found high rates of premarital intercourse and concluded that men who could not marry until well into their twenties could not remain virgins until marriage.[8] This assumption that young men "needed" sexual intercourse led Irving Tebor at Oregon State to examine the "problem" of male virgins, who, he stated, experienced teasing and a lack of support from family and friends.[9]

Ehrmann described sexual desire as one of the most important defining characteristics of manhood. This desire began to develop in early adolescence or even before. Since middle-class young women did not respond sexually until they fell in love and, ideally, married, this posed a problem for their male counterparts. Ehrmann described his male respondents as solving this by having "sexual relations" with lower-class women and "social relations," which might include sex, with women of their own social strata. His college men reported much higher rates of heterosexual intercourse than his female respondents, and Ehrmann explained this as due to a few sexually active young women who were not college students. Thus Ehrmann assumed a double standard of behavior among middle-class youth. Men would have extensive sexual experience with women other than their future spouses, but women would save sexual intercourse for the men they married. This was normal.

A rare study of young men from more varied social backgrounds provided a contrasting picture of these sexually active women and suggested that working-class Americans were less committed to the double standard. During World War II the physicians Leslie Hohman and Bertram Schaffner interviewed 4,600 army inductees. They asked these men to describe both their own sexual behavior and that of the women they knew. Eighty percent of the white inductees had engaged in sexual intercourse, and 71 percent evaluated their partners as "nice girls." In addition, "practically all Negroes have had sexual relations by the time they are twenty one years old, and; in practically all cases they regarded the girls as nice, that is as girls they would have married." In the eyes of these young men, sexually active young working-class women were not "sexual outlets" to be discarded after taking care of a man's sexual needs.[10]

Ehrmann's idea, that the sexual needs of college men were satisfied by lower-class women, received a blow from a study showing that college men did not, in fact, practice restraint with women from their own social backgrounds. In two studies Eugene Kanin, a sociologist at Purdue University, found rampant sexual aggression against college women by their dates.[11] Approximately 60 percent of women described an offensive episode during the previous year, and in about 30 percent of cases this involved attempted intercourse. Far from protecting women they wished to marry, men were more likely to attempt intercourse with women if they were a "regular date," "pinned," or "engaged." Perhaps this was why the most offensive episodes were the very ones young women had discussed the least.

Not only did Ehrmann argue that college men satisfied themselves sexually with the type of women they would not marry; his work and other work like it uninteritionally encouraged young men to think of themselves as sexually "needy." Perhaps a shortage of exploitable young working-class women was one reason men turned to those of their own class. Ironically, women kept the myth of male protection alive through their silence, which partly explained Ehrmann's finding of lower rates of sexual intercourse among college women than among college men.

Besides defining the double standard, Ehrmann made another lasting "discovery." On the basis of his interviews, he described normal sex as following a predictable progression of behaviors that built excitement and defined the experience: "Heterosexual behavior falls into highly compartmentalized *stages* of increasing degrees of intensity, as judged by the young people of our society, both with respect to physical intimacy and to moral judgement. These stages range from no physical contact, at the one extreme, on through holding hands, kissing, general body embrace, and the fondling of various portions of the body, to sexual intercourse at the other."[12] In 1954 Lawrence Podell and John Perkins arranged these behaviors into a fifteen-item ordered scale of sexual experience. From then on, surveys of college students assumed the existence of such a progression, and young people knew that this was the way a proper seduction proceeded.[13] Neither the researchers nor the young understood the social creation of this progression. Like young men's urgent need for sexual outlets, it was simply "natural."

By 1960 the exploitative nature of the double standard began to bother researchers. Since they could see no way to contain young men's sexual needs, they tried to redirect them. If premarital sex could be confined to serious love relationships, young men would gain their sexual experience with women they respected, not those they denigrated. This would have positive consequences for the way middle-class men treated women and therefore for marriage. Professors who took this position could use moral justifications for their arguments and avoid the dangers inherent in advocating premarital sex. This would also endear them to their largely female classes. Two works in particular promoted this view, and these aroused great interest and debate: Kirkendall's second study, some time before 1961, of 200 male students, and Ira Reiss's series of surveys of students' premarital sexual attitudes, which he undertook between 1959 and 1963.[14]

Both men remained cautious about surveying youthful sexual behavior. The turn of the decade was still a time of conservatism and quiet on American college campuses. Researchers who asked what students were doing sexually could be accused of promoting promiscuity. Kirkendall confined his survey to those respondents least likely to take offense, men reporting coital experience, and he used only volunteers, many from his classes. Reiss was more daring. Early in his career he challenged the assumption that premarital sexual intercourse was wrong for women but excusable for men. He noted that this created a predatory attitude among young men, making them eager to classify women as "bad" or potentially so. This caused problems for marriage, since "double standard premarital sexual intercourse leads to many maladjustments: there is male selfishness and female inhibitions; there is past association of thrills and sex, and restraints due to 'bad' associations. Finally we may add that a double standard male may carry over this standard to extramarital sex relations and thereby risk an increase in overall marital maladjustment by engaging in extramarital sex conduct."[15] Even so, Reiss cautiously added that, as a scientist, he was not taking a moral position on the double standard.

Reiss was among the first sex researchers to use random samples, which meant that he could not select whom to interview or use only those who volunteered. This took courage, but he was careful to confine his questions to relatively safe topics such as sexual attitudes. He asked questions about behavior only of a volunteer sample of University of Iowa students, and even then his language was cautious. He asked a series of questions about "kissing," "petting," and "full sexual relations." For example:

- During the time that you have accepted your present standard [of sexual behavior], have you engaged in *full sexual relations?*
- In regard to full sexual relations, would you say you have done less than your standard would allow you to do?

  as much as your standard would allow you to do?

  or would you say your behavior with regard to full sexual relations has exceeded your standard?[16]

He went on to ask how frequently standards had been violated, why this had happened, the level of guilt, and which partner was more to blame for the violation. The framing of these questions told students that decisions about sexual activity were serious, and allowed Reiss to conclude that students were increasingly permissive, but not approving of "promiscuity." This protected Reiss and was in line with his goal of abolishing the double standard.

Both Reiss and Kirkendall maintained that when serious young people satisfied their normal sexual desires in emotionally committed relationships, these relationships developed in an atmosphere of mutual trust and would create lasting marriages. Young men whose sexual needs were met in this way would be less likely to exploit women they had no intention of marrying. Still, Reiss warned that, given differences in male and female roles, such behavior would continue.

In spite of his precautions, Kirkendall felt it necessary to assure readers of his opposition to frivolous unmarried sex by labeling most premarital sex reported in his survey as "highly exploitative," since it involved sexual intercourse without serious commitment. His 200 respondents described 668 different sexual liaisons, only 18 of which were with fiancées. If sex was permissible only under Kirkendall's restrictive criteria, students might not listen. Reiss was more realistic about college professors' ability to manage the behavior of the young, so he had more influence on other researchers. Still, he was careful to coat his sexual liberalism with science, because, as he noted thirty years later, "I was taking a straight mainstream science stance, so I could say 'Look, don't kill the messenger. I'm just telling you what's happening.' I think it was clear that I liked what was happening, since I was constantly describing all these trends without a word of warning. But I didn't make that crystal clear. I did not think of it as 'protect yourself by playing the scientific role,' but had I come out and said, 'I love what is happening, isn't this great?' I would have got a lot of criticism."[17]

Reiss asserted that the double standard was being replaced by "permissiveness with affection." He reached this conclusion on the basis of his widely used sexual attitude scale, which consisted of a series of sexual scenarios. For example: "John and Mary have no particular affection for each other. They engage in full sexual relations, since they both feel that having full sexual relations does not require any particular affection between the couple." Respondents evaluated John's and Mary's behavior and answered a series of questions on their own values about kissing, petting, and "full sexual relations" under a variety of circumstances.[18]

These options allowed student respondents to take a position in favor of premarital sexual intercourse. At the same time, most indicated that they approved only when emotional bonds were strong. Reiss was able to stay on high moral ground by concluding that while women were becoming more permissive, young men's promiscuity was declining. Furthermore, permissive young women were still "good." They felt guilty about past sexual practices and had only accepted this behavior when in strong relationships: three-fifths of engaged women thought sexual intercourse appropriate for themselves, compared with only one-quarter of those not emotionally involved. Reiss justified his caution in asking students about their sexual standards, rather than about what they were actually doing, by contending that no evidence existed of a sexual revolution. He doubted that students were more sexually active than in earlier years. Instead, their values were increasingly consistent with their behavior. This positive interpretation of the sexual realities family sociologists heard daily in their classes further allowed them to present themselves as not promoting sex.

One way of showing that sexually active college women were "good girls" was to demonstrate their continued sexual difficulties. In the late 1950s and early 1960s some researchers began claiming that, in addition to having repressive childhoods, young women were apprehensive about becoming too responsive to erotic overtures.[19] They had well-grounded fears of bad-girl reputations, so they crushed their spontaneous sexual desires when engaging in premarital petting. Such habits, once acquired, were difficult to break. Reiss noted that women supported the double standard more strongly than men. He warned that "years of developing inhibitions in accord with the double standard view of women cannot be discarded at will," and that such women needed "understanding and time to chip away the veneer of culturally imposed inhibition." His caution paid off when Reiss obtained three of the first government grants awarded for sexual surveys. In applying to the National Institute of Mental Health (NIMH), he was warned not to put sex in the title, so he called his proposal "A Study of Attitudes." His funders assured him, "No-one's going to pick this out because it doesn't have the word 'sex' in it."[20]

These early surveys of college students created a new vocabulary to describe sexual problems between women and men. In the lectures on female sexual response, the double-standard woman whose inability to become a fully orgasmic partner arose from a discrepancy between her values and her behavior replaced the sexually unresponsive one. Where before all sex outside of marriage was "extramarital sex," students now learned of the still-forbidden "extramarital sex" plus the ambivalently regarded "premarital sex," terms rapidly picked up by the media. "Premarital" assumed that marriage would follow, so such experience might prove functional for middle-class marriages rather than exploitative. Just as the marital adjustment researchers had seen the middle class as the standardbearers for sexual intimacy in marriage, so the premarital-sex researchers thought educated middle-class students would negotiate a new courtship standard based on mutual trust and respect. In 1960 Reiss predicted that, led by college students, permissiveness with affection would become the dominant societal ethic for premarital behavior.

In the years that followed Reiss's reports, most surveyors of college students' sexual behavior cautiously promoted permissive standards. Rather than risk random sampling, professors kept control of their respondents by conducting surveys in their own classes. This allowed them to show students their own sexual standards and to define these as appropriate. It had the effect of encouraging behavior the surveys purported merely to document while safeguarding the professors against the potentially negative consequences of undertaking sex surveys.

Even if they were more directive than they acknowledged, researchers did not completely control their findings. Their research involved listening to students, not just telling them what to do. In contrast, textbooks intended for marriage courses in the early 1960s often selected their findings carefully to produce more conservative messages. For example, in a widely distributed 1963 text Judson T. Landis and Mary G. Landis asserted that young couples should concentrate on learning how compatible they were but should avoid sexual intimacy: "Normally well-adjusted young people will suffer no ill effects from following a plan which includes self-control and emphasizes avoidance of excessive sex interest until they can marry. The advantages are all on the side of this course of action. Here, as in many other phases of marital and post-marital experience, the long-time view point is of fundamental importance. What is most desirable for life as a whole? Permanent satisfaction in marriage must outweigh other considerations."[21]

But this advice was increasingly falling on deaf ears. In the first five years of the 1960s, surveyors found a growing indifference to their elders' opinions among college students, especially young women. In addition, while students were learning sexual values in college, these were not coming from the classroom. Harrop Freeman and Ruth Freeman's study of 1,100 women plus a few men at a variety of colleges between 1962 and 1965 was typical.[22] Parents, they contended, rarely knew about their daughters' sexual activity and would be horrified if they did. College replaced parental influence with the peer group's standards, and, since two-thirds of respondents viewed their campuses as sexually liberal, it was not surprising that young women's own attitudes had become more liberal too. The Freemans also noted that the double standard continued: half their female respondents agreed with it, and many who did not gave men more permission than women to have premarital relations. In spite of more liberal attitudes, the Freemans assured readers that young women were not irresponsible. Away from home, and pressured by the men they loved, they simply learned that their mothers' sexual standards no longer applied.

By the early 1960s research on this sexual revolution began in earnest. Vance Packard, in his bestselling *The Sexual Wilderness*, concluded that a revolution was occurring because women now allowed sexual intercourse outside of marriage as long as they were in a committed relationship.[23] And, he continued, many women had had sex in a relationship that had since ended. It seemed that young women moved from one commitment to another because "commitment" justified sex. Horrified by this, Packard proposed a voluntary code of conduct for unmarried youth. They should agree to abstain from sexual intercourse unless they first finished a year of college and were "known to hope" to marry their partner. This was not quite the same reassuring picture as that of Reiss, but it was a picture portrayed in many surveys in the first years of the 1960s.

During this time college students themselves began to change, at least in the eyes of others. The first sign occurred with the civil rights movement. In the summer of 1963 many student activists went south with the Student Non-Violent Coordinating Committee. At first most of this political activity took place off campus, and those who became involved appeared in the media as heroes risking their lives for democracy. But the media soon began to describe another change. A *Newsweek* story in the spring of 1964 entitled "The Morals Revolution on Campus" was typical.[24] Announcing that students now believed that a couple who had a "meaningful relationship" had a "moral right to sleep together," *Newsweek* provided a defense of the Reiss position. Men, the magazine claimed, no longer expected to marry virgins. But since "Sex with anyone except 'Mr. Right' is largely frowned upon, as is out-and-out promiscuity," the magazine gave a warning to young women enjoying their new freedom: "The question is, how many 'Mr. Rights' make a wrong?"

Even though young men continued to report more heterosexual partners than young women, only one survey, published in 1966, questioned whether students were telling the truth about their sexual behavior. In a questionnaire distributed to male students in an undergraduate sociology course at the University of Illinois, John Clark and Larry Tifft asked about a variety of socially disapproved behaviors, including nonmarital sexual intercourse, pregnancy, sex with prostitutes, masturbation, rape or attempted rape, and same-sex relations.[25] They then offered students eight dollars to do a second interview, at which they announced that the students would have to take a polygraph test. Before this, they could review their questionnaires (which were anonymous and identified with a number known only to the student) and make any corrections they wished. Faced with the likelihood of being caught lying, students changed many of their responses. The two sexual items most often changed were masturbation, which more students acknowledged, and premarital sex, which students were as likely to decrease as increase. This small study was evidence that respondents did not always tell the truth and that men might exaggerate their sexual experience. Its implications for what researchers could learn by asking questions were largely ignored. It was easier to assume that survey respondents told the truth.

Editor's Note: *References and Notes for this reading can be found in the original source.*

5 Courtship and Marriage

■ READING 12

Dating Scripts Revisited

Mary Riege Laner and Nicole A. Ventrone

During the past decade, several studies of heterosexual dating attitudes and behaviors (Alksnis, Desmarais, & Wood, 1996; Ross & Davis, 1996) have been published as well as some investigations of homosexual dating attitudes and behaviors both of gay men and of lesbian women (Klinkenberg & Rose, 1994; Rose, Zand, & Cini, 1993). Most of these have focused primarily on scripts for first dates (Laner & Ventrone, 1998; Rose & Frieze, 1989, 1993). The latter group of studies found that prescriptions for dating have changed little from the traditional thinking of the 1950s and that despite young adults' claims to egalitarian attitudes, their behaviors on first dates continue to reflect traditional practices. Ganong, Coleman, Thompson, and Goodwin-Watkins (1996) pointed out that

> young people are trained from an early age to seek romantic partners with certain characteristics. The traditional model presents the ideal heterosexual relationship as one in which the man is older, more capable, and more successful than the woman. The media and other social institutions present this model unrelentingly, and eventually young people internalize these values. . . . Of course, in a large and diverse culture such as . . . the United States, other models are also presented . . . such as the ideal of egalitarian relationships . . . and some internalize these other relationship models. (p. 759)

Laner and Ventrone (1998) asserted that economic factors also play a part in the continuation of traditionalist practices: "Although our society may be moving toward greater equality of opportunity for women, it is still the case that women, by and large, earn less than men, especially younger, single women" (p. 475). Talking with friends about dates may also reinforce culturally scripted notions about expected behaviors and dating activities.

Authors' Note: *We wish to thank Professors Sampson Lee Blair and Peter A. Padilla for assistance with data collection for this study.*

One approach to enhancing understanding of dating and courtship is script theory. Scripts are types of schema used to organize our experiences and are usually composed of a set of stereotypical actions (Ginsberg, 1988). These scripts allow us to predict the actions of others and serve as guides for our decisions about how to act. Sexual scripts refer to the cognitive models used in choosing and evaluating behavior in sexual or relationship contexts (Simon & Gagnon, 1986). These scripts operate on three levels—cultural, interpersonal, and intrapsychic. As described in Klinkenberg and Rose (1994),

> Cultural scripts are shared, collective guides that instruct members on appropriate behaviors and emotions in specific roles (e.g., driving a car or interviewing for a job). The use of a cultural script in a specific situation constitutes an interpersonal script. Interpersonal scripts combine the actions present in cultural scripts with ones individuals typically add through experience. As a result, interpersonal scripts are more detailed and individualized than cultural ones. For example, a cultural script for eating in a restaurant may include having a beverage, whereas an interpersonal one may specify white wine for one person and cola for another. Lastly, intrapsychic scripts are those which represent our private wishes and desires. (p. 24)

Given this perspective, along with Ganong et al.'s (1996) comments and the findings of the studies mentioned earlier, two empirical questions suggest themselves. First, what are contemporary popular sources of direct information about dating, and what advice do they offer? Second, would the traditionalist bent found in respondents to earlier surveys still appear if the method of studying first-date behavior were changed? We review the findings of earlier studies briefly and then turn to contemporary sources of advice to daters.

EARLIER STUDIES

Alksnis et al. (1996) used scripts to assess how men and women differ, in determining what constitutes a bad, a good, and a typical date, finding that with regard to the latter, men's and women's ideas agreed. Ross and Davis (1996) compared samples of Black and White respondents regarding their expectations in terms of who pays for dates. They reported that Blacks were less flexible and more traditional than Whites on several aspects of dating-related attitudes and experiences. Suzanna Rose and her colleagues used scripts in several studies to assess what scripts guide dates—especially first dates. Rose and Frieze (1993) asked college students to list 20 actions or events that would occur on a hypothetical first date. Those actions identified by 25% or more of the respondents constituted a script. First-date scripts, they found, are explicit, formal, and have changed little since the 1950s. Dating etiquette is strongly gender stereotyped, showing the traditional dominant/subordinate relationship between the sexes. Furthermore, men and women were both familiar with the script, and Rose and Frieze commented that given their findings, first-date scripts are highly predictable. Perhaps their most surprising finding was that respondents with the most dating experience most strongly emphasized gender-stereotypical behaviors.

In a second study, Rose and Frieze (1993) asked college students to describe an actual first date and found that the actual and hypothetical first dates were highly similar. Klinkenberg and Rose (1994) examined both hypothetical and actual first dates among gay and lesbian respondents, arguing that for homosexuals, a public and well-defined cultural script for dates does not exist as it does for heterosexuals. They found, however, that cultural and interpersonal scripts were clearly defined and that they parallel heterosexual scripts. Subsequently, Laner and Ventrone (1998) replicated Rose and Frieze's 1989 study with a larger sample and found essentially the same script for a first date as the original authors had identified.

As a suggestion for further study, Klinkenberg and Rose (1994) advanced the notion that using a checklist of actions (instead of free recall or hypothesizing what might happen on a date) might help to assess script components more fully. In a personal communication, Rose (October 17, 1996) suggested the same idea to us following our earlier study. That suggestion and Rose and Frieze's (1993) examination of dating guides gave rise to the study reported here.

ADVICE GUIDES ABOUT DATING

Ganong et al. (1996) pointed out that various media provide a steady stream of information about what values should guide interpersonal relationships. When Rose and Frieze (1989) examined dating guides from 1957 through 1983 in an effort to locate cultural norms about dates, they found that the norms of the late 1980s were about the same as in the 1950s—strongly gender stereotyped and, as mentioned earlier, formal and explicit. Recent popular sources of information about dating include the bestselling *The Rules: Time-Tested Secrets for Capturing Mr. Right* (Fein & Schneider, 1995), which a *Time* magazine reviewer contended "sets the dating game back 30 years" (Gleick, 1996, p. 58). Somewhat less one-sided sources are the humorously titled *Dating for Dummies* (Browne, 1997) and *The Complete Idiot's Guide to Dating* (Kuriansky, 1996). Although the latter two "manuals" suggest to readers that egalitarian thinking and relating are currently in, closer inspection reveals a different view.

The *Idiot's Guide,* for example, notes that although women can ask men for a date (egalitarian), it is still the case that "men and women definitely approach the dating scene differently" (Kuriansky, 1996, p. 105) and offered male and female readers different points of view about what the other sex purportedly wants them to know. As it happens, the advice given to men could as easily be given to women (presented here in abbreviated form): Be romantic, listen attentively, agree to do things with her family/friends, build her trust, spend time cuddling, do not expect or demand sex, learn about her body, and do not expect her to date you exclusively while you play around yourself. Similarly, the advice to women could as easily be given to men (again presented here in abbreviated form): Do not expect him to profess love for you soon, do not push him into commitment, do not snoop, do not nag him into talking about his feelings, take the initiative sometimes, do not take everything personally, loosen up your inhibitions, do not compare him to other lovers, do not bad-mouth him to your friends, think of dating as fun, let him withdraw now and then, and accept him without judgment.

These caveats (Kuriansky, 1996) imply that men and women behave and think differently, and yet merely substituting *him or her* for *her or him* reveals their applicability to either sex. Moreover, an examination of the subtopics shown in the index under men/male and women/female reveals that the same subject matter is treated for both sexes with very few exceptions. Thus, the Mars/Venus[1] dichotomy is maintained and traditionalism reinforced despite claims of egalitarian views.

Dating for Dummies (Browne, 1997) also provided "guy stuff" and "girl stuff" sections throughout. In fairness, some of these dealt with biological differences between the sexes (e.g., one guy stuff section discusses impotence), but most support the idea of social differences between the sexes. In addition, the sexist language here and there indicates the author's traditionalist views. For example, in a guy stuff section, the text reads "*Girls* [italics added], if you want to understand *men* [italics added] a little better, take a peek at this stuff" (p. 8).

Have young adult daters internalized more traditionalism than egalitarianism, some of both, or more egalitarianism than traditionalism? We adopted Klinkenberg and Rose's (1994) suggestion and undertook another study of first-date behaviors, this time providing a list of all behaviors that at least 20% of respondents to our earlier study (Laner & Ventrone, 1998) had identified. We then asked participants to indicate what actions or events on the list (expanded from the 25% criterion used in previous studies for inclusion in a script) would or would not occur on a first date.

THE PRESENT STUDY

Our reexamination of the data collected for Laner and Ventrone (1998) revealed 41 possible first-date behaviors—a considerably longer list than previous studies have reported. We asked 103 college men and 103 college women—all students in upper division classes at a large Southwestern university, matched for age, and about 90% Caucasian—to indicate whether those behaviors would occur on a typical first date and if so whether they would typically be something that the man or that the woman would do. An "either or both" option was provided as well as a "neither" option. The behaviors were arranged in a rough time sequence (i.e., from the start of the date until its ending).

The classes from which participants for the study were drawn were all service courses taught in the sociology department. That is, they typically attract a very wide variety of majors, and few students in them are sociology majors.

Respondents ranged in age from 19 to 40 years, with the mean age of 23.19 for both sexes (22 modal age). Questionnaires were distributed on the first day of class. Students were instructed to take the survey home, to fill it out thoughtfully and in private, and to return it at the second class meeting anonymously. Students identified themselves on the questionnaire only by sex and by age at nearest birthday and were assured of confidentiality of response.

Given the apparent strength of first-date scripts found in earlier studies, we hypothesized that despite the revised method for ascertaining the content of a script for first dates, our findings would not differ substantially from those of earlier studies.

Table 1 shows how men and women responded to this task, presenting the 34 main items from the list of 41. (The 7 remaining items are discussed separately in a following section.)

Inspection of Table 1 reveals a high level of agreement between men and women about who typically does what on a first date.[2] In view of this, we were less interested in any statistically significant differences between the sexes than in the general patterns produced by our respondents. Consistent with the findings of previous studies, first dates, as assessed by the current method, are traditional (i.e., male dominated) from start to finish.

TABLE 1 *Proportions of 103 Men and 103 Women Who Identify First-Date Behaviors as Most Likely to Be Done by Men, Women, or Either/Both ("Neither" Category Omitted)*

Behavior	Men's Responses (%)			Women's Responses (%)		
	Man	Woman	Either or Both	Man	Woman	Either or Both
1. Ask someone for a date	83	2	16	68	1	29
2. Wait to be asked far a date	4	86	10	2	87	8
3. Decide on plans by yourself	71	3	17	52	9	26
4. Discuss plans with date	43	16	38	17	26	54
5. Talk to friends about date	11	29	60	1	53	44
6. Buy new clothes for date	3	69	22	0	80	17
7. Select/prepare clothes for date	7	31	61	1	41	57
8. Groom for date (shave or put on makeup)	6	9	84	1	4	94
9. Take extra time to prepare	5	45	48	2	53	43
10. Call date on day of date	53	10	22	47	15	23
11. Prepare car (get gas, etc.)	83	1	13	69	8	18
12. Prepare house/apartment	24	18	56	7	44	47
13. Get money; collect keys	63	5	30	44	1	52
14. Get flowers to bring to date	83	7	8	79	4	2
15. Wait for date to arrive	13	82	5	11	76	11
16. Pick up your date	84	7	8	81	4	14
17. Greet/introduce date to family	16	50	33	5	58	35
18. Go to dinner	13	10	75	6	5	87
19. Eat light	5	78	16	0	87	5
20. Make small talk	31	13	54	15	20	60
21. Pay the bill	91	0	8	77	0	21
22. Open doors for date	88	5	4	89	1	3
23. Go somewhere else (e.g., movie)	22	4	71	11	1	86
24. Pay the bill	88	6	5	67	6	22
25. Go to bathroom to primp	4	76	17	2	73	17
26. Go somewhere else (e.g., drinks)	21	11	59	10	12	73
27. Have a deeper conversation	16	43	37	3	50	38
28. Pay the bill	82	3	15	67	4	23
29. Make affectionate move (e.g., hug)	60	6	30	52	7	39
30. Make sexual move	75	2	12	67	2	15
31. Take date home/walk to door	90	2	7	88	0	7
32. Discuss possible second date	59	5	34	38	5	53
33. Thank date for a good time	9	18	72	4	30	65
34. Call a friend to discuss date	9	54	36	0	67	31
Equalitarianism scores:	Men = 31.85[a]			Women = 35.85		

NOTE: Both authors scored each of the response groups (men and women) separately, achieving an interrater reliability of 95% or greater for all but 3 items. These were rescored and then reached agreement. Among men, fewer than 10% answered "neither" on all items except 3, 10, and 30. Among women, fewer than 10% answered "neither" on all items except 3, 10, 14, and 30.

a. We calculated an equalitarianism score by adding the "either or both" columns for men and for women and dividing by the 34 items.

Both men and women, who are well acquainted with their own scripts as well as with the scripts for the other sex, agree that it is the man who asks someone out (B1),[3] decides on the plans (B3), calls the woman on the day of the date (B10), prepares his car for the date (B11), buys flowers for the woman (B14), picks her up (B16), opens the door for her during the date (B22), and pays all the bills (B21, B24, and B28). It is he who is likely to make both affectionate moves (hugging or kissing) and any sexual moves (B29 and B30) and who returns his partner to her home (B31). Male respondents saw it appropriate for either the man or both partners to discuss a second date. Women, on the other hand, reversed the order—both discuss or man discusses (B32).

We also find, as have earlier studies, that the woman's role on the first date is a reactive one. Moreover, she is more likely to be concerned with appearances (paralleling the male focus on finances). Thus, the woman waits to be asked for a date (B2), buys new clothes (B6), waits for the man to pick her up for the date (B15), introduces him to her family or roommate(s) (B17), eats lightly at dinner (B19)—as one student wrote on her questionnaire, the woman "purposely takes longer to eat so she doesn't eat as much"—primps in the bathroom during the evening (B25), has the leading edge in terms of deeper conversation (B27), and finally, calls a friend after the date to discuss the date or her partner or both (B34).

Some responses, however, indicate a level of similarity between the sexes. For example, both men and women are likely to talk with friends about the date beforehand (B5), although women think that men are somewhat less likely to do so. Men and women are both likely to take care in selecting and preparing their clothes for the date (B7) and in grooming for it (B8). Taking extra time to prepare can characterize either sex (B9), although women think that men are less likely to do this than are women. The evening's activities are shared by both—dinner (B18), making small talk (B20), going to a movie or some other activity (B23), going somewhere for a nightcap or coffee (B26), and finally, both are likely to thank each other for the date (B33).

Some curious aspects of our findings have to do with the two items regarding communication (B20 and B27). Because about half of the men and about a third of the women implicate one sex or the other (but not both), the conversation appears to be more of a monologue on B20 and even more so on B27 where about half of that conversation is being created by either the man only or the woman only—a concern that may be related to the failure of dates to produce satisfactory outcomes. These items might seem to be naturals for an either/both response, but they were not for quite a few of our respondents.

Another curious finding is the distribution of responses to B18. Both persons on a date go to dinner. Although most respondents agreed, we are at a loss to explain why around 10% of men and somewhat fewer women indicated that one or the other partner goes, apparently alone. At first, we thought it possible that, for instance, the questions were understood by some not as going to dinner but as directing the activity (e.g., taking the woman to dinner), but that idea failed in view of the proportion of those who marked this item as related to women (see also Items B23 and B26). In this case, it might still imply something one-sided such as the woman is taken to dinner. In any event, the oddity of this response and a few others lead to the concern that a small proportion of our respondents may not have fully understood the meaning of some items or the directions for responding.

Our egalitarianism scores (see bottom of Table 1) show that on the average, women are slightly (but very slightly) more egalitarian than men. This can easily be seen in the items about asking for a date and paying for the various date activities.[4] Women respondents thought that either sex could do the inviting almost twice as much as did our male respondents. Still, an average of only 9% of the men thought that either partner could pay the bills in contrast to an average of 22% of women who thought so. Nonetheless, as we have seen for both sexes, responses to this question indicate a predominantly traditionalist orientation.

Note that both men and women expect there to be talk with friends about the date both before and after it. These conversations, it is likely, reinforce the traditionalist dating scripts. All in all, what this and other studies on the same topic show is that dating—in particular, first dates—looks very much like what Bailey (1989) described as standard practices starting in the 1920s. With the widespread use of cars and the commercialization of dating, men took control over what had previously been a domain under women's guidance. The initiative and the responsibility for payment, then, became the province of men.

Both the *Idiot's Guide* (Kuriansky, 1996) and *Dating for Dummies* (Browne, 1997) urged readers to see a first date not as a formal outing but as a casual time to be used to get to know one another. It appears, however, that the guidelines governing first dates are quite formal and well-known. In addition, even our personal behavior toward one another tends to be programmed. From our prior survey (Laser & Ventrone, 1998), we took items that respondents had told us would be involved in a first date (not shown in Table 1) having to do with how we treat one another on such occasions. These are behaviors that do not easily fit into the time sequence in that with the exception of the final item, they might occur at any time during the date. We discuss them next. Men and women differed somewhat in their allocations of who would do what, but the fact that these behaviors were predicted to occur indicates that actions we might think of as spontaneous expressions are actually built into our expectations and experiences.

Would partners be polite to one another? Men said that either or both partners would. Women spread their votes across response categories, although not as much for men as for others (men, 27%; women, 36%; and either/both, 36%). Would partners compliment one another? Here, men gave fewer of their votes to women (20%) and more to either/both; women thought that either/both would compliment the partner (81%). Would partners try to impress one another? Again, men gave fewer votes to women (15%) and more to men or to either/ both. Women, however, saw this as something that either or both partners would do (74%). We also asked about holding hands and being flirtatious. Men saw these behaviors as the likely activity of either or both partners. Women, however, spread their responses evenly across categories for holding hands but saw flirtatiousness as a woman's behavior. Finally, at the end of the evening, who would hug or kiss goodnight? According to women, either/both might be involved in the hug, but the kiss split evenly between the man and either/both. According to men, both behaviors were either/both activities (73% and 67%, respectively). Thus, as noted, even our affectionate displays are preprogrammed.

SUMMARY AND DISCUSSION

Using a method that differs from earlier approaches to the study of first-date scripts, we found that 103 male and 103 female college student respondents did not differ in their views from those expressed by participants in prior surveys. Given the consistency of findings in earlier studies of this phenomenon, we anticipated that our results would not differ. Our method generated 41 activities that might take place on a first date, and respondents endorsed them all, mostly in a traditionalist mode. Fourteen activities are indicated as being "the man's," 8 are "the woman's," 7 could be behaviors of either sex, and 5 comprise the activities of the date itself. Women in this study are only slightly more egalitarian than our male respondents.[5] As previous studies have found, men and women appear to know these dating scripts for themselves and for their partners, making first dates highly predictable events. Contemporary advice books for daters, selected for their popularity (two were best-sellers and the others are "very good" sellers according to Teresa Harris [personal communication, 1999]),[6] teach/reinforce the appropriate behaviors (e.g., under "dos and dont's" young adults are told to smile, pay compliments, look their best and the like and are reminded that men and women have different expectations for dating behavior) (see the *Idiot's Guide*, 1996).

Men and women may be far more alike than they are different (Laser, 1995), but neither advice books nor student responses to surveys of this kind would give that impression. The effects of socialization and other life conditions keep the high level of similarity between the sexes something of a secret, when it comes to their first, and perhaps ongoing, dating interactions. Who profits from the seemingly endless focus on male/female differences? Quite an industry has been built around promoting this idea, one guru of which is John Gray whose books, articles, lectures, workshops, and more have continued to spread the Mars/Venus traditionalist message (see also *Mars and Venus on a Date*, another best-seller) (Gray, 1998).

Because Gray and others promise success in the mating process (i.e., finding and "capturing" Mr. or Ms. Right), it is little wonder that there is an extensive market for such materials. Moreover, as we have noted elsewhere (Laner & Ventrone, 1998), if these traditionalist behaviors are involved in making a good first impression and if further dates perpetuate that style of relating (Rose & Frieze, 1993), little can be said for the likelihood of spontaneity or openness between men and women—qualities that are involved in getting to know one another in a realistic way and thus in forming the basis for successful relationships. Ganong et al. (1996) commented that despite many changes,

> today's college students have grown up in a traditional family in which women have had to assume the majority of household tasks whether they worked outside the home or not. . . . Rather than true egalitarian models . . . neither they nor their partners are relinquishing the value they place on women's domestic and nurturing activities. (p. 772)

Ganong et al.'s (1996) own findings with regard to expectations men and women hold for themselves and their partners reflect what the authors call a "semi-egalitarian, semi-traditional mind set," and ultimately, the traditional behaviors coupled with egalitarian expectations may "contribute to the gradual decrease in satisfaction with relationships that occurs over time" (pp. 772–773).

Peer or egalitarian marriages (Schwartz, 1994) are unlikely to be the outcomes of traditionalist dating and courtship. Schwartz pointed out that traditional couples "sacrifice the elemental goals of intimacy, deep friendship and (whether they know it or not) mutual respect, goals that peer marriage better serves" (p. 3). This is because, as Rubin (1983) warned some years ago, "intimacy, as we think of it, is possible only between equals—between two people who have both the emotional development and the verbal skills to share their inner life with each other" (p. 140). Studies of early dating behavior among young, college-educated adults give us little reason for sanguinity in this regard.

Future research in this area might profitably continue to examine dating scripts in a same-age community sample and in upper- and lower-class samples for comparison with these college student studies. Work has begun in studying racial/ethnic dating scripts (Ganong et al., 1996; Ross & Davis, 1996), although to date, these studies have made only African American and European American comparisons. Hispanic and other racial/ethnic groups await study. A beginning has also been made in studying the scripts of gay men and lesbian women (Klinkenberg & Rose, 1994; Rose et al., 1993). It is important to better understand the process by which people come to know their potential mates because it may contain long-term implications—for breakups, for cohabitation, and for more permanent pairings such as marriage.

Notes

1. The first author provides her Courtship and Marriage class with a copy of John Gray's advice to women about "supergluing" their marriages (Manske, 1997), in which 20 suggestions are offered. Students are asked to substitute *he* for *she* wherever it makes sense. They are typically surprised to find that men may be from Venus and women from Mars despite Gray's claims to the contrary.

2. There is a modicum of disagreement between men and women on 2 of the 34 items. Regarding discussing the evening's plans with one's date (B4), most men think that men would do this or that either partner could, whereas women saw this much more as an either/both matter. Similarly, regarding getting money and collecting house and car keys (B13), men saw this primarily as something men would do, whereas women thought that both partners and men only secondarily would do this.

3. *B1* refers to the first item on the list of behaviors in Table 1, *B2* to the second, item and so on.

4. The *Idiot's Guide* (Kuriansky, 1996) advised that women can ask men for a date. However, *Dating for Dummies* (Browne, 1997) asserts that whoever invites, pays.

5. We found it interesting that of 206 respondents, only 1 man and 1 woman mistook the questionnaire as a task with forced choices. The man wrote, "Talk about stereotyping. Let's teach these kids to break down gender barriers, not promote them." The woman wrote, "I feel most things on the survey were applicable to either men or women and that the questions were leaning in a stereotypical fashion." She in fact answered the items in stereotypical fashion, although the either/both option was available for all the behavioral items.

6. Ms. Harris manages a Barnes and Noble store in Phoenix, Arizona.

References

Alksnis, C., Desmarais, S., & Wood, E. (1996). Gender differences in scripts for different types of dates. *Sex Roles, 34,* 499–509.

Bailey, B. L. (1989). *From front porch to back seat: Courtship in twentieth-century America.* Baltimore: Johns Hopkins University Press.

Browne, J. (1997). *Dating for dummies.* Foster City, CA: IDG Books.

Fein, E., & Schneider, S. (1995). *The rules: Time-tested secrets for capturing the heart of Mr. Right.* New York: Warner.

Ganong, L. H., Coleman, M., Thompson, A., & Goodwin-Watkins, C. (1996). African American and European American college students' expectations for self and for future partners. *Journal of Family Issues, 17,* 758–775.

Ginsberg, G. (1988). Rules, scripts and prototypes in personal relationships. In S. W. Duck (Ed.), *Handbook of personal relationships.* New York: John Wiley.

Gleick, E. (1996, September 30). Playing hard to get. *Time,* 58.

Gray, J. (1998). *Mars and Venus on a date.* New York: HarperCollins.

Klinkenberg, D., & Rose, S. (1994). Dating scripts of gay men and lesbians. *Journal of Homosexuality, 26*(4), 23–35.

Kuriansky, J. (1996). *The complete idiot's guide to dating.* New York: Alpha Books.

Laner, M. R. (1995). *Dating: Delights, discontents, and dilemmas* (2nd ed.). Salem, WI: Sheffield.

Laner, M. R., & Ventrone, N. A. (1998). Egalitarian daters/traditionalist dates. *Journal of Family Issues, 19*, 468–477.

Manske, L. (1997, June). 25 ways to superglue your marriage. *McCalls*, pp. 57–59.

Rose, S., & Frieze, I. H. (1989). Young singles' scripts for a first date. *Gender and Society, 3*, 258–268.

Rose, S., & Frieze, I. H. (1993). Young singles' contemporary dating scripts. *Sex Roles, 28*, 499–509.

Rose, S., Zand, D., & Cini, M. A. (1993). Lesbian courtship scripts. In E. D. Rothblum & K. T. Brehony (Eds.), *Boston marriages: Romantic but asexual relationships among contemporary lesbians* (pp. 70–85). Amherst: University of Massachusetts Press.

Ross, L. E., & Davis, A. C. (1996). Black-White college student attitudes and expectations in paying for dates. *Sex Roles, 35*, 43–56.

Rubin, L. (1983). *Intimate strangers: Men and women together.* New York: Harper & Row.

Schwartz, P. (1994). *Peer marriage: How love between equals really works.* New York: Free Press.

Simon, W., & Gagnon, J. H. (1986). Sexual scripts: Permanence and change. *Archives of Sexual Behavior, 15*, 97–120.

■ READING 13

Modern Marriage: From Meal Ticket to Best Friend

Paula Kamen

> *A vibrant marriage has to be more than just problem-free. When a marriage is strong and healthy, it is a powerful vehicle for personal growth.*
>
> —"Steps to a More Spiritual Marriage," *Ladies' Home Journal*, March 1998

When I asked women what the most important part of a marriage was, no one brought up the leading answer in the past: to be financially supported by a man. Instead, the reasons I heard most often (in order of frequency) were "communication," "friendship," "equality" "honesty" "partnership," "compromise," and "openness."

"I kind of feel that for a lot of this generation, it's really not a question: 'Is he a good provider?' I always assumed I'd be working at some point; my mother worked," said Leah, 26, a graduate student at the University of Texas. "But I was looking for someone who was just going to treat me as an equal in a lot of ways: in the kitchen, with housecleaning, with everything. A partnership. That's our marriage." Today, women's roles in marriage are more equal, and as a result of their greater power in marriage, women today are happier with it. In a 1995 CBS News poll, women were more likely than men (63 to 49 percent) to say that their marriages were better than their parents'. When both genders compared themselves with their parents, 56 percent said their marriages were better, 36 percent were the same, and only 3 percent were worse (Bowman 1999).

Today, even for the most traditional couples, marriage, like the American family, has changed. Just as young women have more choices about their sexual behavior and principles, they also have more freedom to tailor their family according to their own personal preferences. In addition, even though marriage and family are still major life goals of most American women, they are not mandatory as they once were. Because women are now less dependent on men as a meal ticket, they can choose not to marry at all, whether they live with a man, have children, or are gay or straight.

"AMERICAN FAMILY VALUES"

The conditions for this move toward a more democratic family have been developing since the turn of the twentieth century. One hundred years ago, the divorce rate began to increase but so slowly that few people took notice. During World War II, an unprecedented number of women entered the workforce. Then after the war, although many women left their jobs to raise families, many kept their jobs, never viewing themselves and their abilities in the same way again. These changes and others became most visible in the 1960s and 1970s, when even more women started pouring into the workforce, getting more education, and initiating divorces. Since the early 1990s, however, this very dramatic change has slowed, and the American family has actually been stabilizing. Statistics indicating the "breakdown" of the American family, based on such factors as divorce and out-of-wedlock children, have plateaued. After skyrocketing in the 1970s and 1980s, rates of divorce, abortion, cohabitation, premarital sex, and single motherhood now are steady, with the figures matching those of other industrialized nations. From 1970 to 1990, the number of married couples with children under 18 shrank from 40 percent of all households to about 25 percent, where it has remained until 2000 (*Household and Family Characteristics* 1998).

In regard to female ideals of commitment, the young women I surveyed were stricter than their counterparts in the late 1970s and most of the 1980s. Indeed, family priorities for women actually resembled the more conservative 1960s levels.[1] And even though more women are attending college than ever before, college women's most ambitious "power career" aspirations have declined to 1970s levels, lower than those of the 1980s but still higher than those of the 1960s and earlier.[2] The result is that women want to "have it all," both marriage and work, but they also expect to sacrifice some of their career or fit it in to family needs (*American Freshman* 1997).

Writing in the *New York Times*, graduate student Elizabeth McGuire talked about young professional women wanting balance, refusing the boomer extremes of having to keep up a "frenetic pace" or quitting their jobs to raise a family. Accordingly, they make career decisions that are more amenable to raising and enjoying children, such as entering more flexible fields and starting their own businesses. In this way, they differ from the career-oriented boomers and even the older Generation Xers, who viewed children as an afterthought, not considering until after establishing their careers the commitment that children require. "Many people may think we are nearing the end of the workplace revolution," McGuire wrote. "In reality, we are only just beginning" (McGuire 1998, A9).

At the same time as they support "family values," young American women have a broader definition of "family." They acknowledge that most women want to work or must work out of necessity and that a family may be different from the white straight suburban nuclear model. For example, when I asked Becky, a New York University graduate student who had been raised by her divorced mother, to define a "family," she stressed that the important thing in the end is that two parents are present. "Does it have to be male/female?" she asked herself. "I have to be perfectly honest and say in the child's interest, it's certainly better if they have a male and female parent. I certainly would have appreciated that. But I'll tell you. I've seen plenty of documentaries about lesbian couples and gay couples, and I think they are fine parents, and are much better than foster care or just shuffling through the different boys' homes or girls' homes." While Becky values the traditional two-parent family, she still resents much of the self-righteous rhetoric about it from conservative politicians. She described her mixed feelings about former Vice President Dan Quayle's insistence that a breakdown in family structure had caused many of society's problems. "He's right to a certain extent. But what's wrong with that is his term 'family values' is loaded in the same way that 'New World Order' is," she explained, using another sound bite from the past Bush administration. "When he's talking about 'family values,' he's talking about a Christian-oriented white family. And that's true. There's no denying that they're talking about Christianity. That bothers me. Because I think that creates its own set of problems."

Throughout history, politicians' narrow definition of the family has lagged behind that of most citizens. The failure to recognize working women proved to be a fatal mistake in the 1992 Republican presidential campaign. At the national convention, in their vague platform of "family values," conservative leaders such as Marilyn Quayle and committee chairman Rich Bond emphasized the worth of only the traditional family of a nonworking mother. In the process, they alienated the majority of American women who do not—or cannot afford to—fit that profile. In response, the Clinton campaign four years later prominently featured the issues of working families.

Even Leslie and Mark, both 24 and religious Baptists, the most traditional couple I interviewed, admitted some modern concessions. Married at 21, they both believe in defined gender roles in marriage. When they have children, Leslie plans to leave her job as a ground-support supervisor at an airline and raise them. She has already lowered her original career expectations by quitting college and moving to Santa Barbara to join Mark, where he is enrolled in a graduate program in engineering. "I'm not like an old-fashioned fifties woman or anything," said Leslie. "But I believe in women's work and men's work. Taking out the garbage is definitely men's work." However, they both emphasized that they respect others' choices and don't "ride a high horse" because of their decision. Leslie views herself not as a conservative but as an individualist by not following one "politically correct" model of womanhood. She pointed out that in the 1970s and 1980s, women had more to prove than they did today. "Instead of showing your independence by being part of the revolution, you show your independence by being your own self," she said. At the same time, however, Mark's and Leslie's marriage is also more flexible than that of their parents. Mark plans to spend much more time with his children than his father did, who was singularly focused on his career, and also he does some of the housework.

MARRIAGE TRADITIONS OLD AND NEW

In this transformed American family, young women still remain devoted to the concept of marriage. Perhaps the greatest testament to its enduring appeal is the booming bridal industry, accounting for $32 billion in retail sales in 1996. Nearly 3 million weddings took place in the United States in 1997, half a million more than in 1995. And people are spending more. The average cost of a wedding in Chicago, for example, climbed from $10,000 in the mid-1980s to about $20,000 today (Kerrill 1997).

While attending a typical American bridal fair in Chicago as a spy for this book, I kept thinking about how, on one hand, so little had changed on the surface. Judging by the overwhelming enthusiasm and open pocketbooks of those in attendance, I saw first-hand that marriage is still romanticized and prized enough to make grown women swoon. The centerpiece of the fair was a fashion show. The crowd, mostly conservatively attired women in their early twenties, some husbands-to-be, and mothers, overflowed into the aisles and sections behind the rows of chairs. With every movement and expression of the models on the runway, the audience clapped and moaned and sighed and often howled, displaying the unswerving attention and devotion usually reserved for fundamentalist revivals.

One of the event's organizers told me that the surest sales are for the big purchases: the dress, the photographer, and the reception. She commented that no matter what their budget, women are not likely to skimp on those three items. Speaking of the bridal industry, she noted, "We pride ourselves on saying that we're a recession-free business." She added that the women will do what it takes to save for these items, commonly delaying the wedding and living at home with parents to save money (as were several young women there whom I interviewed).

Still, while so many women continue to pay homage (along with large sums of money) to wedding and family tradition, much has changed under the surface. The once fringe idea of marriage as a partnership has become utterly mainstream. A large part of the reason that marriage has changed is that women have changed. With more power and higher expectations, young women enter marriage on an entirely different footing than did the generation before the baby boomers. A majority of women (55 percent) now earn at least half their household's income (1995 Whirlpool Foundation study, "Women: The New Providers," *Glamour*, October 1995, 124). The proportion of women working to support their families doubled in the past twenty years, from 19 percent in 1980 to 46 percent in 2000 (Virginia Slims Poll 2000). Now that they have less need of men to support them financially (and know that they can't necessarily count on them, anyway, for life), women are making other, more intimate demands of their husbands for partnership. Although finances are still important and a major source of marital strife, they aren't the only one. According to the 2000 Virginia Slims/Roper Starch Opinion Poll, in response to the question "What makes a good marriage?" women and men rated "respect for each other" at the top of the list (selected by 85 percent of women and 83 percent of men).[3] Following that, selected by seven in ten women and men, were being in love, the spouse's sexual fidelity, communication about feelings, and keeping romance alive-all rated above "financial security" by a slim majority, 59 percent each of men and women.

The ideals of the women's movement, on society's fringes in the 1970s, have become those of the nation. This current young generation as a whole seems to have more progressive attitudes toward women's place in society and marriage. Using the 1972 Attitudes toward Women Scale, University of Michigan researcher Jean Twenge (1997a) compared seventy-one subjects from 1970 to 1995 and found a steady trend toward more liberal/feminist attitudes. Women changed most in the late 1970s and early 1980s, but men lagged a generation behind. (It was not until 1986 to 1990 that they equaled the attitudes toward greater gender equality that women had in the 1970s.) Twenge's findings reflect the results of the past thirty years of surveys of college freshmen by the UCLA Higher Education Research Institute. Over the years, student attitudes have become much more liberal and accepting of married women's roles outside the home, even though other attitudes (such as toward marijuana and the death penalty) became more conservative during the 1980s (*American Freshman* 1997). In an interview, Professor Ilsa Lottes of the University of Maryland remarked that more egalitarian values were the key force separating young women from the boomers of her generation, that in the 1970s, these values were new and not as widely and fully absorbed. "It [the women's movement] was just coming into being," she said. "I wasn't raised to think I could do anything. I'm 53. I was raised to be a teacher so that it wouldn't interfere in my more important roles as a wife and mother. Now I would be called sexist for saying the same thing to my women students."

Just as more Americans approve of women's having a career, professional career women also have a more positive view of marriage. Building on boomer patterns, they feel free to marry later, when it won't interfere with their career, and to have fewer children later in life.[4] Younger men are willing to share housework and child rearing. A woman's marriage vow no longer signifies a total retreat from the outside world into the traditionally womanly sphere of the home and family. She no longer is assumed to be forming her entire identity as a Mrs. Somebody, an accessory to a man, sacrificing all her own ambitions. And thanks to the pioneering efforts of the boomer career women, the workplace, at least for the more affluent, is more family friendly and accepting of women.

BEYOND RACE AND RELIGION

As new ideals for marriage emerge, some of the old ones disappear. Consistent with young women's individualist philosophies, they are less likely to base relationships on religion or race, more traditional concerns. (This is true even though marriage partners still tend to have similar backgrounds.) In the 2000 Virginia Slims Opinion Poll, more than 90 percent of the women said that marriage between people of different religions is acceptable, and 85 percent agreed that interracial marriage was acceptable. Accordingly, the number of such marriages has skyrocketed. Between 1960 and 1990, the number of interracial marriages increased by 800 percent. Roughly, one in twenty-five married couples today are of different races. In 1990, according to a study by the American Enterprise Institute, nearly 2 million children lived in homes in which the primary adults were of different races; this number doubled in 1980 and rose more than four times the number in 1970 (Holmes 1996).

The figures for intermarriage vary by race. Although they still account for only 1 percent of all marriages, the pace of marriage between whites and blacks is rapidly accelerating. According to the U.S. Bureau of the Census, in 1993, of all new marriages by blacks, 12.1 percent were to white partners, up from 2.6 percent in 1970 (most of these were black men marrying white women). This is dramatic considering that just forty years ago, these marriages were illegal in many states. The intermarriage rate is much higher for Hispanics, Asians, and Native Americans, of which at least 30 percent marry outside their race. In fact, with higher intermarriage rates than their male counterparts, Asian American women are just as likely to marry a white man as they are another Asian. A majority of both Native American men and Native American women (53.9 percent) marry whites (Lind 1998).

Young adults also more often marry persons of different religions, with about three-quarters marrying and about one-half dating or cohabiting within their religion (Michael et al. 1994, 46). Only one-third of mainline Protestants marry persons of their own religious identification, compared with 61 percent of evangelical Protestants and 68 percent of Catholics (Laumann et al. 1994, 244). The intermarriage rate for Jews has more than quintupled, from 9 percent for Jews married before 1965 to at least 52 percent for those married after 1965 (Steinfels 1991).

In addition to finding a different partner than they would have in the past, young women also have other expectations about the relationship itself. The women I interviewed indicated that communication was essential, just as it was for their sexual relationships. In contrast, in the past when women were expected to fill predetermined passive and subservient roles, they had no need for such communication with their partner. Although fundamentalists were more insistent than most on maintaining traditional gender roles and male domination of marriage, they also promoted communication between the partners to help support their commitments.

Also observing these changes was Mary Ann Hanlon, 54, who was perhaps the most experienced social observer of modern marriage whom I interviewed. For the past twenty years, she and her husband have held pre-canna classes (premarriage counseling sessions) for working- and middle-class Catholic couples in their Queens, New York, home. Even though the format differs from parish to parish, a course on marriage is a standard requirement for couples taking vows in the Catholic Church. Hanlon's six-week course has always emphasized the importance of communication. She has noticed that couples now more fully accept and absorb these lessons because they have better and "more realistic" communication skills. "They actually talked to each other about the things that were going to have an impact on their lives. The nitty-gritty of how they were going to share the chores, or who is going to handle the money."

In my interviews, women of all classes and educational backgrounds emphasized the importance of communication. Lana, 29, a student at Alladin Beauty College in Denton, Texas, emphasized communication when discussing her faith in marriage and family. "I think you have to work hard at it," said Lana. "Very hard. We work hard at it. I mean, communication, that's the biggest work." A student at Plymouth State University, Ann, 23, also listed "communication as key to a good relationship," explaining that "it shows the person you care enough about them to talk to them about, 'What's going on?' Or work something out when you're having a disagreement." Such themes animated my conversation with three mothers on public aid in the University Settlement on the Lower East Side of New York. I first asked them about challenges that are part of their lives but that their parents did not face. The women, two African Americans and one Latina, elaborated on their greater expectations for communication and partnership. Vernadette, 33, who is married and has an 11-year-old daughter, observed, "The challenge for me is communicating and negotiating with family. That would be breaking the pattern that I've gotten from my mother and father. . . . In my family, feelings were not expressed. They were denied. . . . And dealing with my daughter, I don't want her to continue in the same cycle. If you have a problem, communicate it. Don't talk like it doesn't exist." Vanessa, 25, who never married, said that a great challenge was communicating with men, along with men's lack of responsibility and commitment. (The father of her child abandoned them and refuses to pay child support.) Like Vernadette, she expected a marriage to be an equal partnership. "It's supposed to be fifty/fifty. There should be an equal thing, not just with sex, but in taking care of the kids, you know, fulfilling each others' needs, being there for each other."

Similarly, the women hoped that the husband and wife would be "best friends," rather than exclusively a "wife" or a "husband." Maintaining this type of relationship is more natural to a generation of women and men that is more likely to cultivate friendships with the opposite gender. As they grew up, today's young men and women shared more of the same values and educational experiences, and in college in the 1990s, they were more likely to live in coed residence halls, where they formed friendships and learned to demystify the opposite sex. Bellinda, 22, said this made a difference when she was a freshman at the University of Texas at Austin. "I went to an all-girls Catholic school, so I didn't have really good interpersonal communication, anything like that. I wasn't used to being around men, so it really helped a lot that I was living with a bunch of guys. I had to learn how to be friends with men and how to be more than friends with men, and how to keep those relationships different." After her dormitory experience, she moved into an apartment with two females and one male friend. After our interview, she planned to move in with her boyfriend at Purdue University, who shares a three-bedroom apartment with his brother and a female friend of theirs.

Several other women I interviewed had male best friends and male roommates, and almost all of them pointed out the difference between themselves and their parents' generation. Karen, 26, who is an accounting clerk at a hospital in southern California and whose best friend is a gay male, said that she had witnessed this difference with older coworkers. When she goes to lunch with a man in her office, the women in their forties and fifties seem confused. "He lives with his girlfriend. I live with my boyfriend. We talk a lot. We eat lunch together and stuff, and they think there's something going on. Because how could you guys just be friends? . . . When they were 22 or 23, most of them were married. I don't think they came from a time where men and women were friends as much. It was like you dated them, that was fine. But you didn't just socialize. When you needed advice, you wouldn't call some guy that you talked to or whatever, some guy that you were friends with. There was always like a sexual conflict or something underlying or some kind of tension."

Sexual fulfillment has also taken on new importance. Now that the wife is not required to "serve" her husband sexually with "wifely duties," her needs have become more prominent. A 1994 EDK/*Redbook* survey of married couples revealed that "married couples value their thriving sex lives, which they nurture with romance, intimacy, sexual variety. Today's married sex is red-hot and experimental, women are every bit as interested as men," stated the report, "Married Sex Sizzles." According to this survey, almost half (47 percent) the married couples rated the sexual aspect of their marriage as "very good," and another 35 percent said that it was "good." To keep the spark alive, the most popular way cited by both men and women (73 percent and 78 percent) was experimenting with different positions. A third were adventurous enough to do things not associated with traditionally tame marital sex, such as acting out fantasies, watching erotic movies, and using massage oil or vibrators. Those rating their sex lives as hottest also reported happier marriages. Eighty percent who gave their marriage a high "sizzle rating" also said their marriages were happy (versus only 42 percent of low sizzlers).

A *Mirabella* magazine article, "Hot Monogamy," about this greater emphasis on sexual pleasure in marriage observed that

> we have entered a radically new era of sexuality. . . . Monogamy is definitely the ideal among young people today. Sticking together. Having kids. Concentrating on family life. You could say things were just like they were back in the Fifties-except for two enormous differences. The fact that women work. And the fact that these young monogamous couples are insisting on good, hot sex. (Wolfe 1995, 127)

Dr. Helen Singer Kaplan, a couples sex therapist quoted in the article, attributes this insistence on good sex to the greater importance of commitment and a fear of risks, such as AIDS. Young people take a dimmer view of adultery and so are more likely to turn to their established partner for experimentation and novelty. Also, now that the double standard has diminished, a man has less of a whore/madonna complex about his wife, seeing her as a sexual being as well as a mother/"good girl." In the past, a man seeking a hotter sex life would be more likely to have an affair with a different kind of woman, a "bad girl." This adultery is evident in films of the 1960s and 1970s, including *Shampoo*, which treated adultery as a joke.

Although people are still having extramarital affairs, statistics show that American adults are becoming less tolerant of cheating.[5] Also, the younger generation of men is having fewer affairs, no longer seeing them as a standard alternative to a tame and lustless marriage. The National Health and Social Life Survey found that older generations of men were more likely to have had additional partners during their marriages. Of the men born between 1933 and 1942, 23 percent said they had had another partner besides their wife. But of the men born between 1963 and 1974, the number reported was only 10 percent (Laumann et al. 1994, 208). Men in their forties and older were twice as likely to have paid for sex in their lives (20 percent) than were men in their twenties (10 percent) (Smith 1994b, 75). (However, the NHSLS charted women's rates of infidelity as remaining more stable through the years, at 7 to 9 percent.)

DEMANDS ON MEN AND FATHERS

As women demand more of marriage, they are also demanding more of men. As a result, the roles of husband and father have been transformed. Women now expect men to share the housework and child rearing, and according to the polls, the men think this is reasonable. In the 2000 Virginia Slims Opinion poll, more than 80 percent of men and women favored men's sharing household responsibilities. (Their record of actually helping out was less commendable, however.)

In the 1980s and 1990s, fathers assumed and enjoyed new involvement at home. A recent study of employed adults by the Families and Work Institute showed a smaller gap between working men's and women's contribution to housework. In 1977, men spent about 30 percent as much time as women did on household work, compared with 75 percent as much in 1997. (The gap in 1997 was 45 minutes.) The same study also found that children received more attention from working parents, mainly because of the change in men (Lewin 1998b).[6] Fathers participate in child care from the very beginning, with 90 percent of married fathers present in the delivery room when their children are born, according to Robert L. Griswold, author of *Fatherhood in America* (see Gibbs 1993). In the 1980s, bookstores introduced titles like *Expectant Father, Father a Successful Daughter,* and *Father's Almanac.* The magazine *Modern Dad* was started in 1997 by a 28-year-old former financial manager who noticed that when his friends became fathers, they wanted to be "very connected to their kids" but didn't know how (*Chicago Tribune*, 26 January 1997, sec. 13, p. 6). In polls, men claim more interest in their children than in their career. In a 1990 survey by the *Los Angeles Times,* 39 percent of fathers said they would "quit their jobs" to spend more time with their kids. Another survey found that 74 percent of men said they would rather have a daddy-track job than a fast-track job (Gibbs 1993, 56).

Only recently has the government noted the growing role of fathers in caring for children. A 1994 U.S. Census Bureau report described them as the central force holding down the need for day care. The study found that the proportion of families paying for child care fell from 40 percent in 1988 to 35 percent in 1991, a trend attributed mainly to the increase in care by fathers. In 1988, 15 percent of preschoolers with working mothers were cared for by their fathers, a figure that rose to 20 percent over the next three years (Vobejda and Cohn 1994).

Like the other aspects of marriage discussed, this dual parenting role is growing for Americans from all walks of life. Beauty school student Lana, of Denton, Texas, is grateful that her mechanic husband helps take care of their two sons. They cannot afford day care, so they each take shifts when the other is working. "I think men are getting more level. They're coming around," she said. "They're trying anyway. I mean, my husband has been babysitting all day today. He's good at that." Much of this change has been voluntary, with fathers regarding involvement with their family as rewarding and not as a sacrifice. Representing this emerging view is Gary, 30, a college administrator in Chicago. Like several others I interviewed, his real father had abandoned the family, and Gary has no memory at all of him. His parents divorced when he was an infant, and he now considers his stepfather his real father. (In fact, he didn't know that his stepfather wasn't his real father until recently when he was going through his mother's papers.)

Gary planned his entire career around being able to make more time for his wife Kerry and year-old daughter, Alyanne. After working his way through law school, he chose his current, more flexible job instead of joining a law firm. When Kerry went back to work, as a high school math teacher, he enthusiastically took a month off for child care, under the new Family Leave Act, which took effect in 1993 and has been used by millions of fathers since. "If I had gone into a law firm," he said, "it was quite clear there would be no taking this leave. To do so would mean sacrifice—you will not be promoted. You will forever be stereotyped and cast in a certain way. Yet at my work, it was so natural. There was absolutely no hesitation, no backlash. It was admired."

Gary noticed some other gaps in society's acceptance of a more involved father. Mainly, he had some clashes with his more traditional stepfather, a mechanic in a small Pennsylvania town. "When we were getting married, my father sat down to tell me how important it was that I take charge and not let Kerry make certain decisions. Because if I let her make any decisions, then she'd probably make all the decisions. . . . And trying to explain to him what my concepts of equal relationship are—the word had no meaning for him." As a result, his father insinuates constantly that Gary is being pushed around by his wife. When he tells his parents something "that they don't want to hear, they'll say, 'Did Kerry make you say that?' " Kerry's parents, who are from Jamaica, also are skeptical. "When I [Gary] go to her house, if I try to help do the dishes, her mom, her pop will joke, 'Oh we have to put a dress on you' because I'm doing 'women's work.' "

Even though men of all classes might wish for this more enlightened role, only a few, like Gary, are able to make it happen. White-collar employers are far more likely than most even to consider making the workplace more family friendly. Despite the fact that the majority of women work, the workplace has been slow to offer child care, family leave, and equal wages for women. In the 2000 Virginia Slims Poll, 63 percent of women surveyed said that employers should give women more flexibility. In addition, men still earn more money than their wives do and most often demand that women be the ones to make the career sacrifices. Many women are grateful, however, just to have fathers involved in their families at all, for about a quarter of households are run by a single parent, almost always the mother.[7]

Editor's Note: References and Notes for this reading can be found in the original source.

■READING 14

Few Good Men: Why Poor Mothers Stay Single

Kathryn Edin

It is no secret that the institution of marriage is in trouble. The median age at first marriage is at its highest since the United States began keeping reliable statistics: 24 for women and 26 for men. Nearly six of every 10 new marriages will end in divorce, and the propensity to remarry has also declined. Though these trends cut across race, ethnic, and class lines, poor adults from disadvantaged minority groups marry and remarry far less than others.

Whether these trends are a cause for concern or celebration is in the eye of the beholder. Some happily take them as an indication that women can now survive without men who beat them, abuse their children, or are otherwise difficult to live with. Others lament the moral effect on the fabric of American society. Still others worry because of the strong association between growing up with a single parent and a host of negative outcomes for children. Sara McLanahan and Gary Sandefur's work reveals that half the disadvantage these children face reflects the poverty so often associated with single parenthood (almost 50 percent of all unmarried mothers have family incomes below the poverty line); the other half reflects such factors as lower parental involvement and supervision, and greater residential mobility in mother-only families. Why, then, do low-income women continue to have and raise children outside marriage, in the face of these daunting circumstances?

In 1990 I began publishing the results of a study of low-income single mothers that showed it was nearly impossible for these women to make ends meet on either a welfare check or a low-wage job [see Kathryn Edin and Christopher Jencks, "The Real Welfare Problem," *TAP*, Spring 1990]. Drawing data from in-depth multiple interviews with nearly 400 low-income single mothers in four U.S. cities, my research collaborator Laura Lein and I documented large monthly budget deficits for single mothers, whether on welfare or in low-wage employment. Even though they were clever at devising strategies to make up their budget shortfalls, these strategies took a great deal of time and energy; they were highly unstable and sometimes illegal. The women's situations resembled a continually unraveling patchwork quilt. Because of the budget gaps and the instability of the strategies used to bridge them, these single mothers and their children often went without items most Americans would consider necessities: adequate food or shelter, clothing, heat, electricity, telephone service, and adequate health care or health insurance.

In the mid-1990s, Lein and I began to appear as guests on radio talk shows around the country. When we told the story of the hardship these single mothers and their children faced, callers invariably asked two questions. First, if things were so bad for these single mothers, callers wondered, why did they have children in the first place? Second, wouldn't these women be better off if they simply got married? For these listeners, both *motherhood* and *singleness* were choices low-income women had made, and these choices had led to the hardships. I had inadvertently touched upon a raw nerve in a large segment of Americans; their anger and incomprehension went very deep. I decided it was worth asking these questions of low-income single mothers themselves.

People's ideas about children and marriage presumably emerge out of interactions they have with one another in a given ecological context (a family, kinship group, or neighborhood)—a context that may have distinctive cultural and structural features. The Philadelphia metropolitan area, where my colleagues and I conducted our most recent interviews, contains many poor neighborhoods that tend to be segregated by race and ethnicity. We tried to ensure a balanced representation of whites, African Americans, and Puerto Ricans, the three main racial and ethnic groups in the area. In Philadelphia single parents headed nearly 23 percent of white family households with children under eighteen in 1990. The rate was 44 percent for Hispanics and 63 percent for African Americans. These rates are not unlike those in the rest of the country (18 percent, 29 percent, and 53 percent respectively).

THEORIES ABOUT MARRIAGE

Four theories of nonmarriage hold currency among scholars. First, Gary Becker and others point to the increasing economic independence of women. According to Becker's economic theory of the family, women who can earn a living on their own will find marriage less attractive than those financially dependent on men. Though this explanation for declining marriage rates makes intuitive sense, the evidence is mixed. While more women have indeed been entering the paid labor force during the years when marriage has been declining, the effect on low-income women may be paradoxical. Some analyses show that for low-income women, marriage and earnings are positively related—as a woman's income rises, so does the probability that she will be married.

Starting from the other side of the relationship, William Julius Wilson has looked at changes in men's economic position, assuming that a man must be stably employed for a woman to consider him marriage material. He points to the declines in unskilled men's employment over the past 30 years and to large decreases in unskilled wages. Wilson argues that shrinking labor force participation and declining wages create an imbalance in marriage markets, particularly among African Americans, whose male employment rates and wages remain lower than those of other groups. While this theory is broadly persuasive, the declines in marriage are even greater than the theory would predict.

Third, Charles Murray and others blame welfare. As welfare became more generous, women increasingly traded dependence on a man for dependence on the government. In the early 1970s, the Supreme Court struck down the man-in-the-house rule (which had prohibited female welfare recipients from cohabiting with a man). In Murray's estimation, cohabiting while remaining unmarried became the rational option for a poor couple because they could combine his earnings with her welfare allotment. Nonmarital childbearing did rise in the 1960s and 1970s. However, welfare benefits shrank in real terms from the mid-1970s to the 1990s, while nonmarital childbearing still continued to increase. And there is not much empirical association between the relative generosity of welfare benefits state by state and changes in marriage rates.

Fourth, some observers cite cultural factors. Arguably, the women's movement and women's entry into the paid labor force have revolutionized women's notions of gender roles. There is certainly evidence that among lower-income adults, women's views have changed far more dramatically than men's, and the result is a mismatch in sex role expectations of poor men and women. Yet I know of no analyses that have looked directly at how changes in sex role expectations have influenced marriage rates per se.

There is even more confusion and disagreement on the question of why poor single women have babies. Some scholars and advocates view this as a dysfunctional act, to be remedied by more intensive education on the wisdom of using birth control and deferring pregnancy. Other research has found that given the available alternatives, having a baby may not be all that irrational for some single poor women. Arlene Geronimous and Sanders Korenman found that comparable women who waited to have babies were no better off economically than those who had babies as teens. The *Prospect* has addressed this issue [see Kristin Luker, "Dubious Conceptions: The Controversy over Teen Pregnancy," *TAP*, Spring 1991.]

LISTENING TO THE POOR

So we are still left with more questions than answers. How do low-income single mothers feel about marriage? What factors do they believe prevent them from marrying? To what extent does the marriage norm still operate in poor communities?

One way to get at the often subtle and complex meanings of marriage in poor communities is to listen to residents at length, observe and take part in their daily routines, and immerse oneself in their world. Thus far, my colleagues and I have talked with over 130 black, white, and Puerto Rican mothers in nine neighborhoods across the Philadelphia metropolitan area. These interviews reveal four major motives for nonmarriage among the poor: affordability, respectability, trust, and control. Some of these motives fit with current theories of nonmarriage, but some do not. Overall, the interviews show that although mothers still aspire to marriage, they feel that it entails far more risks than rewards—at least marriage to the kind of men who fathered their children and live in their neighborhoods. Mothers say these risks may be diminished if they can find the "right" man—and they define "rightness" in both economic and noneconomic terms. In sum, they say they are willing and even eager to wed if the marriage represents substantial economic upward mobility and their husband doesn't beat them, abuse their children, insist on making all the decisions, or "fool around" with other women. If they cannot find such a man, most would rather remain single.

AFFORDABILITY

Mothers see economic stability on the part of a prospective partner as a necessary precondition for marriage. Welfare-reliant and low-wage working mothers worry a great deal about money simply because they have to. The price for not balancing their budgets is high: the stability of the household and the well-being of their children. Though men frequently contribute to mothers' households, their employment situations are often unstable and their contributions vary. Mothers' consistent needs for supplemental income, combined with men's erratic employment and earnings, mean that couples often break up over money or fail to marry because of it.

Mothers aren't completely cold and calculating when they weigh the costs and benefits of keeping a man around. Many say they try to take into account the effort their men put into finding and keeping a job. But if the man quits or loses his job for reasons the woman views as his own fault, he often loses the right to co-reside in the household, share in family meals, or even to maintain any romantic relationship with her. Mothers whose boyfriends live with them almost always told us they impose a "pay and stay" rule—if the men are out of work and not contributing to household expenses, they eventually lose the right to co-reside. One Puerto Rican mother said,

> I didn't want to be mean or anything, [but when he didn't work], I didn't let him eat my food. I would tell him, "If you can't put any food here, you can't eat here. These are your kids, and you should want to help your kids, so if you come here, you can't eat their food." Finally, I told him he couldn't stay here either.

Since these men can seldom afford their own apartment and are not eligible for housing subsidies because they have no custodial children, they are often powerfully motivated to try and maintain a place in their girlfriend's household. Often, their only alternatives are to move back in with their own mother or to live on the streets. No low-income single mother we have spoken to has allowed a nonpaying male partner to sponge off her welfare or paycheck for any substantial length of time simply because neither welfare nor low-wage employment pay enough to make this an affordable option.

One might expect that, given their economic needs, mothers would pressure their men into engaging in any form of employment available, including the drug trade. But virtually all tell us that "drug money" cannot buy marriage or even long-term co-residence. In fact, it is often a father's entry into the drug trade that breaks young couples up (except when the woman herself is addicted, in which case she usually loses custody of the children). Mothers fear that if their man gets involved in drug dealing, he might stash weapons, drugs, or drug proceeds in the household, that the violence of street life might follow him into the household, that he will end up in prison, or that he will start "using his product." Mothers consider these outcomes inevitable for anyone who participates in the drug trade for long. Even more worrisome for mothers is the negative role model a drug-dealing husband would provide their children. One African-American mother recounted, "The baby came home and [my child's father] was still selling drugs. I kept on telling him, 'Well, it's time for you to get a job now. . . . The kid's home now, and its time for you to get a job . . . and a job where you're not gonna get hurt or you're not gonna get locked up.' "

The somewhat mercenary nature of mothers' marriage views does not mean they do not care deeply about the men in their lives. Indeed, holding men to economic standards even the mothers recognize are hard to attain is often emotionally wrenching. One Puerto Rican mother admitted,

> There was a struggle going on inside of me. I mean, he lost his job at the auto body shop when they went [bankrupt] and closed down. Then he couldn't find another one. But it was months and months, and I was trying to live on my welfare check and it just wasn't enough. Finally, I couldn't do it anymore [because] it was just too much pressure on me [even though] he is the love of my life. I told him he had to leave even though I knew it wasn't really his fault that [he wasn't working]. But I had nothing in the house to feed the kids, no money to pay the bills, nothing. And he was just sitting there not working. I couldn't take it, so I made him leave.

This dilemma is particularly stark in the neighborhoods we are studying, where unemployment rates are three or four times higher than the national average. Deferring or avoiding marriage allows mothers to substitute an economically productive male for an unproductive one, should the need arise. Divorce takes both time and money, both of which these mothers find in short supply.

RESPECTABILITY

Many middle-class Americans, like the talk-show callers, believe that the marriage norm no longer operates within poor communities because these men and women think too *little* of marriage. Our interviews revealed the opposite. Women often said they avoid marriage because they think too *much* of it. Indeed, marriage often had a kind of sacred significance in the communities we studied, a marker of respectability. However, marriage signals respectability for low-skilled mothers only if accompanied by financial stability and some measure of upward mobility. As one young African-American mother declared, "I'm not marrying nobody until they can move me into my own apartment or my own house." Marriage to an economically unproductive or erratically employed man, on the other hand, makes the mother a "fool" in the eyes of her friends and neighbors. Mothers find it somewhat more respectable to remain single and hold out hope that they will eventually make a respectable match. Even for mothers who could technically afford to marry a "low-class" man, such a union would entail a diminished level of class respectability. Like the young white mother in the following quote, our respondents tended to group marriage together with other status markers such as diplomas, careers, savings accounts, and houses:

> I want a big wedding. I want to be set—out of school, have a career, and then go from there. . . . Yeah, my friends that have children, my one girlfriend, she's engaged, but they're not getting married . . . until they have some money put aside. My other girlfriend, she wants to get a house first and be ready with that and then decide.

In these communities (as in much of America), a wife appropriates the class standing of her husband. Marriage to an economically unproductive male means, in these mothers' view, permanently taking on his very low status. A woman who marries a poor or economically unstable man makes a profound statement to the larger community (and to herself): "This is the best I can do." Such a choice will garner the ridicule rather than the respect of neighbors and kin. By avoiding marriage to men with attributes similar to their own, mothers hope they will someday find a man through whom they can gain enhanced class standing and respectability. As one white mother succinctly put it, "I just want [a marriage] that will take me up to where I want to go."

TRUST

Though many of our respondents have given up on marriage altogether, this is more because of their low view of the men they know than because they reject the institution of marriage itself. Among the low-income couples we observed, the battle between the sexes often looks more like outright war, and many women say that they regard men simply as "children," "no good," or "low-down dirty dogs." Women tend to believe men are untrustworthy in several respects. First, they fear that the men will not (or cannot, in some women's view) be sexually faithful. One young African-American mother stated, "I feel like this: A married man, a single man, a man that's in a relationship for a certain amount of time—they're still gonna run around. A man is gonna be a man." Another said, "There's a shortage of men, so they think, 'I can have more than one woman. I'm gonna go around to this one or that one, and I'm gonna have two or three of them.' " Like these mothers, many women view infidelity as almost inevitable (part of men's "nature"), but they are not willing to accept it as a natural part of marriage.

Women believe the best way to avoid being deceived by an unfaithful spouse is to either avoid marriage altogether (being cheated on by a boyfriend generally entails less loss of face because the woman has not publicly tied herself to the man "for life") or delay marriage while observing and evaluating a potential spouse's behavior over time. If he fails to confirm her fears after several years or shows improvement, she might consider him "marriage material." A white respondent admitted, "Living with [a man] would be fine. If after I lived with him for a couple of years and I see that nothing's gonna change in the relationship, then maybe I'll marry him. But he's gotta be somebody that's got [enough] money to take care of me."

Mothers also mistrust men's ability to handle money. While mothers are hard-pressed to pay their bills each month and therefore budget their money carefully, many view men as prone toward wasteful or selfish spending. An African-American mother recounted, "I gave [my child's father] the money to go buy my son's Pampers. He went on some street with his cousin [and] they were down there partying, drinking, everything. He spent my son's Pamper money [on partying]."

Most mothers understand that a married couple has joint responsibility for either party's debt, while unmarried partners need not assume such responsibility. When a mother considers marriage, she usually begins to demand financial accountability of her partner (which not only ensures that the bills get paid but also makes it harder for him to maintain a relationship with a woman "on the side"). Perhaps not surprisingly, a prospective husband may resent these financial demands and might not always comply, thus confirming her view of his financial irresponsibility.

Additionally, mothers often do not trust men with their children. Respondents tell us stories about men (both their children's fathers and other boyfriends) who leave children home alone, engage in unsuitable activities (heavy drinking or smoking crack, for example) in front of them, neglect to feed or otherwise care for a child in their charge, or even physically or sexually abuse a child. A white respondent recounted a time when she let her children's father take them on a short trip: "I let him take them down the shore. He got into a fight with his girlfriend, beat her up, got locked up. I didn't know where my kids were [and] I didn't find out until 9:00 [the next morning]."

While mothers feel that the experience of parenthood has matured them, fathers without primary custody have never been forced to stop "rippin' and runnin' the streets" and to "settle down." Indeed, most mothers we talk with say their children's fathers have not perceptibly "changed their ways" since they became parents. When asked about her baby's father, one white mother said, "He's 25, but he still likes to run the streets and go out with his friends all the time. I just can't be bothered with that." An African-American mother stated, "Sometimes men don't grow up as fast as women. He's still a kid in part—a kid, period, to be honest with you." Another white mother was even more caustic: "They're stupid. They're still little boys. You think you can get one and mold him into a man, [but] they turn out to be assholes. All men are. They're good for one thing and one thing only, and it ain't supporting me."

While mothers express profound distrust toward men in many ways, they have not always held these attitudes. Many described loving and even committed relationships to their children's fathers or other male partners in the past, and often used the terms "love of my life" or "first love" to describe how they felt (and sometimes still feel) about these relationships. The story differs somewhat for the divorced mothers and those who never married.

Many never-married mothers often related that, prior to their pregnancy, relationships with their children's fathers were warm, romantic, and loving; a good number said they had even planned to marry. But as the pregnancy progressed, many mothers say that their boyfriend's behavior changed dramatically: Boyfriends who had been warm and loving often became panicked, hostile, and uncommunicative. One African-American mother said, "That first stage of me being pregnant was so stressful. . . . He would call up [and say that] I was cheating on him and it wasn't his baby. I went through that the whole [pregnancy, with him calling me a] cheater." A startling number of women tell us that their boyfriends beat them while they're pregnant (often by punching them in the stomach or pushing them down the stairs). One young white mother recalled,

> He started really beating me up. I was pregnant and he beat the shit out of me. . . . I must have been like four, five months pregnant. . . . By then I had a belly. . . . He's on top of me—a grown six-foot-two man, 205 pounds, [and] I'm five feet and maybe 120 pounds because of the fact that I was pregnant—him on top of me, beating me up, punching me, hitting me. And I got a belly [with] his child.

These relationships deteriorate partly because, as the woman's pregnancy advances, her sense of what she and the baby will need materially grows more concrete. Though an intermittently employed boyfriend might have adequate funds to play the role of boyfriend, a pregnant girlfriend quickly realizes that these meager earnings cannot support a family. A young man who may have been completely acceptable six months prior is suddenly viewed as "no good" by his girlfriend, even when his behavior may not have changed in any way.

Mothers often describe a golden period in their relationship with the child's father once their child is born. Often, the father comes to the hospital during or after the birth, and the couple renews their desire to stay together and perhaps marry. However, the new mother, who necessarily begins to deal with the practical demands of raising the child, again places increased financial demands on the father. One African-American mother recalled that after the baby was born,

> That's when everything started blowing up. I didn't wanna be with him no more 'cause he wasn't working and he was getting on my nerves. . . . He just never gave me no money. I would tell him, you know, "Well, the baby needs diapers." "Well, I don't have no money." "The baby needs milk." "Well, I don't have no money." I just started getting mad. I had to buy milk and diapers so I just told him to leave me alone.

Fathers in tight economic straits grow increasingly resentful, and the relationship quickly deteriorates—sometimes within days of the birth. Many of the same fathers that talked of romance and marriage at the hospital often deny that they are the father of the child soon after. They accuse their baby's mother of "stepping out," "sleeping around," or "whoring" behind their back. Some demand a blood test before buying anything for the baby. Not surprisingly, these scenarios increase women's mistrust. One African-American mother said, "[When] a woman gets pregnant, right away the man [says], 'It's not mine.' I mean, if you're together eight years, how come it's not yours all of a sudden?"

For married women, the devastation is perhaps deeper because their expectations are often higher. Most say they had expected their marriages to last "forever" and had often given up educational or occupational goals to wed and to raise children. These women seldom suffer through the harsh pregnancy experiences and subsequent denial of paternity the unmarried women report, but the public humiliation that relational failure can bring is perhaps greater. Separated or divorced mothers described painful breakups due to infidelity, financial irresponsibility, domestic violence, alcoholism or drug abuse, or child abuse—precisely echoing the fears of the unmarried women. These mothers' experiences also leave them unwilling or unable to trust men.

CONTROL

When we ask mothers what they like best about being a single mother, many tell us that they enjoy being in control. Some of the previously married women have at one time been almost completely dependent on a man, having moved directly from their natal household to their husband's with little or no work experience in between. Having not worked full time for years, these women have forgone investments in human capital that might have resulted in higher wages. The period of economic shock and near-destitution that oftentimes follows the marital breakup is a painful one, and mothers say that every inch of economic independence they currently enjoy has been hard won. These lessons convince most mothers that it simply isn't safe to completely depend on a man again. One divorced African-American woman said, "One guy was like, 'Marry me, I want a baby.' I don't want to have to depend on anybody. No way. I [would rather] work. [If I married him and had his baby], I'd [have to quit work and] be dependent again. It's too scary."

For never-married mothers, the story is somewhat different. Some of these women are taught life's hard lessons by their own mothers, older sisters, aunts, and other older female kin, whose boyfriends or husbands beat them, cheat on them, abuse their children, or "drink or smoke up their paychecks." For others, enrollment in the school of hard knocks began during pregnancy or after childbirth, for reasons described above. Having and caring for a child often reveals in unmarried mothers competencies they did not know that they possessed. Yet they feel that men often do not respect these competencies and want to be in control. Unmarried male partners cannot fully exert this control because they know their female partners can get rid of them at any time. As one white woman asserted, "I can kick him out whenever I want to kick him out. This is my life. No one can tell me what to do." Once marriage vows are taken, mothers are afraid all that might change. A divorced white mother stated,

> They think that piece of paper says they own you. You are their personal slave. Cook their meals, clean their house, do their laundry. Who did it before I came along, you know? That's why they get married. A man gets married to have somebody to take care of them cause their mommy can't do it anymore.

Most low-income single mothers don't want to be owned or to "slave" for their husbands. They want marriages that are partnerships of equals. Most believe that the best way to maintain power in a romantic relationship is to make sure they are contributing financially to the household economy. A white woman described an ideal marriage this way: "It will be me and my husband [both] working. We both work, [while] the children are in school." A good marriage from the woman's point of view is one where she contributes financially so that she has a say in the decision making. The greater her financial contribution, the more say she believes she is entitled to.

Since mothers also believe that childbearing and the early child-rearing years mandate at least a partial withdrawal from the labor market, mothers equate the early child-rearing years with relational vulnerability. A marriage that occurs prior to or during the prime family-building years, when the mother is least able to contribute financially to the household, is likely to leave a mother quite powerless in her relationship with her husband. Waiting until all of the children are in school (or even out on their own) means that mothers can focus more of their energies on paid labor and increase their chances of entering into a marital relationship with more control. Such marriages, they feel, are more likely to be both satisfying and sustainable over time. As a young African-American mother said,

> I want to have a nice job, [so] that I know if he walked out I have something to fall back on. The mortgage [and] everything [else] is going to be in my name. That's how I want it to be. . . . I do want to get married, but I'm going to get myself stabilized and get everything together with me and [my daughter] before I even take that route.

Since the 1970s, a sharply declining proportion of unskilled men has been able to earn enough to support a family. As the accounts of Philadelphia-area, low-income, single mothers illustrate, these trends have had a profound influence on marriage: Women simply cannot afford to keep an economically unproductive or intermittently employed man around the house. Unless a prospective marriage partner has the resources to ensure a mother some level of social mobility, she will not generally consider marriage even if she could "afford" to do so. I know of no data that demonstrate that gender mistrust has grown over time, but certainly the risk of divorce—and the economic destitution for women that so often accompanies it—has grown.

Beyond affordability, respectability, and trust, these interviews suggest a wide gap between low-income men and women's expectations in regard to gender roles. Women who have proven their competencies though the hard lessons of single parenthood aren't generally willing to enter subservient roles—they want to maintain power in subsequent relationships. Those who plan on marrying generally assume they will put off marriage until their children are in school, and until they are working steadily. By waiting to marry until after early child-rearing and the temporary labor market withdrawal that accompanies it, mothers feel they can minimize these risks and enhance their bargaining power within marriage.

In relation to theories of the retreat from marriage, I find little support for the argument that these women are eschewing marriage because of their enhanced prospects for economic independence outside of marriage (though the theory could well be true for higher-skilled women). Indeed, poor women seem to view economic independence almost as a *prerequisite* for marriage. I also find virtually no support for the welfare disincentives argument, since very few mothers say that they have avoided marriage or remarriage to maintain eligibility for welfare, even when asked directly.

In short, these low-income single mothers believe that marriage will probably make their lives more difficult. They do not, by and large, perceive any special stigma to remaining single. If they cannot enjoy economic stability and respectability from marriage, they see little reason to expose themselves or their children to men's lack of trustworthiness and sometimes violent behavior, or to risk the loss of control they fear marriage might exact from them. Unless low-skilled men's economic situations improve and they begin to change their behaviors toward women, it is quite likely that large numbers of low-income women will continue to resist marriage.

■ READING 15

The Future of Marriage

Frank F. Furstenberg, Jr.

It's clear that the institution of family is undergoing a major overhaul. Perhaps you've recently been to a wedding where the bride and groom have invited their former spouses to join the festivities. Or maybe a family member told you that your 37-year-old unmarried cousin is pregnant by artificial insemination. Or you heard that your 75-year-old widowed grandfather just moved in with his 68-year-old woman friend. To those of us who grew up in the 1950s, the married-couple family is beginning to look like the Model T Ford.

Public concern over changes in the practice of marriage is approaching hysteria. An avalanche of books and articles declares that the American family is in a severe state of crisis. Yet little agreement exists among experts on what the crisis is about, why it has occurred, or what could be done to restore confidence in matrimony. I believe that the current situation falls somewhere between those who embrace the changes with complete sanguinity and an increasingly vocal group who see the meltdown of the so-called traditional family as an unmitigated disaster.

Social scientists agree that we have seen a startling amount of change in nuptial practices in the past half century. The shift is producing an especially striking contrast from the 1940s, because the period just after World War II was a time of remarkable domestication. The post-war period followed several decades of turbulence in marriage patterns initiated by rapid urbanization during World War I, and the Great Depression.

Many of the complaints about family life in the 1990s sound an awful lot like those voiced in the 1950s, an era we look upon with nostalgia. We often forget that the current gold standard of family life—the family built upon an intimate marital relationship—was regarded with great suspicion when it made its debut. The middle-class nuclear family that became the norm at mid-century was a stripped-down version of the extended families of previous decades. Kingsley Davis observed that a host of social ills could be traced to this new form of family: " . . . The family union has been reduced to its lowest common denominator—married couple and children. The family aspect of our culture has become couple-centered with only one or two children eventually entering the charmed circle," he wrote.

Ernest Burgess, one of the most respected sociologists of his generation, wrote in 1953 that urbanization, greater mobilization, individualization, increased secularization, and the emancipation of women had transformed the family from an institution based on law and custom to one based on companionship and love. Despite believing that the changes taking place in the family were largely beneficial to society, Burgess acknowledged that enormous pressure would be placed on the marital relationship to meet new expectations for intimacy. Burgess and Davis correctly predicted that divorce would rise because of the tremendous strain placed on couples to manage the growing demands for congeniality and cooperation.

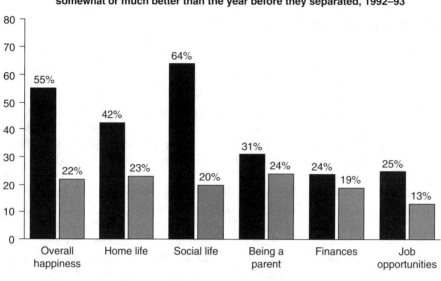

Percent of separated women who say selected aspects of their life are somewhat or much better than the year before they separated, 1992–93

FIGURE 1   *The Trade-Offs of Ending a Marriage.*
Recently separated women are more likely to perceive improvement in their parenting and social lives than in their financial well-being. *Note:* Separated women are those who split from their husbands since the last survey was taken in 1987–88.
Source: National Survey of Families and Households, 1992–93.

Marriage is not in immediate danger of extinction, though. In 1960, 94 percent of women had been married at least once by age 45. The share in 1994 was 91 percent. In other words, the vast majority of Americans are still willing to try marriage at some point. What has changed from the 1960s is when, how, and for how long.

The median age at marriage has risen from a low of 20.3 for women and 22.5 for men in 1960, to 24.5 for women and 26.7 for men in 1994. The proportion of women never married by their late 20s tripled from a historical low of 11 percent in 1960 to a high of 33 percent in 1993. The divorce rate among ever-married women more than doubled between the early 1960s and late 1980s, although it has since leveled off.

The number of children living in married-couple families dropped from 88 percent in 1960 to 69 percent in 1994. Divorce plays a role in this decline, but much of the rise in single-parent families results from the sharp increase in nonmarital childbearing. The proportion of births occurring out of wedlock jumped from 5 percent in 1960 to 31 percent in 1993. While some of these births occur among couples who are living together, the vast majority are to single parents.

The increase in single-parenthood due to divorce and out-of-wedlock births may be the most telling sign that Americans are losing confidence in marriage. Ironically, some of today's most vitriolic political rhetoric is directed toward gay couples who want the right to marry, just as the cultural legitimacy of marriage has been declining.

WHAT WE GET OUT OF MARRIAGE

What has transformed societal attitudes toward marriage so that young people delay it, older people get out of it, and some skip it altogether? Before attempting to answer these questions, a few cautions are in order. Demographers and sociologists, like climatologists, are pretty good at short-term forecasts, but have little ability to forecast into the distant future. In truth, no one can predict what marriage patterns will look like 50 years from now.

Virtually no one foresaw the "marriage rush" of the 1940s that preceded the baby boom. And few predicted the sudden decline of the institution in the 1960s. If our society alternates periods of embracing and rejecting marriage, then we could be poised on the cusp of a marriage restoration. It's doubtful, however, because most of the forces that have worked to reduce the strength of marital bonds are unlikely to reverse in the near future.

The biggest stress on marriage in the late 20th century is a transition from a clearcut gender-based division of labor to a much less focused one. For a century or more, men were assigned to the work force and women to domestic duties. This social arrangement is becoming defunct. Women are only moderately less likely than men to be gainfully employed. Even women with young children are more likely than not to be working. In 1994, 55 percent of women with children under age 6 were currently employed, compared with 19 percent in 1960.

Women's participation in the labor force has reduced their economic dependency on men. The traditional bargain struck between men and women—financial support in exchange for domestic services—is no longer valid. Men now expect women to help bring home the bacon. And women expect men to help cook the bacon, feed the kids, and clean up afterward. In addition, the old status order that granted men a privileged position in the family is crumbling.

These dramatic alterations in the marriage contract are widely endorsed in theory by men and women alike. The share of both who say their ideal marriage is one in which spouses share household and work responsibilities has increased since the 1970s, according to the 1995 Virginia Slims Opinion Poll. Yet in practice, moves toward gender equality have come with a price. Both men and women enter marriage with higher expectations for interpersonal communication, intimacy, and sexual gratification. If these expectations are not met, they feel freer than they once did to dissolve the relationship and seek a new partner.

Being out of marriage has its downside, too, of course. About four in ten recently separated women say they are worse off financially than they were while married, according to the 1992–93 National Survey of Families and Households. This longitudinal study asked women who separated from their husbands since the previous survey in 1987–88 to evaluate several aspects of their lives. At the same time, 43 percent of separated women say their finances are better than during marriage.

Ending an unhappy marriage obviously brings about other positive changes. If it didn't, people wouldn't divorce. Being a single parent isn't easy. Yet more than half of

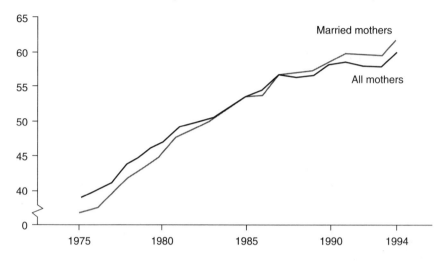

Labor force participation rate of mothers with children younger than age 6 at home for all women aged 16 and older and for married women, 1975–94

FIGURE 2   *Mom Learns to Juggle.*
Married mothers of preschoolers are more likely than all mothers to be in the labor force.
Source: Bureau of Labor Statistics.

separated women say that being a parent is better than before their split-up; 52 percent say care of children is better. Sixty-five percent say their overall home life is better, and 49 percent say their leisure time has improved. This may not mean they have more leisure time than while married, but perhaps the quality of that time is more fulfilling.

The increase in the share of women who work is not the only reason why Americans readily leave marriages that don't suit them. Legal reform and social trends have made divorce and nonmarital childbearing easier and more acceptable. Safe, affordable contraception enables couples to engage in sex outside of marriage with minimal risk of pregnancy. Women's college-enrollment rates have risen sharply in the past two decades, while public policies and societal attitudes have helped increase their involvement in politics and government. These changes have spurred women to greater autonomy. Each has affected marriage in a different way, but they have all worked in concert toward the same result: to make marriage less imperative and more discretionary.

Some Americans vigorously object to this "take-it-or-leave-it" approach to marriage on moral grounds, hoping to reverse the course of recent history by restoring "traditional" family values. Yet changes in the practice of marriage are not peculiar to the U.S. The decline of marriage as it was practiced in the 1940s in the United States has occurred in virtually all Western societies.

MARRIAGE AS A LUXURY ITEM

The rise of delayed marriage, divorce, and out-of-wedlock childbearing disturbs the moral sensibilities of many observers. Others may not object on moral grounds, but they fear that the byproducts of intimate relationships—children—are no longer safeguarded by the family. Their fears are well-founded. A great deal of research shows that children are disadvantaged by our society's high level of marital flux.

A wealth of data shows that married men and women have lower incidences of alcohol related problems and other health risks than do divorced and widowed people. Men especially seem to enjoy health benefits from marriage. Experts believe this is because wives often monitor health behavior, and because marriage provides incentives for men to avoid high-risk behaviors.

Marriage gives all parties involved an economic boost. In fact, stable marriages could be perpetuating the growing division in American society between the haves and have-nots. Marriage, quite simply, is a form of having. Children growing up with both of their biological parents are likely to be more educated, and to have better job skills and a more secure sense of themselves. Thus, they enter adulthood with greater chances of success and a greater likelihood of finding a mate with a similar profile.

This does not mean, however, that children are better off with married parents. Some think that men and women today lack the capacity to sacrifice for children as they did a generation ago. Maybe they do. But if sacrifice means remaining in stressful, hostile, and abusive environment, it's not necessarily worth it. Even so, I doubt if failure to compromise one's own needs for the good of others is the main reason why fewer couples are getting married and staying married.

In my research on low-income families, I hear men and women talking about the virtues of marriage. Nearly all endorse the idea that children are better off when they grow up with both biological parents, although this is probably said in the context of assuming that the marriage is a "good" one.

Plenty of young people have seen "bad" marriages as they've grown up, which has given them an understandable fear of committing themselves and children to such a situation. "Most of my girlfriends, they got married when they was 20," says one woman. "Now they divorced. They got children. Fathers don't do nothing for them, so then, it was a toss-up. Either to go ahead and start out on the wrong foot or get on the right foot and then fall down." In other words, if you plan to have children, it may not matter too much whether you get married first, because you may not get anything out of the marriage, either financially or emotionally.

Although women may not depend on men's economic support as much as they used to, they still expect something out of the bargain. Young adults in low-income populations feel that they don't have the wherewithal to enter marriage. It's as if marriage has become a luxury consumer item, available only to those with the means to bring it off. Living together or single-parenthood has become the budget way to start a family. Most low-income people I talk to would prefer the luxury model. They just can't afford it.

Marriage is both a cause and a consequence of economic, cultural, and psychological stratification in American society. The recent apparent increase in income inequality in the U.S. means that the population may continue to sort itself between those who are eligible for marriage and a growing number who are deemed ineligible to marry.

There is little to suggest that marriage will become more accessible and enduring in the next century. The unpredictability and insecurity of the job market is likely to have an unsettling effect on marriage in the short term by making marriage a risky proposition, and in the long term by generating larger numbers of people who are the products of unstable family situations. Men are making some progress in taking on household tasks, including child care, but women still shoulder most of the burden in families, causing continued marital stress.

While this may sound unduly pessimistic, marriage may change for the better if people are committed to making the institution work, albeit in a new format. The end of the 20th century may eventually be recognized as the period when this new form of family—the symmetrical marriage—first appeared.

It's no longer noteworthy to see a man pushing a stroller or for preschoolers to be just as curious about mommy's job as daddy's. As with many social trends, well-educated couples appear to be leading the way in developing marriages based on equal sharing of economic and family responsibilities. It may be a little easier for them, too, because they are more likely to have the resources to hire people to do the things they choose not to do themselves.

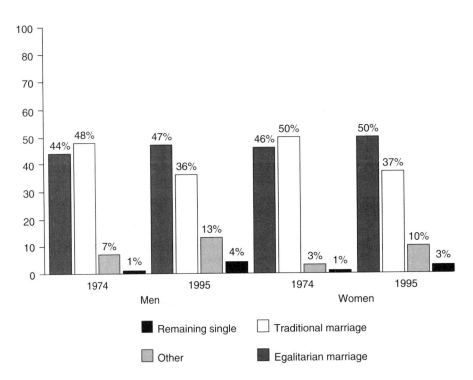

FIGURE 3   *The Perfect Family, 1974–95.*
Both men and women are more likely now than 20 years ago to say an egalitarian marriage is ideal, but they are also more likely to favor alternatives to marriage.

Source: Virginia Slims Opinion Poll.

The move toward symmetry may be more challenging for average Americans of more modest means. Couples who work split shifts because they can't afford child care may be sharing the economic and household load, but they don't spend much time with their spouses.

Single parents who have no one with whom to share the load might have little sympathy for couples who argue about whose turn it is to do the dishes, but at least they are spared the arguing. Single people supporting themselves may feel that their finances are strapped, but when a married person loses his or her job, more than one person is adversely affected.

I am often struck by the fact that we have generous ways—both public and private—of aiding communities beset by natural disasters. Yet we do practically nothing for the same communities when a private industry abandons them, or when their young people can't find work, no matter how hard they look. Restoring marriage to an institution of enduring, compassionate relationships will require more than sanctimonious calls for traditional, communitarian, and family values. We should back up our words with resources. This includes moving toward a society that offers secure, remunerative jobs, as well as better child-care options and more flexible schedules so people can accept those jobs. Otherwise, the institution of marriage as we knew it in this century will in the 21st century become a practice of the privileged. Marriage could become a luxury item that most Americans cannot afford.

6 Divorce and Remarriage

Divorce Culture: A Quest for Relational Equality in Marriage

Karla B. Hackstaff

When people marry they do not simply tie a knot, but weave a complex of relationships according to pre-existing patterns. In U.S. history, the institution of marriage has been like a loom through which several threads of social relations have been woven. Marriage has been a monogamous, lifelong commitment that has regulated gender, sexuality, and the physical and social reproduction of the generations. This Western marital pattern is being redesigned. We are still responding to the tapestry of old, but the various threads are being disaggregated and rewoven. Our society is deeply divided regarding the value and meaning of these new and partially woven designs.

Over the past decade, family scholars have debated whether we should be optimistic or pessimistic about marital and family life (Glenn 1987, 349).[1] Optimistic theorists have argued that families are not falling apart, but simply changing and adapting to new socioeconomic conditions (Riley 1991; Scanzoni 1987; Skolnick 1991). They stress the value of embracing family diversity and removing structural obstacles for the well-being of all families. Optimists emphasize the oppression that has attended women's sacrifices in marriage and point to the potential for greater self-determination and happier relationships today (Cancian 1987; Coontz 1992, 1997; Riessman 1990; Skolnick 1991; Stacey 1990, 1996). These theorists are concerned about threads that have regulated gender and sexuality and have subordinated women in marriage.

Pessimistic theorists have argued that the institution of marriage is a cause for concern—that divorce rates signify an unraveling of social bonds (Bellah et al. 1985; Glenn 1987; Lasch 1979; Popenoe 1988; Popenoe, Elshtain, and Blankenhorn 1996; Spanier 1989; Whitehead 1997a). Above all, pessimists argue that divorce suggests an increasingly tenuous thread of commitment and a growing "individualism" among today's adults, particularly since marital dissolution by divorce, rather than death, entails individual choice. In this view, marriage represents the singular commitment that sustains intergenerational family relationships, especially parenthood. Indeed, several recent books urge a return to lifelong marriage for the sake of children (Blankenhorn 1995a, 1995b; Popenoe, Elshtain, and Blankenhorn 1996; Whitehead 1997a).

Pessimists fear that with the advent of divorce culture we have forsaken nurturance, commitment, and responsibility. Because these are the very virtues that have tradition- ally been valorized in women, these divorce debates are always implicitly, if not explic- itly, about gender. As one optimistic scholar has argued, "when commentators lament the collapse of traditional family commitments and values, they almost invariably mean the uniquely female duties associated with the doctrine of separate spheres for men and women" (Coontz 1992, 40). Critics of divorce do not always or necessarily reject gender equality in marriage, but they do tend to set it apart. Many scholars assume that the thread of gender ideology can be easily disentangled from the thread of commitment.

The middle-class '50s and '70s couples in this study, in combination with those in other studies, enhance our knowledge of the newly constructed meanings of marriage. Among the '70s spouses, I found a reproduction of divorce culture among the married, a growth in a marital work ethic, and fluid, even contradictory, beliefs regarding mari- tal and gender ideologies. These findings validate the concerns of both optimists and pessimists.

Pessimists may be dismayed by the sense of contingency in the talk of married cou- ples and may be confirmed in their belief that commitments are unraveling. On the other hand, optimists may feel validated in their views that spouses do not take divorce lightly; rather, "working" on marriages is the prevailing belief among spouses—though wives are still trying to equalize this work. A full-blown marital work ethic has arisen because of divorce anxiety and marital instability, yet it has also arisen because of instabilities in be- liefs about gender. Spouses must be reflexive about the nature of marriage since the au- thority of marriage culture and male dominance have lost their hegemonic hold. The fluid beliefs among '70s spouses suggest that spouses do not wholly embrace either mar- riage or divorce culture. This may disturb pessimists more—at least those who would like to see marriage culture regain the hegemony of generations past.

At this point in time, marriage does not seem to be forever for almost half of all marriages. Is this a result of culture and the decline of values such as commitment, or are there other factors contributing to marital contingency today? Could divorce culture be transitional—a means to the goals of equality and new tapestries of commitment, rather than an end in itself? While the individualism of divorce culture has brought new prob- lems, we should neither overlook the structural sources of these troubles nor forget the costs of marriage culture, particularly to women.

THE COSTS OF MARRIAGE CULTURE

Women's greater participation in the labor force, increased activity in the political sphere, and greater initiation of divorces suggest that women like Mia Turner and Roxanne Kason-Morris are claiming their rights and appropriating a model of individualism. However, my research suggests that women's increasing "individualism" needs to be un- derstood in context. Because we proceed from a history of male-dominated marriages, individualism does not *mean* the same thing for women as for men.

Historically, we know that as heads of the household, even when not primary bread-winners, most husbands have had greater authority, and therefore greater freedom to be independent, than wives. Economic and legal structures have not only firmly anchored a white man's family authority in the public sphere, but have recognized and applauded his individualism. His autonomy, integrity, rights, and self-expression were never con-strained to the same degree as those of wives, though he carried heavy financial respon-sibilities. Not all men have been able to accomplish or benefit from the provider role—working-class men and men of color have often been thwarted by economic and racial injustice. However, for those able to realize the ideal of the male provider role, these responsibilities have optimized men's freedoms and prerogatives.

Wives who are more individualistic are often trying to counter the legacy of male dominance in marriage. At face value, "contingent marriage" dilutes commitment by making it conditional. Marital commitment and contingency stand in an uneasy relation to one another. The unconditional commitment requires flexibility and a long-range view of reciprocity and rewards over time; it permits conflict, serendipity, and unforeseen developments without threatening the commitment; it builds trust that only a sustained history can provide. Yet, "marriage as forever" can also obscure the latent terms of com-mitment that have prevailed under conditions of male dominance. Paradoxically, a sense of contingency can enable wives to elicit values such as commitment, responsibility, care-taking, and equality. In short, it provides a powerful lever to set the terms of marriage.[2]

Of course, both men and women can use the lever of contingency in heterosexual marriage. Indeed, a male-dominated divorce culture may be a greater threat to the val-ues of responsibility, caretaking, and equality than a male-dominated marriage culture. Yet, as I have suggested, securing power through individualism is not a new means for men within divorce culture. Thus, this lever is more important for women, who have had less economic and political power in the marital relationship. In fact, contingent mar-riage may be crucial for redefining marriage in an egalitarian direction. Most women are hungry not for power but for "the absence of domination" (M. Johnson 1988, 261). Yet, how can wives challenge domination without engaging the power of individualism?

A belief in equality is more widespread today—the '70s spouses did not generally embrace male dominance as their '50s counterparts did, but rather voiced support for gender equality.[3] Yet, ongoing conflicts over gender equality are apparent in husbands' and wives' "hidden agendas." When there is evidence of rights equality—such as a wives' participation in the labor force—husbands tend to assume that equality has been achieved; they are unaware of ongoing inequalities, such as marital work, and their en-during privileges to set the terms of marriage. Rights equality has more often been a mas-culinist discourse in U.S. law and culture (Arendell 1995; Coltrane and Hickman 1992; Weitzman 1985).

Many wives also embrace rights equality, yet women's conventional responsibilities for caretaking, child rearing, kin work, and marital work continue to incline women to-ward a vision of equality that focuses upon relational responsibilities, expressiveness, eq-uity, and interdependence. Relational equality has been more often feminized in U.S. society (Cancian 1987; Riessman 1990). It is not that women are "essentially" relational, but rather that they have been expected and positioned to accomplish relationality. While some women are undoubtedly more individualistic today, as critics of divorce culture argue (Hewlett and West 1998, 200; Whitehead 1997a, 172, 181), more women increasingly want to share the marital and family labors that optimists have documented. Women are frustrated by men's lack of participation in marital work—and the emotion work, kin work, and housework that such reflexive assessment encompasses (Blaisure and Allen 1995; Cancian 1987; DeVault 1987; di Leonardo 1987; Goldscheider and Waite 1991; Hochschild 1983; Hochschild with Maching 1989; Oliker 1989; Thompson and Walker 1989; Thompson 1991).

These gendered marital visions are also apparent in the retrospective accounts of the divorced. Among divorced women and men, Riessman (1990, 164–65, 184) found that "freedom" encapsulated the positive meaning of divorce, but this gateway to freedom did not necessarily hold the same meaning. Women reported a freedom from subordination and the freedom for self-development—reflecting limits to equality in marriage; men reported freedom from obligations demanded by wives and a freedom from wives' scrutiny—reflecting some dissatisfaction with marital labors. Also, while former wives described their "transformations in identity" as learning to balance relatedness with self-reliance, former husbands discovered the value of "talk" and becoming more relational (199). This latter change by some husbands is ironic for former wives if, as I have argued, relational inequality contributes to marital instability and contingency.

In their suburban divorced sample, Kitson and Holmes (1992) found that ex-husbands and ex-wives similarly ranked a "lack of communication or understanding" as the top marital complaint (though wives ranked this higher) and similarly ranked "joint conflict over roles" as a key complaint.[4] Most interesting, however, was a notable gender difference on the marital complaint "not sure what happened"; for ex-husbands it ranked third, for ex-wives it ranked 28th (123). This suggests that men were less attuned to what the marriage lacked—a prerequisite for doing marital work.

Some '70s husbands—such as Robert Leonetti, Gordon Walker, and Paul Nakato—do marital work. Yet, more often than not, wives initiate and try to redistribute the actual "marital work" of communicating, caring, fulfilling needs, adjusting, and planning for marital well-being. To advocate shared marital work is to de-gender the rights and responsibilities conventionally attached to marital practices, to challenge male authority, and to disrupt power relations. Recent research that aims to predict marital happiness and divorce, as well as to improve the efficacy of marital therapy, reveals that a husband's refusal to accept influence from his wife is a key factor for predicting divorce (Gottman et al. 1998, 14, 19).

The above research suggests that marital work and the relational equality that it entails may be as important as rights equality for wives in a culture of divorce. The cultural irony is that even though wives may want a relational marriage, they may need to draw upon individualism to secure it. If secured, that is, if husbands keep up with wives' changes, wives may change the power dynamics of their marriage. Yet, ultimately what many wives want is not freedom from commitment, but freedom within an egalitarian and relational marriage. However, if relationality is unsecured, these wives may choose the gateway of divorce.

It is worth recalling that it was primarily the wives and not the husbands who thought about divorce among '50s couples ensconced in marriage culture. What does this reveal about the gendered costs of marriage culture? Writing about marriage and the nuclear family, Stacey (1996, 69) noted: "It seems a poignant commentary on the benefits to women of that family system that, even in a period when women retain primary responsibility for maintaining children and other kin, when most women continue to earn significantly less than men with equivalent cultural capital, and when women and their children suffer substantial economic decline after divorce, that in spite of all this, so many regard divorce as the lesser of evils." In light of women's postdivorce commitments to children, to charge such mothers with an egoistic or self-centered individualism reveals a refusal to recognize the costs of marriage culture to women.

Are there no costs for men in marriage culture? While research continues to find that marriage is better for men than women in terms of overall health and mortality rates (Hu and Goldman 1990), men are adjusting to new gender ideologies and practices too. Historically, the ability to provide and the ability to head a household have rooted men's identities. Working women and growing beliefs in equality are increasingly uprooting these means to manhood, as distinct from womanhood. As Furstenberg (1988, 239) has observed: "Men looking at marriage today may sense that it offers them a less good deal than it once did. This is the inevitable result of reducing male privileges, female deference to men, and a range of services that were customarily provided as part of the conjugal bargain. The loss of these privileges has persuaded some men to opt out of family life altogether." Paul Nakato's observation that some '70s men would rather be "right" than "married"—echoes Goode (1992, 124) on the sociology of superordinates: "Men view even small losses of deference, advantages, or opportunities as large threats and losses." Craig Kason-Morris felt increasingly underappreciated for all his work; yet his solution was to devote more energy to breadwinning, risking the relational needs of his marriage.

If we ignore the emotional costs of marriage culture and its connection to gender inequality, we will fail to see that divorce culture is a transitional phenomenon. We will also advance the costs of divorce culture—the impoverished single mothers, estranged fathers, and affected children—of concern to pessimists and optimists alike.

THE COSTS OF DIVORCE CULTURE

The gendered patterns of divorce follow from those of marriage. Just as women usually do the primary parenting during a marriage, they generally obtain custody of children after divorce. Fathers are overwhelmingly noncustodial parents—only 14 percent of custodial parents are fathers (Sugarman 1998, 15). Just as fathers help support children during marriage, they are expected to contribute to child support upon divorce. Yet, many noncustodial fathers have become estranged from their children and delinquent on child support. Single, custodial mothers must often raise children on one slim paycheck. More widespread divorce seems to have increased women's and children's impoverishment, undermined fathers' economic and emotional commitment to children, and deprived children of the emotional and economic goods that two parents can provide.

Pessimists acknowledge structural impediments to marital commitments—the decline of the male wage and the need for two wage earners in a postindustrial economy. Yet, they see the decline in cultural and family values, such as commitment, as the more pivotal factor fostering these new social problems. On the other hand, optimists regularly argue that our failure to respond to the new global and postindustrial economy—the low priority given to families by corporate and government entities—is more basic to these problems, and that these new conditions demand solutions that do not discriminate on the basis of marital status. Although structural solutions are central, optimists are also concerned with cultural and family values—though the values of equality or justice are of greater concern than commitment.

Optimists and pessimists alike are concerned about the economic costs of divorce for mothers and their children. About a third of female-headed households are in poverty—six times the rate of married-couple households (U.S. Bureau of the Census 1995, P60-187). A re-evaluation of one study's claims about the economic consequences of divorce a year after divorce, finds that women's standard of living declines by 27 percent and men's increases by 10 percent (Peterson 1996, 534).[5]

A key solution to poverty for many pessimistic family scholars is reinforcing marriage and the nuclear family structure (Blankenhorn 1995b; Hewlett and West 1998; Popenoe et al. 1996; Whitehead 1997a). Marriage has functioned to redistribute economic resources in the past.[6] Also, today more than ever, two earners are necessary to secure a middle-class standard of living. However, to imply that unmarried motherhood or divorce are the *cause* of poverty among women and children, and marriage the only solution, is to use family structure to solve problems generated by the social structure. Such an approach overlooks the enduring gender inequality in economic structures. Also, marriage does not necessarily reverse poverty, particularly for working-class women and women of color. For instance, Brewer (1988, 344) noted that "an emphasis on female-headed households misses an essential truth about black women's poverty: black women are also poor in households with male heads." Higher wages in female-dominated jobs may be a more effective solution than marriage. This would not only help married, nuclear family households, but all families and households.

Similarly, marriage culture will not solve the larger economic problem of declining wages for working- and middle-class men brought by a postindustrial, service, and global economy.[7] Indeed, we could transform divorce culture by repairing wage declines for those most disadvantaged by this postindustrial economy—including many working-class men, especially men of color. This could remove sources of conflict and resentment within and across family groups. Yet, to address structural sources of inequality would only mitigate, and not reverse, divorce culture unless we attend to cultural beliefs about gender as well.

Pessimists advocate marriage culture in part because it would seem to solve so many problems of divorce culture at once, most especially divorced men's failure to provide and care for their children. Of all policies, child support has received the most attention by legislators and media over the last two decades. Only about half of custodial mothers with child support orders receive the full amount (Arendell 1995, 39). In 1991 the "average monthly child support paid by divorced fathers contributing economic support" was only $302 (for an estimated 1.5 children), and "child support payments amounted to only about 16% of the incomes of divorced mothers and their children" (Arendell 1997, 162). As a result of the Family Support Act of 1988, the mechanisms for securing child support from fathers have become more rigorous (Furstenberg and Cherlin 1991, 109); there are established formulas for calculating child support payments and, since 1994, all new child support payments are withheld from the paychecks of absent parents (mostly fathers). Yet, as Hewlett and West (1998, 180) observe, in spite of all the policies and prison terms, "the number of deadbeat dads has declined only slightly since 1978."[8]

We need new ways to address fathers' "failure to provide"—clearly, some fathers partly withdraw from marriage and children because they cannot be "good providers."[9] Yet, to focus on the provider role is to limit fatherhood to a model that evolved during the industrial era and is at odds with a postindustrial economy. One could say that this approach merely exchanges a "fragmented" fatherhood for its predecessor: a "shrinking" fatherhood (Blankenhorn 1995a).[10] Indeed, to focus on providing alone will only sustain men's detachment from parenting. "Studies do show that fathers who visit more regularly pay more in child support" (Furstenberg and Cherlin 1991, 274). Whether these payments are due to visiting or greater commitment, attention to the relational aspects of fathering would seem crucial.

Both optimistic and pessimistic scholars are concerned about the lack of paternal participation in children's lives. Most research shows a substantial and unacceptable decline over time in father-child contact after a divorce (Furstenberg and Cherlin 1991). Data from the recent National Survey of Families and Households reveals that about 30 percent of children of divorce have not seen their fathers at all in the preceding year and many more see their fathers irregularly and infrequently (Arendell 1995, 38). Speaking of unmarried as well as divorced fathers, Hewlett and West (1988, 168) report that "close to half of all fathers lose contact with their children."

Thus, all family scholars see a need to revitalize and redefine fatherhood. For example, a supporter of divorce culture, Arendell (1995, 251) protests: "Why should it be so difficult to be a nurturing, engaged father? Where are the institutional and ideological supports for parenting?" Arendell adds: "That caring fathers are subject to criticism and stigmatization points to a seriously flawed ideological system" (251). Also, advocates of marriage culture Hewlett and West (1998, 173) assert that "a withering of the father-child bond devastates children, stunts men, and seriously erodes our social capital." In spite of shared concerns, the means to a revitalized fatherhood are contested.

Just as critics of divorce culture suggest that marriage will alleviate the impoverishment of single mothers, they argue that fathers cannot be effective parents outside of the marriage structure (Blankenhorn 1995a; Hewlett and West 1998; Popenoe 1996; Wallerstein and Blakeslee 1989; Whitehead 1997a). For example, Hewlett and West (1998, 171–72) note that single males are more likely to die prematurely due to self-neglect, more likely to abuse drugs and alcohol, and are responsible for a disproportionate share of violence—including murder, robbery, and rape. They reason, like Durkheim, that marriage and children have a "civilizing" effect upon men.[11] In Blankenhorn's (1995a) view, both co-residence and a parental alliance with the mother are preconditions for effective fatherhood.

Undoubtedly, co-residence assists in the building of relationships—including, and especially, parent-child relationships. Yet, there is evidence to suggest it is not a precondition for effective fatherhood. In her study of divorced fathers, Arendell (1995) describes "innovative" divorced fathers (not all of whom had single custody) who were able to detach being a father from being a partner, separate anger at an ex-wife from their love for their children, focus on the children's needs rather than adult rights, and combine breadwinning with caretaking in ways that developed their nurturing and relational skills. While such fathers are too rare, fathers who parent effectively after divorce suggest that marriage or co-residence are not prerequisites—though alliances between parents do seem to be important whether outside or inside the marriage structure. Further, studies on nonresidential mothers show they are more active participants in their children's lives (Maccoby and Mnookin 1992, 212; Arendell 1997, 170). Finally, even if custody determinations were divided equally between women and men, co-residence would not always be an option for father and child. Suggesting marriage as the solution for divorce—and effective fathering—is empty advice for those compelled to divorce.[12]

Divorced fathers' flagging commitment seems to have exposed a tenuous responsibility for children in the first place. This may represent a "male flight from commitment" that started in the 1950s (Ehrenreich 1984); even so, this too should be understood as a legacy of separate spheres that identified masculinity with the provider role and devalued men's caretaking capacities (Bernard 1981; Coontz 1992). Since women still do the bulk of child rearing during a marriage, many divorced fathers have to learn how to be a primary parent after divorce (Arendell 1997, 163). As optimists and pessimists alike have observed, men appear to depend upon wives to mediate their relationship to their children (Arendell 1995, 33; Furstenberg and Cherlin 1991, 275; Wallerstein and Blakeslee 1989; Whitehead 1997b).[13] This may explain why marriage seems like the only solution for effective fathering for the pessimists.

Another route for expanding paternal participation—and overcoming the historical equivalence between breadwinning and masculinity[14]—would be to construct men as nurturers, caretakers, and responsible fathers. Arendell (1995, 251) calls for "a more vocal and widespread critique of the conventions of masculinity." A construction of masculinity that goes beyond putting all of men's eggs into one "breadwinner" basket (Bernard 1981) is long overdue. Perhaps marriage has an important "civilizing function" for men because of a flawed construction of masculinity in the first place; men have been deprived of the expectation or opportunity to advance their relationality—from boyhood to manhood.

Reinforcing marriage by compelling "divorce as a last resort" would obscure, not solve, this paternal disability. Rather than advocating marriage or reinforcing the provider role as pessimists do, many optimists argue that men need to combine providing with caretaking just as women have combined caretaking with providing. In the aggregate, women are changing faster than men. To keep up with wives' changes means that husbands must be willing to recognize the legitimacy of a wife's relational concerns, embrace what has been largely a devalued sphere, and to share power with their wives.

If a redistribution of relational responsibilities were to take place in marriage, this might extend fathers' involvement with their children in the event of divorce. More important, this could prevent divorces based on relational inequalities in the first place.[15] Indeed, in my research, paternal participation is part of the "marital labor" that egalitarian wives wanted to share. Reconstructing masculinity (and therefore gender in marriage) might provide the stronger deterrent to divorce for which pessimists have been searching.

IS DIVORCE EVER A GATEWAY FOR CHILDREN?

Given children's attenuated relations with their fathers and the downward mobility most children share with their mothers, is divorce ever a gateway for children? Not only do two-thirds of divorces involve children (U.S. Bureau of the Census 1995, P60-187), but few people object to divorce by childless couples today. Because it is children that electrify the divorce debates, I only sampled married parents. Are children paying the price for adults' individualism and lapsed family values, as the critics of divorce culture would argue? Or, could they be paying the costs of marriage culture and the quest for equality—interpersonal and institutional—that I have described?

Divorce is rarely experienced as a "gateway" for children—even perhaps, when it should be. It is, however, a turning point that is distinct from the adult experience. There is a tendency in the debates about the effects of divorce upon children to project adult experiences and capacities onto children. One recent study found that parents' and children's experiences were generally "out of synch" (Stewart et al. 1997, cited in Arendell 1998, 227). Parents may overestimate their child's well-being. Kitson with Holmes (1992, 227) found that most parents attribute very low levels of distress to their children, even though we know that the early period is hard for children. Whether divorce is due to a spouse's adultery, violence, or self-centeredness, the decision is not the child's to make. Of course, children survive and thrive after the temporary crisis of parental divorce, just as they survive other crises. Yet, the assumption that children are resilient should be tempered with the view that the endurance of parental relationships (even if they divorce) matters to children. Neither "divorce as a last resort" nor "divorce as a gateway" capture the divorce turning point for children, because they both presume some choice in the matter.[16]

Many studies agree upon some costs borne by children after a parental divorce, yet the source, extent, and meaning of these costs are fiercely debated (Wallerstein and Kelly 1980; Wallerstein and Blakeslee 1989; Amato and Booth 1997; Maccoby and Mnookin 1992; Hetherington, Law, and O'Connor 1993; Furstenberg and Cherlin 1991; Whitehead 1997a). The conditions preceding, surrounding, and following divorce matter a great deal, including the quality of parent-child relationships, custodial arrangements, the quality of the ex-spousal and coparenting relationships, the economic and social supports available, and the child's own psychological strengths (Furstenberg and Cherlin 1991; Kelly 1988, 134). The age and gender of the child may matter—though gender effects have been questioned (Arendell 1997, 175; Wallerstein and Kelly 1980; Kelly 1988; Wallerstein and Blakeslee 1989). Remarriage and new stepfamily relations affect a child's adjustment over time; indeed, some research suggests remarriage may be more of an adjustment than divorce (Ahrons and Rodgers 1987, 257).

Drawing upon an analysis of 92 studies involving 13,000 children, Amato (1994, 145) reports consistent findings that children of divorce experience "lower academic achievement, more behavioral problems, poorer psychological adjustment, more negative self-concepts, more social difficulties, and more problematic relationships with both mothers and fathers. Also, children of divorce are reported to become pregnant outside of marriage, marry young, and divorce upon becoming adults (McLanahan and Bumpass 1988; Glenn and Kramer 1987).

Taken together, these findings would seem to be alarming. The pessimists are alarmed. Yet, we should not assume that divorce is the "cause" when divorce is correlated with undesirable effects among children. Research on the adverse effects of divorce for children consistently finds that other factors that accompany divorce may be more important than the divorce itself. For example, "income differences account for almost 50 percent of the disadvantage faced by children in single-parent households" (McLanahan and Sandefur 1994; Coontz 1997, 101). Changes of residence and schools help to explain the other 50 percent of disadvantage. Above all, prospective and longitudinal studies of families suggest that marital conflict is more crucial than divorce in explaining behavioral and emotional problems for those children who are troubled (Amato and Booth 1996, 1997; Block, Block, and Gjerde, 1986; Coontz 1997, 102). Longitudinal studies have discovered that children's problems are apparent over a decade before the parents' divorce. Thus, in some cases, divorce and a single-parent household is better for children than continued marital conflict (Amato, Loomis, and Booth 1995).

Furthermore, Amato's (1994) analysis of multiple studies also reveals that the effects of divorce are very weak and that differences between children of divorce and children in continuously intact families are quite small (Amato and Keith 1991; Amato 1994; Amato and Booth 1996, 1997). As the optimist Coontz (1997, 99) clarifies, this research does not suggest that children of divorced parents have *more problems*, rather that *more children* of divorced parents have problems than do children of married parents. Yet, children of divorce show greater variability in their adjustment (Amato 1994). This means that some children of divorce do better thin children of married parents. Children from all kinds of families fare well and poorly. When we focus on the difference between family structures, we overlook the extensive overlap in children's well-being across family structures. Further, research increasingly suggests that the quality and consistency of family life, and not family structure, influences children's well-being (Arendell 1997, 187).

Most of the '70s couples I interviewed did not believe in staying together "for the sake of the children" if there was marital conflict. Parents sense that if their marriage is continuously in conflict, then this harms children too. Divorce is not a singular solution to conflict or violence since both can be exacerbated upon separation and divorce (Arendell and Kurz, 1999). Yet the gateway is crucial for such troubled marriages. Recall that the '50s Dominicks stayed together miserably for thirty years in spite of extramarital affairs, separation, and indications of violence—all for the sake of the children. These were justifiable conditions under the terms of marriage culture. One wonders to what degree the "sake of the children," among other deterrents, inhibited divorces that should have been when marriage culture reigned uncontested.[17]

Kurz's (1995, 52) random sample of divorced mothers revealed that 19 percent pursued divorce specifically because of violence; however, an astonishing 70 percent reported at least one incident of violence during the marriage or separation. Most research shows that violence remains a graver problem for wives than husbands—particularly in terms of injuries (Gelles and Straus 1988; Kurz 1989; Straton 1994). Also, research increasingly finds that witnessing spouse abuse *is* child abuse—even when a child is not physically violated (Holden, Geffner, and Jouriles 1998). Thus, removing children from the perpetrator, however much he (or she) is loved, is arguably for the sake of the children.

Believers in "divorce as a gateway" may want to make parental happiness equivalent to children's happiness when it is not. Pessimists correctly stress that the child's experience of divorce is distinct from the parents' experience. Thus, scholars are increasingly advocating parenting education classes for divorcing parents (Arendell 1995; Wallerstein 1998). Yet, believers in "divorce as a last resort" also mistakenly presume that the maintenance of marriage and a nuclear family is equivalent to children's happiness. We should not ignore the injuries that have attended marriage culture—particularly a male-dominated marriage culture. When egalitarian spouses become parents there is often a shift toward "increased traditionality of family and work roles in families of the 1980s and 1990s," and this "tends to be associated with *more* individual and marital distress for parents" (Cowan and Cowan 1998, 184). This represents the pinch between egalitarian beliefs and the structural impediments to equality in practice. Further, to the degree that we idealize a male-dominated, nuclear family model we cannot fail to reproduce such constructions of inequality among children. While some children are paying a price for the quest for equality, children also pay a price when the thread of commitment is tangled with the thread of male dominance. Moreover, children do find happiness and another vision of equality in alternative family forms.

THE FUTURE OF DIVORCE CULTURE

From Durkheim (1961) to Giddens (1979, 1991), sociologists have regularly addressed transitional periods such as our own. Norms, ideals, and authorities that guided our marital practices in the past are inadequate to families' needs in today's socioeconomic context. Could divorce culture represent a new tapestry of ideals and norms for guiding today's family lives? Even as the practices of '70s spouses are shaped by novel conditions, spouses attempt to shape them in turn—drawing alternatively, selectively, and even haphazardly on available ideologies and practices. Although divorce culture seems to be replacing marriage culture, it should be seen as a transitional means for "people to make sense of the circumstances in which they find themselves" (Mullings 1986), providing alternative strategies for action when marriage culture falls short. Still, like the '70s spouses, many people are ambivalent about divorce culture. Moreover, marriage culture endures.

Because divorce culture is new and unsettling there is a tendency to inflate its power and prevalence. Marriage culture is widely embraced. "Marriage as forever" is a belief that is not only sustained by married couples, but also the divorced (Riessman 1990). The reintroduction of grounds in "covenant marriages" represents a political effort to value the old tapestry that sustained "divorce as a last resort." Finally, "marrying as a given" lives on. While rates of marriage and remarriage have decreased since the mid-1960s (U.S. Bureau of the Census, 1992, P23-180, 8)—suggesting that fewer people experience marriage as an imperative—the majority of people eventually marry. Also, the two-parent family continues to be the predominant family form—so concern with its decline can be overstated (Cowan and Cowan 1998, 189).

Marriage culture also lives on in the next generation's aspirations. The majority of young people say they value marriage and plan to marry (Landis-Kleine et al. 1995). A 1992 survey showed that of all extremely important goals in life, the most valued by 78 percent of the high school respondents was "having a good marriage and family life" (Glenn 1996, 21). "Being able to find steady work" was ranked a close second by 77 percent of these students, and "being successful in my line of work" and "being able to give my children better opportunities than I've had" tied for third, at 66 percent.

Will the '90s spouses continue, reverse, or transcend the advance of divorce culture? How will they cope with the rise of divorce culture and its problems? Because a culture of divorce creates "divorce anxiety," premarital counseling would seem to be increasingly important. One valuable component of "covenant marriage" advanced by pessimists (in spite of critiques of therapeutic culture) has been to encourage religious or secular premarital counseling. Instituting therapy before marriage might prepare '90s spouses for the reflexive process and the marital work that characterizes marriage in an era of change, choice, and uncertainty.[18] Such counseling should not only attune spouses to one another's hopes, dreams, and desires, but should also provide information on the social conditions faced by married couples today. For example, the arrival of children is a vulnerable period of transition in marriage even when children are deeply desired (Cowan and Cowan 1998). Also, '90s spouses should know that aspirations for lifetime marriage, for thriving children, and a good job are not new; most people getting married share these hopes for themselves even as they harbor doubts about others. What thwarts their resolve and aspirations? Do they simply become individualistic?

This analysis of divorce culture has tried to situate the charges that a high divorce rate represents increased individualism in recent generations. On the one hand, like the pessimists, I agree that divorce culture is marked by individualism. Individualism clearly links and underlies the tenets of divorce culture: the choice to marry, to set conditions, and the chance to unmarry all speak to the primacy of the individual to redesign his or her life. However, my research complicates these claims. Individualism is not in a zero-sum relationship with commitment. It can be morally responsible rather than egoistic, it has not been absent for men in marriage culture, and it is not necessarily an end in itself. Divorce culture exposes how the terms of marital commitment reflect a legacy of male dominance. For married women, individualism can be a tool to resist old and enforce new terms of marital commitment—including nurturance, commitment, and relational responsibility shared by both spouses. When mothers use the power of individualism for relational ends—by working to provide, by removing children from violent households, or by refusing to be subordinated—individualism is neither an end in itself nor easily severed from committed responsibility. The meaning of pulling the individualistic lever of divorce culture cannot be stripped from interactional or institutional contexts. Thus '90s spouses would also do well to take the insights of optimists into account. Our quest for equality is ongoing.

Finally, an overemphasis on the individualism of women or men diverts our attention from the ways our social structures obstruct this quest for equality. The variety of families today may not represent a failure of commitment as much as individuals' valiant struggles to sustain commitments in a society that withholds structural supports from workers and families. Indeed, until the 1993 Family and Medical Leave Act, the United States had no family policy at all.[19] Other scholars have suggested an array of family policies—from easing work and family conflicts to providing economic and social supports—for today's burdened families, which I will not repeat here (see Arendell 1995; Burggraf 1997; Hewlett and West 1998; Hochschild 1997; Mason, Skolnick, and Sugarman 1998). Yet, two things are clear—when we allow corporate and government policies to neglect the needs of working parents, we are undermining marriage culture, and when we ignore enduring gender inequalities we advance divorce culture.

While divorce culture is flawed, I see it as a means to propel marital and family relationships in an egalitarian direction. Both "optional marriage" and "divorce as a gateway" recognize commitments apart from marriage, expose the costs of marriage culture, and legitimate diverse family arrangements. Critics of divorce culture advocate a return to the singular design of the nuclear family structure; however, in many ways this sustains a white, middle-class ethnocentrism,[20] and a heterosexism[21] that has marked our family ideals. By challenging "marriage as a given" and "divorce as a last resort," divorce culture helps to destigmatize unmarried families.

As we reconstruct the terms of marriage culture with the tool of divorce culture, we risk sacrificing relationality for rights equality. Rights language is essential for justice, dignity, and self-determination. Yet, it is not an unmitigated good, and only the young, childless, wealthy, or powerful can indulge in a sense of independence and obscure interdependence by relying upon others to sustain the illusion. Only when the relational responsibilities, still constructed as "feminine," are practiced and valued by men, and by the society at large, will we be able to move beyond the individualism of divorce culture and beyond a notion of equality limited to individual rights and obscuring relational responsibilities. Whether divorce culture eventually supplants rather than contests marriage culture, or generates "family cultures" that transcend this contestation, will depend upon social structural change and the quest for relational equality in the next generation.

Editors' Note: References and Notes for this reading can be found in the original source.

■READING 17

The Consequences of Divorce for Adults and Children

Paul R. Amato

I use a divorce-stress-adjustment perspective to summarize and organize the empirical literature on the consequences of divorce for adults and children. My review draws on research in the 1990s to answer five questions: How do individuals from married and divorced families differ in well-being? Are these differences due to divorce or to selection? Do these differences reflect a temporary crisis to which most people gradually adapt or stable life strains that persist more or less indefinitely? What factors mediate the effects of divorce on individual adjustment? And finally, what are the moderators (protective factors) that account for individual variability in adjustment to divorce? In general, the accumulated research suggests that marital dissolution has the potential to create considerable turmoil in people's lives. But people vary greatly in their reactions. Divorce benefits some individuals, leads others to experience temporary decrements in well-being, and forces others on a downward trajectory from which they might never recover fully. Understanding the contingencies under which divorce leads to these diverse outcomes is a priority for future research.

Of all the changes in family life during the 20th century, perhaps the most dramatic—and the most far-reaching in its implications—was the increase in the rate of divorce. Near the middle of the 19th century, only about 5% of first marriages ended in divorce

(Preston & McDonald, 1979). In contrast, demographers estimate that about half of first marriages initiated in recent years will be voluntarily dissolved (Cherlin, 1992). Observers have attributed this change to a number of factors, including the increasing economic independence of women, declining earnings among men without college degrees, rising expectations for personal fulfillment from marriage, and greater social acceptance of divorce (Cherlin, 1992; Furstenberg, 1994; White, 1991).

Remarriage following divorce is common, and nearly one-half of current marriages involve a second (or higher order) marriage for one or both partners (U.S. Bureau of the Census, 1998, Table 157). Second (and higher order) marriages, however, have an even greater likelihood of dissolution than first marriages. As a result, about one out of every six adults endures two or more divorces (Cherlin, 1992). The shift from a dominant pattern of lifelong marriage to one of serial marriage punctuated by periods of being single represents a fundamental change in how adults meet their needs for intimacy over the life course.

The increase in marital dissolution has had major implications for the settings in which children are nurtured and socialized. Slightly more than half of all divorces involve children under the age of 18. More than one million children experience parental divorce every year (U.S. Bureau of the Census, 1998, Table 160), and about 40% of all children will experience parental divorce before reaching adulthood (Bumpass, 1990). The high rate of marital disruption, combined with an increase in births outside marriage, means that about half of all children will reside at least temporarily in single-parent households, usually with their mothers (Castro & Bumpass, 1989). Because of remarriage, about one in seven children currently lives with a parent and a stepparent (Cherlin, 1992), and about one in three children will live with a stepparent for some time prior to reaching age 19 (Glick, 1989). These patterns vary by race. For example, compared with Whites, African Americans are more likely to bear children outside of marriage, more likely to divorce, and more likely to cohabit rather than remarry following divorce (Cherlin, 1992). Nevertheless, regardless of race, the decline in two-parent households, the increase in nonresident parents, and the introduction of parents' new partners (whether married or cohabiting) into the home represent major transformations in the lives of America's children.

The increase in divorce—and the implications of this increase for the lives of adults and children—has generated a high level of interest among social scientists. Indeed, a search of the SOCIOFILE database revealed 9,282 articles published (and dissertations completed) between 1990 and 1999 in which "divorce" appeared in the title or abstract. The authors of these works represent a variety of disciplines, including developmental psychology, clinical psychology, family therapy, sociology, demography, communication studies, family science, history, economics, social work, public health, social policy, and law. The extent and diversity of divorce scholarship pose a sobering challenge to any reviewer attempting to synthesize current knowledge on this topic.

Reviewing the literature on divorce also is challenging because of the ongoing, contentious debate over the consequences of marital disruption for adults and children. Some scholars see the two-parent family as the fundamental institution of society—the setting in which adults achieve a sense of meaning, stability, and security and the setting in which children develop into healthy, competent, and productive citizens. According to this view, the spread of single-parent families contributes to many social problems, including poverty, crime, substance abuse, declining academic standards, and the erosion of neighborhoods and communities (Blankenhorn, 1995; Glenn, 1996; Popenoe, 1996). In contrast, other scholars argue that adults find fulfillment, and children develop successfully, in a variety of family structures. According to this view, divorce, although temporarily stressful, represents a second chance for happiness for adults and an escape from a dysfunctional home environment for children. Poverty, abuse, neglect, poorly funded schools, and a lack of government services represent more serious threats to the well-being of adults and children than does marital instability (Coontz, 1992; Demo, 1992; Skolnick, 1991; Stacey, 1996).

The polemical nature of divorce scholarship makes it difficult to write on this topic without being identified as either a conservative or a liberal voice. Nevertheless, although complete objectivity is impossible, my goal in this article is to assess the state of knowledge on divorce in a balanced and relatively nonpartisan manner. Indeed, a review of current literature might help to inform the debate between those who see divorce as a major social problem and those who see divorce as a necessary and beneficial alternative to mandatory lifelong marriage.

Because it is impossible to cover the full breadth of divorce scholarship in the 1990s in a single article, my review focuses on the consequences of divorce for the well-being of adults and children. I chose this focus because it encompasses, either directly or indirectly, much of the research in this field and because it is central to debates about the rise in marital instability. I omit (or touch only briefly on) many other aspects of divorce, such as legal issues related to custody determination and child support. I also exclude material on the dissolution of cohabiting relationships (including those with children) because we know relatively little about this topic. Readers should note that my review draws on qualitative as well as quantitative research, although I do not usually identify individual studies on the basis of their methodology.

THEORY

Researchers in the 1990s have employed a variety of theories and conceptual perspectives to explain how divorce affects adults and children; these include feminist theory (Carbonne, 1994), attachment theory (Hazan & Shaver, 1992), attribution theory (Grych & Fincham, 1992), symbolic interactionism (Orbuch, 1992), systems theory (Emery, 1994), the social capital perspective (Teachman, Paasch, & Carver, 1996), and the life-course perspective (Amato & Booth, 1997). The largest number of studies, however, begin with the assumption that marital disruption is a stressful life transition to which adults and children must adjust. Many researchers link their work to established stress perspectives, such as family stress and coping theory (Hill, 1949; McCubbin & Patterson, 1983; Plunkett, Sanchez, Henry, & Robinson, 1997), general stress theory (Pearlin, Menaghan, Lieberman, & Mullan, 1981; Thoits, 1995), and the risk and resiliency perspective (Cowan, Cowan, & Schulz, 1996; Hetherington, 1999; Rutter, 1987). Because stress frameworks dominate the literature on divorce, I give them particular attention here. And because these frameworks have much in common, I combine their various elements into a general divorce-stress-adjustment perspective. This conceptual model integrates the assumptions found in many discrete pieces of research, helps to summarize and organize specific research findings from the 1990s, and provides a guide for future research on divorce. This perspective also is useful because it can be applied to children as well as adults.

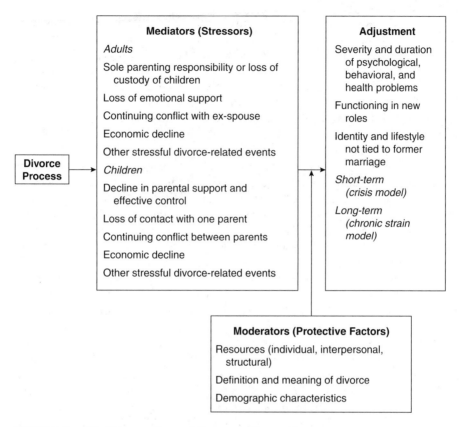

FIGURE 1 *The Divorce-Stress Adjustment Perspective*

The Divorce-Stress-Adjustment Perspective

The divorce-stress-adjustment perspective, outlined in the Figure, views marital dissolution not as a discrete event but as a process that begins while the couple lives together and ends long after the legal divorce is concluded. The uncoupling process typically sets into motion numerous events that people experience as stressful. These stressors, in turn, increase the risk of negative emotional, behavioral, and health outcomes for adults and children. The severity and duration of these negative outcomes varies from person to person, depending on the presence of a variety of moderating or protective factors. Successful adjustment occurs to the extent that individuals experience few divorce-related symptoms, are able to function well in new family, work, or school roles, and have developed an identity and lifestyle that is no longer tied to the former marriage (Kitson, 1992; Kitson & Morgan, 1990).

Thinking of divorce as a process leads to several useful insights. Uncoupling begins with feelings of estrangement—feelings that typically emerge after a period of growing dissatisfaction with the relationship (Kayser, 1993). Because virtually all people enter marriage with the expectation (or the hope) that it will be a mutually supportive, rewarding, lifelong relationship, estrangement from one's spouse is typically a painful experience. Estranged spouses might spend considerable time attempting to renegotiate the relationship, seeking advice from others, or simply avoiding (denying) the problem. Consequently, the first negative effects of divorce on adults can occur years prior to final separation and legal dissolution. In addition, overt conflict between parents during this period might lead to behavior problems in children—problems that can be viewed as early effects of marital dissolution (Davies & Cummings, 1994).

Furthermore, it is often the case that one spouse wants the marriage to end more than the other spouse does (Emery, 1994). When this happens, the spouse who is considering divorce might mourn the end of the marriage even though it is still legally and physically intact. Indeed, when the marriage is legally terminated, the initiating spouse often experiences a great deal of relief. The spouse who wanted the marriage to continue, in contrast, might not mourn the end of the marriage until the legal divorce is completed. Spouses, therefore, often experience the greatest degree of emotional distress at different points in the divorce process (Emery, 1994). The same principle applies to children. For example, an older child might experience stress prior to the divorce, during the period when the parents' marriage is unraveling. For this older child, the physical separation of constantly warring parents might come as a relief. For a younger child in the same family, however, the departure of one parent from the household might be a bewildering event that generates considerable anxiety. In other words, members of divorcing families can experience different trajectories of stress and adjustment.

Legal divorce does not necessarily bring an end to the stress associated with an unhappy marriage, even for the partner who initiates the divorce. Instead, during the time in which the marriage is ending, and in the immediate postdivorce period, new events and processes (mediators) emerge that have the potential to affect people's emotions, behavior, and health. For adults, mediators include: having sole responsibility for the care of children (among custodial parents); losing contact with one's children (among noncustodial parents); continuing conflict with the ex-spouse over child support, visitation, or custody; loss of emotional support due to declining contact with in-laws, married friends, and neighbors; downward economic mobility (especially for mothers); and other disruptive life events, such as moving from the family home into less expensive accommodation in a poorer neighborhood. With regard to children, divorce can result in less effective parenting from the custodial parent, a decrease in involvement with the noncustodial parent, exposure to continuing interparental discord, a decline in economic resources, and other disruptive life events such as moving, changing schools, and additional parental marriages and divorces. These mediating factors represent the mechanisms through which divorce affects people's functioning and well-being. (For discussions of mediators, see Amato, 1993; Kitson, 1992; McLanahan & Booth, 1989; McLanahan & Sandefur, 1994; Rodgers & Pryor, 1998; Simons and Associates, 1996.)

It is important to recognize that mediators can be viewed as outcomes in their own right. For example, a particular study might focus on the impact of divorce on single mothers' standard of living. But a declining standard of living, in turn, can have consequences for single mothers' sense of financial security, children's nutrition, and older adolescents' opportunities to attend college. Mediators, therefore, represent short- or medium-term outcomes of divorce that can have additional long-term consequences for adults' and children's well-being.

Moderators introduce variability into the manner in which divorce and mediating factors are linked to personal outcomes. Protective factors act like shock absorbers and weaken the links between divorce-related events and people's experience of stress, and hence the extent to which divorce is followed by negative emotional, behavioral, or health outcomes (Rutter, 1987). Resources that lessen the negative impact of divorce might reside within the individual (self-efficacy, coping skills, social skills), in interpersonal relationships (social support), and in structural roles and settings (employment, community services, supportive government policies). For example, although divorce often brings about an initial decline in emotional support, people vary in their ability to reconstruct social networks following divorce, including how quickly they are able to form new, supportive intimate relationships. Another moderator refers to the manner in which people regard divorce, with some individuals viewing it as a personal tragedy (typically the partner who is left behind) and others viewing it as an opportunity for personal growth or as an escape from an aversive or dysfunctional marriage (typically the partner who initiates the divorce). Finally, a number of demographic characteristics, such as gender, age, race, ethnicity, and culture can moderate the effects of divorce. As a result of the particular configuration of moderating factors, some individuals are resilient and others are vulnerable following divorce, resulting in a diversity of outcomes. (For discussions of these and other moderators see Bloom, Asher, & White, 1978; Booth & Amato, 1991; Pearlin et al., 1981; Wheaton, 1990).

Imbedded within the divorce-stress-adjustment perspective are two contrary models. The first, a crisis model, assumes that divorce represents a disturbance to which most individuals adjust over time. According to the crisis model, factors such as personal resources and definitions determine the speed with which adjustment occurs. But given a sufficient amount of time, the great majority of individuals return to their predivorce level of functioning. The second model, a chronic strain model, assumes that being divorced involves persistent strains, such as economic hardship, loneliness, and, for single parents, sole parenting responsibilities. Because these problems do not go away, declines in well-being associated with divorce might continue more or less indefinitely. According to the chronic strain model, factors such as personal resources and definitions determine the level of distress that individuals experience, but divorced individuals do not, in general, return to the same level of well-being they experienced early in the marriage.

Some researchers have argued that stress perspectives tend to focus exclusively on the negative aspects of divorce and ignore positive outcomes for adults (Ahrons, 1994; Wheaton, 1990) and children (Barber & Eccles, 1992; Gately & Schwebel, 1991). For example, women (as well as their children) might feel that they are substantially better off when a relationship with an abusive husband ends. The notion that divorce can be beneficial, however, is not inconsistent with the divorce-stress-adjustment perspective. Many stress theorists, such as Thoits (1995) and Wheaton (1990), have argued that potentially stressful events, such as divorce, can have positive long-term consequences when people resolve their problems successfully. Indeed, the divorce-stress-adjustment perspective explicitly focuses on the contingencies that lead to negative, positive, or mixed outcomes for individuals. Nevertheless, the divorce-stress-adjustment perspective assumes that for most people, the ending of a marriage is a stressful experience, even if much of the stress occurs prior to the legal divorce, is temporary, or is accompanied by some positive outcomes.

The Selection Perspective

The main alternative to the divorce-stress-adjustment perspective is based on the notion that poorly adjusted people are selected out of marriage. According to the selection perspective, certain individuals possess problematic personal and social characteristics that not only predispose them to divorce, but also lead them to score low on indicators of well-being after the marriage ends. Consequently, the adjustment problems frequently observed among the divorced might be present early in the marriage or might predate the marriage. Some evidence is consistent with the assumption that people bring traits to marriage that increase the risk of divorce, including antisocial personality traits, depression, and a general history of psychological problems (Capaldi & Patterson, 1991; Davies, Avison, & McAlpine, 1997; Hope, Power, & Rodgers, 1999; Kitson, 1992; Kurdek, 1990). Whereas the divorce-stress-adjustment perspective assumes that marital disruption causes adjustment problems, the selection perspective assumes that adjustment problems cause marital disruption. Selection also can occur if the best adjusted divorced individuals are especially likely to remarry. If this is true, then the mean level of functioning in the divorced (and not remarried) population should decline over time.

The selection perspective, as applied to children, assumes that at least some child problems observed following divorce are present during the marriage—an assumption consistent with several longitudinal studies (Amato & Booth, 1996; Cherlin et al., 1991; Elliot & Richards, 1991; Hetherington, 1999). Many researchers assume that these problems are caused by parents' marital discord or by inept parenting on the part of distressed or antisocial parents. Of course, to the extent that dysfunctional family patterns are reflections of the unraveling of the marriage, then these early effects on children can be viewed as part of the divorce process. But the selection perspective goes one step further and argues that inherent characteristics of parents, such as antisocial personality traits, are direct causes of dysfunctional family patterns and divorce, as well as child problems. The discovery that concordance (similarity between siblings) for divorce among adults is higher among monozygotic than dizygotic twins suggests that genes might predispose some people to behaviors that increase the risk of divorce (McGue & Lykken, 1992; Jockin, McGue, & Lykken, 1996). Consequently, some children from divorced families might exhibit problems because they have inherited genetic traits from their (presumably troubled) parents. According to this perspective, to the extent that parents' personalities and genetically transmitted predispositions are causes of divorce as well as child problems, the apparent effects of divorce on children are spurious.

RESEARCH ON THE CONSEQUENCES OF DIVORCE FOR ADULTS

Comparisons of Divorced and Married Individuals

A large number of studies published during the 1990s found that divorced individuals, compared with married individuals, experience lower levels of psychological well-being, including lower happiness, more symptoms of psychological distress, and poorer self-concepts (Aseltine & Kessler, 1993; Davies et al., 1997; Demo & Acock, 1996b; Kitson,

1992; Lorenz et al., 1997; Marks, 1996; Mastekaasa, 1994a, 1994b, 1995; Robins & Regier, 1991; Ross, 1995; Shapiro, 1996; Simon, 1998; Simon & Marcussen, 1999; Simons & Associates, 1996; Umberson & Williams, 1993; White, 1992). Compared with married individuals, divorced individuals also have more health problems and a greater risk of mortality (Aldous & Ganey, 1999; Hemstrom, 1996; Joung et al., 1997; Lillard & Waite, 1995; Murphy, Glaser, & Grundy, 1997, Rogers, 1996; Zick & Smith, 1991). Although the direction of these differences is consistent, their magnitude varies across studies. For example, Hope, Power, and Rodgers (1999) compared the depression scores of married and divorced mothers in a large, national British sample and found an effect size of .56, which translates into a 188% increase in the odds of depression. Other studies suggest smaller differences, however. Because no one has carried out a systematic evaluation of effect sizes in this literature, it is difficult to make claims about the magnitude of group differences on average.

Research also shows that divorced and married individuals differ on a number of variables that can be viewed not only as outcomes in their own right, but also as mediators of the long-term effects of marital dissolution on well-being. Compared with married individuals, divorced individuals report more social isolation (Joung et al., 1997; Marks, 1996; Mastekaasa, 1997; Peters & Leifbroer, 1997; Ross, 1995; Umberson, Chen, House, Hopkins, & Slaten, 1996), less satisfying sex lives (Laumann, Gagnon, Michael, & Michaels, 1994), and more negative life events (Kitson, 1992; Lorenz et al., 1997; Simons and Associates, 1996). Divorced individuals also have a lower standard of living, possess less wealth, and experience greater economic hardship than married individuals (Hao, 1996; Marks, 1996; Ross, 1995, Teachman & Paasch, 1994), although this particular difference is considerably greater for women than men. For parents, divorce is associated with more difficulties in raising children (Fisher, Fagor, & Leve, 1998; Hetherington & Clingempeel, 1992), less authoritative parenting (Ellwood & Stolberg, 1993; Simons & Associates, 1996; Thomson, McLanahan, & Curtin, 1992), and greater parental role strain among noncustodial as well as custodial parents (Rogers & White, 1998; Umberson & Williams, 1993). Of course, this literature contains some null findings. But the general conclusion that emerges from studies published in the 1990s—that the divorced are worse off than the married in multiple ways—is consistent with research conducted in the 1980s (Kitson & Morgan, 1990) and in earlier decades (Bloom et al., 1978).

Although the divorce-stress-adjustment perspective assumes that marital dissolution increases the risk of negative outcomes, it allows for the possibility that some individuals experience positive changes. Consistent with this notion, several studies show that divorced individuals report higher levels of autonomy and personal growth than do married individuals (Kitson, 1992; Marks, 1996). Acock and Demo (1994) found that many divorced mothers reported improvements in career opportunities, social lives, and happiness following divorce. Similarly, in a qualitative study, Riessmann (1990) found that women reported more self-confidence and a stronger sense of control following marital dissolution, and men reported more interpersonal skills and a greater willingness to self-disclose. In summary, although the majority of studies document the negative consequences of divorce, a small number of studies indicate that divorce also has positive consequences for many individuals. If more studies explicitly searched for positive outcomes, then the number of studies documenting beneficial effects of divorce would almost certainly be larger.

Causation or Selection?

Studies in the 1990s indicate that divorce is associated with a variety of problematic outcomes. But does divorce lower people's well-being, or are poorly functioning people especially likely to divorce? Consistent with the divorce-stress-adjustment perspective, and contrary to the selection perspective, longitudinal studies show that people who make the transition from marriage to divorce report an increase in symptoms of depression, an increase in alcohol use, and decreases in happiness, mastery, and self-acceptance (Aseltine & Kessler, 1993; Hope, Rodgers, & Power, 1999; Marks & Lambert, 1998; Power, Rodgers, & Hope, 1999). Given that divorce is a process rather than a discrete event, declines in well-being are likely to begin prior to the legal divorce. In fact, Kitson's (1992) respondents reported (retrospectively) that they had experienced the greatest level of stress prior to making the decision to divorce, the second highest level of distress at the time of the decision, and the least stress following the final separation. Consistent with Kitson's data, longitudinal studies (Booth & Amato, 1991; Johnson & Wu, 1996; Mastekaasa, 1994b, 1997) show that reports of unhappiness and psychological distress begin to rise a few years prior to marital separation. Furthermore, Johnson and Wu (1996) used a fixed-effects model to control for all time-invariant individual variables, thus making it unlikely that selection could account for the increase in distress.

Some longitudinal studies, however, suggest that selection effects operate alongside divorce effects. For example, Mastekaasa (1997) observed personal problems (such as greater alcohol consumption among wives) as early as 4 years prior to divorce. Hope, Rodgers, and Power (1999) found that depression at age 23 predicted becoming a single mother at age 33. Similarly, Davies and colleagues (1997) found that many divorced mothers had a history of depression that predated the marriage. These mothers also reported high levels of adversity in their families of origin, including weak attachment to parents and parental depression. Controlling for these family-of-origin factors decreased the estimated effect of divorce on adult depression (suggesting a selection effect), although the association between divorce and depression remained significant (suggesting divorce causation).

In general, studies support the notion of divorce causation, but a degree of selection also might be operating. This combination can occur in two ways. First, some individuals might be prone to psychological or interpersonal problems prior to divorce but exhibit additional problems following divorce. That is, long-standing differences between those who divorce and those who remain married might be amplified as divorce becomes imminent. For example, a husband's aggression might contribute to the dissolution of the relationship, but the dissolution of the relationship, in turn, might generate even more serious levels of aggression. Second, some individuals might have long-standing problems that disrupt their marriages, whereas others might be relatively symptom-free until confronted with the stress of marital dissolution. In other words, selection explanations might apply to some groups of people more than others.

Divorce as Crisis or Chronic Strain?

An unresolved issue in the literature of the 1990s is whether divorce represents a temporary crisis to which most individuals adapt or a source of chronic strains that persist indefinitely. Several studies found that unhappiness, distress, depression, alcohol consumption, and health problems had largely subsided 2 or 3 years afterseparation—a result that supports the crisis model (Booth & Amato, 1991; Goldberg, Greenberger, Hamill, & O'Neil, 1992; Kitson, 1992; Lorenz et al., 1997). In contrast, other studies failed to find improvements in people's functioning during the time since divorce, unless they remarried—a result that supports the chronic strain model (Aseltine & Kessler, 1993; DeGarmo & Kitson, 1996; Gray & Silver, 1990; Johnson & Wu, 1996; Mastekaasa, 1995; Neff & Schluter, 1993; Wang & Amato, in press). Furthermore, Umberson and Williams (1993) found that parental strain among divorced fathers increased, rather than decreased, over time. Of course, both the crisis and the chronic strain models might contain some truth. Kitson (1992) found that although half of her respondents improved over time, about one fourth got worse. These results suggest that a crisis model (implying gradual adjustment) might be appropriate for some individuals, and a chronic strain model (implying persistent long-term problems) might be appropriate for others.

Mediators of Divorce Effects

Researchers attempting to identify the mediators of divorce effects have adopted two strategies. Some researchers have examined associations between mediators and measures of well-being using samples composed entirely of divorced individuals. Other researchers have tried to make the mean differences in well-being between divorced and married individuals "disappear" by controlling for presumed mediators. Although within-group studies are useful, between-group studies provide stronger evidence of mediation. Nevertheless, the various types of studies generally yield consistent results.

With regard to parenting, adjustment among custodial mothers is negatively associated with difficulty in finding child care (Goldberg et al., 1992), children's misbehavior (Simons and Associates, 1996), and the number of children in the household (Garvin, Kalter, & Hansell, 1993; Kitson, 1992). Correspondingly, loss of contact with children is associated with increased distress among noncustodial fathers (Lawson & Thompson, 1996; Umberson & Williams, 1993). Other studies have shown that poor adjustment is associated with conflict between ex-spouses (Goodman, 1993; Masheter, 1991), lack of emotional support from others (Marks, 1996; O'Connor, Hawkins, Dunn, Thorpe, & Golding, 1998; Ross, 1995), low income (Booth & Amato, 1991; Garvin et al., 1993; Kitson, 1992; Ross, 1995; Shapiro, 1996; Simons & Associates, 1996; Thabes, 1997), and the number and severity of stressful life changes following divorce (DeGarmo & Kitson, 1996; Kitson, 1992; Lorenz et al., 1997; Miller, Smerglia, Gaudet, & Kitson, 1998; O'Connor et al., 1998; Simons & Associates, 1996). Although some exceptions appear in the literature, research in the 1990s generally demonstrated that difficulties associated with solo parenting, continuing discord with the former spouse, declines in emotional support, economic hardship, and other stressful life events account for much of the gap in well-being between divorced and married adults.

Moderating Factors

What factors make some individuals more vulnerable than others to divorce-induced stress? With regard to resources, several studies show that adjustment among divorced individuals is positively associated with education (Booth & Amato, 1991; Demo & Acock, 1996b; Goldberg et al., 1992), employment (Bisagni & Eckenrode, 1995; Booth & Amato,

1991; Demo & Acock, 1996b; Kitson, 1992; Wang & Amato, in press), and large networks of supportive kin and friends (Aseltine & Kessler, 1993; Cotton, 1999; DeGarmo & Forgatch, 1999; Garvin et al., 1993; Goldberg et al., 1992; Lawson & Thompson, 1996; Thabes, 1997). Support from a new partner appears to be especially beneficial, because studies consistently show that adjustment is higher among divorced individuals who have formed a new romantic relationship (Funder, Harrison, & Weston, 1993; Garvin et al., 1993; Mastekaasa, 1995; Thabes, 1997; Wang & Amato, in press) or have remarried (Demo & Acock, 1996; Hemstrom, 1996; Marks & Lambert, 1998; Shapiro, 1996; Wang & Amato, in press). Remarriage also improves people's standard of living (Kitson, 1992; Teachman & Paasch, 1994) and accumulation of wealth (Hao, 1996).

One particular resource—having a large network of friends and kin—is not always a blessing, however. Miller and colleagues (1998) found that having someone to confide in decreased distress, but receiving material assistance (such as money or housing) increased distress. Of course, people receiving material assistance might be most in need and therefore most distressed. But support also might come with costs, such as feelings of inadequacy or indebtedness on the part of the receiver. Kitson (1992) found that receiving help with services, finances, or information was associated with lower distress; receiving these forms of assistance in conjunction with advice, however, was associated with higher distress. These findings suggest that aid might be more (rather than less) stressful when it comes with strings attached.

Another protective factor involves the manner in which people cognitively appraise the divorce. Longitudinal studies by Booth and Amato (1991) and by Simon and Marcussen (1999) found that people who strongly believed that marriage is a lifelong commitment reported especially high levels of distress following divorce. Adjustment among these individuals might have been difficult because they were troubled by the moral contradiction involved in seeing their own marriages end. Similarly, DeGarmo and Kitson (1996) found that divorce adjustment was easier for women who were not heavily invested in their marital identity. Other studies show that individuals who initiate divorce, compared with those who do not want the marriage to end, tend to be better adjusted in the postdivorce period (Kitson, 1992; Gray & Silver, 1990; Wang & Amato, in press). Consistent with these findings, individuals who report a large number of problems during the marriage tend to function relatively well in the post-divorce period (Booth & Amato, 1991). Indeed, for individuals who are very distressed during the marriage, divorce appears to decrease symptoms of depression (Aseltine & Kessler, 1993; Wheaton, 1990). As noted earlier, initiators of divorce and their partners are often on different trajectories of divorce adjustment. These results suggest, therefore, that people who initiate divorce might experience distress, but they do this mainly prior to, rather than following, marital dissolution.

RESEARCH ON THE CONSEQUENCES OF DIVORCE FOR CHILDREN

Comparisons of Children from Divorced and Two-Parent Families

Early in the decade, Amato and Keith (1991) published a meta-analysis of 92 studies that compared the well-being of children whose parents had divorced with that of children whose parents were married to each other. Their meta-analysis showed that children from divorced families scored significantly lower on a variety of outcomes, including academic achievement, conduct, psychological adjustment, self-concept, and social competence. The differences between groups of children (effect sizes) were small, however, ranging from .08 of a standard deviation for psychological adjustment to .23 of a standard deviation for conduct. For some outcomes, studies conducted in the 1980s yielded smaller effect sizes than earlier studies conducted in the 1960s and 1970s. Amato and Keith (1991) speculated that the gap in well-being between children with divorced and nondivorced parents might have narrowed either because divorce became more socially accepted or because parents were making greater efforts to reduce the potentially disruptive impact of divorce on their children.

During the 1990s, the number of people touched by divorce increased, school-based programs for children of divorce became common, and mediation and education courses for divorcing parents became mandatory in many states (Emery, Kitzmann, & Waldron, 1999). Given these trends, one might expect studies conducted in the 1990s to reveal a continued closing of the gap in well-being between children with divorced parents and children with married parents. An examination of studies conducted in the 1990s, however, does not support this hypothesis.

A large number of studies in the 1990s continued to find that children with divorced parents score lower than children with continuously married parents on measures of academic success (Astone & McLanahan, 1991; Teachman, Paasch, & Carver, 1996), conduct (Doherty & Needle, 1991; Simons and Associates, 1996), psychological adjustment (Forehand, Neighbors, Devine, & Armistead, 1994; Kurdek, Fine, & Sinclair, 1994), self-concept (Wenk, Hardesty, Morgan, & Blair, 1994), social competence (Beaty, 1995; Brodzinsky, Hitt, & Smith, 1993), and long-term health (Tucker et al., 1997). Furthermore, effect sizes in the 1990s appear comparable to those of earlier decades. For example, across 32 studies of children's conduct published in the 1990s, the mean effect size was –.19, which is not appreciably different from the mean value of –.18 for studies conducted in the 1980s, as reported in Amato and Keith (1991). Similarly, across 29 studies of psychological adjustment published in the 1990s, the mean effect size was –.17, which is slightly larger than the mean value of –.10 for studies conducted in the 1980s, also as reported in Amato and Keith. In general, the small but consistent gap in well-being between children from divorced and two-parent families observed in earlier decades persisted into the 1990s.

As with studies of adults, a few studies suggest that divorce also has positive consequences for some children. For example, a qualitative study by Arditti (1999) found that many offspring from divorced families, especially daughters, reported developing especially close relationships with their custodial mothers—a finding that is consistent with some quantitative work (Amato & Booth, 1997). In addition, Amato, Loomis, and Booth (1995), Amato and Booth (1997), Hanson (1999), and Jekielek (1998) found that offspring were better off on a variety of outcomes if parents in high-conflict marriages divorced than if they remained married. When conflict between parents is intense, chronic, and overt, divorce represents an escape from an aversive home environment for children. Only a minority of divorces, however, appear to be preceded by a high level of chronic marital conflict (Amato & Booth, 1997). For this reason, divorce probably helps fewer children than it hurts.

Causation or Selection?

The selection perspective holds that differences between children from divorced and nondivorced families are due to factors other than marital disruption, including parents' personality characteristics, inept parenting, predivorce marital discord, or genetic influence. Consistent with a selection perspective, Capaldi and Patterson (1991) found that mothers' antisocial personalities accounted for the association between mothers' marital transitions and boys' adjustment problems. In contrast, other studies found significant estimated effects of divorce even after controlling for aspects of parents' personalities, including depression (Demo & Acock, 1996a) and antisocial personality traits (Simons and Associates, 1996).

Longitudinal studies provide another type of evidence. Cherlin and colleagues (1991) found that children from maritally disrupted families had more postdivorce behavior problems than children from nondisrupted families. These differences, however, were apparent several years prior to divorce, especially for boys. Amato and Booth (1996) found that problems in parent-child relationships (including parents' reports that their children had given them more than the usual number of problems) were present as early as 8 to 12 years before divorce. Aseltine (1996) and Hetherington (1999) obtained comparable results with regard to children's internalizing behavior, externalizing behavior, social competence, and self-esteem, and Doherty and Needle (1991) found comparable results for substance abuse among daughters. These longitudinal studies suggest that some of the negative outcomes observed among children with divorced parents are present years before the marriage ends and hence might be due to parental or family problems other than marital dissolution.

Nevertheless, as noted earlier, marital dissolution is a process that usually begins long before the legal divorce, so the existence of elevated levels of child problems prior to parental separation does not necessarily provide evidence of selection. Furthermore, several longitudinal studies show that many postdivorce child problems cannot be traced to a point in time prior to the divorce (Doherty & Needle, 1991; Forehand, Armistead, & Corinne, 1997; Morrison & Cherlin, 1995). For example, Doherty and Needle found that substance abuse and psychological problems among adolescent boys were elevated after, but not prior to, divorce. Consistent with these findings, Hanson (1999) found that differences in behavior and well-being between children from divorced and nondivorced families continued to be significant even after controlling for children's predivorce levels of behavior problems. And Morrison and Coiro (1999) found that parental divorce was followed by an increase in children's behavior problems above predivorce levels. Similarly, two follow-up studies of the 1991 work by Cherlin and colleagues (Chase-Lansdale, Cherlin, & Kiernan, 1995; Cherlin, Chase-Lansdale, & McRae, 1998) found that the gap in psychological well-being between offspring with divorced and married parents increased between adolescence and young adulthood. A noteworthy aspect of the latter study was the use of a random-effects model, which provides strong evidence for divorce rather than selection as the cause of the gap.

With regard to possible genetic influence, one study found that the association between parental divorce and child problems was similar for adopted and biological children (Brodzinsky, Hitt, & Smith, 1993)—a finding that cannot be explained by genetic transmission. Another study based on a large sample of twins (Kendler, Neale, Kessler,

Heath, & Eaves, 1992) found that parental divorce predicted offspring depression in adulthood even with genetic resemblance controlled statistically. These studies suggest that even if predivorce family factors (including genetic factors) predispose children to certain emotional and behavioral problems, divorce itself brings about new conditions that exacerbate these differences.

Divorce as Crisis or Chronic Strain?

The crisis perspective holds that children from divorced families, although distressed at the time of marital disruption, show improvements in functioning in the years following divorce. Consistent with this view, some studies show that children's problems decline with time following divorce (Bussell, 1995; Frost & Pakiz, 1990; Goldberg et al., 1992; Jekielek, 1998). Other studies provide contrary evidence. For example, McLanahan and Sandefur (1994) found that the length of time in a single-parent family was not related to children's graduation from high school or risk of a teenage birth. Similar null results were reported by Hetherington and Clingempeel (1992), Machida and Holloway (1991), and Mauldon (1990) for different child outcomes.

Furthermore, the longitudinal studies of Cherlin and colleagues (Chase-Lansdale et al., 1995; Cherlin et al., 1998) found that the gap in psychological well-being between offspring from divorced and nondivorced families grew larger—not smaller—with the passage of time. Consistent with this finding, a large number of studies have demonstrated that parental divorce is a risk factor for multiple problems in adulthood, including low socioeconomic attainment, poor subjective well-being, increased marital problems, and a greater likelihood of seeing one's own marriages end in divorce (see Amato, 1999, for a review). Why might these problems persist into adulthood? Two mechanisms seem likely. First, economic hardship due to parental divorce might lead some children to abandon plans to attend college, resulting in lower occupational attainment and wages throughout adulthood. Other offspring who were exposed to poor parental models of interpersonal behavior might have difficulty forming stable, satisfying, intimate relationships as young adults. These considerations suggest that even if some children show improvements in functioning a year or two after marital disruption, delayed effects of divorce might appear only when offspring have reached young adulthood.

Mediators of Divorce Effects

A number of studies indicate that divorced custodial parents, compared with married parents, invest less time, are less supportive, have fewer rules, dispense harsher discipline, provide less supervision, and engage in more conflict with their children (Astone & McLanahan, 1991; Hetherington & Clingempeel, 1992; Simons and Associates, 1996; Thompson et al., 1992). Many of these deficits in parenting presumably result from the stress of marital disruption and single parenting. Congruent with this perspective, Larson and Gillman (1999) found that negative emotions were more likely to be transmitted from single mothers to adolescent children than vice versa, especially when mothers were under stress. The quality of parental functioning is one of the best predictors of children's behavior and well-being. Several within-group studies show that either a conflicted relationship with the custodial parent or inept parenting on the part of the custodial parent are linked with a variety of negative child outcomes, including lower academic achievement, internalizing problems, externalizing problems, reduced self-esteem, and poorer social competence (Aseltine, 1996; Buchanan, Maccoby, & Dornbush, 1996; Clark & Clifford, 1996; DeGarmo & Forgatch, 1999; Demo & Acock, 1996; Ellwood & Stolberg, 1993; Hetherington & Clingempeel, 1992; McLanahan & Sandefur, 1994; Simons and Associates, 1996; Tschann, Johnston, Kline, & Wallerstein, 1990). Other studies show that depression among custodial mothers, which is likely to detract from parenting, is related to poor adjustment among offspring (Demo & Acock, 1996a; Mednick, Baker, Reznick, & Hocevar, 1990; Silitsky, 1996; Simons & Associates, 1996).

Although the role of the custodial parent (usually the mother) in promoting children's well-being is clear, the role of the noncustodial parent (usually the father) is ambiguous. A variety of studies conducted in the 1970s and 1980s suggest that contact with noncustodial fathers is not related in a consistent manner with children's behavior or well-being (Amato, 1993). However, in a recent meta-analysis of 63 studies of nonresident fathers and their children, Amato and Gilbreth (1999) found that authoritative parenting on the part of noncustodial fathers consistently predicted children's higher academic achievement and lower internalizing and externalizing problems. Amato and Gilbreth also found that studies of noncustodial fathers in the 1990s (e.g., Simons and Associates, 1996; Barber, 1994) were more likely than studies from earlier decades to report positive effects of father contact. These results tentatively suggest that noncustodial fathers might be enacting the parent role more successfully now than in the past, with beneficial consequences for children.

Interparental hostility and lack of cooperation between parents following divorce is a consistent predictor of poor outcomes among offspring (Bolgar, Zweig-Frank, & Parish, 1995; Buchanan, Maccoby, & Dornbusch, 1996; Clark & Clifford, 1996; Ellwood & Stolberg, 1993; Healy, Malley, & Stewart, 1990; Pearson & Thoennes, 1990; Silitsky, 1996; Simons & Associates, 1996; Tschann et al., 1990; Vandewater & Lansford, 1998). Hetherington (1999) found that direct conflict between divorced parents, but not encapsulated conflict (that is, conflict to which children are not exposed), was related to behavior problems among adolescents. Conflict was especially aversive if it involved physical violence or made children feel as if they were caught in the middle. Interparental conflict is not only a direct stressor for children, but also might interfere with children's attachments to parents, resulting in feelings of emotional insecurity (Davies & Cummings, 1994).

Postdivorce economic hardship also is associated with negative outcomes among children (Aseltine, 1996; Bronstein, Stoll, Clauson, Abrams, & Briones, 1994; Mauldon, 1990; McLanahan & Sandefur, 1994; Morrison & Chertin, 1995; Pearson & Thoennes, 1990; Simons and Associates, 1996). One study found that income stability, rather than total income, predicts children's well-being (Goldberg et al., 1992). Research showing that fathers' payment of child support is positively related to children's school attainment and behavior provides additional support for the importance of income in facilitating children's postdivorce adjustment (e.g., King, 1994; McLanahan, Seltzer, Hanson, & Thompson, 1994).

Finally, the number of negative life events to which children are exposed is a consistent predictor of children's divorce adjustment (Aseltine, 1996, Buchanon, Maccoby, & Dornbusch, 1996; Ellwood & Stolberg, 1993; Pearson & Thoennes, 1990; Sandler,

Wolchik, Braver, & Fogas, 1991; Sheets, Sandler, & West, 1996; Silitsky, 1996). Events such as moving (Amato & Booth, 1997; McLanahan & Sandefur, 1994, Simons & Associates, 1996) and changing schools (Mednick et al., 1990; Teachman, Paasch, & Carver, 1996) appear to be especially disruptive. Unfortunately, moving to poorer neighborhoods is common following divorce as custodial parents are forced to live on smaller household incomes (South, Crowder, & Trent, 1998). Overall, in spite of the fact that some null findings appear in this literature, the majority of studies conducted in the 1990s document the importance of the mediators outlined in the divorce-stress-adjustment model and also are consistent with research trends from the 1970s and 1980s (Amato, 1993).

Moderating Factors

What factors facilitate children's adjustment to divorce? In relation to resources, one study found that children who use active coping skills (such as problem solving and gathering social support) tend to adjust to divorce more quickly than children who rely on avoidance or distraction as coping mechanisms (Sandler, Tein, & West, 1994). Social support appears to be another protective factor. Samera and Stolberg (1993) found that children's social support from peers was positively related to adjustment as rated by children, teachers, and parents. Comparable findings were obtained by Silitsky (1996) and Teja and Stolberg (1993). Access to therapeutic interventions also appears to improve children's postdivorce well-being. For example, school-based support programs for children with divorced parents are widespread, and evidence suggests that these interventions are beneficial (Emery et al., 1999; Kalter, & Schreier, 1993; Lee, Picard, & Blain, 1994). Programs aimed at divorcing parents also are common. Although parents who attend these programs tend to rate them positively, it is not clear whether these programs benefit children (Beuhler, Betz, Ryan, Legg, & Trotter, 1992; Braver, Salem, Pearson, & DeLuse, 1996).

With regard to cognition, children who place some of the blame for the divorce on themselves tend to be more poorly adjusted (Bussell, 1995). Healy, Stewart, and Copeland (1993), in a study of primary school children 6 months after parental separation, found that one third reported some feelings of self-blame; self-blame, in turn, was related to a variety of child problems, including depression, externalizing problems, and lowered feelings of self-competence. In addition to self-blame, Kim, Sandler, and Jenn-Yum (1997) found that children's perceived lack of control over events mediated some of the impact of divorce-related stress on adjustment.

Studies focusing on custody arrangements following divorce tend to show that children fare better under joint physical custody rather than sole mother or father custody (Buchanan, Maccoby, & Dornbush, 1996). This conclusion should be treated cautiously, however, because especially cooperative parents are more likely to choose and maintain joint physical custody than are other parents. Consequently, it is difficult to determine whether it is joint physical custody or some characteristic of parents or their postdivorce relationship that is responsible for children's functioning. Children in sole mother custody and sole father custody show few differences (Downey, Ainsworth-Darnell, & Dufur, 1998; McLanahan & Sandefur, 1994). Although many children in single-mother households are disadvantaged by a lack of economic resources, some children in single-father households are disadvantaged by a lack of interpersonal resources (such as single fathers' relatively low level of involvement in school activities), resulting in roughly equal outcomes (Downey, 1994). Furthermore, it appears to matter little whether children reside with a same-gender or opposite-gender parent (Downey & Powell, 1993). A reasonable conclusion is that no particular custody arrangement is best for all children. Indeed, custody arrangements often require modification as children develop and their relationships with parents change (Buchanan, Maccoby, & Dornbusch, 1996).

Research yields mixed results with regard to parental remarriage. A meta-analytic review of studies (mostly from the 1970s and 1980s) found that children in stepfamilies were no better off, and in some ways worse off, than children living in single-parent households following divorce (Amato, 1994b). In contrast, several recent studies found that offspring with remarried custodial parents were less depressed (Aseltine, 1996) or had fewer interpersonal problems (Bolgar et al., 1995) than children with single custodial parents. McLanahan and Sandefur (1994) found that parental remarriage appeared to benefit African Americans more than Whites. Interestingly, Buchanan, Maccoby, and Dornbusch (1996) found that parental remarriage was associated with fewer child problems, whereas parental cohabitation was associated with more problems, especially among boys. Hetherington and Clingempeel (1992) found few differences, overall, between children in divorced single-parent families and stepfamilies. It might be difficult to reach broad generalizations about the role of parental remarriage in children's adjustment, because these effects vary with children's ages, children's gender, the time since divorce, and other factors (Hetherington & Jodl, 1994). Additional parental divorces, however, appear to be more stressful for offspring than first divorces (Amato & Booth, 1991).

In conclusion, I return to the contentious debate over divorce that has continued throughout the 1990s. On one side are those who see divorce as an important contributor to many social problems. On the other side are those who see divorce as a largely benign force that provides adults with a second chance for happiness and rescues children from dysfunctional and aversive home environments. Based on the accumulated research of the 1990s—and of earlier decades—it is reasonable to conclude that both of these views represent one-sided accentuations of reality. The increase in marital instability has not brought society to the brink of chaos, but neither has it led to a golden age of freedom and self-actualization. Divorce benefits some individuals, leads others to experience temporary decrements in well-being that improve over time, and forces others on a downward cycle from which they might never fully recover. Continuing research on the contingencies that determine whether divorce has positive, neutral, or negative long-term consequences for adults and children is a high priority. Work on these issues is likely to progress in the next decade. As long as nearly half of all marriages in the United States end in divorce, there will be an enduring need to understand and monitor the implications of marital dissolution for adults, children, and the larger society.

Note

I thank Alan Booth, Stacy Rogers, and Lynn White for useful comments on an earlier version of this article.

References

Acock, A. C., & Demo, D. H. (1994). *Family diversity and well-being.* Thousand Oaks, CA: Sage.
Ahrons, C. (1994). *The good divorce.* New York: HarperCollins.

Aldous, J., & Ganey, R. F. (1999). Family life and the pursuit of happiness: The influence of gender and race. *Journal of Family Issues, 20,* 155–180.

Amato, P. R. (1993). Children's adjustment to divorce: Theories, hypotheses, and empirical support. *Journal of Marriage and the Family, 55,* 23–38.

Amato, P. R. (1994a). The impact of divorce on men and women in India and the United States. *Journal of Comparative Family Studies, 25,* 207–221.

Amato, P. R. (1994b). The implications of research findings on children in stepfamilies. In A. Booth & J. Dunn (Eds.), *Stepfamilies: Who benefits? Who does not?* (pp. 81–87). Hillsdale, NJ: Erlbaum.

Amato, P. R. (1996). Explaining the intergenerational transmission of divorce. *Journal of Marriage and the Family, 58,* 628–641.

Amato, P. R. (1999). Children of divorced parents as young adults. In E. M. Hetherington (Ed.), *Coping with divorce, single parenting, and remarriage: A risk and resiliency perspective* (pp. 147–164). Mahwah, NJ: Erlbaum.

Amato, P. R., & Booth, A. (1991). Consequences of parental divorce and marital unhappiness for adult well-being. *Social Forces, 69,* 895–914.

Amato, P. R., & Booth, A. (1996). A prospective study of parental divorce and parent-child relationships. *Journal of Marriage and the Family, 58,* 356–365.

Amato, P. R., & Booth, A. (1997). *A generation at risk: Growing up in an era of family upheaval.* Cambridge, MA: Harvard University Press.

Amato, P. R., & Gilbreth, J. (1999). Nonresident fathers and children's well-being: A meta-analysis. *Journal of Marriage and the Family, 61,* 557–573.

Amato, P. R., & Keith, B. (1991). Consequences of parental divorce for children's well-being: A meta-analysis. *Psychological Bulletin, 110,* 26–46.

Amato, P. R., Loomis, L. S., & Booth, A. (1995). Parental divorce, marital conflict, and offspring well-being in early adulthood. *Social Forces, 73,* 895–916.

Arditti, J. A. (1999). Rethinking relationships between divorced mothers and their children: Capitalizing on family strengths. *Family Relations, 48,* 109–119.

Aseltine, R. H. (1996). Pathways linking parental divorce with adolescent depression. *Journal of Health and Social Behavior, 37,* 133–148.

Aseltine, R. H., & Kessler, R. C. (1993). Marital disruption and depression in a community sample. *Journal of Health and Social Behavior, 34,* 237–251.

Astone, N., & McLanahan, S. S. (1991). Family structure, parental practices, and high school completion. *American Sociological Review, 56,* 309–320.

Barber, B. L. (1994). Support and advice from married and divorced fathers: Linkages to adolescent adjustment. *Family Relations, 43,* 433–438.

Barber, B. L., & Eccles, J. S. (1992). Long-term influence of divorce and single parenting on adolescent family- and work-related values, behavior, and aspirations. *Psychological Bulletin, 111,* 108–126.

Beaty, L. A. (1995). Effects of paternal absence on male adolescents' peer relations and self-image. *Adolescence, 30,* 873–880.

Beuhler, C., Betz, P, Ryan, C. M., Legg, B. H., & Trotter, B. B. (1992). Description and evaluation of the orientation for divorcing parents: Implications for postdivorce prevention programs. *Family Relations, 41,* 154–162.

Bianchi, S. M., Subaiya, L., & Kahn, J. R. (1999). The gender gap in the economic well-being of nonresident fathers and custodial mothers. *Demography, 36,* 195–203.

Bisagni, G. M., & Eckenrode, J. (1995). The role of work identity in women's adjustment to work. *American Journal of Orthopsychiatry, 65,* 574–583.

Blankenhorn, D. (1995). *Fatherless America: Confronting our most urgent social problem.* New York: Basic Books.

Block, J. H., Block, J., & Gjerde, P. F. (1986). The personality of children prior to divorce: A prospective study. *Child Development, 57,* 827–840.

Bloom, B. L., Asher, S. J., & White, S. W. (1978). Marital disruption as a stressor: A review and analysis. *Psychological Bulletin, 85,* 867–894.

Bolgar, R., Zweig-Frank, H., & Parish, J. (1995). Childhood antecedents of interpersonal problems in young adult children of divorce. *Journal of the American Academy of Child and Adolescent Psychiatry, 34,* 143–150.

Booth, A., & Amato, P. R. (1991). Divorce and psychological stress. *Journal of Health and Social Behavior, 32,* 396–407.

Braver, S. L., Salem, P., Pearson, J., & DeLuse, S. R. (1996). The content of divorce education programs: Results of a survey. *Family and Conciliation Courts Review, 34,* 41–59.

Brodzinsky, D., Hitt, J. C., & Smith, D. (1993). Impact of parental separation and divorce on adopted and nonadopted children. *American Journal of Orthopsychiatry, 63,* 451–461.

Bronstein, P., Stoll, M. E., Clauson, J., Abrams, C. L., & Briones, M. (1994). Fathering after separation or divorce: Factors predicting children's adjustment. *Family Relations, 43,* 469–479.

Buchanan, C. M., Maccoby, E. E., & Dornbush, S. M. (1996). *Adolescents after divorce.* Cambridge, MA: Harvard University Press.

Bumpass, L. L. (1990). What's happening to the family? Interactions between demographic and institutional change. *Demography, 27,* 483–498.

Bumpass, L. L., Sweet, J. A., & Cherlin, A. (1991). The role of cohabitation in declining rates of marriages. *Journal of Marriage and the Family, 53,* 913–927.

Bussell, D. A. (1995). A pilot study of African American children's cognitive and emotional reactions to parental separation. *Journal of Divorce and Remarriage, 25,* 3–15.

Capaldi, D. M., & Patterson, G. R. (1991). The relation of parental transitions to boys' adjustment problems: I. A linear hypothesis, and II. Mothers at risk for transitions and unskilled parenting. *Developmental Psychology, 27,* 489–504.

Carbonne, J. R. (1994). A feminist perspective on divorce. *The Future of Children, 4,* 183–209.

Castro, M. T., & Bumpass, L. L. (1989). Recent trends in marital disruption. *Demography, 26,* 37–51.

Chase-Lansdale, P. L., Cherlin, A. J., & Kiernan, K. E. (1995). The long-term effects of parental divorce on the mental health of young adults: A developmental perspective. *Child Development, 66,* 1614–1634.

Cherlin, A. J. (1992). *Marriage, divorce, remarriage.* Cambridge, MA: Harvard University Press.

Cherlin, A. J., Chase-Lansdale, P. L., & McRae, C. (1998). Effects of divorce on mental health throughout the life course. *American Sociological Review, 63,* 239–249.

Cherlin, A. J., Furstenberg, E. E., Jr., Chase-Lansdale, P. L., Kiernan, K. E., Robins, P. K., Morrison, D. R., & Teitler, J. O. (1991). Longitudinal studies of effects of divorce on children in Great Britain and the United States. *Science, 252,* 1386–1389.

Clark, J., & Barber, B. L. (1994). Adolescents in post-divorce and always-married families: Self-esteem and perceptions of father interest. *Journal of Marriage and the Family, 56,* 608–614.

Clark, R., & Clifford, T. (1996). Toward a resources and stressors model: The psychological adjustment of adult children of divorce. *Journal of Divorce and Remarriage, 25,*

Coontz, S. (1992). *The way we never were: American families and the nostalgia trap.* New York: Basic Books.

Cooper, H., & Hedges, L. V. (Eds.). (1994). *Handbook of research synthesis.* New York: Russell Sage Foundation.

Cotton, S. R. (1999). Marital status and mental health revisited: Examining the importance of risk factors and resources. *Family Relations, 48,* 225–233.

Cowan, P. A., Cowan, C. P., & Schulz, M. S. (1996). Thinking about ask and resilience in families. In E. M. Hetherington & E. A. Blechman (Eds.), *Stress, coping, and resiliency in children and families* (pp. 1–38). Mahwah, NJ: Erlbaum.

Davies, L., Avison, W. R., & McAlpine, D. D. (1997). Significant life experiences and depression among single and married mothers. *Journal of Marriage and the Family, 59,* 294–308.

Davies, P. T., & Cummings, E. M. (1994). Marital conflict and child adjustment: An emotional security hypothesis. *Psychological Bulletin, 116,* 387–411.

DeGarmo, D. S., & Forgatch, M. S. (1999). Contexts as predictors of changing maternal parenting practices in diverse family structures. In E. M. Hetherington (Ed.), *Coping with divorce, single parenting, and remarriage: A risk and resiliency perspective* (pp. 227–252). Mahwah, NJ: Erlbaum.

DeGarmo, D. S., & Kitson, G. C. (1996). Identity relevance and disruption as predictors of psychological distress for widowed and divorced women. *Journal of Marriage and the Family, 58,* 983–997.

Demo, D. H. (1992). Parent-child relations: Assessing recent change. *Journal of Marriage and the Family, 54,* 104–114.

Demo, D. H., & Acock, A. C. (1996a). Family structure, family process, and adolescent well-being. *Journal of Research on Adolescence, 6,* 457–488.

Demo, D. H., & Acock, A. C. (1996b). Motherhood, marriage, and remarriage: The effects of family structure and family relationships on mothers' well-being. *Journal of Family Issues, 17,* 388–407.

Doherty, W. J., & Needle, R. H. (1991). Psychological adjustment and substance use among adolescents before and after a parental divorce. *Child Development, 62,* 328–337.

Downey, D. B. (1994). The school performance of children from single-mother and single-father families: Economic or interpersonal deprivation? *Journal of Family Issues, 15,* 129–147.

Downey, D. B., Ainsworth-Darnels, J. W., & Dufur, M. J. (1998). Sex of parent and children's well-being in single-parent households. *Journal of Marriage and the Family, 60,* 878–893.

Downey, D. B., & Powell, B. (1993). Do children in single-parent households fare better living with same-sex parents? *Journal of Marriage and the Family, 55,* 55–71.

Elliot, B. J., & Richards, M. P. M. (1991). Children and divorce: Educational performance and behaviour before and after parental separation. *International Journal of Law and the Family, 5,* 258–276.

Ellwood, M. S., & Stolberg, A. L. (1993). The effects of family composition, family health, parenting behavior and environmental stress on children's divorce adjustment. *Journal of Child and Family Studies, 2,* 23–36.

Emery, R. E. (1994). *Renegotiating family relationships: Divorce, child custody, and mediation.* New York: Guilford Press.

Emery, R. E., Kitzmann, K. M., & Waldron, M. (1999). Psychological interventions for separated and divorced families. In E. M. Hetherington (Ed.), *Coping with divorce, single parenting, and remarriage: A risk and resiliency perspective* (pp. 323–344). Mahwah, NJ: Erlbaum.

Fisher, P. A., Fagor, B. I., & Leve, C. S. (1998). Assessment of family stress across low-, medium-, and high-risk samples using the family events checklist. *Family Relations, 47,* 215–219.

Forehand, R., Armistead, L., & Corinne, D. (1997). Is adolescent adjustment following parental divorce a function of predivorce adjustment? *Journal of Abnormal Child Psychology, 25,* 157–164.

Forehand, R., Neighbors, B., Devine, D., & Armistead, L. (1994). Interparental conflict and parental divorce. *Family Relations, 43,* 387–393.

Frost, A. K., & Pakiz, B. (1990). The effects of marital disruption on adolescents: Time as a dynamic. *American Journal of Orthopsychiatry, 60,* 544–555.

Funder, K., Harrison, M., & Weston, R. (1993). *Settling down: Pathways of parents after divorce.* Melbourne, Australia: Australian Institute of Family Studies.

Furstenberg, F. E., Jr. (1994). History and current status of divorce in the United States. *The Future of Children, 4,* 29–43.

Garvin, V., Kalter, N., & Hansell, J. (1993). Divorced women: Individual differences in stressors, mediating factors, and adjustment outcomes. *American Journal of Orthopsychiatry, 63,* 232–240.

Gately, D. W., & Schwebel, A. I. (1991). The challenge model of children's adjustment to parental divorce: Exploring favorable postdivorce outcomes in children. *Journal of Family Psychology, 5,* 60–81.

Glenn, N. (1996). Values, attitudes, and the state of American marriage. In D. Popenoe, J. B. Elshtain, & D. Blankenhorn (Eds.), *Promises to keep: Decline and renewal of marriage in America* (pp. 15–34). Lanham, MD: Rowman and Littlefield.

Glick, P. C. (1989). Remarried families, stepfamilies, and stepchildren: A brief demographic profile. *Family Relations, 38,* 24–27.

Goldberg, W. A., Greenberger, E., Hamill, S., & O'Neil, R. (1992). Role demands in the lives of employed single mothers with preschoolers. *Journal of Family Issues, 13,* 312–333.

Goodman, C. C. (1993). Divorce after long-term marriages: Former spouse relations. *Journal of Divorce and Remarriage, 20,* 43–61.

Gray, J. D., & Silver, R. C. (1990). Opposite sides of the same coin: Former spouses' divergent perspectives in coping with their divorce. *Journal of Personality and Social Psychology, 59,* 1180–1191.

Grych, J. H., & Fincham, F. D. (1992). Marital dissolution and family adjustment: An attributional analysis. In T. L. Orbuch (Ed.), *Close relationship loss: Theoretical approaches* (pp. 157–173). New York: Springer-Verlag.

Hanson, T. L. (1999). Does parental conflict explain why divorce is negatively associated with child welfare? *Social Forces, 77,* 1283–1316.

Hao, L. (1996). Family structure, private transfers, and the economic well-being of families with children. *Social Forces, 75,* 269–292.

Hazan, C., & Shaver, P. R. (1992). Broken attachments: Relationship loss from the perspective of attachment theory. In T. L. Orbuch (Ed.), *Close relationship loss: Theoretical approaches* (pp. 90–110). New York: Springer-Verlag.

Healy, J. M., Malley, J. E., & Stewart, A. J. (1990). Children and their fathers after parental separation. *American Journal of Orthopsychiatry, 60,* 531–543.

Healy, J. M., Stewart, A. J., & Copeland, A. P. (1993). The role of self-blame in children's adjustment to parental separation. *Personality and Social Psychology Bulletin, 19,* 279–289.

Hemstrom, O. (1996). Is marriage dissolution linked to differences in mortality risks for men and women? *Journal of Marriage and the Family, 58,* 366–378.

Hetherington, E. M. (1999). Should we stay together for the sake of the children? In E. M. Hetherington (Ed.), *Coping with divorce, single parenting, and remarriage: A risk and resiliency perspective* (pp. 93–116). Mahwah NJ: Erlbaum.

Hetherington, E. M., & Clingempeel, W. G. (1992). Coping with marital transitions. *Monographs of the Society for Research in Child Development, 57,* (2–3). Chicago: University of Chicago Press.

Hetherington, E. M., & Jodl, K. M. (1994). Stepfamilies as settings for child development. In A. Booth & J. Dunn (Eds.), *Stepfamilies: Who benefits? Who does not?* 55–79 Hillsdale, NJ: Erlbaum.

Hill, R. (1949). *Families under stress.* New York: Harper and Row.

Hope, S., Power, C., & Rodgers, B. (1999). Does financial hardship account for elevated psychological distress in lone mothers? *Social Science and Medicine, 29,* 381–389.

Jekielek, S. M. (1998). Parental conflict, marital disruption and children's emotional well-being. *Social Forces, 76,* 905–935.

Jockin, V., McGue, M., & Lykken, D. T. (1996). Personality and divorce: A genetic analysis. *Journal of Personality and Social Psychology, 71,* 288–299.

Johnson, D. R., & Wu, J. (1996). *An empirical test of crisis, social selection and role explanations of the relationship between marital disruption and psychological distress: A pooled time-series analysis of four-wave panel data.* Paper presented at the International Conference on Social Stress Research, Paris, France.

Joung, I. M. A., Stronks, K., van de Mheen, H., van Poppel, E. W. A., van der Meer, J. B. W., & Mackenbach, J. P (1997). The contribution of intermediary factors to marital status differences in self-reported health. *Journal of Marriage and the Family, 59,* 476–490.

Kalter, N., & Schreier, S. (1993). School-based support groups for children of divorce. *Special Services in the Schools, 8,* 39–66.

Kayser, K. (1993). When love dies: *The process of marital disaffection.* New York: Guilford Press.

Kendler, K. S., Neale, M. C., Kessler, R. C., Heath, A. C., & Eaves, L. J. (1992). Childhood parental loss and adult psychopathology in women. *Archives of General Psychiatry, 49,* 109–116.

Kim, L., Sandler, I. N., & Jenn-Yum, T. (1997). Locus of control as a stress moderator and mediator in children of divorce. Journal of *Abnormal Child Psychology, 25,* 145–155.

King, V. (1994). Nonresident father involvement and child well-being: Can dads make a difference? *Journal of Family Issues, 15,* 78&-96.

Kitson, G. C. (1992). *Portrait of divorce: Adjustment to marital breakdown.* New York: Guilford Press.

Kitson, G. C., & Morgan, L. A. (1990). The multiple consequences of divorce: A decade review. *Journal of Marriage and the Family, 52,* 913–924.

Kurdek, L. A. (1990). Divorce history and self-reported psychological distress in husbands and wives. *Journal of Marriage and the Family, 52,* 701–708.

Kurdek, L. A., Fine, M. A., & Sinclair, R. J. (1994). The relation between parenting transitions and adjustment in young adolescents. *Journal of Early Adolescence, 14,* 412–432.

Larson, R. W., & Gillman, S. (1999). Transmission of emotions in the daily interactions of single-mother families. *Journal of Marriage and the Family, 61,* 21–37.

Laumann, E. O., Gagnon, J. H., Michael, R. T., & Michaels, S. (1994). *The social organization of sexuality.* Chicago: University of Chicago Press.

Lawson, E. J., & Thompson, A. (1996). Black men's perceptions of divorce-related stressors and strategies for coping with divorce. *Journal of Family Issues, 17,* 249–273.

Lee, C. M., Picard, M., & Blain, M. D. (1994). A methodological and substantive review of intervention outcome studies for families undergoing divorce. *Journal of Family Psychology, 8,* 3–15.

Lillard, L. A., & Waite, L. J. (1995). 'Til death do us part: Marital disruption and mortality. *American Journal of Sociology, 100,* 1131–1156.

Lorenz, E. O., Simons, R. L., Conger, R. D., Elder, G. H., Johnson, C., & Chao, W. (1997). Married and recently divorced mothers' stressful events and distress: Tracing change over time. *Journal of Marriage and the Family, 59,* 219–232.

Machida, S., & Holloway, S. D. (1991). The relationship between divorced mothers' perceived control over child rearing and children's post-divorce adjustment. *Family Relations, 40,* 272–278.

Marks, N. E. (1996). Flying solo at midlife: Gender, marital status, and psychological well-being. *Journal of Marriage and the Family, 58,* 917–932.

Marks, N. F., & Lambert, J. D. (1998). Marital status continuity and change among young and midlife adults. *Journal of Family Issues, 19,* 652–686.

Masheter, C. (1991). Postdivorce relationships between ex-spouses: The roles of attachment and interpersonal conflict. *Journal of Marriage and the Family, 53,* 103–110.

Mastekaasa, A. (1994a). Marital status, distress, and well-being: An international comparison. *Journal of Comparative Family Studies, 25,* 183–206.

Mastekaasa, A. (1994b). Psychological well-being and marital dissolution. *Journal of Family Issues, 15,* 208–228.

Mastekaasa, A. (1995). The subjective well-being of the previously married: The importance of unmarried co-habitation and time since widowhood or divorce. *Social Forces, 73,* 665–692.

Mastekaasa, A. (1997). Marital dissolution as a stressor: Some evidence on psychological, physical, and behavioral changes during the preseparation period. *Journal of Divorce and Remarriage, 26,* 155–183.

Mauldon, J. (1990). The effect of marital disruption on children's health. *Demography, 27,* 431–446.

McCubbin, H. I., & Patterson, J. M. (1983). Stress and the family. In H. I. McCubbin & C. R. Figley (Eds.), *Family stress, coping, and social support* (pp. 5–25). Springfield, IL: Thomas.

McGue, M., & Lykken, D. T. (1992). Genetic influence on risk of divorce. *Psychological Science, 3,* 368–373.

McLanahan S. S., & Booth, K. (1989). Mother-only families: Problems, prospects, and politics. *Journal of Marriage and the Family, 51,* 557–580.

McLanahan, S., & Sandefur, G. (1994). *Growing up with a single parent: What hurts, what helps.* Cambridge, MA: Harvard University Press.

McLanahan, S. S., Seltzer, J. A., Hanson, T. L., & Thompson, E. (1994). Child support enforcement and child well-being: Greater security or greater conflict) In I. Garfinkel, S. S. McLanahan, & P. K. Robins (Eds.), *Child support and child well-being* (pp. 239–256). Washington, DC: Urban Institute Press.

Mednick, B. R., Baker, R. L., Reznick, C., & Hocevar, D. (1990). Long-term effects of divorce on adolescent academic achievement. *Journal of Divorce, 13,* 69–88.

Miller, N. B., Smerglia, V. L., Gaudet, D. S., & Kitson, G. C. (1998). Stressful life events, social support, and the distress of widowed and divorced women. *Journal of Family Issues, 19,* 181–203.

Morrison, D. R., & Cherlin, A. J. (1995). The divorce process and young children's well-being: A prospective analysis. *Journal of Marriage and the Family, 57,* 800–812.

Morrison, D. R., & Coiro, M. J. (1999). Parental conflict and marital disruption: Do children benefit when high-conflict marriages are dissolved? *Journal of Marriage and the Family, 61,* 626–637.

Murphy, M., Glaser, K., & Grundy, E. (1997). Marital status and long-term illness in Great Britain. *Journal of Marriage and the Family, 59,* 156–164.

Neff, J. A., & Schluter, T. D. (1993). Marital status and depressive symptoms: The role of race/ethnicity and sex. *Journal of Divorce and Remarriage, 20,* 137–160.

O'Connor, T. G., Hawkins, N., Dunn, J., Thorpe, K., & Golding, J. (1998). Family type and depression in pregnancy: Factors mediating risk in a community sample. *Journal of Marriage and the Family, 60,* 757–770.

Orbuch, T. L. (1992). A symbolic interactionist approach to the study of relationship loss. In T. L. Orbuch (Ed.), *Close relationship lass: Theoretical approaches* (pp. 90–110). New York: Springer-Verlag.

Pearlin, L. L., Menaghan, E. G., Lieberman, M. A., & Mullan, J. T. (1981). The stress process. *Journal of Health and Social Behavior, 22,* 337–356.

Pearson, J., & Thoennes, N. (1990). Custody after divorce: Demographic and attitudinal patterns. *American Journal of Orthopsychiatry, 60,* 233–249.

Peters, A., & Liefbroer, A. C. (1997). Beyond marital status: Partner history and well-being in old age. *Journal of Marriage and the Family, 59,* 687–699.

Peterson, R. R. (1996). A re-evaluation of the economic consequences of divorce. *American Sociological Review, 61,* 528–536.

Plunkett, S. W., Sanchez, M. G., Henry, C. S., & Robinson. L. C. (1997). The double ABCX model and children's post-divorce adaptation. *Journal of Divorce and Remarriage, 27,* 17–33.

Popenoe, D. (1996). *Life without father.* New York: Free Press.

Power, C., Rodgers, B., & Hope, S. (1999). Heavy alcohol consumption and marital status: Disentangling the relationship in a national study of young adults. *Addictions, 94,* 1477–1497.

Preston, S. H., & McDonald, J. (1979). The incidence of divorce within cohorts of American marriages contracted since the Civil War. *Demography, 16,* 1–26.

Riessmann, C. K. (1990). *Divorce talk: Women and men make sense of personal relationships.* New Brunswick, NJ: Rutgers University Press.

Robins, L. N., & Regier, D. A. (1991). *Psychiatric disorders in America: The epidemiologic catchment area study.* New York: Free Press.

Rodgers, B. (1994). Pathways between parental divorce and adult depression. *Journal of Child Psychology and Psychiatry, 35,* 1289–1308.

Rodgers, B., & Pryor, J. (1998). *Divorce and separation: The outcomes for children.* York, England: Joseph Rowntree Foundation.

Rogers, R. G. (1996). The effects of family composition, health, and social support linkages on mortality. *Journal of Health and Social Behavior, 37,* 326–338.

Rogers, S. J., & White, L. K. (1998). Satisfaction with parenting: The role of marital happiness, family structure, and parents gender. *Journal of Marriage and the Family, 60,* 293–308.

Ross, C. E. (1995). Reconceptualizing marital status as a continuum of social attachment. *Journal of Marriage and the Family, 57,* 129–140.

Rutter, M. (1987). Psychosocial resilience and protective mechanisms. *American Journal of Orthopsychiarty, 57,* 316–331.

Samera, T., Stolberg, A. L. (1993). Peer support, divorce, and children's adjustment. *Journal of Divorce and Remarriage, 20,* 45–64.

Sandler, I. N., Tein, J. Y., & West, S. G. (1994). Coping, stress, and the psychological symptoms of children of divorce: A cross-sectional and longitudinal study. *Child Development, 65,* 1744–1763.

Sandler, I., Wolchik, S., Braver, S., & Fogas, B. (1991). Stability and quality of life events and psychological symptomatology in children of divorce. *American Journal of Community Psychology, 19,* 501–520.

Shapiro, A. M. (1996). Explaining psychological distress in a sample of remarried and divorced persons. *Journal of Family Issues, 17,* 186–203.

Sheets, V., Sandler, I., & West, S. G. (1996). Appraisals of negative events by preadolescent children of divorce. *Child Development, 67,* 2166–2182.

Silitsky, D. (1996). Correlates of psychosocial adjustment in adolescents from divorced families. *Journal of Divorce and Remarriage, 26,* 151–169.

Simon, R. W. (1998). Assessing sex differences in vulnerability among employed parents: The importance of marital status. *Journal of Health and Social Behavior, 39,* 38–54.

Simon, R. W., & Marcussen, K. (1999). Marital transitions, marital beliefs, and mental health. *Journal of Health and Social Behavior, 40,* 111–125.

Simons, R. L. and Associates. (1996). *Understanding differences between divorced and intact families.* Thousand Oaks, CA: Sage.

Skolnick, A. (1991). *Embattled paradise: The American family in an age of uncertainty.* New York: Basic Books.

Smith, T. E. (1997). Differences between Black and White students in the effects of parental separation on school grades. *Journal of Divorce and Remarriage, 27,* 25–42.

Smock, P. J. (1994). Gender and the short-run economic consequences of marital disruption. *Social Forces, 73,* 243–262.

South, S. J., Crowder, K. D., & Trent, K. (1998). Children's residential mobility and neighborhood environment following parental divorce and remarriage. *Social Forces, 77,* 667–693.

Stacey, J. (1996). *In the name of the family: Rethinking family values in the postmodern age.* Boston: Beacon Press.

Stack, S., & Eshleman, J. R. (1998). Marital status and happiness: A 17-nation study. *Journal of Marriage and the Family, 60,* 527–536.

Sweet, J. A., & Bumpass, L. L. (1987). *American families and households.* New York: Russell Sage Foundation.

Teachtuan, J. D., & Paasch, K. M. (1994). Financial impact of divorce on children and the family. *Future of Children, 4,* 63–83.

Teachman, J. D., Paasch, K., & Carver, K. (1996). Social capital and dropping out of school early. *Journal of Marriage and the Family, 58,* 773–783.

Teja, S., & Stolberg, A. L. (1993). Peer support, divorce, and children's adjustment. *Journal of Divorce and Remarriage, 20,* 45–64.

Thabes, V. (1997). A survey analysis of women's long-term postdivorce adjustment. *Journal of Divorce and Remarriage, 27,* 163–175.

Thoits, P. A. (1995). Stress, coping, and social support processes: Where are we? What next? *Journal of Health and Social Behavior, 36,* (Ext), 53–79.

Thomson, E., McLanahan, S. S., & Curtin, R. B. (1992). Family structure, gender, and parental socialization. *Journal of Marriage and the Family, 54,* 368–378.

Tschann, J. M., Johnston, J. R., Kline, M., & Wallerstein, J. (1990). Conflict, loss, change and parent-child relationships: Predicting children's adjustment during divorce. *Journal of Divorce and Remarriage, 13,* 1–22.

Tucker, J. S., Friedman, H. S., Schwartz, J. E., Critiqui, M. H., Tomlinson-Keasey C., Wingard, D. L., & Martin, L. R. (1997). Parental divorce: Effects on individual behavior and longevity. *Journal of Personality and Social Psychology, 73,* 381–391.

Umberson, D., Chen, M. D., House, J. S., Hopkins, K., & Slaten, E. (1996). The effect of social relationships on psychological well-being: Are men and women really so different? *American Sociological Review, 61,* 837–857.

Umberson, D., & Williams, C. L. (1993). Divorced fathers: Parental role strain and psychological distress. *Journal of Family Issues, 14,* 378–400.

U.S. Bureau of the Census (1998). *Statistical Abstract of the United States* (118th ed.) Washington, DC: U.S. Government Printing Office.

Vandewater, E. A., & Lansford, J. E. (1998). Influences of family structure and parental conflict on children's well-being. *Family Relations, 47,* 323–330.

Wang, H., & Amato, P. R. (in press). Predictors of divorce adjustment. *Journal of Marriage and the Family.*

Wenk, D., Hardesty, C. L., Morgan, C. S., & Blair, S. L. (1994). The influence of parental involvement on the well-being of sons and daughters. *Journal of Marriage and the Family, 56,* 229–234.

Wheaton, B. (1990). Life transitions, role histories, and mental health. *American Sociological Review, 55,* 209–223.

White, J. M. (1992). Marital status and well-being in Canada. *Journal of Family Issues, 13,* 390–409.

White, L. K. (1991). Determinants of divorce. In A. Booth (Ed.), *Contemporary families* (pp. 141–149). Minneapolis, MN: National Council on Family Relations.

Zick, C. D., & Smith, K. R. (1991). Marital transitions, poverty, and gender differences in mortality. *Journal of Marriage and the Family, 53,* 327–336.

III Parents and Children

No aspect of childhood seems more natural, universal, and changeless than the relationship between parents and child. Yet historical and cross-cultural evidence reveals major changes in conceptions of childhood and adulthood and in the psychological relationships between children and parents. For example, the shift from an agrarian to an industrial society over the past 200 years has revolutionized parent–child relations and the conditions of child development.

Among the changes associated with this transformation of childhood are: the decline of agriculture as a way of life; the elimination of child labor; the fall in infant mortality; the spread of literacy and mass schooling; and a focus on childhood as a distinct and valuable stage of life. As a result of these changes, industrial-era parents bear fewer children, make greater emotional and economic investments in them, and expect less in return than their agrarian counterparts. Agrarian parents were not expected to emphasize emotional bonds or the value of children as unique individuals. Parents and children were bound together by economic necessity: children were an essential source of labor in the family economy and a source of support in an old age. Today, almost all children are economic liabilities. But they now have profound emotional significance. Parents hope offspring will provide intimacy, even genetic immortality. Although today's children have become economically worthless, they have become emotionally "priceless" (Zelizer, 1985).

No matter how eagerly an emotionally priceless child is awaited, becoming a parent is usually experienced as one of life's major "normal" crises. In a classic article, Alice Rossi (1968) was one of the first to point out that the transition to parenthood is often one of life's difficult passages. Since Rossi's article first appeared more than three decades ago, a large body of research literature has developed, most of which supports her view that the early years of parenting can be a period of stress and change as well as joy.

Parenthood itself has changed since Rossi wrote. As Carolyn and Phillip Cowan observe, becoming a parent may be more difficult now than it used to be. The Cowans studied couples before and after the births of their first children. Because of the rapid and dramatic social changes of the past decades, young parents today are like pioneers in a new, uncharted territory. For example, the vast majority of today's couples come to parenthood with both husband and wife in the workforce, and most have expectations of a more egalitarian relationship than their own parents had. But the balance in their lives and their relationship has to shift dramatically after the baby is born. Most couples cannot afford the traditional pattern of the wife staying home full time; nor is this arrangement free of strain for those who try it. Young families thus face more burdens than in the past, yet supportive family policies such as visiting nurses, paid parental leave, and the like that exist in other countries are lacking in the United States.

Mothers are still the principal nurturers and caretakers of their children, but the norms of parenthood have shifted—as the growing use of the term "parenting" suggests. Views of fatherhood in the research literature are changing along with the actual behavior of fathers and children in real life. Until recently, a father could feel he was fulfilling his parental obligations merely by supporting his family. He was expected to spend time with his children when his work schedule permitted, to generally oversee their upbringing, and to discipline them when necessary. Even scholars of the family and of child development tended to ignore the role of the father except as breadwinner and role model. His family participation did not call for direct involvement in the daily round of child rearing, especially when the children were babies. By contrast, scholars expressed the extreme importance of the mother and the dangers of maternal deprivation. Today, however, the role of father is beginning to demand much more active involvement in the life of the family, especially with regard to child rearing. Rosanna Hertz reports on the different ways dual-earner couples arrange for the care of their young children. In her study, she found three different patterns. In the "mothering approach," the couple agree that it is best for the mother to care for the children in the home; even if the mother must work outside the home, she arranges her schedule so as to maximize her time with the children. In the "parenting approach," both parents share the care of the children, and organize their work lives so as to maximize the time they have with their children. In the "market approach," the couple uses professional caregivers to look after their children. Hertz observes that only the shared parenting approaches challenge traditional gender roles and the traditional demands of the workplace.

Of all the family changes of the past several decades, the adoption revolution is one of the most dramatic, yet least discussed. In her article, Mary L. Shanley describes how transracial and open adoption have replaced the older model based on the idea of making the adoptive family as much like a "natural family" as possible. This made adoption a secretive process; the identity of the birth parents was unknown, and even the fact of being adopted was often kept from the child. Shanley discusses the implications of the new openness for the people involved, as well for the meaning of family itself.

Although most of us tend to overestimate the amount of change in families since the 1960s, we tend to think that the lives of parents and children were fairly stable in earlier times. But Donald Hernandez shows that there have been revolutionary transformations in children's lives since the country was founded. The first major change was the shift away from the working farm family to the father-as-breadwinner, mother-as-homemaker arrangement. The second major change, linked to the first, was a dramatic decline in the number of large families. In 1865, the median adolescent had more than seven siblings, whereas by 1930, most children had only one or two. The third revolution in children's lives was an enormous increase in years of education. Most recently, childhood in the United States has been transformed by the entrance of mothers into the workplace, along with the increase in single-parent families and the increasing ethnic and cultural diversity of the child population.

In her article, Ellen Galinsky addresses the issue of work-and-parenting through a research method that is remarkably rare in studies of family life—going to the children and asking them. Among her many findings, perhaps the most surprising is a discrepancy between the opinions of working parents and their children as to whether they are spending too little time together. Most people assume that the issue of time spent with children is about mothers. But although a majority of working mothers feel they are spending too little time with their offspring, the children themselves have a different view. A majority feel they have enough time with their mothers, but not enough with their fathers. These findings, Galinsky argues, show why it is so important to ask children directly about how family issues affect them, rather than rely on our own assumptions.

Since the early 1990s, the effect of family change on children has been a hotly debated political issue. In particular, shifts in family structure—that is, the high proportion of children growing up in single-parent families—has caused concern among social scientists and policy makers. But, as Andrew Cherlin argues in his article, public discussion of the issue takes the form of an argument in which one extreme position is debated against the opposite extreme. This pattern of debate, he argues, makes it hard for the public to understand social problems and is a poor guide to making public policy.

*References*_____

Rossi, A. 1968. Transition to parenthood. *Journal of Marriage and the Family* 30, 26–39.
Zelizer, V. A. 1985. *Pricing the Priceless Child*. New York: Basic Books.

7 Parenthood

■ READING 18

Becoming a Parent

Carolyn P. Cowan and Phillip A. Cowan

Sharon: I did a home pregnancy test. I felt really crummy that day, and stayed home from work. I set the container with the urine sample on a bookcase and managed to stay out of the room until the last few minutes. Finally, I walked in and it looked positive. And I went to check the information on the box and, sure enough, it *was* positive. I was so excited. Then I went back to look and see if maybe it has disappeared; you know, maybe the test was false. Then I just sat down on the sofa and kept thinking, "I'm pregnant. I'm really pregnant. I'm going to have a baby!"

Daniel: I knew she was pregnant. She didn't need the test as far as I was concerned. I was excited too, at first, but then I started to worry. I don't know how I'm going to handle being there at the birth, especially if anything goes wrong. And Sharon's going to quit work soon. I don't know when she's going to go back, and we're barely making it as it is.

Sharon: My mom never worked a day in her life for pay. She was home all the time, looking after *her* mother, and us, and cleaning the house. My dad left all of that to her. We're not going to do it that way. But I don't know how we're supposed to manage it all. Daniel promised that he's going to pitch in right along with me in taking care of the baby, but I don't know whether that's realistic. If he doesn't come through, I'm going to be a real bear about it. If I put all my energy into Daniel and the marriage and something happens, then I'll have to start all over again and that scares the hell out of me.

Sharon is beginning the third trimester of her first pregnancy. If her grandmother were to listen in on our conversation with Sharon and her husband, Daniel, and try to make sense of it, given the experience of her own pregnancy fifty years ago, she would surely have a lot of questions. Home pregnancy tests? Why would a woman with a newborn infant *want* to work if she didn't have to? What husband would share the house-work and care of the baby? Why would Sharon and Daniel worry about their marriage not surviving after they have a baby? Understandable questions for someone who made the transition to parenthood five decades ago, in a qualitatively different world. Unfortunately, the old trail maps are outmoded, and there are as yet no new ones to describe the final destination. They may not need covered wagons for their journey, but Sharon and Daniel are true pioneers.

Like many modern couples, they have two different fantasies about their journey. The first has them embarking on an exciting adventure to bring a new human being into the world, fill their lives with delight and wonder, and enrich their feeling of closeness as a couple. In the second, their path from couple to family is strewn with unexpected obstacles, hazardous conditions, and potential marital strife. Our work suggests that, like most fantasy scenarios, these represent extreme and somewhat exaggerated versions of what really happens when partners become parents. . . .

THE FIVE DOMAINS OF FAMILY LIFE

The responses of one couple to our interview questions offer a preview of how the five domains in our model capture the changes that most couples contend with as they make their transition to parenthood. Natalie and Victor have lived in the San Francisco Bay Area most of their lives. At the time of their initial interview, Natalie, age twenty-nine, is in her fifth month of pregnancy. Victor, her husband of six years, is thirty-four. When their daughter, Kim, is six months old, they visit us again for a follow-up interview. Arranged around each of the five domains, the following excerpts from our second interview reveal some universal themes of early parenthood.

Changes in Identity and Inner Life

After settling comfortably with cups of coffee and tea, we ask both Natalie and Victor whether they feel that their sense of self has shifted in any way since Kim was born. As would be typical in our interviews, Mother and Father focus on different aspects of personal change:

> *Natalie:*   There's not much "me" left to think about right now. Most of the time, even when I'm not nursing, I see myself as attached to this little being with only the milk flowing between us.

> *Victor:*   I've earned money since I was sixteen, but being a father means that I've become the family breadwinner. I've got this new sense of myself as having to go out there in the world to make sure that my wife and daughter are going to be safe and looked after. I mean, I'm concerned about advancing in my job—and we've even bought insurance policies for the first time! This "protector" role feels exciting *and* frightening.

Another change that often occurs in partners' inner lives during a major life transition is a shift in what C. Murray Parkes (1971) describes as our "assumptive world." Men's and women's assumptions about how the world works or how families operate sometimes change radically during the transition from couple to family.

> *Natalie:*   I used to be completely apathetic about political things. I wasn't sure of my congressman's name. Now I'm writing him about once a month because I feel I need to help clean up some of the mess this country is in before Kim grows up.

> *Victor:*   What's changed for me is what I think families and fathers are all about. When we were pregnant, I had these pictures of coming home each night as the tired warrior, playing with the baby for a little while and putting my feet up for the rest of the evening. It's not just that there's more work to do than I ever imagined, but I'm so much more a part of the action every night.

Clearly, Natalie and Victor are experiencing qualitatively different shifts in their sense of self and in how vulnerable or safe each feels in the world. These shifts are tied not only to their new life as parents but also to a new sense of their identities as providers and protectors. Even though most of these changes are positive, they can lead to moments when the couple's relationship feels a bit shaky.

Shifts in the Roles and Relationships within the Marriage

> *Victor:*   After Kim was born, I noticed that something was bugging Natalie, and I kept saying, "What is bothering you?" Finally we went out to dinner without the baby and it came out. And it was because of small things that I never even think about. Like I always used to leave my running shorts in the bathroom . . .

> *Natalie:*   He'd just undress and drop everything!

> *Victor:*   . . . and Nat never made a fuss. In fact she *used* to just pick them up and put them in the hamper. And then that night at dinner she said, "When you leave your shorts there, or your wet towel, and don't pick them up—I get furious." At first I didn't believe what she was saying because it never used to bother her at all, but now I say, "OK, fine, no problem. I'll pick up the shorts and hang them up. I'll be very conscientious." And I have been trying.

> *Natalie:*   You have, but you still don't quite get it. I think my quick trigger has something to do with my feeling so dependent on you and having the baby so dependent on me—and my being stuck here day in and day out. You at least get to go out to do your work, and you bring home a paycheck to show for it. I work here all day long and by the end of the day I feel that all I have to show for it is my exhaustion.

In addition to their distinctive inner changes, men's and women's roles change in very different ways when partners become parents. The division of labor in taking care of the baby, the household, the meals, the laundry, the shopping, calling parents and friends, and earning the money to keep the family fed, clothed, and sheltered is a hot topic for couples (C. Cowan and P. Cowan 1988; Hochschild 1989). It seems to come as a great surprise to most of them that changes in some of their major roles affect their feelings about their overall relationship.

In a domino effect, both partners have to make major adjustments of time and energy as individuals during a period when they are getting less sleep and fewer opportunities to be together. As with Natalie and Victor, they are apt to find that they have less patience with things that didn't seem annoying before. Their frustration often focuses on each other. For couples who thought that having a baby was going to bring them closer together, this is especially confusing and disappointing.

> *Natalie:* It's strange. I feel that we're much closer *and* more distant than we have ever been. I think we communicate more, because there's so much to work out, especially about Kim, but it doesn't always feel very good. And we're both so busy that we're not getting much snuggling or loving time.
>
> *Victor:* We're fighting more too. But I'm still not sure why.

Victor and Natalie are so involved in what is happening to them that even though they can identify some of the sources of their disenchantment, they cannot really make sense of all of it. They are playing out a scenario that was very common for the couples in our study during the first year of parenthood. Both men and women are experiencing a changing sense of self *and* a shift in the atmosphere in the relationship between them. The nurturance that partners might ordinarily get from one another is in very short supply. As if this were not enough to adjust to, almost all of the new parents in our study say that their other key relationships are shifting too.

Shifts in the Three-Generational Roles and Relationships

> *Victor:* It was really weird to see my father's reaction to Kim's birth. The week before Natalie's due date, my father all of a sudden decided that he was going to Seattle, and he took off with my mom and some other people. Well, the next day Natalie went into labor and we had the baby, and my mother kept calling, saying she wanted to get back here. But my dad seemed to be playing games and made it stretch out for two or three days. Finally, when they came back and the whole period was past, it turned out that my father was *jealous* of my mother's relationship with the baby. He didn't want my mother to take time away from him to be with Kim! He's gotten over it now. He holds Kim and plays with her, and doesn't want to go home after a visit. But my dad and me, we're still sort of recovering from what happened. And when things don't go well with me and Dad, Natalie sometimes gets it in the neck.
>
> *Natalie:* I'll say.

For Victor's father, becoming a first-time grandfather is something that is happening *to* him. His son and daughter-in-law are having a baby and he is becoming grandfather, ready or not. Many men and women in Victor's parents' position have mixed feelings about becoming grandparents (Lowe 1991), but rarely know how to deal with them. As Victor searches for ways to become comfortable with his new identity as a father, like so many of the men we spoke to, he is desperately hoping that it will bring him closer to his father.

As father and son struggle with these separate inner changes, they feel a strain in the relationship between them, a strain they feel they cannot mention. Some of it spills over into the relationship between Victor and Natalie: After a visit with his parents, they realize, they are much more likely to get into a fight.

Changing Roles and Relationships Outside the Family

Natalie: While Victor has been dealing with his dad, I've been struggling with my boss. After a long set of negotiations on the phone, he reluctantly agreed to let me come back four days a week instead of full-time. I haven't gone back officially yet, but I dropped in to see him. He always used to have time for me, but this week, after just a few minutes of small talk, he told me that he had a meeting and practically bolted out of the room. He as much as said that he figured I wasn't serious about my job anymore.

Victor: Natalie's not getting much support from her friends, either. None of them have kids and they just don't seem to understand what she's going through. Who ever thought how lonely it can be to have a baby?

Although the burden of the shifts in roles and relationships outside the family affects both parents, it tends to fall more heavily on new mothers. It is women who tend to put their jobs and careers on hold, at least temporarily, after they have babies (Daniels and Weingarten 1982, 1988), and even though they may have more close friends than their husbands do, they find it difficult to make contact with them in the early months of new parenthood. It takes all of the energy new mothers have to cope with the ongoing care and feeding that a newborn requires and to replenish the energy spent undergoing labor or cesarean delivery. The unanticipated loss of support from friends and co-workers can leave new mothers feeling surprisingly isolated and vulnerable. New fathers' energies are on double duty too. Because they are the sole earners when their wives stop working or take maternity leave, men often work longer hours or take on extra jobs. Fatigue and limited availability means that fathers too get less support or comfort from co-workers or friends. This is one of many aspects of family life in which becoming a parent seems to involve more *loss* than either spouse anticipated—especially because they have been focused on the gain of the baby. Although it is not difficult for us to see how these shifts and losses might catch two tired parents off guard, most husbands and wives fail to recognize that these changes are affecting them as individuals and as a couple.

New Parenting Roles and Relationships

Natalie and Victor, unlike most of the other couples, had worked out a shared approach to household tasks from the time they moved in together. Whoever was available to do something would do it. And when Kim was born, they just continued that. During the week, Victor would get the baby up in the morning and then take over when he got home from work. Natalie put her to bed at night. During the weekends the responsibilities were reversed.

It was not surprising that Natalie and Victor expected their egalitarian system—a rare arrangement—to carry over to the care of their baby. What is surprising to us is that a majority of the couples predicted that they would share the care of their baby much more equally than they were sharing their housework and family tasks *before* they became parents. Even though they are unusually collaborative in their care of Kim, Natalie and Victor are not protected from the fact that, like most couples, their different ideas about what a baby needs create some conflict and disagreement:

> *Victor:*   I tend to be a little more . . . what would you say?
>
> *Natalie:*   Crazy.
>
> *Victor:*   A little more crazy with Kim. I like to put her on my bicycle and go for a ride real fast. I like the thought of the wind blowing on her and her eyes watering. I want her to feel the rain hitting her face. Natalie would cover her head, put a thick jacket on her, you know, make sure she's warm and dry.
>
> *Natalie:*   At the beginning, we argued a lot about things like that. More than we ever did. Some of them seemed trivial at the time. The argument wouldn't last more than a day. It would all build up, explode, and then be over. One night, though, Victor simply walked out. He took a long drive, and then came back. It was a bad day for both of us. We just had to get it out, regardless of the fact that it was three A.M.
>
> *Victor:*   I think it was at that point that I realized that couples who start off with a bad relationship would really be in trouble. As it was, it wasn't too pleasant for us, but we got through it.

Despite the fact that their emotional focus had been on the baby during pregnancy and the early months of parenthood, Victor and Natalie were not prepared for the way their relationship with the baby affected and was affected by the changes they had been experiencing all along as individuals, at work, in their marriage, and in their relationships with their parents, friends, and co-workers—the spillover effects. They sometimes have new and serious disagreements, but both of them convey a sense that they have the ability to prevent their occasional blowups from escalating into serious and long-lasting tensions.

As we follow them over time, Victor and Natalie describe periods in which their goodwill toward each other wears thin, but their down periods are typically followed by genuine ups. It seems that one of them always finds a way to come back to discuss the painful issues when they are not in so much distress. In subsequent visits, for example, the shorts-in-the-bathroom episode, retold with much laughter, becomes a shorthand symbol for the times when tensions erupt between them. They give themselves time to cool down, they come back to talk about what was so upsetting, and having heard each other out, they go on to find a solution to the problem that satisfies both of their needs. This, we know, is the key to a couple's stable and satisfying relationship (Gottman and Krokoff 1989).

Compared to the other couples, one of the unusual strengths in Natalie and Victor's life together is their ability to come back to problem issues after they have calmed down. Many couples are afraid to rock the boat once their heated feelings have cooled down. Even more unusual is their trust that they will both be listened to sympathetically when they try to sort out what happened. Because Natalie and Victor each dare to raise issues that concern them, they end up feeling that they are on the same side when it comes to the most important things in life (cf. Ball 1984). This is what makes it possible for them to engage in conflict and yet maintain their positive feelings about their relationship.

Most important, perhaps, for the long-term outcome of their journey to parenthood is that the good feeling between Victor and Natalie spills over to their daughter. Throughout Kim's preschool years and into her first year of kindergarten, we see the threesome as an active, involved family in which the members are fully engaged with one another in both serious and playful activities.

WHAT MAKES PARENTHOOD HARDER NOW

Natalie and Victor are charting new territory. They are trying to create a family based on the new, egalitarian ideology in which both of them work *and* share the tasks of managing the household and caring for their daughter. They have already embraced less traditional roles than most of the couples in our study. Although the world they live in has changed a great deal since they were children, it has not shifted sufficiently to support them in realizing their ideals easily. Their journey seems to require heroic effort.

Would a more traditional version of family life be less stressful? Couples who arrange things so that the woman tends the hearth and baby and the man provides the income to support them are also showing signs of strain. They struggle financially because it often takes more than one parent's income to maintain a family. They feel drained emotionally because they rely almost entirely on their relationship to satisfy most of their psychological needs. Contemporary parents find themselves in double jeopardy. Significant historical shifts in the family landscape of the last century, particularly of the last few decades, have created additional burdens for them. As couples set foot on the trails of this challenging journey, they become disoriented because society's map of the territory has been redrawn. Becoming a family today is more difficult than it used to be.

In recent decades there has been a steady ripple of revolutionary social change. Birth control technology has been transformed. Small nuclear families live more isolated lives in crowded cities, often feeling cut off from extended family and friends. Mothers of young children are entering the work force earlier and in ever larger numbers. Choices about how to create life as a family are much greater then they used to be. Men and women are having a difficult time regaining their balance as couples after they have babies, in part because the radical shifts in the circumstances surrounding family life in America demand new arrangements to accommodate the increasing demands on parents of young children. But new social arrangements and roles have simply not kept pace with these changes, leaving couples on their own to manage the demands of work and family.

More Choice

Compared with the experiences of their parents and grandparents, couples today have many more choices about whether and when to bring a child into their lives. New forms of birth control have given most couples the means to engage in an active sex life with some confidence, though no guarantee, that they can avoid unwanted pregnancy. In addition, despite recent challenges in American courts and legislatures, the 1973 Supreme Court decision legalizing abortion has given couples a second chance to decide whether to become parents if birth control fails or is not used.

But along with modern birth control techniques come reports of newly discovered hazards. We now know that using birth control pills, intrauterine devices, the cervical cap, the sponge, and even the diaphragm poses some risk to a woman's health. The decision to abort a fetus brings with it both public controversy and the private anguish of the physical, psychological, and moral consequences of ending a pregnancy (see Nathanson 1989). Men and women today may enjoy more choice about parenthood than any previous generation, but the couples in our studies are finding it quite difficult to navigate this new family-making terrain.

Sharon, who was eagerly awaiting the results of her home pregnancy test when we met her at the beginning of this reading, had not been nearly as eager to become a mother three years earlier.

> **Sharon:** Actually, we fought about it a lot. Daniel already had a child, Hallie, from his first marriage. "Let's have one of our own. It'll be easy," he said. And I said, "Yeah, and what happened before Hallie was two? You were out the door."
>
> **Daniel:** I told you, that had nothing to do with Hallie. She was great. It was my ex that was the problem. I just knew that for us a baby would be right.
>
> **Sharon:** I wasn't sure. What was I going to do about a career? What was I going to do about me? I wasn't ready to put things on hold. I wasn't even convinced, then, that I wanted to become a mother. It wouldn't have been good for me, and it sure wouldn't have been good for the baby, to go ahead and give in to Daniel when I was feeling that way.

In past times, fewer choices meant less conflict between spouses, at least at the outset. Now, with each partner expecting to have a free choice in the matter, planning a family can become the occasion for sensitive and delicate treaty negotiations. First, couples who want to live together must decide whether they want to get married. One partner may be for it, the other not. Second, the timing of childbirth has changed. For couples married in 1950–54, the majority (60 percent) would have a baby within two years. Now, almost one-third of couples are marrying *after* having a child, and those who marry before becoming parents are marrying later in life. Only a minority of them have their first child within two years. Some delay parenthood for more than a decade (Teachman, Polonko, and Scanzoni 1987).

Couples are also having smaller families. The decline in fertility has for the first time reduced the birthrate below the replacement level of zero population growth—less than two children per family.* And because couples are having fewer children and having

*There are indications, however, that the birthrate of the United States is now on the rise.

them later, more seems to be at stake in each decision about whether and when to have a child. What was once a natural progression has become a series of choice points, each with a potential for serious disagreement between the partners.

Alice is in the last trimester of her pregnancy. In our initial interview, she and Andy described a profound struggle between them that is not over yet.

> *Alice:*   This pregnancy was a life and death issue for me. I'd already had two abortions with a man I'd lived with before, because it was very clear that we could not deal with raising a child. Although I'd known Andy for years, we had been together only four months when I became pregnant unexpectedly. I loved him, I was thirty-four years old, and I wasn't going to risk the possibility of another abortion and maybe never being able to have children. So when I became pregnant this time, I said, "I'm having this baby with you or without you. But I'd much rather have it with you."

> *Andy:*   Well, I'm only twenty-seven and I haven't gotten on track with my own life. Alice was using a diaphragm and I thought it was safe. For months after she became pregnant, I was just pissed off that this was happening to me, to us, but I gradually calmed down. If it was just up to me, I'd wait for a number of years yet because I don't feel ready, but I want to be with her, and you can hear that she's determined to have this baby.

Clearly, more choice has not necessarily made life easier for couples who are becoming a family.

Isolation

The living environments of families with children have changed dramatically. In 1850, 75 percent of American families lived in rural settings. By 1970, 75 percent were living in urban or suburban environments, and the migration from farm to city is continuing.

We began our own family in Toronto, Canada, the city we had grown up in, with both sets of parents living nearby. Today we live some distance from our parents, relatives, and childhood friends, as do the majority of couples in North America. Increasingly, at least in the middle- and upper-income brackets, couples are living in unfamiliar surroundings, bringing newborns home to be reared in single-family apartments or houses, where their neighbors are strangers. Becoming a parent, then, can quickly result in social isolation, especially for the parent who stays at home with the baby.

John and Shannon are one of the younger couples in our study. He is twenty-four and she is twenty-three.

> *John:*   My sister in Dallas lives down the block from our mother. Whenever she and her husband want a night out, they just call up and either they take the baby over to Mom's house or Mom comes right over to my sister's. Our friends help us out once in a while, but you have to reach out and ask them and a lot of times they aren't in a position to respond. Some of them don't have kids, so they don't really understand what it's like for us. They keep calling us and suggesting that

we go for a picnic or out for pizza, and we have to remind them that we have this baby to take care of.

Shannon: All the uncles, aunts, and cousins in my family used to get together every Sunday. Most of the time I don't miss that because they were intrusive and gossipy and into everybody else's business. But sometimes it would be nice to have someone to talk to who cares about me, and who lived through all the baby throw-up and ear infections and lack of sleep, and could just say, "Don't worry, Shannon, it's going to get better soon."

Women's Roles

Since we began our family thirty years ago, mothers have been joining the labor force in ever-increasing numbers, even when they have young babies. Women have always worked, but economic necessity in the middle as well as the working classes, and increased training and education among women, propelled them into the work force in record numbers. In 1960, 18 percent of mothers with children under six were working at least part-time outside the home. By 1970, that figure had grown to 30 percent, and by 1980 it was 45 percent. Today, the majority of women with children under *three* work at least part-time, and recent research suggests that this figure will soon extend to a majority of mothers of one-year-olds (Teachman, Polonko, and Scanzoni 1987).

With the enormous increase in women's choices and opportunities in the work world, many women are caught between traditional and modern conceptions of how they should be living their lives. It is a common refrain in our couples groups.

Joan: It's ironic. My mother knew that she was supposed to be a mom and not a career woman. But she suffered from that. She was a capable woman with more business sense than my dad, but she felt it was her job to stay home with us kids. And she was *very* depressed some of the time. But I'm *supposed* to be a career woman. I feel that I just need to stay home right now. I'm really happy with that decision, but I struggled with it for months.

Tanya: I know what Joan means, but it's the opposite for me. I'm doing what I want, going back to work, but it's driving me crazy. All day as I'm working, I'm wondering what's happening to Kevin. Is he OK, is he doing some new thing that I'm missing, is he getting enough individual attention? And when I get home, I'm tired, Jackson's tired, Kevin's tired. I have to get dinner on the table and Kevin ready for bed. And then I'm exhausted and Jackson's exhausted and I just hit the pillow and I'm out. We haven't made love in three months. I know Jackson's frustrated. *I'm* frustrated. I didn't know it was going to be like this.

News media accounts of family-oriented men imply that as mothers have taken on more of a role in the world of paid work, fathers have taken on a comparable load of family work. But this simply hasn't happened. As Arlie Hochschild (1989) demonstrates, working mothers are coming home to face a "second shift"—running the household and caring for the children. Although there are studies suggesting that fathers are taking on a little more housework and care of the children than they used to (Pleck 1985), mothers who are employed full-time still have far greater responsibility for managing the family work and child rearing than their husbands do (C. Cowan 1988). It is not simply that men's and women's roles are unequal that seems to be causing distress for couples, but rather that they are so clearly discrepant from what both spouses expected them to be.

Women are getting the short end of what Hochschild calls the "stalled revolution": Their work roles have changed but their family roles have not. Well-intentioned and confused husbands feel guilty, while their overburdened wives feel angry. It does not take much imagination to see how these emotions can fuel the fire of marital conflict.

Social Policy

The stress that Joan and Tanya talk about comes not only from internal conflict and from difficulties in coping with life inside the family but from factors outside the family as well. Joan might consider working part-time if she felt that she and her husband could get high-quality, affordable child care for their son. Tanya might consider working different shifts or part-time if her company had more flexible working arrangements for parents of young children. But few of the business and government policies that affect parents and children are supportive of anything beyond the most traditional family arrangements.

We see a few couples, like Natalie and Victor, who strike out on their own to make their ideology of more balanced roles a reality. These couples believe that they and their children will reap the rewards of their innovation, but they are exhausted from bucking the strong winds of opposition—from parents, from bosses, from co-workers. Six months after the birth of her daughter, Natalie mentioned receiving a lukewarm reception from her boss after negotiating a four-day work week.

> ***Natalie:***   He made me feel terrible. I'm going to have to work *very* hard to make things go, but I think I can do it. What worries me, though, is that the people I used to supervise aren't very supportive either. They keep raising these issues, "Well, what if so-and-so happens, and you're not there?" Well, sometimes I wasn't there before because I was traveling for the company, and nobody got in a snit. Now that I've got a baby, somehow my being away from the office at a particular moment is a problem.
>
> ***Victor:***   My boss is flexible about when I come in and when I leave, but he keeps asking me questions. He can't understand why I want to be at home with Kim some of the time that Natalie's at work.

It would seem to be in the interest of business and government to develop policies that are supportive of the family. Satisfied workers are more productive. Healthy families drain scarce economic resources less than unhealthy ones, and make more of a contribution to the welfare of society at large. Yet, the United States is the only country in the Western world without a semblance of explicit family policy. This lack is felt most severely by parents of young children. There are no resources to help new parents deal with their anxieties about child rearing (such as the visiting public health nurses in England), unless the situation is serious enough to warrant medical or psychiatric attention. If both parents want or need to work, they would be less conflicted if they could expect to have adequate parental leave when their babies are born (as in Sweden and other countries), flexible work hours to accommodate the needs of young children, and access to reasonably priced, competent child care. These policies and provisions are simply not available in most American businesses and communities (Catalyst 1988).

The absence of family policy also takes its toll on traditional family arrangements, which are not supported by income supplements or family allowances (as they are in Canada and Britain) as a financial cushion for the single-earner family. The lack of supportive policy and family-oriented resources results in increased stress on new parents just when their energies are needed to care for their children. It is almost inevitable that this kind of stress spills over into the couple's negotiations and conflicts about how they will divide the housework and care of the children.

The Need for New Role Models

Based on recent statistics, the modern family norm is neither the Norman Rockwell *Saturday Evening Post* cover family nor the "Leave It to Beaver" scenario with Dad going out to work and Mom staying at home to look after the children. Only about 6 percent of all American households today have a husband as the sole breadwinner and a wife and two or more children at home—"the typical American family" of earlier times. Patterns from earlier generations are often irrelevant to the challenges faced by dual-worker couples in today's marketplace.

After setting out on the family journey, partners often discover that they have conflicting values, needs, expectations, and plans for their destination. This may not be an altogether new phenomenon, but it creates additional strain for a couple.

> *James:*   My parents were old-school Swedes who settled in Minnesota on a farm. It was cold outside in the winters, but it was cold inside too. Nobody said anything unless they had to. My mom was home all the time. She worked hard to support my dad and keep the farm going, but she never really had anything of her own. I'm determined to support Cindy going back to school as soon as she's ready.

> *Cindy:*   My parents were as different from James's as any two parents could be. When they were home with us, they were all touchy-feely, but they were hardly ever around. During the days my mom and dad both worked. At night, they went out with their friends. I really don't want that to happen to Eddie. So, James and I are having a thing about it now. He wants me to go back to school. I don't want to. I'm working about ten hours a week, partly because he nags at me so much. If it were just up to me, I'd stay home until Eddie gets into first grade.

Cindy and James each feel that they have the freedom to do things differently than their parents did. The problem is that the things each of them wants to be different are on a collision course. James is trying to be supportive of Cindy's educational ambitions so his new family will feel different than the one he grew up in. Given her history, Cindy does not experience this as support. Her picture of the family she wanted to create and James's picture do not match. Like so many of the couples in our study, both partners are finding it difficult to establish a new pattern because the models from the families they grew up in are so different from the families they want to create.

Increased Emotional Burden

The historical changes we have been describing have increased the burden on both men and women with respect to the emotional side of married life. Not quite the equal sharers of breadwinning and family management they hoped to be, husbands and wives now expect to be each other's major suppliers of emotional warmth and support. Especially in the early months as a family, they look to their marriage as a "haven in a heartless world." Deprived of regular daily contact with extended family members and lifelong friends, wives and husbands look to each other to "be there" for them—to pick up the slack when energies flag, to work collaboratively on solving problems, to provide comfort when it is needed, and to share the highs and lows of life inside and outside the family. While this mutual expectation may sound reasonable to modern couples, it is very difficult to live up to in an intimate relationship that is already vulnerable to disappointment from within and pressure from without.

The greatest emotional pressure on the couple, we believe, comes from the culture's increasing emphasis on self-fulfillment and self-development (Bellah et al. 1985). The vocabulary of individualism, endemic to American society from its beginnings, has become even more pervasive in recent decades. It is increasingly difficult for two people to make a commitment to each other if they believe that ultimately they are alone, and that personal development and success in life must be achieved through individual efforts. As this individualistic vocabulary plays out within the family, it makes it even more difficult for partners to subordinate some of their personal interests to the common good of the relationship. When "my needs" and "your needs" appear to be in conflict, partners can wind up feeling more like adversaries than family collaborators.

The vocabulary of individualism also makes it likely that today's parents will be blamed for any disarray in American families. In the spirit of Ben Franklin and Horatio Alger, new parents feel that they ought to be able to make it on their own, without help. Couples are quick to blame themselves if something goes wrong. When the expectable tensions increase as partners become parents, their tendency is to blame each other for not doing a better job. We believe that pioneers will inevitably find themselves in difficulty at some points on a strenuous journey. If societal policies do not become more responsive to parents and children, many of them will lose their way.

Editor's Note: *References for this reading can be found in the original source.*

■READING 19

A Typology of Approaches to Child Care: The Centerpiece of Organizing Family Life for Dual-Earner Couples

Rosanna Hertz

Child rearing tends to be regarded as an individualistic concern for parents in the United States. Society may purport to be so-called profamily but, judging by the small number of policies and programs that pertain to child care, society largely ignores how young children spend their days despite widespread recognition that women's labor force participation has increased dramatically over the past several decades.[1] Indeed, it has become quite popular for political contenders to voice support for family values but to sidestep the sticky questions about how children are being cared for when mothers (and fathers) must work for pay outside the home.

With the exception of Head Start programs, when compared with other industrialized nations, the United States has little government-sponsored or subsidized day care (Benin & Chong, 1993; Kamerman & Kahn, 1991; Zigler, 1990). We lack the extensive system of day care that exists in other industrialized countries (Ferber & O'Farrell, 1991; Moen, 1989) because of ideological conflicts over the government's involvement in family life (Hartmann & Spalter-Roth, 1994).[2] The invocation of family values to indicate a belief in the strength of families to organize independently their lives to maximize the care and nurturance of the young (and elderly) rings hollow when studies find that affordable good quality day care arrangements would reduce both economic hardships and distress couples face in trying to balance the simultaneous child care and workplace demands (Bird, 1995). The lack of affordable child care in the United States is a serious problem for all social classes (Bianchi & Spain, 1986); but its consequences for low-income families are perhaps the greatest of all (Ferber & O'Farrell, 1991, pp. 74–84).[3]

Child care should be a leading social issue addressed at workplaces, in communities and at the state and federal levels of government. But without an array of good solutions to preschool child care (e.g., quality, affordability, certification, etc.), couples attempt to resolve this work/family dilemma through individual solutions. This article explores in a systematic way the different approaches dual-earner couples implement to care for their children. It also seeks to understand in context the critical factors that explain couples' choice of day care arrangements. The data presented suggest that a combination of a priori beliefs and economic resources explains the choice of child care practice. Only in rare instances do beliefs or resources alone play the determining role in selecting child care

Author's Note: I thank Faith I. T. Ferguson, who helped interview some of the couples with me, and I thank Wellesley College for a faculty award for tape transcriptions. I also thank Robert J. Thomas for helpful comments on this manuscript. A version of this article was presented at the British Psychological Society, London, 1996.

practices. However, there is no clear-cut relationship between beliefs and economic resources. In the absence of strong evidence regarding the relationship between beliefs and economic resources, I propose a typology of approaches to child care that reflects the interaction of ideology and economic factors. From a sample of dual-earner couples, I suggest that there are three general approaches to child care: (a) the "mothering" approach, (b) the parenting approach, and (c) the market approach. In addition to exploring diverse views of child rearing that exist in the United States, I will analyze how sentiments about mothering influence the ways couples organize and integrate family and work lives.

THE STUDY AND THE INTERVIEW SAMPLE

This article is part of an in-depth study of 95 dual-earner couples, with the majority (88 couples) having at least one child still living in the home in eastern Massachusetts. Each husband and wife was individually interviewed; the majority of couples were also interviewed simultaneously (Hertz, 1995).[4] Husbands and wives were told that we were interested in studying how couples make decisions about child care, finances, and work. The interviews lasted a minimum of 2 hours, with a smaller number of interviews lasting up to 4 hours. There are two parts to the interview: a longer-in-depth open-ended guide with extensive probes and then a shorter division of labor survey adapted from Huber and Spitzer (1983).

Because the primary focus of the study was looking at how women's labor force participation has altered family life—particularly authority surrounding decision making in the home—I decided to use a stratified quota sample. Different strategies were used to find different segments of the study's population. In general, access to individual couples was obtained either through other professionals who identified couples fitting the study's parameters or through mailings to day care parents in several communities.

I used a combination of factors to decide who belongs in each social class stratum; these included the income of both spouses combined. Families in the upper middle class had a combined income of at least $100,000 annually and professional or managerial occupations; middle-class couples had a combined income of between $40,000 and $100,000, and most were in white-collar jobs in service professions or middle-management occupations; and working-class couples had incomes that overlapped those earned by the middle class, but these couples were distinguished by their occupations. I tried to locate couples for this segment employed in traditional working-class occupations or trades, such as painter, policeman, nurse, waitress, factory worker.

A total of 36% of the couples are working class; the other three fifths are middle and upper middle class. Within the working class, 30 couples are White and 4 couples are of other races. Within the middle and upper middle class, 35 couples are White and 21 couples are of other races. An additional 5 couples do not share the same race as their spouse; they are all middle- to upper middle-class couples. There are no "cross-class" couples (husbands and wives who differ in occupational prestige). For purposes of this article, social class is only mentioned. Racial differences in the three approaches to mothering appear not to be as important for this article as social class. For instance, upper middle-class African American families were as likely to have a professional approach to child rearing as their White counterparts. Racial differences are relevant when it comes to deciding between types of non-kin care and selecting between settings, which I have discussed in another article (Hertz & Ferguson, 1996). Therefore, I have not used race as a way of identifying respondents; I have instead used occupations as a signifier of the social class of each respondent.

At the time of the interview, each spouse within a couple had a minimum of one job. This does not mean, however, that at the time of having young children (preschool or elementary age) there were two full-time jobs. In most cases, women did not leave the labor force for more than 1 year; but in a small number of cases, women were not employed in the labor force when their children were preschool age or younger. More likely among this small group of couples, women worked outside the home for fewer hours than a full-time job. The decision to stay home longer than a year is not related to social class. That is, regardless of social class, it is possible to organize family life around a mothering approach (discussed below) provided that there are enough economic resources to live on one salary for a period of time. It is questionable whether younger couples can afford to do this today except perhaps among the upper middle and upper classes. At the time of the interviews, just over 60% of the couples were between their late 30s and middle 40s.[5] But there is great variation within this group as to the age when they had their first children. For those couples who had children in early decades, having children may have led to greater economic ability for the wife to stay at home. There were also fewer day care services available then; the growth of day care in the United States has mushroomed in the last 10 years. For those couples who have had children in the last 5 years, most remain in the paid labor force, with wives typically taking only brief maternity leaves.[6]

Independent of what age couples are now, I am interested in the relationship between child care beliefs and practices and social class at the time each couple had young children. At the time of the interview, 63 couples (66%) had at least one child age 5 or younger. An additional 25 couples (26%) had children living at home older than age 5. I indicate age of the respondents and their children's ages as part of the lead-ins to quotes so the reader can assess the historical factors (labor force and day care options) that inform each couple's story. I have deliberately selected quotes and respondents in each type who presently have young children as well as those whose children are older to give the reader information about couples presently undergoing child care decision making and couples who are reflecting back to this period in their family lives.

The focal points of this article are based on an analysis of responses to one open-ended question: "Tell me a history of your child care arrangements." Probes included likes and dislikes about child care arrangements but not anything about motherhood. Other topics emerge from the dialogue between interviewer and interviewee. Demographic facts and information are also used to analyze the responses to this question. Because I am particularly interested in the women's and men's views, I have relied heavily on their words and descriptions of family life to demonstrate the diverse beliefs about caring for young children in the United States today.

THE MOTHERING APPROACH

The mothering approach assumes that the person who is best suited to raise the couple's children is the wife, who should be with them at home. According to this approach, only the family can give its children the right values and moral upbringing. These couples uniformly believe that what will create successful adults is a childhood steeped in love, caring, and nurturing properly provided only by the insular world of the family. In this regard, the child's future is tied to a certain kind of early mothering practice.[7]

To maximize wives' abilities to devote themselves to the upbringing of the children, husbands work either overtime or they supplement a primary job with a second one, sacrificing their own leisure and time with children and spouses. But even the additional work hours were insufficient to pay the bills and keep wives out of the paid labor force. For the few lucky families who 15 years ago could get by financially on his earnings, as men reached their late 30s and early 40s, "burn-out" and being physically forced to slow down commonly occurred. Some worked less overtime; others found less strenuous work with less income. Even these men's wives eventually went back to paid work to take the pressure off him and to make their family's life less of an economic struggle to pay bills on time and to perhaps put a little money aside for a vacation. In 53% of working-class couples at the time of the interview, at least one spouse, typically the husband, worked overtime or held a second part-time job, totaling at minimum 60 hours a week.

This ideological belief about child rearing rarely exists for long in practice. Few couples could economically afford to have wives at home and out of the paid labor force. Yet, this central family belief in mother as the best person to raise children fuels how they arrange their work schedules and jobs to attempt not to compromise their children's upbringing. Child rearing—and keeping children within the family circle—is the priority, and work schedules of wives are critical to meeting this approach. Most of these women were employed even when their children were infants and toddlers, but talk about that only emerges once the conversation shifts to paid employment.

Beyond the early childhood years, even mothers who stayed out of the paid workforce, returned to paid employment at least part-time when the youngest entered kindergarten. In other families, however, wives remained in the paid workforce but changed to working shifts (Presser & Cain, 1983; Presser, 1988). To be available to young children, women worked nights giving the appearance of stay-at-home traditional moms to make highly visible their identities as mothers (Garey, 1995). Wives adjusted their work schedules, changing shifts as their children aged, placing their ability to care for children over spending time with husbands (Hertz & Charlton, 1989). Scheduling of work hours for both spouses to maximize mother care is more important than the wife's job mobility or workplace loyalty.

To permit a continued belief in a division of labor in which wives raise children, couples redefine their circumstances. That is, it is not the husband's fault that he does not earn enough. The economy is to blame. Placing blame on an external force does not damage their views of masculinity as tied to being a good provider. Economic explanations also become more congruent with couples' expectations that wives are picking up overtime because of cutbacks or due to erosion of wages so that families can avoid a decline in their standard of living (Ferber & O'Farrell, 1991). Put differently, locating blame external to the couple exempts husbands from feeling they are not good providers and wives from resenting their husbands for having jobs that do not pay enough, forcing them to seek paid employment.

It is interesting that these couples have yet to adjust their ideal view of family life to the reality they are living. But there is reason for this nested in a set of beliefs about family primacy. Even though these couples speak a language of traditional gender roles whereby spouses share the belief that child rearing is the wife's primary responsibility, their practices contradict these beliefs. For the most part, husbands strongly favor their wives' paid employment. It not only relieves the men of economic pressure but also means that the family is not living as tightly. They continue to live paycheck to paycheck but without worrying—especially for wives who typically pay the bills—about meeting monthly payments. But the ideological emphasis for them is not on gender equality as a larger value; instead, family is the critical variable. As a result of wives' paid employment, couples discuss parenting while emphasizing mothering. In this regard, there has been a shift by White working-class couples with traditional values of exclusive mothering to now resemble more the mother practices of earlier generations of minority working-class couples in this study;[8] now family values are about the family doing for itself in terms of raising its children, and whatever couples can do for themselves (without external supports, including everything from day care to welfare) is achieving family values.

Constructing Family Life to Maximize the Mother at Home

Despite hardship at times, keeping the mother/child dyad together is an organizing principal belief of these families. Sometimes, respondents phrased this belief as the mother's need to be with her child; other times, the belief appears as part of what is essential to so-called good mothering in addition to the glue that keeps the family unit strong. Put differently, the wife's status as mother becomes the pivotal point around which all other statuses (e.g., employee) revolve. Because the work of caring for family members is ignored (DeVault, 1991) or regarded as part of what might be called the invisible work (Daniels, 1988) of family life that women do, women's visible presence elevates mothering and other aspects of household work.

This wife, who once managed an office, thought when she was pregnant that she would return to work full-time. But becoming a mother is different than fantasizing about what it might feel like. Now 42 years old and the mother of two children, ages 1 and 10, she reflects back to how dramatically her beliefs changed about the kind of mother she wanted to be:

> I can remember, I always laugh with a girl friend who had a baby a year before me, and she'd say to me, "Are you still going back [to work]?" I go, "Oh ya, I'm gonna go back. No offense Ann, I really don't mean any offense, I really don't know what you do all day." And then once I had my baby, and was home for a couple of weeks with her, I never went back. (Interviewer: Really?) All of a sudden this thing took over me and it was there was no one in this world that could possibly raise this child like I was going to.

Other couples talked quite candidly about this division of labor as a taken-for-granted aspect of their marriage. Another husband, a policeman, age 44 with three children between the ages of 10 and 17, gave a typical response to why it was essential for mothers to be home:

> She's never worked full-time since we had our children. That's a decision we made. She took a maternity leave and decided not to go back to her job. Raising our children was too important. . . . We had had a firm commitment to my children's being raised by my wife.

Because we're firm believers in a strong foundation for children. I mean first through age 6. To me, it's like a building. If the foundation isn't strong, you're asking for trouble later, as you build.

His wife, age 42, who presently works part-time as a secretary and cares for a relative's child in her home 2 days a week, told us that it was an implicit part of their marriage that she stay home when the children were born.

(Interviewer: Why did you make the decision to stay home?)
Oh God. I guess because that was just the way it was. I guess I figured when I had children, I'd stay home with them. I had a great job. And I actually probably made more money than my husband did at the time, but it wasn't a question.
(Was it something the two of you talked about at all?)
Not really, it was just I would stay home. . . .
(Were there any family members who could have watched the children?)
My husband's mother never worked, so she probably could have, if I had decided to ever do that, but I really enjoy being here. I really didn't—I wanted to be with them.

In another family, with children ages 10 and 18, the husband, age 37, had been a factory worker since he was 19 years old. High school sweethearts, he and his 36-year-old wife (presently a medical transcriber who has had a series of different jobs) have both always had to work to make ends meet. He explains the couple's philosophy about raising children even though these beliefs were at times thwarted, as is often the case among working-class couples when the inability to pay bills forces the wife back to work—even part-time—and someone else watches the child, which is less of a concern when older siblings or relatives help out:

It's very important to both of us that one, mainly that she should be—you know, because I was the primary breadwinner, I had the steady job—that she be home with our son [the second child], especially. With our daughter, it was hard because when she was born, I was making a lot less money. . . . We always tried to put both our kids first. But when my daughter was a baby we had someone watching her—we've always both felt very strongly that if we're going to have children, that we should be with them, it's as simple as that. Not shuffling him off—it was never a "you have to go here [day care] every single day when you get home from school." . . . My daughter sometimes gets him [the son] in the afternoon, she helps a lot or his grandfather who lives down the street or we try to always have someone home for him in the afternoons.

In a fourth example, this mother, age 37, with three children between the ages of 10 and 16, returned to work waitressing after a 3-month maternity leave. Below, she explains why she shifted from working day hours to night hours:

I really didn't want to leave my kids with someone else. You know . . . I did try to go to work during the day when Eric was about 3 months old. When I decided I want—needed to go back to work for the money. And an old job was available that I had had, and they really wanted me to come back. It was waitressing again. I worked 4 days and couldn't do it. I cried and it was just too much, I just couldn't be away from him during the day. Didn't bother me to go in the evening when I knew he was with Mark [his father], sleeping most of the time and that was fine. Actually I've always liked working, but um . . . no, it wasn't for me. And it was tough when I just went to work a few years ago during the day. You know, because I wasn't here in the morning to get them off to school and it was difficult for my youngest. They've done great.

Night work did not compete with being a good mother in ways that being a day-working mom did (Garey, 1995). To meet the ideology of the stay-at-home mom, women are employed outside the home during hours that do not count: when children are in school and asleep. This allows these families to meet this kind of mothering expectation without challenging women's primary identities. Further, child care decisions (and the choice to limit paid child care services) define the boundaries of what is necessary for them to retain their sense of being good mothers as well as an important part of their families' lives (Hertz & Ferguson, 1996).

Her husband, age 36, a factory worker who leaves home at 6:00 a.m. and returns at 3:30 in the afternoon, during periods when there is no overtime also works as a custodian for a restaurant before his factory job on Thursdays and Fridays. He simplified all his wife's job arrangements to make his point about their shared beliefs regarding child raising as a family-centered activity. Note that his identity is not tied to fathering but his talk is about what is critical to children's upbringing:

> She got a job at night, I worked during the day. The key to good parenting is one parent being with the child at ALL times. That's what we always thought. . . . Cause kids like to see their parents when they get home. I mean, cause they run through the door and they got so many things to tell you. They just, they don't have anybody to blab it out to.

As their family grew, neighbors watched the children in the transition from mom's leaving to work and dad's returning home from work. Neighbors continue to be a source of help during transition points in the day. At the time of the interview, her oldest children were teenagers and she went back to working the dayshift. Below, she describes why she shifted back:

> Because I always hated . . . I hated when I worked nights and weekends. Um, because it was the weekends. I mean I went to work when everybody else was home, basically. And especially when all of the kids were in school, they would come home, even though it was only a couple nights a week, Thursday and Friday.

She felt like an invisible part of the family. Even though much of the evening and weekend time is devoted to team sports that her husband coaches and that she admits to not really enjoying, it was important to her to be a spectator and cheer the family on rather than work during this time. Being visible represents good mothering. Similarly, the woman above who does secretarial work part-time, in addition to caring for a niece 2 days a week, had just filled out an application to work during the day at a store part-time at the time of the interview. Worried about how they will pay the tuition so their oldest daughter can commute to college to study nursing, she explains why she is applying for this particular job:

> So, I recently put in an application at a candy shop. See if I could sort of have two part-time jobs. I really still want to be home when my youngest gets out of school [elementary].

I FIRMLY believe that somebody needs to be home. As a matter of fact, even as they get older I really want to be around. I'm there for my older two [in high school].

The medical transcriber, who has a skill in high demand, requested hours to complement her children's school schedule. Flexibility in work scheduling allows women to assert the salience of their identity as mothers who place a priority on a particular kind of child rearing. Below, she explains the work arrangement she negotiated:

Now I work days. But once summer vacation comes, I may end up working second shift again. Once again, I don't want to put him in a day care home. . . . I stressed with my boss that I needed flexibility. [She told her boss,] "Yes, I will go full-time, but school vacations, summer vacations, I may have to completely change my schedule and you'll have to go along with that." And that was fine with him.

Even though couples articulate the importance of the wife's being the central care provider, all the women quoted above worked some hours each week from the birth of the first child. But what they did was leave well-paying jobs, often earning more than husbands, to find work with better hours, meaning hours that allowed their husbands (or if possible another relative) to watch the children for at least part of her shift while she went to her job. Neighbors or acquaintances, often members in the same church, cared for children during transition times as part of the patchwork of child care coverage. These "custodial" caregivers did not compete with the mother as the central nurturer (Uttal, 1996). The woman above, who was once an office manager, never really stayed home. This couple needed her income to qualify for a mortgage, so she took a night job as a tax auditor briefly and since then has worked steadily as a phone service operator during weekend evenings and some week nights. He said,

I'd get out of work at 3:30. Then she'd leave for work. I think she worked 4 to midnight. We might pass in the driveway or my mother-in-law would take care of the baby until I got home at night.

When their mortgage was approved, he was laid off. Finally, finding work as a truck driver, she needed weekend work hours because he was gone during the week. She took her present job as an answering service operator because she needed both a flexible schedule and some time out of the house. Below, she tells about this and her perfect job hours:

It's probably the lowest paying job I've ever had and the most abusive in that people who call want to get whomever they want to get, not you. But it's the only thing that fits into my schedule. But my ideal is that I'd like to work for 5 nights a week—Sunday to Thursday night—and I'd like to work 6–11. You know, if I could. That's what I'd like to do.

Work histories for more than one third of the women in this group included several years as child care providers. Economically, couples noted this was a way not to have to place several children in the care of others and, equally important, it continued to position women in the world of the home, not the external labor force (Fitz Gibbon, 1993; Nelson, 1994). Some were licensed as family providers; others, such as the secretary quoted earlier, were paid to care for relatives' or friends' children (and for a brief period, even the medical transcriber watched children). Between shifting from a night schedule to a day one, the waitress above also worked out of her home, a culturally desirable place for her to be, to approximate a full-time homemaker mom caring for her children:

> When my youngest was born, I did day care myself. I did day care for two years. . . . I said to my girlfriend, "I don't know what I'm gonna DO, I don't really want to go back to work with three kids and leaving them. It's just too much." And she said, "Well, you know, I was thinking about getting back into day care and doing it up here. Why don't you get licensed?" So I ended up in day care and ah. It was okay. It served the purpose, you know, with Ann a baby and Eric only 2, being able to be home. But, um, I got burnt out really fast. Really fast, cause I had so many babies. . . . And actually when I gave it up and decided that I wanted to work outside the home, I did keep one little girl and my niece. I kept them and still babysat during the day time and waitressed a couple nights a week. . . . Four years that I babysat. It was the hardest work I ever did.

But it is not simply mothers who do all the nurturing. Fathers are active participants in these households, particularly when it comes to scheduling their work so wives can earn as well. The police officer mentioned earlier followed up his comment about his wife's staying at home with the following comment:

> I work nights now. I've worked days. If she has something to go to, we work it out so one of us is around. I mean, we had babysitters, but there's never been a time when both of us worked that we needed day care.

The waitress described her husband's involvement with the children:

> Mark actually does more of the after-school activities than I do. He is the one who takes them to all their meets and practices and spends afternoons hearing about their day. Since I wasn't home during dinner, he gave them supper but now I do it.

According to the medical transcriber's detailed account, her husband is now doing the thinking work of running their household, instead of simply serving the meals she prepared when she worked nights and her first child was young. When she was asked to commit to full-time hours by her employer, they had a long conversation about how the division of labor between them would change:

> But we did talk about it a lot and he was very well aware of the added responsibility that he would have, not just with my son but with the household things. Because when I was working evenings, I would do everything in the house during the day. . . . I was always the one responsible for the housework, cooking, laundry. And now, especially now that I'm working full-time, my husband does just as much, maybe more sometimes, than I do. . . . In fact, my husband did all the laundry last night. He left it for me to fold and put away, but it was clean and dry. . . . Normally, I work 10:30 to 7:00 at night. He gets home at 3:30 or 4:00. So my husband does the majority of the cooking during the week. . . . But if I'm going to be late, then he'll eat. And him and my daughter play cribbage or yahtzee to see who does the dishes. And on the weekends, if the house is a real pit, it's like "let's get up Saturday morning and clean the house." We just all chip in.

Finally, the good mother is juxtaposed to leaving children with strangers. Below, the trucker driver husband explains a common reason why the mother is preferred:

> We feel that we see the difference in the children that are being raised by their parents and children that are being raised by, you know, an outside entity. (Interviewer: In what ways?) Mostly, I think the way they do it is to let their kids do everything and anything. And ah, my wife is, I have to say, she's home with the children more and she does the disciplinary measures 90% of the time. Only because she's there when it's needed and I have very well-behaved children I am told. I feel they are. I'm not ashamed to take my children anywhere . . . my nephew is in day care and they can't go out to dinner unless there are special provisions because he can't sit in a restaurant. . . . (You think that's because he's in day care?) They, they're not spending, he's not getting the quality motherhood. I don't feel he is, ya. And I don't feel it's the day care people's job to, to instill these things in them. She's being paid to watch this child. She'd gonna do what she has to do to get through her day in a sane manner. She's not going to be a disciplinarian, or she shouldn't be there to, ah, to teach everything . . . my wife places our children in the playpen for several hours each day so she can get things done and the children learn to play by themselves. Other children who are in day care come here to play and they don't know how to entertain themselves.

Beliefs about motherhood remain entrenched in an essentialist argument that the only person qualified to care for young children is either the biological or adoptive mother (Hertz & Ferguson, 1996). Not only are strangers problematic as nurturers but they are less likely, these couples believe, to instill a strong foundation of values they share and believe to be necessary for adulthood. Even though fathers are essential to providing round-the-clock home care for children, it is the mother's visible presence that continues to be at the core of this construction of family life.

THE PARENTING APPROACH

The parenting approach is exemplified in the belief that the family ought to be organized around caring for the children with the critical distinction that both parents are full participants. Couples who adopt the parenting approach create new ways of combining family and work by seeking less demanding jobs or by negotiating more flexible arrangements with present employers (at least during the early years of their children's lives.) Some couples, particularly those who have middle-class occupations, are choosing to push employment in new directions. But for others, particularly those with working-class occupations, underemployment becomes a catalyst for rethinking traditional gender-based divisions of labor. These couples are crafting strategic responses to a shrinking labor market.

Regardless of how they came to share parenting, at the time of the interviews, these couples did not essentialize the mother as the only parent capable of nurturing children. For couples who chose to modify rigid work structures out of a belief that the responsibility for child rearing must be shared between mother and father, they talk about parenting with expectations that both parents are essential as nurturers and providers, though parents are not androgynous. Even among those couples wherein the men have lost full-time jobs and are presently doing less challenging work or working part-time, they also come to admit that men can care for children, throwing into question prior ideological beliefs about the dichotomy that conflates manhood and fatherhood with economic provision and womanhood and motherhood with nurturing activities. (Even though new practices of work/family divisions emerge, it does not necessarily follow that underemployed men view caring for their children as a substitute for their present employment situations.)

Emphasizing the sharing of child rearing between parents limits the need to use external child care providers. When it is used, they attempt to control the kind of child care that supplements their own involvement with children prior to their children's entry into the public schools. Some use only a few hours a week of day care or babysitters; others find cooperative exchanges between families with young children.

Restructuring Employment to Maximize Parenting

This group of parents shares a belief about parental superiority in raising children. They believe that men and women should work outside and inside the home and also share responsibility for child rearing. Individuals attempt to modify their jobs and employment commitments to regulate on their own terms the demands that paid work makes and thus restore some semblance of control, even if it means loss of income (Hertz & Ferguson, 1996).

Couples emphasize that men have historically been short-changed as nurturers, and they are seeking parity with wives in their desire to experience fatherhood (cf. Coltrane, 1989). Men explained their efforts to modify their work schedules to be actively involved in child care. One man, age 37, employed in a social service agency, explains why he decided to reorganize his work schedule to have 1 day a week at home when his first child was born. He was able to reorganize which 40 hours he worked to not cut back on his pay, to have 1 day a week at home and occasionally to hold staff meetings in his home with his infant daughter present:

> Why did I do it? I think I was a new father, I wanted to spend time with my child, first year of life. I also sort of figured I might not have this opportunity again. I thought this was unique. I knew I wasn't going to forever stay at this job and I just had immense flexibility. I still was working very hard, but I had immense flexibility and control because I was the director, so I could really set the policy, and I did. But it was just important to me to spend some time and not have either a professional caregiver or have it so my wife had some time.
>
> It also worked in terms of our hours. Partly there was some pragmatism here in terms of—we wanted to minimize the day care she was in, maximize our time with her, certainly in that first year.

Another unusual arrangement that highlights the prioritizing of family togetherness over full-time work is a middle-class couple who both work part-time day hours: she as a social worker and he as a patient advocate. The wife, age 33, explains that initially she thought she would remain at home, but they each negotiated part-time work hours in their respective jobs to share child rearing. Understanding her husband's desire to be with their child, she reported that they figured out the following solution:

I had negotiated, at my job, to go back part-time after my maternity leave, but I thought in my heart that I might not go back at all. Then when Andy went back to work, he missed Sam so much that he felt like he really wanted to be home more. And what we were able to figure out was that if I went back part-time and he cut back his hours—so he decided he'd work 30 hours and I'd work 20 hours. And we could always be home with him. So that was what we did, and that's what we've done. . . . He worked 3 mornings and 2 afternoons and I worked 3 afternoons and 2 mornings. He worked 6 hours a day and I worked 4 hours a day.

Below, she explains why parental child rearing and part-time jobs better matched their desires:

I don't have criticisms of people who use day care. I just couldn't bear the thought. But it just felt, for me, that I really wanted to be with Sam and I wanted Andy to be with Sam and I feel like I got the absolute best of all possible worlds. Because I think it would have been really hard for me to be home full-time and have Andy work full-time. And working part-time is just the perfect balance. So to be able to work, and to have Sam home with Andy, we just couldn't ask for more. . . . I thought it was better for him to be with one of his parents.

The husband, age 39, explains the price he has paid and the confusion this arrangement has caused at the agency where he is employed:

I felt really stressed out initially. When I started working part-time, it was incredibly difficult because the expectations of myself were that I could do what I used to do just in less time. . . . I think more than anybody else at my office, I have had to scale back my expectations of myself. And I feel like people have been very supportive. . . . But it was frustrating. I'd post my schedule for everybody and give them a list. We'd try to set up a staff meeting and if we're going to do it on a Tuesday, do we do it in the morning or the afternoon? . . . And initially I'd have to scratch my own head and wonder when I was going to be in.

Some middle-class couples find a way to implement even more atypical arrangements, such as mutual exchanges, whereby families swap child care and keep track of hours. Administering part-time two different social services, the couple quoted below, ages 47 and 42, are making ends meet, placing themselves at the economic fringes of the middle class and conscious of their own downward mobility relative to their own parents. They know they could earn more money but as she put it,

We want to maximize as much as possible these first 5 years of being with him. So I would say the first thing is values about the amount of day care. It is also more expensive and it makes you work more. . . . I would say the driving factor was about values. We didn't want him to be in a lot of day care. I figured the longer he had more intimate settings, the better.

Their present arrangements are described below:

Now what we do is on Mondays I take care of a little girl in the morning and then her mom takes care of Mark in the afternoon. On Tuesdays and Thursdays, I bring Mark to a friend's house and that little girl's dad takes care of Mark and walks him to preschool with his little daughter and then picks them up and takes care of him. Then on Wednesdays, I take care of both little girls: the little girl whose mom takes care of Mark on Monday and the little girl whose dad takes care of Mark on Tuesdays and Thursdays. Then on Fridays, I take care of the little girl whose dad walked Mark to preschool. I take care of her on Friday mornings. So that evens out that because we get 2 afternoons and we give a day in the mornings. And then Friday afternoon, I pay the little girl's mother $20 to take care of him.

It is more common in this study sample for women to be the part-time worker or ask for special arrangements for them to combine motherhood and work, trading a solid middle-class standard of living for a more modest one. One woman, age 36, found a job working part-time as a lawyer. Below, she explains why:

> I've seen the way other people's lives had been crazy and I wanted to have a good time with my kids. I just kept hearing from people all the time: "These are the most precious years, don't give them up, hold onto them." . . . There's some truth to that and I really wanted to cherish the time I had with them. . . . I wanted to go back to work because I needed the intellectual stimulation and the respect.

But in many ways, the couples quoted above are labor force elites: They can shift the number of hours they work or change jobs without facing permanent career penalties. Eventually, the men and some of the women in these families shifted back to full-time work when their children entered preschool or grade school. But at least during the early years, they restructured the gender system to make fathering and mothering essential to childhood socialization.

Underemployment as a Route to Shared Parenting

For others, the downward economy and downsizing by corporations beginning in the 1980s (Hodson & Sullivan, 1990) led couples to piece together new work arrangements with active fathering a by-product. These latter couples did not make conscious choices to work less (and earn less) to do more for their children directly. They worry about spiraling downward even further. One father, age 39, with two children and presently working part-time as a home health aid, explains how his employment history has devolved:

> No. I think like MANY of the long-term unemployed, people like me who don't show up in the statistics, life goes on. So you do other things, you work part-time, either delivering pizza, which I did for 3 years, or bundling mail for the post office, whatever. But life goes on, so you have to adjust yourself because first of all, no one's gonna hire you. Once you're over 30, no one's gonna hire you for any real job. So what's the sense? . . . Your buddy who mows lawns for a living is offering you $10 an hour. So you do what you have to do. And you just fall into a whole other world that you forget exists when you worked for a large company, working 9–5 for 6 years.

The wife, age 35, a nurse who typically works the 7:00 P.M. to 7:00 A.M. night shift, worries that if she loses her overtime she will have to find a second nursing job. She added to her husband's comments her thoughts on how underemployment has affected her husband's sense of masculinity: "And of course his ego was all shot to hell. He's not the family provider he wants to be and he's not doing exactly what he wanted, what he set in his mind. All his goals are rearranged."

Couples in which the wife was working full-time and the husband part-time often wished that the wife could opt to work fewer hours. Whereas middle-class White women continue to think about their lives as having the option of staying at home or working full-time, ideological and structural barriers prevent men from having similar choices (Gerson, 1993). Another mother, age 40, an office manager with two children ages 5 and 9, assumed that there would be two full-time paychecks. She now carries the economic burden and wishes she could have a more flexible work schedule.

> When I decided I would have children, I knew I would always be working, but I thought there would be more flexibility in my work schedule that would allow me to take extended vacations with my children, sometimes come home, be available after school to go to a school function with my son, sometimes be able to go to a soccer practice in the afternoon on a Thursday, be able to go to my daughter's ballet classes with her, that kind of thing. I don't feel like I have that kind of flexibility in my life. . . . In the nicer part of the year, I'll arrive home at 6:30 and they've just come from a baseball practice and they're rosy cheeked and they're laughing about what happened, and I'm not a part of that. So I guess over a period of time you do build up a little resentment. It goes away. But that's what I'm missing.

Another man, age 37, who presently works part-time as a postal worker, was laid off from a factory job after a dozen years at his company. His inability to find a full-time job for the past several years made it necessary for his wife to remain employed full-time. Because she is the carrier of the medical benefits, they feel unable to reduce her work to part-time because they would lose these benefits. Despite his positive experiences caring for his 3-year-old son since he was an infant, this father describes the deep ambivalence he feels about contributing in atypical ways to family life:

> I was sort of thrust into the role. Thrust into it by job circumstances. . . . Sometimes it does bother me [not to be the main breadwinner]. . . . I just don't feel like I'm with the crowd. Not that I have to be with the crowd. . . . I realize that most men my age are probably established in careers now and I'm not. But, I just have that vague sense that, ah . . . like the world is going on out there and I'm here.
>
> I know it's more accepted now in society, but still I feel like I'm in the vast minority when it comes to my role. . . . I've more or less settled into the routine of taking care of my son. At first, it was quite an adjustment. . . . It's been kind of a metamorphosis for me. I've gone from being scared to death of it, to, ah, being actually quite comfortable now. Maybe that's why I stopped looking for full-time work, I don't know.

His wife, age 31, explains how her fantasies of the kind of family life she thought about have not materialized:

> It's funny because I guess we all have an idea of what's going to happen when you get married and all this. All my friends had it easy, you know, got married and then they did have the kids and then they stayed home. So I figured that would just happen to me, too. But it was tough. The first year that I was at work it was hard. I think we had a lot of argu-

ments. And I didn't think he could do anything right. When we were both with him it was like, "What are we DOING now?" There was no set of instructions or anything that come with a baby. I always felt I was better with him. As an infant, he felt very awkward with him. And actually, he's done very well with him. I can't, you know, knock him now. But you know, at that time I was very resentful. VERY resentful. And the thing is I had a job I didn't like and I had a manager I didn't like, he was terrible to me, very demanding, and he was very chauvinistic about women.

Even though mothering is a kind of craft or practice (Ruddick, 1980), the ideology that only mothers are really capable of maternal thinking is powerful and, as a result, many women do not necessarily want to share the work of mothering. The last woman quoted admits that mothering does not come naturally and it is only through practice that we learn how to do it. She concedes that her husband has mastered maternal practice; that is, he is engaged in sharing the work of parental love, a kind of work he never imagined himself doing. It is ironic that the couples who are on the cutting edge of transforming maternal thinking are doing so not because of an ideological belief as much as structural constraints of a shrinking labor force that catapult men into learning the work of child rearing. In the process, couples rethink family life, particularly caring for children, as they cobble together identities that are no longer unidimensional. Underemployed couples continue to wish their home and work time could be more evenly divided but not because they wish wives would become full-time mothers.

The Rise of Fathering

Fathering emerges but without a separate language from mothering, although the practice of it is markedly different from the White middle-class breadwinning fathers of a past generation (Bernard, 1981; Goode, 1982). Regardless of the route to sharing child care, the practice of fathering transformed these men into more nurturing and sensitive caregivers who are teaching their young children how to navigate the world (Coltrane, 1989). These men report wanting to be different than their own fathers. The husband of the couple who swap child care put it this way: "I didn't want to be the same kind of father my father had been. I wanted to be a more involved father. So, it seemed to me the way to do that was that I would work less and spend more time with [my child]."

The patient advocate quoted earlier talked about what he feels he has gained by taking care of his child:

When James was born, I was smitten, I was blown away by the strong feelings I had toward him. It was kind of like falling in love with a lover for me. I was really—I was shocked by that feeling, by how strong my feelings are and were. . . . But I also feel that I really—it's been a window for me, it's been watching him learn about the world and how much of an influence I have over that. I feel a tremendous amount of responsibility and I feel really eager to help him explore the world. I want him to do it on his own, but I know that I also have a lot of say in how things get set up, presentations that are made. But it's exciting to be part of that and I really love his discovery of things.

Even though the home health worker quoted above wishes he could return to full-time work to take some of the work pressure off his wife, he also was very eloquent about what it meant to be a father. The detailed response about infants he gives was once reserved for mothers only:

Let's see. I don't think it's that different than being a mother. It's very stressful, very, at the same time it's very rewarding. And . . . but I think to have a lot of your father's influence is a good experience for a lot of children. Because I would take her places that my wife normally wouldn't take her. Like down to the auto parts store. . . . It got a lot harder when my second was born. It's twice as hard, ya. Especially right now, he is cutting teeth. He can't walk and he can't talk and so he can't TELL you anything. And he's at that time when he's trying to rearrange his clock to sleep at night so he's up, like last night he was up at midnight. So I brought him to bed with me. And I put him back to bed around 2 and he was up at 4, so like 3 or 4 times a night. And lack of sleep more than anything else gets you. Then the older one wakes up. Sometimes ARGGGGHHHH. I feel like a lioness with cubs crawling all around. . . . Fatherhood, it's a lot of hard work but it can also be a lot of fun too. . . . As they get older, you can play more and you can put them in a car and go for a ride and it's a lot easier once they're older.

The father, who presently works part-time as a postal worker, explains that what he feels is most important is making a difference in his child's life:

Mr. Mom? Um . . . it's frus . . . it's rewarding, but it's also very frustrating. It's, it's ah . . . it seems like after a day of being with my son all day, it's fun and all that, but sometimes, some days it just wears thin, and I need some adult interaction if you know what I mean? . . . But I feel like I'm in the role of teacher and ah . . . which is I think the most fun part. And just watching him develop and learn new things . . . to see the difference that I can sort of shape and mold my son's life it gives me some personal satisfaction. Nobody told me that.

In sum, the members of this group are testing and contesting the limits of their work environments. Whereas there are certainly career costs and unwanted underemployment, these couples are altering the landscape of traditional ways that couples have attempted to integrate work and family and, in the process, altering the gender system that locates women according to a primary identity as mother and men as economic providers. Men's caring work undermines the belief that mothering comes naturally to women. Further, caring for children elevates the status of parenting as a source of primary identity for both mothers and fathers; it even takes priority over workplace goals and job advancement. In short, changing labor force patterns and creating flexible jobs forced new family practices and in the process altered beliefs about child care and nurturing.

THE MARKET APPROACH

The market approach to caring for children involves hiring other people to care for one's own children. Both wife and husband are career oriented and they emphasize profes-sional caregivers who replace mothers. Unlike the two approaches discussed in preced-ing sections, wherein the use of non-kin child care is minimized, among these couples children spend their days with adult caregivers who are not family members.[9] Often, cou-ples have a combination of care providers[10] and commonly they shift from one type of arrangement to another, ostensibly in response to the child's developmental needs. As I and my coauthor, Faith Ferguson, have argued (Hertz & Ferguson, 1996), regardless of whether children are placed in center-based care or in family day care or a woman is hired to provide individual care, in using day care the mother has hired someone to replace herself at least part of the time and her essential contribution to the family has become *deskilled* (Braverman, 1974). But the new middle-class model for women continues to emphasize the achievements of the individual (i.e., the mother); women achieve this by deskilling motherhood, breaking apart a once presumed holistic pattern of practices.[11] In this study, it is typical for couples in which both are professionals working full-time with more than one child to have multiple child care arrangements. Below is a striking example of deskilling the mother role into several components: the woman who is loving and good with infants and drives the children and the woman who provides developmental stimulation and reads to her children:

> But once the kids were 2 or something, when they like to be read to, that sort of thing, I have sent them to a play group, which is a family day care, really down the street from me. They've each gone there 2 days a week. . . . The reason for this is that my babysitter, as lovely and caring a person as she is, is functionally illiterate, which is the downside of what I have. . . . By the time I figured out that she could barely manage to write a phone message, it was clear that she was so good with my infant that it really didn't matter at that point.
>
> Now, she is driving my daughter to . . . Brownies, ballet, that sort of thing. . . . And we don't have family in the area, so she's sort of a surrogate mother to them in that sense. She has a large family of her own, and my kids know all of the members of her family. . . . I think I have been incredibly lucky. The kids love her and she loves them.

The woman above, pregnant with her third child at age 36 and a doctor with a doctor husband, is quite typical of this group whose caregiving role is tied to finding surrogates. Because the mother remains responsible for patching together child care arrangements, she uses different criteria to select different women to replace herself. The love of one's child becomes the major criteria for how couples select providers, particularly nannies, but also family-based day care settings. These kinds of providers are a substitute for mother love (Hertz, 1986; Hertz & Ferguson, 1996; Wrigley, 1995). Yet, often conflicts emerge around dissimilar values between the provider and the couple because couples tend to hire women of different social class and racial backgrounds to care for their children (Hertz, 1986; Wrigley, 1995). Center-based day care providers (or preschool or nursery school programs) are termed *teachers* and they are expected to expose the child to a first learning environment. This enrichment experience is supposed to supplement parental teaching, though often it is also a substitute for early education the mother once provided. Credentials and professionalism are ways couples assess whether a program shares their views on learning (Hertz & Ferguson, 1963).[12] After-school programs are now the new neighborhoods. These institutional settings provide adult supervision, replacing the mom with milk and cookies but also replacing no-longer-safe neighborhoods where children once freely rode bikes and played pick-up games.

Whereas initially women believe that continuity of care is the best replacement for not being at home themselves, they eventually abandon this idea. In this study and in my prior work (Hertz, 1986), not one family kept the same child care arrangements for the first years of a child's life. Dissatisfaction materializes on either side of the provider/couple relationship: Sometimes the child care provider quits, but other times the reason for a change is couched in a language of child development and the need for a new kind of arrangement, as predicted by the child care professional mother of the woman quoted below:

> At 2 years old, it was clear there was way too much TV. I didn't care about it as an infant, I didn't care about it at 1 year old because they watch some of it but they run around. They are too interested in their own motor stuff. And my mom had told me when she saw Janie [the provider]—a lot of my education about child care has come from my mom [a nursery school director]—I said, "Isn't it great because Janie promised me she'll take care of the kid until she is in kindergarten if I want." And there were kids there until 4 years old. So, I kept thinking that would be continuity I wasn't providing my child by working. And my mom said, "You're not going to want her at Janie's after 2 [years old]." And I didn't know at that time, but how right she was.

Couples speak a new language of quasi-psychology that emphasizes developmentally appropriate educational experiences for preschoolers who are introduced to the rudiments of a structured day, develop positive peer group experiences, and begin to develop a positive relationship to learning. Professionals are looked toward to provide these enrichment experiences. In sum, former child care providers are discarded and new child care workers rationalized on the changing developmental stages of the child.

Women do feel guilty for not being with their child and they worry about the cost to their children. The woman below, age 37, when she had her first child 9 years ago, describes the kind of work hours she was expected to keep.

> I had two people coming in, 6-hour shifts. And then when Kyle was 6 months old, I just sat down with my husband and I just felt like this was really hurting Kyle. So, I decided that my career was interfering with my family. And I actually quit my internship. I came home distraught and I just said, "That's it." At that point I was working 100 hours a week, I would leave at 6:00 one morning and come home at 10:00 the next night if I was on call. I was on call every third to fourth night. It was very hard with a newborn, although I had my husband who was here taking care of the baby at night and other family members. I said to myself, "What are you doing? Is it worth it?"

This woman was lucky because a sister volunteered to come and care for her infant son, which lessened her guilt about not caring for her own child. But when she became pregnant with a second child, the sister said two children was one too many to watch and this couple eventually found non-relative live-in help.

But guilt was not shared by husbands who had similar occupations or male colleagues, as a woman doctor, age 31, reported:

> But you know, I've been a mother for 9 years so I've worked on the guilt a lot. . . . And I used to ask all these men I worked with, I said, "You know, when you go out the door in the morning, do you feel guilty when you say goodbye to your children?" And they would look at me as if to say, "What a dumb question that is." But every time I would go out it would tear me apart. So I've tried to lessen the guilt as the years go by.

Men did not mention feeling guilty about working full-time, which underscores the cultural asymmetry in the emphasis placed on the unique role of the mother/child dyad. The husbands of these women did mention the guilt their wives felt by not being available to their children. A professor with more flexible work hours, married to the doctor quoted above, began his discussion on day care with the following:

> My wife was essentially gone [the first year of the child's life]. I used to take the baby into the hospital in the middle of the night to see her mother. It was a rough year. I had a very free year—on sabbatical—which helped enormously and we had my in-laws close by. But my wife still feels that was a desertion, that she essentially deserted her baby 2 weeks after it was born.

The mothers who exemplify this approach are not the only ones in this study who feel guilty. Women in all three approaches feel guilty when they are unable to match their conception of motherhood and family life: Some try to alter shift scheduling; others try cutting back hours or find another type of work. But the ideal work load is rarely attained. I note the guilt in this section because the most career-oriented women have the least options because their work environments remain entrenched in a male trajectory despite recent claims of organizations' becoming more so-called family friendly (Gilbert, 1985; Hertz, 1986; Hochschild, 1971; Slater & Glazer, 1987). These women report that short of quitting professions in which they have invested heavily through years of school and training, hiring surrogates to replace themselves or deskilling motherhood are the only rational solutions.[13] Most mentioned wishing they could become part-time employees at least for a few years (the added income from their full-time employment was not essential to these families) but few employers agreed to experiment with such work arrangements. Some feel trapped as successful professionals wishing for more leisure time for themselves and time with their children.

Couples who select a market approach to child care also have a division of labor between themselves in which the wife does the work of finding the care, making the arrangements, and thinking through the various possibilities (Hertz, 1986; Hochschild & Machung, 1989; Nock & Kington, 1988). Husbands become sounding boards and only marginal participants in arranging the schedules of children. In this regard, women replace themselves and, in the process, the deskilling of tasks leaves mothers with changed relationships to their children, popularly dubbed "quality time" motherhood. Men's lives remain unaltered in these cases. Of the three approaches to child care, the men in this group are the least involved in child care. Masculinity remains tied to economic achievements and career goals. The mother/child dyad is altered by the insertion of another woman or professional day care setting. However, unlike the mothering approach, women's identities remain split between family and career. Gender relations between spouses are altered only because women buy out family commitments, not because men assume more responsibility (Hertz, 1986). Further, both mothers and fathers become primarily economic providers within their children's lives. During the week, it is others who love, nurture, and care for the children, and on weekends they become a family in which the mother might resume the craft of mothering while the men continue to devote themselves to career advancement.

CONCLUSIONS

Mothering does not mean that wives stop working for pay completely (i.e., they do not necessarily devote 100% of their time to caring for their children). It does mean, however, that a wife's status as mother becomes the pivotal point around which all other statuses (e.g., employee) revolve. Indeed, for many couples the arrival of children creates a paradox: One paid worker leaves the labor force at a time when the family's expenses increase dramatically. To maintain a (pre-child) standard of living, adjustments have to be made: Either (a) the husband increases the number of hours he works (which reduces his ability to share parenting) or (b) the wife continues to work but adjusts her job or hours to accommodate the children. In both instances, the basic parameters of work and family go unchallenged: (a) couples adjust their activities to sustain a pre-child standard of living; (b) they make little claim against employers or ask them to adjust in response to family needs; (c) they invoke mothering as either cause or a correlate of their actions.

The detailed exploration of couples who embrace the mothering approach suggests that the organization of gender conflates motherhood and womanhood. Not only does motherhood supersede all other dimensions of identity, it also allows women to claim a special place in the gender system. Just as couples ignore the wife's permanent labor force employment, they minimize the husband's involvement as co-participant in caring for children. Whereas child care work may be conceptualized as the wife's turf, and therefore the language of mothering dominates these interviews, fathers are not absent from the home nor solely economic providers. The emphasis is on an ideological presentation of family life that masks the present practices and a new division of labor between spouses.

Couples who adopt the parenting approach come to reorganize their work in response to placing family first. They are challenging and restructuring the workplace even if it is only temporary: (a) These couples attempt to restructure work to accommodate their family needs by making demands on employers; (b) both women and men are restructuring their work to be active parents at the expense of job mobility, career success, and economic sacrifice; (c) in the process, they are altering the organization of gender in ways that challenge mothering as the exclusive territory of women. In short, they are crafting new ways of parental thinking about child rearing. These couples personify family values as they attempt to push workplaces to care about families as much as they care about organizational goals.

A smaller group of couples back into the parental approach—forced into this reorganization of family and two jobs due to economic constraints. Decreasing jobs will lead more men to rethink their contributions to family life and to adapt to a shrinking economy by staying home or sharing child care, or both. Although the circumstances of their fathering may not be based on their own choice, these men are potential models for a future in which job uncertainty is likely to increase. On one hand, structural workforce constraints for men may alter motherhood ideals, giving rise to equally compelling arguments for men's greater involvement in sharing the work of child care. On the other hand, these data suggest that gender ideology is a powerful countervailing force to a shrinking labor market. Husbands and wives are not willing to agree that parenting is a substitute for men's paychecks. These couples craft shared parenting models but hope that this is a temporary family/work arrangement.

The market approach in many ways resembles the mothering approach in that couples resolve work/family dilemmas by parceling out the job of mothering. They rationalize this (with ambivalence) by placing a premium on professional child care knowledge over old-fashioned folk wisdom; these couples do not make claims against employers who continue to adhere to a masculine prototype of career trajectories, creating, at best, "mommy tracks"—as the major response to family needs. In this respect, husbands and wives may have more equal marriages but do little to alter the organization of gender between men and women. In fact, they only further inequalities between women whom they hire and themselves (Hertz, 1986; Rollins, 1985).

In addition to giving substance to a typology of alternative approaches to child care, the interviews conducted in this study provide valuable insights into the process through which choices among those alternatives are made. That is, as has been noted repeatedly in recent research on changing gender ideologies and child care (e.g., Hochschild & Machung, 1989; Uttal, 1996), it is vital to better understand the meaning women give to child care practices and the division of labor between spouses. By focusing on meaning (both supportive and contradictory), we are in a better position to assess how durable an approach might be or, if it creates conflicts (e.g., between traditional and nontraditional family gender ideologies), who will have to bend to resolve the conflict. A focus on child care choices helps us see what conflicts arise, how they are given meaning, and how they are resolved.

However, recent research in this area (including Garey, 1995; McMahon, 1995; Uttal, 1996) has overlooked the fact that these choices are rarely made by women alone. Whereas this new research is conceptually interesting, by focusing on the changing meaning of motherhood without considering the possibility of similar changes for the partners of these women, we learn little about the position of the partner as a participant or facilitator for social change in the family or workplace. As I have shown in this article, husbands often play an important role in the decision process. Yet, because most prior studies have tended to neglect husbands (e.g., by not interviewing them), they cannot realistically tell us a great deal about men's involvement in child care choices at either the levels of ideology or practice or about how couples may jointly decide or be forced to alter ideology or practice.

Thus, when we look back at the three different approaches to child care described in this article, it is not surprising that in many respects the parenting approach appears the most novel. Unlike mothering and market approaches, husbands play a visible and different role in child care choice. Their involvement is visible and different because they consciously challenge a traditional familial division of labor and a traditional definition of job and career. Neither the mothering nor the market approaches challenge tradition: The former reinforces tradition and the latter merely integrates another service into the family menu of consumption.

Notes

1. In 1993, fully 60% of all women with children under 6 were in the paid labor force. For those with children aged 6 to 17 years, 75% of all women were employed, representing a marked increase from 1966 when 44% of women with children this age were employed (Hayghe & Bianchi, 1994). For women between 15 and 44 who have had a child for the year 1994, 53% were in the labor force (Bachu, 1995).

2. Day care is regulated by individual states, which vary in licensing regulations and in enforcement (Benin & Chong, 1993). In Massachusetts, lists exist by town, giving the names of all licensed providers. We have no good information on how many family day care providers are illegal. But this assumes that a family would know enough to request a list from the town or know enough to realize that not all providers are licensed.

The vast majority of U.S. workplaces do not have child care provisions. Those that do have huge wait lists and most employees must go elsewhere for day care. Families in eastern Massachusetts who use center-based care put their children into either for-profit commercial day care and nonprofit centers housed within religious sites or universities and private nonprofit centers. In this area, after kin, family day care is the most often used type of care (Marshall et al., 1988).

3. Day care is also the second largest cost all couples have in this study after mortgages or rents. In 1995, for a preschooler in full-day center-based care in the greater Boston area, couples could expect to pay $12,000 per year for one child. Infant and toddler center-based care is even more costly.

4. See Hertz (1995) for a lengthy discussion of making sense of separate interviews and the rationale for this method.

5. The majority of couples in this study have been married to their present spouses at least 10 years. For the vast majority of individuals, these are first marriages. I note that I did not select couples on length of present marriage. I did, however, deliberately seek couples who still had children at home, when possible, so that child care and labor force decisions would not be distant memories.

6. With the exception of the upper middle-class professional women in this study, few women could afford to take a 12-week unpaid leave, which Massachusetts has had for quite some years. Most women did take a leave, but they were able to afford this by using their paid vacation time and sick days. In this study, few couples had enough money to cover the paychecks of a maternity leave. No man in this study took a formal paternity leave, though some men (the parental approach) did work out various arrangements with employers.

7. Because this is a study of dual-earner couples, there are no full time stay-at-home moms at the time of the interview who clearly favor this approach to early childhood care. There are a few women in the middle class who were home for a number of years until their youngest child entered elementary school. It is also possible for professional women to decide to leave the labor force permanently and stay home. I feature, in this section, women in working-class or lower middle-class jobs because they are more likely in this study to advance that approach.

8. White working-class mothers of both husbands and wives were typically in and out of the labor force. Mothers of minority spouses were overwhelmingly always in the labor force. Historically, women of color are more likely to work outside the home (Goldin, 1990, p. 18). In this study, working-class mothers of respondents are essential to the household. In addition to the importance of income contribution to the household for middle-class mothers of respondents, using talents and degrees to advance their race was also essential (Perkins, in press).

9. Children are collectively raised by professionally trained women in kibbutzim, which today resemble full-time center-based U.S. child care. Whereas economic necessity was the catalyst for the creation of the children's collective raising, the historical belief in professional knowledge as the best route to child rearing persists. My point here is two-fold: (a) The professional approach is not always tied to two-earner families, even though in the United States case, the emergence of (and rapidly growing) family and center-based day care is tied to the inability of most families to live on one wage as the family wage eroded; and (b) mothers are not essentialized in the kibbutz as the best caregivers of their own children. Professionally trained women are seen as more knowledgeable and suitable and, until recently, expertise superseded parents' wishes. Categorically, however, women rather than men do this work, gendering the job within the kibbutz and within the U.S. context.

10. Two national surveys indicate that approximately two fifths of preschool children with mothers in the paid labor force had multiple child care arrangements (Folk & Belier, 1993; Hofferth, Brayfield, Diech, & Holcomb, 1991).

11. Hertz and Ferguson (1996) argue that for Black couples in this study, deskilling of motherhood does not promote the same kind of crisis that it does for their White professional counterparts because historically Black women have always been employed outside the home and have had to work out arrangements for the care of children that did not permit nonexclusive mothering practices (Collins, 1990). However, even in this study Black women felt at times like they were the titular wives and mothers (Hertz

& Ferguson, 1996). The woman who solved her child care problems and returned to her internship when her sister volunteered to help was a Black woman whose mother had worked her entire life. The solutions to child care for the first child often included kin for women of color, which was less likely to occur among White women whose mothers (or other immediate relatives) were not willing to leave their own lives if they did not live locally. Even among White women whose mothers lived locally, it was less often in this study that they became the primary child care providers.

12. Regardless of race, the majority of families had multiple arrangements; however, there are differences between White women and women of color in how they found child care providers and how race factors into the selection of a particular arrangement (see Hertz & Ferguson, 1996, for a full discussion).

13. See especially Uttal (1996), who is interested in the meaning mothers assign to caregivers. The women who restructure the dominant cultural ideology of the mother as primary provider conceptualize the child care provider as either a surrogate or they define the child care provider as co-mothering in a coordinated effort that the mother orchestrates between herself and the provider.

References

Bachu, A. (1995). *Fertility of American women: June 1994* (P20-482, p. XVII). Washington, DC: U.S. Bureau of the Census.

Benin, M., & Chong, Y. (1993). Childcare concerns of employed mothers. In J. Frankel (Ed.), *The employed mother and the family context* (pp. 229–244). New York: Springer.

Bernard, J. (1981). The good-provider role: Its rise and fall. *The American Psychologist, 36*, 1–12.

Bianchi, S. M., & Spain, D. (1986). *American women in transition.* New York: Russell Sage Foundation.

Bird, C. E. (1995, March). *Gender parenthood and distress: Social and economic burdens of parenting.* Paper presented at the Eastern Sociological Society annual meetings, Philadelphia.

Braverman, H. (1974). *Labor and monopoly capital: The degradation of work in the twentieth century.* New York: Monthly Review Press.

Collins, P. H. (1990). *Black feminist thought: Knowledge, consciousness and the politics of empowerment.* New York: Routledge.

Coltrane, S. (1989). Household labor and the routine production of gender. *Social Problems, 36*, 473–490.

Daniels, A. K. (1988). *Invisible careers: Women civic leaders from the volunteer world.* Chicago: University of Chicago Press.

DeVault, M. L. (1991). *Feeding the family: The social organization of caring as gendered work.* Chicago: University of Chicago Press.

Ferber, M., & O'Farrell, B. (1991). Family-oriented programs in other countries. In M. Ferber, B. O'Farrell, & L. R. Allen (Eds.), *Work and family: Policies for a changing work force* (pp. 155–178). Washington, DC: National Academy Press.

Fitz Gibbon, H. (1993, August). Bridging spheres: The work of home daycare providers. Paper presented at the American Sociological Association Meetings, Miami.

Folk, K. F., & Beller, A. H. (1993). Part-time work and childcare choices for mothers of preschool children. *Journal of Marriage and the Family, 55*, 146–157.

Garey, A. I. (1995). Constructing motherhood on the night shift: "Working mothers" as "stay at home mom." *Qualitative Sociology, 18*, 415–437.

Gerson, K. (1993). *No man's land: Men's changing commitments to family and work.* New York: Basic Books.

Gilbert, L. (1985). *Men in dual career families.* Hillsdale, NJ: Lawrence Erlbaum.

Goldin, C. (1990). *Understanding the gender gap: An economic history of American women.* New York: Oxford University Press.

Goode, W. J. (1982). Why men resist. In B. Thorne & M. Yalom (Eds.), *Rethinking the family: Some feminist questions* (pp. 131–150). New York: Longman.

Hartmann, H., & Spalter-Roth, R. (1994, March). A feminist approach to policy making for women and families. Paper prepared for the Seminar on Future Directions for American Politics and Public Policy.

Hayghe, H. V., & Bianchi, S. M. (1994). Married mothers' work patterns: The job-family compromise. *U.S. Department of Labor Bureau of Labor Statistics, Monthly Labor Review, 117*, 24–30.

Hertz, R. (1986). *More equal than others: Women and men in dual-career marriages.* Berkeley: University of California Press.

Hertz, R. (1995). Separate but simultaneous interviewing of husbands and wives: Making sense of their stories. *Qualitative Inquiry, 1,* 429–451.

Hertz, R., & Charlton, J. (1989). Making family under a shiftwork schedule: Air Force security guards and their wives. *Social Problems, 36,* 491–507.

Hertz, R., & Ferguson, F.I.T. (1996). Childcare choices and constraints in the United States: Social class, race, and the influence of family views. *Journal of Comparative Family Studies, 27,* 249–280.

Hochschild, A., (1971). Inside the clockwork of male careers. In F. Howe (Ed.), *Women and the power to change* (pp. 47–80). New York: McGraw-Hill.

Hochschild, A., & Machung, A. (1989). *The second shift.* New York: Viking.

Hodson, R., & Sullivan, T. (1990). *The social organization of work.* Belmont, CA: Wadsworth.

Hofferth, S. L., Brayfield, A., Diech, S., & Holcomb, P. (1991). *National Childcare Survey 1990* (Urban Institute Report 91–5). Washington, DC: Urban Institute Press.

Huber, J., & Spitzer, G. (1983). *Sex stratification: Children, housework, and jobs.* New York: Academic Press.

Kamerman, S. B., & Kahn, A. J. (1991). Trends, issues and possible lessons. In S. B. Kamerman & A. J. Kahn (Eds.). *Childcare, parental leave, and the under three's: Policy innovation in Europe* (pp. 201–224). Westport. CT: Auburn House.

Marshall, N., Witte, A., Nichols, L., Marx, F., Mauser, E., Laws, B., & Silverstein, B. (1988). *Caring for our commonwealth: The economics of childcare in Massachusetts.* Boston: Office for Children.

McMahon, M. (1995). *Engendering motherhood: Identity and self-transformation in women's lives.* New York: Guilford.

Moen, P. (1989). *Working parents: Transformations in gender roles and public policies in Sweden.* Madison: University of Wisconsin Press.

Nelson, M. K. (1994). Family day care providers: Dilemmas of daily practice. In N. Glenn, G. Chang, & L. R. Forcey (Eds.), *Mothering ideology, experience and agency* (pp. 181–209). New York: Routledge.

Nock, S. L., & Kington, P. W. (1988). Time with children: The impact of couples' work-time commitments. *Social Forces, 67,* 59–85.

Perkins, L. M. (in press). For the good of the race: Married African American academics, a historical perspective. In M. A. Ferber & J. W. Loeb (Eds.), *Academic couples: Problems and promises.* Urbana-Champaign and Chicago: University of Illinois Press.

Presser, H. B. (1988). Shiftwork and childcare among young dual-earner American parents. *Journal of Marriage and the Family, 50,* 133–148.

Presser, H. B., & Cain, V. (1983). Shiftwork among dual-earner couples with children. *Science, 219,* 876–879.

Rollins, J. (1985). *Between women: Domestics and their employers.* Philadelphia: Temple University Press.

Ruddick, S. (1980). Maternal thinking. *Feminist Studies, 6,* 343–367.

Slater, M., & Galzer, P. M. (1987). Prescriptions for professional survival. *Daedalus, 116,* 119–135.

Uttal, L. (1996). Custodial care, surrogate care, and coordinated care: Employed mothers and the meaning of child care. *Gender & Society, 10,* 291–311.

Wrigley, J. (1995). *Other people's children.* New York: Basic Books.

Zigler, E. (1990). Shaping child care policies and programs in America. *American Journal of Community Psychology, 18,* 183–215.

■READING 20

Transracial and Open Adoption: New Forms of Family Relationships

Mary Lyndon Shanley

Thinking about adoption is a good place to begin rethinking the ethics that should guide family formation and the relationships among family members. The dominant cultural image of family in the United States is that of a heterosexual couple, their offspring, and relatives by blood or marriage—aunts, uncles, nieces, nephews, grandparents and grandchildren. Even now when tradition is giving way to a variety of family forms, traditional discourse suggests that family ties are created "by nature." Adoption complicates this picture by allowing the severing of family ties given by nature, and the voluntary assumption of parental rights and responsibilities for children by adults who are not their biological parents. Adoption concerns both ending an existing set of family relationships or potential relationships, and establishing new ones.

Although most people regard adoption as an important way to make certain that children are well cared for, strong disagreement exists over two issues: whether children should be placed across ethnic or racial lines, and whether adoption records should be open and parties to an adoption should be able to know one another's identities or even meet. Should a Catholic child be placed only with Catholic parents, a Muslim child only with Muslim parents; should a black child be placed only with black parents, a Filipino child only with Filipino parents? Should adoptees have access to their original birth certificates, and should birth parents be able to know who adopted their children? Should the infant available for adoption be understood as an individual who can be moved without constraint from one family to another, or as someone with ties to persons outside the adoptive family—genetic kin or a racial group—that deserve some kind of social and legal recognition?[1]

Traditional policy and practice have assumed that adoptive families should resemble as closely as possible biological families, and that infants relinquished for adoption (older children are regarded differently) should be regarded as freestanding individuals with no relevant links to either their birth parents or the racial, ethnic, or religious groups to which their birth parents belong. These policies formed adoptive families to be "as if" families, that is, families in which children to all appearances might have been born to the adoptive parents. Typically, children were placed with adoptive parents with the same racial features. Birth records were sealed, and the birth parents disappeared from the child's life. The result was to ratify a family based on biological ties to both parents as the desirable norm.

Recent pressures from several sources, however, have posed serious challenges to the "as if" model of the adoptive family. In transracial adoptions the parents' and child's differences in physical appearance publicly announce that they are not biologically related. Proponents of transracial adoption argue that an infant awaiting adoption should be placed without regard to race so that neither the child nor the adoptive parents will experience discrimination.[2] opponents of transracial placement insist that being a member of a racial minority gives the child an interest in being raised by others of that minority, and gives the group an interest in raising the child.[3] The movements for unsealed adoption records and for open adoption are another challenge to the tradition of the "as if" adoptive family. Unsealed records make original birth information available to adult adoptees, and open adoption brings birth parents and adoptive parents into contact, sometimes even before the child is born. Proponents of secrecy in adoption tend to regard the infant as an individual and worry that unsealed records and open adoption place too much emphasis on biological relationships, and may impede the forging of strong bonds in the adoptive family.[4] People who advocate doing away with secrecy argue that knowledge of the genetic link between biological parents and child is part of the identity of each of them and should not be permanently hidden or inaccessible.[5] Those who favor either transracial adoption or open adoption assert that there is no overriding need to make all aspects of an adoptive family conform exactly to those of families formed biologically.

The debates on these topics have for the most part taken place quite separately. People discussing whether or not adoption records should be accessible by the adult adoptee have by and large not talked about ethnic identity and minority group rights. People discussing whether or not children should be placed for adoption across racial lines have rarely focused on the issue of sealed records. I bring these discussions into dialogue with one another because together they illuminate the values expressed—and the values excluded—when policy is based on the presumption that there is only one normative model of family. The debates over transracial and open adoption are part of a more general recognition that there are a number of kinds of families in which parents (or one parent) and child are not genetically related, including blended families, heterosexual families that use donated eggs or sperm, and gay and lesbian families. Juxtaposing these discussions also brings to light, and suggests ways to ameliorate, the effects of gender and racial hierarchy that have marked aspects of adoption and the use of reproductive technologies alike.

Transracial adoption pits values of integration or assimilation against multiculturalism, and individuality against racial-ethnic community.[6] Disputes about secrecy, for their part, pit values of privacy against those of knowledge and freedom of information. All of these values are fundamental to pluralist democracy in the United States. The complex moral and policy issues involved in open and transracial adoption are, in Janet Farrell Smith's words, "not resolvable without remainder." That is, in situations involving "a complex set of conflicting practical demands, each tied to a set of apparently morally reasonable supports, taking up one of these positions will not nullify moral demands of the alternatives not taken."[7] But in the real world where all of us must act, we cannot avoid judgments and policy choices that will favor one side or the other: the law will either prohibit or allow the disclosure of identifying information about the parties to an adoption; and the law will either prohibit or allow the placement of children across racial lines.

My own thinking is that both unsealed records and transracial adoption allow greater room for expression of the values of liberty, equality, relationship, and care in the functioning of families than did the older approach. In developing new family policies, it is crucial to place children at the center of analysis, and to remember that children's need for care requires social policy that supports parents in their caregiving efforts.[8] By challenging the dominance of the norm of the biological family, transracial adoption and unsealed records represent an opening for a plurality of forms that I see as necessary for a more humane family policy. Developing an ethical basis for family law and policy requires carefully weighing multiple values and interests, not adhering to a single principle alone; that balancing guides this discussion of adoption and of the topics that follow.

TRADITIONAL ADOPTION POLICY AND PRACTICE

While new reproductive technologies have made the separation of genetic and social parenthood seem like a relatively recent development, legal convention, and not biology alone, has always determined who would enjoy status as a legal parent. As Thomas Hobbes pointed out, while maternity could be observed at the time of birth, knowledge of paternity depended on the not always reliable word of the mother. Bastardy laws proclaimed that biological fathers would be recognized as legal fathers only if they were married to the mother of their child. Not all women who gave birth were regarded as the legal mothers of their offspring: slave mothers (along with slave fathers) did not have parental rights.

The creation of legal adoption in the mid-nineteenth century was a radical innovation because it dissolved the "natural" (blood) ties that bound families together and replaced them with "artificial" (legal) ties of kinship.[9] In the American understanding of kinship, recounted by anthropologist David Schneider, "family" means biological parents and their children, and "[t]he relationship which is 'real' or 'true' or 'blood' or 'by birth' can never be severed, whatever its legal position. Legal rights may be lost, but the blood relationship cannot be lost. It is culturally defined as being an objective fact of nature, of fundamental significance and capable of having profound effects, and its nature cannot be terminated or changed.'[10] Although children were sometimes adopted by members of their extended family, the primary model of formal adoption was "stranger adoption." Statutes allowing legal adoption undermined the traditional understanding of the indestructible and involuntary nature of family bonds by severing the legal tie between original parents and their offspring and creating a new legal tie by convention and choice.

Despite the fact that adoptive families were created "artificially" by a legal procedure, however, from the mid-nineteenth to the mid-twentieth century most adoptive families gave the *appearance* of having resulted from sexual relations between the parents. Parents were of the age to have borne the child, and of the same race and often the same religion as the biological parents. The dissolution of the child's legal ties to its original parents made it possible for the adoptive family to simulate a biological family, "reflecting the deeply embedded notion in the ideology of American kinship that the only 'real' relation is a blood relation and, by extension, the only experience of authentic identity is bestowed by blood ties."[11]

Adoption law assumed that the family of which the child would become a member would have a particular configuration. There would be two (and only two) parents, of different sexes, and of the same race as the child. The sealing of adoption records reflected the legal assumption that parenthood is an exclusive status that can belong only to two persons at a time with respect to any one child. Underlying the policy of placing children with adoptive parents of the same race was the social fact that interracial marriage has been the exception rather than the rule in the United States (only in 1967 did the Supreme Court rule that state prohibitions on interracial marriage violated the Constitution). Adoption laws and policies were designed to make adoptive families imitate what was seen as a norm given by nature.

The creation of an "as-if" adoptive family incorporated a model of the individual and social ties consonant with the assumptions of liberal individualism and liberal political theory. Infant adoption, in particular, seemed to rest on the notion that at least for a brief period of time after birth, the child could be regarded as an individual who could be moved from one family to another and expected to take on an identity shaped by the roles, status, and obligations that membership in the new family entailed. Legal discourse about adoption focused on the right of a child to a permanent home, and the obligation of the state to protect children by placing them with adults who were financially and emotionally capable of providing care. The intermediary role performed by the adoption agency, which accepted the child from the birth parents and then placed her with adoptive parents, reflected the fact that for a moment the child was a ward of the state not bound to any other specific persons, an individual awaiting the creation of lasting family ties by an adoption decree.

Society dealt with unmarried motherhood differently depending on the race of the mother. Prior to World War II, adoption was not common among whites in the United States.[12] During the first two decades of the twentieth century, a woman who bore a child outside of marriage was considered a "fallen woman," shamefully weak or immoral. A child born out of wedlock was stigmatized, labeled "illegitimate" and a "child of sin;" and considered likely to grow up to be a delinquent. Society expected the mother to raise the child herself as punishment for her transgression and as a "lesson" to other women who might be tempted to engage in illicit (that is unmarried) sex. In the 1930s, extramarital pregnancy continued to be socially condemned, but the advice about what to do changed. An unmarried white woman was now counseled to hide her pregnancy, give the child up for adoption, and never see the child again. It was hoped that by keeping the adoption secret she could "get on with her life" by marrying and eventually bearing "legitimate" children.

In the United States, blacks' experiences and attitudes toward adoption have typically been different from whites. Both during and after slavery, black children who were orphaned or separated from their parents were often taken in by other families. There is a long history of informal adoption in black communities with roots in some West African cultural practices.[13] By contrast, to formally relinquish a child for adoption because of an unwed pregnancy was rare. Because of the rape and sexual exploitation of black women by their white masters during slavery, black communities have tended not to stigmatize black children born out of wedlock.[14] Many black infants were raised by members of their mother's extended family, often without being legally adopted. Raising such a child was regarded not only as caring for an individual child, but as contributing to the well-being of the black community. Black women who bore children out of wedlock were labeled by white society as loose or immoral, and they were not offered the services of maternity homes and adoption agencies to help them in their pregnancies and with the placement of their children. In addition, many black families could not meet some of the criteria agencies used (for example, stipulating family income or number of bedrooms in the house) to select adoptive homes.

After World War II, the stigma and embarrassment about sexual or reproductive inadequacy still haunted infertile couples, while the stigma attached to out of wedlock pregnancy for the white mother became more complex. Some social workers (influenced by psychoanalytic theory and by the scarcity of newborn white infants to adopt) began to shift their view of the unwed mother from someone morally deficient and incorrigible to someone caught in the throes of a psychological conflict that led her (unconsciously) to seek to bear a child.[15] By and large the stigma that had been attached to white children born out of wedlock disappeared, and they began to be regarded as innocent and desirable. This acceptance did not extend to the black mother or infant, however.

> Public and private agencies and government policies viewed both black and white women as breeders, but with a major and consequential distinction. The former were viewed as socially unproductive breeders, constrainable only by punitive, legal sanctions. . . . White unwed mothers in contrast were viewed as socially productive breeders whose babies, unfortunately conceived out of wedlock, could offer infertile couples their only chance to construct proper families.[16]

Race significantly influenced the status of birth mothers and the estimation of their mothering capabilities.

These factors contributed to a change in adoption practices meant to make it easier both to relinquish and to adopt white infants. During the 1940s many jurisdictions began to seal adoption records, making it impossible for *anyone* to discover the identity of the biological parents of an adopted child.[17] E. Wayne Carp has argued that what he calls the move from confidentiality (records closed to all but "the parties of interest," i.e. birth parents, adoptive parents, and child) to secrecy (records inaccessible to everyone except by a court order) was in response to a complex set of factors, including the adoptive parents' fear that the birth parents might reappear, unwed mothers' desire to avoid social condemnation, and social workers' efforts to "increase their own influence and power, and bolster social work professionalism."[18] Adoptive parents pushed for secrecy to avoid the stigma of infertility and the possibility that the birth parents might reappear. Unwed mothers sought secrecy in order to be spared social condemnation. Seeking to avoid an investigation of their life circumstances and the six-month wait for a placement that were often standard in state agencies, unwed mothers turned to private, unlicensed adoption agencies that promised them privacy. As a result, state agencies changed their procedures and urged legislatures to mandate that adoption records be sealed.

The sealed records' concealment of the child's biological parents smoothed the way for the construction of an "as-if" biological family by adoptive parents "who, by physical appearance and age could have conceived the infant"[19] Various secretive practices developed that promoted the construction of the "as if" family. Unwed white pregnant women would often leave home, telling friends and neighbors that they were traveling or visiting relatives, and stay in homes for unwed mothers during their pregnancies. Upon the birth of the child, the birth mother signed a document in which she irrevocably severed her rights and responsibilities to the child. The adoption agency took custody of the child and attempted to match the characteristics of the adoptive and original parents. Statutes and court decisions "used tests of adoptive parental fitness, and strict eligibility standards to make the artificial family approximate the legal ideal of a proper natural one in age, race, affection, and legal authority."[20] When the adoption became final, usually after a probationary period of six months to a year, the court sealed the original birth certificate and adoption records and entered into the public record a new birth certificate, which contained only the names of the adoptive parents. The sealed records could be opened only by court order after a showing of "good cause." (In some states, a petitioner could establish good cause by demonstrating medical necessity; in others, a strongly felt psychological need to discover one's genetic identity came to constitute cause.) The general exclusion of single persons and of gay and lesbian couples from the pool of adoptive parents also made the adoptive family resemble a biological family.

These practices in both U.S. and international adoptions have become known as the "clean break" approach to adoption, in which the integration of a child into an adoptive family "is premised on the complete severance of ties with the biological family." In an intercountry adoption, the clean break model also involves the child's assumption of a new "national identity—as 'Swedish' or 'American' rather than 'South Korean,' 'Colombian,' or 'Chinese.' "[21] Paradoxically, as Barbara Yngvesson notes, the clean break model, which incorporates an individualistic view of the child who can be moved from one family to another across all kinds of cultural and geopolitical lines, also implies that the ties between child and birth parent are so strong that unless the child becomes "parentless" (for example by being legally abandoned), new ties cannot be created.[22]

Many factors, both sociological and ideological, have in recent years challenged the idea that an adoptive family has to simulate a biological family, or that an infant voluntarily relinquished for adoption is a "parentless" child. One consequence of the relatively low number of white babies available for adoption, due in part to contraception and abortion, and in part to the decreasing stigmatization of unwed motherhood, has been the increasing openness of many people's efforts to find healthy infants through ads or public notices seeking women interested in placing their babies for adoption. Single persons and gay and lesbian couples have found ways to adopt children. Some people have adopted across racial lines, making the constructed nature of at least some adoptive families readily visible. Some people have entered into open adoptions, in which members of both the family of origin and the adoptive family are known to everyone involved.

The variety of new forms of families being created through open and transracial adoptions, then, has thrown into question the traditional assumptions about adoption. In the case of nonsecret or open adoption, the birth parents' and the child's right to know one another's identities is at issue; in transracial adoption, both the child's right to a particular cultural identity and the group's right to raise "its own" are at issue. I bring the policy debates over secrecy vs. nonsecrecy and same-race vs. transracial adoption together here because both raise the question of whether or to what extent the law should treat an infant available for adoption as an autonomous individual in need of a family, or as an individual in part defined by relationships to persons or groups beyond the adoptive family.

THE "AS IF" ADOPTIVE FAMILY: NONSECRECY AND OPEN ADOPTION

Both open adoption and transracial adoption challenge the notion that adoptive families should mirror the nuclear family composed of a heterosexual couple and their biological offspring. David Schneider has pointed out how strongly the possibility of having biological offspring a couple could raise together influenced the American understandings both of "family" and of legitimate sexual relations.

> Sexual intercourse between persons who are not married is fornication and improper; between persons who are married but not to each other is adultery and is wrong; between blood relatives is incest and is prohibited; between persons of the same sex is homosexuality and is wrong; with animals is sodomy and is prohibited; with one's self is masturbation and wrong; and with parts of the body other than the genitalia themselves is wrong. All of these are defined as "unnatural sex acts" and are morally, and in some cases, legally, wrong in American culture.[23]

Schneider might have noted that intercourse across racial lines was also prohibited by both cultural and legal rules, on the grounds that it was "unnatural" and an offense to both custom and morality. Interracial marriage was a crime in some states until the Supreme Court struck down antimiscegenation statutes in *Loving v. Virginia* in 1967. As late as 1984, Florida argued before the Supreme Court that a divorced white woman should be denied custody of her white child because the mother's new marriage to a black man would create social difficulties for the child as she grew up. The Court rebuffed Florida's reasoning, saying that "The question . . . is whether the reality of private biases and the possible injury they might inflict are permissible considerations for removal of an infant child from the custody of its natural mother. . . . The Constitution cannot control such prejudices [against interracial marriage], but neither can it tolerate them."[24] Even as the Court rejected any legal validity to the notion that families had to be racially homogeneous, it acknowledged the power of such an idea in Americans' imaginations and social practice.

The primacy of blood ties in many Americans' understanding of family deeply affected the practice of secrecy in adoption. Initially, adoption records were kept confidential in order to protect the privacy of all parties, particularly the birth mother, from outsiders; confidentiality was not meant to block the exchange of nonidentifying information among parties to the adoption. Carol Sanger has pointed out the stigma attached to *all* birth mothers, married and unmarried alike, who decided not to raise their children or who were forced by circumstance or social pressure not to do so.[25] The shame attached to unmarried women bearing children did great harm to individual women and children and played a large role in the subordination of women as a group. Women were often "ruined" by an act from which men might walk away unscathed. Fear of such dire social consequences increased the pressure on women to marry and surrounded premarital sexual activity with fear and anxiety. The practice of hiding one's pregnancy and childbirth in order to resume a "normal" life was the best many women could do in the face of these social pressures, but the toll such secrecy exacted was tremendous.

Open adoption developed in response to the realization of white birth mothers that "the agencies needed them, rather than birth mothers needing the agencies," and it has received considerable support from the adoptees' rights movement. This movement is made up of adult adoptees and others who contend that to be denied access to knowledge of one's genetic history may impede the development of a person's identity and sense of self-worth. In a typical formulation, Vermont state senator Richard Sears (Democrat—Bennington), who was adopted as a child, argued in favor of a proposed statute to open

Vermont's adoption records that adoptees "are the only people in the nation who are denied the basic right of knowing who they are."[26] Most people take knowledge of their genetic origins for granted; members of the adoptees' rights movement maintain that access to such information is a basic civil and human right.

Notwithstanding the development of the practice of open adoption and pressure from various quarters to abandon sealed records, not everyone agrees that *all* adult adoptees should have access to their adoption records. In their eyes, the right of the birth parents to anonymity is very strong and may override the adoptee's right to know the identity of his or her birth parents, particularly if the birth records were sealed at the time of the adoption. State laws vary quite a bit in their provisions for disclosure and secrecy.[27] Some advocates of secrecy worry that if birth parents cannot be guaranteed confidentiality, some birth mothers will choose to terminate the pregnancy or retain custody. Even birth parents who might go through with adoption will face the dilemma of acknowledging the pregnancy and adoption to a future spouse and children, and some may live in dread of being contacted by the grown child later in life.

It seems to me, however, that except in cases in which knowledge that she had once borne and relinquished a child would put a woman in grave danger, the adult adoptee's right to know his or her specific history overrides the birth parents' right to privacy (particularly eighteen years after the birth). The original parents are under no obligation to meet their offspring, much less develop a social relationship (although they may do so if they all agree to); indeed, original parents may get legal protection from attempts at contact that are harassing or threatening.[28] The adoptee does not have a right to an actual social relationship with the original parents; but adult adoptees should not be deprived of the information they need to construct a coherent story of origin, an explanation of how they came into the world.

Editor's Note: *Notes for this reading can be found in the original source.*

8 *Childhood*

■ READING 21

Revolutions in Children's Lives

Donald Hernandez, with David E. Myers

INTRODUCTION

Revolutionary changes in the life course, the economy, and society have transformed childhood, and the resources available to children, during the past 150 years. A revolutionary decline in the number of siblings in the families of children occurred during the past 100 years. Historically, a substantial minority of children did not spend their entire childhood in a two-parent family, but this will expand to a majority for children born during the past decade. The role of grandparents in the home, as surrogate parents filling the gap left by absent parents, has been important but limited during at least the past half century.

The family economy was revolutionized twice during the past 150 years, first as fathers and then mothers left the home to spend much of the day away at jobs as family breadwinners. With these changes, with instability in fathers' work, and with increasing divorce and out-of-wedlock childbearing, never during the past half century were a majority of children born into "Ozzie and Harriet" families in which the father worked full-time year-round, the mother was a full-time homemaker, and all of the children were born after the parents' only marriage.

Corresponding revolutions in child care occurred first as children over age 5 and then as younger children began to spend increasing amounts of time in formal educational or other settings in the care of someone other than their parents. Since today's children are tomorrow's parents, the spread of universal compulsory education led to revolutionary increases in the educational attainments of parents during the past half century, to the benefit of successive cohorts of children. But as opportunities to complete at least a high school education became substantially more equal for children during the past century, opportunities to go beyond high school and complete at least one year of college became less equal.

The absolute income levels of families increased greatly after the Great Depression and World War II through the 1960s but have changed comparatively little since then. Meanwhile, childhood poverty and economic inequality declined after World War II through the 1960s, then increased mainly during the 1980s. Most poor children throughout the era lived in working-poor families, and only a minority of poor children were fully welfare-dependent.

FAMILY COMPOSITION

Because siblings are the family members who are usually closest in age, needs, and activities, they may be among a child's most important companions and most important competitors for family resources. The typical child born in 1890 lived, as an adolescent, in a family in which there were about 6.6 siblings, but the typical child born in 1994 is expected to live in a family that is only one-third as large—with 1.9 children.

About one-half of this decline in family size had occurred by 1945, and the typical child born during that year lived in a family that had 2.9 siblings. Subsequently, during the postwar baby boom that occurred between 1945 and 1957, the annual number of births jumped by 55 percent (from 2.7 to 4.3 million births per year) and the Total Fertility Rate jumped by 52 percent (from 2.4 to 3.7 births per woman), but the family size of the typical adolescent increased by only 17 percent (from 2.9 to 3.4 siblings).

Changes in the distribution of adolescents by family size tell a similar story. The proportion living in families in which there are 5 or more siblings is expected to decline from 77 percent for children born in 1890 to only 6 percent for children born in 1994. Again, about one-half of the decline had occurred for children born in 1945, 32 percent of whom as adolescents lived in families in which there were 5 or more children, and again the increase during the baby boom was comparatively small at about 6 percentage points. At the opposite extreme, the proportion of adolescents living in families in which there are only 1–2 children is expected to increase from only 7 percent for children born in 1890 to 57 percent for children born in 1994. Among children born in 1945, about 30 percent lived in such small families, and this fell by 10 percentage points to 20 percent during the baby boom.

Historically, black children have tended to live in families in which there were substantially larger numbers of siblings than did white children, but trends in the family sizes of both black and white children were generally similar between the Civil War and 1925. Then for about 20 years, however, the racial gap expanded, apparently because the comparatively large decline in tuberculosis and venereal disease led to increased family sizes among blacks. Since about 1945, the number of siblings in the families of both black and white children have been converging.

Among children born in 1994, family-size differences between blacks and whites, as well as between Hispanic children (of any race) and non-Hispanic children, are expected to essentially vanish. Of the racial convergence in family size that is expected to occur for children born between 1945 and 1994, more than two-thirds had occurred among children born in 1973 who are now about 18 years old and approaching college age.

What are the consequences of this decline for children? First, children with larger numbers of siblings have greater opportunities to experience caring, loving sibling companionship. Hence, the family-size revolution drastically reduced the number of siblings who were available as potential companions during childhood and through adulthood. On the other hand, childhood family size appears to have little effect on psychological well-being later during adulthood. But because children growing up in large families—especially families with 5 or more siblings—tend to complete fewer years of schooling than do children from smaller families, they are less likely to enter high-status occupations with high incomes when they reach adulthood. Hence, the family-size revolution led to greatly improved opportunities for educational, occupational, and economic advancement among successive cohorts of children. . . .

Most children depend mainly on the parents in their homes for financial support and day-to-day care. Hence, it would be surprising if important differences in current welfare and future life chances were not found when children who do spend their entire childhood in a two-parent family are compared with those who do not.

In the short run, for many children the separation or divorce of their parents brings a sharp drop in family income and substantial psychological trauma. When the lone parent in a one-parent family marries to form a stepfamily, however, the children often experience a sharp jump in family income. Still, children in stepfamilies are more likely to have a low family income than are children in intact two-parent families. In addition, since one parent is absent from the home in one-parent families, children in these families may receive substantially less day-to-day care and attention from parents than do children in two-parent families.

Children in one-parent families are more likely, on average, to be exposed to parental stress than are children in two-parent families, more likely to exhibit behavioral problems, more likely to receive or need professional psychological help, more likely to perform poorly in school, and more likely to have health problems. In addition, on average, stepchildren are virtually indistinguishable from children in one-parent families in their chances of having behavioral, psychological, academic, and health problems.

Over the long run, children who do not spend most of their childhood in an intact two-parent family tend, as they reach adulthood, to complete fewer years of schooling, enter lower-status occupations, and earn lower incomes than do adults who did spend most of their childhood in an intact two-parent family. Some children from one-parent families may finish fewer years of school because fathers who can afford to provide financial support in college do not in fact do so when the child reaches college age. Many of the disadvantages associated with living in a one-parent family may result from the low family incomes of many children who live in such families.

In view of the potential disadvantages of not living with two parents, how typical has it become for children not to spend their entire childhood in a two-parent family? Historically, about 90 percent of newborn children under age 1 have lived with both biological parents. Still, between the late 1800s and 1950, a large and nearly stable minority of about 33 percent spent part of their childhood before age 18 with fewer than two parents in the home. Little change occurred during the first half of the twentieth century, despite the rise in parental separation and divorce, because this rise was counterbalanced by declining parental mortality.

Since about 1950 the link between marriage and the bearing and rearing of children has loosened. Because of the rise in out-of-wedlock childbearing that occurred between 1950 and 1980, the proportion of newborn children under age 1 who did not live with two parents doubled, climbing from 9 to 19 percent. Combined with the rise in separation and divorce, the proportion of children who will ever live with fewer than two parents is expected to increase from about 33 percent for the era between the late 1800s and 1950 to about 55–60 percent of children born in 1980.

Since at least the Civil War, white and black children have been quite different in their chances of spending part of their childhood living with fewer than two parents. For example, in 1940 the proportion of newborn children under age 1 who did not live with two parents was about 25 percent for blacks, compared with 7 percent for whites. Historically, it appears that for children born between the late 1800s and 1940, a majority of blacks (55–60 percent) spent part of their childhood in families in which there were fewer than two parents. For whites born between the late 1800s and 1940, a minority (but a large minority of approximately 29–33 percent) spent part of their childhood in families in which there were fewer than two parents. . . .

FAMILY WORK AND EDUCATION

As children were experiencing a revolutionary decline in family size and a large increase in one-parent family living, they also were experiencing two distinct transformations in parents' work and living arrangements. On the family farm, economic production, parenting, and child care were combined, as parents and children worked together to support themselves. This changed with the Industrial Revolution, however. Fathers became breadwinners who took jobs located away from home in order to support the family, and mothers became homemakers who remained at home to personally care for the children as well as to clean, cook, and perform other domestic functions for the family. Following the Great Depression, parents' work and the family economy were again transformed. Today most children live either in dual-earner families in which both parents work at jobs away from home or in one-parent families.

More specifically, between about 1840 and 1920 the proportion of children who lived in two-parent farm families fell from at least two-thirds to about one-third, while the proportion who lived in breadwinner-homemaker families climbed from 15–20 percent to 50 percent. Although a majority of children lived in breadwinner-homemaker families between about 1920 and 1970, this figure never reached 60 percent.

In fact, even during the heyday of the breadwinner-homemaker family, a second transformation in parents' work was under way. Between 1920 and 1970, as the proportion of children living in two-parent farm families continued to fall, the proportion who had breadwinner mothers working at jobs that were located away from home increased, and after 1960 the proportion living in one-parent families with their mothers also increased. The rise in the proportion of children living in dual-earner or one-parent families was extremely rapid, since the increase from 15–20 percent to 50 percent required only 30 years—about one-third as long as the time required for the same rise in the breadwinner-homemaker family to take place.

By 1980, nearly 60 percent of children lived in dual-earner or one-parent fami-lies, by 1989 about 70 percent lived in such families, and by the year 2000, only 7 years from now, the proportion of children living in such families may exceed 80 percent. Equally striking is the fact that even between 1920 and 1970, only a minority of chil-dren aged 0–17 lived in families that conformed to the mid-twentieth century ideal por-trayed, for example, on the "Ozzie and Harriet" television program (that is, a nonfarm breadwinner-homemaker family in which the father works full-time year-round, the mother is a full-time homemaker, and all of the children were born after the parents' only marriage).

In fact, only a minority of newborn children under age 1 lived in such families in any year between 1940 and 1980. During these years a large majority of newborns (75–86 percent) did live with employed fathers, but only 42–49 percent lived with two parents in families in which the father worked full-time year-round and all of the children were born after the parents' only marriage. Still smaller proportions of newborns lived with two parents in families in which the father worked full-time year-round, all of the chil-dren were born after the parents' only marriage, and the mother was a full-time home-maker. Between 1940 and 1960, 41–43 percent of newborns lived in such families, and with rising mothers' labor-force participation this fell to only 27 percent in 1980. By age 17, children were even less likely, historically, to live in such families, as the proportion declined from 31 to 15 percent between 1940 and 1980.

These estimates imply that for children born between 1940 and 1960, an average of 65–70 percent of their childhood years were spent in a family situation that did not conform to the mid-twentieth century ideal. Looking ahead, it appears that children born in 1980 may spend an average of 80 percent of their childhood in families that do not conform to this ideal. In addition, children who lived on farms were likely, historically, to experience a parental death or other parental loss, or the economic insecurity associ-ated with drought, crop disease, collapse of commodity prices, and similar catastrophes. Consequently, it is clear that neither historically nor during the industrial era have a ma-jority of children experienced the family stability, the economic stability, and the home-making mother that was idealized in mid-twentieth century America.

For white children, the chances of living in an idealized "Ozzie and Harriet," bread-winner-homemaker family were only slightly larger than for children as a whole. Among newborn black children at least since 1940, however, no more than 25 percent lived in such idealized families, and this figure fell to only 8 percent for black newborns in 1980. By the end of childhood, among blacks born in 1922, only 15 percent still lived in such families by age 17, and among blacks born in 1962, only 3 percent still lived in such families by age 17. Looking across the entire childhood experience of black children, the average pro-portion of childhood years not spent in idealized "Ozzie and Harriet" families increased from about 70–80 percent for the 1920s cohort to at least 95 percent for the 1980s cohort.

In 1980 Hispanic children (of any race) were roughly midway between black and white children in their chances of living in an idealized "Ozzie and Harriet" family. Only 10 percent of Hispanic 17-year-olds (of any race) lived in such families in 1980, only 21 percent of Hispanic newborns (of any race) lived in such families in 1980, and among these newborns more than 85 percent of the childhood years will be spent in families that do not conform to the mid-twentieth century ideal.

With these two historic transformations in parents' work and living arrangements, children simultaneously experienced two revolutionary increases in nonparental care, first among those over age 5 and then among younger children.

As farming became overshadowed by an industrial economy in which fathers worked for pay at jobs located away from home, compulsory school attendance and child labor laws were enacted to ensure that children were protected from unsafe and unfair working conditions, that they were excluded from jobs that were needed for adults, and that they received at least a minimal level of education. Also, as time passed increasing affluence allowed families to support themselves without child labor, and higher educational attainments became increasingly necessary in order to obtain jobs that offered higher pay and higher social prestige.

Hence, in 1870 only 50 percent of children aged 5–19 were enrolled in school, and their attendance averaged only 21 percent of the total days in the year. But 70 years later, in 1940, 95 percent of children aged 7–13 were enrolled in school, 79 percent of children aged 14–17 were enrolled in school, and the average attendance amounted to 42 percent of the days in the year. Even as mothers were increasingly viewed as full-time child care providers and homemakers, the need for them to act as full-time child care providers was diminishing, both because of the revolutionary decline in family size and because of the quadrupling in the amount of nonparental child care provided by teachers in school.

Since a full adult workday amounted to about 8 hours per day, 5 days per week (plus commuting time) after 1940, a full adult work year amounted to about 65 percent of the days in a year. But by 1940, school days of 5–6 hours (plus commuting time) amounted to about two-thirds of a full workday for about two-thirds of a full work year. As of 1940, then, childhood school attendance had effectively released mothers from personal child care responsibilities for a time period equivalent to about two-thirds of a full-time adult work year, except for the few years before children entered elementary school.

By reducing the time required for a mother's most important homemaker responsibility—the personal care of her children—this first child care revolution contributed to the large increase in mothers' labor-force participation after 1940, not only for school-age children but for preschoolers as well. Increasing mothers' labor-force participation and the rise in one-parent families then ushered in the second child-care revolution for preschool children aged 0–5. Between 1940 and 1989, the proportion of children who had no specific parent at home full-time tripled for school-age children (from roughly 22 to 66 percent) and quadrupled for preschoolers (from about 13 percent to about 52 percent).

Today these proportions are probably fairly typical for children in industrial countries, since by 1980 labor-force participation rates for women who were in main parenting ages in the United States were average when compared with other industrial countries. For example, the labor-force participation rates for women aged 30–39 were 70–90 percent in Sweden, Denmark, and Norway, 60–70 percent in the United States, France, and Canada, and 45–60 percent in the United Kingdom, West Germany, Italy, Belgium, Switzerland, Australia, and Japan.[1]

---

[1]Data from the U.S. Bureau of the Census for the following years: 1985 (Norway), 1984 (France), 1983 (Sweden), 1982 (U.S.), 1981 (Canada, Denmark, United Kingdom, Italy, Australia), 1980 (Japan, West Germany, Switzerland), 1977 (Belgium).

The increase in the proportion of preschoolers who had no specific parent at home full-time effectively reduced the amount of parental time that was potentially available to care for preschoolers and effectively increased the need for nonparental care. Yet the proportion of preschoolers who had a relative other than a parent in the home who might act as a surrogate parent also declined. For preschoolers living in dual-earner families, the proportion with a potential surrogate parent in the home declined from 19–20 percent in 1940 to only 4–5 percent in 1980. Meanwhile, the proportion of preschoolers living in one-parent families in which there was a potential surrogate parent in the home declined from 51–57 to 20–25 percent.

Time-use studies of nonemployed mothers indicate that the actual time devoted to child care as a primary activity probably increased by about 50–100 percent between 1926–1935 and 1943 and may have increased a bit more during the 20 years that followed. But between the 1960s and the early 1980s, the average amount of time that all mothers of preschoolers devoted to child care as a primary activity declined because an increasing number of mothers were employed outside the home and because employed mothers of preschoolers devote about one-half as much time to child care as a primary activity as do nonemployed mothers (1.2 vs. 2.2 hours per day during the mid-1970s).

By 1989, then, about 48 percent of preschoolers had a specific nonemployed parent at home on a full-time basis (usually the mother), another 12 percent had dual-earner parents who personally provided for their preschoolers' care (often by working different hours or days), and the remaining 40 percent were cared for by someone other than their parents for a large portion of time. Since the proportion of preschoolers who have a specific parent at home full-time declined from about 80 to about 48 percent during the 29 years between 1960 and 1989, we appear to be halfway through the preschool child-care revolution, and we are probably within 30–40 years of its culmination and will then see a very large proportion of preschool children spending increasingly more time in the care of someone other than their parents.

Overall, black children in 1940 were 24 percentage points less likely to have a specific parent at home full-time than were white children, but this racial gap had narrowed to 12 percentage points by 1980. Essentially all of this convergence occurred among older children, since the racial gap among adolescents declined from 27 to 6 percentage points, while the racial gap among preschoolers remained nearly constant at 18–23 percentage points. In 1980, about one-half of the racial gap among preschoolers was accounted for by differences in parental employment, and about one-half was accounted for by differences in the proportion of preschoolers who have no parent in the home.

Also in 1980, Hispanic children (of any race) were generally quite similar to non-Hispanic white children in their parental working and living arrangements, except that Hispanics (of any race) were somewhat more likely to live in one-parent families in which the parent was not employed and somewhat less likely to live in dual-earner families in which at least one parent worked part-time.

The importance of mothers' employment in contributing to family income is discussed below, but what other consequences do mothers' employment and nonparental care have for preschoolers? Past research suggests, broadly, that mothers' employment and nonparental care are neither necessarily nor pervasively harmful to preschoolers. This research also suggests that nonparental care is not a form of maternal deprivation, since children can and do form attachments to multiple caregivers if the number of caregivers is limited, the child-caregiver relationships are long-lasting, and the caregivers are responsive to the individual child.

Available evidence also suggests that the quality of care that children receive is important, and that some children, especially those from low-income families, are in double jeopardy from psychological and economic stress at home as well as exposure to low-quality nonparental child care. Additional potentially beneficial and detrimental effects of mothers' employment and nonparental care for preschoolers have been identified, but most of the results must be viewed as preliminary and tentative. Overall, research on the consequences of nonparental care for preschoolers is itself in its infancy, and much remains to be done.

The first revolution in child care—that is, the advent of nearly universal elementary and high school enrollment between ages 6 and 17—as well as large increases in high school and college graduation, led in due course to a revolutionary increase in parents' education. For example, among children born during the 1920s, the proportions whose fathers completed only 0–8 years of schooling or 4 or more years of high school were 73 and 15 percent, respectively, but these proportions were nearly reversed (at 5 and 85 percent, respectively) among children born only 60 years later during the 1980s. For the same children, those with fathers who had completed 4 or more or 1 or more years of college climbed from 4 and 7 percent, respectively, to 28 and 47 percent. Increases were generally similar for mothers' education, except for a somewhat smaller rise in the proportion with mothers who were college-educated.

Black children, as well as white children, experienced revolutionary increases in parents' education, but blacks continued to lag behind whites, as the black disadvantage effectively shifted higher on the educational ladder but constricted substantially in size. For example, among the 1920s cohort, the maximum racial disadvantages of 38–43 percentage points were in the proportions whose fathers or mothers had completed at least 7–8 years of schooling. But among the 1980s cohort, the maximum racial gaps were only two-fifths as large at 15–16 percentage points, and were in the proportions whose fathers or mothers had completed 13–15 years of schooling.

Measured in terms of the number of decades by which blacks lagged behind whites, the 2–3 decades by which black children born during the 1940s and the 1950s lagged behind whites in having parents who received at least 8 years of education had essentially vanished for the 1970s cohort. But despite a temporary racial convergence among children born during the 1960s and the 1970s, black children born during the 1980s, like black children born during the 1940s and the 1950s, lagged about 2–3 decades behind whites in the proportion whose fathers and mothers had completed at least 4 years of college.

Old-family Hispanic children (of any race) born during the 1960s and the 1970s were fairly similar to non-Hispanic black children in their parents' educational attainments. But first-generation Hispanic children (of any race) were much less likely (by 32–42 percentage points) to have parents who had completed at least 8 years of schooling, presumably because many of their parents had immigrated from countries in which the general educational levels were much lower than those in the United States.

This revolution in parents' education, and continuing differentials by race and Hispanic origin, are important for children both in the short run and throughout their adult years. In the short run, parents with higher educational attainments are more likely to have higher incomes than those with lower educational attainments. In the long run, children whose parents have comparatively high educational attainments also tend, when they reach adulthood, to complete more years of education and thus obtain jobs that offer higher social prestige and income.

Consequently, successive cohorts of children benefited from increasing parents' education both because it contributed to the large increases in family income for children that occurred between World War II and approximately 1970, as described below, and because it contributed to increasing educational levels among children and therefore to higher prestige and income for successive cohorts of children when they reached adulthood. At the same time, the continuing disadvantage of black and Hispanic children (of any race) in their parents' educational attainments tends to limit their current family incomes and their future chances of achieving occupational and economic success during adulthood. . . .

FAMILY INCOME, POVERTY, AND WELFARE DEPENDENCE

Family income, another major feature of family origins, also has important consequences for children's current well-being and future life chances. On a day-to-day basis, whether children live in material deprivation, comfort, or luxury depends mainly on their family's income level. Of particular interest are children in low-income families because they may experience marked deprivation in such areas as nutrition, clothing, housing, or healthcare.

During the 1940s, 1950s, and 1960s, the absolute income levels of American families increased greatly, as real median family income jumped by 35–45 percent per decade, bringing corresponding decreases in absolute want. Associated with this rapid expansion in the ability to purchase consumer products was an unprecedented proliferation in the number and kinds of products that became available, as well as remarkable increases in the quality of these products. By the 1970s the typical American lived in a world of abundance that Americans 30 years earlier could hardly have imagined. Since the beginning of the 1970s, however, real family income has increased comparatively little, despite the ongoing revolution in labor force participation by wives and mothers, and during the 1970s and the 1980s median family income increased by only 5 and 1 percent, respectively.

Despite large improvements in absolute income levels between 1939 and 1969, however, these statistics tell us little about the extent to which children lived in relative deprivation or luxury compared with the standards of the time in which they grew up, because at a specific point in history, the measure of whether a family is judged to be living in deprivation or luxury is that family's income and whether it is especially low or especially high compared with typical families in the same historical period.

Measuring economic deprivation in comparison with median family income in various years, the "relative poverty rate" for children dropped sharply during the 1940s (from 38 to 27 percent) but then much more slowly (to 23 percent in 1969). Subsequently, the relative poverty rate for children increased—mostly during the 1980s—to 27 percent in 1988, reaching the same level experienced almost 40 years earlier in 1949. . . .

CONCLUSION

America's children experienced several interrelated revolutions in their life course, as the family, economy, and society were transformed during the past 150 years. Family size plummeted. One-parent family living jumped. Family farms nearly became extinct, as first fathers and then mothers left the home for much of the day in order to serve as family breadwinners. Formal schooling, nonparental care for children, and parents' educational attainments have increased greatly, although educational opportunities to go beyond high school have become less equal since the turn of the century.

Absolute family incomes multiplied, but the past two decades brought little change in average income and increasing economic inequality among children, despite increasing mothers' labor-force participation. Relative and official poverty rates for children climbed during the past decade. Welfare dependence increased during recent decades, but most poor children historically and today live in working-poor families.

Currently, it appears that many of these revolutionary changes will be most extreme among children born within a decade of this writing. By historical standards, family size can decline comparatively little below the level expected for children born in the mid-1990s. Divorce, the major contributor to one-parent family living, has changed little since the late 1970s. By the year 2000, a large majority of children will live in dual-earner or one-parent families, a majority of preschoolers will receive substantial nonparental care while parents work, and only a small minority, even among newborns, will live in idealized "Ozzie and Harriet" families. Future changes in parents' education, in real income, poverty, and income inequality, and in welfare recipiency appear less certain, partly because they may be more responsive to specific public policies than are family size, divorce, and whether fathers and mothers work outside the home.

Regardless of future public policies, however, it seems likely that the fundamental transformations that have occurred during the past 150 years in the family, the economy, and the society will not be undone. Today, as throughout America's history, most children live with their parents and rely on them to provide for their economic support and day-to-day care. Yet a majority of children—both historically and today—have experienced either the loss of a parent from the home or economic insecurity, or both. Nevertheless, as a result of 150 years of revolutionary change in parents' work, in the family economy, and in the broader economy and society, America's children have entered a new age.

■ READING 22

What Children Think about Their Working Parents

Ellen Galinsky

Despite all they hear and read proclaiming that working is okay or even good for children, if parents feel there is a problem about work and family life, they define the solution as *simply* having more time with their child.

We asked parents in our Ask the Children survey, "If *you* were granted one wish to change the way that your work affects your child's life, what would that wish be?" The largest proportion of parents—22 percent—wished to "have more time with their child." An additional 16 percent wished to "work less time."

We also asked parents another open-ended question: "If *your child* were granted one wish to change the way that your work affects his/her life, what would that wish be?" The largest proportion of parents—21 percent—thought their child would want "more time with me." An additional 19 percent thought their child would want them to work less time, and 16 percent thought their children would want them "not to have to go to work." Taken together, 56 percent of parents mentioned time.

In this chapter, we explore the issue of time. Why does the debate about quality time versus quantity time persist? Does the amount of time that children say that they have with their parents affect how they feel about their parents' parenting? Do other aspects of time matter, such as the kinds of activities parents and children do together and whether children's time with parents is rushed or calm? What does the research say about the impact of time together on children's development? Is this another either/or debate—quality time *or* quantity time—as many have portrayed it? And finally and very importantly, do children and parents feel the same way about having time together?

WHY WON'T THE DEBATE ABOUT QUALITY TIME VERSUS QUANTITY TIME GO AWAY?

This debate reminds me of a punching bag that is slugged, even beaten down, but rebounds right back up. For four decades, this debate has had real staying power. Clearly it strikes a resonant cord.

In the 1960s, researchers looked at children in orphanages who failed to thrive and extrapolated this result to children who experienced daily separations from their employed mothers. Others countered that it is not the *quantity* of time that matters, but what happens in that time—the *quality* of time—that is important. And besides, they noted, the prolonged separations children experience from parents in orphanages are not the same as daily separations. The embers of this debate were fanned into flame again in the 1980s when findings from a few studies found that infants whose mothers were away from them for more than 20 hours a week were at risk for being insecurely attached.

Many parents don't seem to like the notion of quality time. In our one-on-one interviews, some described it as a rationalization for parents to spend less time with their children. A cellular phone advertisement that ran in the late 1990s became a symbol—in fact, a lightning rod—for the issue of quality versus quantity time. In this ad, a child approaches her mother just before the mother is to leave for work. She and her siblings want to go to the beach. When the mother refuses, the child asks when she can be a "client." The mother pauses—then tells her children that they have 3 minutes to get ready to go the beach. The last shot shows the mother sitting on the beach making a conference call on her cellular phone while her children play nearby in the sand.

A mother of a 9-week-old child, who has just returned to work from maternity leave, comments:

> I would say that in general this generation of children may be getting signals that my generation didn't get—that they come in second. It is in this ad about this woman on the phone and the kid wants to go to the beach [and says to her mother,] "When am I going to be a client?" [The mother] gives such a mixed message. Instead of saying, "You're right. We are going to the beach," it's "We are going to the beach and I'm doing my conference call while you play around. And I'll [at least] make sure that you don't cut your foot on shells."

It is clear to many parents that one shouldn't make a distinction between the amount of time one spends with his or her children and what happens in that time. Both the quality and quantity of the time that parents and child share are important. Yet, when asked about their *one* wish to change the way their work affects their child, parents emphasize the *quantity* of time per se: They wish for "more time." What is going on?

WHAT IS GOING ON ABOUT TIME IN TODAY'S FAMILIES?

How Much Time Are Employed Parents Spending with Their Children?

To answer the question of time employed parents spend, let's compare two studies that were conducted 20 years apart: the Families and Work Institute's 1997 National Study of the Changing Workforce and the U.S. Department of Labor's 1977 Quality of Employment Survey (QES).[1]

My colleagues Terry Bond and Jennifer Swanberg and I find—no surprise—that in dual-earner families[2] with children under 18, mothers spend more time doing things and caring for children than fathers on workdays (3.2 hours for mothers versus 2.3 hours for fathers). We also find—again no surprise—that mothers today spend more time than fathers with their children on days off work (8.3 hours for mothers versus 6.4 hours for fathers).

But we find—to the surprise of many—that the gap between mothers and fathers in dual-earner families has narrowed considerably in the past 20 years. Although the amount of time that mothers spend with their children on workdays has not changed in a statistically significant way, fathers have increased the amount of time they spend with children by a half hour.

The 1997 National Study of the Changing Workforce also found that over the past 20 years fathers have increased the time they spend with their children by slightly more than 1 hour on nonwork days, whereas mothers' time has again remained the same.

When the Families and Work Institute released these findings in 1998, the media and public reactions were swift and strong. A few women wrote prominent editorials skeptical of the veracity of the findings, stating, for example, in *The New York Times* that "super dads need a reality check,"[3] whereas many men, like Matt Lauer, host of the *Today* show, gave the findings a high five sign. At last, good news for dads, he said to me.

The public reaction echoes the private fault line between men and women on the subject of time with children. Women ask, "Is he really caring for the children or is he just 'Dad, the helper,' 'Dad, the babysitter?'" "Why does he always wait until I ask him to be with the kids?" "Why doesn't he know what they like to eat for lunch and who their friends are?" Men ask, "Why does she always criticize what I do? When I try to do more, all I get are complaints, complaints, complaints." Or, "I am doing more, but nobody seems to notice."

Are men exaggerating? Are they really spending more time with their children? The 1997 National Study of the Changing Workforce didn't ask parents to keep time diaries, but it did have a reality check, as *The York Times* called it: We asked fathers and mothers how much time their *partners* spent with the children. Although of course our findings are estimates, we found—again a surprise to many—that mothers' estimates of their husbands parallel the amount of time fathers report spending with their children. So fathers do not seem to be exaggerating—at least according to wives.

Furthermore, because employed mothers have managed to keep constant the amount of time they spend with their children, because fathers have increased their time, and because families have fewer children today than they did 20 years ago, it appears that employed parents indeed are spending somewhat more time with their children than they were two decades ago.

Where do parents get more time? Certainly not from their workdays. For employed fathers with children under 18, the 40-hour workweek is a myth. On average, including paid and unpaid time and including part-time and full-time work, fathers work 50.9 hours per week and mothers work 41.4 hours. By our calculations, fathers' total work time has increased by 3.1 hours per week in the past 20 years, and mothers' time has increased by 5.2 hours.[4]

There has also been an increase in the amount of time that parents spend on their jobs while at home. Almost one in three parents spends time on a weekly basis doing work at home that is directly related to his or her job. The proportion of parents who take work home from the job once a week or more has increased 10 percent since 1977, while the proportion who never take work home from the job has decreased by 16 percent.

So if parents are spending more time at work and fathers are spending more time with their children, where has this increased time come from? Employed parents know the answer to that question. They are spending less time on themselves:

> I haven't set aside time for myself all these years. That's one thing I really need to start working on, just for my own sanity.

On average, fathers in dual-earner families report they have 1.2 hours for themselves on workdays. Mothers have about 18 minutes less—0.9 hour per workday. This figure has decreased quite significantly over the past 20 years. On average, fathers in dual-earner families in 1997 had 54 fewer minutes for themselves on workdays than fathers did in

1977, while mothers have 42 fewer minutes for themselves on workdays today than mothers did in 1977.[5]

Even on days off work, fathers' time for themselves has also decreased—from 5.1 hours to 3.3 hours, a change of 1.8 hours over the past 20 years. Mothers' time for themselves on days off work has also decreased from 3.3 hours to 2.5 hours, a change of 0.8 hour.[6] So while both parents are sacrificing "time for themselves" to spend more time with their children, fathers have done so more than mothers (who, granted, were spending more time with their children to begin with).

WHAT DID WE FIND ABOUT TIME, EMPLOYED PARENTS, AND CHILDREN?

How Much Time Are Employed Parents Spending with Individual Children?

In the Ask the Children study,[7] we looked at how much time employed parents spend with just one of their children, randomly selected. Overall, employed mothers report spending about an hour more with their child than employed fathers on workdays (3.8 hours for mothers compared with 2.7 hours for fathers). On nonworkdays, mothers also report spending about an hour more with their child than employed fathers: 7.7 hours for mothers and 6.6 hours for fathers.[8]

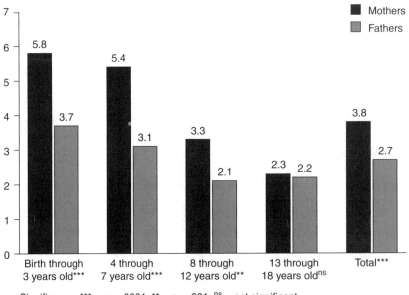

Significance: *** = p < .0001; ** = p < .001; ns = not significant

FIGURE 1   *Employed Parents: Hours Spent with Their Child on Workdays*

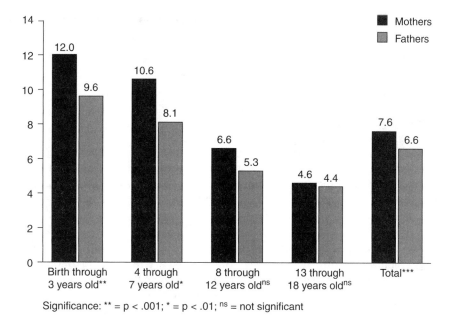

Significance: ** = p < .001; * = p < .01; ns = not significant

FIGURE 2 *Employed Parents: Hours Spent with Their Child on Nonworkdays*

When we look at the amount of time parents spend with children of different ages, there are shifts over time. Mothers spend more time with younger children than fathers do. By the teenage years, the amount of time that both parents spend declines—mothers' time more sharply than fathers'—to the point where there are no statistical differences in the amount of time mothers and fathers spend.

The same pattern applies to nonworkdays: Mothers reduce the amount of time they spend considerably as children age, dropping from 12 hours a day with a very young child to 4.6 hours with a teenager. Again, the difference in the amount of time mothers and fathers spend narrows and then disappears as the child grows up.[9] It is not simply that parents with an older child don't pay attention to that child; rather, children of these ages can be quite busy, doing their own thing. A mother with a teenage daughter says:

> I would like to be with my teenage daughter more, but she is so involved with schoolwork, activities, and her friends. Inevitably I will hang around the house weekend after weekend, and the one day that I make plans, she will come up to me and say, "Let's do something together today."

Since a few studies have found differences between how boys and girls are affected by their mothers' and fathers' work, I wondered whether there are gender differences here. I found that mothers spend more time with their daughters on workdays: 42.5 percent of mothers report spending 4.5 hours or more with their daughters on workdays compared with 24 percent who spend this much time with their sons. These differences occur during the teenage years, not when children are very young. In contrast, there is no difference in the amount of time mothers report spending with their daughters and their sons on nonworkdays. Moreover, there are no differences in the amount of time that fathers report spending with their sons and their daughters of all ages on workdays and nonworkdays.

How Much Time Do Children Say They Spend with Their Mothers and Fathers?

Now we turn full circle and look at children's estimates of the time they spend with their parents. Children in the third through twelfth grades were asked about how much time they spend with each of their parents—just the two of them or with other people—on a typical workday and on a typical nonworkday.[10]

Time Spent with Employed Parents on Workdays.   The majority of children report spending considerable time with their mothers on workdays, although the amount of time fluctuates, depending on the age of the child. Twenty-nine percent of younger children (8 through 12 years old) say they spend 2 hours or less compared with 35 percent of older children (13 through 18 years old). At the other end of the spectrum, 47 percent of younger children and 35 percent of older children spend 5 hours or more with their mothers on workdays.

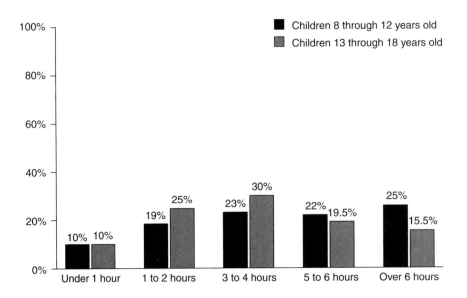

Significance: * = p < .01.

FIGURE 3   *Children Third through Twelfth Grades with Employed Mothers: Time Spent with Mother on Workdays*

There is no difference in the amount of time that sons and daughters report spending with their mothers on workdays (although recall that mothers report spending more time with their teenage daughters than their teenage sons). It is not clear to me why there is a discrepancy between children's and parents' viewpoints, though children have less reason to overestimate than parents.

Children spend less time with their fathers than their mothers on workdays. Overall, 44 percent of children ages 8 through 18 years old report spending 2 hours or less with their fathers on workdays while 27 percent spend 5 hours or more. Interestingly, there is no significant difference in the amount of time younger and older children report spending with their fathers. Neither are there differences between boys and girls

Time Spent with Parents on Nonworkdays.   An impressive 68.5 percent of both younger and older children say that they spend 5 hours or more with their mothers on nonworkdays. Although mothers do not report spending any more time with their daughters on nonworkdays than with their sons, children do report differences—girls say they spend more time with their mothers on nonworkdays than boys do. Here again, the discrepancy is hard to figure out.

Although children spend less time with their fathers than their mothers on nonworkdays, the amount of time they report spending with their fathers is still high: 66 percent of children—boys and girls alike—say that they spend 5 hours or more with their fathers on nonworkdays.

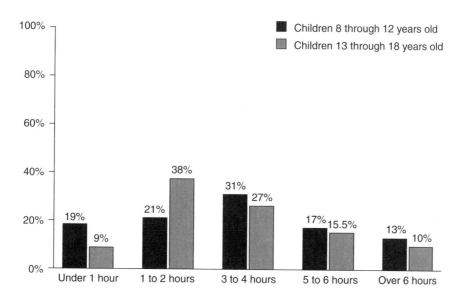

Significance: ns = not significant.

FIGURE 4   ***Children Third through Twelfth Grades with Employed Fathers: Time Spent with Father on Workdays***

Do Parents and Children Feel They Have Enough Time Together?

Enough Time—According to Parents.   It is one thing to know the *amount* of time that parents and children report spending together, but it is another to know the *psychological meaning* of that time. Do parents feel they have enough time with their child? Do children concur? I especially wondered about fathers. Since fathers spend less time with their children—both by their own and by their children's estimates—are they more likely than mothers to want more time?

Overall, 50 percent of parents with children, birth through 18 years old, say that they have too little time with their child; however, beneath this overall figure *fathers*—much more so than mothers—seem to be yearning to be with their child: 56 percent of fathers versus 44 percent of mothers feel deprived of time with their child!

Because fathers work longer hours, they have less time for their lives off the job. One father of a 9-year-old boy reflects on the fleeting nature of time:

> Time is something, once it's gone, it's gone forever. So, you can look back and think, "Well, gee, I wish I would have spent more time with my kids when they were younger, I wish I would've spent more time with them when they were in high school," whatever. But once time is gone, that's it.

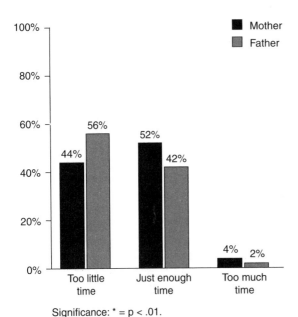

Significance: * = p < .01.

FIGURE 5   *Employed Parents with a Child Birth through 18: Enough Time with Their Child*

Mothers and fathers with a son or a daughter are equally likely to feel that they have too little time with this child. Moreover, parents of children of different ages—from infants to teenagers—are also equally likely to feel they have too little time.

Enough Time—According to Children. The majority of children 8 through 18 years old feel that they have enough time with their employed mothers and fathers: 67 percent say that they have enough time with their mothers and 60 percent say they have enough time with their fathers. Paralleling the overall difference in the amount of time fathers and mothers spend with their children, children are more likely to feel that they have too little time with their *fathers* than with their mothers.

In our one-on-one interviews, a number of children talked about wanting more time with their fathers. One 12-year-old girl whose father takes frequent business trips says:

> I miss him. He's gone for short times. He calls from where he is. I'd rather have him at home during that time, but I know he has to do it because it's part of his job.

We heard a similar story from another girl whose father often works hard, including on weekends:

> I can't spend much time with him because he's working. Sometimes I go with him to work on the weekends. But I just wish that he wouldn't work so much.

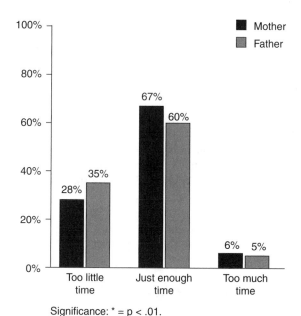

Significance: * = p < .01.

FIGURE 6 *Children Third through Twelfth Grades with Employed Parents: Enough Time with Mothers and Fathers*

Moreover, as has been the pattern thus far, children are far, far more likely to feel that they spend too little time with nonresident fathers (67 percent) than with resident fathers (35 percent).

These findings illustrate why it is so important to ask the children rather than to rely on our own assumptions. The issue of time with children has typically been framed in the public debate as mothers' issue. But when we ask the children, we see that fathers need to be front and center in this discussion as well.

Enough Time—Comparing Children's Views of Employed and Nonemployed Mothers.   All of the analyses in this chapter focus on employed mothers, but we also asked the question about having enough time with parents of children who have non-employed mothers. Children with employed mothers are no more likely to feel they have too little time with their mothers than children with nonemployed mothers. Stated differently, children with mothers at home and children with mothers who work are equally likely to feel they have enough time with their mother.

Enough Time—Comparing Children and Mothers.   What is also striking—and I must say unanticipated—is the discrepancy between the views of children and those of their mothers on whether they have enough time together. Almost half of mothers (49 percent) with a child 13 through 18 years old feel that they have too little time with their child, whereas less than one third of children (30 percent) this age concur. The results comparing mothers and younger children do not reach statistical significance but follow the same pattern. Perhaps mothers of teenagers anticipate the soon-to-occur loss of everyday contact with their child as the child grows up, goes to college, moves out. So they often long for more time, whereas children may be more eager (though ambivalently so) to separate from their mothers.

Enough Time—Comparing Children and Fathers.   Teenagers are more likely than their younger counterparts to want more time with their fathers. Thirty-nine percent of children 13 through 18 years old feel they have too little time with their fathers compared with 29 percent of children 8 through 12 years old. On the other hand, children do not feel as strongly about this issue as fathers. For example, almost two thirds of fathers (64 percent) with a child 13 through 18 years feel that they have too little time with this child, but only 39 percent of children this age feel the same way about time with their fathers.

Unexpected Findings about Employed Parents and Time

In sum, while 53 percent of employed parents with a child 8 through 18 feel they have too little time with their child, only 31 percent of children with employed parents feel the same way.

Typically, when issues of employed parents and time are discussed, the focus is on comparing children with employed versus nonemployed mothers. When we "ask the children," however, we find that there is no statistically significant difference between these two groups of children in feeling that they have too little time with their mothers.

Second, the public discussion has been more concerned with mothers than with fathers. When we turn to children, we find that children 8 through 18 years old are more

TABLE 1 *Employed Mothers and Children with Employed Mothers: Enough Time Together*

	Children 8 through 12 years old	Children 13 through 18 years old
Too little time		
Mother	31%	49%
Child	24.5	30
Just enough time		
Mother	68%	50%
Child	69	65
Too much time		
Mother	1.5%	1%
Child	6.5	5
Significance:	*ns = not significant;*	*** = p < .0001.*

TABLE 2 *Employed Fathers and Children with Employed Fathers: Enough Time Together*

	Children 8 through 12 years old	Children 13 through 18 years old
Too little time		
Father	64%	64%
Child	29	39
Just enough time		
Father	35%	34%
Child	65	56
Too much time		
Father	1%	2%
Child	5.5	5
Significance:	*** = p < .0001;*	** = p < .001.*

likely to feel that they have too little time with their employed *fathers* than with their employed mothers. We also find that fathers—more so than mothers—feel they have too little time with their child.

Third, the public discussion about employed parents and time has centered on younger children, but we find that older children are more likely than younger children to feel that they have too little time with their fathers. Asking the children helps us see that the hidden story about working parents and time is about fathers and teenagers.

Editor's Note: *Notes for this reading can be found in the original source.*

■ **R E A D I N G   2 3**

Going to Extremes: Family Structure, Children's Well-Being, and Social Science

Andrew J. Cherlin

In this article I argue that public discussions of demographic issues are often conducted in a troubling pattern in which one extreme position is debated in relation to the opposite extreme. This pattern impedes our understanding of social problems and is a poor guide to sound public policies. To illustrate this thesis I use the case of social scientific research examining how children are affected by not living with two biological parents while they are growing up. Over the last decade, I maintain, most of the public, and even many social scientists, have been puzzled and poorly informed by this debate. In particular I consider Judith Wallerstein's clinically based claims of the pervasive, profound harm caused by divorce and, at the other extreme, Judith Rich Harris's reading of behavioral genetics and evolutionary psychology, which leads her to dismiss the direct effects of divorce. Neither extreme gives a clear picture of the consequences of growing up in a single-parent family or a stepfamily.

Beginning in the early 1960s, there occurred a series of events that Samuel Preston, in a memorable phrase from his 1984 PAA presidential address, called "the earthquake that [has] shuddered through the American family in the past 20 years" (Preston 1984:451). The divorce rate in the United States began an ascent in which the risk of divorce doubled by the mid-1970s and has remained at a high plateau (or perhaps in a slight decline) since about 1980. At current rates, about half of all marriages would end in divorce (Cherlin 1992). The proportion of children born to unmarried mothers also increased; unlike the divorce rate, it continued to rise through the 1980s and the first half of the 1990s before reaching the current plateau of just under one-third (U.S. Department of Health and Human Services 1998; U.S. National Center for Health Statistics 1998). Cohabitation, once common only among the poor, became a widespread and acceptable living arrangement; about half of all young adults cohabit with a partner before marrying (Bumpass and Lu 1998). In addition, between 1960 and 1998 the median age at first marriage rose 4.7 years for women and 3.9 years for men (U.S. Bureau of the Census 1999).

As a result of these changes, the proportion of children who spend time in a single-parent family while growing up has increased dramatically: It now stands at about 50% (Bumpass and Raley 1995). That increase has caused concern, and even alarm, among social scientists, social commentators, and policy makers. A lively debate continues about the consequences of these changes for children and about the proper public response; all sides cite the research of social demographers.

Social demographic research is cited about many other controversial topics as well. Demographers study things that are close to people's lives and about which there is great public debate, such as population growth, immigration, adolescent pregnancy and childbearing, racial segregation, the labor market, and gender equity. Consequently the public often pays attention to our findings. Most of us value this aspect of our research. We want our findings to be widely disseminated; we want our research to inform important public discussions.

Too often, however, these public discussions are played out in a troubling pattern in which one extreme position is debated in relation to the opposite extreme. As I will show, that certainly has been the case in the recent debate about family structure and children's well-being. In this article I review that debate and discuss what conclusions we are justified in drawing from the research literature on this subject.

The pattern I am talking about, however, applies broadly to a number of social issues. It passes through three stages. In the first stage, a social scientist presents an extreme view of a particular problem—it is either a total disaster or completely benign—and his or her work receives great media attention. In the next stage, another social scientist, taking a different perspective, presents evidence for the opposite extreme. This viewpoint also receives great attention. And in the third stage, news coverage and public debates lurch back and forth between these extremes as if there were no middle position worth contemplating. I believe that this pattern of going to extremes impedes our understanding of social problems and that it is also a poor guide to sound public policies.

One could argue that extreme statements are useful precisely because they attract so much attention to social issues. One could argue that, in an era of wall-to-wall special interest groups, extreme statements are needed to mobilize a constituency. One could even argue that at a time when hundreds of television channels and millions of web sites compete for people's attention, extreme statements are necessary if one is even to be heard.

I would argue, however, that extreme statements invite counterextremes, with unexpected and often undesirable results. The best-known example in population research occurred during the debates about rapid population growth in the 1960s and 1970s. Some regard that time as the glory period of demography, and indeed demographic research helped to raise public awareness of a pressing global problem. But even in that era, extreme positions sometimes backfired. I would suggest that the exaggerated predictions made by Paul Ehrlich (1968) and others in the 1960s, foretelling widespread famine and soaring mortality rates, contributed to the rise of the opposite extreme in the late 1970s and 1980s: the Panglossian claims of Julian Simon (1981) and others that population growth, far from being a problem, was a positive element. Simon's arguments, I believe, had more force because he could easily refute some of Ehrlich's exaggerated claims (see Tierney 1990).

I see an echo of that pattern in the current literature on the consequences of adolescent childbearing. According to the old wisdom of population research, adolescent childbearing led almost inevitably to poorer outcomes in adulthood. In the 1990s, a newer literature sometimes seems to suggest that teenage childbearing per se is hardly a problem at all—a conclusion sharply at variance with the perceptions of service providers who work with teen mothers (Hoffman, Foster, and Furstenberg 1993).

In this article, however, I want to illustrate my argument by focusing on the example I am most familiar with: the social scientific research on the short- and long-term effects, on children, of not living with two biological parents while they are growing up. On this topic, the past decade has witnessed a grand swing of the pendulum from one extreme to the other, which has left most of the public, and even many social scientists, puzzled and poorly informed.

During the 1980s and early 1990s, data on family structure and on child and adolescent well-being became available to social demographers from high-quality longitudinal surveys such as the Child Supplement to the National Longitudinal Survey of Youth, the Panel Study of Income Dynamics, the High School and Beyond Study, and the National Survey of Families and Households. As these data were analyzed, they yielded substantial evidence that growing up in a single-parent family or a stepfamily is associated with a lower level of well-being and poorer life outcomes than living in a family with two biological parents. The best-known set of studies was conducted by Sara McLanahan and Gary Sandefur, and was reported in 1994 in the book *Growing up With a Single Parent* (McLanahan and Sandefur 1994). These researchers found strong associations between growing up in a single-parent or stepparent family and a higher probability of dropping out of high school, of giving birth as a teenager, and, for young men, of being "idle"— that is, neither employed nor in school in the first few years after high school.

But two important questions remain. First, how much of this association is truly cause and effect, as opposed to merely reflecting unmeasured factors that influence both the likelihood of growing up without two biological parents and outcomes such as high school graduation? And second, even if the association is causal, what proportion of children in single-parent families experience harmful outcomes? There is still strong disagreement on these questions; let us turn to them now.

PARENTS MAKE ALL THE DIFFERENCE

Over the past decade, the public has been exposed to two extreme positions—two highly publicized treatments of the subject that have reached diametrically opposed conclusions. Both were put forward initially by psychologists but were embraced by scholars from other disciplines. The first treatment came from clinical psychologist Judith Wallerstein. On the basis of a long-term study of 60 families who came to her divorce clinic in northern California, Wallerstein concluded that divorce harms most of the children who experience it, and that the harm is clearly caused by the divorce and by how the divorced parents act.

Wallerstein had been writing insightful clinical case studies for a decade when she suddenly leaped to the conclusion that the families she studied were typical American families. She then coauthored a book with science writer Sandra Blakeslee, in which she described the sorry state of the children 10 years after their parents' divorces. Then she suggested to her readers that their children would likely respond to a divorce in the same way. The book, *Second Chances: Men, Women, and Children a Decade After Divorce* (Wallerstein and Blakeslee 1989), became a best seller and probably the most widely read book on divorce ever published. More recently, Wallerstein has begun to release information from a 25-year follow-up of the youngest children in the families she studied, who were 2 to 6 years old when the study began.

Does divorce actually cause the problems displayed by children in single-parent families? Definitely so, conclude Wallerstein and her coauthors. Moreover, according to the 25-year follow-up study, the effects continue or even worsen over time. In a 1997 paper on the results of that follow-up, Wallerstein and Julia Lewis (1997) wrote that divorce is a cumulative experience for the children. They argued that the effect of divorce gains new strength at late adolescence, when the adolescents, in some cases, don't receive the financial support they need to attend college. Many of the now-grown children in their study had attained less education than their parents. Wallerstein and Lewis claimed that when these children reach young adulthood, many fear that their own adult relationships will fail, as did those of their parents.

What proportion of children are harmed by divorce? Wallerstein's writings clearly imply that most children are harmed. At the 25-year mark, she and Lewis wrote, one respondent after another spoke of their lost childhood. They told of an anxiety about intimate adult relationships that was as severe among those whose parents had undergone a conflicted divorce as among those whose parents had remained cordial—and was as severe among those who had seen their fathers regularly as among those who saw little of their fathers.

But how do we know that the parents' divorce, as opposed to other individual and family problems, caused these difficulties? No comparison group is presented. Moreover, Wallerstein's claims that her families were healthy and typical are unconvincing. To be sure, she screened out families in which the children had seen mental-health professionals before the beginning of the study. Wallerstein and Lewis (1997) asserted that the children were a psychologically sturdy group; they reminded the reader that none had ever been referred for psychological help.

Wallerstein, however, neglects to say that she did not screen out families in which the parents had seen mental-health professionals. As Frank Furstenberg and I noted a decade ago (Cherlin and Furstenberg 1989), only the appendix to Wallerstein's first book about the study, published in 1980 (Wallerstein and Kelly 1980), informs the reader that 50% of the fathers and close to half of the mothers were "moderately troubled" individuals when the study began: "Here were the chronically depressed, sometimes suicidal individuals, men and women with severe neurotic difficulties" in personal relationships or with "longstanding problems in controlling their rage or sexual impulses" (p. 328). Furthermore, an additional 15% of the fathers and 20% of the mothers were "severely troubled during their marriages." These individuals "had histories of mental illness including paranoid thinking, bizarre behavior, manic-depressive illnesses, and generally fragile or unsuccessful attempts to cope with the demands of life, marriage, and family" (p. 328).

Typical American families? No, these were largely troubled families—and troubled parents often raise troubled children. This is why Wallerstein's long-term reports are so grim. There is no question that her conclusions exaggerate the harm typically caused by divorce.

PARENTS DON'T MAKE ANY DIFFERENCE

Had I written this article five years ago, I would have spent more time arguing against Wallerstein's doomsday view of divorce. Now, however, Wallerstein is the *old* extremist in this debate. In 1998 a new extremist appeared in print: Her book was touted in a *New Yorker* article (Gladwell 1998) and featured on the cover of *Newsweek* (Begley 1998). She is psychologist Judith Rich Harris, who is influenced not by clinical case studies but by behavioral genetics and evolutionary psychology. In her startling book *The Nurture Assumption: Why Children Turn Out the Way They Do* (Harris 1998), she proposes that what parents do makes little difference in how their children's lives turn out. Rather, she asserts, about half of the variation in children's personalities and behavior is due to genetic inheritance; the other half is due mainly to the influence of children's peer groups. Unlike Wallerstein, Harris argues that growing up in a single-parent family does not actually cause the negative outcomes we see in children from single-parent families. It follows that relatively few children are harmed by living in a single-parent family per se.

Harris is greatly influenced by the subfield of behavioral genetics, which has created a revolution in developmental psychology but is not well known to most demographers. Its practitioners infer the effects of heredity on personality and behavior mainly from studies of pairs of individuals who differ in genetic relatedness (Plomin, DeFries, and McClearn 1990). The most common design is to compare pairs of identical twins with pairs of fraternal twins. The former have 100% of their genes in common; the latter, like any pair of full siblings, have, on average, 50% in common. The researchers assume, crucially, that the family environments of identical twins while they are growing up are no more similar than those of fraternal twins. This assumption is unlikely to be completely true, strictly speaking, but studies indicate enough similarity to justify taking the results seriously (Kendler et al. 1994). Under this assumption, if identical twins are more similar than fraternal twins in personality or behavior, this must be due to their greater genetic similarity or to the interaction of their genetic tendencies with their environment.

Using this logic, behavioral geneticists have published hundreds of articles that suggest a genetic contribution to personality and behavior. In a study of 1,516 same-sex adult twin pairs in which both twins in each pair had ever married, McGue and Lykken (1992) reported the following: A fraternal twin's odds of divorce were twice as high if his or her co-twin had divorced, but an identical twin's odds of divorce were six times higher if his or her co-twin had divorced. Although the authors reject any simplistic notion of a "divorce gene," they argue that genes contribute to personality traits and behaviors; these, in turn, influence the likelihood that a person's marriage will end in divorce. Commenting on this study, Harris writes, "Heredity, not their experiences in their childhood home, is what makes the children of divorce more likely to fail in their own marriages" (1998:308).

Could it be, Harris argues, that divorce is simply a marker for genetically transmitted characteristics, such as vulnerability to depression, that make parents more likely to divorce and also make their children more likely to suffer unwanted life outcomes? In other words, if children whose parents divorced are more depressed, could that be the case because depression runs in their family and partially caused both the parents' divorce and the children's depressive symptoms? Harris states that more behavioral genetic studies of divorce are needed; these studies, she predicts, will show that "parental divorce has no lasting effects on the way children behave when they're not at home, and no lasting effects on their personalities" (1998:311).

Along the way, Harris trashes much social demographic research for assuming cause and effect in studies that exclude heredity. She subjects the book by McLanahan and Sandefur (1994) to particular criticism, probably, she acknowledges, because it is the leading study of its type. The writer for *Newsweek* was even less kind to social scientists. In the cover story on Harris's book, she wrote:

> To reach her parents-don't-matter conclusion, Harris first demolishes some truly lousy studies that have become part of the scientific canon. (Begley 1998:55)

Later she stated:

> Even [Harris's] detractors like the way she's blown the lid off dumb studies that can't tell the difference between parents' influencing their kids through genes and influencing them through actions. (Begley 1998:56)

These are fighting words. How should demographers respond? Unfortunately, the major way in which sociology—my discipline—has responded to genetic arguments has been to deny that genetics makes any difference at all for human personality and behavior. The denial comes from two sources. First, sociologists study the ways in which society shapes individuals, and they tend to believe that what they study is the most important source of influences. Consequently they assume that social structure and culture can easily override genetic predispositions. The second source is political: Sociologists are wary of genetic arguments because they have been used in the past to deny equal rights and opportunities to women and minorities. The political concern is understandable: One must use care in stating the implications of behavioral genetic research. Yet these two sources of denial have led to an unfortunate rejection of the importance of genetic inheritance to the study of human society. In view of the accumulating evidence, most sociologists' steadfast refusal to consider heredity is becoming an embarrassment to sociologists who reach out to other disciplines.

The situation is somewhat better among social scientists who identify themselves as demographers. Many listeners agreed with Richard Udry when he argued, in his 1994 presidential address to the Population Association of America, that gender differences have both genetic and environmental components (Udry 1994). The program at the 1999 PAA annual meetings included sessions titled "Evolutionary Perspectives on Fertility" and "The Biodemography of Aging," both of which represent growing areas of inquiry. I would guess that a substantial number of demographers would accept the idea that genetic inheritance plays a role in shaping human behavior.

In any case, I believe that demographers should not react to Harris's critique by denying the importance of genetic inheritance. The more appropriate response is that genetics in fact may be important, but parents' actions still make a difference for outcomes of children in single-parent families. Behavioral genetic studies show clearly that heredity does *not* account for all—or anywhere near all—of the variance in human behavior. In the typical behavioral genetic study of a characteristic such as major depression, heredity appears to account for about half of the variance in the twin pairs studied (Dunn and Plomin 1990).

What accounts for the rest? The most controversial part of Harris's argument is her claim that children's peer groups, rather than treatment by parents, produce the environmental effects on children's development. Harris says, in effect, that half of the variation in children's behavior and personality is due to genes and most of the rest is due to peer groups; what parents do doesn't affect children's development very much. The claim that peers make a big difference and parents don't—not the genetic argument, which many psychologists accept—is drawing the most fire.

To be sure, peer groups have an important influence on children's development, but evidence suggests that what parents do also matters greatly. As I noted above, Harris uses divorce as an example showing why parents don't matter much. Because of her focus on peer groups, however, she claims that one of the few ways in which parental divorce affects children is that the decline in mothers' incomes after separating sometimes forces them to move to a new neighborhood. Harris acknowledges that McLanahan and Sandefur (1994) also discuss post-separation moves, but her own twist is the argument that the move hurts children only because it disrupts their peer groups. They must find and join a new group, which is difficult and which could introduce new, unwanted influences.

What is the evidence? Research suggests that frequent moves *can* lead to poorer adjustment among children in single-parent families. Consider a study by C. Jack Tucker, Jonathan Marx, and Larry Long (1998). These authors used data from the Child Health Supplement to the 1988 National Health Interview Survey to investigate the effects of residential moves on academic and behavior problems in school. As shown in Figure 1, they found that, among children not living with both biological parents, those whose families had moved several times were doing less well in school than children whose families had moved less often. So far, so good for Harris. The authors, however, also found that, among children living with both biological parents, those whose families moved several times were *not* doing significantly worse in school than those whose families moved

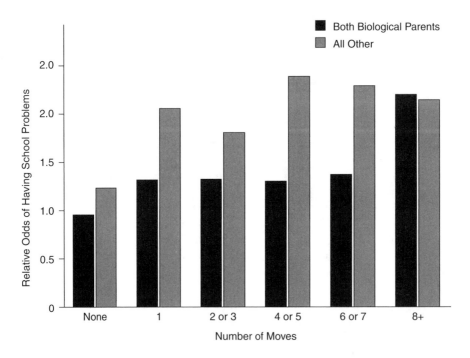

FIGURE 1 *Relative Odds of Having School Problems, by Number of Moves and Family Type*

Source: Tucker, Marx, and Long (1998).

less often (unless the parents had moved eight or more times). The presence of a second, biological parent in the household seemed to buffer children from the potentially disruptive effects of frequent moves. Apparently the task of finding new peer groups and adjusting to new schools was not a problem for most children in families with two biological parents. These findings suggest that parental divorce or being born to a single parent increases the risk that residential moves will hurt school performance, whereas the risk is reduced by living with two biological parents. In other words, even if peer groups make a difference, parents also make a difference in moderating their effects.

Or consider an article that Lindsay Chase-Lansdale, Christine McRae Battle, and I published (Cherlin, Chase-Lansdale, and McRae 1998) as part of a larger study on the effects of divorce on children. We studied the records of 11,759 British children who were born in 1958 and followed until 1991, when they were 33 years old. All lived in families with two biological parents until at least age 7. Indicators of emotional problems were obtained from the children at ages 7, 11, 16, 23, and 33. We standardized those measures and conducted an analysis of the trajectory of emotional problems from age 7 to age 33, according to whether the children's parents divorced. We used growth-curve modeling, a variant of the models known among demographers as multilevel models and among econometricians as random-effects models.

We found that children whose parents would later divorce *already* showed more emotional problems at age 7 than children from families that would stay together. This can be seen in Figure 2 in the gap, at age 7, between children whose parents would later divorce and those whose parents would remain together. This preexisting gap is consistent

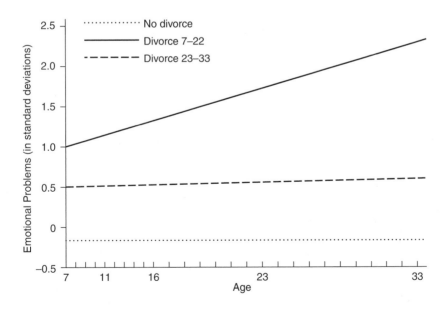

FIGURE 2   *Growth Curve Model of Emotional Problems from Age 7 to 33, by Age at Parental Divorce*

Source: Cherlin, Chase-Lansdale, and McRae (1998).

with the argument that divorce occurs in families that are already troubled. The gap between those whose parents will divorce and those whose parents will not is ignored by the Wallersteinian extreme. In fact, several other researchers have reported evidence that precursors of the difficulties associated with divorce are visible in children, to some extent, years before the breakup (Block, Block, and Gjerde 1986; Doherty and Needle 1991; Elliott and Richards 1991). I would submit that this is now a well-established finding. It suggests that studies that do not take into account the preexisting difficulties of children and their families overstate the effect of growing up in a single-parent family.

That's only part of the story, however. The gap continues to widen between the no-divorce group and the group whose parents divorced when the children were between ages 7 and 22. This finding indicates that, when a divorce did occur, it coincided with a further increase in emotional problems—a pattern suggesting that family breakup also may affect mental health. In fact, it recalls Wallerstein and Lewis's statement that the effects of divorce are cumulative rather than time-limited. This pattern also was confirmed by a fixed-effects model that we estimated. Even so, partisans of genetic explanations could argue that the widening gap also may be due to differences in inherited characteristics that change over time. The onset of clinical depression, for example, which may have a genetic component, typically does not occur until early adulthood.[1]

What about evidence from behavioral genetic studies themselves—the kind of study that, according to Harris, should show little or no effect of divorce? I am aware of only one: a study of female twin-pairs published in 1992 (Kendler et al. 1992). The authors examined whether a parental divorce contributed to the variance in major depression (and other mental health outcomes) between identical and fraternal twin-pairs, once the degree of genetic resemblance was taken into account. They did find a statistically significant association: A parental separation or divorce increased the risk of major depression for members of a twin-pair by 42%, even after making allowance for genetic relatedness.[2] This finding suggests that divorce indeed has an effect on mental health—that the variation is not due only to genes.[3]

In sum, the evidence suggests that Harris's position is too extreme when she tells parents, in the final paragraph of the penultimate chapter, "Relax. How they turn out is not a reflection on the care you have given them" (Harris 1998:349). The danger in the heavy media coverage of Harris's book is that parents will believe this overstatement, and will conclude that an ill-considered divorce will do no harm or that saving to pay for college tuition will do no good. Genes and peers notwithstanding, we have strong evidence that parents still make a major difference.

HOW MANY CHILDREN WILL EXPERIENCE DIFFICULTIES?

This is not to say that all children, or even most, will suffer long-term problems due to a parental divorce. Consider the responses, at age 23, of the British sample we studied. They answered a 24-question index of mental health developed by British psychiatrist Michael Rutter. The yes-or-no questions include "Do you often feel miserable and depressed?" "Are you constantly keyed up and jittery?" and "Do you often get worried about things?" Clinical use of the scale suggests that people who answer "yes" to seven or more questions may need mental health services (Rutter, Tizard, and Whitmore 1970).

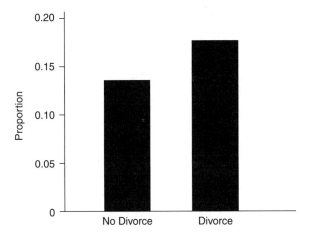

FIGURE 3 *Proportion Scoring above the Clinical Cutoff at Age 23, by Parental Marital Status*
Source: Chase-Lansdale, Cherlin, and Kiernan (1995).

Figure 3, which is taken from a 1995 study (Chase-Lansdale, Cherlin, and Kiernan 1995), shows the proportion scoring above this clinical cutoff for the divorce group and the no-divorce group for 23-year-old women, with controls for social class and childhood behavior problems. One can look at this figure in two ways. In an absolute sense, relatively few individuals in either group scored above the cutoff, this finding suggests that the majority of individuals who experienced parental divorce do not experience long-term mental health problems. In a relative sense, however, the risk of experiencing mental health problems was 31% higher in the divorce group (.180 versus .137), which suggests that parental divorce raises the risk of mental health problems. Thus the data suggest that divorce increases the risk of problems but that most people whose parents divorce do not experience those problems.

CONCLUSION

What, then, can we conclude about the effects of growing up in a single-parent family? We know enough to clearly reject one extreme view: that family structure causes all of the problems we see in children who don't live with two biological parents while growing up. Studies of parental divorce show that some of these problems, or at least their precursors, were present before the parents separated—and not merely a year or two beforehand, but sometimes five or ten. These findings strongly suggest (although they do not prove) that some of the children's problems following disruption reflect personal characteristics or family dysfunction which are not simply part of the divorce process. Evidence suggests that these characteristics could be partly genetic in origin, or could involve the interaction of genetic predispositions with environmental influences. Overall this set of findings implies that some of the problems might have occurred even if the biological parents had not divorced.

By scientific standards, we cannot wholly reject the other extreme view: that none of the problems we see were caused by the divorce, that they were caused completely by genetics and peer groups, and that they all would have occurred anyway. Without the possibility of a controlled experiment, it is difficult to reject the null hypothesis that family structure counts for almost nothing. Even so, some of the evidence seems inconsistent with this extreme. According to the one high-quality twin study that has been conducted on this topic, a parental divorce appears to increase the risk of depression, even with controls for inherited characteristics (Kendler et al. 1992). In addition, other social-scientific studies that I have reviewed here have produced patterns of findings that are difficult to reconcile with a "parents make no difference" view. Recall that children seem to handle residential moves more easily when they live with two parents (Tucker et al. 1998).

In summary, the long-term mental health of adults who experienced parental divorce as children or adolescents appears to deteriorate in relation to the mental health of those who grew up with two biological parents, even after the initial gap between the two groups in early childhood is taken into account (Cherlin et al. 1998).

To make further progress in examining the extreme "family structure makes no difference" position, it would be useful to have access to large genetic samples embedded in high-quality longitudinal studies of randomly selected populations. This need is beginning to be met: The National Longitudinal Study of Adolescent Health, for example, which is being conducted by researchers at the University of North Carolina Population Center, includes an embedded genetic sample in its large, longitudinal survey. I hope there will be other studies with similar designs.

Yet on the basis of current evidence, imperfect though it may be, I think there are strong grounds for being nearly as skeptical about the "no difference" extreme as about the "all the difference" extreme. The former view does not fit the facts at our disposal. Rather, the evidence suggests that genetic inheritance and its interaction with the environment are part of the story but far from the whole story. Thus the lesson I draw is that the actual effect of family structure lies between the extremes. Whether a child grows up with two biological parents, I conclude, makes a difference in his or her life; it is not merely an epiphenomenon. Not having two parents at home sometimes leads to short- and long-term problems, but not all the differences we see in outcomes are the results of family structure. Some of the differences would have occurred anyway. Moreover, parental divorce or being born to unmarried parents does not automatically lead to problems. Many (perhaps most) children who grow up in single-parent families or in stepfamilies will not be harmed seriously in the long term.

Fortunately I see signs that observers, despite Harris and Wallerstein, are turning away from the extremes. Consider Barbara Defoe Whitehead, who stirred up concern in a now famous article published in 1993 in the *Atlantic Monthly*. The title of the article, "Dan Quayle Was Right," referred to the then vice-president's criticism of the television program *Murphy Brown* for scripting its main character to have a child outside marriage (Whitehead 1993). Drawing heavily on Wallerstein, Whitehead left the impression that divorce badly scars most children and, as the cover line on the magazine warned, that it "dramatically undermines our society."

In *The Divorce Culture*, however, a more recent, book-length treatment of the same topic, Whitehead (1997) apparently has backed away from that position. She seems to accept the evidence that the majority of children whose parents divorce do not suffer serious long-term harm from the divorce. Yet she still argues that divorce is a serious problem even if only a minority of children suffer long-term harm. After all, she argues, if 40% to 50% of all American children are experiencing divorce, then a "minority" is still a lot of kids—and she is right. We have here a troubling social problem that does not "dramatically undermine our society" but nevertheless warrants our attention and concern. Growing up in a single-parent family is not a sentence to life at emotional hard labor, but it sometimes has consequences that parents would not wish upon their children.

As I hope this example shows, backing off from extremes doesn't mean backing away from moral concern or social commentary. Rather, it means helping the lay audience and the media to avoid oversimplifying the causes of complex phenomena such as children's well-being. It means moving away from seesaw debates between those who think a particular social issue is a disaster and those who think it's not a problem at all. For social scientists, it also means recognizing how unlikely it is that a single social science discipline could provide a complete understanding of these changes. Consequently, researchers can avoid extremes by taking an interdisciplinary approach to research. Here social demographers are at an advantage because of the increasingly interdisciplinary nature of the field. They have the inclination and the opportunity to exchange findings across disciplinary boundaries.

One could argue that the tendency to advance extreme arguments is built into the scientific method, which most demographers attempt to follow. The simplification of a complex problem is essential to a solid scientific theory: Unless your research allows you to simplify reality to some degree, you have not said anything of importance. Other approaches to the social world, however, do not emphasize simplification so strongly. Anthropologists, for example, with their grounded, ethnographic perspective, are much more concerned with thick description and broad understandings. In fact, this difference is a major reason why the introduction of an anthropological perspective into demography has been so beneficial.

But I am not arguing that we should back away from the scientific research enterprise, nor that we should hesitate to identify important pathways when we find them. Rather, I am suggesting that we not overstate the importance of our perspectives. In attempting to learn the origins of complex social phenomena, perhaps the best advice we could follow comes from Albert Einstein, who said, "Everything should be made as simple as possible, but not simpler" (Jones 1996).

Notes

1. Blankenhorn (1999) cites our article as evidence that researchers are becoming more pessimistic about the effects of family disruption on children. He is correct that our conclusion about the widening gap represents a modification of an earlier article that examined the British cohort only through age 11 (Cherlin et al. 1991). Blankenhorn, however, ignores the initial gap we found at age 7, which indicates the existence of a substantial predisruption effect. In fact, he ridicules predisruption effects, arguing that "this whole exercise of trying to isolate the effects of predivorce marital problems from the effects of divorce is largely a waste of time. Often, it's fraud" (p. 8) because the problems are merely part of the divorce process. Yet some of the divorces in the British cohort took place five or 10 years after our initial measures at age 7, and the results were similar. It seems unlikely that the gap at age 7 is due only to the imminent onset of divorce.

2. Sec Kendler et al. (1992), Table 1.

3. The authors note that presumably genetic differences between identical and fraternal twin-pairs accounted for far more of the variance in major depression in the sample than did parental separation and divorce (Kendler al. 1992). The composition of the sample, however, increased the likelihood of obtaining this result: Only 12% of the twin-pairs had experienced parental separation or divorce, whereas their variation in genetic relatedness (zygosity) was much greater: 57% were identical (monozygotic) and 43% were fraternal (dizygotic).

References

Begley, S. 1998. "The Parent Trap." *Newsweek*, September 7, pp. 55–59.

Blankenhorn, D. 1999. "The Shift (Cont.)." 1999. *Propositions* (Winter, No. 3):4–8.

Block, J. H., J. Block, and P. F. Gjerde. 1986. "The Personality of Children Prior to Divorce: A Prospective Study." *Child Development* 57:827–40.

Bumpass, L. L. and H. -H. Lu. 1998. "Trends in Cohabitation and Implications for Children's Family Contexts in the U.S." Working Paper 98–15, Center for Demography and Ecology, University of Wisconsin, Madison.

Bumpass, L. L. and R. K. Raley, 1995. "Redefining Single-Parent Families: Cohabitation and Changing Family Reality." *Demography* 32:97–109.

Chase-Lansdale, P. L., A. J. Cherlin, and K. E. Kiernan. 1995. "The Long-Term Effects of Parental Divorce on the Mental Health of Young Adults: A Developmental Perspective." *Child Development* 66:1614–34.

Cherlin, A. J. 1992. *Marriage, Divorce, Remarriage.* Cambridge: Harvard University Press.

Cherlin, A. J., P. L. Chase-Lansdale, and C. McRae. 1998. "Effects of Parental Divorce on Mental Health Throughout the Life Course." *American Sociological Review* 63:239–49.

Cherlin, A. J. and F. F. Furstenberg, Jr. 1989. "Divorce Doesn't Always Hurt the Kids." *The Washington Post*, March 19, p. C1.

Cherlin, A. J., F. F. Furstenberg, Jr., P. L. Chase-Lansdale, K. E. Kiernan, P. K. Robins, D. R. Morrison, and J. O. Teitler. 1991. "Longitudinal Studies of Effects of Divorce on Children in Great Britain and the United States." *Science* 252(June 7):1386–89.

Doherty, W. and R. Needle. 1991. "Psychological Adjustment and Substance Use Among Adolescents Before and After Parental Divorce." *Child Development* 62:328–37.

Dunn, J. and R. Plomin. 1990. *Separate Lives: Why Siblings Are So Different.* New York: Basic Books.

Ehrlich, P. R. 1968. *The Population Bomb.* New York: Ballantine.

Elliott, B. J. and M. P. Richards. 1991. "Children and Divorce: Educational Performance and Behaviour Before and After Parental Separation." *International Journal of Law and the Family* 5:258–76.

Gladwell, M. 1998. "Do Parents Matter?" *The New Yorker*, August 17, pp. 54–64.

Harris, J. R. 1998. *The Nurture Assumption: Why Children Turn Out the Way They Do.* New York: Free Press.

Hoffman, S. E., M. Foster, and F. F. Furstenberg, Jr. 1993. "Reevaluating the Costs of Teenage Childbearing." *Demography* 30:1–13.

Jones, A., ed. 1996. *Chambers Dictionary of Quotations.* New York: Chambers.

Kendler, K. S., M. C. Neale, R. C. Kessler, A. C. Heath, and J. J. Eaves. 1992. "Childhood Parental Loss and Adult Psychopathology in Women: A Twin Study Perspective." *Archives of General Psychiatry* 49:109–16.

Kendler, K. S., M. Neale, R. Kessler, A. Heath, and L. Eaves. 1994. "Parental Treatment and the Equal Environment Assumption in Twin Studies of Psychiatric Illness." *Psychological Medicine* 24:579–90.

McGue, M. and D. T. Lykken. 1992. "Genetic Influence on Risk of Divorce." *Psychological Science* 3:368–73.

McLanahan, S. and G. Sandefur. 1994. *Growing Up With a Single Parent: What Hurts, What Helps.* Cambridge: Harvard University Press.

Plomin, R., J. C. DeFries, and G. E. McClearn. 1990. Behavioral Genetics: A Primer. 2nd ed. New York: Freeman.

Preston, S. H. 1984. "Children and the Elderly: Divergent Paths for America's Dependents." *Demography* 21:435–57.

Rutter, M., J. Tizard, and K. Whitmore. 1970. *Education, Health, and Behavior.* London: Longman.

Simon, J. L. 1981. *The Ultimate Resource.* Princeton, NJ: Princeton University Press.

Tierney, J. 1990. "Betting the Planet." *New York Times Magazine,* December 2, pp. 52 ff.

Tucker, C. J., J. Marx, and L. Long. 1998. " 'Moving On': Residential Mobility and Children's School Lives." *Sociology of Education* 71:111–29.

U.S. Bureau of the Census. 1999. "Table MS-2." Retrieved May 11, 1999 (www.census.gov).

U.S. Department of Health and Human Services. 1998. *Trends in the Well-Being of America's Children and Youth.* Washington, DC: U.S. Government Printing Office.

U.S. National Center for Health Statistics. 1998. *Births and Deaths: Preliminary Data for 1997.* Washington, DC: U.S. Government Printing Office.

Udry, J. R. 1994. "The Nature of Gender." *Demography* 31:561–73.

Wallerstein, J. S. and S. Blakeslee. 1989. *Second Chances: Men, Women, and Children a Decade After Divorce.* New York: Ticknor and Fields.

Wallerstein, J. S. and J. B. Kelly. 1980. *Surviving the Breakup: How Children and Parents Cope With Divorce.* New York: Basic Books.

Wallerstein, J. S. and J. Lewis. 1997. "The Long-Term Impact of Divorce on Children: A First Report From a 25-Year Study." Presented at the Second World Congress of Family Law and the Rights of Children and Youth, June 2–7, San Francisco.

Whitehead, B. D. 1993. "Dan Quayle Was Right." *The Atlantic,* April, pp. 47–84.

———. 1997. *The Divorce Culture.* New York: Knopf.

IV *Families in Society*

During the 1950s and 1960s, family scholars and the mass media presented an image of the typical, normal, or model U.S. family. It included a father, a mother, and two or three children living a middle-class existence in a single-family home in an area neither rural nor urban. Father was the breadwinner, and mother was a full-time homemaker. Both were, by implication, white.

No one denied that many families and individuals fell outside the standard nuclear model. Single persons, one-parent families, two-parent families in which both parents worked, three-generation families, and childless couples abounded. Three- or four-parent families were not uncommon, as one or both divorced spouses often remarried. Many families, moreover, neither white nor well-off, varied from the dominant image. The image scarcely reflected the increasing ratio of older people in the empty nest and retirement parts of the life cycle. But like poverty before its "rediscovery" in the mid-1960s, family complexity and variety existed on some dim fringe of semi-awareness.

When they were discussed, individuals or families who departed from the standard model were analyzed in a context of pathology. Studies of one-parent families or working mothers, for example, focused on the harmful effects to children of such "deviant" situations. Couples childless by choice were assumed to possess some basic personality inadequacy. Single persons were similarly interpreted, or else thought to be homosexual. Homosexuals symbolized evil, depravity, degradation, and mental illness.

Curiously, although social scientists have always emphasized the pluralism of U.S. society in terms of ethnic groups, religion, and geographic region, the concept of pluralism had rarely been applied to the family. In the wake of the social upheavals of the 1960s and 1970s, middle-class "mainstream" attitudes toward women's roles, sexuality, and the family were transformed. Despite the backlash that peaked in the 1980s, the "traditional" family did not return. U.S. families became increasingly diverse, and Americans were increasingly willing to extend the notion of pluralism to family life.

The selections in this part of the book discuss not only diversity in families, but also the reality that families are both embedded in and sensitive to changes in the social structure and economics of U.S. life. As Lillian B. Rubin writes in "Families on the Fault Line," words such as *downsizing, restructuring*, and *reengineering* have become all too familiar and even terrifying to blue-collar workers and their families. Rubin had carried out a similar study of working-class families two decades earlier. In the 1970s, she found that while these families were never entirely secure, they felt they had a grasp of the American dream. Most owned their own homes, and expected that their children would do even better. In the more recent study, the people Rubin interviewed perceived a discontinuity between past and present, a sense that something had gone very wrong in the country.

Thirty-five percent of the men in the study were either unemployed at the time or had experienced bouts of unemployment. Parents and children had given up hope of upward mobility, or even that the children could own homes comparable to the one they had grown up in. The families, particularly the men, were angry, yet perplexed about who or what to blame—the government, high taxes, immigrants, minorities, women—for displacing men from the workplace.

The economic pressures on families since the mid-1970s have done as much as feminism to draw women into the paid workforce. The two-parent family in which both parents work is the form that now comes closest to being the "typical American family." In the 1950s, the working mother was considered deviant, even though many women were employed in the labor force. It was taken for granted that maternal employment must be harmful to children; much current research on working mothers still takes this "social problem" approach to the subject.

Katherine S. Newman's article reports on her ethnographic studies of family life among the working poor in America's inner cities. She contrasts media images of "the underclass"—with its drug-addicted mothers and swaggering, criminal men who father children by as many different women as possible—with the realities she observed. She found that while there are families that unfortunately fit this description, they are a small minority. Moreover, such families are despised by the majority of inner-city residents and do not reflect the dominant family values of those communities. Nevertheless, despite their values, these families are not carbon copies of mainstream, middle-class ones. Newman shows how economic pressures at the bottom of the income scale affect the psychological and social functioning of people who are trying to "play by the rules."

Cynthia Fuchs Epstein discusses how escalating time pressures in the professional workplace have created barriers to women's equality. A *true professional* is now defined by a willingness to commit oneself to overtime. As a result, today's lawyers, doctors, and managers, both men and women, are finding it difficult to build a career and a family at the same time. In addition, persisting stereotypes about gender roles influence both individual decision making and workplace policy. Epstein also argues that these continuing cultural stereotypes of gender roles are reinforced by the brand of feminism that emphasizes women's "difference."

In their article, Kathleen Gerson and Jerry A. Jacobs challenge widespread notions about families and work; first, the notion that people are putting in more time at work than earlier generations did, and second, that there has been a cultural shift in which people have come to prefer the workplace to the home. Gerson and Jacobs have found that average working time has not changed all that much, but that this average is misleading. Rather, the workforce has come to be divided; one group of workers is putting in very long work weeks, while another group is unable to find enough work to meet their needs. In fact, given a choice, both men and women, especially those with young children, would prefer more time at home and greater flexibility at work.

The next group of articles address family diversity along a number of dimensions—economic status, race, ethnicity, and sexual orientation. In recent years, family researchers have recognized that diversity is more complicated than previously thought. It's too simple to sort people into distinct categories—African Americans, Hispanics, Asians, European Americans, or gays. These aspects of diversity cross-cut one another, along with many other aspects of difference—such as social class, religion, region, family structure (e.g., stepfamilies), and many more.

There is also great diversity within groups. In his article Ronald L. Taylor explores diversity among African American families. He recalls being troubled that the stereotypes of black Americans that appeared in the media as well as in social science did not reflect the families he knew growing up in a small southern city. The dominant image of black families remains the low-income, single-parent family living in a crime-ridden inner-city neighborhood. Yet only a quarter of African American families fits that description. All African Americans share a common history of slavery and segregation, and they still face discrimination in housing and employment. Taylor discusses the impact of these past and present features on African American family life.

Latino families are now emerging as America's largest "minority." They are more diverse than other groups, as Maxine Baca Zinn and Barbara Wells show in their article. Mexican Americans are the largest group among Latinos and have been the most studied. But Puerto Ricans, Cubans, and Central and South Americans differ from those of Mexican background, and among themselves. These differences are not just cultural, but reflect the immigrants' social and economic status in their home country as well as the reasons for and the timing of their departure for the United States.

Sexual orientation—whether one is gay or straight—is an identity that cuts across all racial, ethnic, and class categories. Recently, homosexuality has become a major battleground in the culture wars, with the issue of gay marriage making headlines. In early 2000, the Vermont legislature debated whether same-sex partners should be granted the same right to marry as heterosexuals, or whether they should be granted "domestic partnerships" instead. These would include all the rights married couples enjoy except the name. In the end, lawmakers voted for domestic partnerships, making Vermont the first state to grant legal recognition of gay couples.

In her article, Laura Benkov analyzes the tension between traditional and emerging definitions of *family*. The first is based on heterosexual, procreative unions; the emerging one, based on the quality of relationships, can encompass gay and lesbian partners choosing to have children. Such children, she argues, should not have fewer legal rights than those born in more traditional families.

Among the grown children of Korean and Vietnamese immigrants, Karen Pyke finds that the image of the "normal American family" serves as a framework for making sense of their own family lives. They tend to see their own parents as deficient in comparison to the image; they seem too strict and emotionally distant. On the other hand, their own cultures seem superior when it comes to children taking care of their aging parents. Pyke concludes that public images of the family serve as ideological templates that can shape the wishes and disappointments experienced by children of immigrants. Indeed, cultural images of families, such as the Cleavers and other TV sitcom families of the 1950s, can have similar emotional effects on all Americans, no matter what their background.

When people grow nostalgic about family life in past times, they rarely think of the higher mortality rates and shorter lives that typified earlier generations. One of the major recent changes in family life because of the longevity revolution is that families have more years of their lives to share across generations. In his article, Vern L. Bengtson argues that bonds between generations are becoming more important than they were in the past. Commentators who talk about "family decline" because of divorce and single parenthood overlook a more cheerful recent trend—the greater availability of grandparents, great-grandparents, aunts, and uncles as a resource for children. For example, for children born in 1900, the chances of being an orphan by the age of 18—of having no parents alive, were 18 percent. In contrast, a child born in 2000 is likely to have all four grandparents alive at age 18. Bengtson argues that kin and even step-kin may represent a latent network of people who may be inactive for long periods, but who may be called on in a crisis. In short, the extended family may be more important in the twenty-first century than in any previous era.

Scientific progress is usually positive, but, as with most things in life, there can be unanticipated and unwanted outcomes. As gender and family roles have changed, and as modern methods of contraception have become available, society has experienced a sexual revolution. Part of it, perhaps the most dramatic part, has been the increasing sexual activity of teenagers, especially of girls. Teenage girls who are having sex are also experiencing more pregnancies. Kristin Luker argues that, while teenage pregnancy is indeed a problem, its causes are often misinterpreted. It is not, she argues, simply an issue of immorality or of young women out of control. Rather, she argues, it makes far more sense to understand that teenage pregnancy partly reflects limited opportunities for realizing personal achievement, fulfillment, and enhancement of self-esteem; and also results from changed cultural expectations about teenage sex and the tendencies of teens to take chances by not using birth control consistently.

The most dramatic and painful kind of family trouble is violence among family members. In their article, Michael P. Johnson and Kathleen J. Ferraro review what has been learned about domestic violence in the 1990s. They emphasize the importance of making distinctions among types of violence. For example, some couples are violent only some of the time, such as when an argument gets out of hand and one or both partners lash out at one another. Such "common couple violence" may not reflect a general pattern of the relationship. On the other hand, "intimate terrorism" is a pattern of both violent and nonviolent behavior on the part of one partner—virtually always the man—to exert control over the partner. Violence is not confined to heterosexual couples, however. Future research is needed on different kinds of partner violence and to the control issue outside male–female relationships.

9 *Work and Family*

■ **READING 24**

Families on the Fault Line

Lillian B. Rubin

THE BARDOLINOS

It has been more than three years since I first met the Bardolino family, three years in which to grow accustomed to words like *downsizing, restructuring*, or the most recent one, *reengineering;* three years in which to learn to integrate them into the language so that they now fall easily from our lips. But these are no ordinary words, at least not for Marianne and Tony Bardolino.

The last time we talked, Tony had been unemployed for about three months and Marianne was working nights at the telephone company and dreaming about the day they could afford a new kitchen. They seemed like a stable couple then—a house, two children doing well in school, Marianne working without complaint, Tony taking on a reasonable share of the family work. Tony, who had been laid off from the chemical plant where he had worked for ten years, was still hoping he'd be called back and trying to convince himself their lives were on a short hold, not on a catastrophic downhill slide. But instead of calling workers back, the company kept cutting its work force. Shortly after our first meeting, it became clear: There would be no recall. Now, as I sit in the little cottage Marianne shares with her seventeen-year-old daughter, she tells the story of these last three years.

"When we got the word that they wouldn't be calling Tony back, that's when we really panicked; I mean *really* panicked. We didn't know what to do. Where was Tony going to find another job, with the recession and all that? It was like the bottom really dropped out. Before that, we really hoped he'd be called back any day. It wasn't just crazy; they told the guys when they laid them off, you know, that it would be three, four months at most. So we hoped. I mean, sure we worried; in these times, you'd be crazy not to worry. But he'd been laid off for a couple of months before and called back, so we thought maybe it's the same thing. Besides, Tony's boss was so sure the guys would be coming back in a couple of months; so you tried to believe it was true."

She stops speaking, takes a few sips of coffee from the mug she holds in her hand, then says with a sigh, "I don't really know where to start. So much happened, and sometimes you can't even keep track. Mostly what I remember is how scared we were. Tony started to look for a job, but there was nowhere to look. The union couldn't help; there were no jobs in the industry. So he looked in the papers, and he made the rounds of all the places around here. He even went all the way to San Francisco and some of the places down near the airport there. But there was nothing.

"At first, I kept thinking, *Don't panic; he'll find something.* But after his unemployment ran out, we couldn't pay the bills, so then you can't help getting panicked, can you?"

She stops again, this time staring directly at me, as if wanting something. But I'm not sure what, so I sit quietly and wait for her to continue. Finally, she demands, "Well, can you?"

I understand now; she wants reassurance that her anxiety wasn't out of line, that it's not she who's responsible for the rupture in the family. So I say, "It sounds as if you feel guilty because you were anxious about how the family would manage."

"Yeah, that's right," she replies as she fights her tears. "I keep thinking maybe if I hadn't been so awful, I wouldn't have driven Tony away." But as soon as the words are spoken, she wants to take them back. "I mean, I don't know, maybe I wasn't that bad. We were both so depressed and scared, maybe there's nothing I could have done. But I think about it a lot, and I didn't have to blame him so much and keep nagging at him about how worried I was. It wasn't his fault; he was trying.

"It was just that we looked at it so different. I kept thinking he should take anything, but he only wanted a job like the one he had. We fought about that a lot. I mean, what difference does it make what kind of job it is? No, I don't mean that; I know it makes a difference. But when you have to support a family, that should come first, shouldn't it?"

As I listen, I recall my meeting with Tony a few days earlier and how guiltily he, too, spoke about his behavior during that time. "I wasn't thinking about her at all," he explained. "I was just so mad about what happened; it was like the world came crashing down on me. I did a little too much drinking, and then I'd just crawl into a hole, wouldn't even know whether Marianne or the kids were there or not. She kept saying it was like I wasn't there. I guess she was right, because I sure didn't want to be there, not if I couldn't support them."

"Is that the only thing you were good for in the family?" I asked him.

"Good point," he replied laughing. "Maybe not, but it's hard to know what else you're good for when you can't do that."

I push these thoughts aside and turn my attention back to Marianne. "Tony told me that he did get a job after about a year," I remark.

"Yeah, did he tell you what kind of job it was?"

"Not exactly, only that it didn't work out."

"Sure, he didn't tell you because he's still so ashamed about it. He was out of work so long that even he finally got it that he didn't have a choice. So he took this job as a dishwasher in this restaurant. It's one of those new kind of places with an open kitchen, so there he was, standing there washing dishes in front of everybody. I mean, we used to go there to eat sometimes, and now he's washing the dishes and the whole town sees him doing it. He felt so ashamed, like it was such a comedown, that he'd come home even worse than when he wasn't working.

"That's when the drinking really started heavy. Before that he'd drink, but it wasn't so bad. After he went to work there, he'd come home and drink himself into a coma. I was working days by then, and I'd try to wait up until he came home. But it didn't matter; all he wanted to do was go for that bottle. He drank a lot during the day, too, so sometimes I'd come home and find him passed out on the couch and he never got to work that day. That's when I was maddest of all. I mean, I felt sorry for him having to do that work. But I was afraid he'd get fired."

"Did he?"

"No, he quit after a couple of months. He heard there was a chemical plant down near L.A. where he might get a job. So he left. I mean, we didn't exactly separate, but we didn't exactly not. He didn't ask me and the kids to go with him; he just went. It didn't make any difference. I didn't trust him by then, so why would I leave my job and pick up the kids and move when we didn't even know if he'd find work down there?

"I think he went because he had to get away. Anyway, he never found any decent work there either. I know he had some jobs, but I never knew exactly what he was doing. He'd call once in awhile, but we didn't have much to say to each other then. I always figured he wasn't making out so well because he didn't send much money the whole time he was gone."

As Tony tells it, he was in Los Angeles for nearly a year, every day an agony of guilt and shame. "I lived like a bum when I was down there. I had a room in a place that wasn't much better than a flop house, but it was like I couldn't get it together to go find something else. I wasn't making much money, but I had enough to live decent. I felt like what difference did it make how I lived?"

He sighs—a deep, sad sound—then continues, "I couldn't believe what I did, I mean that I really walked out on my family. My folks were mad as hell at me. When I told them what I was going to do, my father went nuts, said I shouldn't come back to his house until I got some sense again. But I couldn't stay around with Marianne blaming me all the time."

He stops abruptly, withdraws to someplace inside himself for a few moments, then turns back to me. "That's not fair. She wasn't the only one doing the blaming. I kept beating myself up, too, you know, blaming myself, like I did something wrong.

"Anyhow, I hated to see what it was doing to the kids; they were like caught in the middle with us fighting and hollering, or else I was passed out drunk. I didn't want them to have to see me like that, and I couldn't help it. So I got out."

For Marianne, Tony's departure was both a relief and a source of anguish. "At first I was glad he left; at least there was some peace in the house. But then I got so scared; I didn't know if I could make it alone with the kids. That's when I sold the house. We were behind in our payments, and I knew we'd never catch up. The bank was okay; they said they'd give us a little more time. But there was no point.

"That was really hard. It was our home; we worked so hard to get it. God, I hated to give it up. We were lucky, though. We found this place here. It's near where we used to live, so the kids didn't have to change schools, or anything like that. It's small, but at least it's a separate little house, not one of those grungy apartments." She interrupts herself with a laugh, "Well, 'house' makes it sound a lot more than it is, doesn't it?"

"How did your children manage all this?"

"It was real hard on them. My son had just turned thirteen when it all happened, and he was really attached to his father. He couldn't understand why Tony left us, and he was real angry for a long time. At first, I thought he'd be okay, you know, that he'd get over it. But then he got into some bad company. I think he was doing some drugs, although he still won't admit that. Anyway, one night he and some of his friends stole a car. I think they just wanted to go for a joyride; they didn't mean to really steal it forever. But they got caught, and he got sent to juvenile hall.

"I called Tony down in L.A. and told him what happened. It really shocked him; he started to cry on the phone. I never saw him cry before, not with all our trouble. But he just cried and cried. When he got off the phone, he took the first plane he could get, and he's been back up here ever since.

"Jimmy's trouble really changed everything around. When Tony came back, he didn't want to do anything to get Jimmy out of juvy right away. He thought he ought to stay there for a while; you know, like to teach him a lesson. I was mad at first because Jimmy wanted to come home so bad; he was so scared. But now I see Tony was right.

"Anyhow, we let Jimmy stay there for five whole days, then Tony's parents lent us the money to bail him out and get him a lawyer. He made a deal so that if Jimmy pleaded guilty, he'd get a suspended sentence. And that's what happened. But the judge laid down the law, told him if he got in one little bit of trouble again, he'd go to jail. It put the fear of God into the boy."

For Tony, his son's brush with the law was like a shot in the arm. "It was like I had something really important to do, to get that kid back on track. We talked it over and Marianne agreed it would be better if Jimmy came to live with me. She's too soft with the kids; I've got better control. And I wanted to make it up to him, too, to show him he could count on me again. I figured the whole trouble came because I left them, and I wanted to set it right.

"So when he got out of juvy, he went with me to my folks' house where I was staying. We lived there for awhile until I got this job. It's no great shakes, a kind of general handyman. But it's a job, and right from the start I made enough so we could move into this here apartment. So things are going pretty good right now."

"Pretty good" means that Jimmy, now sixteen, has settled down and is doing well enough in school to talk about going to college. For Tony, too, things have turned around. He set up his own business as an independent handyman several months ago and, although the work isn't yet regular enough to allow him to quit his job, his reputation as a man who can fix just about anything is growing. Last month the business actually made enough money to pay his bills. "I'll hang onto the job for a while, even if the business gets going real good, because we've got a lot of catching up to do. I don't mind working hard; I like it. And being my own boss, boy, that's really great," he concludes exultantly.

"Do you think you and Marianne will get together again?"

"I sure hope so; it's what I'm working for right now. She says she's not sure, but she's never made a move to get a divorce. That's a good sign, isn't it?"

When I ask Marianne the same question, she says, "Tony wants to, but I still feel a little scared. You know, I never thought I could manage without him, but then when I was forced to, I did. Now, I don't know what would happen if we got together again. It wouldn't be like it was before. I just got promoted to supervisor, so I have a lot of responsibility on my job. I'm a different person, and I don't know how Tony would like that. He says he likes it fine, but I figure we should wait a while and see what happens. I mean, what if things get tough again for him? I don't ever want to live through anything like these last few years."

"Yet you've never considered divorce."

She laughs, "You sound like Tony." Then more seriously, "I don't want a divorce if I can help it. Right now, I figure if we got through these last few years and still kind of like each other, maybe we've got a chance."

* * *

In the opening pages of this book, I wrote that when the economy falters, families tremble. The Bardolinos not only trembled, they cracked. Whether they can patch up the cracks and put the family back together again remains an open question. But the experience of families like those on the pages of this book provides undeniable evidence of the fundamental link between the public and private arenas of modern life.

No one has to tell the Bardolinos or their children about the many ways the structural changes in the economy affect family life. In the past, a worker like Tony Bardolino didn't need a high level of skill or literacy to hold down a well-paying semiskilled job in a steel mill or an automobile plant. A high school education, often even less, was enough. But an economy that relies most heavily on its service sector needs highly skilled and educated workers to fill its better-paying jobs, leaving people like Tony scrambling for jobs at the bottom of the economic order.

The shift from the manufacturing to the service sector, the restructuring of the corporate world, the competition from low-wage workers in underdeveloped countries that entices American corporations to produce their goods abroad, all have been going on for decades; all are expected to accelerate through the 1990s. The manufacturing sector, which employed just over 26 percent of American workers in 1970, already had fallen to nearly 18 percent by 1991. And experts predict a further drop to 12.5 percent by the year 2000. "This is the end of the post–World War boom era. We are never going back to what we knew," says employment analyst Dan Lacey, publisher of the newsletter *Workplace Trends.*

Yet the federal government has not only failed to offer the help working-class families need, but as a sponsor of a program to nurture capitalism elsewhere in the world it has become party to the exodus of American factories to foreign lands. Under the auspices of the U.S. Agency for International Development (AID), for example, Decaturville Sportswear, a company that used to be based in Tennessee, has moved to El Salvador. AID not only gave grants to trade organizations in El Salvador to recruit Decaturville but also subsidized the move by picking up the $5 million tab for the construction of a new plant, footing the bill for over $1 million worth of insurance, and providing low-interest loans for other expenses involved in the move.

It's a sweetheart deal for Decaturville Sportswear and the other companies that have been lured to move south of the border under this program. They build new factories at minimal cost to themselves, while their operating expenses drop dramatically. In El Salvador, Decaturville is exempted from corporate taxes and shipping duties. And best of all, the hourly wage for factory workers there is forty-five cents an hour; in the United States the minimum starting wage for workers doing the same job is $4.25.

True, like Tony Bardolino, many of the workers displaced by downsizing, restructuring, and corporate moves like these will eventually find other work. But like him also, they'll probably have to give up what little security they knew in the past. For the forty-hour-a-week steady job that pays a decent wage and provides good benefits is quickly becoming a thing of the past. Instead, as part of the new lean, clean, mean look of corporate America, we now have what the federal government and employment agencies call "contingent" workers—a more benign name for what some labor economists refer to as "disposable" or "throwaway" workers.

It's a labor strategy that comes in several forms. Generally, disposable workers are hired in part-time or temporary jobs to fill an organizational need and are released as soon as the work load lightens. But when union contracts call for employees to join the union after thirty days on the job, some unscrupulous employers fire contingent workers on the twenty-ninth day and bring in a new crew. However it's done, disposable workers earn less than those on the regular payroll and their jobs rarely come with benefits of any kind. Worse yet, they set off to work each morning fearful and uncertain, not knowing how the day will end, worrying that by nightfall they'll be out of a job.

The government's statistics on these workers are sketchy, but Labor Secretary Robert Reich estimates that they now make up nearly one-third of the existing work force. This means that about thirty-four million men and women, most of whom want steady, full-time work, start each day as contingent and/or part-time workers. Indeed, so widespread is this practice now that in some places temporary employment agencies are displacing the old ones that sought permanent placements for their clients.

Here again, class makes a difference. For while it's true that managers and professionals now also are finding themselves disposable, most of the workers who have become so easily expendable are in the lower reaches of the work order. And it's they who are likely to have the fewest options. These are the workers, the unskilled and the semiskilled—the welders, the forklift operators, the assemblers, the clerical workers, and the like—who are most likely to seem to management to be interchangeable. Their skills are limited; their job tasks are relatively simple and require little training. Therefore, they're able to move in and perform with reasonable efficiency soon after they come on the job. Whatever lost time or productivity a company may suffer by not having a steady crew of workers is compensated by the savings in wages and benefits the employment of throwaway workers permits. A resolution that brings short-term gains for the company at the long-term expense of both the workers and the nation. For when a person can't count on a permanent job, a critical element binding him or her to society is lost.

THE TOMALSONS

When I last met the Tomalsons, Gwen was working as a clerk in the office of a large Manhattan company and was also a student at a local college where she was studying nursing. George Tomalson, who had worked for three years in a furniture factory, where he laminated plastic to wooden frames, had been thrown out of a job when the company went bankrupt. He seemed a gentle man then, unhappy over the turn his life had taken but still wanting to believe that it would come out all right.

Now, as he sits before me in the still nearly bare apartment, George is angry. "If you're a black man in this country, you don't have a chance, that's all, not a chance. It's like no matter how hard you try, you're nothing but trash. I've been looking for work for over two years now, and there's nothing. White people are complaining all the time that black folks are getting a break. Yeah, well, I don't know who those people are, because it's not me or anybody else I know. People see a black man coming, they run the other way, that's what I know."

"You haven't found any work at all for two years?" I ask.

"Some temporary jobs, a few weeks sometimes, a couple of months once, mostly doing shit work for peanuts. Nothing I could count on."

"If you could do any kind of work you want, what would you do?"

He smiles, "That's easy; I'd be a carpenter. I'm good with my hands, and I know a lot about it," he says, holding his hands out, palms up, and looking at them proudly. But his mood shifts quickly; the smile disappears; his voice turns harsh. "But that's not going to happen. I tried to get into the union, but there's no room there for a black guy. And in this city, without being in the union, you don't have a chance at a construction job. They've got it all locked up, and they're making sure they keep it for themselves."

When I talk with Gwen later, she worries about the intensity of her husband's resentment. "It's not like George; he's always been a real even guy. But he's moody now, and he's so angry, I sometimes wonder what he might do. This place is a hell hole," she says, referring to the housing project they live in. "It's getting worse all the time; kids with guns, all the drugs, grown men out of work all around. I'll bet there's hardly a man in this whole place who's got a job, leave alone a good one."

"Just what is it you worry about?"

She hesitates, clearly wondering whether to speak, how much to tell me about her fears, then says with a shrug, "I don't know, everything, I guess. There's so much crime and drugs and stuff out there. You can't help wondering whether he'll get tempted." She stops herself, looks at me intently, and says, "Look, don't get me wrong; I know it's crazy to think like that. He's not that kind of person. But when you live in times like these, you can't help worrying about everything.

"We both worry a lot about the kids at school. Every time I hear about another kid shot while they're at school, I get like a raving lunatic. What's going on in this world that kids are killing kids? Doesn't anybody care that so many black kids are dying like that? It's like a black child's life doesn't count for anything. How do they expect our kids to grow up to be good citizens when nobody cares about them?

"It's one of the things that drives George crazy, worrying about the kids. There's no way you can keep them safe around here. Sometimes I wonder why we send them to school. They're not getting much of an education there. Michelle just started, but Julia's in the fifth grade, and believe me she's not learning much.

"We sit over her every night to make sure she does her homework and gets it right. But what good is it if the people at school aren't doing their job. Most of the teachers there don't give a damn. They just want the paycheck and the hell with the kids. Everybody knows it's not like that in the white schools; white people wouldn't stand for it.

"I keep thinking we've got to get out of here for the sake of the kids. I'd love to move someplace, anyplace out of the city where the schools aren't such a cesspool. But," she says dejectedly, "we'll never get out if George can't find a decent job. I'm just beginning my nursing career, and I know I've got a future now. But still, no matter what I do or how long I work at it, I can't make enough for that by myself."

George, too, has dreams of moving away, somewhere far from the city streets, away from the grime and the crime. "Look at this place," he says, his sweeping gesture taking in the whole landscape. "Is this any place to raise kids? Do you know what my little girls see every day they walk out the door? Filth, drugs, guys hanging on the corner waiting for trouble.

"If I could get any kind of a decent job, anything, we'd be out of here, far away, someplace outside the city where the kids could breathe clean and see a different life. It's so bad here, I take them over to my mother's a lot after school; it's a better neighborhood. Then we stay over there and eat sometimes. Mom likes it; she's lonely, and it helps us out. Not that she's got that much, but there's a little pension my father left."

"What about Gwen's family? Do they help out, too?"

"Her mother doesn't have anything to help with since her father died. He's long gone; he was killed by the cops when Gwen was a teenager," he says as calmly as if reporting the time of day.

"Killed by the cops." The words leap out at me and jangle my brain. But why do they startle me so? Surely with all the discussion of police violence in the black community in recent years, I can't be surprised to hear that a black man was "killed by the cops."

It's the calmness with which the news is relayed that gets to me. And it's the realization once again of the distance between the lives and experiences of blacks and others, even poor others. Not one white person in this study reported a violent death in the family. Nor did any of the Latino and Asian families, although the Latinos spoke of a difficult and often antagonistic relationship with Anglo authorities, especially the police. But four black families (13 percent) told of relatives who had been murdered, one of the families with two victims—a teenage son and a twenty-two-year-old daughter, both killed in violent street crimes.

But I'm also struck by the fact that Gwen never told me how her father died. True, I didn't ask. But I wonder now why she didn't offer the information. "Gwen didn't tell me," I say, as if trying to explain my surprise.

"She doesn't like to talk about it. Would you?" he replies somewhat curtly.

It's a moment or two before I can collect myself to speak again. Then I comment, "You talk about all this so calmly."

He leans forward, looks directly at me, and shakes his head. When he finally speaks, his voice is tight with the effort to control his rage. "What do you want? Should I rant and rave? You want me to say I want to go out and kill those mothers? Well, yeah, I do. They killed a good man just because he was black. He wasn't a criminal; he was a hard-working guy who just happened to be in the wrong place when the cops were looking for someone to shoot," he says, then sits back and stares stonily at the wall in front of him.

We both sit locked in silence until finally I break it. "How did it happen?"

He rouses himself at the sound of my voice. "They were after some dude who robbed a liquor store, and when they saw Gwen's dad, they didn't ask questions; they shot. The bastards. Then they said it was self-defense, that they saw a gun in his hand. That man never held a gun in his life, and nobody ever found one either. But nothing happens to them; it's no big deal, just another dead nigger," he concludes, his eyes blazing.

It's quiet again for a few moments, then, with a sardonic half smile, he says, "What would a nice, white middle-class lady like you know about any of that? You got all those degrees, writing books and all that. How are you going to write about people like us?"

"I was poor like you once, very poor," I say somewhat defensively.
He looks surprised, then retorts, "Poor and white; it's a big difference."

* * *

Thirty years before the beginning of the Civil War, Alexis de Tocqueville wrote: "If ever America undergoes great revolutions, they will be brought about by the presence of the black race on the soil of the United States; that is to say they will owe their origin, not to the equality, but to the inequality of condition." One hundred and sixty years later, relations between blacks and whites remain one of the great unresolved issues in American life, and "the inequality of condition" that de Tocqueville observed is still a primary part of the experience of black Americans.

I thought about de Tocqueville's words as I listened to George Tomalson and about how the years of unemployment had changed him from, as Gwen said, "a real even guy" to an angry and embittered one. And I was reminded, too, of de Tocqueville's observation that "the danger of conflict between the white and black inhabitants perpetually haunts the imagination of the [white] Americans, like a painful dream." Fifteen generations later we're still paying the cost of those years when Americans held slaves—whites still living in fear, blacks in rage. "People see a black man coming, they run the other way," says George Tomalson.

Yet however deep the cancer our racial history has left on the body of the nation, most Americans, including many blacks, believe that things are better today than they were a few decades ago—a belief that's both true and not true. There's no doubt that in ending the legal basis for discrimination and segregation, the nation took an important step toward fulfilling the promise of equality for all Americans. As more people meet as equals in the workplace, stereotypes begin to fall away and caricatures are transformed into real people. But it's also true that the economic problems of recent decades have raised the level of anxiety in American life to a new high. So although virtually all whites today give verbal assent to the need for racial justice and equality, they also find ways to resist the implementation of the belief when it seems to threaten their own status or economic well-being.

Our schizophrenia about race, our capacity to believe one thing and do another, is not new. Indeed, it is perhaps epitomized by Thomas Jefferson, the great liberator. For surely, as Gordon Wood writes in an essay in the *New York Review of Books*, "there is no greater irony in American history than the fact that America's supreme spokesman for liberty and equality was a lifelong aristocratic owner of slaves."

Jefferson spoke compellingly about the evils of slavery, but he bought, sold, bred, and flogged slaves. He wrote eloquently about equality but he was convinced that blacks were an inferior race and endorsed the racial stereotypes that have characterized African-Americans since their earliest days on this continent. He believed passionately in individual liberty, but he couldn't imagine free blacks living in America, maintaining instead that if the nation considered emancipating the slaves, it must also prepare for their expulsion.

No one talks seriously about expulsion anymore. Nor do many use the kind of language to describe African-Americans that was so common in Jefferson's day. But the duality he embodied—his belief in justice, liberty, and equality alongside his conviction of black inferiority—still lives.

THE RIVERAS

Once again Ana Rivera and I sit at the table in her bright and cheerful kitchen. She's sipping coffee; I'm drinking some bubbly water while we make small talk and get reacquainted. After a while, we begin to talk about the years since we last met. "I'm a grandmother now," she says, her face wreathed in a smile. "My daughter Karen got married and had a baby, and he's the sweetest little boy, smart, too. He's only two and a half, but you should hear him. He sounds like five."

"When I talked to her the last time I was here, Karen was planning to go to college. What happened?" I ask.

She flushes uncomfortably. "She got pregnant, so she had to get married. I was heartbroken at first. She was only nineteen, and I wanted her to get an education so bad. It was awful; she had been working for a whole year to save money for college, then she got pregnant and couldn't go."

"You say she had to get married. Did she ever consider an abortion?"

"I don't know; we never talked about it. We're Catholic," she says by way of explanation. "I mean, I don't believe in abortion." She hesitates, seeming uncertain about what more she wants to say, then adds, "I have to admit, at a time like that, you have to ask yourself what you really believe. I don't think anybody's got the right to take a child's life. But when I thought about what having that baby would do to Karen's life, I couldn't help thinking, *What if . . . ?*" She stops, unable to bring herself to finish the sentence.

"Did you ever say that to Karen?"

"No, I would *never* do that. I didn't even tell my husband I thought such things. But, you know," she adds, her voice dropping to nearly a whisper, "if she had done it, I don't think I would have said a word."

"What about the rest of the kids?"

"Paul's going to be nineteen soon; he's a problem," she sighs. "I mean, he's got a good head, but he won't use it. I don't know what's the matter with kids these days; it's like they want everything but they're not willing to work for anything. He hardly finished high school, so you can't talk to him about going to college. But what's he going to do? These days if you don't have a good education, you don't have a chance. No matter what we say, he doesn't listen, just goes on his smart-alecky way, hanging around the neighborhood with a bunch of no-good kids looking for trouble.

"Rick's so mad, he wants to throw him out of the house. But I say no, we can't do that because then what'll become of him? So we fight about that a lot, and I don't know what's going to happen."

"Does Paul work at all?"

"Sometimes, but mostly not. I'm afraid to think about where he gets money from. His father won't give him a dime. He borrows from me sometimes, but I don't have much to give him. And anyway, Rick would kill me if he knew."

I remember Paul as a gangly, shy sixteen-year-old, no macho posturing, none of the rage that shook his older brother, not a boy I would have thought would be heading for trouble. But then, Karen, too, had seemed so determined to grasp at a life that was different from the one her parents were living. What happens to these kids?

When I talk with Rick about these years, he, too, asks in bewilderment: What happened? "I don't know; we tried so hard to give the kids everything they needed. I mean, sure, we're not rich, and there's a lot of things we couldn't give them. But we were always here for them; we listened; we talked. What happened? First my daughter gets pregnant and has to get married; now my son is becoming a bum."

"Roberto—that's what we have to call him now," explains Rick, "he says it's what happens when people don't feel they've got respect. He says we'll keep losing our kids until they really believe they really have an equal chance. I don't know; I knew I had to *make* the Anglos respect me, and I had to make my chance. Why don't my kids see it like that?" he asks wearily, his shoulders seeming to sag lower with each sentence he speaks.

"I guess it's really different today, isn't it?" he sighs. "When I was coming up, you could still make your chance. I mean, I only went to high school, but I got a job and worked myself up. You can't do that anymore. Now you need to have some kind of special skills just to get a job that pays more than the minimum wage.

"And the schools, they don't teach kids anything anymore. I went to the same public schools my kids went to, but what a difference. It's like nobody cares anymore."

"How is Roberto doing?" I ask, remembering the hostile eighteen-year-old I interviewed several years earlier.

"He's still mad; he's always talking about injustice and things like that. But he's different than Paul. Roberto always had some goals. I used to worry about him because he's so angry all the time. But I see now that his anger helps him. He wants to fight for his people, to make things better for everybody. Paul, he's like the wind; nothing matters to him.

"Right now, Roberto has a job as an electrician's helper, learning the trade. He's been working there for a couple of years; he's pretty good at it. But I think—I hope—he's going to go to college. He heard that they're trying to get Chicano students to go to the university, so he applied. If he gets some aid, I think he'll go," Rick says, his face radiant at the thought that at least one of his children will fulfill his dream. "Ana and me, we tell him even if he doesn't get aid, he should go. We can't do a lot because we have to help Ana's parents and that takes a big hunk every month. But we'll help him, and he could work to make up the rest. I know it's hard to work and go to school, but people do it all the time, and he's smart; he could do it."

His gaze turns inward; then, as if talking to himself, he says, "I never thought I'd say this but I think Roberto's right. We've got something to learn from some of these kids. I told that to Roberto just the other day. He says Ana and me have been trying to pretend we're one of them all of our lives. I told him, 'I think you're right.' I kept thinking if I did everything right, I wouldn't be a 'greaser.' But after all these years, I'm still a 'greaser' in their eyes. It took my son to make me see it. Now I know. If I weren't I'd be head of the shipping department by now, not just one of the supervisors, and maybe Paul wouldn't be wasting his life on the corner."

* * *

We keep saying that family matters, that with a stable family and two caring parents children will grow to a satisfactory adulthood. But I've rarely met a family that's more constant or more concerned than the Riveras. Or one where both parents are so involved with their children. Ana was a full-time homemaker until Paul, their youngest, was twelve. Rick has been with the same company for more than twenty-five years, having worked his way up from clerk to shift supervisor in its shipping department. Whatever the conflicts in their marriage, theirs is clearly a warm, respectful, and caring relationship. Yet their daughter got pregnant and gave up her plans for college, and a son is idling his youth away on a street corner.

Obviously, then, something more than family matters. Growing up in a world where opportunities are available makes a difference. As does being able to afford to take advantage of an opportunity when it comes by. Getting an education that broadens horizons and prepares a child for a productive adulthood makes a difference. As does being able to find work that nourishes self-respect and pays a living wage. Living in a world that doesn't judge you by the color of your skin makes a difference. As does feeling the respect of the people around you.

This is not to suggest that there aren't also real problems inside American families that deserve our serious and sustained attention. But the constant focus on the failure of family life as the locus of both our personal and social difficulties has become a mindless litany, a dangerous diversion from the economic and social realities that make family life so difficult today and that so often destroy it.

THE KWANS

It's a rare sunny day in Seattle, so Andy Kwan and I are in his backyard, a lovely showcase for his talents as a landscape gardener. Although it has been only a few years since we first met, most of the people to whom I've returned in this round of interviews seem older, grayer, more careworn. Andy Kwan is no exception. The brilliant afternoon sunshine is cruel as it searches out every line of worry and age in his angular face. Since I interviewed his wife the day before, I already know that the recession has hurt his business. So I begin by saying, "Carol says that your business has been slow for the last couple of years."

"Yes," he sighs. "At first when the recession came, it didn't hurt me. I think Seattle didn't really get hit at the beginning. But the summer of 1991, that's when I began to feel it. It's as if everybody zipped up their wallets when it came to landscaping.

"A lot of my business has always been when people buy a new house. You know, they want to fix up the outside just like they like it. But nobody's been buying houses lately, and even if they do, they're not putting any money into landscaping. So it's been tight, real tight."

"How have you managed financially?"

"We get by, but it's hard. We have to cut back on a lot of stuff we used to take for granted, like going out to eat once in a while, or going to the movies, things like that. Clothes, nobody gets any new clothes anymore.

"I do a lot of regular gardening now—you know, the maintenance stuff. It helps; it takes up some of the slack, but it's not enough because it doesn't pay much. And the competition's pretty stiff, so you've got to keep your prices down. I mean, everybody knows that it's one of the things people can cut out when things get tough, so the gardeners around here try to hold on by cutting their prices. It gets pretty hairy, real cutthroat."

He gets up, walks over to a flower bed, and stands looking at it. Then, after a few quiet moments, he turns back to me and says, "It's a damned shame. I built my business like you build a house, brick by brick, and it was going real good. I finally got to the point where I wasn't doing much regular gardening anymore. I could concentrate on land-scaping, and I was making a pretty good living. With Carol working, too, we were doing all right. I even hired two people and was keeping them busy most of the time. Then all of a sudden, it all came tumbling down.

"I felt real bad when I had to lay off my workers. They have families to feed, too. But what could I do? Now it's like I'm back where I started, an ordinary gardener again and even worrying about how long that'll last," he says disconsolately.

He walks back to his seat, sits down, and continues somewhat more philosophically, "Carol says I shouldn't complain because, with all the problems, we're lucky. She still has her job, and I'm making out. I mean, it's not great, but it could be a lot worse." He pauses, looks around blankly for a moment, sighs, and says, "I guess she's right. Her sister worked at Boeing for seven years and she got laid off a couple of months ago. No notice, noth-ing; just the pink slip. I mean, everybody knew there'd be layoffs there, but you know how it is. You don't think it's really going to happen to you.

"I try not to let it get me down. But it's hard to be thankful for not having bigger trouble than you've already got," he says ruefully. Then, a smile brightening his face for the first time, he adds, "But there's one thing I can be thankful for, and that's the kids; they're doing fine. I worry a little bit about what's going to happen, though. I guess you can't help it if you're a parent. Eric's the oldest; he's fifteen now, and you never know. Kids get into all kinds of trouble these days. But so far, he's okay. The girls, they're good kids. Carol worries about what'll happen when they get to those teenage years. But I think they'll be okay. We teach them decent values; they go to church every week. I have to believe that makes a difference."

"You say that you worry about Eric but that the girls will be fine because of the val-ues of your family. Hasn't he been taught the same values?"

He thinks a moment, then says, "Did I say that? Yeah, I guess I did. I think maybe there's more ways for a boy to get in trouble than a girl." He laughs and says again, "Did I say *that?*" Then, more thoughtfully, "I don't know. I guess I worry about them all, but if you don't tell yourself that things'll work out okay, you go nuts. I mean, so much can go wrong with kids today.

"It used to be the Chinese family could really control the kids. When I was a kid, the family was law. My father was Chinese-born; he came here as a kid. My mother was born right here in this city. But the grandparents were all immigrants; everybody spoke Chinese at home; and we never lived more than a couple of blocks from both sides of the family. My parents were pretty Americanized everywhere but at home, at least while their parents were alive. My mother would go clean her mother's house for her because that's what a Chinese daughter did."

"Was that because your grandmother was old or sick?"

"No," he replies, shaking his head at the memory. "It's because that's what her mother expected her to do; that's the way Chinese families were then. We talk about that, Carol and me, and how things have changed. It's hard to imagine it, but that's the kind of control families had then.

"It's all changed now. Not that I'd want it that way. I want my kids to know respect for the family, but they shouldn't be servants. That's what my mother was, a servant for her mother.

"By the time my generation came along, things were already different. I couldn't wait to get away from all that family stuff. I mean, it was nice in some ways; there was always this big, noisy bunch of people around, and you knew you were part of something. That felt good. But Chinese families, boy, they don't let go. You felt like they were choking you.

"Now it's *really* different; it's like the kids aren't hardly Chinese any more. I mean, my kids are just like any other American kids. They never lived in a Chinese neighborhood like the one I grew up in, you know, the kind where the only Americans you see are the people who come to buy Chinese food or eat at the restaurants."

"You say they're ordinary American kids. What about the Chinese side? What kind of connection do they have to that?"

"It's funny," he muses. "We sent them to Chinese school because we wanted them to know about their history, and we thought they should know the language, at least a little bit. But they weren't really interested; they wanted to be like everybody else and eat peanut butter and jelly sandwiches. Lately it's a little different, but that's because they feel like they're picked on because they're Chinese. I mean, everybody's worrying about the Chinese kids being so smart and winning all the prizes at school, and the kids are angry about that, especially Eric. He says there's a lot of bad feelings about Chinese kids at school and that everybody's picking on them—the white kids and the black kids, all of them.

"So all of a sudden, he's becoming Chinese. It's like they're making him think about it because there's all this resentment about Asian kids all around. Until a couple of years ago, he had lots of white friends. Now he hangs out mostly with other Asian kids. I guess that's because they feel safer when they're together."

"How do you feel about this?"

The color rises in his face; his voice takes on an edge of agitation. "It's too bad. It's not the way I wanted it to be. I wanted my kids to know they're Chinese and be proud of it, but that's not what's going on now. It's more like . . . , " he stops, trying to find the words, then starts again. "It's like they have to defend themselves *because* they're Chinese. Know what I mean?" he asks. Then without waiting for an answer, he explains, "There's all this prejudice now, so then you can't forget you're Chinese.

"It makes me damn mad. You grow up here and they tell you everybody's equal and that any boy can grow up to be president. Not that I ever thought a Chinese kid could ever be president; any Chinese kid knows that's fairy tale. But I did believe the rest of it, you know, that if you're smart and work hard and do well, people will respect you and you'll be successful. Now, it looks like the smarter Chinese kids are, the more trouble they get."

"Do you think that prejudice against Chinese is different now than when you were growing up?"

"Yeah, I do. When I was a kid like Eric, nobody paid much attention to the Chinese. They left us alone, and we left them alone. But now all these Chinese kids are getting in the way of the white kids because there's so many of them, and they're getting better grades, and things like that. So then everybody gets mad because they think our kids are taking something from them."

He stops, weighs his last words, then says, "I guess they're right, too. When I was growing up, Chinese kids were lucky to graduate from high school, and we didn't get in anybody's way. Now so many Chinese kids are going to college that they're taking over places white kids used to have. I can understand that they don't like that. But that's not our problem; it's theirs. Why don't they work hard like Chinese kids do?

"It's not fair that they've got quotas for Asian kids because the people who run the colleges decided there's too many of them and not enough room for white kids. Nobody ever worried that there were too many white kids, did they?"

* * *

"It's not fair"— a cry from the heart, one I heard from nearly everyone in this study. For indeed, life has not been fair to the working-class people of America, no matter what their color or ethnic background. And it's precisely this sense that it's not fair, that there isn't enough to go around, that has stirred the racial and ethnic tensions that are so prevalent today.

In the face of such clear class disparities, how is it that our national discourse continues to focus on the middle class, denying the existence of a working class and rendering them invisible?

Whether a family or a nation, we all have myths that play tag with reality—myths that frame our thoughts, structure our beliefs, and organize our systems of denial. A myth encircles reality, encapsulates it, controls it. It allows us to know some things and to avoid knowing others, even when somewhere deep inside we really know what we don't want to know. Every parent has experienced this clash between myth and reality. We see signals that tell us a child is lying and explain them away. It isn't that we can't know; it's that we won't, that knowing is too difficult or painful, too discordant with the myth that defines the relationship, the one that says: *My child wouldn't lie to me.*

The same is true about a nation and its citizens. Myths are part of our national heritage, giving definition to the national character, offering guidance for both public and private behavior, comforting us in our moments of doubt. Not infrequently our myths trip over each other, providing a window into our often contradictory and ambivalently held beliefs. The myth that we are a nation of equals lives side-by-side in these United States with the belief in white supremacy. And, unlikely as it seems, it's quite possible to believe both at the same time. Sometimes we manage the conflict by shifting from one side to the other. More often, we simply redefine reality. The inequality of condition between whites and blacks isn't born in prejudice and discrimination, we insist; it's black inferiority that's the problem. Class distinctions have nothing to do with privilege, we say; it's merit that makes the difference.

It's not the outcome that counts, we maintain; it's the rules of the game. And since the rules say that everyone comes to the starting line equal, the different results are merely products of individual will and wit. The fact that working-class children usually grow up to be working-class parents doesn't make a dent in the belief system, nor does it lead to questions about why the written rule and the lived reality are at odds. Instead, with perfect circularity, the outcome reinforces the reasoning that says they're deficient, leaving those so labeled doubly wounded—first by the real problems in living they face, second by internalizing the blame for their estate.

Two decades ago, when I began the research for *Worlds of Pain*, we were living in the immediate aftermath of the civil rights revolution that had convulsed the nation since the mid-1950s. Significant gains had been won. And despite the tenacity with which this headway had been resisted by some, most white Americans were feeling good about themselves. No one expected the nation's racial problems and conflicts to dissolve easily or quickly. But there was also a sense that we were moving in the right direction, that there was a national commitment to redressing at least some of the worst aspects of black-white inequality.

In the intervening years, however, the national economy buckled under the weight of three recessions, while the nation's industrial base was undergoing a massive restructuring. At the same time, government policies requiring preferential treatment were enabling African-Americans and other minorities to make small but visible inroads into what had been, until then, largely white terrain. The sense of scarcity, always a part of American life but intensified sharply by the history of these economic upheavals, made minority gains seem particularly threatening to white working-class families.

It isn't, of course, just working-class whites who feel threatened by minority progress. Wherever racial minorities make inroads into formerly all-white territory, tensions increase. But it's working-class families who feel the fluctuations in the economy most quickly and most keenly. For them, these last decades have been like a bumpy roller coaster ride. "Every time we think we might be able to get ahead, it seems like we get knocked down again," declares Tom Ahmundsen, a forty-two-year-old white construction worker. "Things look a little better; there's a little more work; then all of a sudden, boom, the economy falls apart and it's gone. You can't count on anything; it really gets you down."

This is the story I heard repeatedly: Each small climb was followed by a fall, each glimmer of hope replaced by despair. As the economic vise tightened, despair turned to anger. But partly because we have so little concept of class resentment and conflict in America, this anger isn't directed so much at those above as at those below. And when whites at or near the bottom of the ladder look down in this nation, they generally see blacks and other minorities.

True, during all of the 1980s and into the 1990s, white ire was fostered by national administrations that fanned racial discord as a way of fending off white discontent—of diverting anger about the state of the economy and the declining quality of urban life to the foreigners and racial others in our midst. But our history of racial animosity coupled with our lack of class consciousness made this easier to accomplish than it might otherwise have been.

The difficult realities of white working-class life not withstanding, however, their whiteness has accorded them significant advantages—both materially and psychologically—over people of color. Racial discrimination and segregation in the workplace have kept competition for the best jobs at a minimum. They do, obviously, have to compete with each other for the resources available. But that's different. It's a competition among equals; they're all white. They don't think such things consciously, of course; they don't have to. It's understood, rooted in the culture and supported by the social contract that says they are the superior ones, the worthy ones. Indeed, this is precisely why, when the courts or the legislatures act in ways that seem to contravene that belief, whites experience themselves as victims.

From the earliest days of the republic, whiteness has been the ideal, and freedom and independence have been linked to being white. "Republicanism," writes labor historian David Roediger, "had long emphasized that the strength, virtue and resolve of a people guarded them from enslavement." And it was whites who had these qualities in abundance, as was evident, in the peculiarly circuitous reasoning of the time, in the fact that they were not slaves.

By this logic, the enslavement of blacks could be seen as stemming from their "slavishness" rather than from the institution of slavery. Slavery is gone now, but the reasoning lingers on in white America, which still insists that the lowly estate of people of color is due to their deficits, whether personal or cultural, rather than to the prejudice, discrimination, and institutionalized racism that has barred them from full participation in the society.

This is not to say that culture is irrelevant, whether among black Americans or any other group in our society. The lifeways of a people develop out of their experiences—out of the daily events, large and small, that define their lives; out of the resources that are available to them to meet both individual and group needs; out of the place in the social, cultural, and political systems within which group life is embedded. In the case of a significant proportion of blacks in America's inner cities, centuries of racism and economic discrimination have produced a subculture that is both personally and socially destructive. But to fault culture or the failure of individual responsibility without understanding the larger context within which such behaviors occur is to miss a vital piece of the picture. Nor does acknowledging the existence of certain destructive subcultural forms among some African-Americans disavow or diminish the causal connections between the structural inequalities at the social, political, and economic levels and the serious social problems at the community level.

In his study of "working-class lads" in Birmingham, England, for example, Paul Willis observes that their very acts of resistance to middle-class norms—the defiance with which these young men express their anger at class inequalities—help to reinforce the class structure by further entrenching them in their working-class status. The same can be said for some of the young men in the African-American community, whose active rejection of white norms and "in your face" behavior consigns them to the bottom of the American economic order.

To understand this doesn't make such behavior, whether in England or the United States, any more palatable. But it helps to explain the structural sources of cultural forms and to apprehend the social processes that undergird them. Like Willis's white "working-class lads," the hip-hoppers and rappers in the black community who are so determinedly "not white" are not just making a statement about black culture. They're also expressing their rage at white society for offering a promise of equality, then refusing to fulfill it. In the process, they're finding their own way to some accommodation and to a place in the world they can call their own, albeit one that ultimately reinforces their outsider status.

But, some might argue, white immigrants also suffered prejudice and discrimination in the years after they first arrived, but they found more socially acceptable ways to accommodate. It's true—and so do most of today's people of color, both immigrant and native born. Nevertheless, there's another truth as well. For wrenching as their early experiences were for white ethnics, they had an out. Writing about the Irish, for example, Roediger shows how they were able to insist upon their whiteness and to prove it by adopting the racist attitudes and behaviors of other whites, in the process often becoming leaders in the assault against blacks. With time and their growing political power, they won the prize they sought—recognition as whites. "The imperative to define themselves as white," writes Roediger, "came from the particular 'public and psychological wages' whiteness offered to a desperate rural and often preindustrial Irish population coming to labor in industrializing American cities."

Thus does whiteness bestow its psychological as well as material blessings on even the most demeaned. For no matter how far down the socioeconomic ladder whites may fall, the one thing they can't lose is their whiteness. No small matter because, as W. E. B. DuBois observed decades ago, the compensation of white workers includes a psychological wage, a bonus that enables them to believe in their inherent superiority over nonwhites.

It's also true, however, that this same psychological bonus that white workers prize so highly has cost them dearly. For along with the importation of an immigrant population, the separation of black and white workers has given American capital a reserve labor force to call upon whenever white workers seemed to them to get too "uppity." Thus, while racist ideology enables white workers to maintain the belief in their superiority, they have paid for that conviction by becoming far more vulnerable in the struggle for decent wages and working conditions than they might otherwise have been. . . .

■ READING 25

Family Values against the Odds

Katherine S. Newman

Rosa Lee Cunningham, the subject of Leon Dash's Pulitzer Prize–winning series in the *Washington Post*, is an epitome of poverty for the end of the twentieth century.[1] Born the eldest girl in a Washington, D.C., family that had been liberated from the privations of southern sharecropping only in the 1930s, Rosa Lee quickly spiraled down into oblivion. Rosa Lee's first child was born when she was a mere fourteen years old. By the time she was twenty-four, Rosa Lee's children numbered eight and their six fathers were nowhere to be seen. She raised her kids on her own by waitressing in nightclubs, selling drugs, and shoplifting. In the wake of her own disillusionment and the overwhelming burden of taking care of her children, Rosa Lee was drawn to heroin. When stealing to support her family and her habit proved unreliable, she sold herself on the street and then turned her own daughter into a hooker to maintain the needed cash flow.

Responses to Dash's series, and the book that followed, have taken a predictable path: reviewers have been as worried as they have been disgusted by the cultural disintegration Rosa Lee and her ilk represent. Rosa Lee, who could not stay away from men of questionable character, and then did disastrously poorly by the children that resulted, takes center stage as the prototypical underclass mother, the prime mover in her own despair. And the crime and degradation that follow are depicted as the inevitable result of a culture of poverty so deep that it defies remedy. No jobs program, no drug program, no heavenly social worker, can rescue someone like Rosa Lee Cunningham. She is a lost soul, with children condemned to repeat her mistakes,[2] while the rest of society suffers the consequences of predatory criminals in its midst.

Powerful portraits of this kind have shaped public impressions of inner-city families. They present implicit explanations for how poor people fall to the bottom of society's heap: by failing to control their impulses. American culture is predisposed to find such an explanation appealing, since it rests upon the view that people are masters of their own destinies, that they can, by dint of individual effort, control the circumstances of their lives. Those that fail fall to the ground where they belong, not because they have been denied opportunity, or are victims of forces larger than anyone could control, but because they have succumbed to temptation or lack the brains to do any better—the story told by Herrnstein and Murray's book *The Bell Curve*. It is a story as old as the Puritans and as resonant today as it was in the seventeenth century.

The inner city does indeed have more than its share of families like the Cunninghams. Their problems reflect the crushing personal costs of living in parts of our country where good jobs have gone the way of the dinosaurs, where schools can be hard to distinguish from penitentiaries, and where holding families together has become women's work, while the means to do so have become the object of a fierce competition. More than a few in central Harlem have found themselves in Rosa Lee's situation.

But they are a minority, and a despised one at that. They are so far from the accepted, approved personification of motherhood and family life that they do not even belong in the same world with the families of Latoya or Carmen. Journalists and scholars who write about the Rosa Lees of this world have focused their energies on those inner-city residents who are the most troubled and who inflict the greatest damage on their neighbors. Their passions are understandable, for in keeping with the spirit that animated the original War on Poverty, they want to reawaken America's conscience and persuade us that we have a cancer growing in the midst of our prosperity. That message worked effectively in the 1960s, when the country was bursting with economic growth, the middle class was secure in its comforts, and faith in the capacity of government to eradicate social ills had not yet been eviscerated.

The same message delivered in the 1990s has had the opposite impact. Focusing on the deviant cases, on the whoring mothers, the criminal fathers, the wilding teenagers, and the abandoned toddlers, merely confirms a knowing hopelessness or worse: a Darwinian conviction that perhaps we should just "let it burn," sacrificing the present generation in the hope of rehabilitating future ghetto dwellers. Attitudes have hardened in part as the litany of broken lives dominates the only "news" in print from the inner city.

It would be absurd to suggest that the downbeat reports are untrue. The "underclass" story is a persistent, intractable, and most of all depressing reality for those who cannot escape it. But there is a war for the soul of the ghetto, and it has two sides. On the other side of deviance lie the families who embrace mainstream values, even if they don't look like Ozzie and Harriet, who push their children to do better, even when they have not progressed far in life themselves. Indeed, these families—the working poor and many a "welfare family" as well—are the first to condemn Rosa Lees of their own neighborhood, to point to them as examples of what they don't want to be.

Who is winning this culture war? What are the *dominant* values of inner-city residents? The sociological emphasis on separated subcultures in the inner city has ignored the power of mainstream models and institutions like schools, the influence of the media, the convictions of poor parents, and the power of negative examples to shape the moral world of the ghetto poor. We must not confuse the irregular social structures of families—which do indeed depart from the canonical forms of middle-class society—with a separate set of values. Structure and culture can diverge in ghetto society as they do elsewhere in this country.

FAMILY VALUES

Latoya has a complicated family tree. Her mother, Ilene, who is on disability because of her diabetes, lives in the Bronx, far enough away to be in another world. Latoya's father, Alvin, has had many jobs in the course of his adult life—working mainly as a truck driver—and has only recently, in his later years, become once again a constant presence in Latoya's life. His problems with alcohol have made him a nuisance at times, but he has been welcomed back into the extended family fold because "he's blood" and has, for now at least, made a sincere effort to leave the booze behind.

Many years ago, Latoya's father began living with Elizabeth, then a recent migrant from rural Georgia, from a sleepy little town where there was nothing much to do and nowhere to go. First chance she got, Lizzie had boarded a bus for New York and begun her lifelong career cleaning houses for wealthy whites on New York's Upper East Side. She has been doing domestic work now for about twenty-five years, during which she gave birth to two daughters, Natasha and Stephanie, Latoya's half sisters through the father they share.

Though Alvin has been only sporadically in the picture, Latoya, Natasha, and Stephanie became a devoted band of sisters who look to Lizzie as the spiritual and practical head of the family. Together they form an extended family of long standing. They live within a few blocks of one another; they attend church together, especially on the important holidays.

Latoya was the first of the sisters to land a job at Burger Barn, but she was able to get Natasha on the crew not long thereafter. The two half sisters have worked together, covering for one another, blowing off the steam generated by confrontational customers, and supporting one another in the face of problem-seeking managers for nearly five years now. Little sister Stephanie, a junior in high school who has also had a summer stint at the Barn, makes it possible for Latoya to maintain a steady presence at work. It falls to Stephanie to retrieve Latoya's children from their city-funded day care center and after-school programs on those days when Latoya has to work late. Stephanie is often the one who stays with her nieces and nephews when Latoya has to work the night shift. Natasha used to do the same for Latoya.

Without the support that Natasha and Stephanie provide, Latoya would have a very hard time holding on to her job. But if we reduced the role these sisters play in Latoya's life to the instrumental need for emergency child care, we would miss the true depth of their interdependence. This is really one family, spread over several physical households in a pattern that will be familiar to readers of Carol Stack's classic book *All Our Kin.* Stack describes the complex exchange relations that characterize the families of the "Flats," a poor community in southern Illinois where goods and people circulate in a never-ending swap system. Reciprocal relations provide mothers with an insurance system against scarcity, unpredictable landlords, jobs that come and go, AFDC checks that get cut off without warning, and men who give what they can but much of the time find they have little to contribute.

FAMILY CIRCLES—SUPPORT STRUCTURES AMONG THE WORKING POOR

No one in Latoya's extended family network is on welfare; the adults are working, even Alvin, drinking problem and all. The children are in school. Yet because they are poor as well, these folk live in clusters of households that are perpetually intertwined. Although Latoya and Lizzie are separate "heads of households" as the Census Bureau might define them, in a very real sense they are one social system with moving parts that cannot stand alone. The older sisters, Natasha and Latoya, go out to clubs together when they can get Stephanie to baby-sit; together they hatch surprise birthday celebrations for Lizzie. Joining forces with their cousins, aunts, and uncles, they haul turkeys and cranberries up the stairs to whichever apartment can hold the largest number of people when it is time to host the Thanksgiving feast. And when Christmas comes, Latoya's children, sisters, and cousins and Lizzie and Alvin dress up in their Sunday best and lay claim to nearly a whole pew in the Baptist church several blocks away. Lizzie complains that her children don't attend church in the regular way she does, a habit born of her southern origins. But like many American families, Latoya and her sisters honor their mother's attachment to the church and participate in this family ritual.

Latoya, Natasha, Stephanie, and Lizzie have deliberately stayed close to one another not only because they need one another for practical support but because they value family above all else. "Family are your best friends," Natasha explains. Latoya is Natasha's closest friend, the person she socializes with, the person she confides in, her defender at work, the woman she goes shopping with when they want to look their best after hours. Danielle, cousin to them both, is part of the same inner circle, and together with her children they all form a tightly knit extended family.

Indeed, Latoya's three children look upon their aunts, Natasha and Stephanie, as permanent members of their household, people they can depend on to braid their hair for church, answer the occasional homework question, and bring them home an illicit burger or two. It was rare to find Latoya and her children at home without one of her half sisters as well.

Public perceptions of America center around middle-class nuclear families as the norm, the goal toward which others should be striving. Yet in those suburban households, it would be rare to find the intensity of relations that knits these sisters and cousins together, keeping them in daily contact with one another. Middle-class Americans value autonomy, including autonomous relations between generations and siblings once they reach adulthood. And, of course, if they have a stable hold on a decent income, there is

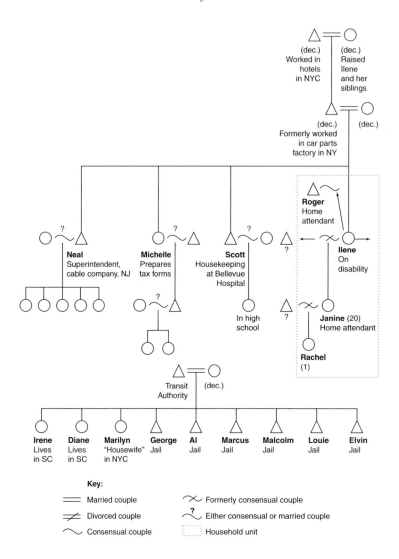

FIGURE 1A

little forcing them together into the sort of private safety net that Latoya and her relatives maintain.

The same could be said, and then some, for the immigrant families who make up a significant part of Harlem's low-wage workforce. Dominicans, Haitians, Jamaicans, West Africans, and South Americans from various countries have settled in Harlem's outer pockets. Immigrant workers in the low-wage economy depend upon extensive family networks—composed of seasoned migrants who have lived in New York for some time and those newly arrived—to organize their housing, child care, and a pool of income that they can tap when the need arises. Streaming into New York in an age-old pattern of chain migration, immigrants are often faced with the need to support family members

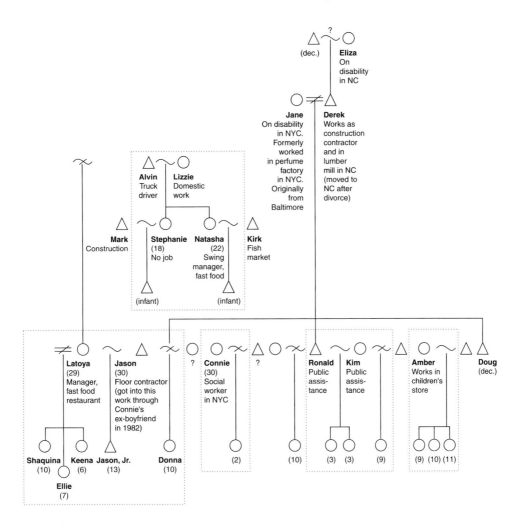

FIGURE 1B

Katherine S. Newman/Catherine Ellis

back home while they attempt to meet the far higher costs of living they encounter in their adopted city. Families that are ineligible for government benefits routinely provided to the native-born must work long hours, pack a large number of people into small apartments, and recruit as many wage earners into the network as possible.

Immigrants cluster into apartment buildings in much the same fashion as the African-American poor do, both because relatives have been instrumental in helping their family members find housing and because proximity makes it that much easier to organize collective child-minding or communal meals. In Carmen's building there are five households linked together by kinship connections. Their members move freely between them, opening the refrigerator door in one to see whether there's anything good to eat, watching television in another because it has a cable hookup, using the one phone that hasn't been cut off for nonpayment. Carmen's grandmother watches her grandchildren, a half-dozen in all now, so that their parents can go to work.

Yet to really understand the meaning of family in Carmen's life, one has to look back to the Dominican Republic, where her mother and one of her sisters still live. Carmen had to leave her mother behind to join her father and his kin, a transition necessitated both by her ambitions and by the declining purchasing power of her mother's paycheck. Carmen sends back money whenever she can, usually once a month, and that remittance spells the difference between a decent standard of living in *La Republica* and a slide into poverty.[3] For Carmen, though, this is a poor substitute for the intimacy she longs for, the daily love and affection of her mother. What she really wants, more than anything in this world, is to obtain a green card so that she can sponsor her mother and younger sister in New York. Now that she is a young parent herself, she wants her own mother close by so that she does not have to depend exclusively on her paternal relatives. That prospect is far off, though, and Carmen has to be content with the occasional trip back to her homeland, something she manages once every two or three years.

For immigrants, then, the meaning of family stretches over the seas and persists through long absences. It is organized into daisy chains of people who have followed each other, one by one, and then settled into pockets that turn into ethnic enclaves dense with interlocking ties. Families that lived next door to one another in Haiti land on adjacent blocks in Harlem. The same pattern organizes the native migrants from America's rural South, who also put down roots in Harlem neighborhoods. One can still find blocks dominated by people from particular towns in Georgia or the Carolinas and their descendants. In this respect, the native-born and the international migrant share common settlement patterns, which, in turn, provide the social structure that is so vital to the survival of the working poor.

Well-heeled families can buy the services they need to manage the demands of work and family. They can purchase child care, borrow from banks when they need to, pay their bills out of their salaries, and lean on health insurance when a doctor is needed. Affluence loosens the ties that remain tight, even oppressive at times, in poor communities. Yet there is an enduring uneasiness in our culture about the degree of independence generations and members of nuclear families maintain from one another, a sense that something has been lost. We look back with nostalgia at the close-knit family ties that were characteristic of the "immigrant generations" of the past and that still bind together newcomers to our shores, for the same reasons immigrants clung together at the turn of the century.[4]

What we fail to recognize is that many inner-city families, especially the majority who work to support themselves, maintain these close links with one another, preserving a form of social capital that has all but disappeared in many an American suburb.[5] These strong ties are the center of social life for the likes of Latoya and Natasha. It is true that these family values compete with other ambitions: the desire for a nice house and a picket fence in a suburb where graffiti doesn't mar the scenery and mothers needn't worry constantly about street violence. They dream about the prospect of owning a home and garden somewhere far away from Harlem. Yet if that miracle day arrived, they would be faced with a serious dilemma: unless they could afford to take everyone near and dear to them along on the adventure, they would find it very hard to live with the distance such a move would put between them and their relatives.

Why do we assume that family values of this kind are a thing of the past in the ghetto? While the answer lies in part on the emphasis that writers have given to people like Rosa Lee, it is just as much an artifact of the way we confuse kinship structures with the moral culture of family life in the inner city. Very few of the people who work for Burger Barn live in households that resemble the Bill Cosby model. Most are adult children in single-parent households, and some are single parents themselves. Latoya, for example, divorced her first husband when he turned to drugs, and has for a number of years now had a common-law relationship with Jason, the father of her son, the youngest child (at age two) in her household. Jason has lived with Latoya's family most of this time, taking on much of the financial responsibility for Latoya's children, since his earnings as a skilled craftsman are much higher than her Burger Barn wages. Still, their relationship has had its ups and downs; they have broken up and reconciled more than once.

Family patterns of this kind certainly do not sound like suburban America, or at least not the middle-class culture we would like to believe defines mainstream life.[6] The instability of family organization in America's ghettos has been the source of much hand-wringing. There can be little doubt that children born out of wedlock face an uphill battle, as they are more likely to be raised in poverty,[7] and that children of divorce, no matter what segment of society they come from, are similarly disadvantaged.[8]

However, we should not assume that "irregular" household structures suggest a diminished regard for the importance of family life, for the closeness of kin. Even though Latoya anguishes over Jason during their rough spots, she is no less attached to or attentive to her children. She draws the rest of her kin, especially her female kin, closer to her and builds a nest of loving relatives who sustain the familial bond and help her create a stable environment for her children. Latoya's values place family, particularly the well-being of her children, at the top of her priorities. Were we to look at the structure of her household and focus only on the ways it deviates from the nuclear family norm, we would miss what is most important about it: the quality of the relationships inside and the links between them and the web of kin who live in nearby apartments. Without them, it is true, Latoya would have a difficult time sustaining order or protecting her children in the dicey neighborhood where they live. But her story is a success in part because it is a story of a family that has pulled together against considerable adversity.

Patty began her career ten years ago at Burger Barn. She worked fulltime for the entire nine months of her first pregnancy and didn't leave work until the baby was born. She continued working and finished high school even though her second child was on the way. Her attachment to the job, through the thick-and-thin of a failed marriage and a stint on welfare, reflects the values her mother instilled. Patty's mother has worked all her life as a home attendant, first with mothers recently home from the hospital with their new babies in tow and then with homebound elderly. Working as a home aide was something of an upward step in the family, for Patty's maternal grandmother spent her whole life as a housekeeper.

> My grandmother, who just passed [away], was my idol all during the time I was growing up. She bought a house in Queens off scrubbing floors. She bought that house and mortgaged it two or three times, so she had to start all over paying it off. But she did it.

Hence Patty and her sister, who also is in home health care, taking care of AIDS patients, have come from a long line of women who have shouldered the burdens of earning a living and raising their children. None of them would have been able to manage these responsibilities were it not for the fact that each in turn has made the extended family the core of her life. Patty's mother lives on the sixth floor of her building and still has her son, Patty's brother, under her wing. Patty's sister lives just a few blocks away. Their proximity has made a big difference in Patty's life, for with their collective help, she has been able to go to work knowing that there are other adults in her family who can help watch her children.

This web of kinship does not supersede the individual household or substitute collective child-rearing for that of the mother-in-charge. Patty remains the main figure around whom her kids' lives revolve. She is the one who feeds and clothes them, watches over their homework, and puts the Band-Aids on when they skin their knees. She keeps them safe from the pitfalls of the streets that surround her apartment in a Harlem public housing complex. She has gone without things she needs for herself so she could afford air-conditioning and a Nintendo machine, items that sound like luxuries but turn out to be the key—or at least one key—to keeping her kids indoors and safe through the hot summer months. They must have something to play with and somewhere to cool off if she is to leave the teenagers to their own devices while she is working. At least equally important, however, is Patty's reliance upon her siblings and her mother as substitute supervisors of her kids, her adjunct eyes and ears, when she is at work. Without them, she would be faced with some unhappy choices.

While family support is critical for working parents, it is no less important in the lives of working youth. Teenagers at Burger Barn are often on the receiving end of the same kind of care from older relatives or "friends of the family" who are so close they constitute what anthropologists call "fictive kin," honorary aunts and uncles. Shaquena, who began working in a gym for little kids sponsored by a local church when she was just eleven, has had a difficult life. Her mother has been in and out of jail on drug convictions; one of her brothers was convicted of murder. Had her grandmother not been willing to take her in, Shaquena might have joined the thousands of New York City children shuffled into foster care.

As it is, she lives with her grandmother, who has raised her since she was ten years old. And Shaquena isn't the only one in the family who has sheltered under Grandma's wing. The household includes Shaquena's aunt, her aunt's two children, a cousin, two unmarried uncles, and an aunt and uncle who have a child as well. The grandmother has taken in her adult children and grandchildren, so that the household is a three-generation affair, albeit with several missing links (like Shaquena's own mother). Together the generations share the burden of supporting this extended household, relying on a combination of earned income and state aid: SSI for the grandmother, unemployment insurance for one of the aunts, the wages brought in by one of the uncles who works in a police station, the underground earnings of another who washes cars, and Shaquena's Burger Barn salary.

The Harlem neighborhood Shaquena calls home is jam-packed with people—kin and friends—who visit one another, eat together, and borrow from one another when the need arises.

My aunt . . . lives right across the street from us. She, like last night, my grandmother ran out of sugar. My grandmother called my aunt and my aunt bought her the sugar. The guy down the hall, he real cool with us, he give us stuff, and my grandmother's cool with a lot of elderly on our floor. She will ask her daughter, my aunt, for things before she asks a friend, but she's got friends [to ask]. If I need something, I go right upstairs, because my best friend lives right upstairs. Her grandmother and my grandmother are friends and they keep a kitchen full of food.

Shaquena can depend upon this circle of friends and relatives to take care of her basic needs, so she can reserve her own earnings for the necessities of teenage life. But she is conscious of the dry periods when funds are tight and often uses her savings to buy toothpaste, soap, and little things for the baby in the house or for her godson who lives across the street with her aunt. It is important to her to pull her own weight and to contribute to the collective well-being of her family whenever she knows it's needed.

The practical side of this arrangement is important. Yet so too is the emotional value of having a big family, especially since Shaquena has had such a rocky relationship with her mother. With her grandmother, aunts, uncles, and cousins, she has a secure place in a situation that is as real and important to her as any nuclear family, suburban-style.

"ABSENT" MEN

Popular accounts of the ghetto world often lament the declining presence of men—especially fathers—in the life of the family. Men are in jail in record numbers; they have no interest in marrying the mothers of their children; they "hit" and run. That men cause grief to the women and children who need them is hardly news. As the divorce statistics remind us, this is a sad story repeated in every class. All over America there are children who need fathers but don't have them. We have developed a culture, both in the ghetto and outside it, that assigns to women the responsibility for raising children, leaving men peripheral to the task.

This is not to minimize the difference between a jailed father and a divorced father, a poor father who has never married the mother of his children and a more affluent father who fails to pay child support. There are differences, and they have consequences. Survey research tells us, for example, that single-parent children of never-married mothers are more likely than those of divorced parents to drop out of high school, and that daughters of never-married mothers are more likely than those of divorced parents to become teen mothers—though, it should be added, the differences are not as large as some pundits might claim.[9]

Yet it would be drawing too broad a brush stroke to suggest that men have absented themselves wholesale from the inner city. Uncles, fathers, brothers, sons, boyfriends—and husbands—are very much in evidence in the daily comings-and-goings of working poor families in Harlem. They help to support the households they live in and often provide regular infusions of cash, food, and time to the mothers of their children with whom they do not live.[10] The Bureau of the Census or a sociologist looking at a survey could easily miss the presence of men in Harlem households where they do not officially live, but to which they are nonetheless important as providers. Juan, father of Kyesha's son, is a case in point. He regularly gives part of his paycheck to his mother, who has several younger children and has been on AFDC for as long as he can remember. Juan also gives money to Kyesha to help take care of their son. Little of this check is left by the time he takes care of everyone who depends on him.

> It is a struggle to make ends meet. Like if I plan on buying something that week, then I got to hold back on that. 'Cause we got cable and you got to help out, you know. Or say the lights got to be paid. So I give a hundred dollars this week, fifty the next week. My mother has a bad habit sometimes. She doesn't think reasonably. So sometimes a lot of money has to come out of my pocket—I pay whole bills so I can get that off my back.

When the welfare authorities discovered that Juan was giving his mother money, they moved to take away some of her grant. He countered by finding a couch to sleep on in a friend's apartment so that his mother could report that he no longer lives in her home.

Reynaldo, whose mother is Puerto Rican and father from Ecuador, is a jack-of-all-trades who worked for a brief time at Burger Barn in between various hustles as a nonunion electrician, car repairman, carpenter, and cellular phone dealer for fellow Latinos in his Dominican neighborhood. A tall, stocky young man with a love of baggy pants and gold chains, Rey is a classic entrepreneur. He mixes and matches his job opportunities, picking up anything he can get on the side. For a time he had a job stocking shelves in a drugstore, but during his off-hours he made money fixing up broken-down cars for neighbors and rewiring a vacant apartment for his landlord. Rey works all the hours that are not consumed by school, his girlfriend, and hanging out with his younger brother.

No doubt he is influenced in his own brand of workaholism by the example of his father, Ernie, who taught him much of what he knows about electrical and machine repair. Ernie has never met a mechanical device he couldn't tear down to the foundation and rebuild just like new. Outside on the street curb sit the broken-down Fords, Dodges, and GM cars that await his attention. His auto repair shop is just the sidewalk in front of their apartment building, but everyone in the neighborhood knows that this is a business venue. Ernie is forever walking around with a cloth in his hands, wiping away the grease and oil from an old car he has torn apart and made whole again. The shelves of the family's back room are crammed with blowtorches, pliers, hammers, wrenches, reels of plastic-coated wiring—all the equipment needed to fix the long line of radios and TV sets that friends and friends of friends have left behind for repair.

As if he weren't busy enough, Ernie has a lively sideline as an off-the-books contractor; renovating apartments destined for immigrant families just like his own. Old apartment buildings in the Dominican neighborhoods have bad plumbing, plaster weeping off the walls, tiles missing, caulking cracked and flaking, windows shattered and taped. Landlords claim to have little money for keeping apartments up to code and in any case prefer to use local workers and avoid union labor. Their preferences keep Ernie in work as the apartments turn over. In turn, Ernie has kept Rey at his side and taught him everything he knows so he can turn over some of the work he has no time for, maintaining the opportunity "in the family."

Rey's mother is a student, working toward an Associate in Arts degree that will, she hopes, make it possible for her to work in computer administration someday. Most of her days are spent going to a community college that is a long subway ride from home. Until Mayor Giuliani canceled the policy, her education was subsidized by the city welfare system (in an effort to further the long-term career prospects of women on AFDC). After many years of working in a bra factory, she has come to understand the importance of credentials and is determined to accumulate them so that she can get a good job with decent pay.

Rey's younger brother, now sixteen, has staked his future on the prospect of going to college, for he seems to have the academic gifts. Where Rey coasts through school and sees little purpose in it, his brother would visit me at Columbia University and look eagerly at the college as heaven. He works during the summers and on the weekends for a print shop that is owned by a friend of the family.

In contrast to the households discussed earlier, whose earnings come mainly from the hard work of women, Rey's family relies largely on the income of the menfolk. While his mother has worked odd factory jobs now and again and hopes to find a real job when she finishes her studies, it is the entrepreneurial spirit of the men in the household that keeps the family going. Between them, father and sons earn enough in the (nontaxed) underground economy and the formal (wage-labor) system to keep the family at a lower-working-class standard of living. They have nothing to spare, they cannot do without any of these sources of income, but they are not starving. They can even hope that the youngest child will be able to get through high school and make it into a public college, something that will require heavy doses of financial aid, but is not an unthinkable goal.

It is tempting to look at Rey's family as an inner-city exception, an icon of middle-class virtue. The two-parent family, the loving brothers, and the entrepreneurial energy all add up to an admirable portrait of a stable, supportive circle of kin pulling together. And there is much truth to the view. Yet, Rey's parents are actually divorced. They broke up years ago in order to qualify the household for welfare. Rey's father maintains an official address elsewhere.

If we were to look at an official government census of Rey's household, we would find that the adults within it are classified as out of the labor force. Indeed, it would be deemed a single-parent household supported by the welfare system. Harlem is populated by thousands of families whose official profiles look just like this. Yet there is a steady income stream coming into Rey's home, because most of the adults are indeed working, often in the mostly unregulated economy of small-scale services and self-employment, including home-based seamstresses, food vendors, gypsy cab drivers, and carpenters.[11] Most of this income never sees the tax man.

Much of what has been written about this underground system focuses on the drug world. But for thousands of poor people in New York who cannot afford a unionized plumber or electrician, unlicensed craftsmen and informal service workers (who provide child care or personal services) are more important exemplars of the shadow economy. Men like Rey and his father provide reasonably priced services and products, making it possible for people who would otherwise have to do without to get their cars fixed, their leaking roofs patched, or their children looked after. Immigrants who lack legal papers find employment in this shadow world, and those who are legal take second jobs in the underground economy.

It has proved extremely hard to estimate the size of this alternative system,[12] but it is so widespread in poor communities that it often rivals the formal economy. The multipurpose shop Rey's father runs from the living room and the street corner is the mainstay of the family's income, and in this they are hardly alone. The thoroughfares of Harlem have, for many years, had an active sidewalk market trade that is largely invisible to the Internal Revenue Service.[13]

Whether we look at employment or "family structure," Rey's household departs from the normative model of the nuclear family. The statistical observer or census-taker might lump this family together with others as dissolved, or as one whose adult members have been out of the labor force for many years. But anyone who is paying closer attention will see that this makes no sense. These people do make up an actively functioning family, and in fact kinship means everything to them. Their values place work and family at the center of their own culture in a form that would be embraced even by conservative forces in American society. And the men of the family are at least as committed to these norms as the women.

Jamal is the only income-earner in his tiny household. His common-law wife, Kathy, once received SSA, a government support provided to her because her father died when she was just a child. But once she ran away to live with Jamal, these funds were appropriated by her mother. Nowadays Jamal spends hours on the bus to reach his job sweeping floors and cleaning toilets in a Burger Barn in another borough. In Jamal's opinion, a real man earns a living and supports his family, and he puts his dictum into practice daily in a job that most Americans wouldn't waste their time on. In this, he follows a path, a cultural definition of manhood, that continues to emphasize responsibility to family, responsibility that is sometimes expressed from a distance (as in Juan's case), while other times defined by coresidence (as is true for Ernie or Jamal).

Black men have been blanketed with negative publicity, excoriated as no good, irresponsible, swaggering in their masculinity, trapped in a swamp of "ghetto-related behavior."[14] Is this simply the force of stereotypes at work on a national psyche predisposed to believe the worst? Of course not. There are men in Harlem who have turned their backs on their mothers, wives, girlfriends, and children. Yet while we deplore the damage these males cause, we may overlook people like Jamal or Juan, or fifteen-year-old James, who brings his paycheck home to his parents to help with the rent, or Salvador, who works two jobs so that his wife, Carmen, and daughter will have a roof over their heads. We will not see the contributions that Latoya's common-law husband has made to the support of her children. And if we are to truly understand the role that men play in sustaining family values, we have to credit the existence of these honorable examples, while recognizing that many of their brethren have failed to follow through.

Some of those "failures" are young blacks who have irregular connections to family, who have no real place to live, whose seasonal labor is so poorly paid that there isn't much they can do to provide for their girlfriends even when they are so inclined.[15] Ron's mother died when he was a teenager. He now lives somewhat uneasily on the sufferance of his girlfriend while working at Burger Barn off and on. Since this relationship also is off and on, his living arrangements are precarious.

> You could say I work and pay my rent. I pay for where I stay at with my girl. My girl is my landlord, but nobody knows that. She does want money. I don't like to say this is my

own bread, 'cause I don't like to be caught up in that "I'm gonna kick you out." So I always stay in contact with my family. That way, if something happens between me and her, my sister lives in Brooklyn and she always has the door open for me until I make me another power move. My sister's household is secure, but me, I'm on the edge when it comes to financial things. 'Cause if Burger Barn falls off, then I'm off.

Ron is so close to the edge that he cannot do anything more than contribute some of his wages to whatever household he lands in for the time being. People in his situation have nothing left over for anyone else, which is one of the reasons they don't behave like people with commitments. This is no excuse for siring children they can't support, but it does point to the importance of steady, reasonably paid employment in encouraging responsibility, a point William Julius Wilson has brought to national attention in *When Work Disappears.* Men who lack the wherewithal to be good fathers, often aren't.

FAMILY FLAWS

In pointing to the continuous importance of family as a set of values expressed in practice, I do not mean to paint the households of the working poor as indistinguishable from the "mainstream model." Seen through middle-class eyes, there is much to worry about. Parents who work at the bottom of the income pyramid are stressed, tired, and stretched to the limit of their ability to cope. The irregularity of the income they receive, whether from low-wage jobs, undependable partners, or both, subjects families like Latoya's to unpredictable shortages, gnawing insecurities. Welfare reform is blowing like an ill wind through many of these kin networks, and because the working poor and the AFDC recipients are interleaved, policy directives aimed at the latter are derailing many of the former. Lacking vacations, having little left over to pamper themselves with after a long day flipping burgers, and seeing so little advancement ahead of them, Burger Barn workers are often short-tempered at home. Economic pressures cannot descend upon families without showing their effects, especially on young kids.

Kyesha's two-year-old son, Anthony, spends much of his day in front of a television set tuned perpetually to soap operas and game shows. Sesame Street crosses the screen on occasion, but the purpose of the tube is not to educate little Anthony but to entertain his grandmother, stuck at home with him and several children of her own. Grandma Dana is not particularly attentive to Anthony's emotional needs, even though she keeps him fed and safe. He is never left alone, he does not run into the street, and his clothes are clean. But the focus stops there, and Anthony's behavior reflects the absence of sustained adult attention.

When Kyesha comes home, she wants to flop down on her bed and skim through movie star magazines. She lacks the energy to play with an active child.[16] She spends a lot of time figuring out how she is going to get to see her boyfriend and works on Dana in the hope that she will babysit Anthony for yet another evening so she can go out. The little boy is given to wandering into the tiny room they share and sounding off in an attempt to get Kyesha's attention. More often than not, she shoos him away so she can relax. If, like any normal two-year-old, he fails to obey, he is likely to be swatted.

Anthony will not start kindergarten knowing his colors and numbers, or the daily drill of communal "circle time" that is thoroughly familiar to any child who has spent time in a quality day care center. He will head down the road with a lack of basic experience that will weigh heavily when his teachers begin to assess his reading readiness or language fluency. There are consequences to growing up poor in a household of people who are pedaling hard just to stay afloat and have no time or reserve capacity left to provide the kind of enrichment that middle-class families can offer in abundance.

Shaquena has a rich array of people to turn to when she needs help. She has a web of kin and family friends living all around her, people who feed her and give her a place to hang out when all is not well at home. Yet her mother is a drug addict and her family broke up long ago under the strain. Had it not been for her grandmother, she would have found herself in foster care, her mother declared unfit. Hanging out with her girlfriends in the public housing project near her apartment in her younger years, she was known for getting into trouble. Fights, retaliation for insults, conflicts over boys—all have escalated to the point of serious violence. Shaquena's attachment to the work world is impressive because of this unlikely background, but the traces of her upbringing are visible enough in her temper, in the difficulty she has getting along with people at work from time to time. Her family cares about her, but to say that they are just as loving and stable in their irregular configuration as any Bill Cosby family in the suburbs would be pure romanticism.

Latoya and her common-law husband have had an on-again-off-again relationship that has caused her no end of grief. He messes up and she kicks him out. Left behind is his ten-year-old daughter by a previous relationship, not to mention the son they have in common. Latoya dreams of having a house in the suburbs, something she could afford if she could get her man to settle down, for he has a well-paid job as a carpenter, a unionized position that gives him benefits and upward of $15 an hour. Together they could make a break for it, but the instability of their relationship renders this fantasy almost unattainable. Latoya's heart bears the scars of his irresponsibility, and her children miss their dad when he is not around. Latoya's salary from Burger Barn barely stretches to meet the mounting expenses of a family of five, even with Jason's contributions. When they are together, though, their joint income puts them well above the poverty line, straight into the blue-collar working class. Hence family stability and standard of living go hand in hand in Latoya's household: when the family is together, everything looks rosy, and when things fall apart, the struggle is monumental.

Middle-class families have their ups and downs too, of course. Television is a babysitter in many families. Suburban marriages break up, leaving children in serious economic straits, with divorced mothers facing a job market that will not allow them to keep a secure hold on their lives their children are accustomed to.[17] The poor have no lock on the pitfalls of modern family life. Yet the consequences of family instability in poor neighborhoods are clearly more devastating because the whole institutional structure that surrounds folks at the bottom—the schools, the low-wage work place, the overcrowded labor market, the potholed streets, the unsavory crack dealers on the front stoop—creates more vulnerability in families that have to deal with internal troubles. Support is more problematic, more likely to depend upon the resources of relatives and friends who are, in turn, also poor and troubled.

Editor's Note: *Notes for this reading can be found in the original source.*

■READING 26

The Family and Part-Time Work

Cynthia Fuchs Epstein, Carroll Seron,
Bonnie Oglensky, and Robert Sauté

THE ROLE OF PARENTS

Many of the issues that part-time professional work raises are linked to society's norms about the role of women and the care of children. Individual time and work priorities for parents, and especially working mothers, are shaped in part by questions of "family values," the sex division of labor, the rights of women, the needs of children, the "ideal family," and, of course, the psychologies of individual mothers and fathers. Although historically child care has been the responsibility of mothers, today fathers also are expected to share some of the obligations and to appreciate the attendant satisfactions of child care. But it continues to be defined as a woman's issue, and, as we have seen, it has generated pressures to institutionalize part-time work in the legal profession.

In the post-World War II era and for a time thereafter (Skolnick, 1991) the model of a stay-at-home, nonwage-earning mother caring for children represented an ideal in American society. Although women were actually moving into the workforce in ever-increasing numbers, the advent of the woman's movement in the late 1960s imbued women's presence in the labor force with a legitimacy that went beyond the economic pressures driving them there. At the same time, restrictions on their participation in high-prestige professions were seriously curbed through Title VII of the Civil Rights Act of 1964 and a series of landmark court cases. In the years that followed, women flocked to the legal profession (Epstein, [1981] 1993) as they did to medicine and other spheres from which they had been excluded in the past. Indeed, mothers all over America have gone back to work after the birth of their children in numbers that have increased sharply in recent years. Fifty-five percent of new mothers returned to the workforce in 1995 within 12 months of giving birth, compared with 31 percent in 1976 when the Bureau of Labor Statistics started to track these figures (Fiore, 1997). Seventy-seven percent of college-educated women ages 30 to 44 juggle work and child rearing.

Of course, this trend conflicts with today's norms of motherhood, which specify standards for "intensive mothering" that have become ever more demanding (Coser and Coser, 1974; Hays, 1996). Standards for "quality time" with children have also escalated the numbers of hours each week parents are supposed to devote to involvement in their children's education, psychological development, and leisure-time activities (Hays, 1996).

At the same time, child care—private and public day-care centers, all-day nurseries, agencies that supply nannies and baby-sitters for those who can afford private solutions—all cater to the child-care needs of working parents. However, there is not enough high-quality child care generally available to meet demand, and there are also cultural perspectives that make the use of surrogates (except for family members) problematic.

The backlash against working mothers has been reflected in a stream of books (Hewlett, 1986; Mack, 1997; Whitehead, 1997), newspaper and magazine articles, and television news stories. From the mainstream press to the publications of right-wing organizations and "foundations," features are published constantly decrying the use of surrogate care. Working women are directly or indirectly chastised for selfishness in articles such as "Day Careless" (Gallagher, 1998) in *National Review*; "Day Care: The Thalidomide of the 1980s" and "Working Moms, Failing Children," in publications of the Rockford Institute; and cover stories in national newsmagazines such as "The Myth of Quality Time: How We're Cheating Our Children" in *Newsweek* and "The Lies Parents Tell About Work, Kids, Money, Day Care and Ambition" in *US. News and World Report*. News coverage focuses on stories about inadequate, inappropriate, and even lethal caregivers (Barnett and Pivers, 1997). Sociologist Arlie Hochschild's (1997) claim that Americans prefer working to dealing with the stresses of parenting received much media attention, including a cover story in the *New York Times Magazine*, and evoked a lively public response faulting American women for their selfishness in preferring the workplace to the home. And the case of Louise Woodward, an English *au pair* worker acquitted in the death of an infant in her care in a Boston suburb, generated an avalanche of hate mail to the mother, a part-time physician, faulting her for not caring for her child herself.

The hostility and indifference expressed by the media to their child-care needs and the arrangements they make fuels guilt in working mothers and reinforces conventional negative attitudes about the advisability of full-time mothers' care for children (Faludi, 1991).

Women have written about the continuing conflict between their roles, seeing it as a war between their "selves." For example, in a book explaining her retreat from a high-powered publishing position to become a more attentive mother, Elizabeth Perle McKenna (1997:85) wrote:

> Every morning the bell would ring and out would come these two identities, sparring with one another, fighting for the minutes on the clock and for my attention.

Research that shows positive effects on the family well-being of dual-career couples (Barnett and Pivers, 1997; Parcel and Menanghan, 1994) does not evoke the same kind of media attention that bad experiences evoke, and virtually no media coverage focuses on the benefits to children of surrogate care or the successful management of roles by worker-mothers.

Thus, cultural contradictions of mothering have deepened rather than resolved concerns about the balancing of work and family obligations (Hays, 1996).

Though all the mothers among the lawyers interviewed for this study rely on at least part-time surrogate care, they are wary about delegating child care and seek to minimize it. Although even full-time working mothers express some ambivalence about assigning part of their mothering role to another person, part-timers have chosen reduced work schedules as a way to express their preferences and reduce their guilt, and, of course, to reduce role strain (Goode, 1960; Merton, 1957). A refrain common in many of the interviews with part-time lawyers was expressed by an associate at a large firm: "No one, no one, not a nanny, not a day-care center, will show my children as much love, and be able to care for my children the way that I can." Josh Leventhal, a supervising attorney in a government agency, worked part time to share in care for his children, as did his wife, Robin, another government attorney. Josh told us he agreed with his wife in thinking "a nonparent would not take the same sort of care that a parent would." Similarly, Sara Wright, an associate in a medium-size law firm whose office shelves were filled with photographs of her two toddlers, expressed concern that her children "have [my] moral values and not the babysitter's" and said this motivated her to take a part-time schedule.

Some of the lawyers interviewed expressed distrust of surrogates. Marina Goff, who cut back her work schedule after moving to a distant suburb so she could spend more time with her two-year-old son and five-year-old daughter, spoke of the "horror stories you hear, even from friends." Several other lawyers also spoke of the "absolute nightmare to find people who can watch your children." Fueled by newspaper accounts of horrible behavior by nannies, two of the attorneys interviewed admitted secretly videotaping their in-home child-care providers. Both were pleasantly relieved to discover that their children had exemplary care.

Of course, this cultural climate has had an effect on attitudes about how much commitment working mothers ought to have to their careers, and how much to the family. These cultural attitudes persuade many women to work less and a few to leave the workplace altogether for the sake of "motherhood," although discontent about the nature of their work may also contribute to retreat from career paths.

McKenna's (1997) study of women who decide to leave work found that when she scratched the surface, "women admitted that, yes, they wanted more flexibility and time for their children, but if they had been happier in their work, they would have figured it out somehow" (164). She pointed to the case of Alicia Daymans, who declared in an early part of an interview that she decided to leave the high-profile magazine she worked for because she wanted to spend more time with her daughter, but revealed later that the "real" reasons were the moral and philosophical differences she had with the publication's owners. Certainly, spending time with her preadolescent daughter was a big concern, but she admitted that this alone would not have prompted her to leave.

Certainly, many women feel it is appropriate to work full time and use child-care surrogates, and do. We interviewed scores of women attorneys in our study of lawyers in large corporate law firms (Epstein *et al.*, 1995) who said they were comfortable with the balance of work and family in their lives and had worked with responsible and loving child-care surrogates who served their families well. This supported David Chambers's (1989) striking findings that women graduates of the Michigan Law School who were mothers showed the highest amount of contentment when compared with childless women (married and single) and with men. Although many of them worked part-time for some period after law school, many either consistently worked full-time or swiftly returned to full-time work after a brief leave. Consistent with our findings, women with children in Chambers's sample made more accommodations to career than men. Most for some period since law school ceased working outside the home or shifted to part-time work. A quarter of the mothers worked part time or took leaves for periods totaling at least 18 months. But even women who do not feel guilty about sharing themselves with career and family must interact with others who question their behavior and punish them.

Several lawyer mothers complained that some "stay-at-home" mothers refused to make playdates with their children, if the nanny brought the child to their home. As a result many women are exposed to multiple and often contradictory messages. The women and the few men who choose part-time work, or the law jobs with "regular hours" considered less than the large-firm norm, are those who hope to reconcile the obligations and satisfactions of both spheres using an alternative equation. Part-timers particularly subscribe to the hands-on parenting norms popular today and are members of socio-emotional communities that foster them. Pressures from spouses, children, coworkers, extended family members, and social acquaintances all affect what they say, believe, and do about balancing familial duties and professional calling.

It appears that the families of the lawyers who use part-time work in law firms to resolve the conflicts of work and child care are not so different structurally than the families of their full-time lawyer colleagues (Epstein *et al.*, 1995). They are about the same size and are headed by spouses who work in similar occupations, for example.

More than 80 percent (62 out of 75) of the lawyers in this study who work or have worked part time chose to do so for child-care reasons. They are mothers (with two exceptions) whose children ranged in age from infancy to 13 years old. Several mothers chose to work reduced hours from the time that they returned to work from maternity leave; others chose it as their children moved beyond infancy, and still others after the birth of a second child. About 40 percent either have returned or plan to return to full-time employment as their children mature (22 of 57), and 12 percent (7) are unsure of their plans. Almost half (28 lawyers) have no present intention of resuming full-time work. Additionally, most lawyers responding to a survey sent out by the Part-Time Network of the Association of the Bar of the City of New York (the LAWWS Network) (Schwab, 1994)—a group promoting part-time options in the legal profession—answered that they did not wish to return to full-time work in the future. A subset of our sample has migrated back and forth between full-time and part-time status as their families have increased in size, grown older, or been affected by other work or family pressures.

DECISIONS TO WORK PART-TIME FOR THE "JOYS OF MOTHERHOOD"

Just as these lawyers reported that their decisions to have children were worked out strategically in terms of their careers, more than half of the women part-timers in this study reported that when they were pregnant they were fairly certain that they would not return to work full-time after giving birth. Yet, of these, many told us that for strategic purposes, they behaved at work "as if" they were unsure about their postpartum plans. They did not want to reveal their intentions to work part-time prior to taking maternity leave because they did not want to lose quality work before they took leave, and they also believed they could negotiate a more favorable reduced-hours arrangement later. For most of the women in the study the decision to work part time was cushioned because they are wives of prosperous men. Thus, they were financially free to act on their feelings that it was necessary to spend more time at home.

Psychological reactions to motherhood compelled a number of lawyers interviewed to choose part-time work. Some reported their decisions to take extended periods of maternity leave or return on a part-time basis were spontaneous and emotionally unpredictable. As Patricia Clarke, a senior associate in a large Wall Street firm, described it:

> I fell madly in love with my son. . . . I just started to feel that I wouldn't be able to leave him every day and feel like someone else was raising my child. I didn't love my job enough to justify that. . . . It wasn't a trade-off worth making.

Cheryl Meany, a government attorney who left a position at a medium-size firm because she could not reduce her work schedule from four to three days a week, was agitated when she remarked, "I just felt desperate to be with my child." She admitted to being more traditional than other lawyers and wishing to stay home to take care of her two preschool-age daughters, but she was not alone in feeling "desperate."

Several mothers noted that the urge to work part time was fueled by jealous competition with their care providers. Gloria Mann, another government attorney, declared that she needed to spend "every waking hour" with her new son because:

> Being a mother to him . . . I felt like every minute, . . . every weekend I would be there for him to know that I was his mother, [not the] . . . baby-sitter.

Another mother admitted that she was heartbroken to find a local store clerk mistake her son's *au pair* for her.

Cultural lore stresses the value of witnessing a child's first steps or first words. The importance of these moments was internalized by many of the women (but was not reported by fathers in the same way). In her interview, Betty Forten, a full-time attorney, wept softly as she described her feelings at missing her son's first successful attempt at walking, a major regret of the women who worked full time. In her study of child-care providers, *Other People's Children* (1995), the sociologist Julia Wrigley found that nannies know the cultural importance of such infant milestones and that many refrain from telling parents when their children utter their first words or take their first steps, so that the mother or father will "discover" these achievements themselves.

The importance of witnessing and participating in the later development of a child was the rationale for their choice as Barbara Friedl, an eighth-year associate in a large, expanding firm, explained:

> I discovered that the more verbal they get, the more incredibly engaging they are. And the more my presence makes a difference to them. And right now, for a five-year-old . . . there is no one in the universe like me. . . . Her baby-sitter is wonderful and she adores her . . . but there is something absolutely extraordinary about having Mommy pick her up from school.

PROFILE OF FAMILIES AND CHILD-CARE ARRANGEMENTS

What do families in which the part-time lawyering choice is made look like? To draw this portrait we rely only on the 84 lawyers in the sample who returned questionnaires asking about their families and other socioeconomic data. The composition of their families and the child-care provisions they have made are as follows:

> *Marital status:* Part-time lawyers typically are married. There is one single mother among the lawyers who answered the questionnaire and one childless single attorney whose part-time arrangement was negotiated to provide time to pursue other interests.
>
> *Employment of spouse:* Most of the part-time lawyers' spouses were employed in law, finance, and other professional work. It seems evident that lawyers who choose to work part time rely on the income of a full-time working spouse. In general, women in households with higher levels of other income, either higher spousal earnings or larger amount of nonearned household income, are more likely to work part time than other women (Blank, 1990).
>
> *Size of family:* The lawyers in this study have small families, with a norm of two children, like other professional families. About half (48 of 84) have two children. Eight of the lawyers in the sample had more than two children, and eight had none (although these were young and anticipated having children). Many of the women had not had children until they were past the age of 30.
>
> *Child-care arrangements:* These lawyers use a wide variety of child-care arrangements. They rely on relatives, daily or live-in nannies, or day care. Almost one-half (32 of 69) of those for whom we have data use live-in or live-out full-time (i.e., full-week) care providers. Twenty-two families employ part-time providers as their primary child care, and the remaining 15 use baby-sitters, relatives, or day care.

A couple's resources of course affect the child-care arrangements they make. The high-income lawyers tend to use the most child care. Among families with high incomes, full-time or live-in nannies predominate. Of the 29 families for whom we have both income and employment sector data, 25 with family incomes of more than $150,000 have live-in nannies. Twenty-two of those lawyers are employed by large private law firms. A number of lawyers in large firms employ housekeepers as well as nannies, and some also have additional staff to take care of their country homes. Nannies were also employed by six lawyers who worked in the legal departments of corporations, by one self-employed lawyer, and by one government agency lawyer. About half (10 of the 22) of those who use part-time care providers work for government agencies, and four of the five using day care work in government agencies.

The nature of the attorneys' work is related closely to their incomes and thus is a determining factor in the type of child care they choose. The nature of the work may be a consideration in another way as well. Not only do attorneys in large firms and in corporate settings have the money to hire a nanny, but the demands on their time for schedule flexibility and the "on-call" nature of their work are believed to require it. Such flexibility typically cannot be put together at the last minute on an *ad hoc* basis. A few husbands have schedules that are predictable or flexible enough to permit them to pick up their children after school or day care or to relieve a sitter at the end of the day, and a small number of these part-time lawyers rely on them or on members of their extended families to do so. The more typical scenario, however, is that the husband's schedule is deemed to be more demanding than that of his wife, and she is expected to fill in the gaps in child care.

Seventeen sets of attorney couples were among the 32 families who employ full-time child-care providers. Five attorneys with full-time help have spouses who work in the financial sector. The lawyers whose spouses are academic professionals do not employ full-time or live-in nannies. But this lack of full-time coverage may be a reflection of the relatively greater flexibility of both spouses' work schedules rather than lower income.

Many lawyers rely on extraordinary flexibility and commitment from their child-care providers. Patricia Borden, a government staff attorney who works three days a week, is married to another attorney. She requires an at-home child-care provider who can stretch her own workday to care for her two children. Day-care centers available to her have strict time limits and are not "flexible the way a human can be." She remarked,

> I have . . . a tremendously flexible arrangement, both the after-school for him [her older son], and a sitter [for her toddler] for as long as I need her. She's tremendously flexible. If she has some appointment, she'll clear it with me. And then I'll know that I absolutely have to be home by then. Otherwise it's easy to sort of bleed into 7 o'clock without trying hard. So my days are generally sort of 9:30 to 7.

"Family-Friendly" Work Settings

Some places of legal employment are more desirable than others because of their "family-friendly" atmosphere. A Westchester, New York, manufacturing concern at which we interviewed part-time attorneys has such a reputation. There, breaking away from work to attend a child's soccer game or ballet recital is considered necessary. In this setting, women with small children often are given work assignments with little or no travel. But official organizational friendliness may not solve the interpersonal problems that develop because of different parental statuses of employees. For instance, questions of fairness were raised by two childless women attorneys when they were asked to increase their work travel so that a woman attorney with children could be freed from travel obligations. When one of them balked she was queried by her supervising attorney, "What's the matter? You don't have any kids."

One government agency has a reputation for being a good place for parents to work because of its flexibility toward part-time commitments and a staff with a large percentage of parents with young children. Patricia Brooke, who moved from a lucrative position at a midsize firm, spelled out why she sought employment there:

> It was very interesting work, a three-day-a-week schedule . . . and mostly the head of this department was very supportive of part-time people and did not consider them to be second-class citizens. At my previous firm, while I was part time. . . . I was certainly a second-class citizen.

Negotiating Part-Time Status with a Spouse

Decisions about childbearing, time off, and part-time work were pondered and made by these lawyers within a broad context that incorporated economics, norms of professional commitment, and ideas about gender roles. The decision about which spouse will work part time is generally made against three criteria: a "rational" economic assessment, the couple's response to traditional sex roles, and their agreed-upon ideology. All of these criteria may be seen as ideological concepts that are intertwined and susceptible to challenge and negotiation.

There are economic repercussions on the family when a spouse cuts back work time and income, but because of the income differentials in the various sectors of the profession the impact on family lifestyle may vary. Usually, when a spouse cuts back on work time, family income falls precipitously. Virtually all families decide jointly whether to reduce paid labor from two full-time jobs, and most couples negotiate over how much their work schedules can be reduced and what child-care arrangements can be made. Many husbands initially were reluctant to accept their wives' working a reduced schedule, but others saw this as the wife's decision. Patricia Brooke said her husband, Tom, was skeptical about her working part time, for financial and professional reasons. "He was . . . thinking, 'Gee, we're now gonna be poor,' " she said. Tom is also a lawyer and has doubts about the seriousness and legitimacy of part-time lawyering.

> The fact that we're both lawyers in many ways makes the relationship difficult, because he has . . . standards, and he doesn't think of part-time lawyers as . . . serious. . . . He would never admit any of this, but I think his reluctance about part-time [makes him see] me as less legitimate as a lawyer because I'm only working three days.

The decision about which spouse will work full-time is rarely couched today in the language of traditional roles, but is usually justified in terms of maximizing income over a long time period. Yet studies show that it is common for men to regard themselves as the "breadwinner" no matter how much income a wife brings into the family (Potuchek, 1997). Indeed, we heard from a male government attorney that many of his colleagues had come to the agency because of idealistic motivations to "help people," but found their salaries could not support growing families, home mortgages, and wives who felt they should cut back in their own careers. Moving to legal work that was more lucrative was, therefore, the "daddy track." Thus we see many decisions are interactive with people's views of appropriate roles and future needs. Couples weigh effort versus return; sacrifices are calculated against potential gains. Many husbands have incomes sufficient to forgo their wives' contributions. When the men are in independent professional practices or are small-business owners, couples usually decide it is more important to invest in his career than hers. Finally, families often use the language of economic rationalization when deciding which spouse should work part time. Karyn Post works four days a week as a senior associate in the corporate department of a prestigious midtown New York firm. She was hired on a part-time basis from a firm where she also had worked a reduced schedule. She has no plans to return to a full-time schedule and does not need to because her husband does very well working in the financial sector. She describes the process through which she and her husband agreed that she should work a reduced schedule:

> We decided that the financial rewards of partnership versus the hours that I would have to work to accomplish that were not worth it, and that it was better for me to go part-time

and take on a bigger role at home. . . . I'm happy I was able to do that because I'd rather be at home and be with the kids. It was better to invest more in his career.

As we have seen, women report that they, together with their husbands, often make the decision to work part-time because they accept the idea that men will ultimately make more money than women. This is based on common knowledge that in general, women workers make less money for equal or similar work. Although this is not really the case for *professional* women who work in the same spheres as men and put in the same amount of time, couples still regard it as logical to invest in the husband's career.

Of course, powerful norms setting appropriate gender roles form a backdrop to all of these decisions even when the stated rationales are economic.

But sometimes, traditional sex-role assignments are a clearly stated factor in such decisions. Fiona Scott, a federal attorney, remarked that she was "more maternalistic than [her] husband was paternalistic." Others reported their husbands were uninterested in child rearing. Carrie Little, an associate at a large firm, explained that her husband did not consider reducing his work schedule because "he didn't really want to stay home and take charge. . . . He's more of a male." The traditional gender roles are not necessarily seen as "natural" but many regard them as inevitable. Jeannette Warren, a part-time partner at a prestigious firm, left her first job in the public interest sector in the early 1970s because it did not permit her to take a reduced schedule. She had the major responsibility for child care, a responsibility she desired. As she outlined her thinking:

> Women have . . . family responsibilities . . . that men just don't have. . . . My husband could do anything that I would do with my girls, but there were times when they just wanted me; and the other side of it is . . . maternal instinct, . . . I wanted to take them to the doctor; I didn't want him to take them to the doctor. . . . Women genetically or instinctively [are different].

Several mothers attributed their husbands' relative disinterest in child care to societal norms. "Of course, I wish my husband were more involved, but he's not. Society just doesn't value that for men, and he's just not that different from other men."

As the husband of a part-time lawyer described it, many attitudes come from the general society about the propriety of men and women taking on certain work and family roles. Philip Smith, an associate in a large firm, talked to us about having considered going part-time himself. He and his wife discussed it "jokingly . . . with an edge of seriousness." Sex roles played a major part in his thinking:

> You're brought up and programmed to think you're supposed to be and do [certain things]. . . . And I guess you're brought up to think that well, if someone works part-time, it's going to be the wife. That's just how it is. And how shocking it would be if it was any other way.

Even if the subject is broached, the mechanisms that persuade people to conform to society's norms are sometimes right on the surface. Sharon Winick, a seventh-year associate in a large firm, recounted a discussion with her husband:

Some of the issues [my husband and I discussed] were: Is it easy for a man to work part time? Is the stigma greater on a man? Can he ever redeem himself if he does that? Is it even possible to do that? He didn't experience the pull to want to be home. He experienced it as wanting to support me.

A part-time attorney whose husband is a lawyer who works at home confronted the cultural view of her husband's decision: "Real men do not work at home."

IDEOLOGICAL RENEGADES

When men chose to work part-time they explained it in ways that seemed a conscious attempt to subvert social norms and to offer themselves as alternative examples. They tended to have a political commitment to a gender-free ideology and a commitment to raising their children with maximum parental involvement. Robert Malcolm worked part-time for two years beginning four months after his first child was born. His father had played a very traditional role as a parent, which made him seek a different role. "I don't understand why men would want it to be any other way in . . . their relationships with their kids," he said. Equality of responsibility in child rearing is also a political issue, as he described it:

> In terms of household responsibilities . . . it's sort of a political issue. I come from the left side of the spectrum, and I'm a fairly strong feminist, and I think it's the proper way to live your life.
>
> . . .
>
> It was important to us that the kids viewed us equally. It was important to us that they didn't view the stereotyped roles for men and women in the household, . . . that the kids basically had parents home with them for most of the time.

His wife, Leila, has worked three days a week in a municipal agency for two years and will continue to do so for the foreseeable future; she supports his decision. She feels that the reward for this political commitment was the way in which their son was socialized. "My son was totally equally bonded to both parents. He didn't have one primary over the other," she said. Their larger political commitment to set themselves as an example was important in this decision:

> We did it [worked part time] for ourselves, but we were really happy [to] set an example. . . . When [only] a few men do it . . . you'll continue to have a situation where women rank behind men. Women will always be doing other things at home, and men will keep advancing their careers. So we both thought that the best thing would be if [we] share child-care responsibility.

In both cases where men worked reduced schedules to be with their children they became dissatisfied, feeling they were missing out on their careers and failing to enjoy their parenting roles. Both male lawyers returned to full-time work, leaving their wives to work part time. One of the men returned to a full-time schedule because he missed the supervisory role that is denied in his department to part-timers; the other, because of a trial that required his full-time participation. As we found in our study of large corporate firms (Epstein *et al.*, 1995), most men find that attempts to adjust their work schedules to accommodate family needs meet extreme resistance from employers, and the costs they face are felt to be too high to pay (Rhode, 1997). It is simply easier for their wives to find accommodation in the workplace.

Furthermore, sometimes knowingly and sometimes quite unconsciously, many women place constraints on their husbands' interest in reducing their workloads and spending more time with their children. Some who have tried it find also that women in the community resist their attempts to participate in parenting that goes beyond the traditional father's role as a soccer or baseball coach. John Spiegel, a government attorney whose wife works for the same agency two days a week on site, two days at home, told us it was clear that his wife "had more of a need" to be with the children. He felt also that if he spent more time at home he would be more isolated because he didn't think he'd be included in the activities arranged by mothers. Several mothers were candid about not encouraging their husbands to reduce their work time, saying they wished to be in charge at home. With a husband whose commitment to child care might be the envy of many working mothers, Sara Atkins found herself feeling quite ambivalent. A woman with two post-graduate degrees from elite schools, she left a full-time, high-demand position in a firm because of health problems and a desire to mother her two children. She intimated that her husband's active involvement with the children threatened her role as "primary parent," and she felt somewhat competitive with him. Her work choice effectively undercut her husband's plan to share the parenting role in an equitable way.

PROFESSIONAL IDEOLOGY

Many factors influence an attorney's choice of part-time work. One of the issues for women in law is the conflict between motherhood and the ideology of professionalism. As noted earlier, many of the profession's leaders regard law as a "calling." It is this sense of vocation that partly differentiates a profession from a craft and sets it above other occupations.

Mothers who choose part-time work must adjust to the perception that they are compromising their calling. Of course, many young lawyers, men and women alike, no longer accept this definition of a professional. (It was only among lawyers in government service that we found a sense of mission to accomplish socially useful objectives. Yet even there the attractions of law were its autonomy, variety of work, and potential for a high income, rather than a grandiose ideal.) Margaret Segrest, a recently laid-off counsel in a multinational corporation's legal department with two boys and an attorney husband, expressed a sentiment that was not uncommon:

> I enjoy practicing law . . . I want to keep my foot in for economic reasons. . . . I like getting dressed and coming to work, and I like thinking, and I did invest a lot in going to law school.

What distinguishes a professional from a nonprofessional, in her view, is the professional's commitment to task without regard to other constraints. In contrast to a job in which one just does the required work within a given time period, a professional is supposed to be dedicated to producing the best she can and to provide service at its highest level.

In balancing physical, emotional, and time demands between lawyering and mothering, the allocation of energies required for mothering becomes less problematic for many part-time attorneys when the practice of law is reduced to "work, money, and prestige" as a lawyer sharing a job put it. The choice between children and career, as one woman expressed it, is a "no-brainer." Or as another joked, "There's a saying that on our deathbed nobody ever says, 'Gee, I wish I'd spent more time at work.' "

THE HOUSEHOLD DIVISION OF LABOR: CONSEQUENCES OF PART-TIME WORK

As Seron (1996) points out, the professions in general and the legal profession in particular depend on a gendered division of labor in the home. Totally dedicated male lawyers depend on their wives to handle household duties whether they stay at home or work full time or part time. As in dual-career families studied by Arlie Hochschild (1989), even an "equal" division of household labor tended to be a division of tasks inside and outside the house with unequal results. Several women reported that their husbands shared equally in household tasks, but when those cases are examined the division of labor follows traditional patterns, with men responsible for being "handy," i.e., caring for the car and yard, making repairs, and filling in with some cooking or household chores. Women will more typically manage recurring household finances, do laundry and household chores, and be responsible for all child-care duties. Moreover, women in this study had a common complaint: Their husbands "just don't notice." Even those men who accepted responsibility for housework and child care had to be supervised, in their wives' view. By doing chores that fit within the definition of being handy or neglecting details of housework, men "do gender," in the words of the sociologists Candace West and Don Zimmerman (1987). The ways in which they divide up household tasks and how they do them allow men to reaffirm their gendered identities. Elsie Marshak works as a part-time associate 35 hours a week, or 70 percent of a 50-hour full-time position, at a large firm in midtown Manhattan. With three daughters ranging in age from two to nine, she and her husband, an executive in the electronics industry, employ a full-time nanny. As she described the division of labor in her household:

> It's hard to pinpoint specific jobs. He helps clean up dinner, he helps prepare dinner sometimes. He helps me with the children in the evening. We have our own division that's hard to put into a two-sentence summary. He does everything outside the house. I do everything inside the house. Like, all the bill paying, the party arrangements, vacations, social planning . . . doctor's appointments, kids. I do everything for the kids, clothing, parties, RSVPs, I mean I delegate some of that to the nanny but, basically, it's my responsibility. Basically, I run my house. I delegate things to him.

Another attorney describes herself as the "hunter-gatherer of the family who does all the shopping, cooking, and arranging of things" while her husband is the handyman. By taking on the lion's share of household duties, women allow their spouses to pursue their careers or develop businesses. Some women work part-time so that they can devote more time to household chores in addition to child-rearing responsibilities. By doing these things on weekdays they free weekends for family social activities.

Not all of the women lawyers in our sample embraced or even fully accepted their role in the gendered division of labor in the household. Charlotte Henry, a government attorney, was deeply resentful that when she went part-time her husband expected her to take on more traditional wifely domestic responsibilities such as cooking, cleaning, and shopping. This was not what she had in mind when she reduced her work schedule. In her view, her husband imposed an old framework—assuming that she would spend her time away from work as his mother did, at household tasks. But Ms. Henry chose to go to the gym and engage in other personal interests when child-care responsibilities did not interfere. "Time for oneself" was an issue for many women.

Men's involvement with their children ranged from the father who worked part-time so that he could be a primary caregiver to those who worked long hours and spent little time with their offspring. Most women think that their husbands spend relatively more time and give more attention to their children than men in previous generations, but they are also aware that the traditional role structure has not changed radically. Caren Petrie, a senior associate at a large firm, said of her husband:

> Actually, he's good. In fact, if I tell him, he'll do [household chores]. I wish sometimes he'd do things without my telling me. He's actually very good with the kids. He'll spend a lot more time than my father did with the kids. And, I think, than what his father did. But he has the *good* time with the kids. He doesn't do the grunt work, which I take care of. All the schools and the insurance stuff.

Cheryl Mobry, who works in a municipal legal department, told how her husband once wanted to work a reduced schedule but changed his mind and instead works long hours. "He loves the kids, and I think he'd certainly like to get home earlier . . . But when he has a day by himself with the kids, he's not all excited about it, which I am." She saw an irony in this situation: Middle- and upper-middle-class women can add to their family income, but it has not significantly changed traditional roles. She expanded on this:

> It was actually a joint decision that it made more sense for us for him to work hard, for me to take more of a responsibility at home—I take care of everything; he does very little. And he is spoiled. I think that because of women's lib the men have made out very well, because the women bring in money, but still do what their mothers did, and the husbands, it takes a lot to get them to move.

PART-TIME WORK AS A SOLUTION FOR ROLE STRAIN AND ROLE INEQUITIES

Faced with cross-pressures to meet the norms of intensive mothering, the problems of surrogate child care, the curtailing of professional identity, and the continued strength of traditional gender roles in the family, what keeps women lawyers, who usually can afford to, from leaving the paid work force altogether?

Two issues predominate: the fatigue and isolation of parenting, and the attempt to maintain power in marital relationships.

Most of the women lawyers interviewed saw their work as a needed respite from domestic responsibilities. Elsie Marshak, the associate described earlier as working 35 hours a week in a large firm, considers work a condition for sanity: "I need to work. I would go crazy staying at home full time. But I was also going to go crazy doing everything at once." Using similar language, Laurie Potempkin, another part-time associate, asserted, "I think that I would go crazy staying at home. I need some structure to my life. I need the intellectual stimulation. And kids are great. But they're very demanding; it's very physically demanding and not as intellectually so in the early years." She went on to describe mothering as lonely and isolating:

> When I was on maternity leave, I found it lonely. There wasn't the camaraderie of working with people, the interaction with colleagues; you just sit with other mothers. But I guess maybe I didn't click with the other mothers. They were just always talking about kids and play days and stuff.

The gendered division of labor exists and persists because of differences in power between men and women. Some women respond to this imbalance by asserting their need for independence. Part-time work allows them to keep some control over their financial resources, social networks, and professional identities. In large part, they are defending a space with both real and symbolic territories. Their social networks and professional identities are reminders that they are more than mothers. Although, with a few notable exceptions, women attorneys do not earn enough in part-time positions to maintain their standard of living, their earnings are considerable compared to what they would earn in other occupations. Further, an independent income offers the possibility of autonomy; its absence means dependence. In negotiating conflicting norms, they often use their mothers' experience as a guide, stressing their continued employment as a safety net. Elsie Marshak reflected:

> My parents . . . had a rocky marriage for 30 years, and my mother always pushed me to be financially independent. . . . I'm not truly independent. Our lives are so intertwined with kids, but [it's important] knowing that, if I want independence, I can have it.

Though Deborah Seinfield, in her 40s, removed herself from the partnership track, staying in the labor force as a part-time associate gives her a sense of independence:

> I never thought I'd be able to depend on somebody else . . . for money. . . . One of the things that's always kept me from quitting, other than the fact that my husband says, "No," was I couldn't imagine asking him for money, for an allowance.

Neither of these attorneys believe their incomes make them self-sufficient, but they are grounds for claiming at least symbolic autonomy.

The integration of work roles and family roles is negotiated by husbands and wives on the basis of their philosophies, traditions, and practical concerns. Financial pressures, the number of children and their ages, and access to good child-care providers are all important factors, but all are weighed and interpreted within frameworks that mark the pair's private worlds and reflect the larger society.

Editors' Note: *References for this reading can be found in the original source.*

■READING 27

Changing the Structure and Culture of Work: Work and Family Conflict, Work Flexibility, and Gender Equity in the Modern Workplace

Kathleen Gerson and Jerry A. Jacobs

Once considered "separate spheres," the domains of work and family can no longer be so easily divided. As women, and especially mothers, have joined the workplace, the notion of distinct but complementary spheres has been replaced by a growing concern that the demands of work are increasingly at odds with the needs of families. Most families now depend on either two earners or one (female) parent. Yet the organization of work remains based on the principle that commitment means uninterrupted, full-time, and even overtime attention for a span of decades. This clash between family needs and workplace demands has produced a new dominant image based not on separate spheres, but on "work-family conflict."

Debate about the rise of work-family conflict has centered on the issue of working time.[1] Analysts such as Schor (1991) argue that Americans today are putting in more time at work than did earlier generations. Hochschild adds that increasing working time reflects basic cultural shifts in which home has become work and work has become home (1997, 38). Others, however, have disputed these claims, pointing to time-use studies that suggest leisure time has actually increased in recent decades (Robinson and Godbey 1997).

We offer a more complicated picture. Our analysis suggests that while average time at work has not increased substantially in the last several decades, this average masks a new dispersion among workers (Jacobs and Gerson 1998, 1999; see also Bluestone and Rose 1997; Rones, Ilg, and Gardner 1997). The labor force appears to be increasingly divided, with a growing group of workers putting in very long workweeks (well beyond the 40-hour standard) and another sizable group unable to find enough work to meet their needs. When the focus shifts from individuals to households, moreover, long workweeks appear to be concentrated among families with two earners (or one parent). These families are experiencing the greatest time crunch, not because they are working more as individuals but rather because their joint working time has become so large.

Working hours are fundamental, but taken alone they cannot tell the whole story of how workers' lives are changing. We also need to understand how in the context of growing work commitments people are coping with new conflicts between family and work. How are workers balancing their multiple obligations, what kinds of balance would they prefer, and what conflicts do they experience? Given the time that most must devote to work, what kind of workplace arrangements make a difference in workers' abilities to resolve the conflicts they face? And, finally, do workers perceive that serious costs and risks are associated with options that are ostensibly designed to ease their plight?

To answer these questions, we draw on the National Study of the Changing Workforce, a survey of the American labor force conducted in 1992.[2] Unique in the range of questions asked about workers' values and preferences and in its focus on the links, conflicts, and tensions between work and family, this survey also asked unusually detailed questions about workplace policies, organization, and culture. For these reasons, the Changing Workforce study makes it possible to untangle how work structures and processes—crucial factors that are usually hidden or overlooked in census and economic surveys—shape and constrain worker outlooks and strategies.

We use this rich material to examine the links between work and family life, paying special attention to the role of workplace structure and culture in mediating conflicts between the home and the workplace. First, we examine workers' views about how they would like to balance family, work, and personal commitments. Who experiences conflict, and how and why does the perception of conflict vary across different groups of workers? Then we turn our attention to the kinds of work arrangements that might help alleviate such difficulties. Indeed, we argue that the current focus on hours spent working neglects an equally important aspect of work-family conflict—the actual conditions of work. Especially for workers who must put in long hours, aspects of the job such is flexibility, autonomy, and control over when one works are as likely to matter as working time. We thus investigate how the structure and culture of the workplace can either exacerbate or alleviate the conflicts workers face.

Finally, we consider a central but typically overlooked aspect of work-family conflict: Even when family-friendly policies are formally available, workers may conclude that taking advantage of them entails unspoken but very real costs. We thus complete our analysis by examining worker perceptions about potential conflicts between family-friendly and high-opportunity work environments. Do workers perceive that having and using policies that provide for family support are at odds with long-term career prospects?

In a social and economic context in which most workers simply cannot choose to work the amount of time they prefer, it is critical to discover if other circumstances at work can alleviate work-family conflicts. For workers in high-demand jobs, flexibility and autonomy are likely to be as or more important than working hours. Although we cannot investigate the innumerable and subtle ways that job conditions influence workers' options, we are able to explore one important aspect of job structure: the degree of flexibility and control a worker possesses in scheduling her or his work hours. Not only is control over scheduling important in its own right, especially for those who put in long hours, but it is also likely to be linked to other workplace circumstances, such as having a sense of personal autonomy and support.

If work arrangements that offer flexibility, autonomy, and control help workers resolve conflicts between family and work, we need to understand how such arrangements can be implemented fairly. The challenge is to develop social and economic policies that alleviate current dilemmas without sacrificing the principles of gender equity and responsible parenthood. Otherwise, new policies run the risk of reinstituting old inequalities in a new form. First, however, we need to know who is experiencing conflict and why.

BALANCING WORK AND FAMILY: PERCEPTIONS OF ACTUAL AND IDEAL ALLOCATIONS

Although most workers do not experience extreme levels of work-family conflict, the Changing Workforce survey suggests that close to half experience some.[3] These figures, however, may underestimate the scope of the problem because, taken alone, they do not tell us how workers would prefer to allocate their time. Do workers wish to spend more time with their families, more time working, or more time pursuing personal avocations beyond the bounds of either family or work?

The answer to this question is not obvious. If workers now perceive that work offers the pleasures once sought at home while home now poses the problems once posed by work, then most would prefer allocating more time to the job. Yet there is good reason to expect that those experiencing conflicts would, if given an opportunity, devote more time to family and personal pursuits. To understand how work-family conflict is experienced by workers, we need to know not only how they are currently balancing the various aspects of their lives but also how they would do so if they had more choice.

Table 1, which compares the actual and desired balance between family, self, and work for women and men, offers some insight.[4] It shows that both women and men would prefer, on average, to devote a larger percentage of their time to family and personal pursuits than they currently do. Similarly, each group would prefer to spend a smaller percentage of time at work. In considering their ideal balance between family, work, and self, women say they wish to spend 13 percent less time at work and 4 percent more time with their families. Men display a similar outlook, wishing for 14 percent less time on the job and 7 percent more time on family activities. Both groups, on average, would also like to have considerably more time available for pursuing individual and personal activities, with women wishing for 20 percent more time and men hoping for 15 percent more.

The gap between the actual and desired balance grows as workers' hours increase. Those who work 50 hours per week or more are most likely to report that their actual distribution of time to work is too high and to family is too low. For both men and women, these are the workers most likely to report that their ideal balance is far from their actual balance. These preferences, moreover, are consistent with other findings, which also show that those men and women who put in the longest hours on the job are most likely to report a preference for working less (Jacobs and Gerson 1999).

It thus appears that if workers could act on their fondest wishes, they would create a new balance in which work would occupy less time and family life would get more attention. While there are surely exceptions, most workers are not working long hours in

TABLE 1   *Ideal versus Actual Balance between Work and Family*

	Women		Men	
	Actual	*Desired*	*Actual*	*Desired*
Total				
Percentage time for:				
Family	44.9	49.2	40.9	47.5
Self	19.5	39.8	21.0	37.5
Work	35.9	22.9	38.5	24.8
Like division	60.2		64.8	
Workweek of 1–34 hours				
Percentage time for:				
Family	50.3	49.3	41.0	47.0
Self	20.5	42.4	26.1	37.1
Work	29.6	23.8	32.8	26.8
Like division	65.8		70.2	
Workweek of 35-49 hours				
Percentage time for:				
Family	44.0	49.1	42.7	48.5
Self	19.5	40.1	21.6	38.9
Work	36.7	22.6	36.3	24.4
Like division	60.1		69.2	
Workweek of 50+ hours				
Percentage time for:				
Family	39.6	49.4	37.1	46.2
Self	17.9	32.8	18.4	34.7
Work	43.5	22.5	44.5	24.8
Like division	50.9		54.4	

Source: National Study of the Changing Workforce.

order to escape their homes and families. Rather, in the competition among work, family, and self, the self appears to be losing. The costs of work-family conflicts appear to have settled on the employed women and men themselves, who in their desire to meet work demands and family needs have less personal time.

FLEXIBILITY AT THE WORKPLACE

Are there social conditions and factors that can help alleviate work-family conflicts? For many workers, flexibility in scheduling work hours and increased control in work conditions may matter as much as actual time spent working. For full-time workers in particular, 45 flexible hours may seem less onerous than 35 rigidly scheduled ones. Indeed, many workers may be willing to work more hours in exchange for greater flexibility.

Flexibility gives workers some sense of control over when (and in some cases, where) they work. It also provides workers with greater discretion over how they meet their family responsibilities and balance the public and private aspects of their lives. Despite the often-criticized notion of "quality time," there are good reasons to believe that workers with flexibility and control over their working conditions will derive greater pleasure from work and also be happier, more supportive family members. Indeed, decades of research have consistently shown that satisfaction with work and good child care arrangements are the critical factors affecting the welfare of employed parents and their children.[5]

It is thus important to know who has flexible schedules and whether flexibility makes a difference. To find out, we examine answers to the question "Overall, how much control would you say you have in scheduling your work hours—none, very little, some, a lot, or complete flexibility?" Surprisingly, the overall perception of personal control remarkably similar for women and men. Forty-four percent of women and 42 percent of men respond that they have "none" or "very little," while another 26 percent of women and 27 percent of men say they have "some." At the other end of the spectrum, 30 percent of women and men report having "a lot" or "complete flexibility." At this general level, gender does not appear to be linked to job flexibility, as some have suggested (e.g., Glass and Camarigg 1992).

Despite the commonsense expectation that flexible schedules might represent an adaptation or accommodation to long work hours, there appears to be no strong or significant link between working time and flexibility. Among men, no relationship emerges between control over scheduling and hours worked.[6] Women who work long hours do report less flexibility than those with less demanding jobs, but the relationship is not strong ($r = -.13$). Work flexibility is thus not simply a reflection of overall hours worked; it deserves attention in its own right.

A closer look reveals some hidden effects of gender beneath the apparently similar and generally weak link between working time and control over scheduling. Figure 1 shows a curvilinear relationship between workers' perceptions of flexibility and the number of hours they usually work in their main job, but the extent of the curve differs by gender. It is not surprising that a high percentage of both women and men with relatively short workweeks report more flexibility. Nor is it surprising that the percentage who enjoy a sense of control declines steadily for both women and men until they reach a level of 40 to 49 working hours. Part-time work, almost by definition, is more flexible. While flexibility may be an unintended by-product of shorter working hours, many may opt for shorter hours as a strategy for obtaining flexibility.

Among workers who work very long hours, however, men and women diverge in unanticipated ways. While men who work 50 or more hours per week report substantial increases in flexibility, women in this situation experience this rebound to a much smaller degree. For men, working relatively short or long hours bestows flexibility, leaving those in the middle relatively squeezed. For women, however, there is no such counterbalancing reward for working longer hours. Women at the high end of the spectrum lack the autonomy and control that similarly situated men enjoy.

The lack of flexibility available to highly committed women workers signals difficulties for women (and their families) on several fronts. Most obviously, it implies that those workers most likely to be shouldering heavy burdens at work and at home are the least likely to have the flexibility they need. Equally problematic, the lack of control at work is also likely to reflect a hidden consequence of the "glass ceiling," which limits

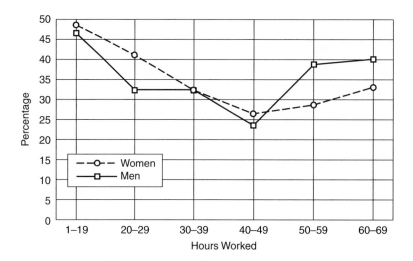

FIGURE 1 *Scheduling Flexibility, by Sex and Hours, 1993: Percentage Reporting Jobs with "A Lot of " or "Complete" Flexibility*

Source: National Survey of the Changing Workforce.

women's upward mobility despite their strong work commitment. While men who put in long hours at work may enjoy the rewards of achieving positions of authority, women who do the same are less likely to attain sufficient status to control their schedules.[7]

Since supportive job and workplace conditions appear as consequential as amount of working time in shaping workers' experiences, it important to ascertain what structural and personal factors either enhance or diminish perceptions of control over work scheduling. Most important, do work conditions remain consequential even when personal attributes, such as family situation, are taken into account? Economists, especially those who emphasize the role of "human capital" in labor market processes, argue that men and women make contrasting work choices because they prefer a different balance between family and work (e.g., Becker 1981). This perspective contends that men prefer to maximize earnings and job success to support their families, while women are willing to sacrifice economic reward and upward mobility in order to invest more time in family pursuits. This argument implies that women, especially married mothers, are more likely to choose more flexible jobs, while men, especially married fathers, are more likely to make work choices based on other criteria.

Gender and Family Situation

Is work flexibility linked to gender and family situation? The answer appears to be no. For women, flexibility at work is not related to family responsibilities, such as being married and having children in the household.[8] For men, this family situation is actually linked to having less flexibility at work. Men with family obligations may feel an increased pressure to work at inflexible jobs, but there is no evidence that women are trading off other job benefits for flexible work. Moreover, having an employed spouse has no influence on either women's or men's own work flexibility, and neither do the work hours of a spouse. For women, there is also no connection between placing a higher importance on a husband's job and choosing flexible work. And men who place more importance on a wife's job are more rather than less likely to experience less flexibility in their own jobs.

There is thus no support for the contention that women choose and men eschew flexible work in order to reproduce a gendered division of labor in the home. Family obligations may increase the pressures oil working parents, but neither mothers nor fathers enjoy more flexibility to meet these demands.

The Relative Importance of Individual, Family, and Workplace Conditions

Since few have the power to choose the conditions of their work based on their private needs, it should come as no surprise that family situation is not linked to flexible work. Despite the rise of dual-earner and single-parent homes, employers, far more than workers, set the conditions under which parents balance work and family obligations.

The crucial importance of work conditions becomes especially clear in Table 2, which presents the multivariate relationships between workplace flexibility and a range of individual, family, and workplace factors. Even after such personal attributes as age, education, job experience, and family situation are taken into account, work structure and culture remain the most consistently important factors linked to job flexibility.

Among men, education enhances flexibility, while children in the household, a long commute, and feeling insecure in a job dampens it. For women, white-collar positions enhance flexibility, while public sector and union jobs dampen it. Most important, work conditions remain influential for men and women alike. Those who have supportive supervisors and workplace cultures are more likely to have flexibility as well. Moreover, autonomy provides the most powerful link with workplace flexibility. Job autonomy increases the explained variance from 13 to 18 percent for men and from 11 to 18 percent for women. When autonomy is taken into account, the relative importance of such factors as workplace culture and supervisor support appears to diminish. However, all of these contextual factors are highly intertwined and tend to occur together. They are actually different aspects of the overall work, environment, and they have similar consequences for men and women in similar situations.

Workplace structure and culture make an important difference in workers' lives. Employers' support for flexible work arrangements, especially in the form of understanding supervisors and a supportive work culture, give both women and men more control over how to balance work and family. While similar work conditions affect female and male workers in similar ways, it remains clear that men are more likely than women to obtain privileges that give them more felicitous work circumstances.

THE AVAILABILITY, USE, AND DESIRABILITY OF FLEXIBILITY AT WORK

There can be little doubt that workers, especially parents with young children and employed partners, benefit from family-supportive arrangements such as work flexibility,

TABLE 2   *Multivariate Associations with Workplace Flexibility*

Demographic Variables	Men		Women	
	Beta	S. E.	Beta	S. E.
Intercept	0.55	(.49)	0.31	(.44)
Age groups:				
Age 25 or under (reference)	—	—	—	—
Age 26–35	–0.27*	(.14)	–0.37*	(.13)
Age 36–45	–0.07	(.16)	–0.32*	(.14)
Age 46–55	–0.22	(.17)	–0.43*	(.15)
Age 56–65	–0.08	(.21)	–0.39*	(.18)
Tenure:				
Firm	–0.003	(.007)	–0.002	(.008)
Job	–0.006	(.009)	0.003	(.010)
Education:				
College graduate	0.42*	(.16)	0.05	(.18)
Some college	0.29*	(.15)	0.12	(.17)
High school graduate	0.17	(.14)	0.08	(.16)
High school dropout	—	—	—	—
Family situation:				
Kids in home under age 18	–0.16	(.12)	–0.12	(.17)
Kids in home under age 6	–0.04	(.13)	0.08	(.12)
Married	0.04	(.12)	0.25	(.14)
Spouse works	–0.58*	(.23)	–0.37	(.26)
Spouse's hours	0.01*	(.005)	0.001	(.004)
Spouse's job importance	–0.01	(.06)	0.02	(0.5)
Workplace culture:				
Demands	–0.06	(.08)	–0.06	(.08)
Autonomy	0.53*	(.07)	0.62*	(.06)
Initiate	0.05	(.04)	0.05	(.04)
Culture	0.18*	(.08)	0.18*	(.07)
Insecure	–0.04	(.05)	–0.02	(.04)
Supervisor support	0.08	(.08)	0.06	(.07)

(continued)

autonomy, and control over scheduling. Yet how widely available are such arrangements? Are workers with access to them willing to use them? Among those without access to such options, how strong is the desire to obtain them? The answers to these questions shed additional light on the larger question of whether the growing time squeezes between work and family reflect workplace constraints or worker preferences. To answer these questions we briefly consider to what extent family-friendly options that provide more flexibility and control at work are available, used, or desired in modern workplaces.[9]

TABLE 2   *(continued)*

Demographic Variables	Men		Women	
	Beta	S. E.	Beta	S. E.
Job attributes:				
Supervisor	0.13	(.09)	0.22	(.09)
Eligible for overtime	−0.23*	(.10)	0.16	(.08)
Union	−0.25	(.10)	−0.42	(.10)
Commute	−0.03*	(.01)	0.01	(.01)
Annual earnings (in thousands)	−0.002	(.002)	0.004	(.002)
Total hours worked	0.002	(.004)	−0.01	(.003)
Occupation:				
Professional/technical worker	0.13	(.12)	0.45	(.16)
Manager	0.08	(.14)	0.70	(.19)
Clerical	0.30	(.20)	0.62	(.15)
Sales/service	0.08	(.12)	0.59	(.16)
Blue-collar (reference)	—	—	—	—
Industry:				
Manufacturing (reference)	—	—	—	—
Retail trade	0.18	(.12)	0.09	(.14)
Business services	0.25	(.13)	−0.05	(.13)
Social services	−0.24	(.13)	−0.07	(.12)
Personal services	0.28	(.16)	0.20	(.18)
Public sector	−0.33*	(.16)	−0.40	(.20)
R^2	0.18		0.18	

Source: National Study of the Changing Workforce.

*$p < .05$

Availability and Use of Flexible Scheduling

While a large proportion of the workforce (almost 86%) has the discretion to change their working hours "as needed," far fewer can set their own hours (29%) or change them daily (40%). Professional men, including those with preschool-age children, are the most likely to be able to set their own working hours (about 40%), but professional men with young children are the least likely to be able to change their hours daily (23%) or to change their hours as needed (74%). Among women, professionals with preschool-age children are the least likely (26%) to be able to set their hours and are also less likely than other employed women to be able to change their hours daily (38%). Again we find that, at least among professional and managerial workers, those most likely to need flexible scheduling face greater obstacles in obtaining it.

There is some good news for some employed parents. Professionals with young children have comparatively more access to such benefits as extended breaks, working at home, and working more one day in order to work less the next. It appears, however, that these benefits accrue to professional status and, to a lesser extent, to gender rather than to family status. In general, professional men fare better than either professional women or nonprofessional workers. Among professional men, 63 percent can take extended breaks at work (compared to 41% for nonprofessional workers), 50 percent can vary the length of the workday (compared to 41% for nonprofessionals), 39 percent can work at home regularly (compared to 13% for nonprofessionals), and 25 percent can do so occasionally (compared to 8% for nonprofessionals). Women professionals fare better than nonprofessionals, but not as well as their male counterparts, who are more likely to be able to take extended breaks and work at home occasionally.

Among those who have the option to shift their work hours and location, a very high proportion of workers choose to do so. When, for example, the option to work more one day and less the next is available, 75 percent of workers take advantage of it (including 81% of professional women and 74% of professional men with preschool-age children). Similarly, among those who are allowed to work at home occasionally, 79 percent choose to do so (including 88% of professional women and 84% of professional men with preschool-age children). It is instructive that women professionals with young children are much less likely to take extended breaks (63%) than to work at home. When given a choice, both women and men with young children seem to prefer more time at home and less time socializing at the office. While this may not seem surprising, it casts additional doubt on the argument that parents are trading time at home to socialize at work. Indeed, the high proportion of workers who take advantage of the options to work at home and to vary the length of their working day suggests a large demand for work arrangements that allow people to integrate work and family life more thoroughly and flexibly.

The Demand for Flexibility among Those Who Lack It

The majority of workers do not enjoy options such as flexible scheduling or working at home. Among these workers we find that many not only desire these benefits but would be willing to trade other benefits and even change their jobs to get them.

Among workers who do not have flexible schedules, about 28 percent would be willing to trade other benefits and 26 percent would be willing change jobs to get such control. The desire among professional women with young children is especially high, with 49 percent of those with preschool-age children stating that they would trade other benefits for flexibility at work and 32 percent saying they would even change jobs. Professional men with young children agree, albeit to a lesser extent. While only 12 percent would be willing to change jobs, 29 percent would trade other benefits for flexibility in scheduling.

The chance to work at home is also in high demand. Among all workers, 21 percent would trade other benefits to obtain such an option, and 22 percent would change jobs. For professional mothers, the percentages rise to 48 percent and 32 percent. For fathers, 18 percent would trade another benefit, and 24 percent would change jobs.

Availability and Desirability of Part-Time Work

The option to work part-time is substantially less popular than flexible scheduling or working at home. While about 55 percent of workers claim the option, among those without it only 16 percent would be willing to trade other benefits and only 11 percent would be willing change jobs to obtain it. Among professionals with young children, the part-time option remains equally unattractive. Professional women, especially those with young children, are the most likely to have this option (59%), but only 45 percent of professional men with young children can choose to work part-time. More noteworthy, however, is the lack of desire to obtain the part-time option when it is not available. While 32 percent of professional women with young children would be willing to give up another benefit, only 15 percent would be willing to change jobs. Among professional fathers, only 9 percent would trade away other benefits and only 5 percent would be willing to change jobs. Women may be more able and willing than men to cut back on their careers, but this difference does not bode well for gender equality in professional careers. As important, the general reluctance to cut back from work, even temporarily when the children are young, suggests that women and men alike perceive that such a choice might exact a high price in the long run.

THE HIDDEN COSTS OF FAMILY-SUPPORTIVE POLICIES: ARE FAMILY-FRIENDLY POLICIES ALSO WOMAN-FRIENDLY?

If given a genuine choice, both women and men, especially those with young children, appear to prefer more flexibility at work and more time at home. When available, a high proportion of workers take advantage of the chances to work at home and to vary the length of their working day. Similarly, when flexible scheduling is not available, a remarkable number of women and men appear willing to make other work sacrifices to obtain it. In contrast to the growing concern that workers pursuing personal gratification at work over the needs of their families and children, this picture suggests instead that they are striving for more flexible and fluid options for integrating these once separate spheres.

Yet despite the large and often unmet desire for family-supportive work arrangements, many workers may be fearful that choosing to use family-friendly policies can be costly to their long-term prospects at work. The relatively low desire for part-time work, for example, suggests that workers are reluctant to take advantage of options that might threaten economic and career opportunities. It is thus crucial to understand whether workers perceive that hidden penalties are attached to making use of family-friendly policies that may be formally available but informally stigmatized. Only by understanding how workers perceive these trade-offs can we gain a clearer picture of not only what workers need but also what obstacles prevent them from meeting these needs or even expressing their concerns to those in a position to help them.

In theory, family-friendly policies are built on the principles of family support and gender equity. Many workers, moreover, appear prepared to make substantial sacrifices in order to obtain them. Yet if such policies target only women and penalize those who use them, they threaten to re-create earlier forms of gender inequality in a new form. "Mommy tracks," for example, ask mothers to forgo upward mobility and thus confront women with an unfair choice between motherhood and a work career (Schwartz 1989).

They also exclude men from the responsibilities and opportunities of parental involvement. Although "gender-neutral" family policies may appear less pernicious, stigmatizing parental involvement in general simply shifts the penalties to both involved mothers *and* involved fathers. It is a dubious social policy that rewards parents of either sex for subordinating family needs to work and career.

In the best of all possible worlds, neither mothers nor fathers would be penalized at work for taking care of their children. And such a world would clearly not exact a higher price from women than from men. Yet in today's world there are good reasons to be concerned that "family-friendly" does not necessarily mean either woman-friendly or parent-friendly. Despite the heralding of policies to ease the plight of employed mothers, options that provide family support at the expense of work advancement exact significant costs to anyone who might choose them. In contrast, policies that not only provide for a fluid balance between family and work but also safeguard the work opportunities of the person who uses them would be more than just family-friendly. By protecting the rights of employed women and acknowledging the needs of work-committed parents of either sex, such policies would be genuinely woman-friendly and parent-friendly. Family-supportive policies, however, have more often been conceived and enacted in ways that reinforce and reproduce both public and private gender inequality by penalizing employed mothers and excluding fathers altogether.

Since employers are reluctant to admit that their policies come with costs attached for those who choose them, it is difficult to ascertain the exact nature of the risks workers take when they seek or use family-supportive options. It is possible, however, to ascertain whether workers perceive that formally available policies contain informal but heavy sanctions. Moreover, the perception of risk, regardless of its objective validity, is crucial to how workers weigh their options and make their choices. We thus examine the relationship between workers' perceptions of whether their workplace culture is family-supportive and their perceptions about whether their work environments offer advancement opportunities.

As Table 3 reveals, workers with supportive workplace cultures typically report having supportive supervisors as well, and for women, the link is especially strong (r = .44). Yet family-friendly workplaces do not appear to provide the best opportunities to advance. Cultural support is thus negatively related to women's perceptions of women's chances for advancement, whether they are white or minority. Equally noteworthy, these women also report that such workplaces do not necessarily provide good opportunities for white or minority men either. Perhaps most significant, women's perceptions of their *own* chances for advancement are negatively related to their perceptions that their workplaces are family-supportive.

When the focus is supervisor support for family-friendly arrangements rather than the level of supportiveness at the workplace as a whole, the same pattern emerges and the relationships are even stronger. The negative link between supervisor support for family-friendly arrangements and women's perceptions of their own chances for advancement is the strongest (r = −.31). Moreover, these patterns are virtually identical for men. Men also perceive that family-supportive supervisors and workplace cultures are less likely to provide chances to advance *any* group. They agree with women that having a supervisor who is supportive of family needs is also less likely to enhance their *own* chances for advancement (r = −.32).

TABLE 3 *Relationship between Family-Friendly Workplace Culture and Self-Reported Chances for Advancement*

	Workplace Culture[a] (p)	Supervisor Support[b] (r)
Women		
Workplace culture	1.00	.44
Supervisor support scale	.44	1.00
Chances to advance:		
White women	–.12	–.21
Minority women	–.17	–.28
White men	–.07	–.07
Minority men	–.15	–.22
Respondent's chances to advance	–.18	–.31
Men		
Workplace culture	1.00	.46
Supervisor support scale	.46	1.00
Chance to advance:		
White women	–.12	–.17
Minority women	–.15	–.18
White men	–.09	–.19
Minority men	–.14	–.21
Respondent's chances to advance	–.18	–.32

Source: National Study of the Changing Workforce.

Note: All correlations statistically significant, $p < .05$.

[a]Workplace Culture is a composite of four items designed to tap whether the respondent's working environment is sensitive to work-family issues.

[b]Supervisor Support is a composite of nine items designed to tap whether the respondent's supervisor is attentive to workers' needs and concerns.

Do these perceptions persist when other factors are taken into account? While a family-supportive workplace culture remains negatively associated with chances for advancement, the effects become attenuated as other factors, such as personal autonomy at work, are added.[10] When supervisor support is included, the effect of workplace culture disappears altogether, but the effect of supervisor support remains. This pattern occurs whether the measure of advancement opportunities refers to the woman herself or to other women, and it holds for men as well.

Women and men alike thus tend to perceive that family-friendly workplace policies come with costly strings attached. If workers feel confronted with a choice between family involvement and career building, their perceptions are probably well founded. The *New York Times* (1996) has reported, for example, that there is no overlap between the companies with the best record for promoting women and those with the most supportive family policies. Genuine family support, however, must move beyond mere tinkering at the edges of organizations to restructure the basic assumptions on which they are built. To be woman-friendly and parent-friendly as well as family-friendly, workplaces must be committed to supporting the careers of those who wish time to care for their families even as they strive at work.

BEYOND WORKING TIME: CREATING FLEXIBLE, EGALITARIAN WORKPLACES

While the debate over changes in work and family in America has focused largely on the issue of overwork, we have found that working time is only one of several important ingredients contributing to the problems of work-family conflict and gender inequality. Workplace structure and culture matter, and workers who enjoy job flexibility and employer support are better off than those who do not. Rather than preferring work over family, most full-time workers desire family-supportive workplace options that offer them ways to better integrate and balance their lives. Unfortunately, they also perceive that these benefits can only be gained at considerable cost.

Gender inequality persists in institutional arrangements, yet women and men find their personal dilemmas converging. As women build ever-stronger ties to the workplace and families confront the time squeezes posed by dual-earning arrangements, mothers and fathers must cope with conflicts that are structured not simply by family demands but more fundamentally by intransigent job constraints. When women and men face similar situations, their responses are also similar. In the struggle to resolve work-family conflicts, however, persisting gender inequality continues to place women at a disadvantage. Women not only shoulder more of the burden of domestic work; they also face larger obstacles at the workplace, including less autonomy and flexibility on the job and more pressure to make career sacrifices by cutting back when children are young.

While the problems workers face take different forms, most workers hold the same desire—to balance gratifying work with family involvement. Beyond economic security and opportunity, women and men alike wish some measure of flexibility in how they choose to integrate the many obligations they shoulder: In a world where both mothers and fathers must work, no group should have to sacrifice opportunity and economic welfare in order to make time for their families.

Since the problem of work-family conflict has institutional roots, the resolutions depend on institutional transformations. To understand the circumstances that can genuinely provide opportunities for committed workers to be involved parents, analysis needs to extend beyond worker preferences or choices to focus on workplace organization and the structure of opportunities that parents (and those who would like to become parents) face. If we fail to acknowledge the social sources of personal dilemmas, we are left blaming ordinary women and men for conditions they did not create and cannot control. A social and institutional focus makes it clear that social policy needs to uphold two important and inextricable principles: equal opportunity for women and unencumbered support for involved parents, regardless of sex.

We cannot afford to build work-family policies on outdated stereotypes that cast women as less committed to work than men. Yet we also cannot afford to create new stereotypes that cast employed mothers, and to a lesser extent fathers, as shortchanging their children. These images place all who would endeavor to balance family and work in an impossible bind in which work commitment is defined as family neglect and family involvement is defined as a lack of work commitment. If our findings are a guide, these are inaccurate images that offer untenable choices. What workers need and want is flexible work in a supportive setting that offers them a way to resolve the double binds they face.

Notes

1. To distinguish clearly between public and private responsibilities, this chapter will use the terms "work" and "worker" to refer to paid work and paid workers only, even though unpaid domestic tasks surely qualify as "work" broadly conceived.
2. Conducted by the Families and Work Institute, this study involved hour-long telephone interviews with a national probability sample of 3,381 employed men and women aged 18 through 64. For a general report on the findings, see Galinsky, Bond, and Friedman (1993).
3. We discuss the data on the extent of work-family conflict elsewhere (Jacobs and Gerson 1997).
4. Unfortunately, the Changing Workforce survey asked only a third of respondents about their ideal balance between family, self, and work or career. Thus, the percentages for actual and ideal time allocations are not strictly comparable. Since the smaller group is a random subset of the entire sample, there is good reason to have confidence in the comparisons.
5. The voluminous literature on comparisons between employed mothers and mothers who do not have a paid job has shown that working, taken alone, has no effect on the well-being of children. What matters are the mother's level of satisfaction with her choices, the involvement of the father, and the degree of satisfaction with child care arrangements. See, for example, Harvey (1999), Hoffman (1987), and Nye (1988).
6. For men, the correlation between working hours at one's main job and control over scheduling is .05, and the correlation between total hours worked and control over one's schedule is .04. Neither correlation is significant. For women, the respective correlations are –.13 and .10.
7. Although the Changing Workforce survey lacks specific information on men's and women's structural positions at work, it is clear from other studies that male managers and professionals are more likely than their female counterparts to occupy high-level positions in organizational and occupational hierarchies.
8. Due to space constraints, the results for the bivariate relationships between workplace flexibility and all the variables included in Table 2 are not shown. They may be found in Jacobs and Gerson (1997).
9. A more detailed analysis of the availability, use, and desire for a wide range of family-supportive workplace options and benefits can be found in Gerson and Jacobs (1999).
10. The detailed results of this analysis are presented in Jacobs and Gerson (1997).

References

Becker, Gary. 1981. *A treatise on the family.* Cambridge, Mass.: Harvard University Press.
Blustone, Barry, and Stephen Rose. 1997. Overworked and underemployed: Unraveling an economic enigma. *American Prospect* 31(March/April):58–69.
Bond, James T., Ellen Galinsky, and Jennifer E. Swanberg. 1998. *The 1997 national study of the changing workforce.* New York: Families and Work Institute.
Galinsky, Ellen, James T. Bond, and Dana E. Friedman, 1993. *The changing workforce: Highlights of the national study.* New York: Families and Work Institute.
Gerson, Kathleen, and Jerry A. Jacobs. 1999. The availability and use of family-friendly workplace policies. Unpublished manuscript.
Glass, Jennifer, and Valerie Camarigg. 1992. Gender, parenthood, and job-family compatability. *American Journal of Sociology* 98(July):131–51.
Harvey, Lisa. 1999. Short-term and long-term effects of early parental employment on children of the national longitudinal survey of youth. *Developmental Psychology* 35(March):445–59.
Hochschild, Arlie R. 1997. *The time bind: When work becomes home and home becomes work.* New York: Metropolitan Books.

Hoffman, Lois. 1987. The effects on children of maternal and paternal employment. In *Families and work*, edited by N. Gerstel and H. Gross, 362–95. Philadelphia: Temple University Press.

Jacobs, Jerry A., and Kathleen Gerson. 1997. The endless day or the office? Working hours, work-family conflict, and gender equity in the modern workplace. Report to the Alfred P. Sloan Foundation.

———. 1998. Who are the overworked Americans? *Review of Social Economy* 56(4):442–59

———. 1999. The overworked American debate: New evidence comparing ideal and actual working hours. In *Work and family: Research informing policy*, edited by T. Parcel and D. B. Cornfield. Thousand Oaks, Calif.: Sage Publications.

New York Times. 1996. Somber news for women on corporate ladder. 6 November, D1, D19.

Nye, F. Ivan. 1988. Fifty years of family research, 1937–1987. *Journal of Marriage and the Family* 50(May):305–16.

Robinson, John P., and Geoffrey Godbey. 1997. *Time for life. The surprising ways Americans use their time.* University Park: Pennsylvania State University Press.

Rones, Philip L., Randy E. Ilg, and Jennifer M. Gardner. 1997. Trends in the hours of work since the mid-1970s. *Monthly Labor Review* 120(4):3–14.

Schor, Juliet. 1991. *The overworked American.* New York: Basic Books.

Schwartz, Felice N. 1989. Management women and the new facts of life. *Harvard Business Review*, January–February, 65–76.

10 Dimensions of Diversity

■ READING 28

Diversity within African American Families

Ronald L. Taylor

PERSONAL REFLECTIONS

My interest in African American families as a topic of research was inspired more than two decades ago by my observation and growing dismay over the stereotypical portrayal of these families presented by the media and in much of the social science literature. Most of the African American families I knew in the large southern city in which I grew up were barely represented in the various "authoritative" accounts I read and other scholars frequently referred to in their characterizations and analyses of such families. Few such accounts have acknowledged the regional, ethnic, class, and behavioral diversity within the African American community and among families. As a result, a highly fragmented and distorted public image of African American family life has been perpetuated that encourages perceptions of African American families as a monolith. The 1986 television documentary *A CBS Report: The Vanishing Family: Crisis in Black America*, hosted by Bill Moyers, was fairly typical of this emphasis. It focused almost exclusively on low-income, single-parent households in inner cities, characterized them as "vanishing" non-families, and implied that such families represented the majority of African American families in urban America. It mattered little that poor, single-parent households in the inner cities made up less than a quarter of all African American families at the time the documentary was aired.

As an African American reared in the segregated South, I was keenly aware of the tremendous variety of African American families in composition, lifestyle, and socioeconomic status. Racial segregation ensured that African American families, regardless of means or circumstances, were constrained to live and work in close proximity to one another. Travel outside the South made me aware of important regional differences among African American families as well. For example, African American families in the

Northeast appeared far more segregated by socioeconomic status than did families in many parts of the South with which I was familiar. As a graduate student at Boston University during the late 1960s, I recall the shock I experienced upon seeing the level of concentrated poverty among African American families in Roxbury, Massachusetts, an experience duplicated in travels to New York, Philadelphia, and Newark. To be sure, poverty of a similar magnitude was prevalent throughout the South, but was far less concentrated and, from my perception, far less pernicious.

As I became more familiar with the growing body of research on African American families, it became increasingly clear to me that the source of a major distortion in the portrayal of African American families in the social science literature and the media was the overwhelming concentration on impoverished inner-city communities of the Northeast and Midwest to the near exclusion of the South, where more than half the African American families are found and differences among them in family patterns, lifestyles, and socioeconomic characteristics are more apparent.

In approaching the study of African American families in my work, I have adopted a *holistic* perspective. This perspective, outlined first by DuBois (1898) and more recently by Billingsley (1992) and Hill (1993), emphasizes the influence of historical, cultural, social, economic, and political forces in shaping contemporary patterns of family life among African Americans of all socioeconomic backgrounds. Although the impact of these external forces is routinely taken into account in assessing stability and change among white families, their effects on the structure and functioning of African American families are often minimized. In short, a holistic approach undertakes to study African American families *in context*. My definition of the *family*, akin to the definition offered by Billingsley (1992), views it as an intimate association of two or more persons related to each other by blood, marriage, formal or informal adoption, or appropriation. The latter term refers to the incorporation of persons in the family who are unrelated by blood or marital ties but are treated as though they are family. This definition is broader than other dominant definitions of families that emphasize biological or marital ties as defining characteristics.

This chapter is divided into three parts. The first part reviews the treatment of African American families in the historical and social sciences literatures. It provides a historical overview of African American families, informed by recent historical scholarship, that corrects many of the misconceptions about the nature and quality of family life during and following the experience of slavery. The second part examines contemporary patterns of marriage, family, and household composition among African Americans in response to recent social, economic, and political developments in the larger society. The third part explores some of the long-term implications of current trends in marriage and family behavior for community functioning and individual well-being, together with implications for social policy.

THE TREATMENT OF AFRICAN AMERICAN FAMILIES IN AMERICAN SCHOLARSHIP

As an area of scientific investigation, the study of African American family life is of recent vintage. As recently as 1968, Billingsley, in his classic work *Black Families in White*

America, observed that African American family life had been virtually ignored in family studies and studies of race and ethnic relations. He attributed the general lack of interest among white social scientists, in part, to their "ethnocentrism and intellectual commitment to peoples and values transplanted from Europe" (p. 214). Content analyses of key journals in sociology, social work, and family studies during the period supported Billingsley's contention. For example, a content analysis of 10 leading journals in sociology and social work by Johnson (1981) disclosed that articles on African American families constituted only 3% of 3,547 empirical studies of American families published between 1965 and 1975. Moreover, in the two major journals in social work, only one article on African American families was published from 1965 to 1978. In fact, a 1978 special issue of the *Journal of Marriage and the Family* devoted to African American families accounted for 40% of all articles on these families published in the 10 major journals between 1965 and 1978.

Although the past two decades have seen a significant increase in the quantity and quality of research on the family lives of African Americans, certain features and limitations associated with earlier studies in this area persist (Taylor, Chatters, Tucker, & Lewis, 1990). In a review of recent research on African American families, Hill (1993) concluded that many studies continue to treat such families in superficial terms; that is, African American families are not considered to be an important unit of focus and, consequently, are treated peripherally or omitted altogether. The assumption is that African American families are automatically treated in all analyses that focus on African Americans as individuals; thus, they are not treated in their own right. Hill noted that a major impediment to understanding the functioning of African American families has been the failure of most analysts to use a theoretical or conceptual framework that took account of the totality of African American family life. Overall, he found that the preponderance of recent studies of African American families are

> (a) fragmented, in that they exclude the bulk of Black families by focusing on only a subgroup; (b) ad hoc, in that they apply arbitrary explanations that are not derived from systematic theoretical formulations that have been empirically substantiated; (c) negative, in that they focus exclusively on the perceived weaknesses of Black families; and (d) internally oriented, in that they exclude any systematic consideration of the role of forces in the wider society on Black family life. (p. 5)

THEORETICAL APPROACHES

The study of African American families, like the study of American families in general, has evolved through successive theoretical formulations. Using white family structure as the norm, the earliest studies characterized African American families as impoverished versions of white families in which the experiences of slavery, economic deprivation, and racial discrimination had induced pathogenic and dysfunctional features (Billingsley, 1968). The classic statement of this perspective was presented by Frazier, whose study, *The Negro Family in the United States* (1939), was the first comprehensive analysis of African American family life and its transformation under various historical conditions—slavery, emancipation, and urbanization (Edwards, 1968).

It was Frazier's contention that slavery destroyed African familial structures and cultures and gave rise to a host of dysfunctional family features that continued to undermine the stability and well-being of African American families well into the 20th century. Foremost among these features was the supposed emergence of the African American "matriarchal" or maternal family system, which weakened the economic position of African American men and their authority in the family. In his view, this family form was inherently unstable and produced pathological outcomes in the family unit, including high rates of poverty, illegitimacy, crime, delinquency, and other problems associated with the socialization of children. Frazier concluded that the female-headed family had become a common tradition among large segments of lower-class African American migrants to the North during the early 20th century. The two-parent male-headed household represented a second tradition among a minority of African Americans who enjoyed some of the freedoms during slavery, had independent artisan skills, and owned property.

Frazier saw an inextricable connection between economic resources and African American family structure and concluded that as the economic position of African Americans improved, their conformity to normative family patterns would increase. However, his important insight regarding the link between family structure and economic resources was obscured by the inordinate emphasis he placed on the instability and "self-perpetuating pathologies" of lower-class African American families, an emphasis that powerfully contributed to the pejorative tradition of scholarship that emerged in this area. Nonetheless, Frazier recognized the diversity of African American families and in his analyses, "consistently attributed the primary sources of family instability to external forces (such as racism, urbanization, technological changes and recession) and not to internal characteristics of Black families" (Hill, 1993, pp. 7–8).

During the 1960s, Frazier's characterization of African American families gained wider currency with the publication of Moynihan's *The Negro Family: The Case for National Action* (1965), in which weaknesses in family structure were identified as a major source of social problems in African American communities. Moynihan attributed high rates of welfare dependence, out-of-wedlock births, educational failure, and other problems to the "unnatural" dominance of women in African American families. Relying largely on the work of Frazier as a source of reference, Moynihan traced the alleged "tangle of pathology" that characterized urban African American families to the experience of slavery and 300 years of racial oppression, which, he concluded, had caused "deep-seated structural distortions" in the family and community life of African Americans.

Although much of the Moynihan report, as the book was called, largely restated what had become conventional academic wisdom on African American families during the 1960s, its generalized indictment of all African American families ignited a firestorm of criticism and debate and inspired a wealth of new research and writings on the nature and quality of African American family life in the United States (Staples & Mirande, 1980). In fact, the 1970s saw the beginning of the most prolific period of research on African American families, with more than 50 books and 500 articles published during that decade alone, representing a fivefold increase over the literature produced in all the years since the publication of DuBois's (1909) pioneering study of African American family life (Staples & Mirande, 1980). To be sure, some of this work was polemical and defensively apologetic, but much of it sought to replace ideology with research and to provide alternative perspectives for interpreting observed differences in the characteristics of African American and white families (Allen, 1978).

Critics of the deficit or pathology approach to African American family life (Scanzoni, 1977; Staples, 1971) called attention to the tendency in the literature to ignore family patterns among the majority of African Americans and to overemphasize findings derived from studies of low-income and typically problem-ridden families. Such findings were often generalized and accepted as descriptive of the family life of all African American families, with the result that popular but erroneous images of African American family life were perpetuated. Scrutinizing the research literature of the 1960s, Billingsley (1968) concluded that when the majority of African American families was considered, evidence refuted the characterization of African American family life as unstable, dependent on welfare, and matriarchal. In his view, and in the view of a growing number of scholars in the late 1960s and early 1970s, observed differences between white and African American families were largely the result of differences in socioeconomic position and of differential access to economic resources (Allen, 1978; Scanzoni, 1977).

Thus, the 1970s witnessed not only a significant increase in the diversity, breadth, and quantity of research on African American families, but a shift away from a social pathology perspective to one emphasizing the resilience and adaptiveness of African American families under a variety of social and economic conditions. The new emphasis reflected what Allen (1978) referred to as the "cultural variant" perspective, which treats African American families as different but legitimate functional forms. From this perspective, "Black and White family differences [are] taken as given, without the presumption of one family form as normative and the other as deviant." (Farley & Allen, 1987, p. 162). In accounting for observed racial differences in family patterns, some researchers have taken a *structural perspective*, emphasizing poverty and other socioeconomic factors as key processes (Billingsley, 1968). Other scholars have taken a *cultural approach*, stressing elements of the West African cultural heritage, together with distinctive experiences, values, and behavioral modes of adaptation developed in this country, as major determinants (Nobles, 1978; Young, 1970). Still others (Collins, 1990; Sudarkasa, 1988) have pointed to evidence supporting both interpretations and have argued for a more comprehensive approach.

Efforts to demythologize negative images of African American families have continued during the past two decades, marked by the development of the first national sample of adult African Americans, drawn to reflect their distribution throughout the United States (Jackson, 1991), and by the use of a variety of conceptualizations, approaches, and methodologies in the study of African American family life (Collins, 1990; McAdoo, 1997). Moreover, the emphasis in much of the recent work

> has not been the defense of African American family forms, but rather the identification of forces that have altered long-standing traditions. The ideological paradigms identified by Allen (1978) to describe the earlier thrust of Black family research—cultural equivalence, cultural deviance, and cultural variation—do not fully capture the foci of this new genre of work as a whole. (Tucker & Mitchell-Kernan, 1995, p. 17)

Researchers have sought to stress balance in their analyses, that is, to assess the strengths and weaknesses of African American family organizations at various socioeconomic levels, and the need for solution-oriented studies (Hill, 1993). At the same time, recent historical scholarship has shed new light on the relationship of changing historical circumstances to characteristics of African American family organization and has underscored the relevance of historical experiences to contemporary patterns of family life.

AFRICAN AMERICAN FAMILIES IN HISTORICAL PERSPECTIVE

Until the 1970s, it was conventional academic wisdom that the experience of slavery decimated African American culture and created the foundation for unstable female-dominated households and other familial aberrations that continued into the 20th century. This thesis, advanced by Frazier (1939) and restated by Moynihan (1965), was seriously challenged by the pioneering historical research of Blassingame (1972), Furstenberg, Hershberg, and Modell (1975), and Gutman (1976), among others. These works provide compelling documentation of the centrality of family and kinship among African Americans during the long years of bondage and how African Americans created and sustained a rich cultural and family life despite the brutal reality of slavery.

In his examination of more than two centuries of slave letters, autobiographies, plantation records, and other materials, Blassingame (1972) meticulously documented the nature of community, family organization, and culture among American slaves. He concluded that slavery was not "an all-powerful, monolithic institution which strip[ped] the slave of any meaningful and distinctive culture, family life, religion or manhood" (p. vii). To the contrary, the relative freedom from white control that slaves enjoyed in their quarters enabled them to create and sustain a complex social organization that incorporated "norms of conduct, defined roles and behavioral patterns" and provided for the traditional functions of group solidarity, defense, mutual assistance, and family organization. Although the family had no legal standing in slavery and was frequently disrupted, Blassingame noted its major role as a source of survival for slaves and as a mechanism of social control for slaveholders, many of whom encouraged "monogamous mating arrangements" as insurance against runaways and rebellion. In fashioning familial and community organization, slaves drew upon the many remnants of their African heritage (e.g., courtship rituals, kinship networks, and religious beliefs), merging those elements with American forms to create a distinctive culture, features of which persist in the contemporary social organization of African American family life and community.

Genovese's (1974) analysis of plantation records and slave testimony led him to similar conclusions regarding the nature of family life and community among African Americans under slavery. Genovese noted that, although chattel bondage played havoc with the domestic lives of slaves and imposed severe constraints on their ability to enact and sustain normative family roles and functions, the slaves "created impressive norms of family, including as much of a nuclear family norm as conditions permitted and . . . entered the postwar social system with a remarkably stable base" (p. 452). He attributed this stability to the extraordinary resourcefulness and commitment of slaves to marital relations and to what he called a "paternalistic compromise," or bargain between masters and slaves that recognized certain reciprocal obligations and rights, including recognition of slaves' marital and family ties. Although slavery undermined the role of African

American men as husbands and fathers, their function as role models for their children and as providers for their families was considerably greater than has generally been supposed. Nonetheless, the tenuous position of male slaves as husbands and fathers and the more visible and nontraditional roles assumed by female slaves gave rise to legends of matriarchy and emasculated men. However, Genovese contended that the relationship between slave men and women came closer to approximating gender equality than was possible for white families.

Perhaps the most significant historical work that forced revisions in scholarship on African American family life and culture during slavery was Gutman's (1976) landmark study, *The Black Family in Slavery and Freedom*. Inspired by the controversy surrounding the Moynihan report and its thesis that African American family disorganization was a legacy of slavery, Gutman made ingenious use of quantifiable data derived from plantation birth registers and marriage applications to re-create family and kinship structures among African Americans during slavery and after emancipation. Moreover, he marshaled compelling evidence to explain how African Americans developed an autonomous and complex culture that enabled them to cope with the harshness of enslavement, the massive relocation from relatively small economic units in the upper South to vast plantations in the lower South between 1790 and 1860, the experience of legal freedom in the rural and urban South, and the transition to northern urban communities before 1930.

Gutman reasoned that, if family disorganization (fatherless, matrifocal families) among African Americans was a legacy of slavery, then such a condition should have been more common among urban African Americans closer in time to slavery—in 1850 and 1860—than in 1950 and 1960. Through careful examination of census data, marriage licenses, and personal documents for the period after 1860, he found that stable, two-parent households predominated during slavery and after emancipation and that families headed by African American women at the turn of the century were hardly more prevalent than among comparable white families. Thus "[a]t all moments in time between 1860 and 1925 . . . the typical Afro-American family was lower class in status and headed by two parents. That was so in the urban and rural South in 1880 and 1900 and in New York City in 1905 and 1925" (p. 456). Gutman found that the two-parent family was just as common among the poor as among the more advantaged, and as common among southerners as those in the Northeast. For Gutman, the key to understanding the durability of African American families during and after slavery lay in the distinctive African American culture that evolved from the cumulative slave experiences that provided a defense against some of the more destructive and dehumanizing aspects of that system. Among the more enduring and important aspects of that culture are the enlarged kinship network and certain domestic arrangements (e.g., the sharing of family households with nonrelatives and the informal adoption of children) that, during slavery, formed the core of evolving African American communities and the collective sense of interdependence.

Additional support for the conclusion that the two-parent household was the norm among slaves and their descendants was provided by Furstenberg et al. (1975) from their study of the family composition of African Americans, native-born whites, and immigrants to Philadelphia from 1850 to 1880. From their analysis of census data, Furstenberg et al. found that most African American families, like those of other ethnic groups, were headed by two parents (75% for African Americans versus 73% for native whites). Similar results are reported by Pleck (1973) from her study of African American family structure in late 19th-century Boston. As these and other studies (Jones, 1985; White, 1985) have shown, although female-headed households were common among African Americans during and following slavery, such households were by no means typical. In fact, as late as the 1960s, three fourths of African American households were headed by married couples (Jaynes & Williams, 1989; Moynihan, 1965).

However, more recent historical research would appear to modify, if not challenge, several of the contentions of the revisionist scholars of slavery. Manfra and Dykstra (1985) and Stevenson (1995), among others, found evidence of considerably greater variability in slave family structure and in household composition than was reported in previous works. In her study of Virginia slave families from 1830 to 1860, Stevenson (1995) discovered evidence of widespread matrifocality, as well as other marital and household arrangements, among antebellum slaves. Her analysis of the family histories of slaves in colonial and antebellum Virginia revealed that many slaves did not have a nuclear "core" in their families. Rather, the "most discernible ideal for their principal kinship organization was a malleable extended family that provided its members with nurture, education, socialization, material support, and recreation in the face of the potential social chaos the slavemasters' power imposed" (1995, p. 36).

A variety of conditions affected the family configurations of slaves, including cultural differences among the slaves themselves, the state or territory in which they lived, and the size of the plantation on which they resided. Thus, Stevenson concluded that

> the slave family was not a static, imitative institution that necessarily favored one form of family organization over another. Rather, it was a diverse phenomenon, sometimes assuming several forms even among the slaves of one community. . . . Far from having a negative impact, the diversity of slave marriage and family norms, as a measure of the slave family's enormous adaptive potential, allowed the slave and the slave family to survive. (p. 29)

Hence, "postrevisionist" historiography emphasizes the great diversity of familial arrangements among African Americans during slavery. Although nuclear, matrifocal, and extended families were prevalent, none dominated slave family forms. These postrevisionist amendments notwithstanding, there is compelling historical evidence that African American nuclear families and kin-related households remained relatively intact and survived the experiences of slavery, Reconstruction, the Great Depression, and the transition to northern urban communities. Such evidence underscores the importance of considering recent developments and conditions in accounting for changes in family patterns among African Americans in the contemporary period.

CONTEMPORARY AFRICAN AMERICAN FAMILY PATTERNS

Substantial changes have occurred in patterns of marriage, family, and household composition in the United States during the past three decades, accompanied by significant alterations in the family lives of men, women, and children. During this period, divorce rates have more than doubled, marriage rates have declined, fertility rates have fallen to record levels, the proportion of "traditional" families (nuclear families in which children live with both biological parents) as a percentage of all family groups has declined, and the proportion of children reared in single-parent households has risen dramatically (Taylor, 1997).

Some of the changes in family patterns have been more rapid and dramatic among African Americans than among the population as a whole. For example, while declining rates of marriage and remarriage, high levels of separation and divorce, and higher proportions of children living in single-parent households are trends that have characterized the U.S. population as a whole during the past 30 years, these trends have been more pronounced among African Americans and, in some respects, represent marked departures from earlier African American family patterns. A growing body of research has implicated demographic and economic factors as causes of the divergent marital and family experiences of African Americans and other populations.

In the following section, I examine diverse patterns and evolving trends in family structure and household composition among African Americans, together with those demographic, economic, and social factors that have been identified as sources of change in patterns of family formation.

Diversity of Family Structure

Since 1960, the number of African American households has increased at more than twice the rate of white households. By 1995, African American households numbered 11.6 million, compared with 83.7 million white households. Of these households, 58.4 million white and 8.0 million African American ones were classified as family households by the U.S. Bureau of the Census (1996), which defines a *household* as the person or persons occupying a housing unit and a *family* as consisting of two or more persons who live in the same household and are related by birth, marriage, or adoption. Thus, family households are households maintained by individuals who share their residence with one or more relatives, whereas nonfamily households are maintained by individuals with no relatives in the housing unit. In 1995, 70% of the 11.6 million African American households were family households, the same proportion as among white households (U.S. Bureau of the Census, 1996). However, nonfamily households have been increasing at a faster rate than family households among African Americans because of delayed marriages among young adults, higher rates of family disruption (divorce and separation), and sharp increases in the number of unmarried cohabiting couples (Cherlin, 1995; Glick, 1997).

Family households vary by type and composition. Although the U.S. Bureau of the Census recognizes the wide diversity of families in this country, it differentiates between three broad and basic types of family households: married-couple or husband-wife families, families with female householders (no husband present), and families with male householders (no wife present). Family composition refers to whether the household is *nuclear*, that is, contains parents and children only, or extended, that is, nuclear plus other relatives.

To take account of the diversity in types and composition of African American families, Billingsley (1968; 1992) added to these conventional categories *augmented* families (nuclear plus nonrelated persons), and modified the definition of nuclear family to include *incipient* (a married couple without children), *simple* (a couple with children), and *attenuated* (a single parent with children) families. He also added three combinations of augmented families: *incipient extended augmented* (a couple with relatives and nonrelatives), *nuclear extended augmented* (a couple with children, relatives, and nonrelatives), and *attenuated extended augmented* (a single parent with children, relatives, and nonrelatives). With these modifications, Billingsley identified 32 different kinds of nuclear, extended, and augmented family households among African Americans. His typology has been widely used and modified by other scholars (see, for example, Shimkin, Shimkin, & Frate, 1978; Stack, 1974). For example, on the basis of Billingsley's typology, Dressler, Haworth-Hoeppner, and Pitts (1985) developed a four-way typology with 12 subtypes for their study of household structures in a southern African American community and found a variety of types of female-headed households, less than a fourth of them consisting of a mother and her children or grandchildren.

However, as Staples (1971) pointed out, Billingsley's typology emphasized the household and ignored an important characteristic of such families—their "extendedness." African Americans are significantly more likely than whites to live in extended families that "transcend and link several different households, each containing a separate . . . family" (Farley & Allen, 1987, p. 168). In 1992, approximately 1 in 5 African American families was extended, compared to 1 in 10 white families (Glick, 1997). The greater proportion of extended households among African Americans has been linked to the extended family tradition of West African cultures (Nobles, 1978; Sudarkasa, 1988) and to the economic marginality of many African American families, which has encouraged the sharing and exchange of resources, services, and emotional support among family units spread across a number of households (Stack, 1974).

In comparative research on West African, Caribbean, and African American family patterns some anthropologists (Herskovits, 1958; Sudarkasa, 1997) found evidence of cultural continuities in the significance attached to coresidence, formal kinship relations, and nuclear families among black populations in these areas. Summarizing this work, Hill (1993, pp. 104–105) observed that, with respect to

> co-residence, the African concept of family is not restricted to persons living in the same household, but includes key persons living in separate households. . . . As for defining kin relationships, the African concept of family is not confined to relations between formal kin, but includes networks of unrelated [i.e., "fictive kin"] as well as related persons living in separate households. . . . [According to] Herskovits (1941), the African nuclear family unit is not as central to its family organization as is the case for European nuclear families: "The African immediate family, consisting of a father, his wives, and their children, is but a part of a larger unit. This immediate family is generally recognized by Africanists as belonging to a local relationship group termed the 'extended family.' "

Similarly, Sudarkasa (1988) found that unlike the European extended family, in which primacy is given to the conjugal unit (husband, wife, and children) as the basic building block, the African extended family is organized around blood ties (consanguineous relations).

In their analysis of data from the National Survey of Black Americans (NSBA) on household composition and family structure, Hatchett, Cochran, and Jackson (1991) noted that the extended family perspective, especially kin networks, was valuable in describing the nature and functioning of African American families. They suggested that the "extended family can be viewed both as a family network in the physical-spatial sense and in terms of family relations or contact and exchanges. In this view of extendedness, family structure and function are interdependent concepts" (p. 49). Their examination of the composition of the 2,107 households in the NSBA resulted in the identification of 12 categories, 8 of which roughly captured the "dimensions of household family structure identified in Billingsley's typology of Black families (1968)—the incipient nuclear family, the incipient nuclear extended and/or augmented nuclear family, the simple nuclear family, the simple extended and/or augmented nuclear family, the attenuated nuclear family, and the attenuated extended and/or augmented family, respectively" (p. 51). These households were examined with respect to their *actual kin networks*, defined as subjective feelings of emotional closeness to family members, frequency of contact, and patterns of mutual assistance, and their *potential kin networks*, defined as the availability or proximity of immediate family members and the density or concentration of family members within a given range.

Hatchett et al. (1991) found that approximately 1 in 5 African American households in the NSBA was an extended household (included other relatives—parents and siblings of the household head, grandchildren, grandparents, and nieces and nephews). Nearly 20% of the extended households with children contained minors who were not the head's; most of these children were grandchildren, nieces, and nephews of the head. The authors suggested that "[t]hese are instances of informal fostering or adoption—absorption of minor children by the kin network" (p. 58).

In this sample, female-headed households were as likely to be extended as male-headed households. Hatchett et al. (1991) found little support for the possibility that economic hardship may account for the propensity among African Americans to incorporate other relatives in their households. That is, the inclusion of other relatives in the households did not substantially improve the overall economic situation of the households because the majority of other relatives were minor children, primarily grandchildren of heads who coresided with the household heads' own minor and adult children. Moreover, they stated, "household extendedness at both the household and extra-household levels appears to be a characteristic of black families, regardless of socioeconomic level" (p. 81), and regardless of region of the country or rural or urban residence.

The households in the NSBA were also compared in terms of their potential and actual kin networks. The availability of potential kin networks varied by the age of the respondent, by the region and degree of urban development of the respondent's place of residence, and by the type of household in which the respondent resided (Hatchett et al., 1991). For example, households with older heads and spouses were more isolated from kin than were younger households headed by single mothers, and female-headed households tended to have greater potential kin networks than did individuals in nuclear households. With respect to region and urbanicity, the respondents in the Southern and North Central regions and those in rural areas had a greater concentration of relatives closer at hand than did the respondents in other regions and those in urban areas. However, proximity to relatives and their concentration nearby did not translate directly into actual kin networks or extended family functioning:

> Complex relationships were found across age, income, and type of household. From these data came a picture of the Black elderly with high psychological connectedness to family in

the midst of relative geographical and interactional isolation from them. The image of fe-male single-parent households is, on the other hand, the reverse or negative of this picture. Female heads were geographically closer to kin, had more contact with them, and received more help from family but did not perceive as much family solidarity or psychological con-nectedness. (Hatchett et al., 1991, p. 81)

The nature and frequency of mutual aid among kin were also assessed in this sur-vey. More than two thirds of the respondents reported receiving some assistance from family members, including financial support, child care, goods and services, and help dur-ing sickness and at death. Financial assistance and child care were the two most frequent types of support reported by the younger respondents, whereas goods and services were the major types reported by older family members. The type of support the respondents received from their families was determined, to some extent, by needs defined by the family life cycle.

In sum, the results of the NSBA document the wide variety of family configura-tions and households in which African Americans reside and suggest, along with other studies, that the diversity of structures represents adaptive responses to the variety of so-cial, economic, and demographic conditions that African Americans have encountered over time (Billingsley, 1968; Farley & Allen, 1987).

Although Hatchett et al. (1991) focused on extended or augmented African Amer-ican families in their analysis of the NSBA data, only 1 in 5 households in this survey con-tained persons outside the nuclear family. The majority of households was nuclear, containing one or both parents with their own children.

Between 1970 and 1990, the number of all U.S. married-couple families with chil-dren dropped by almost 1 million, and their share of all family households declined from 40% to 26% (U.S. Bureau of the Census, 1995). The proportion of married-couple fam-ilies with children among African Americans also declined during this period, from 41% to 26% of all African American families. In addition, the percentage of African Ameri-can families headed by women more than doubled, increasing from 33% in 1970 to 57% in 1990. By 1995, married-couple families with children constituted 36% of all African American families, while single-parent families represented 64% (U.S. Bureau of the Census, 1996). The year 1980 was the first time in history that African Ameri-can female-headed families with children outnumbered married-couple families. This shift in the distribution of African American families by type is associated with a num-ber of complex, interrelated social and economic developments, including increases in age at first marriage, high rates of separation and divorce, male joblessness, and out-of-wedlock births

Marriage, Divorce, and Separation

In a reversal of a long-time trend, African Americans are now marrying at a much later age than are persons of other races. Thirty years ago, African American men and women were far more likely to have married by ages 20–24 than were white Americans. In 1960, 56% of African American men and 36% of African American women aged 20–24 were never married; by 1993, 90% of all African American men and 81% of African American women in this age cohort were never married (U.S. Bureau of the Census, 1994).

The trend toward later marriages among African Americans has contributed to changes in the distribution of African American families by type. Delayed marriage tends to increase the risk of out-of-wedlock childbearing and single parenting (Hernandez, 1993). In fact, a large proportion of the increase in single-parent households in recent years is accounted for by never-married women maintaining families (U.S. Bureau of the Census, 1990).

The growing proportion of never-married young African American adults is partly a result of a combination of factors, including continuing high rates of unemployment, especially among young men; college attendance; military service; and an extended period of cohabitation prior to marriage (Glick, 1997; Testa & Krogh, 1995; Wilson, 1987). In their investigation of the effect of employment on marriage among African American men in the inner city of Chicago, Testa and Krogh (1995) found that men in stable jobs were twice as likely to marry as were men who were unemployed, not in school, or in the military. Hence, it has been argued that the feasibility of marriage among African Americans in recent decades has decreased because the precarious economic position of African American men has made them less attractive as potential husbands and less interested in becoming husbands, given the difficulties they are likely to encounter in performing the provider role in marriage (Tucker & Mitchell-Kernan, 1995).

However, other research has indicated that economic factors are only part of the story. Using census data from 1940 through the mid-1980s, Mare and Winship (1991) sought to determine the impact of declining employment opportunities on marriage rates among African Americans and found that although men who were employed were more likely to marry, recent declines in employment rates among young African American men were not large enough to account for a substantial part of the declining trend in their marriage rates. Similarly, in their analysis of data from a national survey of young African American adults, Lichter, McLaughlin, Kephart, and Landry (1992) found that lower employment rates among African American men were an important contributing factor to delayed marriage—and perhaps to nonmarriage—among African American women. However, even when marital opportunities were taken into account, the researchers found that the rate of marriage among young African American women in the survey was only 50% to 60% the rate of white women of similar ages.

In addition to recent declines in employment rates, an unbalanced sex ratio has been identified as an important contributing factor to declining marriage rates among African Americans. This shortage of men is due partly to high rates of mortality and incarceration of African American men (Kiecolt & Fossett, 1995; Wilson & Neckerman, 1986). Guttentag and Secord (1983) identified a number of major consequences of the shortage of men over time: higher rates of singlehood, out-of-wedlock births, divorce, and infidelity and less commitment among men to relationships. Among African Americans, they found that in 1980 the ratio of men to women was unusually low; in fact, few populations in the United States had sex ratios as low as those of African Americans. Because African American women outnumber men in each of the age categories 20 to 49, the resulting "marriage squeeze" puts African American women at a significant disadvantage in the marriage market, causing an unusually large proportion of them to remain unmarried. However, Glick (1997) observed a reversal of the marriage squeeze among African Americans in the age categories 18 to 27 during the past decade: In 1995, there were 102 African American men for every 100 African

American women in this age range. Thus, "[w]hereas the earlier marriage squeeze made it difficult for Black women to marry, the future marriage squeeze will make it harder for Black men" (Glick, 1997, p. 126). But, as Kiecolt and Fossett (1995) observed, the impact of the sex ratio on marital outcomes for African Americans may vary, depending on the nature of the local marriage market. Indeed, "marriage markets are local, as opposed to national, phenomena which may have different implications for different genders . . . [for example,] men and women residing near a military base face a different sex ratio than their counterparts attending a large university" (Smith, 1995, p. 137).

African American men and women are not only delaying marriage, but are spending fewer years in their first marriages and are slower to remarry than in decades past. Since 1960, a sharp decline has occurred in the number of years African American women spend with their first husbands and a corresponding rise in the interval of separation and divorce between the first and second marriages (Espenshade, 1985; Jaynes & Williams, 1989). Data from the National Fertility Surveys of 1965 and 1970 disclosed that twice as many African American couples as white couples (10% versus 5%) who reached their 5th wedding anniversaries ended their marriages before their 10th anniversaries (Thornton, 1978), and about half the African American and a quarter of the white marriages were dissolved within the first 15 years of marriage (McCarthy, 1978). Similarly, a comparison of the prevalence of marital disruption (defined as separation or divorce) among 13 racial-ethnic groups in the United States based on the 1980 census revealed that of the women who had married for the first time 10 to 14 years before 1980, 53% of the African American women, 48% of the Native American women, and 37% of the non-Hispanic white women were separated or divorced by the 1980 census (Sweet & Bumpass, 1987).

Although African American women have a higher likelihood of separating from their husbands than do non-Hispanic white women, they are slower to obtain legal divorces (Chertin, 1996). According to data from the 1980 census, within three years of separating from their husbands, only 55% of the African American women had obtained divorces, compared to 91% of the non-Hispanic white women (Sweet & Bumpass, 1987). Cherlin speculated that, because of their lower expectations of remarrying, African American women may be less motivated to obtain legal divorces. Indeed, given the shortage of African American men in each of the age categories from 20 to 49, it is not surprising that the proportion of divorced women who remarry is lower among African American than among non-Hispanic white women (Glick, 1997). Overall, the remarriage rate among African Americans is about one fourth the rate of whites (Staples & Johnson, 1993).

Cherlin (1996) identified lower educational levels, high rates of unemployment, and low income as importance sources of differences in African American and white rates of marital dissolution. However, as he pointed out, these factors alone are insufficient to account for all the observed difference. At every level of educational attainment, African American women are more likely to be separated or divorced from their husbands than are non-Hispanic white women. Using data from the 1980 census, Jaynes and Williams (1989) compared the actual marital-status distributions of African Americans and whites, controlling for differences in educational attainment for men and women and for income distribution for men. They found that when differences in educational attainment were taken into account, African American women were more likely to be "formerly married than White women and much less likely to be living with a husband" (p. 529). Moreover, income was an important factor in accounting for differences in the marital status of African American and white men. Overall, Jaynes and Williams found that socio-economic differences explained a significant amount of the variance in marital status differences between African Americans and whites, although Bumpass, Sweet, and Martin (1990) noted that such differences rapidly diminish as income increases, especially for men. As Glick (1997) reported, African American men with high income levels are more likely to be in intact first marriages by middle age than are African American women with high earnings. This relationship between income and marital status, he stated, is strongest at the lower end of the income distribution, suggesting that marital permanence for men is less dependent on their being well-to-do than on their having the income to support a family.

As a result of sharp increases in marital disruption and relatively low remarriage rates, less than half (43%) the African American adults aged 18 and older were currently married in 1995, down from 64% in 1970 (U.S. Bureau of the Census, 1996). Moreover, although the vast majority of the 11.6 million African Americans households in 1995 were family households, less than half (47%) were headed by married couples, down from 56% in 1980. Some analysts expect the decline in marriage among African Americans to continue for some time, consistent with the movement away from marriage as a consequence of modernization and urbanization (Espenshade, 1985) and in response to continuing economic marginalization. But African American culture may also play a role. As a number of writers have noted (Billingsley, 1992; Cherlin, 1996), blood ties and extended families have traditionally been given primacy over other types of relationships, including marriage, among African Americans, and this emphasis may have influenced the way many African Americans responded to recent shifts in values in the larger society and the restructuring of the economy that struck the African American community especially hard.

Such is the interpretation of Cherlin (1992, p. 112), who argued that the institution of marriage has been weakened during the past few decades by the increasing economic independence of women and men and by a cultural drift "toward a more individualistic ethos, one which emphasized self-fulfillment in personal relations." In addition, Wilson (1987) and others described structural shifts in the economy (from manufacturing to service industries as a source of the growth in employment) that have benefited African American women more than men, eroding men's earning potential and their ability to support families. According to Cherlin, the way African Americans responded to such broad sociocultural and economic changes was conditioned by their history and culture:

> Faced with difficult times economically, many Blacks responded by drawing upon a model of social support that was in their cultural repertoire. . . . This response relied heavily on extended kinship networks and deemphasized marriage. It is a response that taps a traditional source of strength in African-American society: cooperation and sharing among a large network of kin. (p. 113)

Thus, it seems likely that economic developments and cultural values have contributed independently and jointly to the explanation of declining rates of marriage among African Americans in recent years (Farley & Allen, 1987).

Single-Parent Families

Just as rates of divorce, separation, and out-of-wedlock childbearing have increased over the past few decades, so has the number of children living in single-parent households. For example, between 1970 and 1990, the number and proportion of all U.S. single-parent households increased threefold, from 1 in 10 to 3 in 10. There were 3.8 million single-parent families with children under 18 in 1970, compared to 11.4 million in 1994. The vast majority of single-parent households are maintained by women (86% in 1994), but the number of single-parent households headed by men has more than tripled: from 393,000 in 1970 to 1.5 million in 1994 (U.S. Bureau of the Census, 1995).

Among the 58% of African American families with children at home in 1995, more were one-parent families (34%) than married-couple families (24%). In 1994, single-parent families accounted for 25% of all white family groups with children under age 18, 65% of all African American family groups, and 36% of Hispanic family groups (U.S. Bureau of the Census, 1995).

Single-parent families are created in a number of ways: through divorce, marital separation, out-of-wedlock births, or death of a parent. Among adult African American women aged 25–44, increases in the percentage of never-married women and disrupted marriages are significant contributors to the rise in female-headed households; for white women of the same age group, marital dissolution or divorce is the most important factor (Demo, 1992; Jaynes & Williams, 1989). Moreover, changes in the living arrangements of women who give birth outside marriage or experience marital disruption have also been significant factors in the rise of female-headed households among African American and white women. In the past, women who experienced separation or divorce, or bore children out of wedlock were more likely to move in with their parents or other relatives, creating subfamilies; as a result, they were not classified as female headed. In recent decades, however, more and more of these women have established their own households (Parish, Hao, & Hogan, 1991).

An increasing proportion of female-headed householders are unmarried teenage mothers with young children. In 1990, for example, 96% of all births to African American teenagers occurred outside marriage; for white teenagers, the figure was 55% (National Center for Health Statistics, 1991). Although overall fertility rates among teenage women declined steadily from the 1950s through the end of the 1980s, the share of births to unmarried women has risen sharply over time. In 1970, the proportion of all births to unmarried teenage women aged 15–19 was less than 1 in 3; by 1991, it had increased to 2 in 3.

Differences in fertility and births outside marriage among young African American and white women are accounted for, in part, by differences in sexual activity, use of contraceptives, the selection of adoption as an option, and the proportion of premarital pregnancies that are legitimized by marriage before the children's births (Trusell, 1988). Compared to their white counterparts, African American teenagers are more likely to be sexually active and less likely to use contraceptives, to have abortions when pregnant, and to marry before the babies are born. In consequence, young African American women constitute a larger share of single mothers than they did in past decades. This development has serious social and economic consequences for children and adults because female-headed households have much higher rates of poverty and deprivation than do other families (Taylor, 1991b).

Family Structure and Family Dynamics

As a number of studies have shown, there is a strong correspondence between organization and economic status of families, regardless of race (Farley & Allen, 1987). For both African Americans and whites, the higher the income, the greater the percentage of families headed by married couples. In their analysis of 1980 census data on family income and structure, Farley and Allen (1987) found that "there were near linear decreases in the proportions of households headed by women, households where children reside with a single parent, and extended households with increases in economic status" (p. 185). Yet, socioeconomic factors, they concluded, explained only part of the observed differences in family organization between African Americans and whites. "Cultural factors—that is, family preferences, notions of the appropriate and established habits—also help explain race differences in family organization" (p. 186).

One such difference is the egalitarian mode of family functioning in African American families, characterized by complementarity and flexibility in family roles (Billingsley, 1992; Hill, 1971). Egalitarian modes of family functioning are common even among low-income African American families, where one might expect the more traditional patriarchal pattern of authority to prevail. Until recently, such modes of family functioning were interpreted as signs of weakness or pathology because they were counternormative to the gender-role division of labor in majority families (Collins, 1990). Some scholars have suggested that role reciprocity in African American families is a legacy of slavery, in which the traditional gender division of labor was largely ignored by slaveholders, and Black men and women were "equal in the sense that neither sex wielded economic power over the other" (Jones, 1985, p. 14). As a result of historical experiences and economic conditions, traditional gender distinctions in the homemaker and provider roles have been less rigid in African American families than in white families (Beckett & Smith, 1981). Moreover, since African American women have historically been involved in the paid labor force in greater numbers than have white women and because they have had a more significant economic role in families than their white counterparts, Scott-Jones and Nelson-LeGall (1986, p. 95) argued that African Americans "have not experienced as strong an economic basis for the subordination of women, either in marital roles or in the preparation of girls for schooling, jobs, and careers."

In her analysis of data from the NSBA, Hatchett (1991) found strong support for an egalitarian division of family responsibilities and tasks. With respect to attitudes toward the sharing of familial roles, 88% of the African American adults agreed that women and men should share child care and housework equally, and 73% agreed that both men and women should have jobs to support their families. For African American men, support for an egalitarian division of labor in the family did not differ by education or socioeconomic level, but education was related to attitudes toward the sharing of family responsibilities and roles among African American women. College-educated women were more likely than were women with less education to support the flexibility and interchangeability of family roles and tasks.

Egalitarian attitudes toward familial roles among African Americans are also reflected in child-rearing attitudes and practices (Taylor, 1991a). Studies have indicated that African American families tend to place less emphasis on differential gender-role socialization than do other families (Blau, 1981). In her analysis of gender-role socialization among southern African American families, Lewis (1975) found few patterned differences in parental attitudes toward male and female roles. Rather, age and relative birth order were found to be more important than gender as determinants of differential treatment and behavioral expectations for children. Through their socialization practices, African American parents seek to inculcate in both genders traits of assertiveness, independence, and self-confidence (Boykin & Toms, 1985; Lewis, 1975). However, as children mature, socialization practices are adapted to reflect "more closely the structure of expectations and opportunities provided for Black men and women by the dominant society" (Lewis, 1975, p. 237)—that is, geared to the macrostructural conditions that constrain familial role options for African American men and women.

However, such shifts in emphasis and expectations often lead to complications in the socialization process by inculcating in men and women components of gender-role definitions that are incompatible or noncomplementary, thereby engendering a potential source of conflict in their relationships. Franklin (1986) suggested that young African American men and women are frequently confronted with contradictory messages and dilemmas as a result of familial socialization. On the one hand, men are socialized to embrace an androgynous gender role within the African American community, but, on the other hand, they are expected to perform according to the white masculine gender-role paradigm in some contexts. According to Franklin, this dual orientation tends to foster confusion in some young men and difficulties developing an appropriate gender identity. Likewise, some young African American women may receive two different and contradictory messages: "One message states, 'Because you will be a Black woman, it is imperative that you learn to take care of yourself because it is hard to find a Black man who will take care of you.' A second message . . . that conflicts with the first . . . is 'your ultimate achievement will occur when you have snared a Black man who will take care of you' " (Franklin, 1986, p. 109). Franklin contended that such contradictory expectations and mixed messages frequently lead to incompatible gender-based behaviors among African American men and women and conflicts in their relationships.

Despite the apparently greater acceptance of role flexibility and power sharing in African American families, conflict around these issues figures prominently in marital instability. In their study of marital instability among African American and white couples in early marriages, Hatchett, Veroff, and Douvan (1995) found young African American couples at odds over gender roles in the family. Anxiety over their ability to function in the provider role was found to be an important source of instability in the marriages for African American husbands, but not for white husbands. Hatchett (1991) observed that marital instability tended to be more common among young African American couples if the husbands felt that their wives had equal power in the family and if the wives felt there was not enough sharing of family tasks and responsibilities. Hatchett et al. (1991) suggested that African American men's feelings of economic anxiety and self-doubt may be expressed in conflicts over decisional power and in the men's more tenuous commitment to their marriages vis-à-vis African American women. Although the results of their study relate to African American couples in the early stages of marriage, the findings may be predictive of major marital difficulties in the long term. These and other findings (see, for example, Tucker & Mitchell-Kernan, 1995) indicate that changing attitudes and definitions of familial roles among young African American couples are tied to social and economic trends (such as new and increased employment opportunities for women and new value orientations toward marriage and family) in the larger society.

African American Families, Social Change, and Public Policy

Over the past three decades, no change in the African American community has been more fundamental and dramatic than the restructuring of families and family relationships. Since the 1960s, unprecedented changes have occurred in rates of marriage, divorce, and separation; in the proportion of single and two-parent households and births to unmarried mothers; and in the number of children living in poverty. To be sure, these changes are consistent with trends for the U.S. population as a whole, but they are more pronounced among African Americans, largely because of a conflux of demographic and economic factors that are peculiar to the African American community.

In their summary of findings from a series of empirical studies that investigated the causes and correlates of recent changes in patterns of African American family formation, Tucker and Mitchell-Kernan (1995) came to several conclusions that have implications for future research and social policy. One consistent finding is the critical role that sex ratios–the availability of mates play in the formation of African American families. Analyzing aggregate-level data on African American sex ratios in 171 U.S. cities, Sampson (1995) found that these sex ratios were highly predictive of female headship, the percentage of married couples among families with school-age children, and the percentage of African American women who were single. In assessing the causal effect of sex ratios on the family structure of African Americans and whites, he showed that the effect is five times greater for the former than the latter. Similarly, Kiecolt and Fossett's (1995) analysis of African American sex ratios in Louisiana cities and counties disclosed that they had strong positive effects on the percentage of African American women who were married and had husbands present, the rate of marital births per thousand African American women aged 20–29, the percentage of married-couple families, and the percentage of children living in two-parent households.

Another consistent finding is the substantial and critical impact of economic factors on African American family formation, especially men's employment status. Analyses by Sampson (1995) and Darity and Myers (1995) provided persuasive evidence that economic factors play a major and unique role in the development and maintenance of African American families. Using aggregate data, Sampson found that low employment rates for African American men in cities across the United States were predictive of female headship, the percentage of women who were single, and the percentage of married-couple families among family households with school-age children. Moreover, comparing the effect of men's employment on the family structure of African American and white families, he found that the effect was 20 times greater for African Americans than for whites. Similar results are reported by Darity and Myers, who investigated the effects of sex ratio and economic marriageability—Wilson and Neckerman's (1986) Male Marriageability Pool Index—on African American family structure. They found that, although both measures were independently predictive of female headship among African Americans, a composite measure of economic and demographic factors was a more stable and effective predictor. Moreover, Sampson found that the strongest independent effect of these factors on family structure was observed among African American families in poverty. That is, "the lower the sex ratio and the lower the male employment rate the higher the rate of female-headed families with children and in poverty" (p. 250). It should be noted that neither rates of white men's employment nor white sex ratios was found to have much influence on white family structure in these analyses, lending support to Wilson's (1987) hypothesis regarding the structural sources of family disruption among African Americans.

Although the findings reported here are not definitive, they substantiate the unique and powerful effects of sex ratios and men's employment on the marital behavior and family structure of African Americans and point to other problems related to the economic marginalization of men and family poverty in African American communities. Some analysts have predicted far-reaching consequences for African Americans and for society at large should current trends in marital disruption continue unabated. Darity and Myers (1996) predicted that the majority of African American families will be headed by women by the beginning of the next decade if violent crime, homicide, incarceration, and other problems associated with the economic marginalization of African American men are allowed to rob the next generation of fathers and husbands. Moreover, they contended, a large number of such families are likely to be poor and isolated from the mainstream of American society.

The growing economic marginalization of African American men and their ability to provide economic support to families have contributed to their increasing estrangement from family life (Bowman, 1989; Tucker & Mitchell-Kernan, 1995) and are identified as pivotal factors in the development of other social problems, including drug abuse, crime, homicide, and imprisonment, which further erode their prospects as marriageable mates for African American women.

In addressing the structural sources of the disruption of African American families, researchers have advanced a number of short- and long-term proposals. There is considerable agreement that increasing the rate of marriage alone will not significantly improve the economic prospects of many poor African American families. As Ehrenreich (1986) observed, given the marginal economic position of poor African American men, impoverished African American women would have to be married to three such men— simultaneously—to achieve an average family income! Thus, for many African American women, increasing the prevalence of marriage will not address many of the problems they experience as single parents.

With respect to short-term policies designed to address some of the more deleterious effects of structural forces on African American families, Darity and Myers (1996) proposed three policy initiatives that are likely to produce significant results for African American communities. First, because research has indicated that reductions in welfare benefits have failed to stem the rise in female-headed households, welfare policy should reinstate its earlier objective of lifting the poor out of poverty. In Darity and Myers's view, concerns about the alleged disincentives of transfer payments are "moot in light of the long-term evidence that Black families will sink deeper into a crisis of female headship with or without welfare. Better a world of welfare-dependent, near-poor families than one of welfare-free but desolate and permanently poor families" (p. 288). Second, programs are needed to improve the health care of poor women and their children. One major potential benefit of such a strategy is an improvement in the sex ratio because the quality of prenatal and child care is one of the determinants of sex ratios. "By assuring quality health care now, we may help stem the tide toward further depletion of young Black males in the future" (p. 288). A third strategy involves improvements in the quality of education provided to the poor, which are key to employment gains.

Although these are important initiatives with obvious benefits to African American communities, in the long term, the best strategy for addressing marital disruptions and other family-related issues is an economic-labor market strategy. Because much of current social policy is ideologically driven, rather than formulated on the basis of empirical evidence, it has failed to acknowledge or address the extent to which global and national changes in the economy have conspired to marginalize significant segments of the African American population, both male and female, and deprive them of the resources to form or support families. Although social policy analysts have repeatedly substantiated the link between the decline in marriages among African Americans and fundamental changes in the U.S. postindustrial economy, their insights have yet to be formulated into a meaningful and responsive policy agenda. Until these structural realities are incorporated into governmental policy, it is unlikely that marital disruption and other adverse trends associated with this development will be reversed.

There is no magic bullet for addressing the causes and consequences of marital decline among African Americans, but public policies that are designed to improve the economic and employment prospects of men and women at all socioeconomic levels have the greatest potential for improving the lot of African American families. Key elements of such policies would include raising the level of education and employment training among African American youth, and more vigorous enforcement of antidiscrimination laws, which would raise the level of employment and earnings and contribute to higher rates of marriage among African Americans (Burbridge, 1995). To be sure, many of the federally sponsored employment and training programs that were launched during the 1960s and 1970s were plagued by a variety of administrative and organizational problems, but the effectiveness of some of these programs in improving the long-term employment prospects and life chances of disadvantaged youth and adults has been well documented (Taylor et al., 1990).

African American families, like all families, exist not in a social vacuum but in communities, and programs that are designed to strengthen community institutions and provide social support to families are likely to have a significant impact on family functioning. Although the extended family and community institutions, such as the church, have been important sources of support to African American families in the past, these community support systems have been overwhelmed by widespread joblessness, poverty, and a plethora of other problems that beset many African American communities. Thus, national efforts to rebuild the social and economic infrastructures of inner-city communities would make a major contribution toward improving the overall health and well-being of African American families and could encourage more young people to marry in the future.

Winning support for these and other policy initiatives will not be easy in a political environment that de-emphasizes the role of government in social policy and human welfare. But without such national efforts, it is difficult to see how many of the social conditions that adversely affect the structure and functioning of African American families will be eliminated or how the causes and consequences of marital decline can be ameliorated. If policy makers are serious about addressing conditions that destabilize families, undermine communities, and contribute to a host of other socially undesirable outcomes, new policy initiatives, such as those just outlined, must be given higher priority.

References

Allen, W. (1978). The search for applicable theories of black family life. *Journal of Marriage and the Family, 40,* 117–129.

Beckett, J., & Smith, A. (1981). Work and family roles: Egalitarian marriage in black and white families. *Social Service Review, 55,* 314–326.

Billingsley, A. (1968). *Black families in white America.* Englewood Cliffs, NJ: Prentice Hall.

Billingsley, A. (1992). *Climbing Jacob's ladder: The enduring legacy of African American families.* New York: Simon & Schuster.

Blassingame, J. (1972). *The slave community.* New York: Oxford University Press.

Blau, Zena. (1981). *Black children/white socialization.* New York: Free Press.

Bowman, P. J. (1989). Research perspectives on black men: Role strain and adaptation across the life cycle. In R. L. Jones (Ed.), *Black adult development and aging* (pp. 117–150). Berkeley, CA: Cobb & Henry.

Bowman, P. J. (1995). Commentary. In M. B. Tucker & C. Mitchell-Kernan (Eds.), *The decline in marriage among African Americans* (pp. 309–321). New York: Russell Sage Foundation.

Boykin, A. W., & Toms, F. D. (1985). Black child socialization: A conceptual framework. In H. P. McAdoo & J. L. McAdoo (Eds.), *Black children* (pp. 33–54). Beverly Hills, CA: Sage.

Bumpass, L., Sweet, J., & Martin, T. C. (1990). Changing patterns of remarriage. *Journal of Marriage and the Family, 52,* 747–756.

Burbridge, L. C. (1995). Policy implications of a decline in marriage among African Americans. In M. B. Tucker & C. Mitchell-Kernan (Eds.), *The decline in marriage among African Americans* (pp. 323–344). New York: Russell Sage Foundation.

Cherlin, A. (1992). *Marriage, divorce, remarriage* (rev. ed.). Cambridge, MA: Harvard University Press.

Cherlin, A. (1995). Policy issues of child care. In P. Chase-Lansdale & J. Brooks-Gunn (Eds.), *Escape from poverty* (pp. 121–137). New York: Cambridge University Press.

Cherlin, A. (1996). *Public and private families.* New York: McGraw-Hill.

Collins, P. (1990). *Black feminist thought.* Boston, MA: Unwin Hyman.

Darity, W., & Myers, S. (1995). Family structure and the marginalization of black men: Policy implications. In M. B. Tucker & C. Mitchell-Kernan (Eds.), *The decline in marriage among African Americans* (pp. 263–308). New York: Russell Sage Foundation.

Demo, D. (1992). Parent-child relations: Assessing recent changes. *Journal of Marriage and the Family, 54,* 104–117.

Dressler, W., Haworth-Hoeppner, S., & Pitts, B. (1985). Household structure in a southern black community. *American Anthropologist, 87,* 853–862.

DuBois, W. E. B. (1898). The study of the Negro problem. *Annals, 1,* 1–23.

DuBois, W. E. B. (1909). *The Negro American family.* Atlanta: Atlanta University Press.

Edwards, G. F. (1968). *E. Franklin Frazier on race relations.* Chicago: University of Chicago Press.

Ehrenreich, B. (1986, July-August). Two, three, many husbands. *Mother Jones,* 8–9.

Espenshade, T. (1985). Marriage trends in America: Estimates, implications, and underlying causes. *Population and Development Review, 11,* 193–245.

Farley, R., & Allen, W. (1987). *The color line and the quality of life in America.* New York: Oxford University Press.

Franklin, C. (1986). Black male-Black female conflict: Individually caused and culturally nurtured. In R. Staples (Ed.), *The black family* (3rd ed., pp. 106–113). Belmont, CA: Wadsworth.

Frazier, E. F. (1939). *The Negro family in the United States.* Chicago: University of Chicago Press.

Furstenberg, F., Hershberg, T., & Modell, J. (1975). The origins of the female-headed black family: The impact of the urban experience. *Journal of Interdisciplinary History, 6,* 211–233.

Genovese, E. (1974). *Roll Jordan roll: The world slaves made.* New York: Pantheon.

Glick, P. (1997). Demographic pictures of African American families. In H. McAdoo (Ed.), *Black families* (3rd ed., pp. 118–138). Thousand Oaks, CA: Sage.

Gutman, H. (1976). *The black family in slavery and freedom, 1750–1925.* New York: Pantheon.

Guttentag, M., & Secord, P. F. (1983). *Too many women.* Beverly Hills, CA: Sage.

Hatchett, S. (1991). Women and men. In J. Jackson (Ed.), *Life in black America* (pp. 84–104). Newbury Park, CA: Sage.

Hatchett, S., Cochran, D., & Jackson, J. (1991). In J. Jackson (Ed.), *Life in black America* (pp. 46–83). Newbury Park, CA: Sage.

Hatchett, S., Veroff, J., & Douvan, E. (1995). Marital instability among black and white couples in early marriage. In M. B. Tucker & C. Mitchell-Kernan (Eds.), *The decline in marriage among African Americans* (pp. 177–218). New York: Russell Sage Foundation.

Hernandez, D. J. (1993). *America's children.* New York: Russell Sage.

Herskovits, M. J. (1958). *The myth of the Negro past* (Beacon Paperback No. 69). Boston: Beacon Press.

Hill, R. (1971). *The strengths of black families.* New York: Emerson Hall.

Hill, R. (1993). *Research on the African American family: A holistic perspective.* Westport, CT: Auburn House.

Jackson, J. (Ed.). (1991). *Life in black America.* Newbury Park, CA: Sage.

Jaynes, G., & Williams, R. (1989). *A common destiny: Blacks and American society.* Washington, DC: National Academy Press.

Johnson, L. B. (1981). Perspectives on black family empirical research: 1965–1978. In H. P. McAdoo (Ed.), *Black families* (pp. 252–263). Beverly Hills, CA: Sage.

Jones, J. (1985). *Labor of love, labor of sorrow: Black women, work, and the family from slavery to the present.* New York: Basic Books.

Kiecolt, K., & Fossett, M. (1995). Mate availability and marriage among African Americans: Aggregate- and individual-level analysis. In M. B. Tucker & C. Mitchell-Kernan (Eds.), *The decline in marriage among African Americans* (pp. 121–135). New York: Russell Sage Foundation.

Lewis, D. (1975). The black family: Socialization and sex roles. *Phylon, 36,* 221–237.

Lichter, D. T., McLaughlin, D. K., Kephart, G., & Landry, G. (1992). Race and the retreat from marriage: A shortage of marriageable men? *American Sociological Review, 57,* 781–799.

Manfra, J. A. & Dykstra, R. P. (1985). Serial marriage and the origins of the black stepfamily: The Rowanty evidence. *Journal of American History, 7,* 18–44.

Mare, R., & Winship, C. (1991). Socioeconomic change and the decline of marriage for blacks and whites. In C. Jencks & P. E. Peterson (Eds.), *The urban underclass* (pp. 175–204). Washington, DC: Brookings Institute.

McAdoo, H. P. (Ed.). (1997). *Black families* (3rd ed.). Thousand Oaks, CA: Sage.

McCarthy, J. (1978). A comparison of the probability of the dissolution of first and second marriages. *Demography, 15,* 345–359.

Moynihan, D. P. (1965). *The Negro family: The case for national action.* Washington, DC: U.S. Government Printing Office.

National Center for Health Statistics. (1991). *Monthly Vital Statistics Report* (Vol. 35, No. 4, Suppl.). Washington, DC: U.S. Department of Health and Human Services.

Nobles, W. (1978). Toward an empirical and theoretical framework for defining black families. *Journal of Marriage and the Family, 40,* 679–688.

Parish, W. L., Hao, L., & Hogan, D. P. (1991). Family support networks, welfare, and work among young mothers. *Journal of Marriage and the Family, 53,* 203–215.

Pleck, E. (1973). The two-parent household: Black family structure in late nineteenth-century Boston. In M. Gordon (Ed.), *The American family in socio-historical perspective* (pp. 152–178). New York: St. Martin's Press.

Sampson, R. J. (1995). Unemployment and unbalanced sex ratios: Race-specific consequences for family structure and crime. In M. B. Tucker & C. Mitchell-Keman (Eds.), *The decline in marriage among African Americans* (pp. 229–254). New York: Russell Sage Foundation.

Scanzoni, J. (1977). *The black family in modern society.* Chicago: University of Chicago Press.

Scott-Jones, D., & Nelson-LeGall, S. (1986). Defining black families: Past and present. In E. Seidman & J. Rappaport (Eds.), *Redefining social problems* (pp. 83–100). New York: Plenum.

Shimkin, D., Shimkin, E. M., & Frate, D. A. (Eds.). (1978). *The extended family in black societies.* The Hague, the Netherlands: Mouton.

Smith, A. W. (1995). Commentary. In M. B. Tucker & C. Mitchell-Kernan (Eds.), *The decline in marriage among African Americans* (pp. 136–141). New York: Russell Sage Foundation.

Stack, C. (1974). *All our kin.* New York: Harper & Row.

Staples, R. (1971). Toward a sociology of the black family: A decade of theory and research. *Journal of Marriage and the Family, 33,* 19–38.

Staples, R., & Johnson, L. B. (1993). *Black families at the crossroads.* San Francisco: Jossey-Bass.

Staples, R., & Mirande, A. (1980). Racial and cultural variations among American families: A decennial review of the literature on minority families. *Journal of Marriage and the Family, 42,* 157–173.

Stevenson, B. (1995). Black family structure in colonial and antebellum Virginia: Amending the revisionist perspective. In M. B. Tucker & C. Mitchell-Kernan (Eds.), *The decline in marriage among African Americans* (pp. 27–56). New York: Russell Sage Foundation.

Sudarkasa, N. (1988). Interpreting the African heritage in Afro-American family organization. In H. P. McAdoo (Ed.), *Black families* (pp. 27–42). Newbury Park, CA: Sage.

Sudarkasa, N. (1997). African American families and family values. In H. P. McAdoo (Ed.), *Black families* (pp. 9–40). Thousand Oaks, CA: Sage.

Sweet, J., & Bumpass, L. (1987). *American families and households.* New York: Russell Sage Foundation.

Taylor, R. L. (1991a). Child rearing in African American families. In J. Everett, S. Chipungu, & B. Leashore (Eds.), *Child welfare: An Africentric perspective* (pp. 119–155). New Brunswick, NJ: Rutgers University Press.

Taylor, R. L. (1991b). Poverty and adolescent black males: The subculture of disengagement. In P. Edelman & J. Ladner (Eds.), *Adolescence and poverty: Challenge for the 1990s* (pp. 139–162). Washington, DC: Center for National Policy Press.

Taylor, R. L. (1997). Who's parenting? Trends and Patterns. In T. Arendell (Ed.), *Contemporary parenting: Challenges and issues* (pp. 68–91). Thousand Oaks, CA: Sage.

Taylor, R. J., Chatters, L., Tucker, M. B., & Lewis, E. (1990). Developments in research on black families: A decade review. *Journal of Marriage and the Family, 52,* 993–1014.

Testa, M., & Krogh, M. (1995). The effect of employment on marriage among black males in inner-city Chicago. In M. B. Tucker & C. Mitchell-Kernan (Eds.), *The decline in marriage among African Americans* (pp. 59–95). New York: Russell Sage Foundation.

Thornton, A. (1978). Marital instability differentials and interactions: Insights from multivariate contingency table analysis. *Sociology and Social Research, 62,* 572–595.

Trusell, J. (1988). Teenage pregnancy in the United States. *Family Planning Perspectives, 20,* 262–272.

Tucker, M. B., & Mitchell-Kernan, C. (1995). Trends in African American family formation: A theoretical and statistical overview. In M. B. Tucker & C. Mitchell Kernan (Eds.), *The decline in marriage among African Americans* (pp. 3–26). New York: Russell Sage Foundation.

U.S. Bureau of the Census. (1990). Marital status and living arrangements: March 1989. *Current Population Reports* (Series P-20, No. 445). Washington, DC: U.S. Government Printing Office.

U.S. Bureau of the Census. (1994). Marital status and living arrangements: March 1993. *Current Population Reports* (Series P-20, No. 478). Washington, DC: U.S. Government Printing Office.

U.S. Bureau of the Census. (1995). Household and family characteristics: March 1994. *Current Population Reports* (Series P-20, No. 483). Washington, DC: U.S. Government Printing Office.

U.S. Bureau of the Census. (1996). *Statistical abstract of the United States: 1996.* Washington, DC: U.S. Government Printing Office.

White, D. G. (1985). *Ain't I a woman? Female slaves in the plantation South.* New York: W. W. Norton.

Wilson, W. J. (1987). *The truly disadvantaged: The inner city, the underclass and public policy.* Chicago: University of Chicago Press.

Wilson, W. J., & Neckerman K. (1986). Poverty and family structure: The widening gap between evidence and public policy issues. In S. Danziger & D. Weinberg (Eds.), *Fighting poverty: What works and what doesn't* (pp. 232–259). Cambridge, MA: Harvard University Press.

Young, V. H. (1970). Family and childhood in a southern Negro community. *American Anthropologist, 72,* 269–288.

■READING 29

Diversity within Latino Families: New Lessons for Family Social Science

Maxine Baca Zinn and Barbara Wells

Who are Latinos? How will their growing presence in U.S. society affect the family field? These are vital questions for scholars who are seeking to understand the current social and demographic shifts that are reshaping society and its knowledge base. Understanding family diversity is a formidable task, not only because the field is poorly equipped to deal with differences at the theoretical level, but because many decentering efforts are themselves problematic. Even when diverse groups are included, family scholarship can distort and misrepresent by faulty emphasis and false generalizations.

Latinos are a population that can be understood only in terms of increasing heterogeneity. Latino families are unprecedented in terms of their diversity. In this chapter, we examine the ramifications of such diversity on the history, boundaries, and dynamics of family life. We begin with a brief look at the intellectual trends shaping Latino family research. We then place different Latino groups at center stage by providing a framework that situates them in specific and changing political and economic settings. Next, we apply our framework to each national origin group to draw out their different family experiences, especially as they are altered by global restructuring. We turn, then, to examine family structure issues and the interior dynamics of family living as they vary by gender and generation. We conclude with our reflections on studying Latino families and remaking family social science. In this chapter, we use interchangeably terms that are commonly used to describe Latino national-origin groups. For example, the terms Mexican American, Mexican, and Mexican-origin population will be used to refer to the same segment of the Latino population. Mexican-origin people may also be referred to as Chicanos.

INTELLECTUAL TRENDS, CRITIQUES, AND CHALLENGES

Origins

The formal academic study of Latino families originated in the late 19th and early 20th centuries with studies of Mexican immigrant families. As the new social scientists of the times focused their concerns on immigration and social disorganization, Mexican-origin and other ethnic families were the source of great concern. The influential Chicago School of Sociology led scholars to believe that Mexican immigration, settlement, and poverty created problems in developing urban centers. During this period, family study was emerging as a new field that sought to document, as well as ameliorate, social problems in urban settings (Thomas & Wilcox, 1987). Immigrant families became major targets of social reform.

Interwoven themes from race relations and family studies gave rise to the view of Mexicans as particularly disorganized. Furthermore, the family was implicated in their plight. As transplants from traditional societies, the immigrants and their children were thought to be at odds with social requirements in the new settings. Their family arrangements were treated as cultural exceptions to the rule of standard family development. Their slowness to acculturate and take on Western patterns of family development left them behind as other families modernized (Baca Zinn, 1995).

Dominant paradigms of assimilation and modernization guided and shaped research. Notions of "traditional" and "modern" forms of social organization joined the new family social science's preoccupation with a standard family form. Compared to mainstream families, Mexican immigrant families were analyzed as traditional cultural forms. Studies of Mexican immigrants highlighted certain ethnic lifestyles that were said to produce social disorganization. Structural conditions that constrained families in the new society were rarely a concern. Instead, researchers examined (1) the families' foreign patterns and habits, (2) the moral quality of family relationships, and (3) the prospects for their Americanization (Bogardus, 1934).

Cultural Preoccupations

Ideas drawn from early social science produced cultural caricatures of Mexican families that became more exaggerated during the 1950s, when structural functionalist theories took hold in American sociology. Like the previous theories, structural functionalism's strategy for analyzing family life was to posit one family type (by no means the only family form, even then) and define it as "the normal family" (Boss & Thorne, 1989). With an emphasis on fixed family boundaries and a fixed division of roles, structural functionalists focused their attention on the group-specific characteristics that deviated from the normal or standard family and predisposed Mexican-origin families to deficiency. Mexican-origin families were analyzed in isolation from the rest of social life, described in simplistic terms of rigid male dominance and pathological clannishness. Although the earliest works on Mexican immigrant families reflected a concern for their eventual adjustment to American society, the new studies virtually abandoned the social realm. They dealt with families as if they existed in a vacuum of backward Mexican traditionalism. Structural functionalism led scholars along a path of cultural reductionism in which differences became deficiencies.

The Mexican family of social science research (Heller, 1966; Madsen, 1964; Rubel, 1966) presented a stark contrast with the mythical "standard family." Although some studies found that Mexican family traditionalism was fading as Mexicans became acculturated, Mexican families were stereotypically and inaccurately depicted as the chief cause of Mexican subordination in the United States.

New Directions

In the past 25 years, efforts to challenge myths and erroneous assumptions have produced important changes in the view of Mexican-origin families. Beginning with a critique of structural functionalist accounts of Mexican families, new studies have successfully challenged the old notions of family life as deviant, deficient, and disorganized.

The conceptual tools of Latino studies, women's studies, and social history have infused the new scholarship to produce a notable shift away from cultural preoccupations.

Like the family field in general, research on Mexican-origin families has begun to devote greater attention to the "social situations and contexts that affect Mexican families" (Vega, 1990, p. 1015). This "revisionist" strategy has moved much Latino family research to a different plane—one in which racial-ethnic families are understood to be constructed by powerful social forces and as settings in which different family members adapt in a variety of ways to changing social conditions.

Current Challenges

Despite important advances, notable problems and limitations remain in the study of Latino families. A significant portion of scholarship includes only Mexican-origin groups (Massey, Zambrana, & Bell, 1995) and claims to generalize the findings to other Latinos. This practice constructs a false social reality because there is no Latino population in the same sense that there is an African American population. However useful the terms *Latino* and *Hispanic* may be as political and census identifiers, they mask extraordinary diversity. The category Hispanic was created by federal statisticians to provide data on people of Mexican, Cuban, Puerto Rican, and other Hispanic origins in the United States. There is no precise definition of group membership, and Latinos do not agree among themselves on an appropriate group label (Massey, 1993). While many prefer the term *Latino*, they may use it interchangeably with *Hispanic* to identify themselves (Romero, 1996). These terms are certainly useful for charting broad demographic changes in the United States, but when used as panethnic terms, they can contribute to misunderstandings about family life.

The labels Hispanic or Latino conceal variation in the family characteristics of Latino groups whose differences are often greater than the overall differences between Latinos and non-Latinos (Solis, 1995). To date, little comparative research has been conducted on Latino subgroups. The systematic disaggregation of family characteristics by national-origin groups remains a challenge, a necessary next step in the development of Latino family research.

We believe that the lack of a comprehensive knowledge base should not stand in the way of building a framework to analyze family life. We can use the burgeoning research on Latinos in U.S. social life to develop an analytical, rather than just a descriptive, account of families. The very complexity of Latino family arrangements begs for a unified (but not unitary) analysis. We believe that we can make good generalizations about Latino family diversity. In the sections that follow, we use a structural perspective grounded in intergroup differences. We make no pretense that this is an exhaustive review of research. Instead, our intent is to examine how Latino family experiences differ in relation to socially constructed conditions.

CONCEPTUAL FRAMEWORK

Conventional family frameworks, which have never applied well to racial-ethnic families, are even less useful in the current world of diversity and change. Incorporating multiplicity into family studies requires new approaches. A fundamental assumption guiding our analysis is that Latino families are not merely an expression of ethnic differences but, like all families, are the products of social forces.

Family diversity is an outgrowth of distinctive patterns in the way families and their members are embedded in environments with varying opportunities, resources, and rewards. Economic conditions and social inequalities associated with race, ethnicity, class, and gender place families in different "social locations." These differences are the key to understanding family variation. They determine labor market status, education, marital relations, and other factors that are crucial to family formation.

Studying Latino family diversity means exposing the structural forces that impinge differently on families in specific social, material, and historical contexts. In other words, it means unpacking the structural arrangements that produce and often require a range of family configurations. It also requires analyzing the cross-cutting forms of difference that permeate society and penetrate families to produce divergent family experiences. Several macrostructural conditions produce widespread family variations across Latino groups: (1) the sociohistorical context; (2) the structure of economic opportunity; and (3) global reorganization, including economic restructuring and immigration.

The Sociohistorical Context

Mexicans, Puerto Ricans, Cubans, and other Latino groups have varied histories that distinguish them from each other. The timing and conditions of their arrival in the United States produced distinctive patterns of settlement that continue to affect their prospects for success. Cubans arrived largely between 1960 and 1980; a group of Mexicans indigenous to the Southwest was forcibly annexed into the United States in 1848, and another has been migrating continually since around 1890; Puerto Ricans came under U.S. control in 1898 and obtained citizenship in 1917; Salvadorans and Guatemalans began to migrate to the United States in substantial numbers during the past two decades.

The Structure of Economic Opportunity

Various forms of labor are needed to sustain family life. Labor status has always been the key factor in distinguishing the experiences of Latinos. Mexicans, Puerto Ricans, Cubans, and others are located in different regions of the country where particular labor markets and a group's placement within them determine the kind of legal, political, and social supports available to families. Different levels of structural supports affect family life, often producing various domestic and household arrangements. Additional complexity stems from gendered labor markets. In a society in which men are still assumed to be the primary breadwinners, jobs generally held by women pay less than jobs usually held by men. Women's and men's differential labor market placement, rewards, and roles create contradictory work and family experiences.

Global Reorganization, Including Economic Restructuring and Immigration

Economic and demographic upheavals are redefining families throughout the world. Four factors are at work here: new technologies based primarily on the computer chip, global economic interdependence, the flight of capital, and the dominance of the information and service sectors over basic manufacturing industries (Baca Zinn & Eitzen,

1998). Latino families are profoundly affected as the environments in which they live are reshaped and they face economic and social marginalization because of underemployment and unemployment. Included in economic globalization are new demands for immigrant labor and the dramatic demographic transformations that are "Hispanicizing" the United States. Family flexibility has long been an important feature of the immigrant saga. Today, "Latino immigration is adding many varieties to family structure" (Moore & Vigil, 1993, p. 36).

The macrostructural conditions described earlier provide the context within which to examine the family experiences of different Latino groups. They set the foundation for comparing family life across Latino groups. These material and economic forces help explain the different family profiles of Mexicans, Puerto Ricans, Cubans, and others. In other words, they enable sociologists to understand how families are bound up with the unequal distribution of social opportunities and how the various national-origin groups develop broad differences in work opportunities, marital patterns, and household structures. However, they do not explain other important differences in family life that cut across national-origin groups. People of the same national origin may experience family differently, depending on their location in the class structure as unemployed, poor, working class or professional; their location in the gender structure as female or male; and their location in the sexual orientation system as heterosexual, gay, lesbian, or bisexual (Baca Zinn & Dill, 1996). In addition to these differences, family life for Latinos is shaped by age, generation living in the United States, citizenship status, and even skin color. All these differences intersect to influence the shape and character of family and household relations.

While our framework emphasizes the social context and social forces that construct families, we do not conclude that families are molded from the "outside in." What happens on a daily basis in family relations and domestic settings also constructs families. Latinos themselves—women, men, and children—have the ability actively to shape their family and household arrangements. Families should be seen as settings in which people are agents and actors, coping with, adapting to, and changing social structures to meet their needs (Baca Zinn & Eitzen, 1996).

Sociohistorical Context for Family Diversity among Mexicans

Families of Mexican descent have been incorporated into the United States by both conquest and migration. In 1848, at the end of the Mexican War, the United States acquired a large section of Mexico, which is now the southwestern United States. With the signing of the Treaty of Guadalupe Hidalgo, the Mexican population in that region became residents of U.S. territory. Following the U.S. conquest, rapid economic growth in that region resulted in a shortage of labor that was resolved by recruiting workers from Mexico. So began the pattern of Mexican labor migration that continues to the present (Portes & Rumbaut, 1990). Some workers settled permanently in the United States, and others continued in cycles of migration, but migration from Mexico has been continuous since around 1890 (Massey et al., 1995).

Dramatic increases in the Mexican-origin population have been an important part of the trend toward greater racial and ethnic diversity in the United States. The Mexican population tripled in size in 20 years, from an estimated 4.5 million in 1970 to 8.7 million in 1980 to 13.5 million in 1990 (Rumbaut, 1995; Wilkinson, 1993). At present, approximately two thirds of Mexicans are native born, and the remainder are foreign born (Rumbaut, 1995). Important differences are consistently found between the social experiences and economic prospects of the native born and the foreign born (Morales & Ong, 1993; Ortiz, 1996). While some variation exists, the typical Mexican migrant to the United States has low socioeconomic status and rural origins (Ortiz, 1995; Portes & Rumbaut, 1990). Recent immigrants have a distinct disadvantage in the labor market because of a combination of low educational attainment, limited work skills, and limited English language proficiency. Social networks are vital for integrating immigrants into U.S. society and in placing them in the social class system (Fernandez-Kelly & Schauffler, 1994). Mexicans are concentrated in barrios that have social networks in which vital information is shared, contacts are made, and job referrals are given. But the social-class context of these Mexican communities is overwhelmingly poor and working class. Mexicans remain overrepresented in low-wage occupations, especially service, manual labor, and low-end manufacturing. These homogeneous lower-class communities lack the high-quality resources that could facilitate upward mobility for either new immigrants or second- and later-generation Mexicans.

The common assumption that immigrants are assimilated economically by taking entry-level positions and advancing to better jobs has not been supported by the Mexican experience (Morales & Ong, 1993; Ortiz, 1996). Today's Mexican workers are as likely as ever to be trapped in low-wage unstable employment situations (Ortiz, 1996; Sassen, 1993). Studies (Aponte, 1993; Morales & Ong, 1993; Ortiz, 1996) have found that high labor force participation and low wages among Mexicans have created a large group of working poor. Households adapt by holding multiple jobs and pooling wages (Velez-Ibañez & Greenberg, 1992).

Mexicans are the largest Latino group in the United States; 6 of 10 Latinos have Mexican origins. This group has low family incomes, but high labor force participation for men and increasing rates for women. Mexicans have the lowest educational attainments and the largest average household size of all Latino groups (See Table 1 and Figure 1 for between-group comparisons.)

Puerto Ricans

The fortunes of Puerto Rico and the United States were joined in 1899 when Puerto Rico became a U.S. possession in the aftermath of Spain's defeat in the Spanish-American War. Puerto Ricans are U.S. citizens and, as such, have the right to migrate to the mainland without regulation. A small stream of migrants increased dramatically after World War II for three primary reasons: high unemployment in Puerto Rico, the availability of inexpensive air travel between Puerto Rico and the United States, and labor recruitment by U.S. companies (Portes & Rumbaut, 1990). Puerto Ricans were concentrated in or near their arrival point—New York City—although migrant laborers were scattered throughout the Northeast and parts of the Midwest. They engaged in a variety of blue-collar occupations; in New York City, they were particularly drawn into the textile and garment industries (Torres & Bonilla, 1993). The unique status of Puerto Rico as a commonwealth of the United States allows Puerto Ricans to engage in a circulating migration between Puerto Rico and the mainland (Feagin & Feagin, 1996).

TABLE 1 *Social and Economic Population Characteristics*

| | Median Income | Poverty | % Female Head of Household | Labor Force Participation | | High School Graduate | Average Household |
				Male	Female		
Mexican	23,609	29.6	19.9	80.9	51.8	46.5	3.86
Puerto Rican	20,929	33.2	41.2	70.6	47.4	61.3	2.91
Cuban	30,584	13.6	21.3	69.9	50.8	64.7	2.56
Central/South American	28,558	23.9	25.4	79.5	57.5	64.2	3.54
Other Hispanic	28,658	21.4	29.5			68.4	
All Hispanic	24,313	27.8	24	79.1	52.6	53.4	2.99
All U.S.	38,782	11.6	12	75	58.9	81.7	2.65
	1994	1994	1995	1995	1995	1995	1995

Sources: U.S. Bureau of the Census, Statistical Abstract of the United States: 1996 (116th ed.) Washington, D.C.: U.S. Government Printing Office, 1996, Tables 53, 68, 241, 615, 622, 723, 738.

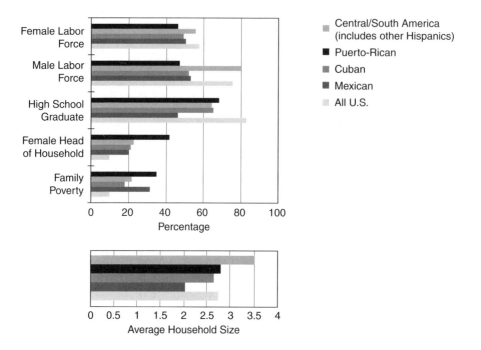

FIGURE 1   Social and Economic Population Characteristics

Puerto Ricans are the most economically disadvantaged of all major Latino groups. The particular context of Puerto Ricans' entry into the U.S. labor market helps explain this group's low economic status. Puerto Ricans with limited education and low occupational skills migrated to the eastern seaboard to fill manufacturing jobs (Ortiz, 1995); their economic well-being was dependent on opportunities for low-skill employment (Aponte, 1993). The region in which Puerto Ricans settled has experienced a major decline in its manufacturing base since the early 1970s. The restructuring of the economy means that, in essence, the jobs that Puerto Ricans came to the mainland to fill have largely disappeared. Latinos who have been displaced from manufacturing have generally been unable to gain access to higher-wage service sector employment (Carnoy, Daly, & Ojeda, 1993).

Compared to Mexicans and Cubans, Puerto Ricans have the lowest median family incomes and the highest unemployment and poverty rates. Puerto Ricans also have a high rate of female-headed households.

Cubans

The primary event that precipitated the migration of hundreds of thousands of Cubans to the United States was the revolution that brought Fidel Castro to power in 1959. This revolution set off several waves of immigration, beginning with the former economic and political elite and working progressively downward through the class structure. Early Cuban immigrants entered the United States in a highly politicized cold-war context as political refugees from communism. The U.S. government sponsored the Cuban Refugee Program, which provided massive supports to Cuban immigrants, including resettlement assistance, job training, small-business loans, welfare payments, and health care (Dominguez, 1992; Perez-Stable & Uriarte, 1993). By the time this program was phased out after the mid-1970s, the United States had invested nearly $1 billion in assistance to Cubans fleeing from communism (Perez-Stable & Uriarte, 1993, p. 155). Between 1960 and 1980, nearly 800,000 Cubans immigrated to the United States (Domiguez, 1992).

The Cuban population is concentrated in south Florida, primarily in the Miami area, where they have established a true ethnic enclave in which they own businesses; provide professional services; and control institutions, such as banks and newspapers (Perez, 1994). The unique circumstances surrounding their immigration help explain the experience of Cubans. U.S. government supports facilitated the economic successes of early Cuban immigrants (Aponte, 1993, Fernandez-Kelley & Schauffler, 1994). High rates of entrepreneurship resulted in the eventual consolidation of an enclave economy (Portes & Truelove, 1987).

Immigrants, women, and minorities have generally supplied the low-wage, flexible labor on which the restructured economy depends (Morales & Bonilla, 1993). However, Cubans "embody a privileged migration" in comparison to other Latino groups (Morales & Bonilla, 1993, p. 17). Their social-class positions, occupational attainments, and public supports have insulated them from the effects of restructuring. Yet Cubans in Miami are not completely protected from the displacements of the new economic order. As Perez-Stable and Uriarte (1993) noted, the Cuban workforce is polarized, with one segment moving into higher-wage work and the other remaining locked in low-wage employment.

Cuban families have higher incomes and far lower poverty rates than do other major Latino groups. Cubans are the most educated major Latino group and have the smallest average household size.

Other Latinos

In each national-origin group discussed earlier, one finds unique socioeconomic, political and historical circumstances. But the diversity of Latinos extends beyond the differences between Mexican Americans, Cuban Americans, and mainland Puerto Ricans. One finds further variation when one considers the experiences of other Latino national-origin groups. Although research on "other Latinos" is less extensive than the literature cited earlier, we consider briefly contexts for diversity in Central American and Dominican families.

Central Americans.   Political repression, civil war, and their accompanying economic dislocations have fueled the immigration of a substantial number of Salvadorans, Guatemalans, and Nicaraguans since the mid-1970s (Hamilton & Chinchilla, 1997). The U.S. population of Central Americans more than doubled between the 1980 and 1990 censuses and now outnumbers Cubans (U.S. Bureau of the Census, 1993). These Latinos migrated under difficult circumstances and face a set of serious challenges in the United

States (Dorrington, 1995). Three factors render this population highly vulnerable: (1) a high percentage are undocumented (an estimated 49% of Salvadorans and 40% of Guatemalans), (2) they have marginal employment and high poverty rates, and (3) the U.S. government does not recognize them as political refugees (Lopez, Popkin, & Telles, 1996).

The two largest groups of Central Americans are Salvadorans and Guatemalans, the majority of whom live in the Los Angeles area. Lopez et al.'s (1996) study of Central Americans in Los Angeles illumined the social and economic contexts in which these Latinos construct their family lives. In general, the women and men have little formal education and know little English, but have high rates of labor force participation. Salvadorans and Guatemalans are overrepresented in low-paying service and blue-collar occupations. Salvadoran and Guatemalan women occupy a low-wage niche in private service (as domestic workers in private homes). Central Americans, especially the undocumented who fear deportation and usually have no access to public support, are desperate enough to accept the poorest-quality, lowest-paying work that Los Angeles has to offer. These immigrants hold the most disadvantageous position in the regional economy (Scott, 1996). Lopez et al. predicted that in the current restructured economy, Central Americans will continue to do the worst of the "dirty work" necessary to support the lifestyles of the high-wage workforce.

Dominicans.   A significant number of Dominicans began migrating to the U.S. in the mid-1960s. What Grasmuck and Pessar (1996) called the "massive displacement" of Dominicans from their homeland began with the end of Trujillo's 30-year dictatorship and the political uncertainties that ensued. Dominican immigrant families did not fit the conventional image of the unskilled, underemployed peasant. They generally had employed breadwinners who were relatively well educated by Dominican standards; the majority described themselves as having urban middle-class origins (Mitchell, 1992).

The Dominican population is heavily concentrated in New York City. They entered a hostile labor market in which their middle class aspirations were to remain largely unfulfilled because the restructured New York economy offers low-wage, marginal, mostly dead-end employment for individuals without advanced education (Torres & Bonilla, 1993). Dominicans lacked the English language competence and educational credentials that might have facilitated their upward mobility (Grasmuck & Pessar, 1996). More than two thirds of the Dominican-origin population in the United States is Dominican born. As a group, Dominicans have high rates of poverty and female-headed families. Approximately 4 in 10 family households are headed by women.

THE STRUCTURE OF ECONOMIC OPPORTUNITY

Latino families remain outside the economic mainstream of U.S. society. Their median family income stands at less than two thirds the median family income of all U.S. families (U.S. Bureau of the Census, 1996). But the broad designation of "Latino" obscures important differences among national-origin groups. In this section, we explore variations in the structure of economic opportunity and consider how particular economic contexts shape the lives of different groups of Latino families.

Class, Work, and Family Life

A number of studies (see, for example, Cardenas, Chapa, & Burek, 1993; Grasmuck & Pessar, 1996; Lopez et al., 1996; Ortiz, 1995; Perez, 1994) have documented that diverse social and economic contexts produce multiple labor market outcomes for Latino families. The quality, availability, and stability of wage labor create a socioeconomic context in which family life is constructed and maintained. Cuban American families have fared far better socioeconomically than have other Latino families. Scholars consistently cite the role of the Cuban enclave in providing a favorable economic context with advantages that other groups have not enjoyed (Morales & Bonilla, 1993; Perez, 1994; Perez-Stable & Uriarte, 1993). Cuban families have the highest incomes, educational attainments, and levels of upper-white-collar employment. Puerto Rican, Mexican, and Central American families cluster below Cubans on these socioeconomic indicators, with Puerto Ricans the most disadvantaged group.

The structure of Mexican American economic opportunity stands in sharp contrast to that of Cubans. Betancur, Cordova, and Torres (1993) documented the systematic exclusion of Mexicans from upward-mobility ladders, tracing the incorporation of Mexican Americans into the Chicago economy to illustrate the historic roots of the concentration of Mexicans in unstable, poor-quality work. Throughout the 20th century Mexican migrants have constituted a transient workforce that has been continually vulnerable to fluctuations in the labor market and cycles of recruitment and deportation. Betancur et al.'s study highlighted the significance of the bracero program of contract labor migration in institutionalizing a segmented market for labor. The bracero program limited Mexican workers to specific low-status jobs and industries that prohibited promotion to skilled occupational categories. Mexicans were not allowed to compete for higher-status jobs, but were contracted to fill only the most undesirable jobs. Although formal bracero-era regulations have ended, similar occupational concentrations continue to be reproduced among Mexican American workers.

The effects of these diverging social-class and employment contexts on families are well illustrated by Fernandez-Kelly's (1990) study of female garment workers—Cubans in Miami and Mexicans in Los Angeles—both of whom placed a high value on marriage and family; however, contextual factors shaped differently their abilities to sustain marital relationships over time. Fernandez-Kelly contended that the conditions necessary for maintaining long-term stable unions were present in middle-class families but were absent in poor families. That is, the marriages of the poor women were threatened by unemployment and underemployment. Among these Mexican women, there was a high rate of poor female-headed households, and among the Cuban women, many were members of upwardly mobile families.

Women's Work

Several studies (Chavira-Prado, 1992; Grasmuck & Pessar, 1991; Lamphere, Zavella, Gonzales & Evans, 1993; Stier & Tienda, 1992; Zavella, 1987) that have explored the intersection of work and family for Latinas have found that Latinas are increasingly likely to be employed. Labor force participation is the highest among Central American women and the lowest among Puerto Rican women, with Mexican and Cuban women equally likely to be employed. Not only do labor force participation rates differ by national origin, but the meaning of women's work varies as well. For example, Fernandez-Kelly's (1990) study demonstrated that for Cuban women, employment was part of a broad family objective to reestablish middle-class status. Many Cuban immigrants initially experienced downward mobility, and the women took temporary jobs to generate income while their husbands cultivated fledgling businesses. These women often withdrew from the workforce when their families' economic positions had been secured. In contrast, Mexican women in Los Angeles worked because of dire economic necessity. They were drawn into employment to augment the earnings of partners who were confined to secondary-sector work that paid less than subsistence wages or worse, to provide the primary support for their households. Thus, whereas the Cuban women expected to work temporarily until their husbands could resume the role of middle-class breadwinner, the Mexican women worked either because their partners could not earn a family wage or because of the breakdown of family relationships by divorce or abandonment.

GLOBAL REORGANIZATION

Economic Restructuring

The economic challenges that Latinos face are enormous. A workforce that has always been vulnerable to exploitation can anticipate the decline of already limited mobility prospects. A recent body of scholarship (see, for example, Lopez et al., 1996; Morales & Bonilla, 1993; Ortiz, 1996) has demonstrated that the restructuring of the U.S. economy has reshaped economic opportunities for Latinos.

Torres and Bonilla's (1993) study of the restructuring of New York City's economy is particularly illustrative because it focused on Puerto Ricans, the Latino group hit hardest by economic transformations. That study found that restructuring in New York City is based on two processes that negatively affect Puerto Ricans. First, stable jobs in both the public and private sectors have eroded since the 1960s because many large corporations that had provided long-term, union jobs for minorities left the New York area and New York City's fiscal difficulties restricted the opportunities for municipal employment. Second, the reorganization of light manufacturing has meant that new jobs offer low wages and poor working conditions; new immigrants who are vulnerable to exploitation by employers generally fill these jobs. The restructuring of the economy has resulted in the exclusion or withdrawal of a substantial proportion of Puerto Ricans from the labor market (Morales & Bonilla, 1993).

Families are not insulated from the effects of social and economic dislocations. Research that has tracked this major social transformation has considered how such changes affect family processes and household composition (Grasmuck & Pessar, 1996; Lopez et al., 1996; Rodriguez & Hagan, 1997). What Sassen (1993) called the "informalization" and "casualization" of urban labor markets will, in the end, shape families in ways that deviate from the nuclear ideal. The marginalization of the Puerto Rican workforce is related not only to high unemployment and poverty rates, but to high rates of nonmarital births and female-headed households (Fernandez-Kelly, 1990; Morrissey, 1987).

Contrasting the experience of Dominicans to that of Puerto Ricans indicates that it is impossible to generalize a unitary "Latino experience" even within a single labor market—New York City. Torres and Bonilla (1993) found that as Puerto Ricans were displaced from manufacturing jobs in the 1970s and 1980s, new Dominican immigrants came into the restructured manufacturing sector to fill low-wage jobs. Dominicans were part of a pool of immigrant labor that entered a depressed economy, was largely ineligible for public assistance, and was willing to accept exploitative employment. Grasmuck and Pessar (1991, 1996) showed how the incorporation of Dominicans into the restructured New York economy has affected families. Although the rate of divorce among early immigrants was high, relationships have become increasingly precarious as employment opportunities have become even more constrained. Currently, rates of poverty and female-headed households for Dominicans approximate those of Puerto Ricans (Rumbaut, 1995).

A Latino Underclass?　Rising poverty rates among Latinos, together with the alarmist treatment of female-headed households among "minorities," have led many policy makers and media analysts to conclude that Latinos have joined inner-city African Americans to form part of the "underclass." According to the underclass model, inner-city men's joblessness has encouraged nonmarital childbearing and undermined the economic foundations of the African American family (Wilson, 1987, 1996). Researchers have also been debating for some time whether increases in the incidence of female-headed households and poverty among Puerto Ricans are irreversible (Tienda, 1989). Recent thinking, however, suggests that applying the underclass theory to Latinos obscures more than it reveals and that a different analytical model is needed to understand poverty and family issues in each Latino group (Massey et al., 1995). Not only do the causes of poverty differ across Latino communities, but patterns of social organization at the community and family levels produce a wide range of responses to poverty. According to Moore and Pinderhughes (1993), the dynamics of poverty even in the poorest Latino barrios differ in fundamental ways from the conventional portrait of the under-class. Both African Americans and Puerto Ricans have high rates of female-headed households. However, Sullivan's (1993) research in Brooklyn indicated that Puerto Ricans have high rates of cohabitation and that the family formation processes that lead to these household patterns are different from those of African Americans. Other case studies have underscored the importance of family organization. For example, Velez-Ibañez (1993) described a distinctive family form among poor Mexicans of South Tucson—cross-class household clusters surrounded by kinship networks that stretch beyond neighborhood boundaries and provide resources for coping with poverty.

Immigration

Families migrate for economic reasons, political reasons, or some combination of the two. Immigration offers potential and promise, but one of the costs is the need for families to adapt to their receiving community contexts. A growing body of scholarship has focused on two areas of family change: household composition and gender relations.

Household Composition.　Immigration contributes to the proliferation of family forms and a variety of household arrangements among Latinos (Vega, 1995). Numerous studies

have highlighted the flexibility of Latino family households. Chavez (1990, 1992) identified transnational families, binational families, extended families, multiple-family households, and other arrangements among Mexican and Central American immigrants.
Landale and Fennelly (1992) found informal unions that resemble marriage more than cohabitation among main-land Puerto Ricans, and Guarnizo (1997) found binational households among Dominicans who live and work in both the United States and the Dominican
Republic. Two processes are at work as families adapt their household structures. First,
family change reflects, for many, desperate economic circumstances (Vega, 1995), which
bring some families to the breaking point and leads others to expand their household
boundaries. Second, the transnationalization of economies and labor has created new opportunities for successful Latino families; for example, Guarnizo noted that Dominican
entrepreneurs sometimes live in binational households and have "de facto binational citizenship" (p. 171).

Immigration and Gender.   Several important studies have considered the relationship
between immigration and gender (Boyd, 1989; Grasmuck & Pessar, 1991; Hondagneu-
Sotelo, 1994). In her study of undocumented Mexican immigrants, Hondagneu-Sotelo
(1994) demonstrated that gender shapes migration and immigration shapes gender relations. She found that family stage migration, in which husbands migrate first and wives
and children follow later, does not fit the household-strategy model. Often implied in
this model is the assumption that migration reflects the unanimous and rational collective decision of all household members. However, as Hondagneu-Sotelo observed, gender hierarchies determined when and under what circumstances migration occurred; that
is, men often decided spontaneously, independently, and unilaterally to migrate north to
seek employment. When Mexican couples were finally reunited in the United States,
they generally reconstructed more egalitarian gender relations. Variation in the form of
gender relations in the United States is partially explained by the circumstances surrounding migration, such as the type and timing of migration, access to social networks,
and U.S. immigration policy.

FAMILY DYNAMICS ACROSS LATINO GROUPS

Familism

Collectivist family arrangements are thought to be a defining feature of the Latino population. Presumably, a strong orientation and obligation to the family produces a kinship
structure that is qualitatively different from that of all other groups. Latino familism,
which is said to emphasize the family as opposed to the individual, "is linked to many of
the pejorative images that have beset discussions of the Hispanic family" (Vega, 1990,
p. 1018). Although themes of Latino familism figure prominently in the social science
literature, this topic remains problematic owing to empirical limitations and conceptual
confusion.

Popular and social science writing contain repeated descriptions of what amounts
to a generic Latino kinship form. In reality, a Mexican-origin bias pervades the research

on this topic. Not only is there a lack of comparative research on extended kinship structures among different national-origin groups, but there is little empirical evidence for all but Mexican-origin families. For Mexican-origin groups, studies are plentiful (for reviews, see Baca Zinn, 1983; Vega, 1990, 1995), although they have yielded inconsistent evidence about the prevalence of familism, the forms it takes, and the kinds of supportive relationships it serves.

Among the difficulties in assessing the evidence on extended family life are the inconsistent uses of terms like *familism* and *extended family system*. Seeking to clarify the multiple meanings of familism, Ramirez and Arce (1981) treated familism as a multidimensional concept comprised of such distinct aspects as structure, behavior, norms and attitudes, and social identity, each of which requires separate measurement and analysis. They proposed that familism contains four key components: (1) demographic familism, which involves such characteristics as family size; (2) structural familism, which measures the incidence of multigenerational (or extended) households; (3) normative families, which taps the value that Mexican-origin people place on family unity and solidarity; and (4) behavioral familism, which has to do with the level of interaction between family and kin networks.

Changes in regional and local economies and the resulting dislocations of Latinos have prompted questions about the ongoing viability of kinship networks. Analyzing a national sample of minority families, Rochelle (1997) argued that extended kinship networks are declining among Chicanos, Puerto Ricans, and African Americans. On the other hand, a large body of research has documented various forms of network participation by Latinos. For three decades, studies have found that kinship networks are an important survival strategy in poor Mexican communities (Alvirez & Bean, 1976; Hoppe & Heller, 1975; Velez-Ibañez, 1996) and that these networks operate as a system of cultural, emotional, and mental support (Keefe, 1984; Mindel, 1980; Ramirez, 1980), as well as a system for coping with socioeconomic marginality (Angel & Tienda, 1982; Lamphere et al., 1993).

Research has suggested, however, that kinship networks are not maintained for socioeconomic reasons alone (Buriel & De Ment, 1997). Familistic orientation among Mexican-origin adults has been associated with high levels of education and income (Griffith & Villavicienco, 1985). Familism has been viewed as a form of social capital that is linked with academic success among Mexican-heritage adolescents (Valenzuela & Dornbusch, 1994).

The research on the involvement of extended families in the migration and settlement of Mexicans discussed earlier (Chavez, 1992; Hondagneu-Sotelo, 1994; Hondagneu-Sotelo & Avila, 1997) is profoundly important. In contrast to the prevailing view that family extension is an artifact of culture, this research helps one understand that the structural flexibility of families is a social construction. Transnational families and their networks of kin are extended in space, time, and across national borders. They are quintessential adaptations—alternative arrangements for solving problems associated with immigration.

Despite the conceptual and empirical ambiguities surrounding the topic of familism, there is evidence that kinship networks are far from monolithic. Studies have revealed that variations are rooted in distinctive social conditions, such as immigrant versus non-immigrant status and generational status. Thus, even though immigrants use kin for assistance, they have smaller social networks than do second-generation Mexican Americans who have broader social networks consisting of multigenerational kin (Vega, 1990). Studies have shown that regardless of class, Mexican extended families in the United States become stronger and more extensive with generational advancement, acculturation, and socio-economic mobility (Velez-Ibañez, 1996). Although an assimilationist perspective suggests that familism fades in succeeding generations, Velez-Ibañez found that highly elaborated second- and third-generation extended family networks are actively maintained through frequent visits, ritual celebrations, and the exchange of goods and services. These networks are differentiated by the functions they perform, depending on the circumstances of the people involved.

Gender

Latino families are commonly viewed as settings of traditional patriarchy and as differ-ent from other families because of machismo, the cult of masculinity. In the past two decades, this cultural stereotype has been the impetus for corrective scholarship on Latino families. The flourishing of Latina feminist thought has shifted the focus from the determinism of culture to questions about how gender and power in families are con-nected with other structures and institutions in society. Although male dominance re-mains a central theme, it is understood as part of the ubiquitous social ordering of women and men. In the context of other forms of difference, gender exerts a powerful influence on Latino families.

New research is discovering gender dynamics among Latino families that are both similar to and different from those found in other groups. Similarities stem from social changes that are reshaping all families, whereas differences emerge from the varied lo-cations of Latino families and the women and men in them. Like other branches of scholarship on Latino families, most studies have been conducted with Mexican-origin populations. The past two decades of research have shown that family life among all Latino groups is deeply gendered. Yet no simple generalizations sum up the essence of power relations.

Research has examined two interrelated areas: (1) family decision making and (2) the allocation of household labor. Since the first wave of "revisionist works" (Zavella, 1987) conducted in the 1970s and 1980s (Baca Zinn, 1980; Ybarra, 1982), researchers have found variation in these activities, ranging from patriarchal role-segregated patterns to egalitar-ian patterns, with many combinations in between. Studies have suggested that Latinas' employment patterns, like those of women around the world, provide them with resources and autonomy that alter the balance of family power (Baca Zinn, 1980; Coltrane & Valdez, 1993; Pesquera, 1993; Repack, 1997; Williams, 1990; Ybarra, 1982; Zavella, 1987). But, as we discussed earlier, employment opportunities vary widely, and the variation produces multiple work and family patterns for Latinas. Furthermore, women's employment, by it-self, does not eradicate male dominance. This is one of the main lessons of Zavella's (1987) study of Chicana cannery workers in California's Santa Clara Valley. Women's cannery work was circumscribed by inequalities of class, race, and gender. As seasonal, part-time workers, the women gained some leverage in the home, thereby creating temporary shifts in their day-to-day family lives, but this leverage did not alter the balance of family power. Fernandez-Kelly and Garcia's (1990) comparative study of women's work and family pat-terns among Cubans and Mexican Americans found strikingly different configurations of power. Employed women's newfound rights are often contradictory. As Repack's study (1997) of Central American immigrants revealed, numerous costs and strains accompany women's new roles in a new landscape. Family relations often became contentious when women pressed partners to share domestic responsibilities. Migration produced a situation in which women worked longer and harder than in their countries of origin.

Other conditions associated with varying patterns in the division of domestic labor are women's and men's occupational statuses and relative economic contributions to their families. Studies by Pesquera (1993), Coltrane and Valdez (1993), and Coltrane (1996) found a general "inside/outside" dichotomy (wives doing most housework, husbands doing outside work and sharing some child care), but women in middle-class jobs received more "help" from their husbands than did women with lower earnings.

"Family power" research should not be limited to women's roles, but should study the social relations between women and men. Recent works on Latino men's family lives have made important strides in this regard (Coltrane & Valdez, 1993; Shelton & John, 1993). Still, there is little information about the range and variety of Latino men's family experiences (Mirande, 1997) or of their interplay with larger structural conditions. In a rare study of Mexican immigrant men, Hondagneu-Sotelo and Messner (1994) discussed the diminution of patriarchy that comes with settling in the United States. They showed that the key to gender equality in immigrant families is women's and men's relative positions of power and status in the larger society. Mexican immigrant men's status is low owing to racism, economic marginality, and possible undocumented status. Meanwhile, as immigrant women move into wage labor, they develop autonomy and economic skills. These conditions combine to erode patriarchal authority.

The research discussed earlier suggested some convergences between Latinos and other groups in family power arrangements. But intertwined with the shape of domestic power are strongly held ideals about women's and men's family roles. Ethnic gender identities, values, and beliefs contribute to gender relations and constitute an important but little understood dimension of families. Gender may also be influenced by Latinos' extended family networks. As Lamphere et al. (1993) discovered, Hispanas in Albuquerque were living in a world made up largely of Hispana mothers, sisters, and other relatives. Social scientists have posited a relationship between dense social networks and gender segregation. If this relationship holds, familism could well impede egalitarian relations in Latino families (Coltrane, 1996; Hurtado, 1995).

Compulsory heterosexuality is an important component of both gender and family systems. By enforcing the dichotomy of opposite sexes, it is also a form of inequality in its own right, hence an important marker of social location. A growing literature on lesbian and gay identity among Latinas and Latinos has examined the conflicting challenges involved in negotiating a multiple minority status (Alarcon, Castillo, & Moraga, 1989; Almaguer, 1991; Anzaldúa, 1987; Carrier, 1992; Moraga, 1983; Morales, 1990). Unfortunately, family scholarship on Latinos has not pursued the implications of lesbian and gay identities for understanding family diversity. In fact, there have been no studies in the social sciences in the area of sexual orientation and Latino families (Hurtado, 1995). But although the empirical base is virtually nonexistent and making *families* the unit of analysis no doubt introduces new questions (Demo & Allen, 1996), we can glean useful insights from the discourse on sexual identity. Writing about Chicanos, Almaguer (1991) identified the following obstacles to developing a safe space for forming a gay or lesbian identity: racial and class subordination and a context in which ethnicity remains a primary basis of group identity and survival. "Moreover Chicano *family life* [italics added] requires allegiance to patriarchal gender relations and to a system of sexual meanings that directly mitigate against the emergence of this alternative basis of self identity" (Almaguer, p. 88). Such repeated references to the constraints of ethnicity, gender, and sexual orientation imposed by Chicano families (Almaguer, 1991; Moraga, 1983) raise important questions. How do varied family contexts shape and differentiate the development of gay identities among Latinos? How do they affect the formation of lesbian and gay families among Latinas and Latinos? This area is wide open for research.

Children and Their Parents

Latinos have the highest concentration of children and adolescents of all major racial and ethnic groups. Nearly 40% of Latinos are aged 20 or younger, compared to about 26% of non-Hispanic whites (U.S. Bureau of the Census, 1996). Among Latino subgroups, the highest proportions of children and adolescents are among Mexicans and Puerto Ricans and the lowest among Cubans (Solis, 1995).

Latino socialization patterns have long held the interest of family scholars (Martinez, 1993). Most studies have focused on the child-rearing practices of Mexican families. Researchers have questioned whether Mexican families have permissive or authoritarian styles of child rearing and the relationship of childrearing styles to social class and cultural factors (Martinez, 1993). Patterns of child rearing were expected to reveal the level of acculturation to U.S. norms and the degree of modernization among traditional immigrant families. The results of research spanning the 1970s and 1980s were mixed and sometimes contradictory.

Buriel's (1993) study brought some clarity to the subject of child-rearing practices by situating it in the broad social context in which such practices occur. This study of Mexican families found that child-rearing practices differ by generation. Parents who were born in Mexico had a "responsibility-oriented" style that was compatible with their own life experience as struggling immigrants. U.S.-born Mexican parents had a "concern-oriented" style of parenting that was associated with the higher levels of education and income found among this group and that may also indicate that parents compensate for their children's disadvantaged standing in U.S. schools.

Mainstream theorizing has generally assumed a middle-class European-American model for the socialization of the next generation (Segura & Pierce, 1993). But the diverse contexts in which Latino children are raised suggest that family studies must take into account multiple models of socialization. Latino children are less likely than Anglo children to live in isolated nuclear units in which parents have almost exclusive responsibility for rearing children and the mothers' role is primary. Segura and Pierce contended that the pattern of nonexclusive mothering found in some Latino families shapes the gender identities of Latinos in ways that conventional thinking does not consider. Velez-Ibañez & Greenberg (1992) discussed how the extensive kinship networks of Mexican families influence child rearing and considered the ramifications for educational outcomes. Mexican children are socialized into a context of "thick" social relations. From infancy onward, these children experience far more social interaction than do children who are raised in more isolated contexts. The institution of education—second only to the family as an agent of socialization—is, in the United States, modeled after the dominant society and characterized by competition and individual achievement. Latino students who have been socialized into a more cooperative model of social relations often experience a disjuncture between their upbringing and the expectations of their schools (Velez-Ibañez & Greenberg, 1992).

Social location shapes the range of choices that parents have as they decide how best to provide for their children. Latino parents, who are disproportionately likely to occupy subordinate social locations in U.S. society, encounter severe obstacles to providing adequate material resources for their children. To date, little research has focused on Latino fathers (Powell, 1995). Hondagneu-Sotelo and Avila's (1997) study documented a broad range of mothering arrangements among Latinas. One such arrangement is transnational mothering, in which mothers work in the United States while their children remain in Mexico or Central America; it is accompanied by tremendous costs and undertaken when options are extremely limited. The researchers found that transnational mothering occurred among domestic workers, many of whom were live-in maids or child care providers who could not live with their children, as well as mothers who could better provide for their children in their countries of origin because U.S. dollars stretched further in Central America than in the United States. Other mothering arrangements chosen by Latinas in the study included migrating with their children, migrating alone and later sending for their children, and migrating alone and returning to their children after a period of work.

Intrafamily Diversity

Family scholars have increasingly recognized that family experience is differentiated along the lines of age and gender (Baca Zinn & Eitzen, 1996; Thorne, 1992). Members of particular families—parents and children, women and men—experience family life differently. Scholarship that considers the internal differentiation of Latino families is focused on the conditions surrounding and adaptations following immigration.

While immigration requires tremendous change of all family members, family adaptation to the new context is not a unitary phenomenon. Research has found patterns of differential adjustment as family members adapt unevenly to an unfamiliar social environment (Gold, 1989). Gil and Vega's (1996) study of acculturative stress in Cuban and Nicaraguan families in the Miami area identified significant differences in the adjustment of parents and their children. For example, Nicaraguan adolescents reported more initial language conflicts than did their parents, but their conflicts diminished over time, whereas their parents' language conflicts increased over time. This difference occurred because the adolescents were immediately confronted with their English language deficiency in school, but their parents could initially manage well in the Miami area without a facility with English. The authors concluded that family members experience "the aversive impacts of culture change at different times and at variable levels of intensity" (p. 451).

Differential adjustment creates new contexts for parent-child relations. Immigrant children who are school-aged generally become competent in English more quickly than do their parents. Dorrington (1995) found that Salvadoran and Guatemalan children often assume adult roles as they help their parents negotiate the bureaucratic structure of their new social environment; for example, a young child may accompany her parents to a local utility company to act as their translator.

Immigration may also create formal legal distinctions among members of Latino families. Frequently, family members do not share the same immigration status. That is, undocumented Mexican and Central American couples are likely, over time, to have children born in the United States and hence are U.S. citizens; the presence of these children then renders the "undocumented family" label inaccurate. Chavez (1992, p. 129) used the term *binational family* to refer to a family with both members who are undocumented and those who are citizens or legal residents.

Not only do family members experience family life differently, but age and gender often produce diverging and even conflicting interests among them (Baca Zinn & Eitzen, 1996). Both Hondagneu-Sotelo's (1994) and Grasmuck and Pessar's (1991) studies of family immigration found that Latinas were generally far more interested in settling permanently in the United States than were their husbands. In both studies, the women had enhanced their status by migration, while the men had lost theirs. Hondagneu-Sotelo noted that Mexican women advanced the permanent settlement of their families by taking regular, nonseasonal employment; negotiating the use of public and private assistance; and forging strong community ties. Grasmuck and Pessar observed that Dominican women tried to postpone their families' return to the Dominican Republic by extravagantly spending money that would otherwise be saved for their return and by establishing roots in the United States.

DISCUSSION AND CONCLUSION

The key to understanding diversity in Latino families is the uneven distribution of constraints and opportunities among families, which affects the behaviors of family members and ultimately the forms that family units take (Baca Zinn & Eitzen, 1996). Our goal in this review was to call into question assumptions, beliefs, and false generalizations about the way "Latino families are." We examined Latino families not as if they had some essential characteristics that set them apart from others, but as they are affected by a complex mix of structural features.

Our framework enabled us to see how diverse living arrangements among Latinos are situated and structured in the larger social world. Although this framework embraces the interplay of macro-and microlevels of analysis, we are mindful that this review devoted far too little attention to family experience, resistance, and voice. We do not mean to underestimate the importance of human agency in the social construction of Latino families, but we could not devote as much attention as we would have liked to the various ways in which women, men, and children actively produce their family worlds. Given the sheer size of the literature, the "non-comparability of most contemporary findings" and the lack of a consistent conceptual groundwork" (Vega, 1990, p. 102), we decided that what is most needed is a coherent framework within which to view and interpret diversity. Therefore, we chose to focus on the impact of social forces on family life.

The basic insights of our perspective are sociological. Yet a paradox of family sociology is that the field has tended to misrepresent Latino families and those of other racial-ethnic groups. Sociology has distorted Latino families by generalizing from the experience of dominant groups and ignoring the differences that make a difference. This is a great irony. Family sociology, the specialty whose task it is to describe and understand social diversity, has marginalized diversity, rather than treated it as a central feature of social life (Baca Zinn & Eitzen, 1993).

As sociologists, we wrote this chapter fully aware of the directions in our discipline that hinder the ability to explain diversity. At the same time, we think the core insight of sociology should be applied to challenge conventional thinking about families. Reviewing the literature for this chapter did not diminish our sociological convictions, but it did present us with some unforeseen challenges. We found a vast gulf between mainstream family sociology and the extraordinary amount of high-quality scholarship on Latino families. Our review took us far beyond the boundaries of our discipline, making us "cross disciplinary migrants" (Stacey, 1995). We found the new literature in diverse and unlikely locations, with important breakthroughs emerging in the "borderlands" between social science disciplines. We also found the project to be infinitely more complex than we anticipated. The extensive scholarship on three national-origin groups and "others" was complicated by widely varying analytic snapshots. We were, in short, confronted with a kaleidoscope of family diversity. Our shared perspective served us well in managing the task at hand. Although we have different family specializations and contrasting family experiences, we both seek to understand multiple family and household forms that emanate from structural arrangements.

What are the most important lessons our sociological analysis holds for the family field? Three themes offer new directions for building a better, more inclusive, family social science. First, understanding Latino family diversity does not mean simply appreciating the ways in which families are different; rather, it means analyzing how the formation of diverse families is based on and reproduces social inequalities. At the heart of many of the differences between Latino families and mainstream families and the different aggregate family patterns among Latino groups are structural forces that place families in different social environments. What is not often acknowledged is that the same social structures—race, class, and other hierarchies—affect *all* families, albeit in different ways. Instead of treating family variation as the property of group difference, recent sociological theorizing (Baca Zinn, 1994; Dill, 1994; Glenn, 1992; Hill Collins, 1990, 1997) has conceptualized diverse family arrangements in *relational* terms, that is, mutually dependent and sustained through interaction across racial and class boundaries. The point is not that family differences based on race, class, and gender simply coexist. Instead, many differences in family life involve relationships of domination and subordination and differential access to material resources. Patterns of privilege and subordination characterize the historical relationships between Anglo families and Mexican families in the Southwest (Dill, 1994). Contemporary diversity among Latino families reveals *new* interdependences and inequalities. Emergent middle-class and professional lifestyles among Anglos and even some Latinos are interconnected with a new Latino servant class whose family arrangements, in turn, must accommodate to the demands of their labor.

Second, family diversity plays a part in different economic orders and the shifts that accompany them. Scholars have suggested that the multiplicity of household types is one of the chief props of the world economy (Smith, Wallerstein, & Evers, 1985). The example of U.S.-Mexican cross-border households brings this point into full view. This household arrangement constitutes an important "part of the emerging and dynamic economic and technological transformations in the region" (Velez-Ibañez, 1996, p. 143). The structural reordering required by such families is central to regional economic change.

Finally, the incredible array of immigrant family forms and their enormous capacity for adaptation offer new departures for the study of postmodern families. "Binational," "transnational," and "multinational" families, together with "border balanced households" and "generational hopscotching," are arrangements that remain invisible even in Stacey's (1996) compelling analysis of U.S. family life at the century's end. And yet the experiences of Latino families—flexible and plastic—as far back as the late 1800s (Griswold del Castillo, 1984), give resonance to the image of long-standing family fluidity and of contemporary families lurching backward and forward into the postmodern age (Stacey, 1990). The shift to a postindustrial economy is not the only social transformation affecting families. Demographic and political changes sweeping the world are engendering family configurations that are yet unimagined in family social science.

These trends offer new angles of vision for thinking about family diversity. They pose new opportunities for us to remake family studies as we uncover the mechanisms that construct multiple household and family arrangements.

References

Alarcon, N., Castillo, A., & Moraga, C. (Eds.). (1989). *Third woman: The sexuality of Latinas.* Berkeley, CA: Third Woman.

Almaguer, T. (1991). Chicano men: A cartography of homosexual identity and behavior. *Differences: A Journal of Feminist Cultural Studies, 3,* 75–100.

Alvirez, D., & Bean, F. (1976). The Mexican American family. In C. Mindel & R. Habenstein (Eds.), *Ethnic families in America* (pp. 271–292). New York: Elsevier.

Angel, R., & Tienda, M. (1982). Determinants of extended household structure: Cultural pattern or economic need? *American Journal of Sociology, 87,* 1360–1383,

Anzaldúa, G. (1987). *Borderlands/La Frontera: The new meztiza.* San Francisco: Spinsters, Aunt Lute Press.

Aponte, R. (1993). Hispanic families in poverty: Diversity, context, and interpretation. *Families in Society: The Journal of Contemporary Human Services, 36,* 527–537.

Baca Zinn, M. (1980). Employment and education of Mexican American women: The interplay of modernity and ethnicity in eight families. *Harvard Educational Review, 50,* 47–62.

Baca Zinn, M. (1983). Familism among Chicanos: A theoretical review. *Humboldt Journal of Social Relations, 10,* 224–238.

Baca Zinn, M. (1994). Feminist rethinking from racial-ethnic families. In M. Baca Zinn & B. T. Dill (Eds.), *Women of color in U.S. society* (pp. 303–312). Philadelphia: Temple University Press.

Baca Zinn, M. (1995). Social science theorizing for Latino families in the age of diversity. In R. E. Zambrana (Ed.), *Understanding Latino families* (pp. 177–187). Thousand Oaks, CA: Sage.

Baca Zinn, M., & Dill, B. T. (1996). Theorizing difference from multiracial feminism. *Feminist Studies, 22,* 321–332.

Baca Zinn, M., & Eitzen, D. S. (1993). The demographic transformation and the sociological enterprise. *American Sociologist, 24,* 5–12.

Baca Zinn, M., & Eitzen, D. S. (1996). *Diversity in families* (4th ed.). New York: HarperCollins.

Baca Zinn, M., & Eitzen, D. S. (1998). Economic restructuring and systems in inequality. In M. L. Andersen & P. H. Collins (Eds.), *Race, class and gender* (3rd ed., pp. 233–237). Belmont, CA: Wadsworth.

Betancur, J. J., Cordova, T., & Torres, M. L. A. (1993). Economic restructuring and the process of incorporation of Latinos into the Chicago economy. In R. Morales & F. Bonilla (Eds.), *Latinos in a changing U.S. economy: Comparative perspectives on growing inequality* (pp. 109–132). Newbury Park, CA: Sage.

Bogardus, A. (1934). *The Mexican in the United States.* Los Angeles: University of Southern California Press.

Boss, P., & Thorne, B. (1989). Family sociology and family therapy. In M. McGoldrick, C. M. Anderson, & F. Walsh (Eds.), *Women in families* (pp. 78–96). New York: W. W. Norton.

Boyd, M. (1989). Family and personal networks in international migration: Recent developments and new agendas. *International Migration Review, 23,* 638–670.

Buriel, R. (1993). Childrearing orientations in Mexican American families: The influence of generation and sociocultural factors. *Journal of Marriage and the Family, 55,* 987–1000.

Buriel, R., & De Ment, T. (1997). Immigration and sociocultural change in Mexican, Chinese, and Vietnamese American families. In A. Booth, A. C. Crouter, & N. Landale (Eds.), *Immigration and the family: Research and policy on U.S. immigrants* (pp. 165–200). Mahway, NJ: Lawrence Erlbaum.

Cardenas, G., Chapa, J., & Burek, S. (1993). The changing economic position of Mexican Americans in San Antonio. In R. Morales & F. Bonilla (Eds.), *Latinos in a changing U.S. economy: Comparative perspectives on growing inequality* (pp. 160–183). Newbury Park, CA: Sage.

Carnoy, M., Daley, H. M., & Ojeda, R. H. (1993). The changing economic position of Latinos in the U.S. labor market since 1939. In R. Morales & F. Bonilla (Eds.), *Latinos in a changing U.S. economy: Comparative perspectives on growing inequality* (pp. 28–54). Newbury Park, CA: Sage.

Carrier, J. (1992). Miguel: Sexual life history of a gay Mexican American. In G. Herdt (Ed.), *Gay culture in America* (pp. 202–224). Boston: Beacon Press.

Chavez, L. R. (1990). Coresidence and resistance: Strategies for survival among undocumented Mexicans and Central Americans in the United States. *Urban Anthropology, 19,* 31–61.

Chavez, L. R. (1992). *Shadowed lives: Undocumented immigrants in American society.* Forth Worth, TX: Holt, Rinehart, & Winston.

Chavira-Prado, A. (1992). Work, health, and the family: Gender structure and women's status in an undocumented migrant population. *Human Organization, 51,* 53–64.

Coltrane, S. (1996). *Family man.* New York: Oxford University Press.

Coltrane, S., & Valdez, E. O. (1993). Reluctant compliance: Work-family role allocation in dual earner Chicano families. In J. Hood (Ed.), *Men, work, and family* (pp. 151–175). Newbury Park, CA: Sage.

Demo, D. H., & Allen, K. R. (1996). Diversity within gay and lesbian families: Challenges and implications for family theory and research. *Journal of Social and Personal Relationships, 13,* 415–434.

Dill, B. T. (1994). Fictive kin, paper sons, and compadrazgo: Women of color and the struggle for survival. In M. Baca Zinn & B. T. Dill (Eds.), *Women of color in U.S. society* (pp. 149–169). Philadelphia: Temple University Press.

Dominguez, J. I. (1992). Cooperating with the enemy? U.S. immigration policies toward Cuba. In C. Mitchell (Ed.), *Western hemisphere immigration and United States foreign policy* (pp. 31–88). University Park, PA: Pennsylvania State University Press.

Dorrington, C. (1995). Central American refugees in Los Angeles: Adjustment of children and families. In R. Zambrana (Ed.), *Understanding Latino families: Scholarship, policy, and practice* (pp. 107–129). Thousand Oaks, CA: Sage.

Feagin, J. R., & Feagin, C. B. (1996). *Racial and ethnic relations.* Upper Saddle River, NJ: Prentice Hall.

Fernandez-Kelly, M. P. (1990). Delicate transactions: Gender, home, and employment among Hispanic women. In F. Ginsberg & A. L. Tsing (Eds.), *Uncertain terms* (pp. 183–195). Boston: Beacon Press.

Fernandez-Kelly, M. P., & Garcia, A. (1990). Power surrendered and power restored: The politics of home and work among Hispanic women in southern California and southern Florida. In L. Tilly & P. Gurin (Eds.), *Women and politics in America* (pp. 130–149). New York: Russell Sage Foundation.

Fernandez-Kelly, M. P., & Schauffler, R. (1994). Divided fates: Immigrant children in a restructured U.S. economy. *International Migration Review, 28,* 662–689.

Gil, A. G., & Vega, W. A. (1996). Two different worlds: Acculturation stress and adaptation among Cuban and Nicaraguan families. *Journal of Social and Personal Relationships, 13,* 435–456.

Glenn, E. N. (1992). From servitude to service work: Historical continuities in the racial division of paid reproductive labor. *Signs: Journal of Women in Culture and Society, 18,* 1–43.

Gold, S. J. (1989). Differential adjustment among new immigrant family members. *Journal of Contemporary Ethnography, 17,* 408–434.

Grasmuck, S., & Pessar, P. R. (1991). *Between two islands: Dominican international migration.* Berkeley: University of California Press.

Grasmuck, S., & Pessar, P. R. (1996). Dominicans in the United States: First- and second-generation settlement, 1960–1990. In S. Pedraza & R. G. Rumbaut (Eds.), *Origins and destinies: Immigration, race, and ethnicity in America* (pp. 280–292). Belmont, CA: Wadsworth.

Griffith, J., & Villavicienco, S. (1985). Relationships among culturation, sociodemographic characteristics, and social supports in Mexican American adults. *Hispanic Journal of Behavioral Science, 7,* 75–92.

Griswold del Castillo, R. (1984). *La familia.* Notre Dame, IN: University of Notre Dame Press.

Guarnizo, L. E. (1997). Los Dominicanyorks: The making of a binational society. In M. Romero, P. Hondagneu-Sotelo, & V. Ortiz (Eds.), *Challenging fronteras: Structuring Latina and Latino lives in the U.S.* (pp. 161–174). New York: Routledge.

Hamilton, N., & Chinchilla, N. S. (1997). Central American migration: A framework for analysis. In M. Romero, P. Hondagneu-Sotelo, & V. Ortiz (Eds.), *Challenging fronteras: Structuring Latina and Latino lives in the U.S.* (pp. 81–100). New York: Routledge.

Heller, C. (1996). *Mexican American youth: Forgotten youth at the crossroads.* New York: Random House.

Hill Collins, P. (1990). *Black feminist thought: Knowledge, consciousness and the politics of empowerment.* Boston: Unwin Hyman.

Hill Collins, P. (1997). African-American women and economic justice: A preliminary analysis of wealth, family, and black social class. Unpublished manuscript, Department of African American Studies. University of Cincinnati.

Hondagneu-Sotelo, P. (1994). *Gendered transitions: Mexican experiences of migration.* Berkeley: University of California Press.

Hondagneu-Sotelo, P., & Avila, E. (1997). "I'm here, but I'm there": The meanings of transnational motherhood. *Gender and Society, 11,* 548–571.

Hondagneu-Sotelo, P., & Messner, M. A. (1994). Gender displays and men's power: The "new man" and the Mexican immigrant man. In H. Brod & M. Kaufman (Eds.), *Theorizing masculinities* (pp. 200–218). Newbury Park, CA: Sage.

Hoppe, S. K., & Heller, P. L. (1975). Alienation, familism and the utilization of health services by Mexican-Americans. *Journal of Health and Social Behavior, 16,* 304–314.

Hurtado, A. (1995). Variations, combinations, and evolutions: Latino families in the United States. In R. E. Zambrana (Ed.), *Understanding Latino families* (pp. 40–61). Thousand Oaks, CA: Sage.

Keefe, S. (1984). Deal and ideal extended familism among Mexican Americans and Anglo Americans: On the meaning of "close" family ties. *Human Organization, 43,* 65–70.

Lamphere, L., Zavella, P., & Gonzales F., with Evans, P. B. (1993). *Sunbelt working mothers: Reconciling family and factory.* Ithaca, NY: Cornell University Press.

Landale, N. S., & Fennelly, K. (1992). Informal unions among mainland Puerto Ricans: Cohabitation or an alternative to legal marriage? *Journal of Marriage and the Family, 54,* 269–280.

Lopez, D. E., Popkin, E., & Telles, E. (1996). Central Americans: At the bottom, struggling to get ahead. In R. Waldinger & M. Bozorgmehr (Eds.), *Ethnic Los Angeles* (pp. 279–304). New York: Russell Sage Foundation.

Madsen, W. (1973). *The Mexican-Americans of south Texas.* New York: Holt, Rinehart & Winston.

Martinez, E. A. (1993). Parenting young children in Mexican American/Chicago families. In H. P. McAdoo (Ed.), *Family ethnicity: Strength in diversity* (pp. 184–194). Newbury Park, CA: Sage.

Massey, D. S. (1993). Latino poverty research: An agenda for the 1990s. Items, *Social Science Research Council Newsletter, 47*(l), 7–11.

Massey, D. S., Zambrana, R. E., & Bell, S. A. (1995). Contemporary issues for Latino families: Future directions for research, policy, and practice. In R. E. Zambrana (Ed.), *Understanding Latino families* (pp. 190–204). Thousand Oaks, CA: Sage.

Mindel, C. H. (1980). Extended familism among urban Mexican-Americans, Anglos and blacks. *Hispanic Journal of Behavioral Sciences, 2,* 21–34.

Mirande, A. (1997). *Hombres y machos: Masculinity and Latino culture.* Boulder, CO: Westview Press.

Mitchell, C. (1992). U.S. foreign policy and Dominican migration to the United States. In C. Mitchell (Ed.), *Western hemisphere immigration and United States foreign policy* (pp. 89–123). University Park: Pennsylvania State University Press.

Moore, J. W., & Pinderhughes, R. (Eds.). (1993). *In the barrios: Latinos and the underclass debate.* New York: Russell Sage Foundation.

Moore, J. W., & Vigil, J. D. (1993). Barrios in transition. In J. W. Moore & R. Pinderhughes (Eds.), *In the barrios: Latinos and the underclass debate* (pp. 27–50). New York: Russell Sage Foundation.

Moraga, C. (1983). *Loving in the war years: Lo que nunca paso por sus labios.* Boston: South End Press.

Morales, E. S. (1990). Ethnic minority families and minority gays and lesbians. In F. W. Bozett & M. B. Sussman (Eds.), *Homosexuality and family relations* (pp. 217–239). New York: Harrington Park Press.

Morales, R., & Ong, P. M. (1993). The illusion of progress: Latinos in Los Angeles. In R. Morales & F. Bonilla (Eds.), *Latinos in a changing U.S. economy: Comparative perspectives on growing inequality* (pp. 55–84). Newbury Park, CA: Sage.

Morales, R., & Bonilla, F. (1993). Restructuring and the new inequality. In R. Morales & F. Bonilla (Eds.), *Latinos in a changing U.S. economy: Comparative perspectives on growing inequality* (pp. 1–27). Newbury Park, CA: Sage.

Morrissey, M. (1987). Female-headed families: Poor women and choice. In N. Gerstel & H. Gross (Eds.), Families and work (pp. 302–314). Philadelphia: Temple University Press.

Ortiz, V. (1995). The diversity of Latino families. In R. Zambrana (Ed.), *Understanding Latino families: Scholarship, policy, and practice* (pp. 18–30). Thousand Oaks, CA: Sage.

Ortiz, V. (1996). The Mexican-origin population: Permanent working class or emerging middle class? In R. Waldinger & M. Bozorgmehr (Eds.), *Ethnic Los Angeles* (pp. 247–277). New York: Russell Sage Foundation.

Perez, L. (1994). Cuban families in the United States. In R. L. Taylor (Ed.), *Minority families in the United States: A multicultural perspective.* Englewood Cliffs, NJ: Prentice Hall.

Perez-Stable, M., & Uriarte, M. (1993). Cubans and the changing economy of Miami. In R. Morales & F. Bonilla (Eds.), *Latinos in a changing U.S. economy: Comparative perspectives on growing inequality* (pp. 133–159). Newbury Park, CA: Sage.

Pesquera, B. M. (1993). In the beginning he wouldn't lift even a spoon: The division of household labor. In A. de la Torre & B. M. Pesquera (Eds.), *Building with our hands* (pp. 181–198). Berkeley: University of California Press.

Portes, A., & Rumbaut, R. G. (1990). *Immigrant America: A portrait.* Berkeley: University of California Press.

Portes, A., & Truelove, C. (1987). Making sense of diversity: Recent research on Hispanic minorities in the United States. *Annual Review of Sociology, 13,* 357–385.

Powell, D. R. (1995). Including Latino fathers in parent education and support programs: Development of a program model. In R. E. Zambrana (Ed.), *Understanding Latino families* (pp. 85–106). Thousand Oaks, CA: Sage.

Ramirez, O. (1980, March). Extended family support and mental health status among Mexicans in Detroit. *Micro, Onda, LaRed, Monthly Newsletter of the National Chicano Research Network,* p. 2.

Ramirez, O., & Arce, C. H. (1981). The contemporary Chicano family: An empirically based review. In A. Baron, Jr. (Ed.), *Explorations in Chicano Psychology* (pp. 3–28). New York: Praeger.

Repack, T. A. (1997). New rules in a new landscape. In M. Romero, P. Hondagneu-Sotelo, & V. Ortiz (Eds.), *Challenging fronteras: Structuring Latina and Latino lives in the U.S.* (pp. 247–257). New York: Routledge.

Rochelle, A. (1997). *No more kin: Exploring race, class, and gender in family networks.* Thousand Oaks, CA: Sage.

Rodriguez, N. P., & Hagan, J. M. (1997). Apartment restructuring and Latino immigrant tenant struggles: A case study of human agency. In M. Romero, P. Hondagneu-Sotelo, & V. Ortiz (Eds.), *Challenging fronteras: Structuring Latina and Latina lives in the U.S.* (pp. 297–309). New York: Routledge.

Romero, M. (1997). Introduction. In M. Romero, P. Hondagneu-Sotelo, & V. Ortiz (Eds.), *Challenging fronteras: Structuring Latina and Latino lives in the U.S.* (pp. xiii–xix). New York: Routledge.

Rubel, A. J. (1966). *Across the tracks: Mexican Americans in a Texas city.* Austin: University of Texas Press.

Rumbaut, R. G. (1995). *Immigrants from Latin America and the Caribbean: A socioeconomic profile* (Statistical Brief No. 6). East Lansing: Julian Samora Research Institute, Michigan State University.

Sassen, S. (1993). Urban transformation and employment. In R. Morales & F. Bonilla (Eds.), *Latinos in a changing U.S. economy: Comparative perspectives on growing inequality* (pp. 194–206). Newbury Park, CA: Sage.

Scott, A. J. (1996). The manufacturing economy: Ethnic and gender divisions of labor. In R. Waldinger & M. Bozorgmehr (Eds.), *Ethnic Los Angeles*. New York: Russell Sage Foundation.

Segura, D. A., & Pierce, J. L. (1993). Chicana/o family structure and gender personality: Chodorow, familism, and psychoanalytic sociology revisited. *Signs, 19*, 62–91.

Shelton, B. A., & John, D. (1993). Ethnicity, race, and difference: A comparison of white, black, and Hispanic men's household labor time. In J. Hood (Ed.), *Men, work, and family* (pp. 1–22). Newbury Park, CA: Sage.

Smith, J., Wallerstein, I., & Evers, H. D. (1985). *The household and the world economy*. Beverly Hills, CA: Sage.

Solis, J. (1995). The status of Latino children and youth: Challenges and prospects. In R. E. Zambrana (Ed.), *Understanding Latino families* (pp. 62–84). Thousand Oaks, CA: Sage.

Stacey, J. (1990). *Brave new families: Stories of domestic upheaval in late twentieth century America*. New York: Basic Books.

Stacey, J. (1995). Disloyal to the disciplines: A feminist trajectory in the border lands. In D. C. Stanton & A. Stewart (Eds.), *Feminisms in the academy* (pp. 311–330). Ann Arbor: University of Michigan Press.

Stacey, J. (1996). *In the name of the family: Rethinking family values in the postmodern age*. Boston: Beacon Press.

Stier, H., & Tienda, M. (1992). Family, work, and women: The labor supply of Hispanic immigrant wives. *International Migration Review, 26*, 1291–1313.

Sullivan, M. L. (1993). Puerto Ricans in Sunset Park, Brooklyn: Poverty amidst ethnic and economic diversity. In J. W. Moore & R. Pinderhughes (Eds.), *In the barrios: Latinos and the underclass debate* (pp. 1–26). New York: Russell Sage Foundation.

Thomas, D., & Wilcox, J. E. (1987). The rise of family theory. In M. B. Sussman & S. Steinmetz (Eds.), *Handbook of marriage and the family* (pp. 81–102). New York: Plenum.

Thorne, B. (1992). Feminism and the family: Two decades of thought. In B. Thorne & M. Yalom (Eds.), *Rethinking the family: Some feminist questions* (pp. 3–30). Boston: Northeastern University Press.

Tienda, M. (1989). Puerto Ricans and the underclass debate. *Annals of the American Association of Political and Social Sciences, 501*, 105–119.

Torres, A., & Bonilla, F. (1993). Decline within decline: The New York perspective. In R. Morales & F. Bonilla (Eds.), *Latinos in a changing U.S. economy: Comparative perspectives on growing inequality* (pp. 85–108). Newbury Park, CA: Sage.

U.S. Bureau of the Census. (1993). *1990 census of the population: Persons of Hispanic origin in the United States*. Washington, DC: U.S. Government Printing Office.

U.S. Bureau of the Census. (1996). *Statistical abstract Of the United States: 1996*. Washington DC: U.S. Government Printing Office.

Valenzuela, A., & Dombusch, S. (1994). Familism and social capital in the academic achievement of Mexican origin and Anglo adolescents. *Social Science Quarterly, 75*, 18–36.

Vega, W. (1990). Hispanic families in the 1980s: A decade of research. *Journal of Marriage and the Family, 52*, 1015–1024.

Vega, W. A. (1995). The study of Latino families: A point of departure. In R. E. Zambrana (Ed.), *Understanding Latino families* (pp. 3–17). Thousand Oaks, CA: Sage.

Velez-Ibañez, C. (1993). U.S. Mexicans in the borderlands: Being poor without the underclass. In J. Moore & R. Pinderhughes (Eds.), *In the barrios: Latinos and the underclass debate* (pp. 195–220). New York: Russell Sage Foundation.

Velez-Ibañez, C. (1996). *Border visions*. Tucson: University of Arizona Press.

Velez-Ibañez, C. G., & Greenberg, J. B. (1992). Formation and transformation of funds of knowledge among U.S.-Mexican households. *Anthropology and Education Quarterly, 23*, 313–335.

Williams, N. (1990). *The Mexican American family: Tradition and change*. Dix Hills, NY: General Hall.

Wilkinson, D. (1993). Family ethnicity in America. In H. P. McAdoo (Ed.), *Family ethnicity: Strength in diversity* (pp. 15–59). Newbury Park, CA: Sage.

Wilson, W. J. (1987). *The truly disadvantaged. The inner city, the underclass, and public policy.* Chicago: University of Chicago Press.

Wilson, W. J. (1996). *When work disappears: The world of the new urban poor.* New York: Alfred A. Knopf.

Ybarra, L. (1982). When wives work: The impact on the Chicano family. *Journal of Marriage and the Family, 44,* 169–178.

Zavella, P. (1987). *Women's work and Chicano families: Cannery workers of the Santa Clara Valley.* Ithaca, NY: Cornell University Press.

■ R E A D I N G 3 0

Reinventing the Family

Laura Benkov

There is a certain distortion that occurs when we look back at the past through the lens of the present. When what once seemed impossible has become reality, it is easy to forget the groping in the dark along an untrodden and sometimes treacherous path. It was with this in mind that in March 1988 I read the clipping a friend had sent me from the *Hartford Advocate.* Underneath the headline "The Lesbian Baby Boom," it said "Even Geraldo's covered it—but the women who are doing it say it's no big deal." Almost a decade had passed since I first dared to ask myself if I, a lesbian, could choose to have children. Now as I read the words "No big deal" I flashed back to those sleepless nights clouded with confusion, shame, trepidation, grief, and longing.

One's perspective on the lesbian baby boom is clearly a matter of whom you talk to. When I finally broke through my isolation and began to speak to lesbians who had chosen to raise children, some—like the women described in the *Hartford Advocate*—told me they had never viewed their desire for parenthood as incompatible with their lesbianism. Andrea, a mother of two, said, "I always knew that I was going to be a mother, and being a lesbian never felt like I was making a choice not to have children. That probably had a lot to do with the fact that I came out during the seventies, amid a sense of all sorts of opportunities for women." Yet Andrea's ease with her status as lesbian mother was only one story. There were many other lesbians who had come to be mothers only after significant personal struggle. It is no wonder that I found myself drawn to their descriptions of arduous journeys. Susan lived years of ambivalence about her sexuality, not because she was uncertain of whom she loved but because she believed that choosing a woman meant giving up her lifelong dream of being a parent. Esther talked of being suddenly overcome by grief on an otherwise ordinary evening as she watched her lover washing her hair, when she recognized for the first time a yearning she could not imagine would ever come to fruition: to raise a child with this person she loved so deeply.

If we were indeed in the midst of a lesbian baby boom, then it *was* a big deal, for it was a painful and often lonely journey past grief that had brought us here.

Somewhere along the way these lesbians stopped assuming they couldn't be parents and began figuring out how to bring children into their lives. As I listened to their tales of transformation, each marked by a unique moment of revelation, the "boom" seemed the social equivalent of spontaneous combustion. So many lesbians struggled to become parents at precisely the same historical moment, yet each experienced herself as unique and alone. Of course, no one was as alone as she might have felt, and the movement certainly hadn't appeared out of the blue. Many social forces had laid the groundwork for its emergence.

As women influenced by second-wave feminism questioned their roles in the traditional family, they discovered possibility where before there had been only closed doors. Raising children without being married emerged as a potentially positive decision, not an unwanted circumstance. It is no accident that the rise of lesbian parenting has coincided with the burgeoning of single heterosexual women choosing to have children. The idea that women could shape their intimate lives according to their own standards and values rather than conform to constricting social norms was powerful in its own right. But the feminist movement was significant beyond the realm of ideas. On a very practical level, women's fight for control over their reproductive capacities created a context in which the choice to bear a child was as significantly opened up as the choice not to bear one; abortion rights and access to reproductive technology such as donor insemination are flip sides of the same coin.

The gay rights movement also contributed greatly to the parenting boom, enabling people to take a less fearful, more assertive stance toward society and yielding more visible communities, with the support and social dialogue that implies. From that supportive base, many began to define the kinds of lives they wanted to live, and to pursue their wish to be parents.

Perhaps most significant of all to what has become known in some circles as the choosing children movement, were the lesbian and gay parents who'd come out of heterosexual marriages. They had stepped out of the shadows, transforming the notion of lesbian and gay parents from a contradiction in terms to a visible reality that society had to contend with.

The fact that in our society women tend more than men to be intensely involved with raising children was reflected in the choosing children movement, just as it had been in the battles of parents coming out of heterosexual marriages. During the late 1970s, the first signs of lesbians choosing to have children were evident. By the mid-1980s, the trend had expanded from its initial West Coast and urban-center origins to throughout the nation. It was not until the late 1980s that a similar movement, smaller in scope, emerged among gay men. Though gay men's efforts overlap in some ways with lesbian endeavors, they are also distinctive. Often societal taboos against homosexuals more strongly burden gay men. And homosexuality aside, the notion of men as primary nurturing parental figures is ill defined in our culture. Many gay men seeking to become fathers, and perhaps to raise children without significant female input, feel out of place simply by virtue of their gender.

Initially, gay men participated in the lesbian baby boom as fathers sought by lesbians who chose to bear children. The advent of AIDS profoundly curtailed the move toward joint parenting arrangements. But in many communities it also brought gay men and lesbians together; and in more recent years, with growing consciousness about HIV prevention and testing available, joint parenting arrangements seem to be on the rise again.

Taking on secondary parenting roles in families headed by lesbians does suit some gay men, but others want, as do their lesbian counterparts, to have a more intensive, primary parental relationship. Increasingly, gay men are choosing to become parents through adoption, surrogacy, or joint parenting arrangements.

Within a decade, the unimaginable became commonplace. This remarkable shift occurred against a backdrop of skepticism and hostility. Society remained fixed on the question of whether homosexuals should be allowed to raise children, even as they were becoming parents in record numbers. The fierce debates that began in the early 1970s only continued as openly gay men and women chose parenthood. By the mid-1980s, a multitude of new controversies clamored for attention. Lesbian and gay parents had pushed Americans to look more closely than ever before at a deceptively simple question: What is a family? If the family is not defined by heterosexual procreative union, then what indeed is it? Perhaps it was the fear of this very question that underlay the hostility toward lesbian and gay parents to begin with. If the capacity to have and raise children does not distinguish heterosexuals from homosexuals, then what does?

In a recent *New York Times* book review, Margaret O'Brien Steinfels posed the following question: Does a married heterosexual couple's "capacity to have children [represent] a differentiating quality in heterosexual relationships?" According to Steinfels:

> Our legislatures and our religious faiths may come up with new ways to regulate or recognize erotically bound relationships beyond the traditional form of marriage: the state may devise practical solutions to problems like insurance and shared property, and religious bodies may try to encourage lasting and exclusive intimacy in a monogamous setting. Nonetheless society has a legitimate interest in privileging those heterosexual unions that are oriented toward the generation and rearing of children. That, at any rate, is the widely held conviction that remains to be debated. . . .

Steinfels's suggestion that heterosexual unions are uniquely bound to childrearing rings false at this historical moment. Heterosexual procreation is only one of many means of family making. This is underscored not only by the fact that lesbian and gay unions can include childrearing but also because heterosexual unions often do not. Many heterosexual couples choose not to raise children, and many others, despite their heterosexuality, cannot procreate. Divorce, adoption, and reproductive technology mean that children often aren't raised by their birth parents, and likewise many parents aren't genetically connected to their kids. Steinfels's query embodies a myth our society clings to despite its distance from reality: that heterosexual unions, by virtue of their potential link to procreation, are somehow necessary to the survival of the species and therefore morally superior. Lesbians and gay men choosing to parent are not unique in challenging this myth, but they do so most explicitly, often sparking heated backlash.

During his 1992 campaign for reelection, George Bush said that "children should have the benefit of being born into a family with a mother and a father," thus citing the number and gender of parents as a pivotal aspect of optimal family life and implicitly privileging biological connection between parents and children by the phrase "born into." In short, he held up as the ideal the traditional family, characterized by heterosexual procreative unions and legal sanction.

Eight-year-old Danielle, the daughter of lesbian and gay parents, vehemently disagreed. "I have two moms and two dads," she said. "A family is people who all love each other, care for each other, help out and understand each other."

In defining the ideal family, Bush emphasized structural characteristics while Danielle, in contrast, highlighted emotions and relationships. Their disagreement aptly reflects this moment in American society: the tension between idealization of the traditional family and the reality of families that don't fit that mold is strongly emerging as a key issue of our times. As lesbians and gay men choose to raise children, the many different kinds of families they create reveal the inadequacy of a definition of family that rests on one particular structure. Increasingly, our society must heed Danielle's idea that family is defined by the quality of relationships, which can exist in many forms.

DONOR INSEMINATION: A MIMICRY OF PROCREATIVE UNION

In 1884, according to one of the earliest accounts of donor insemination in America, a woman lay unconscious on an examining table while, without her knowledge much less her consent, a doctor inseminated her with sperm from the "handsomest medical student" in his class. It was only after the insemination that the doctor informed the woman's infertile husband, who, pleased by the news, asked that his wife never be told what had occurred. The insemination resulted in the birth of a baby boy, who, presumably along with his mother, wasn't informed of the circumstances of his conception. A little over a century later, though women who are inseminated are neither unconscious nor uninformed, much of this early account remains salient. Donor insemination has evolved as a medically controlled practice, largely restricted to infertile heterosexual couples and shrouded in secrecy. Where then do lesbians fit in?

In the beginning of its use in this country, donor insemination was seen solely as a solution to infertility among married heterosexual couples. As such, donor insemination practices were structured to produce families that mimicked in every way possible the traditional heterosexual family. Both medical practitioners and the law geared donor insemination toward creating families that looked like, and had the legal status of, a family consisting of a married man and woman and their biological offspring.

This attempt to mimic the traditional heterosexual family included an effort to hide the very fact that donor insemination was used. The appearance of a biological connection was painstakingly constructed by matching the donor's physical traits with the husband's. By and large, the fact that a child had been conceived through donor insemination was rarely disclosed within families and was barely discussed in the larger cultural arena. In one major text of the 1960s, a doctor noted that one of the advantages of donor insemination, as compared to adoption, was that its use need never be revealed. He further suggested that screening criteria for couples receiving donor insemination include an assessment of how well they could keep a secret. Now, thirty years later, donor characteristics are still most often matched to that of the husband and secrecy continues.

The effort to hide the use of donor insemination parallels past approaches to adoption. There, too, great pains were taken to match the physical characteristics of children with those of their adoptive parents, and adoption was held as a secret around which much anxiety revolved. More recently, adoption practices have shifted: there is much less emphasis on matching physical characteristics, and experts encourage parents to speak openly about adoption, with the idea that talking to children about their origins from an early age is key to their overall well-being. Unlike earlier practices, this way values honesty in family life over the appearance of a biological family unit. Along with more honesty within adoptive families has come more open discussion of adoption in society. While much thinking about adoption continues to reflect a cultural bias that elevates biological families over all others, adoption practices have begun to move beyond this ideology by coming out of the closet. In contrast, the secrecy surrounding donor insemination points up the continuing emphasis on the appearance of a biological family unit.

The painstaking attention to appearance and the secrecy surrounding donor insemination stem from an insidious ideology: heterosexual procreation is the ideal basis of a family, one which if not achieved in actuality should at least be aspired to in appearance. With this as an undercurrent, donor insemination is characterized by a contradictory view of genetics. On the one hand, the practice distinguishes genetic and social parent roles, relegating genetics to an inconsequential position by severing all ties between donors and their offspring, and by recognizing those who take on the social role of parenthood as fathers of those children. On the other hand, hiding the fact that this process has occurred reveals an almost superstitious belief in the power of genetics. The implication is that biological connection is such a crucial aspect of parenting that its absence is shameful and should be hidden. The social role of a nonbiological parent is not highly valued in its own right, and instead must be bolstered by the illusion of a genetic connection. In this pervasive view, a "real" parent is the biological parent. If you have to, donor insemination is okay to do, but it's not okay to talk about.

THE LEGAL CONSTRUCTIONS OF FAMILY IN DONOR INSEMINATION PRACTICES

As with the secrecy and matching practices, the laws surrounding donor insemination reinforce efforts to make these families look like the standard nuclear model. Children conceived through donor insemination in the context of a heterosexual marriage are deemed the legal children of the recipient and her husband. Donors, on the other hand, waive all parental rights and responsibilities. The complex reality of such families—that there are both a biological and a social father involved—is set aside in favor of a simpler one. Severing the donor tie and sanctioning the husband's parental relationship serve the purpose of delineating one—and only one—father.

As donor insemination was more widely practiced in this country, legal parameters developed that, like the practices themselves, value the traditional family over all others. Among the first legal questions posed about donor insemination was whether it constituted adultery and, along with that, whether the child so conceived was "illegitimate." As the courts decided these initial cases they exhibited a strong conviction that children need to be "legitimate"—that is, to have fathers. From this premise the law constructed the husbands of inseminated women as the legal fathers of the resulting children. Father status thus hinged on marriage— that is, children were considered to be the "issue of the marriage." This was automatic, with no mediating process such as adoption needed to complete the arrangement. Initially these parameters were outlined only when disputes arose, but as the use of donor insemination grew more widespread, legislation was enacted that explicitly delineated what the courts had implicitly held all along: families that, in fact, were not created through the procreative union of a married heterosexual couple were given the legal status of this traditional unit. The state threw a safety net around the families created through donor insemination when, and only when, those families were headed by married heterosexual couples. On a state-by-state basis, the law carved out a distinction between donors and fathers: donors, in surrendering their sperm to doctors, waived parental rights and responsibilities, while the men married to inseminating women took on the legal rights and responsibilities of fatherhood.

Significantly, in many states, the donors' lack of parental status hinges on medical mediation. That is, donors who directly give sperm to women can be, and often are, legally considered parents. Thus, not only is heterosexuality a prerequisite to the legal delineation of families constituted through donor insemination but medical control of the process is built into the law. People creating families through donor insemination do so most safely—that is, with least threat to their integrity as a family unit—if they utilize medical help.

LESBIANS AND SINGLE WOMEN SEEK DONOR INSEMINATION

The extent to which donor insemination practices emphasize the appearance of a procreative heterosexual union has, of course, great implications for lesbians and unmarried heterosexual women—most especially with respect to access to the technology. In conceiving through donor insemination, these women have little possibility of creating "pretend father" relationships that would obscure the fact that donor insemination has occurred. Indeed, when lesbians and single heterosexual women use donor insemination, they bring the practice out of the closet, revealing it to be a way that women can bear children in the absence of any relationship to men. It is no wonder that unmarried women, regardless of their sexual orientation, have been barred from using donor insemination, given the challenge their access poses to deeply held beliefs. To be inseminated as a single straight woman or lesbian is to boldly acknowledge that the resulting child has no father and that women can parent without input from men beyond the single contribution of genetic material. Such inseminations also highlight the separation between social and genetic parenting roles. This last aspect is especially obvious when lesbian couples use donor insemination: a nonbiological mother, clearly not a father, becomes the child's other parent.

For many years, the medical profession would not grant unmarried women access to insemination. A study done in 1979 found that over 90 percent of doctors wouldn't inseminate unmarried women. The doctors gave several reasons for their decision, the most central being their beliefs that lesbians and single women are unfit parents and that all children need fathers. However, some doctors refused to inseminate unmarried women, not out of deep personal conviction, but because they mistakenly believed that it was illegal. Though the statutory language about donor insemination often includes mention of marriage, it does not require it. A number of doctors also feared future wrongful-life suits, assuming that children raised by lesbians or single women would ultimately be unhappy enough to sue those responsible for their existence.

In the late 1970s, into the context of medically controlled, heterosexual-marriage–oriented donor insemination practices, came single heterosexual women and lesbians wanting to have children. The technology was an obvious choice for these women, not only in its most basic sense as a source of sperm, but also as a way of forming families whose integrity would be legally protected. Many want to establish families as couples or individuals without having to negotiate parenting responsibilities with an outside adult. Lesbians choosing to have children are much more vulnerable than married heterosexual couples to disputes about the boundaries of their families. Homophobia in the legal system renders them generally more subject to custody problems. Furthermore, since lesbians are unable to marry, and the female partners of inseminating women by and large can't adopt the resulting children, nonbiological lesbian mothers have no protected legal parent status. In this social context, creating families through known donors poses tremendous legal risks if those donors ever make custody claims. For lesbians, therefore, the legal protection of a family unit created through anonymous donor insemination is crucial.

But since access to the most legally safe source of insemination—that is, medically controlled—was highly restricted in the early days of the lesbian baby boom, many of the first lesbians to have children did so on the margins of mainstream donor insemination practices. Some women created their own alternatives. They inseminated themselves and, in an effort to protect the integrity of their families, created their own systems of anonymity, using go-betweens to conceal the identity of the sperm donors. However, this means of anonymity didn't provide firm protection against the possibility of custody disputes. In practice, the anonymity of donors would often be hard to maintain in small communities, and legally—especially in the absence of medical mediation—an identified donor would have parental rights. Matters became more complicated with the advent of AIDS, which made this way of inseminating a highly risky business. Ultimately, the self-created system gave way to another approach.

Some lesbians moved in a different direction, attempting to change the exclusionary practices themselves. During the late 1970s and early 1980s, as the feminist health-care movement grew and women fought to gain reproductive freedom, unmarried women made headway with demands for access to medically controlled donor insemination. The Sperm Bank of California in Oakland was established in 1982 by women running the Oakland Feminist Women's Health Center in response to the rising number of unmarried women seeking advice about insemination. The Sperm Bank of California led the way in establishing an insemination program that didn't screen out women on the basis of sexual orientation or marital status. Currently there are several such sperm banks throughout the country, and increasingly doctors are willing to inseminate unmarried women. However, access remains restricted in certain areas, and many insurance companies will cover insemination expenses only for married women.

During the last fifteen years, lesbians choosing to be parents have been charting a course through society that began on the margins and has increasingly moved into the mainstream, yielding social changes along the way.

In the realm of donor insemination, the reciprocal influence of heterosexual, nuclear family ideology and lesbian parenthood is strikingly apparent. Lesbians choosing to have children shape their families along parameters stemming from the idealization of the traditional nuclear family, but by the same token they significantly transform many of those parameters. Donor insemination has shifted from a completely medically dominated, heterosexually defined technology to a practice that serves unmarried women, both straight and gay, and thereby yields many different sorts of families. As lesbians and single heterosexual women make more use of donor insemination, the practice itself is changing: by necessity, donor insemination is coming out of the closet. In our culture there are few stories of conception through donor insemination. Despite the fact that approximately a million Americans have been conceived this way, we continue to behave as though conception occurs only through heterosexual union. Ultimately, lesbians will write the stories of donor insemination, as they speak openly to their children about another way that people come into the world.

Choices: Known or Unknown Donors

As the doors to donor insemination opened for lesbians, a new era began. Having access to the technology is not synonymous with wanting to use it. Most lesbian mothers-to-be spend considerable time deciding whether to do so through a known or unknown donor. The complexity of this decision was a theme in many of my talks with lesbian mothers. In December 1991, as I was trying to sort through the many layers of this decision, both for myself and in relation to this book, I decided to visit the sperm bank in Oakland. I was not prepared for the intensity of my response. Barbara Raboy, the director, explained the process of freezing and storing sperm as I stared at hundreds upon hundreds of specimens neatly ordered in dozens of large metal tanks. It was about what I'd expected to see, except for the names scribbled in marker across the outside of the tanks and in smaller letters on the compartments within each tank. In front of me was the Artist tank, with Fuchsia, Chartreuse, and Amber as its subdivisions. Next to it was the Universe tank, with Mars, Pluto, and Jupiter; and behind that, the Landscape tank, with Rocky Mountain, Grand Canyon, and Yellowstone. Barbara noticed my puzzlement and explained: "We thought names would be more fun than a strict number and letter filing system, so the staff take turns naming the tanks and the subdivisions within them—it's how we locate any particular specimen—you know donor number 5003 is in the A row in the Fuschia section of the Artist tank." I was disappointed that the tank names had no more salient correspondence to the sperm inside, but the knowledge freed me from the mind-boggling task of imagining what distinguished a Rocky Mountain sperm specimen from a Jupiter one.

Instead, I began to imagine the people who dreamed up these names: huddled among the slides and test tubes, who had been most pleased by colors, who by mountain vistas or thoughts of intergalactic travel? As the namers became more real to me, so too did the men whose sperm was sequestered in the tiny vials. Several pages listed donor characteristics—no. 2017, Dutch descent, blue eyes, brown wavy hair, 6 feet tall, athletic student of computer technology. If you wanted to know more about a particular donor, there were additional sheets—medical history and some personal information. But when all was said and done, the wish to know would remain just that. To see these vials was to glimpse the unknown. Throughout the country women were waiting—some whose male partners were infertile, some who were single, some who were lesbian. What they had in common was a strong yearning for children. This is what I was thinking as I looked at vial no. 2017. Then my ears rang with the voices of children, and I knew that I was standng in a place of beginnings, surrounded by mystery.

My initial puzzlement about the tank labels was a clue to my state of mind. I'd entered the sperm bank as I would a foreign country, imagining the tank names held some crucial meaning as unintelligible to me as a street sign in China. It struck me as odd that I could feel this way despite the fact that for years I'd thought about becoming a mother through this very process. Donor insemination was potentially a key element of my future, one that would involve my body and my most intimate relationships; yet simultaneously, I experienced it as a strange, foreign, and mystifying process.

I was not alone in this contradictory place. Though donor insemination has been practiced in this country for over a century, as a culture we have barely begun to grapple with the meaning it holds for us. Standing amid the vials of semen at the sperm bank, I could not help but be aware of the unique historical moment in which we are living. The very fact that I, a lesbian, could consider insemination is remarkable. Just ten years earlier I would have been shut out of any insemination program. But choices bring great complexity. Layers of thinking make up the decision about whether to become pregnant through a donor, known or unknown. How do lesbians aspiring to be mothers respond to society's constraints? What ways of forming a family will be safe in a culture that doesn't recognize our primary intimate connections? Because society as yet barely acknowledges donor insemination, an air of mysteriousness pervades the practice. How then do lesbians sort out the meanings donor insemination has for us and may have for our children?

From the language of "illegitimacy" and "bastards" to the tales of adopts searching for their birth parents, we are inundated with ideas that a father's absence is always problematic and knowledge of our genetic roots always essential. What do we accept of these stories? What do we reject? All of this is filtered through our most intensely personal experiences and histories. Ultimately it is from these many layers that lesbians create their families. Self-consciously exploring the meaning of family, each woman writes her own story. But no one writes it alone: each family is shaped by the culture it is embedded in, and in turn, the culture is changed by these emerging families.

The Role of the State

After twelve years together, Jasmine and Barbara agreed they were ready to raise children. Other than the gender of their partners, they envisioned family life in rather traditional terms. Their household would define the boundaries of their family; as a couple, they would jointly share parenting. Jasmine saw their decision to inseminate with an unknown donor as stemming clearly from the surrounding social context.

Jasmine explains: "We were very stuck on the method of conception—a known versus an unknown donor. One of the things that happened around the time we were thinking about this question was the foster-care issue in Massachusetts. We knew women who had adopted young children through foreign adoptions, and I listened to their descriptions of the home-study process. I felt very uncomfortable with the idea that somebody was judging you, and that you in a sense had to give them this little drama that 'I'm the one who's adopting and this woman is my roommate.'

"Not only did we feel angry about the injustice of it, but we also felt frustrated by the fact that as a couple we had so much more to offer in terms of the structure of our lives than this fallacy would indicate. When the foster-care uproar happened, we were very indignant about the idea that we could be judged that way. If we had gone along with the little drama of who we were supposed to be, it wouldn't have barred us from adopting, so it was really our decision that we wanted as few external people as possible out there judging us or making decisions about our lives.

"We didn't want that interference. That spilled over into the issue of the donor. We really needed to feel in control. The thing was, we were the parents and we wanted to make the decisions as the child grew up about other adults in the child's life. It's not that we wanted to shelter the child from other people, but we certainly didn't want an obligation ready-set. So given that we wanted integrity as a family unit, we decided to go with an unknown donor."

The influence of homophobia and heterosexist constructions of the family is apparent in Jasmine's explanation for their decision to use an anonymous donor. Jasmine and Barbara shied away from adoption because they didn't want to be subjected to state scrutiny that would have failed to recognize the value of their relationship. The homophobia unleashed during the Massachusetts foster-care battle was a bitter reminder of their vulnerability. A known donor was also someone who could potentially bring the state to bear on their family life—someone who in the eyes of the law would have parental rights in contrast to the nonbiological mother. Protecting the integrity of their family unit as they defined it meant using an unknown donor.

Though all prospective lesbian parents face the same legal constraint—a definition of family that gives privilege to genetic connection and heterosexual parenting—people see the state's potential role in their lives quite differently. Unlike Jasmine and Barbara, Susan and Dana chose to have a child with a man they knew who would be involved as a parent but in a secondary role. Each had a close relationship with her own father, and they wanted the same for their children. Though concerned about how legally vulnerable the nonbiological mother would be, Susan and Dana proceeded on the assumption that they could work out a trusting relationship with the father, one which would not ultimately bring them face-to-face with the state's ill-fitting definition of family.

Susan, explaining their decision, says: "The legal line obviously is 'don't take risks, therefore don't use a known father who would then have the possibility of having rights.' I agree that that's one way to avoid the particular risk of a custody fight and control issues over the child. But I think it's one of the most personal choices in the world—anything about reproductive issues and how one wants to raise one's children are very intimate and individual, and I think you shouldn't make decisions frankly just on the legal basis.

"You should make them on your whole world view and your values and what you want for your child. Maybe the risk of a custody fight could be minimized by choosing a person carefully and by choosing a gay man rather than a person who would have the gay issue to use against you."

Jasmine and Barbara's thinking diverges from Susan and Dana's along several lines. First, the two couples position themselves very differently in relation to the state. Jasmine and Barbara are acutely focused on the threat the state poses to the integrity of their family unit. Susan and Dana, on the other hand, feel that threat less acutely because they believe that recourse to the state's definition can most likely be avoided through establishing trustworthy relationships. Marie, another lesbian who chose a known donor, explains the position:

I don't have the kind of fears around the legal stuff that some people do. You have to pick really carefully. Obviously there are certainly men out there whom you could enter into this kind of relationship with and it would be a disaster. But I don't think it's impossible to find a situation where you can have some confidence that this guy will do what he says he'll do. I understand legally you leave yourself open. I think it would be dangerous to do this with a man who is conflicted and who's doing this because he wishes he had kids. Then, ten years down the line he might turn around and say, "I want the child."

These women are grappling with the question of whether you can create a family that defies the state's definition and feel safe that its boundaries will remain as you intended them to be. In part, the different choices lesbians make about family structure stem from different perspectives on the state's ultimate power in their lives.

What Makes a Family?

There is another important dimension to the decision of choosing between known and unknown donors: what should constitute the boundaries of a family? Many women, like Marie and her lover, Jana, choose a donor who will be known to the child but won't take on a parental role. Essentially, except for the fact that the child can know the donor, these families closely resemble families like Jasmine and Barbara's, where the women are the child's sole parents. However, often lesbians choosing known donors draw the boundaries around their families a little differently. Though frequently the men aren't primary parents, they do have a parental role. Susan and Dana created this type of family. While they define their family primarily within the bounds of their own household, their arrangement with their children's father is similar to an extended family. Though at first they were most concerned about maintaining their status as primary parents, as the family became securely established, Susan and Dana wanted the father to be more rather than less involved. They encouraged him to develop a strong relationship with the children. Susan says, "You realize that there are so many things to do. There's never enough time in a day. So additional people to help out is wonderful. We should all have bigger extended families, especially when we're all working. We've been lucky that not just our children's biological father but his choice of partners and his family have been a very rich source of additional good people in the kids' lives."

Opening boundaries in this way can be challenging, however. For a while, Dana, who was to be the nonbiological mother struggled with her lack of society-recognized parent status. "I think for a lot of Susan's pregnancy I was obsessed that this child might be born and this father would have more rights than I would. I had this image that he would never be doing the dirty work of everyday parenting. He'd show up as this knight on a white horse and get all this affection and admiration."

Susan and Dana were deeply committed to the idea that Dana was as much a mother as Susan, and Dana's feelings of doubt dissipated soon after their daughter's birth. "Once Danielle was born it was bizarre to think that. Her father is an important part of her life, but there's a whole 'nother ball game in terms of who her parents are who raise her. My fears were so far from reality. Before Danielle and I had this bond I imagined, in the naiveté of someone who's not a parent, that someone who shows up once a week could be an equal parent to someone who's with you twenty-four hours a day."

Deciding who will be part of one's family is, of course, a highly personal endeavor. The decision regarding a known or unknown donor is partly a decision about what kind of intimate relationships to create. Some are comfortable sharing parenting with people outside a romantic relationship, while others find this a complicated and unrewarding situation.

The Ties that Bind?—The Meaning of Genetic Connections

Beyond thinking about the relationships they want for themselves, lesbians choosing between known and unknown donors must consider how their choice will affect their children. As lesbians think about this, beliefs about the importance of genetic connections take center stage. These beliefs come partly from personal history and partly from ideas that dominate our culture. When women consider whether to use a known or unknown donor, complex, intense, and often conflicting feelings arise. Esther, for instance, originally tried to find a man who would be willing to be a sperm donor but maintain a minimal role in the child's life. The men she approached either wanted more involvement or were worried that they would be asked to take on more responsibility than they bargained for. Esther reconciled herself to conceiving with an anonymous donor, but her feelings about her son Ian's origins intensely color her relationship with him. She says, "I'm consumed by the connections. I look at Ian and see my grandmother's hands. He's an incredible dancer and my father was, too. I don't know if there's a dancing gene. That's why I wanted a Jewish donor. I wanted the history and culture. A known donor would have embodied more of that. Ian's relation to the donor has been a presence for me since he was born. It's hard to sort out my own sadness about my father's death and my sadness for Ian in not having that relationship."

It is hard also to separate Esther's personal history from the culture we are immersed in. As a society, we tend to emphasize intergenerational biological connections and pay scant attention to nonbiological relationships. For example, we continually hear stories about adopted children who feel an absence in their lives and need to search for their birth parents. We rarely hear about the adopted children—of whom there are also many—who don't feel a need for this contact. Hearing these stories of searches for genetic roots, many lesbians are uncomfortable with anonymous donor insemination. As Marie put it, "I don't think an anonymous donor is the best thing for a kid. I'm sure that kids conceived that way will manage and will be okay if their parents handle it levelly and matter-of-factly. But we don't really know. We haven't had a generation of kids growing up without knowing anything about half of their genetic material. What we do know about is kids who were adopted and don't have that kind of information. Most of them go through something about it whether they end up searching or not. It just makes sense to me that if you can provide a child with that basic information, then you should."

While many like Marie see children as better off with access to genetic information, even if the donor is uninvolved as a parent, a good case can be made for the opposite decision. Jenny, for instance, chose a sperm bank, in part to protect her child from possibly feeling rejected by a known but uninvolved donor. "I'd rather take responsibility for my choice to have him this way," she said. "He can be angry at me for my decision, rather than feel hurt because there's a man he can identify who doesn't behave as a father."

As important as it is for lesbians to think through their decisions, the reality all ultimately may have to come to terms with is not a singular model. Instead, we must come to recognize and appreciate pluralism: children who are loved and given opportunities to grow can thrive in many different family contexts. Knowing this, we can discard a determination of which family structure is "best" in favor of finding ways to make all the different structures work.

GAY MEN HAVE A DIFFERENT SET OF DECISIONS

Gay men are often in the position of parenting children who are primarily raised by lesbians. This family model fits in a culture in which women are socialized toward primary childrearing and men toward a secondary role. While there are many gay men for whom this arrangement works well, there are also those who, like their lesbian counterparts, want more involvement with their children. But men do not have the same options as lesbians. There is no equivalent of donor insemination. Surrogacy comes the closest, but it is a much more biologically, ethically, legally, financially, and psychologically complex process. Similarly, gay men are considerably less likely to find women willing to be the equivalent of a known donor—that is, to have babies with whom they will be minimally involved (though on occasion people do make such arrangements). For gay men who want to be primary parents, adoption is often a more feasible option than biological parenting. Given all this, the issues faced by gay men who choose to become fathers through biological conception are quite distinct from lesbians' concerns.

Becoming a Father through Surrogacy

Eric and Jeff were college sweethearts who came out together. Though each had imagined they would get married and have children, it was clear early on in their relationship that their futures were bound together. Jeff never gave up the idea of having children, though he didn't actively pursue it until he hit his thirties. At that point, he approached Eric with the idea of advertising for a surrogate mother. Though he thought about adoption, he wanted to have a child who was biologically connected to him. Eric was doubtful that they would find someone willing to be a surrogate. "Everything you read about surrogacy is these women who are married who have several kids, who want to give this to another couple who can't have kids—it's all portrayed in a straight, heterosexual way."

They discussed the possibility of co-parenting with lesbians, but that wasn't an appealing arrangement. Jeff says, "I wanted this to be our child—for this to be a family of three." Eric says, "We've structured a life for ourselves that we feel very comfortable with, that we like a lot, and we set the parameters for that. We don't let others set the parameters, and that's important to us. A co-parenting relationship would just be way too complicated, and too many people who we know don't approach life the way we do." Jeff adds, "Being dependent on someone else would be very frustrating." They placed an ad that specified they were two gay men wanting to raise a child. They got one response, which they pursued.

Paid surrogacy is a complicated social and personal step. It is fundamentally a financial arrangement through which a child comes into the world. The biological parameters, including a woman's efforts to conceive and nine months of carrying a child, are much more extensive than for donor insemination. For these reasons, the social and psychological issues that surround the process are complex.

One of the most troubling aspects of surrogacy is the class imbalance: Eric and Jeff wanted a child and were well off financially; Donna, who responded to their ad, did not want a child, but needed money. Eric and Jeff hoped that they could work out a friendly arrangement, one that would benefit all concerned. At first it seemed they were on their way to doing just that. An agreement was hammered out with lawyers, and the insemination and pregnancy went smoothly. In less than two years since Jeff first proposed parenting, he and Eric had a baby girl, Leah.

Eric, Jeff, and Donna were on friendly terms and had agreed on limited visitation, but this eventually became a source of strife. Jeff and Eric wanted the visits to be supervised and to occur in their home; Donna wanted to take the baby on her own. Communication broke down when Eric and Jeff refused Donna's request. There was a series of exchanges in letters, through which Jeff and Eric tried to establish ground rules for Donna's visitation. Ultimately, Donna didn't respond and contact ceased.

Despite the problems that arose, Eric feels that, "If there wasn't a whole lot of emotional baggage involved on the part of the mother, contact would be preferable. It would be easier for Leah to understand more of her background and her heritage, and who she is as a person if she had that contact, but I could be wrong."

Jeff doesn't quite agree. "I've changed my opinion. Now I feel that other than curiosity, it would be a lot easier for them to have next to no involvement with each other. We have very little in common with her mother . . . . I think those relationships where a gay man helps out two women and stays involved and all are friends are wonderful, but they're unrealistic in these circumstances. Surrogacy is just this bizarre thing where you're dealing with different financial statuses. Because there's such disparity, there's so little in common to base that kind of friendship on."

Like some women who conceive through unknown donors, Jeff is ambivalent about his wish that there be no contact between his child and her biological mother. "I do worry sometimes, like when I see people on television who've been adopted and haven't seen their biological parents, and are freaked out. But I think that doesn't have to happen—that often those people have a lot of other emotional baggage." Eric points out the different positions of gay men and lesbians. "I feel kind of envious of women who go to sperm banks. Once they make that decision, it's over. They may still agonize over not being able to provide that connection for their child, but it's done." In contrast, surrogacy often involves a process of negotiation and the formation of a relationship. As it was for Eric, Jeff, and Donna, surrogacy can be an intense and complex undertaking. What it will ultimately mean to children like Leah is yet to be seen.

As the nonbiological parent, Eric was in a vulnerable position. Like most lesbian and gay couples raising children, Eric and Jeff had to rely on mutual trust. Jeff says, "We can't conceive of ourselves breaking up. If for some unknown reason we ever did, it would have to be amicable—it's just we can't not be that way. We have a relationship where we talk and communicate better than almost anyone we know." Eric adds, "If you can't work out your differences, I believe you have no right to take this kind of adventure. Because we are trailblazing, we take the responsibility very seriously."

Legally, the surrogacy process is not complete until an adoption has occurred. In the case of heterosexual couples, the biological mother terminates her parental rights, and the spouse of the biological father adopts the child, making the couple the child's only legal parents. In their attempt to "close the circle" of the surrogacy arrangement, Jeff and Eric attempted a second-parent adoption. When Donna agreed to terminate her parental rights, it was Eric who would adopt Leah. The legal question revolved around whether he could do that without Jeff giving up his parental rights. If he had not been able to, the couple considered having Eric become the sole legal parent, as a source of balance. However, shortly before Leah's second birthday, Eric and Jeff were successful in their adoption attempt—their particular circumstances making them a first in the country. When Leah was two years old, Jeff and Eric initiated another surrogacy arrangement through which they had a son.

For the most part, access to surrogacy—like access to other alternative modes of bringing children into one's life—is much more available to heterosexual infertile couples than to gay men. However, surrogacy is much like independent adoption, with access strongly related to financial resources. Surrogacy is far less popular among gay men than donor insemination is among lesbians. Its high cost, along with the social complexity it involves, render it a less frequent approach than adoption or joint-family arrangements.

Surrogacy has been practiced since biblical times—in some informal sense, there have always been women bearing children for friends or family members. But formal, paid contracts for surrogacy arrangements first emerged in this country around 1976, and have been on the rise ever since. Though in any given case surrogacy can work well for all involved, it poses major ethical issues not just for its participants but for society as well. It involves much more than a separation between genetic and social parenting roles, since gestation and birth are processes involving not only a woman's body but also her relation to the child she bears. For the most part, these arrangements involve large sums of money, and bring wealthy people who want children together with poor women in need of money. Out of these issues—the psychological ramifications and the financial exchange—arise many crucial questions.

The major societal quandaries about surrogacy fall into two categories: is it baby selling? and is it exploitative of women? These questions came most vividly to public attention in 1987, when Mary Beth Whitehead, having given birth to the child the courts would refer to as Baby M after signing a surrogacy contract for William and Betsy Stem, changed her mind and wanted to keep the baby. Was she bound by the contract she'd signed? Was the contract, in which there was an exchange of money and an exchange of human life, legal? Was it ethical? And, most important, who should get the child? Mary Beth Whitehead argued that the contract was invalid; she captured the complexity of the surrogacy issue in her statement that she'd "signed on an egg, not on a baby." After a much publicized trial, the Stems were awarded full custody of the one-year-old child. However, along with that decision came a ruling that made surrogacy illegal in the state of New Jersey, where the case had occurred.

While there is little legislation explicitly applying to surrogacy, after the Whitehead case, seventeen states enacted some form of applicable legislation. For the most part, these laws make surrogacy contracts unenforceable. The legal reasoning is drawn from several other areas of law. One argument is that a woman cannot consent to adoption before the birth of a child, and hence cannot be bound by a surrogacy contract drawn up at the time of conception. Another is that in every state baby selling is illegal. Here though, much of surrogacy bypasses this idea, treating compensation not as money in exchange for a human life but as payment for the mother's expenses or for her work in gestation—akin to rent. Some of the laws have focused on money as the key issue, strictly forbidding any exchange other than expenses; a few states prohibit mediators (that is, brokers) from accepting fees. Even with the contracts legally unenforceable, many of the problems that arise when mothers change their minds remain unresolved. Since surrogacy arrangements by and large involve men with substantial resources and women in need of money, if a child is born from such an arrangement and the surrogate changes her mind, most often a typical custody battle ensues, with the best-interests-of-the-child standard applied by the courts. Here, surrogate mothers are at a considerable disadvantage, often not well off enough to pursue a court battle. Surrogacy practices contain a major potential for the exploitation of women in desperate financial circumstances. The guidelines that minimize the risk of such exploitation include making contracts unenforceable (that is, permanently decided only after birth, as in adoption) and giving, as only New York does, the woman custody without a court battle in the event that she changes her mind.

Another Kind of Extended Family

Not all surrogacy arrangements involve a financial exchange. At the other end of the spectrum from the tradition of women as primary and men as secondary parents are the more rare arrangements of women who bear children for men to raise. Such was the case with Kevin, John, and Toni. Kevin had always wanted to be a father and had thought seriously about adopting a child, but he was ultimately discouraged by the foster-care debate in Massachusetts. He was a publicly gay man who would neither have nor want the option of passing as straight in order to adopt a child, so he worried that his chances of getting a child were minimal. Over many years, Kevin had become very close friends with Toni, a single bisexual mother. Kevin had been present at the birth of Toni's second child, and he and John were now like uncles to the children. A close-knit extended-family relation was well established by the time Toni shocked Kevin with the offer to bear a child for him and John to raise. Toni felt she could offer a child no better parents than Kevin and John. For his part, Kevin was overwhelmed by Toni's offer. "I would never have asked a woman to have a baby for me—it's way too much to ask. But I was thrilled."

John was skeptical, feeling strongly still that adopting an existing child was a better way to go. But as the foster-care battle raged, "biological parenting began to seem more appealing because of the legal protection it provided." The three carefully hammered out an agreement, one that included a clear commitment on John and Kevin's part not to challenge Toni if she changed her mind and wanted the baby. For her part, however, Toni was far more worried about the opposite occurrence; she did not want to raise another child, and wanted John and Kevin to have primary responsibility. Her involvement with now two-year-old Amber is substantial, and the group does function as an extended family, with Toni's other children clearly Amber's siblings. Though the arrangement thus bears some resemblance to the familiar family, it is also highly unusual, especially because, simultaneously to being Amber's mother, Toni is not her parent; both the power and the responsibility of parenting fall equally on John and Kevin's shoulders.

JOINT PARENTING—LESBIANS AND GAY MEN TOGETHER

Arrangements such as Kevin and John's with Toni, or Susan and Dana's with their children's father, bring lesbians and gay men together to form families. Most commonly these arrangements involve a division into primary and secondary parenting centered in one household, most often the woman or women involved. These setups resemble amicable custody arrangements in cases of divorce, but they are in reality quite different because they are planned this way and from the outset fall outside of the law's definitions.

Lesbians and gay men also come together in a different family form, that of equally shared parenting. Though it has much in common with the arrangement described above, this particular version deserves separate consideration. Joint-parenting arrangements bring lesbians and gay men together in ways that push even further beyond the nuclear family model, creating an altogether new family form. Truly joint-parenting arrangements decenter family life, creating strong bonds between lesbians and gay men established around parenting itself and independent of primary erotic and romantic unions. Such was the family Barry and Adria established.

"I always say this is the longest pregnancy in the world because it took thirteen years of actively trying to become a dad 'til the time Ari was born," Barry said. He had always seen himself as someone who would have children and, though he didn't know how it would happen, that vision didn't change when he came out at age twenty-two. In his late twenties, he began to discuss the possibility of shared parenting with a heterosexual female friend. But over the course of their conversations, it became clear to Barry that the relationship wouldn't work; much as he wanted a child, he decided not to pursue that possibility.

Then he began to look into adoption as a single man, getting as far as the home-study stage. But at that point he backed away from the process. "It was not a time I wanted to invite the state into my home to scrutinize the way I lived. Also I didn't really want to raise a child alone. I really did want to have another parent."

Shortly after that, he was approached by an acquaintance. "She had had a child when she was really young and felt both trapped in her life and not able to figure out how she could get out of the trap in terms of getting more money and some skills. She had seen me interact with her son who was three at the time, and she knew I was trying to become a father and thought it was really unfair that gay men had such a hard time doing it. She offered to be a surrogate mom if I would help her get some kind of training so that she could get a better kind of job. She still wanted to be friends, and thought maybe an appropriate arrangement would be that she would relate to this child like a distant relative. We hadn't worked out the details, but it was '81 and AIDS was happening. There were no tests, and I didn't feel like I could responsibly inseminate so I decided not to do it."

With his third attempt to become a father failing to pan out, and AIDS on the horizon, Barry put the question of children on the back burner for the next four years. Once the HIV test was available and he tested negative, he decided he could continue his quest.

On New Year's Eve, 1986, Barry was introduced by a mutual friend to Adria, a lesbian who was looking for someone with whom to raise a child. In her early adulthood, Adria had assumed she would adopt children. But as she became focused on her work and community, the idea of becoming a parent faded into the background. Unlike Barry, Adria hadn't spent years engrossed in the pursuit of parenthood. At age forty-two, her world view shifted dramatically when a close friend was diagnosed with AIDS and moved into her home. During the process of caring for him while he was dying, Adria became possessed with an intense desire to be pregnant. What had previously been a source of ambivalence and questioning became definitive. Living through her friend's illness, Adria felt, "If I can do this, I can do anything." The catch was, that Adria had been in a relationship with Marilyn for eight years and Marilyn was not keen on the idea of raising a child. Adria, for her part, wanted her child to have an involved father. This proved to be a good fit, since from Marilyn's perspective it would be more comfortable if Adria had a co-parent other than herself.

Barry describes the tumble of feelings and questions he encountered during their first meetings: "We'd been part of overlapping communities with the same kind of political history, so we knew things about each other and felt very familiar when we actually met, but we had never met before we sat down to ask questions like, 'Would you like to make a commitment for the rest of your life with this stranger and have a very intimate relationship—not sexual, but as close as you can be?' It was very awkward, like going through a series of courting behaviors—checking each other out, putting your best foot forward, and there are these flirtations going on. Our process was that we couldn't say, 'Yes, this is working, let's do it.' It was more like looking for why it wouldn't work until we could find nothing more, then saying, 'Is there any reason why we couldn't do this?' " Adria, on the other hand, immediately impressed by Barry's integrity and level of commitment to parenting, knew at their first encounter that she and Barry would become family.

During the next five months, they let each other into their lives. "It became clear that our sensibility around child-rearing was very similar even though we're very different people," Barry remembers. "Our personalities and backgrounds are very different. Starting this process at an older age, we were both clear about what we wanted and what we didn't want. We wanted to build family with each other. I think we both hoped that ideally that could happen, but if we could find someone close enough, with a similar enough world-view, we knew enough not to expect everything on our list. We introduced each other to our circle of friends, celebrated our birthdays together, gradually doing some of those kinds of family things."

A month after Barry and Adria decided to go ahead with the plan, Barry met Michael. "Here I am, not looking for a relationship, because I'm clear I want kids. You know, if a relationship happens that's fine, that can come later. And then, here's Michael to integrate into this picture. Part of his attraction to me was that I was building a family and he loves children—so we have this dynamic of Michael who is outside wanting in as much as he could, and Marilyn, who is inside wanting to have boundaries as much as she could. And there's Adria and me in the middle, trying to make this happen."

During the next two years, Barry and Adria went through a very intense period that included difficulty conceiving and four miscarriages. The process was particularly discouraging, given Adria's age. One doctor dismissed them completely, chalking up the difficulties to approaching menopause. Adria feared that Barry would abandon the effort to have a baby with her since he so badly wanted a child. But there was never any question in Barry's mind. "We were clear that we really wanted to parent together. That had already been born in this process. We were already really close friends and had this thing that was starting to cross all the traditional lines between gay men and lesbians—building the most physical, intimate relationship you can. Being in the medical part of this process, which was very unpleasant, was really one of the things that pulled us together. Those miscarriages, though I don't recommend this as a strategy, turned out to be a way to find out how you are together. Going through hard times, what we learned is that our instincts pull us together—that's how we deal with hardship. And so that brought us even closer." Barry and Adria supported each other through each episode and were very much partners in the effort. Eventually they saw a fertility specialist, who prescribed Clomid and took over the insemination process. Barry became an expert at assisting the doctor in ultrasound and follicle measuring. At age forty-four, Adria became pregnant and carried to term.

Throughout this process a complicated dynamic developed among the four adults. In many ways Adria and Barry developed a primary intimate relationship, one that had to be balanced with their respective partner relationships. It was the beginning of what was to be their particular sort of family—not a uniform, single entity but more like concentric circles, with four overlapping intimate adult relationships. Though Barry and Adria were at the center of this parenting unit, their approach was inclusive, embracing Michael and Marilyn. This was evident as they moved about the world. Barry remembers the day Adria was late for her first Lamaze class: "So in this room are all these straight couples with very pregnant women, and in walk Barry, Michael, and Marilyn, who is an Olympic athlete, with a very slender toned body—I mean, this woman is not pregnant. It's an awkward threesome. The teacher looks at us and says, "This is the birthing class." And we say, "Great, we're in the right place." Now they're really confused, and we go around the room to introduce ourselves. You have to say your name and the magic due date, so I say 'My name is Barry and I'm the father of this child that Adria, who's not here, is carrying,' and then Michael says, 'My name is Michael and I'm Barry's partner, and I'm going to help parent this child that Adria, who's not here, is carrying,' and then Marilyn, 'I'm Marilyn and I'm Adria's partner.' Their eyes are getting bigger and their mouths are falling open, and finally Adria comes, not having a clue what she was walking into."

Ari was delivered through cesarean section in 1989—Marilyn, Barry, and Michael were all present at his birth. Adria and Barry had agreed to share parenting equally. This is difficult to achieve in the context of two separate households. Each can be with Ari whenever he or she wants and also whenever he is needing one of them. Though they have free access to each other's homes, separation is a key issue in this family. From the very beginning of his life, Ari has gone back and forth between the households almost every other day. Barry and Adria also do a lot of traveling. In the first couple of months, before Ari began to travel back and forth, Barry slept at Adria's house. After that, while Adria was nursing Ari, she would come to Barry's house on the days he wasn't with her. At six months of age, Ari began to take a bottle as well, which somewhat eased the stress.

As they look toward the future, both Barry and Adria have some trepidation about their own feelings regarding separations. They are beginning to feel that Ari, now a preschooler, needs longer stretches in each household. Barry anticipates this. "It's hard for me to imagine him not being home for three days in a row. I just can't—not that I'm not totally comfortable and happy with where he is, because he's at home being loved by his wonderful mother and other parent, and nothing could please me more, but he's not home with me. I find myself wandering into his room a lot when he's not there, looking for him."

Adria has been known to appear at Barry's house in the middle of the night, needing to check in with Ari. Speculating about Ari's responses to the constant comings and goings, Adria says, "I think he suffers as any being would suffer from everything changing all the time. It's the same two houses, it's the same people, and he has everything at both places. He always has his little shopping bag and he carries his blanket with him wherever he goes. I think he'll either grow up to be a person who will only be in one place and will be kind of rigid about it because he's had enough of this, or he'll be someone who any place he hangs his hat will be his home. I think he'll have a certain kind of autonomy and confidence, because he seems to now, but I think he'll also have some issues about being left—people always come back, but they also always leave." One of the issues Barry and Adria are currently trying to address is their desire to have more time together with Ari rather than being on separate shifts.

The complexities of the four-way relationship take a lot of energy to navigate. Though decisions are essentially a matter of consensus, the family's communication about Ari is primarily channeled through Barry and Adria. In a sense, Michael and Marilyn have become the keepers of their respective couple relationships. As Adria sees it, "they watch over the intimacy of the couples—and they help each couple to separate from the other." For Marilyn, Barry's and Michael's involvements with Ari have freed her to be his parent. "The fact that she's not the only other parent besides me, the fact that there's someone else who's fifty percent responsible for him has allowed her a lot of room, to in fact be a very important parent. In our family, because she doesn't want to be a mother, there's not much competition like you'll see in some lesbian couples. And she doesn't want to be his father; there's not competition with Michael and Barry, either. She has her place with Ari. She's the only athlete among us. He's a little talking boy—he's not very athletic. She teaches him how to jump. That's where they live together, in this sort of playful world and he's very close to her."

Michael, unlike Marilyn, has much more interest in a primary parenting role, and has had to grapple with that in the context of a family unit that is clearly centered on Barry and Adria as primary parents. He and Barry think about expanding the family—through having Michael father a child. "When Ari's at our house he's there with both of us and it's fairly equal in terms of day-to-day doing things," Barry says. "Michael has stepped in as the cook. He likes to do it and he cooks for Ari all the time, so he's Ari's best cook and when he's hungry he looks to Michael. I know Michael has felt unseen and unrecognized but not by me or our family. My father, for instance, was watching Michael put Ari to bed one night and he just said 'it's so amazing—he is a father to this child.' But even though Michael gets recognition from our family and community, there's so much in this culture that in basic ways doesn't recognize his role. We try to be especially conscious of it and name it when it's happening."

As with the Lamaze class, as they move about the world this family shakes people's attitudes. Once, Ari closed a car door on his hand. In the emergency room, Barry and

Michael met Adria and Ari at the hospital. Barry remembers that day vividly; "So I'm holding Ari and he's telling me the story, saying 'Daddy, I cried a little but it's okay now,' and we go together but they keep trying to separate us all. Then we get to the point of registering, and I'm holding Ari and the clerk is asking me all these questions that I'm answering while Michael and Adria stand behind me. Then the clerk says to me, 'Okay, Michael, so you're the father,' and Michael says 'No, I'm Michael and he's on my plan.' Meanwhile, Ari is pointing to me saying, 'This is the father.' So, okay, this is the father, but Michael learned that in order to get his work to pay these bills—to not raise red flags—he says he's the stepfather. And the clerk must be thinking—well, okay, this is a very friendly divorce—here's the mom, dad, stepfather, and kid. Then he asks Michael for his address. I'd already given him my address as the father and, of course, it's the same address. At this point we're all fidgeting, and Adria says, 'I bet you want to know my address next.' So we have these funny experiences, but we make it work."

Of his family life, Barry says, "It's made us all look at how we do relationships. I think our mode of operating now is basically to act out of the basic goodness that's there in all of these relationships and to let go of a lot of the petty stuff about each other that drives each of us crazy. We pick and choose what we have to deal with. It works incredibly well, and it's also complicated trying to manage these multiple needs." Looking back at his original decision to become a parent in this way, Barry says, "It's important to try to imagine every situation you can before you do something like this, 'cause it gets you thinking, but there's no way to know what the reality will be. No matter how much we talked, there was no way I could be prepared for the instant of Ari's birth, when I went from one primary relationship with Michael to three. And of course it doesn't matter what the adults decide in advance; once the child is born, their needs are going to determine—and should determine—what happens. Sometimes that can bear no relation to all these plans."

Amid all the complexity, Ari seems to thrive. He makes families out of everything, one of his favorites being clothes hangers. The blue one is always himself, and then there is a Mommy, a Daddy, a Marilyn, and a Michael. He wonders why his best friend has no Marilyn or Michael.

THE REINVENTED FAMILY

Lesbian and gay parents essentially reinvent the family as a pluralistic phenomenon. They self-consciously build from the ground up a variety of family types that don't conform to the traditional structure. In so doing, they encourage society to ask, "What is a family?" The question has profound meaning in both the culture at large and the very heart of each of our intimate lives. It is like a tree trunk from which many branches extend: What is a mother, a father, a parent, a sibling? Can a child have two or more mothers or fathers? Is one more "real" by virtue of biological or legal parent status? How does society's recognition (or its absence) foster or impede parent-child relationships? To what extent does the state shape family life? To what extent can nontraditional families alter the state's definition of family?

These questions go well beyond the issue of whether families headed by lesbians and gay men should exist. There emerges a complex reciprocal tension between lesbian and gay family life on the one hand and homophobia and the idealization of the traditional family on the other. Clearly, lesbian and gay parents don't create their families in a vacuum. Their choices are shaped by the institutions that mediate family formation, most notably the legal and medical systems, and adoption agencies. Lesbian and gay parents vary with respect to how they view the state. While some let legal definitions inform their choices, others feel they can probably keep the state out of their lives by relying on trust and goodwill. Sometimes families who've taken this route end up, to their dismay, in the courts, challenging prevailing legal thought.

However they choose to form their families, lesbians and gay men do so in the context of the idealization of the traditional model; their families are inevitably shaped by this fact. Yet at the same time, over the past decade, many changes have been wrought by lesbian and gay family formation itself—ranging from unmarried women's increased access to donor insemination to the particular challenges that lesbian and gay families bring to the law. Though our society is a long way from embracing eight-year-old Danielle's deceptively simple statement that a "family is people who all love each other, care for each other, help out, and understand each other," her words may yet prove to be our most crucial guide to the future.

■**READING 31**

"The Normal American Family" as an Interpretive Structure of Family Life among Grown Children of Korean and Vietnamese Immigrants

Karen Pyke

This article examines the ways that children of Korean and Vietnamese immigrants describe growing up in their families and their plans for filial care. Based on an analysis of 73 in-depth interviews, this study finds that respondents repeatedly invoked a monolithic image of the "Normal American Family" as an interpretive framework in giving meaning to their own family life. The Family served as a contrast structure in respondents' accounts of parents—and Asian parents in general—as overly strict, emotionally distant, and deficient. However, when discussing plans for filial care, respondents relied on favorable images of the close family ties associated with Asian immigrants, such as those depicted in "model minority" stereotypes. In so doing they generated positive descriptions of their families, particularly in contrast to mainstream American families. The findings suggest that narrow and ethnocentric images of the Family promulgated throughout mainstream culture compose an ideological template that can shape the desires, disappointments, and subjective realities of children of immigrant minorities.

The use of monolithic images of the "Normal American Family" as a stick against which all families are measured is pervasive in the family wars currently raging in political and scholarly discourses (Holstein & Gubrium, 1995). The hotly contested nature of these images—consisting almost exclusively of White middle-class heterosexuals—attests to their importance as resources in national debates. Many scholars express concern that hegemonic images of the Normal American Family are ethnocentric and that they denigrate the styles and beliefs of racial–ethnic, immigrant, gay–lesbian, and single-parent families while encouraging negative self-images among those who do not come from the ideal family type (Bernades, 1993; Dilworth-Anderson, Burton, & Turner, 1993; Smith, 1993; Stacey, 1998; Zinn, 1994). Yet we still know little about how the Family ideology shapes the consciousness and expectations of those growing up in the margins of the mainstream. This study examines the accounts that grown children of Korean and Vietnamese immigrants provide of their family life and filial obligations. The findings suggest that public images of the Normal American Family constitute an ideological template that shapes respondents' familial perspectives and desires as new racial–ethnic Americans.

FAMILY IDEOLOGY AS AN INTERPRETIVE STRUCTURE

Images of the Normal American Family (also referred to as the Family) are pervasive in the dominant culture—part of a " 'large-scale' public rhetoric" (Holstein & Miller, 1993, p. 152). They are found in the discourse of politicians, social commentators, and moral leaders; in the talk of everyday interactions; and in movies, television shows, and books. Smith (1993, p. 63) describes these ubiquitous images as an "ideological code" that subtly "inserts an implicit evaluation into accounts of ways of living together." Such images serve as instruments of control, prescribing how families ought to look and behave (Bernades, 1985). Most scholarly concern centers on how this ideology glorifies and presents as normative that family headed by a breadwinning husband with a wife who, even if she works for pay, is devoted primarily to the care of the home and children. The concern is that families of diverse structural forms, most notably divorced and female-headed families, are comparatively viewed as deficient and dysfunctional (Fireman, 1995; Kurz, 1995; Stacey, 1998). Scholars concerned about the impact of such images point to those who blame family structures that deviate from this norm for many of society's problems and who suggest policies that ignore or punish families that don't fit the construct (e.g., Blankenhorn, 1995; Popenoe, 1993, 1996).

In addition to prescribing the structure of families, the Family ideal contains notions about the appropriate values, norms, and beliefs that guide the way family members relate to one another. The cultural values of "other" families, such as racial–ethnic families, are largely excluded. For example, prevailing family images emphasize sensitivity, open honest communication, flexibility, and forgiveness (Greeley, 1987). Such traits are less important in many cultures that stress duty, responsibility, obedience, and a commitment to the family collective that supercedes self-interests (Chung, 1992; Freeman, 1989). In further contrast to the traditional family systems of many cultures, contemporary American family ideals stress democratic rather than authoritarian relations, individual autonomy, psychological well-being, and emotional expressiveness (Bellah, Madsen, Sullivan, Swidler, & Tipton, 1985; Bernades, 1985; Cancian, 1987; Coontz, 1992; Skolnick, 1991). Family affection, intimacy, and sentimentality have grown in importance in the United States over time (Coontz, 1992), as evident in new ideals of fatherhood that stress emotional involvement (Coltrane, 1996).

These mainstream family values are evident in the therapeutic ethic, guiding the ways that those who seek professional advice are counseled and creating particular therapeutic barriers in treating immigrant Asian Americans (Bellah et al., 1985; Cancian, 1987; Tsui & Schultz, 1985). Family values are also widely disseminated and glorified in the popular culture, as in television shows like *Ozzie and Harriet, Leave It To Beaver, The Brady Bunch, Family Ties, and The Cosby Show,* many of which are rerun on local stations and cable networks (Coontz, 1992). Parents in these middle-class, mostly White, television families are emotionally nurturing and supportive, understanding, and forgiving (Shaner, 1982; Skill, 1994). Indeed, such shows tend to focus on the successful resolution of relatively minor family problems, which the characters accomplish through open communication and the expression of loving concern. Children in the United States grow up vicariously experiencing life in these television families, including children of immigrants who rely on television to learn about American culture. With 98% of all U.S. households having at least one television set, Rumbaut (1997, p. 949) views TV as an immense "assimilative" force for today's children of immigrants. Yet, he continues, it remains to be studied how their world views are shaped by such "cultural propaganda." The images seen on television serve as powerful symbols of the "normal" family or the "good" parent—and they often eclipse our appreciation of diverse family types (Brown & Bryant, 1990; Greenberg, Hines, Buerkel-Rothfuss, & Atkin, 1980). As the authors of one study on media images note, "The seductively realistic portrayals of family life in the media may be the basis for our most common and pervasive conceptions and beliefs about what is natural and what is right" (Gerbner, Gross, Morgan, & Signorielli, 1980, p. 3). Family scholars have rarely displayed analytic concern about the emphasis on emotional expressiveness and affective sentimentality that pervades much of the Family ideology, probably because the majority—who as middle-class, well-educated Whites live in the heartland of such values—do not regard them as problematic. As a result, this Western value orientation can seep imperceptibly into the interpretive framework of family research (Bernades, 1993; Dilworth-Anderson et al., 1993; Fineman, 1995; Smith, 1993; Thorne & Yalom, 1992).

The theoretical literature on the social construction of experience is an orienting framework for this study (Berger & Luckmann, 1966; Holstein & Gubrium, 1995). According to this view, cultural ideologies and symbols are integral components of the way individuals subjectively experience their lives and construct reality. The images we carry in our heads of how family life is supposed to be frame our interpretation of our own domestic relations. This is evident in the different ways that Korean and Korean American children perceived their parents' childrearing behavior in a series of studies. In Korea, children were found to associate parental strictness with warmth and concern and its absence as a sign of neglect (Rohner & Pettengill, 1985). These children were drawing on Korean family ideology, which emphasizes strong parental control and parental responsibility for children's failings. In this interpretive framework, parental strictness is a positive characteristic of family life and signifies love and concern. Children of Korean immigrants living in the United States, on the other hand, viewed their parents' strictness in negative terms and associated it with a lack of warmth—as did American children in general (Pettengill & Rohner, 1985). Korean American children drew on American family ideology, with its emphasis on independence and autonomy, and this cast a negative shadow on their parents' strict practices.

Although pervasive images of the Normal American Family subtly construct Asian family patterns of interaction as "deviant," countervailing images of Asians as a "model minority" are also widely disseminated. News stories and scholarly accounts that profile the tremendous academic success among some immigrant Asian children or describe the upward economic mobility observed among segments of the Asian immigrant population credit the cultural traditions of collectivist family values, hard work, and a strong emphasis on education. Such images exaggerate the success of Asian immigrants and mask intraethnic diversity (Caplan, Choy, & Whitmore, 1991; Kibria, 1993; Min, 1995; Zhou & Bankston, 1998). Meanwhile, conservative leaders use model minority images as evidence of the need to return to more traditional family structures and values, and they blame the cultural deficiency of other racial minority groups for their lack of similar success, particularly African Americans and Latinos (Kibria, 1993; Min, 1995; Zhou & Bankston, 1998). The model minority construct thus diverts attention from racism and poverty while reaffirming the Family ideology. In the analysis of the accounts that children of immigrants provided of their family life, references to such cultural images and values emerged repeatedly as a mechanism by which respondents gave meaning to their own family lives.

KOREAN AND VIETNAMESE IMMIGRANT FAMILIES

This study focuses on children of Vietnamese and Korean immigrants because both groups constitute relatively new ethnic groups in the United States. Few Vietnamese and Koreans immigrated to the United States before 1965. However, from 1981 to 1990, Korea and Vietnam were two of the top five countries from which immigrants arrived (*Statistical Yearbook*, 1995, table 2, pp. 29–30). Thus adaptation to the United States is a relatively new process for large groups of Koreans and Vietnamese, one that is unassisted by earlier generations of coethnic immigrants. The children of these immigrants, located at the crossroads of two cultural worlds, offer a good opportunity to examine the familial perspectives and desires of new racial–ethnic Americans.

Most in-depth study of children of immigrants examines only one ethnic group, which makes it difficult to know which aspects of adaptation are shared with other ethnic groups and which are distinct. Studying only one Asian ethnic group also contributes to a tendency to over-generalize the findings to all Asian ethnic groups. Thus this study was designed to compare two Asian ethnicities so that ethnic differences and similarities could be noted. The author selected Koreans and Vietnamese because, in addition to being new American ethnic groups, their economic status and pathways to immigration differ. Whereas Koreans have immigrated voluntarily, in search of better economic opportunities and educations for their children, most Vietnamese arrived as political refugees or to rejoin family members, some doing so after spending time in Vietnam's prisons or "reeducation camps" (Gold, 1993; Hurh, 1998; Kibria, 1993; Min, 1998). Vietnamese immigrants have been, overall, less educated and from more rural and poorer backgrounds than Korean immigrants. Only 12% of first-generation Vietnamese heads of household have a college degree, compared with 45% for Koreans (Oropesa & Landale, 1995). Family socioeconomic status is important to the study of adaptation because it affects the kinds of neighborhoods where immigrant children grow up and attend school (Zhou, 1997). However, equally important are the cultural practices that organize family relationships, including parental values and childrearing practices, and the expectations that parents have of their children. It is here that ethnic differences among Koreans and Vietnamese appear more subtle.

Due to the relatively short history of massive Asian immigration, Asian American family research has been fragmented and limited. As Uba (1994) points out, most of the research has been descriptive rather than explanatory, has focused on Chinese Americans and Japanese Americans, and has given little attention to between-group differences. Thus the empirical picture of Korean and Vietnamese family systems is incomplete. What we do know is that the philosophical values of Chinese Confucianism have influenced the traditional family systems of Korea and Vietnam. These values emphasize solidarity, hierarchal relations, and filial piety (Kibria, 1993; Hurh, 1998; Min, 1998; Sue & Morishima, 1982). Confucianism provides a firm set of rules about how family members are supposed to behave toward one another (Cha, 1994; Chung, 1992; Kim & Choi, 1994; Min, 1998; Zhou & Bankston, 1998). Priority is placed on family interests over individual desires and needs in order to maintain stability and harmony. Status distinctions guide the way in which members are to interact with one another. Younger members are expected to display respect, deference, and obedience to elders (including to older siblings, especially brothers), and wives are expected to show the same to their husbands and parents-in-law. Children—including adult offspring—are forbidden from expressing dissenting opinions or confronting parents, which is viewed as disrespectful (Chung, 1992; Kibria, 1993; Min, 1998; Pettengill & Rohner, 1985). Emotional expressiveness, including displays of affection, is discouraged, while self-control is emphasized (Hurh, 1998; Uba, 1994). Family ties and roles are central from birth until death, with a strong emphasis on family devotion. In general, parents are expected to rely on their children's support in later life. Confucianism assigns the care and financial support of aging parents to the eldest son and his wife, who are expected to live under the same roof as the parents. Korean and Vietnamese cultures also derive from Confucianism a respect for the well educated, and education is considered the primary means for social mobility. This undergirds the great importance that many Asian parents place on their children's education (Min, 1998; Zhou & Bankston, 1998). The economic hardships of many immigrant parents strengthen their emphasis on the education of their children, whom they expect to forge success in the United States (Kibria, 1993; Min, 1998).

There are, of course, ethnic differences between Korean and Vietnamese families, as well as differences in the degree to which they conform to traditional family practices. Although the comparative research is scant, Confucianism appears to have a stronger influence on the traditional family system in Korea than in Vietnam. For example, in Vietnamese families there is a greater tendency for siblings to pool resources in providing filial care rather than relying on the elder son alone, which might be related to their poorer economic circumstances. Additionally, Vietnamese women are permitted stronger kinship ties to their family of origin upon marriage than are Korean women, who are expected to live with their in-laws if they marry an elder son (Hurh, 1998; Kibria, 1993).

Although more research is needed that closely examines Asian ethnic differences in family practices, the existing literature reveals patterns of similarities among the family systems of Koreans and Vietnamese that differentiate them from American family patterns. The role prescriptions, family obligations, hierarchal relations, lack of emotional expressiveness, and collectivist values associated with the traditional family systems of Korea and Vietnam contrast sharply with the emphasis on individualism, self-sufficiency, egalitarianism, expressiveness, and self-development in mainstream U.S. culture (Bellah et al., 1985; Cancian, 1987; Chung, 1992; Hurh, 1998; Kim & Choi, 1994; Min, 1998; Pyke & Bengtson, 1996; Tran, 1988; Uba, 1994). Immigrant children tend to quickly adopt American values and standards, creating generational schisms and challenges to parental control and authority. That parent–child conflict and cultural gaps exist in many Asian immigrant families is well documented (Gold, 1993; Freeman, 1989; Kibria, 1993; Min, 1998; Rumbaut, 1994; Zhou & Bankston, 1998; Wolfe, 1997). However, no study to date has closely examined the cultural mechanisms at play in this process. This study begins that task.

METHOD

The data are from an interview study of the family and social experiences of grown children of Korean and Vietnamese immigrants. Respondents were either located at a California university where 47% of all undergraduates are of Asian descent (Maharaj, 1997) or were referred by students from that university. In-depth interviews were conducted with 73 respondents consisting of 34 Korean Americans (24 women, 10 men) and 39 Vietnamese Americans (23 women, 16 men). Both parents of each respondent were Korean or Vietnamese, except for one respondent, whose parents were both Sino-Vietnamese. Respondents ranged in age from 18–26 and averaged 21 years. Only one respondent was married, and none had children.

Respondents were either born in the United States (second generation) or immigrated prior to the age of 15 (1.5 generation), except for one Vietnamese American woman who immigrated at 17. The foreign born accounted for 77% of the sample and immigrated at an average age of 5 years. The remaining 23% were born in the United States. Most respondents in this sample spent their entire adolescence in the United States, and a majority lived in the United States for most, if not all, of their childhood. Eight percent of the Vietnamese American respondents were born in the United States, compared to 38 percent of Korean American respondents (see Table 1 for gender and ethnic differences). All study participants were college graduates or students and all resided in California, where one-third of U.S. legal immigrants arrive and 45% of the nation's immigrant student population lives (Zhou, 1997). Thus the sample over-represents those who are academically successful. Because the respondents have endured sustained exposure to assimilation pressures from the educational system, higher levels of assimilation were expected in this sample than in the larger immigrant population. As a result, these respondents were perhaps more likely to invoke American cultural ideals

TABLE 1   *Sample Characteristics*

Ethnicity	n	Average Age (years)	Foreign Born (%)	Average Age at Immigration (years)
Korean American women	24	21	62	5
Korean American men	10	21	60	7
Vietnamese American women	23	21	96	5
Vietnamese American men	16	22	81	5
Total for sample	73	21	77	5

in describing their family life than a more representative sample that included the less educated and those who immigrated at older ages.

The author gathered the 73 individual interviews analyzed here in the preliminary phase of data collection for a larger ongoing project sponsored by the National Science Foundation (#SBR-9810725). The larger study includes a sample of 184 who participated in individual and focus group interviews. Only the initial phase of data collection was designed to prompt respondents' extensive descriptions of family life. The purpose of the larger study is to compare the dynamic complexities and structural contexts of adaptation and ethnic identity among children of immigrants, with special attention to their subjective experiences in mediating different cultural worlds. Because ethnic identity development differs for males and females (Espiritu, 1997; Waters, 1996), I also stratified the sample by gender.

As previously discussed, I stratified the sample by ethnicity, as well, in order to compare the effects of structural and cultural factors on adaptation processes. Despite Korean and Vietnamese distinctions in socioeconomic status, pathways to immigration, and cultural practices, I did not observe ethnic differences relevant to the central focus of this analysis. Although this is surprising, ethnic differences in the specific areas of family life that I was investigating are probably relatively subtle, particularly from the viewpoint of American children of Asian immigrant parents. More specifically, because respondents relied on American family ideology in giving meaning to their domestic relations, their focus was on how immigrant family life differs from the American ideal rather than from other Asian ethnic groups. This can blur ethnic distinctions and serve as a basis for shared personal experiences across ethnic groups. In fact, the rise of an Asian American ethnic identity among Asian-origin individuals is believed to result, in part, from the shared experiences of growing up American in an Asian home (Kibria, 1997).

Gender differences observed in these data focused on the nature of respondents' criticisms of parents, with females complaining that parents grant more freedom and respect to sons. Males also complained of strict parents, but when asked, acknowledged receiving more respect and freedom than sisters. These observed differences are not central to this analysis and are presented elsewhere (Pyke & Johnson, 1999).

A five-page interview guide with open-ended questions and follow-up probes concerning the familial and social experiences of respondents directed the intensive interview process. All respondents were asked what being a child of immigrants was like, how they think immigration affected their family, what their parents were like when the respondent was growing up, what communication was like with their parents, what their parents' marriage was like, how close they feel to their parents, whether they ever felt embarrassed by their parents, whether they ever deceived their parents, what kinds of things their parents would do to get them to obey, whether they have ever disappointed their parents in any way, how they would change their parents if they could change anything about them they wanted, what kinds of assistance they plan to provide for their parents, and how they feel about providing assistance. The author conducted about one-third of the interviews, and several trained student assistants conducted the remainder. The student assistants took a qualitative methods course with the author, in which they learned interviewing skills and conducted practice interviews. They also received extensive training and practice with the interview guide prior to collecting project data. Most trained student interviewers were children of Asian immigrants near in age to the respondents. They were therefore able to establish rapport with respondents, and they typically received candid responses, as revealed by respondents' frequent use of colloquialisms and profanity in interviews. Interviews were conducted in 1996 and 1997 and lasted between 1½ and 3 hours. They were tape-recorded and transcribed for analysis.

This research began with the general goal of learning about the subjective family experiences of children of Asian immigrants. I used a grounded research approach that emphasized an inductive method of generating explanation from the data (Glaser & Strauss, 1967; Strauss & Corbin, 1990). Except for the general assumption that respondents are active agents in the construction of their family experiences, I imposed no apriori assumptions, hypotheses, or specific theoretical frames on the research process. This allowed unanticipated data to emerge. Interviews focusing on family dynamics were conducted until a point of saturation was reached, as indicated by the recurring nature of the data and the emergence of clear trends (Ambert, Adler, Adler, & Detzner, 1995; Glaser & Strauss, 1967).

The overwhelming majority of respondents provided negative descriptions of their parents and upbringing in at least one domain, such as discipline, emotional closeness, or communication; only a small minority provided wholly positive accounts. Despite such intergenerational strain or distance, most respondents were strongly committed to caring for their parents in later life. In order to more closely examine the interview data, and thus to uncover deeper layers of understanding to these prominent patterns, two research assistants coded data into topical categories that corresponded with the questions asked. These coded segments were extracted for ease in theoretical sorting. I then analyzed the data, moving back and forth between emerging theoretical categories of the extracted data and the full interviews in order to check the validity of the findings. Because I am a native-born White American and wanted both to guard against the introduction of personal bias in the analysis and to acquire greater awareness of ethnic meanings, I shared my interpretive understandings of the data with Asian American students and student assistants. I then incorporated their insights into the analysis.

During the analysis, I noted recurring references in one form or another to notions about so-called normal families. Respondents used such references for one purpose only—as a point of contrast to life in their families. Three categorical expressions of this theme emerged in the data: (a) comparisons with television families; (b) comparisons with families of non-Asian friends; and (c) contrasts with specific family behavior or characteristics described as normal or American. I did not anticipate the importance of such family imagery when I devised the interview guide; thus I never asked respondents about family life on TV or among friends, or what they regarded as a normal or ideal family. Rather this theme emerged unexpectedly in the interviews. The unprompted and recurring nature of these references indicates their importance as resources in respondents' construction of their family experiences. In the following discussion, I present a sample of the qualitative data, in the form of quotes, to illustrate the observed patterns (Ambert et al., 1995). Respondents chose the pseudonyms used here.

RESULTS

I examine two ways in which respondents commonly used the typification of American family life as a contrast structure against which behavior in immigrant Asian families was juxtaposed and interpreted (Gubrium & Holstein, 1997). When describing relations with their parents, most respondents provided negative accounts of at least one aspect of their relationship, and they criticized their parents for lacking American values that emphasize psychological well-being and expressive love. Recurring references to a narrow Americanized notion of what families ought to look like were woven throughout many such accounts. However, when respondents described the kinds of filial care they planned to provide for their parents, the respondents switched to an interpretive lens that values ethnic family solidarity. In this context, respondents' references to notions of the Normal American Family became a negative point of comparison that cast their own immigrant families, and Asian families in general, in positive terms.

Viewing Parental Relations Through an Americanized Lens

Respondents were asked to fantasize about how they would change their parents if they could change anything about them that they wanted to change. The three areas of desired change that respondents mentioned most often reveal their adoption of many mainstream American values. They wished for parents who: (a) were less strict and gave them more freedom; (b) were more liberal, more open-minded, more Americanized, and less traditional; (c) were emotionally closer, more communicative, more expressive, and more affectionate. These three areas are interrelated. For example, being more Americanized and less traditional translates into being more lenient and expressive. A small minority of respondents presented a striking contrast to the dominant pattern by describing, in terms both positive and grateful, parents who had liberal attitudes or Americanized values and parenting styles.

The communication most respondents described with parents focused on day-to-day practical concerns, such as whether the child had eaten, and about performance in school and college, a major area of concern among parents. Conversations were often limited to parental directives or lectures. For the most part, respondents were critical of the emotional distance and heavy emphasis on obedience that marked their relations with their parents. Chang-Hee, an 18-year-old who immigrated from Korea at 8, provided a typical case. When asked about communication, she disparaged her parents for not talking more openly, which she attributed to their being Asian. Respondents typically linked parental styles with race and not with other factors such as age or personality. Like many other respondents, Chang-Hee constructed an account not only of her family relations, but also of Asian families in general.

> To tell you the truth, in Asian families you don't have conversations. You just are told to do something and you do it. . . . You never talk about problems, even in the home. You just kind of forget about it and you kind of go on like nothing happened. Problems never really get solved. That's why I think people in my generation, I consider myself 1.5 generation, we have such a hard time because I like to verbalize my emotions. . . . [My parents] never allowed themselves to verbalize their emotions. They've been repressed so much [that] they expect the same out of me, which is the hardest thing to do because I have so many different things to say and I'm just not allowed.

Some respondents volunteered that their parents never asked them about their well-being, even when their distress was apparent. Chang-Hee observed, "If I'm sad, [my mom] doesn't want to hear it. She doesn't want to know why. . . . She's never asked me, 'So what do you feel?' " This lack of expressed interest in children's emotional well-being, along with the mundane level of communication, was especially upsetting to respondents because, interpreted through the lens of American family ideology, it defined their parents as emotionally uncaring and distant.

Several respondents longed for closer, more caring relationships with their parents that included expressive displays of affection. Thanh, a married 22-year-old college student who left Vietnam when she was 6, said, "I'd probably make them more loving and understanding, showing a bit more affection. . . . A lot of times I just want to go up and hug my parents, but no, you don't do that sort of thing."

Research indicates that the desire for greater intimacy is more common among women than men (Cancian, 1987). Thus it was surprising that many male respondents also expressed strong desires for more caring and close talk—especially from their fathers, who were often described as harsh and judgmental. Ralph, 20, a Korean American man born in the United States, said:

> My dad, he's not open. He is not the emotional type. So he talks . . . and I would listen and do it. It's a one-way conversation, rather than asking for my opinions. . . . I would think it'd be nicer if he was . . . much more compassionate, caring, because it seems like he doesn't care.

Similarly, Dat, a 22-year-old biology major who left Vietnam when he was 5, said:

> I would fantasize about sitting down with my dad and shooting the breeze. Talk about anything and he would smile and he would say, "Okay, that's fine, Dat." Instead of, you know, judge you and tell me I'm a loser. . . .

A definition of love that emphasizes emotional expression and close talk predominates in U.S. culture (Cancian, 1986). Instrumental aspects of love, like practical help, are ignored or devalued in this definition. In Korean and Vietnamese cultures, on the other hand, the predominant definitions of love emphasize instrumental help and support. The great divide between immigrant parents who emphasize instrumental forms of love and children who crave open displays of affection was evident in the following conversation, which occurred between Dat and his father when Dat was 7 or 8 years old. Dat recalled, "I tried saying 'I love you' one time and he looked at me and said, 'Are you American now? You think this is *The Brady Bunch?* You don't love me. You love me when you can support me.'" These different cultural definitions of love contributed to respondents' constructions of immigrant parents as unloving and cold.

The Family as a Contrast Structure in the Negative Accounts of Family Life

Many of the images of normal family life that respondents brought to their descriptions came in the form of references to television families or the families of non–Asian American friends. Although these monolithic images do not reflect the reality of American family life, they nevertheless provided the basis by which respondents learned how to be American, and they served as the interpretive frame of their own family experiences. By contrasting behavior in their immigrant families with mainstream images of normalcy, the respondents interpreted Asian family life as lacking or deficient. Dat referred to images of normal family life in America, as revealed on television and among friends, as the basis for his desire for more affection and closeness with his father:

> Sometimes when I had problems in school, all I wanted was my dad to listen to me, of all people. I guess that's the American way and I was raised American. . . . That's what I see on TV and in my friends' family. And I expected him to be that way too. But it didn't happen. . . . I would like to talk to him or, you know, say "I love you," and he would look at me and say, "Okay." That's my ultimate goal, to say, "I love you." It's real hard. Sometimes when I'm in a good mood, the way I show him love is to put my hands over his shoulders and squeeze it a little bit. That would already irritate him a little. . . . You could tell. He's like, "What the fuck's he doing?" But I do it because I want to show him love somehow. Affection. I'm an affectionate person.

Similarly, Hoa, a 23-year-old Vietnamese American man who immigrated at age 2, referred to television in describing his own family: "We aren't as close as I would like . . . We aren't as close as the dream family, you know, what you see on TV. Kind of like. . . . *Leave It To Beaver.* You know, stuff I grew up on."

Paul, a 21-year-old Korean American born in the United States, also criticizes his father, and Asian fathers in general, in relation to the fathers of friends and those on television:

> I think there is somewhat of a culture clash between myself and my parents. They are very set on rules—at least my father is. He is very strict and demanding and very much falls into that typical Asian father standard. I don't like that too much and I think it is because . . . as a child, I was always watching television and watching other friends' fathers. All the relationships seemed so much different from me and my father's relationship. . . . I guess it's pretty cheesy but I can remember watching *The Brady Bunch* reruns and thinking Mike Brady would be a wonderful dad to have. He was always so supportive. He al-

ways knew when something was wrong with one of his boys. Whenever one of his sons had a problem, they would have no problem telling their dad anything and the dad would always be nice and give them advice and stuff. Basically I used what I saw on television as a picture of what a typical family should be like in the United States. I only wished that my family could be like that. And friends too—I used to see how my friends in school would be in Little League Baseball and their dad would be like their coaches or go to their games to cheer their sons on and give them support. I could not picture my father to be like that kind of man that I saw on TV, or like my friends' fathers.

Respondents did not refer to non–Asian American friends who had distant, conflict-ridden family relationships. Yet many respondents likely did have contact with such individuals. It appears as though respondents see only in ways permitted by the Family ideology. That is, as Bernades argued, "the image or idol of 'The Family' rather than the reality of people's lives is taken as the object of attention" (1985, p. 288). Looking at "American" families through this ideological lens determines which families are "seen." Those that do not fit the cultural imagery are not seen or are viewed as atypical. "Atypical" families are not referenced in these accounts, even though, in actuality, they are probably closer to the empirical reality of American family life. Friends whose families do comply, on the other hand, loom large as symbols that verify the existence of the Family ideal.

In comparison to this ideal, even parents who had adopted more American parenting practices fell short. For example, the parents of Mike, 22, who had immigrated to the United States from Vietnam as an infant, were less strict than the parents of most respondents. Nevertheless, Mike said:

My parents were really easy. They let me hang out with my friends, they had no problem with me sleeping over or other people sleeping over. So having friends in high school wasn't hard at all, and going out wasn't a problem at all. It was just, you know, you go over to your friend's house and he just talks to his parents about everything. So I got a little bit jealous. You know, I wished I could talk to my parents about stuff like that but I couldn't.

Sometimes respondents simply made assumptive references to normal or American families, against which they critically juxtaposed Asian immigrant families. Being American meant that one was a member of the Normal American Family and enjoyed family relations that were warm, close, and harmonious. Being Asian, on the other hand, meant living outside such normality. Thuy, a 20-year-old Vietnamese American woman who had immigrated when 13, said:

If I could, I would have a more emotional relationship with my parents. I know they love me, but they never tell me they love me. They also are not very affectionate. This is how I've always grown up. It wasn't really until we came to the United States that I really noticed what a lack of love my parents show. *American* kids are so lucky. They don't know what it's like to not really feel that you can show emotion with your own parents.

Similarly, Cora, 20, a Korean American woman born in the United States, remarked:

I would probably want [my parents] to be more open, more understanding so I could be more open with them, 'cause there's a lot of things that I can't share with them because they're not as open-minded as *American* parents. . . . 'Cause I have friends and stuff. They talk to their parents about everything, you know?

When asked how he was raised, Josh, 21, a Vietnamese American man who immigrated when 2, responded by calling up a construction of the "good" American Family and the "deficient" Asian Family. He said, "I'm sure that for all *Asian* people, if they think back to [their] childhood, they'll remember a time they got hit. *American* people, they don't get hit."

Respondents repeatedly constructed American families as loving, harmonious, egalitarian, and normal. Using this ideal as their measuring stick, Asian families were constructed as distant, overly strict, uncaring, and not normal. In fact, respondents sometimes used the word "normal" in place of "American." For example, Hoa, who previously contrasted his family with the one depicted in *Leave It To Beaver,* said, "I love my dad but we never got to play catch. He didn't teach me how to play football. All the stuff a *normal* dad does for their kids. We missed out on that." Thomas, 20, a Korean American who arrived in the United States at age 8, said, "I always felt like maybe we are not so normal. Like in the real America, like Brady Bunch normal. . . . I always felt like . . . there was something irregular about me." Similarly, after describing a childhood where she spoke very little to her parents, Van, 24, who immigrated to the United States from Vietnam at 10, began crying and noted, "I guess I didn't have a *normal* childhood." To be a normal parent is to be an American parent. Asian immigrant parents are by this definition deficient. Such constructions ignore diversity within family types, and they selectively bypass the social problems, such as child abuse, that plague many non–Asian American families. It is interesting, for example, that respondents did not refer to the high divorce rate of non–Asian Americans (Sweet & Bumpass, 1987) to construct positive images of family stability among Asian Americans. This may be because, applying an Americanized definition of love, many respondents described their parents' marriage as unloving and some thought their parents ought to divorce.

Respondents relied on the Family not only as an interpretive framework, but also as a contrast structure by which to differentiate Asian and American families. This juxtaposition of American and Asian ignores that most of the respondents and the coethnics they describe are Americans. "American" is used to refer to non–Asian Americans, particularly Whites. The words "White" and "Caucasian" were sometimes used interchangeably with "American." Indeed, the Normal American Family *is* White. This Eurocentric imagery excludes from view other racial minority families such as African Americans and Latino Americans. It is therefore not surprising that racial–ethnic families were not referenced as American in these interviews. In fact, respondents appeared to use the term "American" as a code word denoting not only cultural differences but also racial differences. For example, Paul, who was born in the United States, noted, "I look Korean but I think I associate myself more with the *American race.*" The oppositional constructions of Asian and American families as monolithic and without internal variation imply that these family types are racialized. That is, the differences are constructed as not only cultural but also racially essential and therefore immutable (Omi & Winant, 1994). By defining American as White, respondents revealed the deep-seated notion that, as Asian Americans, they can never truly be American. Such notions dominate in mainstream depictions of Asian Americans as perpetual foreigners. For example, in a speech about foreign donations, Ross Perot read the names of several Asian American political donors and commented, "So far we haven't found an American name" (Nakao, 1996). When respondents centered Whites as a point of reference in these accounts, they reaffirmed the marginalized position of racial–ethnic minorities in the Family ideology and in U.S. culture writ large.

These data illustrate how Eurocentric images of normal family relationships promulgated in the larger society served as an ideological template in the negative accounts that respondents provided of their immigrant parents. However, as described next, when respondents discussed their plans for filial care, they presented positive accounts of their immigrant families.

Maintaining Ethnic Values of Filial Obligation

Respondents were not consistent in their individual constructions of Asian and American families as revealed in their interviews. When discussing future plans for filial care, most respondents positively evaluated their family's collectivist commitment to care. Such an interpretation is supported by model minority stereotypes in mainstream U.S. culture that attribute the success enjoyed by some Asian immigrants to their strong family values and collectivist practices (Kibria, 1993; Zhou & Bankston, 1998).

The majority of respondents valued and planned to maintain their ethnic tradition of filial care. For example, Josh, who criticized his parents (and Asian parents in general) for using physical forms of punishment, nonetheless plans to care for his parents in their old age. He said, "I'm the oldest son, and in Vietnamese culture the oldest son cares for the parents. That is one of the things that I carry from my culture. I would not put my parents in a [nursing] home. That's terrible." In contrast to White Americans who condition their level of filial commitment on intergenerational compatibility (Pyke, 1999), respondents displayed a strong desire to fulfill their filial obligation and—especially among daughters—were often undeterred by distant and even conflict-ridden relations with parents. For example, after describing a strained relationship with her parents, Kimberly, 20, who came to this country from Vietnam when 7, added, "I would still take care of them whether I could talk to them or not. It doesn't matter as long as I could take care of them." Similarly, in Wolf's study of 22 grown children of Filipino immigrants, respondents who complained of tension and emotional distance with parents nonetheless experienced family ties and responsibilities as a central component of their daily lives and identities (1997).

Most respondents expected to begin financially supporting their parents prior to their elderly years, with parents in their 50s often regarded as old. A few respondents had already begun to help out their parents financially. Many planned on living with parents. Others spoke of living near their parents, often as neighbors, rather than in the same house, as a means of maintaining some autonomy. The tradition of assigning responsibility for the care of parents to the eldest son was not automatically anticipated for many of these families, especially those from Vietnam. Respondents most often indicated that responsibility would be pooled among siblings or would fall exclusively to the daughters. Several said that parents preferred such arrangements, because they felt closer to daughters. Although the tendency for daughters to assume responsibility for aging parents is similar to the pattern of caregiving common in mainstream American families (Pyke &

Bengtson, 1996), several respondents noted that such patterns are also emerging among relatives in their ethnic homeland.

The Importance of Collectivism as an Expression of Love

Respondents typically attributed their future caregiving to reciprocation for parental care in the past and a cultural emphasis on filial respect and support. Yet the enthusiasm and strong commitment that pervades their accounts suggests that they are motivated by more than obligation. For example, Vinh, 26, a graduate student who immigrated from Vietnam at age 5, said about his parents:

> They are my life. They will never be alone. I will always be with them. When I was growing [up] as a child, my parents were always with me. And I believe . . . when you grow up, you should be with them; meaning, I will take care of them, in my house, everything. Your parents didn't abandon you when you were a kid. They did not abandon you when you [were] pooping in your diaper. Then when they do, I will not abandon them. . . . Whatever it takes to make them comfortable, I will provide it. There is no limit.

Unable to express love via open displays of affection and close talk, filial assistance becomes a very important way for adult children to symbolically demonstrate their affection for their parents and to reaffirm family bonds. Blossom, 21, who immigrated to the United States from Korea when 6, described the symbolic value of the financial assistance her father expects. She said, "Money is not really important, but it's more about our heart that [my dad] looks at. Through money, my dad will know how we feel and how we appreciate him." Remember that Dat's father told him, "You love me when you can support me." Because instrumental assistance is the primary venue for expressing love and affection in these immigrant families, adult children often placed no limits on what they were willing to do. For example, John, 20, who immigrated from Vietnam when 3, remarked "I'm willing to do anything (for my parents), that's how much I care."

Parental financial independence was not always welcomed by those children who gave great weight to their role of parental caregivers. For example, it was very important to Sean, 19, an only child, to care for his Sino-Vietnamese parents. Sean, who planned to become a doctor, commuted from his home to a local university. He said, "I want my parents to stay with me. I want to support them. . . . I'll always have room for my parents. . . . When I get my first paycheck, I want to support them financially." As reflected in the following exchange with the interviewer, Sean viewed his parents' retirement plan with some hurt.

> ***Sean:***   They have their own retirement plan, and they keep track of it themselves, so they're all prepared for me to be the disobedient son and run away.
>
> ***Interviewer:***   Is that how you feel?
>
> ***Sean:***   Yes I do. . . . Or if I don't succeed in life, they'll be taken care of by themselves.
>
> ***Interviewer:***   So is that how you see their retirement plan, as a kind of symbol that they're . . . ?
>
> ***Sean:***   They're ready for me to mess up.

The emotional centrality of family ties is also apparent in Sean's description of his hurt when his father—who worries that the time Sean spends away from home studying or at his job is pulling him away from the family—occasionally tests his son's commitment by suggesting that he leave the family home and "fly away." With tear-filled eyes, Sean explained:

> It hurts me because I've never had that idea to fly away. . . . I don't want to go and that's what hurts me so bad. I mean, I could cry over things like that. And this is a 19-year-old kid that's crying in front of you. How seldom do you get that?

The Family as a Contrast Structure in the Positive Accounts of Filial Obligation

Many respondents distinguished their ethnic collectivist tradition of filial obligation from practices in mainstream American families, which they described as abandoning elderly parents in retirement or nursing homes. The belief that the elderly are abandoned by their families is widespread in U.S. society and very much a part of everyday discourse. Media accounts of nursing home atrocities bolster such views. Yet most eldercare in this country is not provided in formal caregiving settings but by family members (Abel, 1991). Nonetheless, respondents used this tenacious myth as a point of contrast in constructing Asian American families as more instrumentally caring. For example, Thuy, who previously described wanting a "more emotional relationship" with her parents, like "American kids" have, explained:

> With the American culture, it's . . . not much frowned upon to put your parents in a home when they grow old. In our culture, it is a definite no-no. To do anything like that would be disrespectful. . . . If they need help, my brother and I will take care of them, just like my mom is taking care of her parents right now.

Similarly, Hien, 21, a Vietnamese American woman who arrived in this country as an infant, noted, "I know a lot of non-Asians have their parents go to the nursing homes . . . but I personally prefer to find a way of trying to keep them at home."

Mike, who wished he could talk to his parents the way his friends do to theirs, plans to care for his Americanized parents even though they have told him they do not want him to. He was not alone in remaining more committed to filial care than his parents required him to be. He said:

> They tell me to just succeed for yourself and take care of your own family. But [referring to filial care] that's just how the Vietnamese culture is. Here in America, once your parents are old, you put them in a retirement home. But not in my family. When the parents get old you take care of them. It doesn't matter if they can't walk, if they can't function anymore. You still take care of them.

When discussing relationships with their parents, respondents used the Family as the ideological raw material out of which they negatively constructed their parents as unloving and distant. However, when the topic changed to filial care, respondents switched to an ethnic definition of love that emphasizes instrumental support and that casts a positive and loving light on their families. As Katie, 21, a Korean American woman born in the United States, observed:

> When you say that you are close to your parents here in America, I think most people would take that as you are affectionate with your parents, you hang out with them, you can talk to them about anything . . . more of a friendship thing. But Korean families are not like that. . . . They do not get close to their children like that. They are not friends with them. The kids of Korea do not open up with their parents. Their parents are really their *parents*. . . . But still, no matter what, they are very close. Here in America . . . Caucasians don't take care of their parents like we do. They just put them in an old people's home and that's it. It's like they say, "You are too old for me. I don't need you anymore and I'm just going to put you here 'cause it's convenient for me and you'd be in the way anyway. . . ." And in that way, Americans are *not* close to their parents. So it really depends on how you define the word "close"—the answer changes. [Note that the words "Caucasian" and "American" are used synonymously here, as previously discussed.]

In describing their plans for parental care, respondents turned their previous construction of Asian and American families on its head. In this context the Family was constructed as deficient and uncaring, while the families of respondents—and Asian families in general—were described as more instrumentally caring and closer. Respondents' view of American families as uncaring should not be interpreted as a departure from mainstream family ideology. There has been much concern in the public discourse that today's families lack a commitment to the care of their elders and children (e.g., Popenoe, 1993; see Coontz, 1992, pp. 189–191). Indeed, the pervasive criticism that "individualism has gone haywire" in mainstream families—bolstered by references to the solidarity of model minority families—provides ideological support for ethnic traditions of filial care. That is, children of immigrants do not face ideological pressure from the dominant society to alter such practices; rather, they are given an interpretive template by which to view such practices as evidence of love and care in their families. In fact, U.S. legislative attempts to withdraw social services from legal immigrants without citizenship, with the expectation that family sponsors will provide such support, structurally mandate collectivist systems of caregiving in immigrant families (Huber & Espenshade, 1997). In other words, the dominant society ideologically endorses and, in some ways, structurally requires ethnic immigrant practices of filial care. Filial obligation thus serves as a site where children of Korean and Vietnamese immigrants can maintain their ethnic identity and family ties without countervailing pressure from the mainstream.

DISCUSSION

Interweaving respondents' accounts with an analysis of the interpretive structure from which those accounts are constructed suggests that the Family ideology subtly yet powerfully influences the children of immigrants, infiltrating their subjective understandings of and desires for family life. Respondents relied on American family images in two ways. When discussing their relations with parents and their upbringing, respondents used the Family ideology as a standard of normal families and good parents, leading them to view their immigrant parents as unloving, deficient, and not normal. However, when respondents discussed filial care, a complete reversal occurred. Respondents referred to negative images of rampant individualism among mainstream American families, specifically in regard to eldercare, to bolster their positive portrayals of the instrumental care and filial piety associated with their ethnic families. Thus the Family ideology was called upon in contradictory ways in these accounts—in the denigration of traditional ethnic parenting practices and in the glorification of ethnic practices of filial obligation.

Findings from this study illustrate how a narrow, ethnocentric family ideology that is widely promulgated throughout the larger culture and quickly internalized by children of immigrants creates an interpretive framework that derogates many of the ethnic practices of immigrant families. As others have argued, the cultural imposition of dominant group values in this form of "controlling images" can lead minorities to internalize negative self-images (Espiritu, 1997). That is, racial–ethnic immigrants can adopt a sense of inferiority and a desire to conform with those values and expectations that are glorified in the mainstream society as normal. Indeed, many respondents explicitly expressed a desire to have families that were like White or so-called American families, and they criticized their own family dynamics for being different. Rather than resist and challenge the ethnocentric family imagery of the mainstream, respondents' accounts reaffirmed the Normal American Family and the centrality of White native-born Americans in this imagery. This research thus reveals a subtle yet powerful mechanism of internalized oppression by which the racial–ethnic power dynamics in the larger society are reproduced. This is a particularly important finding in that racial–ethnic families will soon constitute a majority in several states, causing scholars to ponder the challenge of such a demographic transformation of the cultural and political hegemony of White native-born Americans (Maharidge, 1996). This study describes an ideological mechanism that could undermine challenges to that hegemony.

This research also uncovered an uncontested site of ethnic pride among the second-generation respondents who drew on mainstream images of elder neglect in their positive interpretation of ethnic filial commitment. As previously discussed, the belief that mainstream American families abandon their elders is tenacious and widespread in the dominant society, despite its empirical inaccuracy. This negative myth has been widely used in popular discourse as an example of the breakdown of American family commitment, and it sometimes serves as a rallying cry for stronger "family values." Such cries are often accompanied by references to the family solidarity and filial piety celebrated in the model minority stereotype. Thus the mainstream glorification of ethnic filial obligation, as contrasted with negative images of abandoned White American elders, provided respondents with a positive template for giving meaning to ethnic practices of filial care. The mainstream endorsement of filial obligation marks it as a locale where respondents can maintain family ties and simultaneously produce a positive self-identity in both cultural worlds. This might explain why some respondents were steadfastly committed to filial care despite parental requests to the contrary.

It remains to be seen, however, whether these young adults will be able to carry out their plans of filial obligation. It is likely that many will confront barriers in the form of demanding jobs, childrearing obligations, geographic moves, unsupportive spouses, competing demands from elderly in-laws, and financial difficulties. Furthermore, parents' access to alternative sources of support such as Social Security and retirement funds could diminish the need for their children's assistance. Some research already finds that elderly Korean immigrants prefer to live on their own and are moving out of the homes of their immigrant children despite the protests of children, who see it as a public accusation that they did not care for their parents (Hurh, 1998). Although this research examined first-generation immigrant adults and their aging parents, it suggests a rapid breakdown in traditional patterns of coresidential filial care that will likely be reiterated in the next generation. Future research is needed to examine these dynamics among second-generation immigrants, to look at how they will cope with inabilities to fulfill ethnic and model minority expectations of filial obligation, and to assess the impact of any such inabilities on their ethnic identity.

This study makes a unique contribution to the small and largely descriptive literature on Asian immigrant families. Rather than simply reiterating as descriptive data the accounts of family life offered by respondents, I examined the ideological underpinnings of those accounts. In so doing, I uncovered a subtle process by which White hegemonic images of the Family infiltrate the ways that children of immigrants think about their own family lives. Although scholars have often assumed that the prescriptive and moralistic characteristics of the Family are hurtful to those whose families do not comply, the findings presented here provide an empirical description of how such ideology negatively biases the family accounts of children of immigrants. It must be noted, however, that because the sample in the study was demographically predisposed to higher levels of assimilation, the respondents are probably more likely than a less assimilated sample to view their families through an Americanized lens. This suggests the need for further study of how variations in acculturation levels affect the accounts that children of immigrants provide of their family lives.

A broader sample of families that do not conform with images of the Normal American Family also needs to be investigated. This sample should include native-born racial minorities and children of single parents, as well as immigrants. Studying a broader sample will allow greater understanding of whether narrow cultural notions of a normal family life influence the subjective experience of diverse groups of children growing up in the margins of the mainstream. It is particularly important, as family scholars begin to respond to the burgeoning numbers of ethnically and structurally diverse family forms, that researchers generate culturally sensitive interpretive frameworks that do not automatically and unconsciously perpetuate existing notions that certain family types and practices are inferior. The effort to develop such frameworks requires researchers to examine not only the values and assumptions they bring to their analyses (Dilworth-Anderson et al., 1993), but also the values and assumptions that respondents bring to their accounts. To summarize, this study suggests the need for family researchers to analytically bracket as problematic the ideological structures that shape the empirical accounts of family life we rely upon in our research.

Note

I am grateful to Katherine Allen, Susan Blank, Francesca Cancian, Tran Dang, Yen Le Espiritu, Joe Feagin, Jaber Gubrium, Nazli Kibria, Pyong Gap Min, Karen Seccombe, Darin Weinberg, Min Zhou, and the reviewers for their suggestions. I also thank Van-Dzung Nguyen and Mumtaz Mohammedi for their research assistance, the Department of Sociology at University of California-Irvine for its support of this research, and the many students who eagerly participated as research assistants or respondents.

References

Abel, E. K. (1991). *Who cares for the elderly?* Philadelphia: Temple University Press.

Ambert, A., Adler, P. Adler, P. & Detzner, D. (1995). Understanding and evaluating qualitative research. *Journal of Marriage and the Family, 57,* 879–893.

Bellah, R. N., Madsen, R., Sullivan, W. M., Swidler, A., & Tipton, S. (1985). *Habits of the heart.* San Francisco: Harper & Row.

Berger, P. L., & Luckmann, T. (1966). *The social construction of reality.* New York: Doubleday.

Bernades, J. (1985). "Family ideology": Identification and exploration. *Sociological Review, 33,* 275–297.

Bernades, J. (1993). Responsibilities in studying postmodern families. *Journal of Family Issues, 14,* 35–49.

Blankenhorn, D. (1995). *Fatherless America.* New York: Basic Books.

Brown, D., & Bryant, J. (1990). Effects of television on family values and selected attitudes and behaviors. In J. Bryant (Ed.), *Television and the American family* (pp. 253–274). Hillsdale, NJ: Erlbaum.

Cancian, E. M. (1986). The feminization of love. *Signs, 11,* 692–708.

Cancian, E. M. (1987). *Love in America.* New York: Cambridge University Press.

Caplan, N., Choy, M. H., & Whitmore, J. K. (1991). *Children of the boat people: A study of educational success.* Ann Arbor: University of Michigan Press.

Cha, J. (1994). Aspects of individualism and collectivism in Korea. In U. Kim, H. C. Triandis, Ç. Kâğitçibaşi, S. Choi, & G. Yoon (Eds.), *Individualism and collectivism: Theory, methods, and applications* (pp. 157–174). Thousand Oaks, CA: Sage.

Chung, D. K. (1992). Asian cultural commonalities: A comparison with mainstream American culture. In S. Furuto, R. Biswas, D. Chung, K. Murase, R. Ross-Sheriff (Eds.), *Social work practice with Asian Americans* (pp. 27–44). Newbury Park, CA: Sage.

Coltrane, S. (1996). *Family man.* New York: Oxford University Press.

Coontz, S. (1992). *The way we never were.* New York: Basic Books.

Dilworth-Anderson, P., Burton, L. M., & Turner, W. L. (1993). The importance of values in the study of culturally diverse families. *Family Relations, 42,* 238–242.

Espiritu, Y. L. (1997). *Asian American women and men.* Thousand Oaks, CA: Sage.

Fineman, M. A. (1995). *The neutered mother, the sexual family, and other twentieth century tragedies.* New York: Routledge.

Freeman, J. M. (1989). *Hearts of sorrow: Vietnamese-American lives.* Stanford, CA: Stanford University Press.

Gerbner, G., Gross, L., Morgan, M., & Signorielli, N. (1980). *Media and the family: Images and impact.* Washington, DC: White House Conference on the Family, National Research Forum on Family Issues. (ERIC Document Reproduction Service No. ED 198 919).

Glaser, B. G., & Strauss, A. L. (1967). *The discovery of grounded theory.* New York: Aldine.

Gold, S. J. (1993). Migration and family adjustment: Continuity and change among Vietnamese in the United States. In H. P. McAdoo (Ed.), *Family ethnicity* (pp. 300–314). Newbury Park, CA: Sage.

Greeley, A. (1987, May 17). Today's morality play: The sitcom. *New York Times,* p. H1.

Greenberg, B. S., Hines, M., Buerkel-Rothfuss, N., & Atkin, C. K. (1980). Family role structures and interactions on commercial television. In B. S. Greenberg (Ed.), *Life on television: Content analyses of U.S. TV drama* (pp. 149–160). Norwood, NJ: Ablex.

Gubrium, J. F. & Holstein, J. A. (1997). *The new language of qualitative method.* New York: Oxford University Press.

Holstein, J. A., & Gubrium, J. F. (1995). Deprivatization and the construction of domestic life. *Journal of Marriage and the Family, 57,* 894–908.

Holstein, J. A., & Miller, G. (1993). Social constructionism and social problems work. In J. A. Holstein & G. Miller (Eds.), *Reconsidering social constructionism* (pp. 151–172). New York: Aldine De Gruyter.

Huber, G. A., & Espenshade, T. J. (1997). Neo-isolationism, balanced-budget conservatism, and the fiscal impacts of immigrants. *International Migration Review, 31,* 1031–1054.

Hurh, W. M. (1998). *The Korean Americans.* Westport, CN: Greenwood Press.

Kibria, N. (1993). *The family tightrope: The changing lives of Vietnamese Americans.* Princeton, NJ: Princeton University Press.

Kibria, N. (1997). The construction of 'Asian American': Reflections on intermarriage and ethnic identity among second-generation Chinese and Korean Americans. *Ethnic and Racial Studies, 20,* 523–544.

Kim, U., & Choi, S. (1994). Individualism, collectivism, and child development: A Korean perspective. In P. Greenfield & R. Cocking (Eds.), *Cross-cultural roots of minority child development* (pp. 227–257). Hillsdale, NJ: Erlbaum.

Kurz, D. (1995). *For richer, for poorer.* New York: Routledge.

Maharaj, D. (1997, July 8). E-mail hate case tests free speech protections. *Los Angeles Times,* pp. Al, A16.

Maharidge, D. (1996). *The coming white minority: California eruptions and America's future.* New York: New York Times Books.

Min, P. G. (1995). Major issues relating to Asian American experiences. In P. G. Min (Ed.), *Asian Americans* (pp. 38–57). Thousand Oaks, CA: Sage.

Min, P. G. (1998). *Changes and conflicts: Korean immigrant families in New York.* New York: Allyn and Bacon.

Nakao, A. (1996, November 17). Asians' political image marred: Fundraising probes' timing "unfortunate." *The San Francisco Examiner,* p. Al.

Omi, M., & Winant, H. (1994). *Racial formation in the United States.* New York: Routledge.

Oropesa, R. S., & Landale, N. S. (1995). *Immigrant legacies: The socioeconomic circumstances of children by ethnicity and generation in the United States.* (Working Paper 95–01R). Population Research Institute, The Pennsylvania State University, State College.

Pettengill, S. M., & Rohner, R. P. (1985). Korean-American adolescents' perceptions of parental control, parental acceptance–rejection and parent–adolescent conflict. In I. R. Lagunes & Y. H. Poortinga (Eds.), *From a different perspective: Studies of behavior across culture* (pp. 241–249). Berwyn, IL: Sweets North America.

Popenoe, D. (1993). American family decline, 1960–1990: A review and appraisal. *Journal of Marriage and the Family, 55,* 527–555.

Popenoe, D. (1996). *Life without father: Compelling new evidence that fatherhood and marriage are indispensable and for the good of the children and society.* New York: Martin Kessler/Free Press.

Pyke, K. D. (1999). The micropolitics of care in relationships between aging parents and adult children Individualism, collectivism, and power. *Journal of Marriage and the Family, 61,* 661–672.

Pyke, K. D., & Bengtson, V. L. (1996). Caring more or less: Individualistic and collectivist systems of family eldercare. *Journal of Marriage and the Family, 58,* 379–392.

Pyke, K. D., & Johnson, D. (1999, November). *Between: two faces of gender: The incongruity of home and mainstream cultures among sons and daughters of Asian immigrants.* Paper presented at the Annual Meeting of the National Council of Family Relations, Irvine, CA.

Rohner, R. P., & Pettengill, S. M. (1985). Perceived parental acceptance–rejection and parental control among Korean adolescents. *Child Development, 56,* 524–528.

Rumbaut, R. G. (1994). The crucible within: Ethnic identity, self-esteem and segmented assimilation among children of immigrants. *International Migration Review, 28,* 748–794.

Rumbaut, R. G. (1997). Assimilation and its discontents: Between rhetoric and reality. *International Migration Review, 31,* 923–960.

Shaner, J. (1982). Parental empathy and family role interactions as portrayed on commercial television. *Dissertation Abstracts International, 42,* 3473A.

Skill, T. (1994). Family images and family actions as presented in the media: Where we've been and what we've found. In D. Zillmann, J. Bryant, & A. C. Huston (Eds.), *Media, children, and the family* (pp. 37–50). Hillsdale, NJ: Erlbaum.

Skolnick, A. (1991). *Embattled paradise: The American family in an age of uncertainty.* New York: Basic Books.

Smith, D. E. (1993). The standard North American family: SNAF as an ideological code. *Journal of Family Issues, 14,* 50–65.

Stacey, J. (1998). The right family values. In K. Hansen & A. Garey (Eds.), *Families in the U.S.* (pp. 859–880). Philadelphia: Temple University Press.

Strauss, A., & Corbin, J. (1990). *Basics of qualitative research.* Newbury Park, CA: Sage.

Sue, S., & Morishima, J. K. (1982). *The mental health of Asian Americans.* San Francisco: Jossey-Bass.

Sweet, J. A., & Bumpass, L. (1987). *American families and households.* New York: Russell Sage Foundation.

Thorne, B., & Yalom, M. (1992). *Rethinking the family: Some feminist questions.* Boston: Northeastern University.

Tran, T. V. (1988). The Vietnamese American family. In C. H. Mindel, R. W. Habenstein, & R. Wright, Jr. (Eds.), *Ethnic families in America: Patterns and variations* (pp. 276–299). New York: Elsevier.

Tsui, P., & Schultz, G. (1985). Failure of rapport: Why psychotherapeutic engagement fails in the treatment of Asian clients. *American Journal of Orthopsychiatry, 55,* 561–569.

Uba, L. (1994). *Asian Americans: Personality patterns, identity, and mental health.* New York: The Guilford Press.

U.S. Immigration and Naturalization Service (1997). *Statistical yearbook of the immigration and naturalization service, 1995.* Washington, DC: U.S. Government Printing Office.

Waters, M. C. (1996). The intersection of gender, race, and ethnicity in identity development of Caribbean American teens. In M. C. Waters (Ed.), *Urban girls: Resisting stereotypes, creating identities* (pp. 65–81) New York: New York University Press.

Wolf, D. (1997). Family secrets: Transnational struggles among children of Filipino immigrants. *Sociological Perspectives, 40,* 457–482.

Zhou, M. (1997). Growing up American: The challenge confronting immigrant children and children of immigrants. *Annual Review of Sociology, 23,* 63–95.

Zhou, M., & Bankston, III, C. (1998). *Growing up American: How Vietnamese children adapt to life in the United States.* New York: Russell Sage Foundation.

Zinn, M. B. (1994). Feminist rethinking of racial–ethnic families. In M. B. Zinn & B. T. Dill (Eds.), *Women of color in U.S. society* (pp. 303–314). Philadelphia: Temple University Press.

■READING 32

Beyond the Nuclear Family: The Increasing Importance of Multigenerational Bonds

Vern L. Bengtson

Family relationships across several generations are becoming increasingly important in American society. They are also increasingly diverse in structure and in functions. In reply to the widely debated "family decline" hypothesis, which assumes a nuclear family model of 2 biological parents and children, I suggest that family multigenerational relations will be more important in the 21st century for 3 reasons: (a) the demographic changes of population aging, resulting in "longer years of shared lives" between generations; (b) the increasing importance of grandparents and other kin in fulfilling family functions; (c) the strength and resilience of intergenerational solidarity over time. I also indicate that family multigenerational relations are increasingly diverse because of (a) changes in family structure, involving divorce and step-family relationships; (b) the increased longevity of kin; (c) the diversity of intergenerational relationship "types." Drawing on the family research legacy of Ernest W. Burgess, I frame my arguments in terms of historical family transitions and hypotheses. Research from the Longitudinal Study of Generations is presented to demonstrate the strengths of multigenerational ties over time and why it is necessary to look beyond the nuclear family when asking whether families are still functional.

During the past decade, sociologists have been engaged in an often heated debate about family change and family influences in contemporary society. This debate in many ways reflects the legacy of Ernest W. Burgess (1886–1966), the pioneer of American family sociology. It can be framed in terms of four general hypotheses, each of which calls attention to significant transitions in the structure and functions of families over the 20th century.

The first and earliest hypothesis concerns the *emergence of the "modern" nuclear family form* following the Industrial Revolution. This transition (suggested by Burgess in 1916 and elaborated by Ogburn, 1932, and Parsons, 1944) proposed that the modal structure of families had changed from extended to nuclear, and its primary functions had changed from social-institutional to emotional-supportive. The second hypothesis concerns the *decline of the modern nuclear family* as a social institution, a decline said to be attributable to the fact that its structure has been truncated (because of high divorce rates) and its functions further reduced (Popenoe, 1993). A third hypothesis can be termed the *increasing heterogeneity of family forms*, relations that extend beyond biological or conjugal relationship boundaries. Growing from the work of feminist scholars (Coontz, 1991; Skolnick, 1991; Stacey, 1990), and research on racial and ethnic minority families (Burton, 1995; Collins, 1990; Stack, 1974), this perspective suggests that family structures and relationships should be redefined to include both "assigned" and "created" kinship systems (Cherlin, 1999). I suggest a fourth hypothesis for consideration: *The increasing importance of multigenerational bonds.* I propose that relations across more than two generations are becoming increasingly important to individuals and families in American society; that they are increasingly diverse in structure and functions; and that in the early 21st century, these multigenerational bonds will not only enhance but in some cases replace nuclear family functions, which have been so much the focus of sociologists during the 20th century.

In this article, I first summarize the "Burgess legacy" in American family sociology and relate it to the four hypotheses summarized above. Then I suggest some foundations for my hypotheses concerning the increasing importance and diversity of multigenerational relationships, starting from a discussion of macrosocial trends (population aging and intergenerational family demography) and moving to microsocial dimensions (solidarity and types of cross-generational relationships). I conclude with some suggestions about future research that will be needed to examine further the role of multigenerational bonds in 21st century society.

THE BURGESS LEGACY: AS FAMILIES HAVE CHANGED, HAVE THEY DECLINED IN IMPORTANCE?

Before beginning to trace this argument—which is a substantial departure from conventional wisdom about the "problems" of American families and their solutions today—I want first to acknowledge my personal and intellectual debt to Ernest W. Burgess, the namesake for this award from the National Council on Family Relations. He was truly a giant in the development of family sociology in America and one of the great lights of the "Chicago school" of sociology from 1915 into the 1960s (Bogue, 1974).

Burgess was briefly my teacher at the University of Chicago, several years after his formal retirement. I remember him as a diminutive and courtly gentleman peering over the lectern as he talked, apparently without notes, about the "roleless role" of the aged in modern societies. Shortly after I first met him, he became increasingly frail and unable to live on his own. This led to a situation of profound irony. This giant of American family studies, who had never married and had outlived his biological kin, had no family to take care of his needs in his declining years. He had lived with his sister, also unmarried, for almost 40 years until her death. In early 1965, he quietly checked himself into a neighborhood board-and-care home for the elderly, which turned out to be in deplorable condition. Discovering this, Bernice Neugarten, Robert Havighurst, and other University of Chicago faculty arranged for his transfer to the Drexel Home for the Aged. He died there in December 1966 at the age of 80, without family except for the "fictive kin" represented by the warm care of the Drexel Home staff and his University of Chicago colleagues. It was an ironic departure for one of the U.S. pioneers in family sociology, a man who had no access himself to the multigenerational family network that is my theme in this paper.

Burgess was truly an innovator in sociology. He inherited a tradition of 19th-century sociological analysis based on political and moral philosophy; he adapted this to focus on the social problems encountered by early-20th-century Americans—social disorganization, crime, delinquency, urbanization, poverty—and to insist on the importance of empirical data in analyzing these problems. Because so little systematic social research had preceded him, he became a pioneer in almost every field he entered, from the methodology of social surveys (Burgess, 1916) to the role of the aged in Western societies (Burgess, 1960). But his most enduring legacy is reflected in the sociology of the family.

Burgess insisted that we must consider both the macrosocial contexts of families over time and their microsocial dynamics if we are to understand the increasing complexity of family life. Starting from Burgess' insight, I think we can identify four major shifts in American families over the 20th century that I will list as hypotheses, the source for future research concerning their utility.

The Emergence of the "Modern" Nuclear Family Form

Burgess' groundbreaking analyses of the American family started from a consideration of macrosocial trends brought about by the Industrial Revolution and continued with his exploration of the microsocial dynamics within families. One of his earliest concerns was the family as an aspect of social organization in the context of social evolution. His first book (Burgess, 1916) would today be regarded as a polemic in support of the traditional extended family and its functions because he argued that this family form was necessary for the socialization of children if social evolution were to continue. Within the next decade, however, he shifted his perspective. From the structural "functions" of families applied to the modernizing societies of the early 20th century, he turned to an emphasis on family members' "interactions."

Burgess' hypothesis was that families had changed. He broke from late-19th-century views of the extended family structure as the bedrock of social organization and progress to say, "The family in historical times has been, and at present is, in transition from an institution to a companionship" (Burgess, 1926, p. 104). He focused on the nuclear family and its changing functions as the consequence of industrialization and modernization, arguments echoed later by Ogbum (1932), Davis (1941), and Parsons (1944).

His thesis was that urbanization, increased individualism and secularism, and the emancipation of women had transformed the family from a social institution based on law and custom to one based on companionship and love.

Burgess advanced his position very quietly in a number of scholarly journal publications. These appeared to have escaped notice by the popular press at that time, quite unlike today's debates about the family. He argued that the family had become more specialized in its functions and that structural and objective aspects of family life had been supplanted by more emotional and subjective functions. This he termed the "companionship" basis of marriage, which he suggested had become the underlying basis of the "modern" family form.

But Burgess went further. He proposed that the most appropriate way to conceptualize and study the family was as "a unity of interacting personalities" (Burgess, 1926). By this he meant three things: First, "the family" is essentially a *process*, an interactional system influenced by each of its members; it not merely a *structure*, or a household. Second, the behaviors of one family member—a troubled child, a detached father—could not be understood except in *relationship* to other family members, their ongoing patterns of interactions, and personalities developing and changing through such interactions. This conceptualization provided the intellectual basis for the first marriage and family counseling programs in the United States. Third, the central *functions* of families had changed from being primarily structural units of social organization to being relationships supporting individuals' needs. Marriage was transformed from a primarily economic union to one based on sentiment and companionship.

Thus, Burgess represented a bridge between 19th-century conceptions of the family as a unit in social evolution to 20th-century ideas of families as supporting individuals' needs. His work also provided a bridge in sociological theory, from structural-functionalism to symbolic interactionism and phenomenology. But in all this, Burgess' focus was on the nuclear family, a White, middle-class, two-generation family; and the family forms emerging in the 21st century will, as I argue below, look much different than the family that Burgess observed.

The Decline of the Modern Nuclear Family Form

The "decline of the family" in American society is a theme that has become the focus of increasingly heated debates by politicians, pundits, and family sociologists during the last decade. David Popenoe (1993), the most articulate proponent of this position, has argued that there has been a striking decline in the family's structure and functions in American society, particularly since 1960. Moreover, his hypothesis is that recent family decline is "more serious" than any decline in the past, because "what is breaking up is the nuclear family, the fundamental unit stripped of relations and left with two essential functions that cannot be performed better elsewhere: Childrearing and the provision to its members of affection and companionship" (Popenoe, p. 527). Supporters of the family decline hypothesis have focused on the negative consequences of changing family structure, resulting from divorce and single parenting, on the psychological, social, and economic well-being of children. Furthermore, they suggest that social norms legitimating the pursuit of individual over collective goals and the availability of alternate social groups for the satisfaction of basic human needs have substantially weakened the social institution of the family as an agent of socialization and as a source of nurturance for family members (Popenoe).

There is much to support Popenoe's hypothesis. There has been a significant change in nuclear family structure over the past 50 years, starting with the growing divorce rate in the 1960s, which escalated to over half of first marriages in the 1980s (Amato & Booth, 1997; Bumpass, Sweet, & Martin, 1990). There also has been an increase in single-parent families, accompanied by an increase in poverty for the children living in mother-headed families (McLanahan, 1994). The absence of fathers in many families today has created problems for the economic and emotional well-being of children (Popenoe, 1996).

At the same time, the "family decline" hypothesis is limited, and to some critics flawed, by its preoccupation with the family as a coresident household and the nuclear family as its primary representation. Popenoe defined the family as "a relatively small domestic group of kin (or people in a kinlike relationship) consisting of at least one adult and one dependent person" (Popenoe, 1993, p. 529). Although this might be sufficient as a demographic definition of a "family household," it does not include important aspects of family functions that extend beyond boundaries of coresidence. There is nothing in Popenoe's hypothesis to reflect the function of multigenerational influences on children—the role of grandparents in socializing or supporting grandchildren, particularly after the divorce of middle-generation parents (Johnson & Barer, 1987; Minkler & Rowe, 1993). Nor is there any mention of what Riley and Riley (1993) have called the "latent matrix of kin connections," a web of "continually shifting linkages that provide the potential for activating and intensifying close kin relationships" in times of need by family members (Riley & Riley, p. 169). And there is no consideration of the longer years of shared lives between generations, now extending into many decades, and their consequences for the emotional and economic support for family members across several generations (Bengtson & Allen, 1993; Silverstein & Litwak, 1993).

The Increasing Heterogeneity of Family Forms

A third hypothesis has been generated by feminist scholars (Coontz, 1991; Osmond & Thorne, 1993; Skolnick, 1991; Stacey, 1993, 1996; Thorne & Yalom, 1992) and researchers studying minority families (Burton, 1995; Collins, 1990; Stack, 1974). This hypothesis can be summarized as follows: Families are changing in both forms and meanings, expanding beyond the nuclear family structure to involve a variety of kin and nonkin relationships. Diverse family forms are emerging, or at least being recognized for the first time, including the matriarchal structure of many African American families. Stacey (1996) argued that the traditional nuclear family is increasingly ill-suited for a postindustrial, postmodern society. Women's economic and social emancipation over the past century has become incongruent with the nuclear "male breadwinner" family form and its traditional allocation of power, resources, and labor. We have also seen a normalization of divorce and of stepparenting in recent years. Many American families today are what Ahrons (1994) has described as "binuclear." Following divorce and remarriage of the original marital partners and parents, a stable, child-supportive family context may emerge. Finally, because some four million children in the United States are being raised by lesbian or gay parents (Stacey & Biblarz, in press), these and other alternative family forms "are here . . . and let's get used to it!" (Stacey, 1996, p. 105).

In responding to Popenoe, Stacey (1996) argued that the family is indeed in decline—if what we mean by "family" is the nuclear form of dad, mom, and their biological or adopted kids. This form of the family rose and fell with modern industrial society. In the last few decades, with the shift to a postindustrial domestic economy within a globalized capitalist system and with the advent of new reproductive technologies, the modern family system has been replaced by what Stacey has called "the postmodern family condition," a pluralistic, fluid, and contested domain in which diverse family patterns, values, and practices contend for legitimacy and resources. Stacey suggested that family diversity and fluidity are now "normal," and the postmodern family condition opens the possibility of egalitarian, democratic forms of intimacy, as well as potentially threatening levels of insecurity.

The Increasing Importance of Multigenerational Bonds

I want to suggest a fourth hypothesis about family transitions during the 20th century that builds on those of Burgess, Popenoe, Stack, and Stacey but reflects the recent demographic development of much greater longevity. It is this: *Relations across more than two generations are becoming increasingly important to individuals and families in American society.* Considering the dramatic increase in life expectancy over the past half century, this is not a particularly radical departure from conventional wisdom. But I suggest a corollary to this hypothesis, which I hope will lead to spirited debate: *For many Americans, multigenerational bonds are becoming more important than nuclear family ties for well-being and support over the course of their lives.*

I will attempt to provide a foundation for this hypothesis in the remainder of this article. First, I argue that changes in intergenerational demography (changing societal and family age structures, creating longer years of "shared lives") have resulted in increased opportunities—and needs—for interaction, support, and mutual influence across more than just two generations. Second, I will note the strength of intergenerational solidarity over time and the diversity of cross-generational types. Third, because the increase in marital instability and divorce over the last several decades has weakened the ability of nuclear families to provide the socialization, nurturance, and support needed by family members, I argue that kin across several generations will increasingly be called upon to provide these essential family functions in 21st-century society.

THE MACROSOCIOLOGY OF INTERGENERATIONAL RELATIONSHIPS

The demographic structure of American families has changed significantly in recent years. We hear most about two trends: The increase in divorce rates since the 1960s, with one out of two first marriages ending in divorce (Cherlin, 1992); and the increasing number of children living in single-parent households, often accompanied by poverty (McLanahan & Sandefur, 1994; Walker & McGraw, 2000). But there is a third trend that has received much less attention: The increased longevity of family members and the potential resource this represents for the well-being of younger generations in the family.

Multigenerational Family Demography: From Pyramids to Beanpoles

First consider how much the age structure of the U.S. population has changed over the past 100 years. Treas (1995b) provided a valuable overview of these changes and their consequences for families. In 1900, the shape of the American population structure by age was that of a pyramid, with a large base (represented by children under age 5) progressively tapering into a narrow group of those aged 65 and older. This pyramid characterized the shape of the population structure by age in most human societies on record, from the dawn of civilization through the early Industrial Revolution and into the early 20th century (Laslett, 1976; Myers, 1990). But by 1990, the age pyramid for American society had come to look more like an irregular triangle. By 2030, it will look more like a rectangle, with strikingly similar numbers in each age category starting from children and adolescents through those above the age of 60. The story here is that because of increases in longevity and decreases in fertility, the population age structure of the United States, like most industrialized societies, has changed from a pyramid to a rectangle in just over a century of human historical experience.

Second, consider the implications of these macrosocietal changes in age distribution for the generational structure of families in American society. At the same time, there have been increases in life expectancy over the 20th century, decreases in fertility have occurred, and the population birth-rate has decreased from 4.1 in 1900 to 1.9 in 1990 (Cherlin, 1999). This means that the age structure of most American families has changed from a pyramid to what might be described as a "beanpole" (Bengtson, Rosenthal, & Burton, 1990), a family structure in which the shape is long and thin, with more family generations alive but with fewer members in each generation. Whether the "beanpole" structure adequately describes a majority of families today has been debated (Farkas & Hogan, 1995; Treas, 1995a). Nevertheless, the changes in demographic distribution by age since 1900 are remarkable, and the progression "from pyramids to beanpoles" has important implications for family functions and relationships into the 21st century.

The changing "kin supply" structure across generations. What might be lost in a review of macrosocial demographic trends are the consequences for individual family members and their chances of receiving family support. For example, the "family decline" hypothesis of Popenoe (1993) suggests that U.S. children are at greater risk today because of the breakdown of the nuclear family structure and the too-frequent disappearance of fathers. The decrease in mortality rates over the last century suggests a more optimistic story, however: The increasing availability of extended intergenerational kin (grandparents, great-grandparents, uncles, and aunts) has become a resource for children as they grow up and move into young adulthood.

Peter Uhlenberg (1996) examined the profound effects that mortality changes over the 20th century have had on the "supply" of kin available for support of family members in American society. He noted that for children born in 1900, the chances of being an orphan (both parents dying before the child reached age 18) were 18%. But for children born in 2000, 68% will have four *grand*parents still living by the time they reach 18. Further along the life course, by the time these children are themselves facing the responsibilities of rearing children, the effects of mortality declines on the availability of older kin for support are even more substantial. For those born in 1900, by age 30 only 21% had *any* grandparent still living. For those born in 2000, by age 30, 76% will still have at least one grand-parent alive. Today it is more likely that 20-year-olds will have a grandmother still living (91%) than 20-year-olds alive in 1900 had a mother still living (83%; Uhlenberg).

Another perspective on this issue is provided by Wachter (1997) in computer sim-ulations about availability of kin for 21st-century family members. He examined impli-cations of longevity, fertility, and divorce for the future. He noted that although low fertility rates in the late 20th century will lead to a shortage of kin for those reaching re-tirement around 2030, the effects of divorce, remarriage, and family blending are ex-panding the numbers and types of stepkin, "endowing the elderly of the future with kin networks that are at once problematic, rich, and varied" (Wachter, p. 1181). The impli-cation is that stepkin are increasing the kin supply across generations, becoming poten-tial sources of nurture and support for family members in need, and that this may compensate, in part, for lower fertility rates (Amato & Booth, 1997).

Longer years of "shared lives" across generations. Other implications of these demo-graphic changes over the 20th century should be noted. First, we now have more years of "cosurvivorship between generations" than ever before in human history (Bengtson, 1996; Goldscheider, 1990). This means that more and more aging parents and grand-parents are available to provide for family continuity and stability across time (Silverstein, Giarrusso, & Bengtson, 1998). This also means a remarkable increase in multigenera-tional kin representing a "latent network" (Riley & Riley, 1993) who can be activated to provide support and well-being for younger family members. The increased longevity of parents, grandparents, great-grandparents, and other older family members in recent decades represents a resource of kin available for help and support that can be, and fre-quently is, activated in times of need (King, 1994; Silverstein, Parrott, & Bengtson, 1995). These older kin will also be in better health (Hayward & Heron, 1999).

At the same time, there are potentially negative consequences of the "longer years of shared lives" across generations. One involves protracted years of caregiving for de-pendent elders (Bengtson, Rosenthal, & Burton, 1995). A second involves protracted conflict—what a 84-year-old mother in the Longitudinal Study of Generations termed a "life-long lousy parent-child relationship." Family researchers have not adequately ad-dressed intergenerational conflicts throughout the adult years (Clarke, Preston, Raskin, & Bengtson,1999). Because of longer years of shared lives, intergenerational relation-ships—in terms of help given or received, solidarity or conflict or both—will be of in-creasing importance for family life in the future.

Finally, to the story of multigenerational family demography and its changes over the 21st century must be added a recognition of "alternative family forms," reflected in gay and lesbian couples raising children (Kurdek & Schmidt, 1987), never-married sin-gles and couples raising children (Smock & Manning, 1997), and other nonbiological but socially significant family forms. We know little about the intergenerational relationships of these variations beyond the White, middle-class, two-generation household in Amer-ica today. What they represent in "latent kin support networks" or "cosurvivorship across generations" must be a focus of future research.

When Parenting Goes Across Several Generations

A function not addressed by Burgess was the importance of grandparents to family 'mem-bers' well-being, an understandable oversight given the historical period when he was writing, when the expected life span of individuals was almost 3 decades shorter than today. Popenoe (1993) also did not discuss the importance of grandparents in the potential support they represent for younger generation members.

Grandparents provide many unacknowledged functions in contemporary families (Szinovacz, 1998). They are important role models in the socialization of grandchildren (Elder, Rudkin, & Conger, 1994; King & Elder 1997). They provide economic resources to younger generation family members (Bengtson & Harootyan, 1994). They contribute to cross-generational solidarity and family continuity over time (King, 1994; Silverstein et al., 1998). They also represent a bedrock of stability for teenage moms raising infants (Burton & Bengtson, 1985).

Perhaps most dramatic is the case in which grandparents (or great-grandparents) are raising grandchildren (or great-grandchildren). Over four million children under age 18 are living in a grandparent's household. Frequently this is because these childrens' parents are incapacitated (by imprisonment, drug addiction, violence, or psychiatric disorders) or unable to care for their offspring without assistance (Minkler & Rowe, 1993). Research by Harris (2000) indicates that about 20,000 children in Los Angeles County alone are now the responsibility of grandparents or great-grandparents because of recent court decisions concerning the parents' lack of competence. In Harris' study, one grandmother had been assigned by the court as guardian to 13 of her grandchildren, born to two of her daughters, each of whom had been repeatedly imprisoned on crack cocaine charges (Harris & Pedersen, 1997). Similar instances are related by Minkler and Rowe in their study of crack-addicted parents in the San Francisco area.

When Parents Divorce and Remarry, Divorce and Remarry

The rising divorce rate over the last half of the 20th century has generated much concern about the fate of children (McLanahan & Sandefur 1994). The probability that a marriage would end in divorce doubled between the 1960s and the 1970s, and half of all marriages since the late 1970s ended in divorce (Cherlin, 1992). About 40% of American children growing up in the 1980s and 1990s experienced the breakup of their parents' marriages (Bengtson, Rosenthal, & Burton, 1995; Furstenberg & Cherlin, 1991), and a majority of these also experienced their parents' remarriage and the challenges of a "blended family."

In the context of marital instability, the breakup of nuclear families, and the remarriage of parents, it is clear that grandparents and step-grandparents are becoming increasingly important family connections (Johnson & Barer, 1987). Two fifths of divorced mothers move during the first year of the divorce (McLanahan, 1983), and most of these move in with their parents while they make the transition to single parenting (Goldscheider & Goldscheider, 1993).

When Help Flows Across Generations, It Flows Mostly Downward

An unfortunate stereotype of the older generation today is of "greedy geezers" who are spending their children's inheritance on their own retirement pleasures (Bengtson, 1993). This myth is not in accord with the facts. Intergenerational patterns of help and assistance flow mostly from the older generations to younger generations in the family. For example, McGarry and Schoeni (1995) have shown that almost one third of U.S. parents gave a gift of $500 or more to at least one of their adult children during the past year; however, only 9% of adult children report providing $500 to their aging parents. Similar results are reported by Bengtson and Harootyan (1994) and Soldo and Hill (1993).

Silverstein et al. (1995) noted that intergenerational support patterns ebb and flow over time. Multigenerational families represent "latent kin networks" of support (Riley & Riley, 1993) that often are enacted only in times of crisis. This is similar to Hagestad's (1996) notion of elders as the "Family National Guard": Although remaining silent and unobserved for the most part, grandparents (and great-grandparents) muster up and march out when an emergency arises regarding younger generation members' well-being.

THE MICROSOCIOLOGY OF INTERGENERATIONAL RELATIONSHIPS

Although there have been important changes in the demography of intergenerational relationships since the 19th century, population statistics about family and household structure tell only one part of the story. At the behavioral level, these changes have more immediate consequences in the ways family members organize their lives and pursue their goals in the context of increasing years of intergenerational "shared lives." How to conceptualize and measure these intergenerational interactions has become increasingly important since Burgess (1926) put forth his definition of the family as "a unity of interacting personalities."

The Solidarity Model: Dimensions of Intergenerational Relationships

In discussing these social-psychological approaches to intergenerational relations, I should first identify the study from which my colleagues and I have examined them, the Longitudinal Study of Generations (LSOG). This study began as a cross-sectional survey of more than 2,044 three-generational family members, sampled from more than 840,000 members of the primary HMO serving Southern California at that time (see Bengtson, 1975 and 1996, for details of the sampling procedures). It has continued as a longitudinal study with data collected at 3-year intervals, adding the great-grandchild generation in 1991.

A concern in the LSOG since it began 3 decades ago has been the conceptualization and measurement of intergenerational relationships. We use the theoretical construct of *intergenerational solidarity* as a means to characterize the behavioral and emotional dimensions of interaction, cohesion, sentiment, and support between parents and children, grandparents and grandchildren, over the course of long-term relationships. We define six conceptual dimensions of intergenerational solidarity (Bengtson & Mangen, 1988; Bengtson & Schrader, 1982; Roberts, Richards, & Bengtson, 1991).

1. Affectual solidarity: the sentiments and evaluations family members express about their relationship with other members (How close do you feel to your father or

mother? How well do you get along with your child or grandchild? How much affection do you feel from them?)

2. Associational solidarity: the type and frequency of contact between intergenerational family members
3. Consensual solidarity: agreement in opinions, values, and orientations between generations
4. Functional solidarity (assistance): the giving and receiving of support across generations, including exchange of both instrumental assets and services as well as emotional support
5. Normative solidarity: expectations regarding filial obligations and parental obligations, as well as norms about the importance of familistic values
6. Structural solidarity: the "opportunity structure" for cross-generational interaction reflecting geographic proximity between family members

The theoretical rationale for these six dimensions and the adequacy (or limitations) of their measurement in survey research have been described at length in a volume by Mangen, Bengtson, and Landry (1988) and in subsequent articles (Roberts & Bengtson, 1990; Roberts et al., 1991; Silverstein et al., 1995). The solidarity paradigm has proven useful in research by other investigators (Amato & Booth, 1997; Lee, Netzer, & Coward, 1994; Marshall, Matthews, & Rosenthal, 1993; Rossi & Rossi, 1990). It can be seen as exemplifying an operational definition of the life course theoretical perspective (Bengtson & Allen, 1993; Elder, Rudkin, & Conger, 1994).

The Strength of Intergenerational Relationships Over Time

Using longitudinal data from the LSOG, we have been able to chart the course of intergenerational solidarity dimensions over time. Our design allows consideration of the development and aging of each of the three and now four generations in our sample, as well as the sociohistorical context of family life as it has changed over the years of the study (Bengtson et al., in press).

One consistent result concerns the high levels of affectual solidarity (reflecting the emotional bonds between generations) that have been found over six times of measurement, from 1971 to 1997 (Bengtson et al., 2000). Three things should be noted. We find that the average solidarity scores between grandparents and parents, parents and youth, grandparents and grandchildren are high, considerably above the expected midpoint of the scale. Second, these scores are remarkably stable over the 26 years of measurement; there are no statistically significant differences by time of measurement, and the scores are correlated over time between .5 and .8. Third, there is a "generational bias" in these reports: Parents consistently report higher affect than their children do over time, as do grandparents compared with grandchildren. This supports the "intergenerational stake" hypothesis first proposed 30 years ago (Bengtson & Kuypers, 1971; Giarrusso, Stallings, & Bengtson, 1995). The older generation has a greater psychosocial investment, or "stake," in their joint relationship than does their younger generation, and this influences their perceptions and evaluations of their common intergenerational relationships.

TABLE 1   *Constructing a Typology of Intergenerational Relationships Using Five Solidarity Variables*

Types of Relationships	Affect (Close)	Consensus (Agree)	Structure (Proximity)	Association (Contact)	Gives Help	Receives Help
Tight-Knit	+	+	+	+	+	+
Sociable	+	+	+	+	−	−
Intimate but Distant	+	+	−	−	−	−
Obligatory	−	−	+	+	(+)	(+)
Detached	−	−	−	−	−	−

These results indicate the high level of emotional bonding across generations and the considerable stability of parent-child affectual relationships over long periods of time.

At the same time, it should be noted that not all intergenerational relationships display such high levels of emotional closeness. We find that about one in five relationships are characterized by either significant conflict (Clarke et al., 1999) or detachment (as discussed next).

The Diversity of Intergenerational Relationships

To gain a better understanding of the complexity and contradictions of cross-generational relationships, we employed latent class analysis (LCA) to examine the typological structure underlying measurements of intergenerational solidarity in a nationally representative sample (Silverstein & Bengtson, 1997). This methodology allowed us to simultaneously contrast five solidarity dimensions, some congruent, others incongruent, in a multidimensional framework. We found five types or classes of intergenerational family relationships (see Table 1). One type we labeled "Tight-Knit," characterized by high emotional closeness, living fairly close to each other, interacting frequently, and having high levels of mutual help and support. This seems similar to what Parsons (1944) described as the ideal "modern family" type of relationship. At the other extreme is the "Detached" type, with low levels of connectedness in all of the observed measures of solidarity. This appears similar to what would be predicted by the "decline of the family" hypothesis. Between the Tight-Knit and the Detached are three classes which we called variegated types (Silverstein & Bengtson, p. 442). The "Sociable" and "Intimate-but-Distant" types seem similar to what Litwak (1960a) described as the "modified extended family" in which functional exchange is low or absent, but there are high levels of affinity that suggest the potential for future support and exchange. The "Obligatory" type suggests a high level of structural connectedness (proximity and interaction) with an average level of functional exchange, but a low level of emotional attachment.

We next assessed the distribution of the five types using a nationally representative sample from the American Association of Retired People Study of Intergenerational Linkages (see Bengtson & Harootyan, 1994, for details). The results suggest considerable diversity of intergenerational relationships in contemporary American society, particularly in terms of gender. When we examined responses from adult children concerning their interactions with parents (older fathers and mothers combined), we found surprisingly similar distributions across the five types of intergenerational relationships. The Tight-Knit and Sociable types each represented 25% of the sample; the Obligatory and Intimate-but-Distant types are each 16%; and the Detached type constitutes 17% (Silverstein & Bengtson, 1997). No one type is dominant, demonstrating the diversity of American family forms and styles.

We then looked at gender differences in these distributions—how relationships with older mothers compared with those with older fathers. Here we found significant contrasts, as indicated in Figure 1. At one extreme, relations with mothers were more likely to be Tight-Knit (31%) than were relations with fathers (20%). At the other, relations with fathers were 4 times as likely to be Detached (27%) that those with mothers (7%). In fact, the Detached represented the second most frequent type of relationship between older fathers and their adult children.

Next, we examined other predictors of differences in the distribution of intergenerational types: ethnicity and race, income (socioeconomic status), age, and gender of the child. There were no differences by income levels, nor were the results different in terms of the age or gender of the child. Nevertheless, we found important racial and ethnic variations. Blacks and Hispanics were less likely than non-Hispanic Whites to have obligatory relationships with mothers, and Blacks were less likely than Whites to have Detached relationships with mothers. This corresponds to other studies that have found stronger maternal attachments in Black and Hispanic families than within White families.

These results suggest the folly of using a "one size fits all" model of intergenerational relationships. There is considerable diversity among the types; there is no one modal type. Our findings reinforce the message of Burton (1995) in her enumeration of 16 structural types of relationships between teenage mothers and older generation family members: Diversity and complexity are inherent features of family networks across generations.

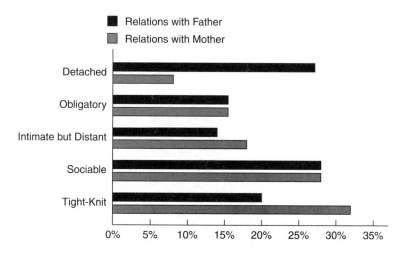

FIGURE 1 *Types of Intergenerational Relationships, by Gender of Parent*

The Effects of Changing Family Forms
on Intergenerational Influence

Situating multigenerational families in sociohistorical context allows us to broaden our inquiry about their importance and functionality. How have intergenerational influences changed over recent historical time? Are families still important in shaping the developmental outcomes of its youth? What have been the effects of changing family structures and roles, the consequences of divorce and maternal employment, on intergenerational influences? We used the 30-year LSOG to explore these issues.

An important feature of the LSOG is that enough time has elapsed since its start in 1971 that the ages at which members of different generations were assessed have begun to overlap. This provides what we call a generation-sequential design. A limitation of existing data sets has been that researchers could not track changes across generations within specific families over decades of time, nor draw conclusions about the relationship between historical change in family structures and intergenerational influence and socialization outcomes. The LSOG is unique because of its accumulation of parallel longitudinal assessments for multiple generations within the same families in different historical periods.

Within a life course framework that focuses on the interplay of macroeconomic and microrelational processes. Bengtson, Biblag, and Roberts (in press) examined the development and cultivation of youth's achievement orientations: Their educational and occupation career aspirations, their values, and their self-esteem. Achievement orientations are viewed as personal attributes that may be passed down, or "transmitted," from generation to generation in families, promoting continuity over multiple generational lines across many decades of history. We also know that parent-child affectual bonds can mediate this process. It is therefore useful to study these intergenerational transmission processes. In so doing, we can empirically examine the hypotheses concerning family decline or intergenerational family importance and diversity.

Our analysis (Bengtson et al., in press) contrasted the achievement orientations of Generation X youth (18- to 22-year-olds) today with their baby-boomer parents when they were about the same age in 1971. We know that Generation Xers have grown up in families that were quite different in structure than their parents' families were. How has this affected their achievement orientations: their aspirations, values, and self-esteem?

Figure 2 illustrates just how different the family context of these two successive generations has been. Generation Xers were much more likely than their baby-boomer parents to have grown up in a family with less than two siblings, with a father and mother who were college graduates, with a mother who was working full time, and, above all, in a divorced household (40% for Generation Xers, 20% for their baby-boomer parents). Given these differences, how do the two generations compare in terms of family solidarity and achievement orientations?

Our analysis suggests that today's Generation Xers are surprisingly similar to what their baby-boomer parents were on these measures at the same age, almost 30 years ago. This suggests that despite changes in family structure and socioeconomic context, intergenerational influences on youths' achievement orientations remain strong. Generation Xers whose parents divorced were slightly less advantaged in terms of achievement orientations than Generation Xers who came from nondivorced families but were nevertheless higher on these outcome measures than were their baby-boomer parents at the same age, regardless of

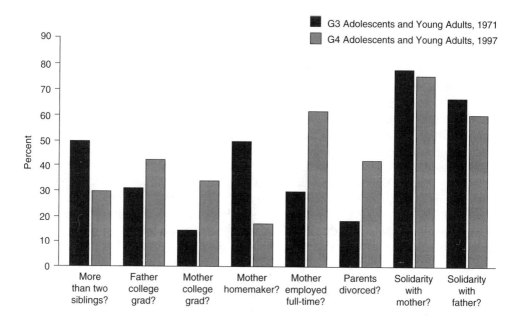

FIGURE 2 *Historical Changes in Family Structure and Parental Attributes: "Generation X" Compared with Their Baby-Boomer Parents at the Same Age*

family structure. We also found that maternal employment has not negatively affected the aspirations, values, and self-esteem of youth across these two generations, despite the dramatic increase in women's labor force participation over the past 3 decades. Finally, we found that Generation X women have considerably higher educational and occupational aspirations in 1997 than did their baby-boomer mothers almost 30 Years before. In Fact, Generation X young women's aspirations were higher than Generation X young men's.

These findings challenge the hypothesis that families are declining in function and influence and that "alternative" family structures spell the downfall of American youth. Multigenerational families continue to perform their functions in the face of recent social change and varied family forms.

Implications for Muitigenerational Family Research

The intergenerational solidarity research model represents only a start at understanding the processes and dynamics of multigenerational relationships over time. Nevertheless, it is a start, and the research that my colleagues and I have been pursuing over the past 2 decades suggests several things about family relationships.

First, intergenerational relationships *are* complex (Amato & Booth 1997; Szinovacz, 1998). They involve not only demographic configurations (the number and availability of kin) but also opportunity structures for interaction (geographic proximity). They reflect not only behaviors (frequency of contact, help given and received) but also emotional-cognitive dimensions (feelings of closeness and bonding, similarity of values and opinions). They concern not only intergenerational exchanges that can be counted (the amount of financial support given to or received from other generation members) but also normative issues (filial obligations and values about the importance of family relationships) that may lead to help given or received in the future. In short, there are multiple dimensions of intergenerational relationships. Most research to date has focused only on the demography of intergenerational relationships (family structures and the proximity of family members to each other) or on behaviors such as contacts and exchanges of tangible assets between generations. Emotional-cognitive and normative dimensions of intergenerational relations deserve equal attention in research, however (Rossi & Rossi, 1990).

Second, our studies suggest that the multifaceted nature of intergenerational relationships can be summarized with a relatively small number of concepts. For example, the five solidarity measures can be examined simultaneously; this results in five multidimensional types ranging from the Tight-Knit to the Detached. Interestingly, these types appear to be distributed fairly evenly across a sample of U.S. adults. No one type predominates: With one fourth of the intergenerational relationships categorized as Tight-Knit and another one sixth categorized as Detached, this suggests considerable diversity in family intergenerational relationships today.

Third, if these data were used to test Popenoe's "family decline" hypothesis, there is little to support it here. In contrast, there is support for the views advanced by feminist scholars concerning significant gender contrasts in family relationships: Relations of adult children with older fathers are much more likely to be Detached, whereas those with mothers are more likely to be Tight-Knit. Moreover, we found that U.S. families continue to perform their socialization function across successive generations, transmitting aspirations, values, and self-esteem, even when parents are divorced.

There are other issues that should be pursued. For example, we must recognize that conflict is another important dimension in intergenerational relationships (Clarke et al., 1999) and the "paradox between conflict and solidarity" (Bengtson et al., 1995, p. 351) is characteristic of most parent-child relations. Others have termed this "intergenerational ambivalence" (Luescher & Pillemer, 1998). Regardless of how we label it, we need more research on the nature and sources of intergenerational conflict, in the context of the extensive solidarity that many families seem to exhibit over time (Richlin-Klonsky & Bengtson, 1996).

Finally, our research paradigm is primarily based on survey data and quantitative analyses. These are ideal for examining central tendencies and distributions over a large sample but mask nuances and individual variation in responses. In addition, survey results are limited to dyads (a parent and a child), making the analysis of "whole" multigenerational families problematic (Hagestad, 1996). We have conducted qualitative studies that parallel our development of the solidarity paradigm, and these have revealed important themes in multigenerational family progress over time. One is the "drifting apart, coming together" history of one multigenerational family over time (Richlin-Klonsky & Bengtson, 1996). A second story is the contrast between "collectivistic and individualistic" family caregiving strategies in 20 multigenerational families (Pyke & Bengtson, 1996). A third story is the contrasting "family narratives" in four-generational families examined over decades of time (Gardner, Preston, & Bengtson, 1998). The insights from these studies suggest to me that the further exploration of multigenerational family issues will be advanced best by a combination of methods: qualitative studies focusing on a few families leading the way in generating new hypotheses, which can then be tested using large-scale survey data.

MULTIGENERATIONAL FAMILY BONDS: MORE IMPORTANT THAN EVER BEFORE?

My hypothesis is that multigenerational family bonds are important, more so than family research has acknowledged to date. I have argued that demographic changes over the 20th century ("from pyramids to beanpoles" and "longer years of shared lives") have important implications for families in the 21st century, particularly with regard to the "latent network" of family support across generations. I have suggested that multigenerational relationships are increasingly diverse in structure and functions within American society. I propose that because the increase in marital instability and divorce have weakened so many nuclear families, these multigenerational bonds will not only enhance but in some cases replace some of the nuclear family functions that have been the focus of so much recent debate.

To test this hypothesis concerning the increasing importance of multigenerational bonds will require research such as the following: First, we will need to examine longitudinal data to trace the salience over time of the multigenerational model. My argument (following Riley & Riley 1993) is that multigenerational relations represent a "latent kin network" that may be inactive and unacknowledged for long periods of time, until a family crisis occurs. Such is the case when grandparents are called to help in the raising of grandchildren; when family elders become incapacitated and adult children and other kin provide caregiving support. Fortunately, by now we have several large ongoing longitudinal studies (such as the National Survey of Families and Households, Health and Retirement Survey, Analysis of Household Economics and Demography, etc.) that can be used to examine the activation of latent kin networks over time.

We will need trend data so as to examine whether multigenerational families are indeed interacting more and fulfilling more functions for members in the 21st century than in the past. We need to explore how trends in longevity, elder health, the bean pole intergenerational structure, and the aging of baby boomers are affecting intergenerational solidarity and support.

Third, we need more data on the ethnic and racial diversity of American family forms. We need to examine multigenerational influences across and within special populations, such as minority families and first- and second-generation immigrants. For example, considerable evidence shows that for many African Americans, extended kin relationships are more salient than they are for White families (Burton, 1995). As has been observed so many times in our recent history, minority patterns can signal changes on the horizon for White majority families.

We also need data reflecting the increasing diversity of American family forms beyond biological and conjugal relationships. We need to examine the multigenerational relationships of gay and lesbian families and of never-married parents.

We need cross-national data to examine how multigenerational relations are changing and the implications of these changes. For example, in the face of rapid industrialization and population aging, we are seeing changes in the meaning and expression of "filial piety" in Asian societies. In Korea and Japan, for example, multigenerational household sharing is becoming less prevalent (Bengtson & Putney, 2000). What does this imply in terms of Confucian norms about caring for one's parents? We need also to examine the changing mix between state and family provisions for the elderly. Paradoxically, it appears that Eastern societies are becoming more dependent on state provisions for the elderly, whereas Western societies are facing declining governmental resources and placing more responsibilities on families (Bengtson & Putney).

Finally, we need to focus on policy implications of the growing importance of multigenerational bonds. What can be done to strengthen multigenerational family supports? Grandparent visitation rights have been challenged recently in the U.S. Supreme Court; what does this mean in light of other court decisions to place more responsibility on grandparents as court-mandated guardians of grandchildren?

CONCLUSION: BEYOND THE NUCLEAR FAMILY

Are families declining in importance within American society? Seven decades ago, Ernest W. Burgess addressed this question from the standpoint of family transformations across the 19th and 20th centuries. His hypothesis was that families and their functions had changed from a social institution based on law and custom to a set of relationships based on emotional affect and companionship (Burgess, 1926). But this did not mean a loss of social importance. He suggested that the modern family should be considered as "a unity of interacting personalities" (Burgess) and that future research should focus on the interactional dynamics within families. In all this, Burgess' focus, and that of those who followed him (Ogburn, 1932; Parsons, 1944), was on the nuclear family form.

Seven decades later, this question—are families declining in importance?—has resurfaced. Some family experts have hypothesized that families have lost most of their social functions along with their diminished structures because of high divorce rates and the growing absence of fathers in the lives of many children (Popenoe, 1993). A contrasting hypothesis is that families are becoming more diverse in structure and forms (Skolnick, 1991; Stacey, 1996).

In this article, I have suggested another hypothesis, one that goes beyond our previous preoccupation with the nuclear or two-generation family structure. This concerns the increasing importance of multigenerational bonds and the multigenerational extension of family functions. I want to be clear about this hypothesis because it differs from contemporary wisdom about the most pressing problems of American families today and because I hope it will generate much debate. I have proposed that (a) multigenerational relationships (these involving three or more generations) are becoming increasingly important to individuals and families in American society; (b) these multigenerational relationships are increasingly diverse in structure and functions; and (c) for many Americans, multigenerational bonds are becoming more important than nuclear family ties for well-being and support over the course of their lives.

Burgess was right, many decades ago: The American family is in transition. But it is not only in transition "from institution to companionship," as he argued. Over the century, there have been significant changes in the family's structure and functions.

Prominent among them has been the extension of family bonds, of affection and affirmation, of help and support, across several generations, whether these be biological ties or the creation of kinlike relationship. But as families have changed, they have not necessarily declined in importance. The increasing prevalence and importance of multigenerational bonds represents a valuable new resource for families in the 21st century.

Note

I want to acknowledge my debt for this award to Roseann Giarrusso, Merril Silverstein, Robert Roberts, and Timothy Biblarz, my coinvestigators in the Longitudinal Study of Generations over many years. I also want to thank my students at the University of Southern California, particularly Stephen Conroy, Mary Gardner, Susan Harris, Anne Marenco, Betty Oswald, Norella Putney, Maria Schmeeckle, Brent Taylor, Ynes Wilson-Hirst, and Dr. Beth Mabry who (with Danielle Zucker from Stanford) have helped me through several drafts of this paper. I appreciate the suggestions of Paul Amato, Alan Booth, Arlene Skolnick, Judith Stacey, and Peter Uhlenberg, from whose work I have learned a great deal. Finally, I want to acknowledge the assistance of Linda Hall and Deborah Weisberg in the preparation of the paper and the administration of our research program. The Longitudinal Study of Generations has been supported for many years by the National Institute on Aging (Grant AG07977), and I want to thank NIA social science administrators Matilda White Riley, Ron Abeles, Jared Jobe, and Richard Suzman for their support at crucial times in this longitudinal investigation. Thanks also to the Spencer Foundation and The James Irvine Foundation for funding some portions of this research.

References

Ahrons, C. R. (1994). *The good divorce.* New York: HarperCollins

Amato, P., & Booth, A. (1997). *A generation at risk: Growing up in an era of family upheaval.* Cambridge, MA: Harvard.

Bengtson, V. L. (1975). Generations and family effects in value socialization. *American Sociological Review, 40,* 358–371.

Bengtson, V L. (1993). Is the "contract across generations" changing? Effects of population aging on obligations and expectations across age groups. In V. L. Bengtson & W. A. Achenbaum (Eds.), *The changing contract across generations* (pp. 3–24). New York: Aldine de Gruyter.

Bengtson, V. L. (1996). Continuities and discontinuities in intergenerational relationships over time. In V. L. Bengtson (Ed.), *Adulthood and aging: Research on continuities and discontinuities.* New York: Springer.

Bengtson, V. L., & Allen, K. R. (1993). The life course perspective applied to families over time. In P. Boss, W. Doherty, R. LaRossa, W. Schumm, & S. Steinmetz (Eds.), *Sourcebook of family theories and methods: A contextual approach* (pp. 469–498). New York: Plenum Press.

Bengtson, V. L., Biblarz, T., Clarke, E., Giarrusso, R., Roberts, R. E. L., Richlin-Klonsky, J., & Silverstein, M. (2000). Intergenerational relationships and aging: Families, cohorts, and social change. In J. M. Claire & R. M. Allman (Eds.), *The gerontological prism: Developing interdisciplinary bridges.* Amityville, NY: Baywood.

Bengtson, V. L., Biblarz, T. L., & Roberts, R. E. L. (in press). *Generation X and their elders.* New York: Cambridge University Press.

Bengtson, V. L., & Harootyan, R. (Eds.). (1994). *Intergenerational linkages: Hidden connections in American society.* New York: Springer.

Bengtson, V. L., & Kuypers, J. A. (1971). Generational difference and the "developmental stake." *Aging and Human Development, 2,* 249–260.

Bengtson, V. L., & Mangen, D. J. (1988). Family intergenerational solidarity revisited. In D. J. Mangen, V. L. Bengtson, & P. H. Landry (Eds.), *Measurement of intergenerational relations* (pp. 222–238). Newbury Park, CA: Sage.

Bengtson, V. L., & Putney, N. (2000). Who will care for the elderly? Consequences of population aging East and West. In K. D. Kim, V. L. Bengtson, G. C. Meyers, and K. S. Eun (Eds.), *Aging in East and West: Families, states and the elderly.* New York: Springer.

Bengtson, V. L., Rosenthal, C. J., & Burton, L. M. (1990). Families and aging: Diversity and heterogeneity. In R. Binstock & L. George (Eds.), *Handbook of aging and the social sciences* (3rd ed., pp. 263–287). New York: Academic Press.

Bengtson, V. L., Rosenthal, C. J., & Burton, L. M. (1995). Paradoxes of families and aging. In R. H. Binstock & L. K. George (Eds.), *Handbook of aging and the social sciences* (4th ed., pp. 253–282). San Diego, CA: Academic Press.

Bengtson, V. L., & Schrader, S. S. (1982). Parent-child relations. In D. Mangen & W. Peterson (Eds.), *Handbook of research instruments in social gerontology,* (Vol. 2, pp. 115–185). Minneapolis: University of Minnesota Press.

Bogue, D. J. (1974). *The basic writing of Ernest W. Burgess.* Chicago: University of Chicago Press.

Bumpass, L. L., Sweet, J., & Martin, C. (1990). Changing patterns of remarriage. *Journal of Marriage and the Family, 52,* 747–756.

Burgess, E. W. (1916). *The function of socialization in social evolution.* Chicago: University of Chicago Press.

Burgess, E. W. (1926). The family as a unity of interacting personalities. *The Family, 7,* 3–9.

Burgess, E. W. (1960). Aging in western culture. In E. W. Burgess (Ed.), *Aging in western societies* (pp. 3–28). Chicago: University of Chicago Press.

Burton, L. (1995). Intergenerational patterns of providing care in African-American families with teenage childbearers: Emergent patterns in an ethnographic study. In V. L. Bengtson, K. W. Schaie, & L. M. Burton (Eds.), *Adult intergenerational relations* (pp. 79–97). New York: Springer.

Burton, L. M., & Bengtson, V. L. (1985). Black grandmothers: Issues of timing and continuity in roles. In V. Bengtson & J. Robertson (Eds.), *Grandparenthood* (pp. 304–338). Beverly Hills, CA: Sage.

Cherlin, A. J. (1992). *Marriage, divorce, remarriage* (rev. and enlarged ed.). Cambridge, MA: Harvard University Press.

Cherlin, A. J. (1999). *Public and private families.* Boston: McGraw-Hill.

Clarke, E., Preston, M., Raksin, J., & Bengtson, V. L. (1999). Types of conflicts and tensions between older parents and adult children. *Gerontologist, 39,* 261–270.

Collins, P. H. (1990). *Black feminist thought.* New York: Routledge.

Coontz, S. (1991). *The way we never were.* New York: Basic Books.

Davis, K. (1941). Family structure and functions. *American Sociological Review, 8,* 311–320.

Elder, G. H., Rudkin, L., & Conger, R. D. (1994). Intergenerational continuity and change in rural America. In K. W. Schaie, V. Bengtson, & L. Burton (Eds.), *Societal impact on aging: Intergenerational perspectives.* New York: Springer.

Farkas, J., & Hogan, D. (1995). The demography of changing intergenerational relationships. In V. L. Bengtson, K. Warner Schaie, & L. M. Burton (Eds.), *Adult intergenerational relations: Effects of societal change* (pp. 1–19). New York: Springer.

Furstenberg, E., & Cherlin, A. (1991). *Divided families: What happens to children when parents part.* Cambridge, MA: Harvard University Press.

Gardner, M., Preston, M., & Bengtson, V. L. (1998, August). For better or worse: A longitudinal comparison of family well-being in two four-generation families. Paper presented at the annual meeting of the American Sociological Association, San Francisco, CA.

Giarrusso, R., Stallings, M., & Bengtson, V. L. (1995). The "intergenerational stake" hypothesis revisited: Parent-child differences in perceptions of relationship 20 years later. In V. L. Bengtson, K. W. Schaie, & L. M. Burton (Eds.), *Adult intergenerational relations: Effects of societal change* (pp. 227–263). New York: Springer.

Goldscheider, F. K. (1990). The aging of the gender revolution: What do we know and what do we need to? *Research on Aging, 12,* 531–545.

Goldscheider, F. K., & Goldscheider, C. (1993). *Leaving before marriage: Ethnicity, familism, and generational relationships.* Madison: University of Wisconsin Press.

Hagestad, G. O. (1996). On-time, off-time, out of time? Reflections on continuity and discontinuity from an process. In V. L. Bengtson (Ed.), *Adulthood and aging: Research on continuities and discontinuities* 204–222), New York: Springer.

Harris, S. C. (2000). *Grandmothers raising grandchildren: An ethnography of family life and life in "The System." Dissertation in progress: University of Southern California, Los Angeles.*

Harris, S. C., & Pedersen, H. L. (1997, October). *Grandparents who parent.* Paper presented at the American Association for Marriage and Family Therapists, Atlanta, GA.

Hayward, M. D., & Heron, M. (1999). Racial inequality in active life among adult Americans. *Demography, 36,* 77–91.

Johnson, C. L., & Barer, B. M. (1987). Marital instability and the changing kinship networks of grandparents. *Gerontologist, 27,* 330–335.

King, V. (1994). Variation in the consequences of non-resident father involvement for children's well-being. *Journal of Marriage and the Family, 56,* 963–972.

King, V., & Elder G. H., Jr. (1997). The legacy of grandparenting: Childhood experiences with grandparents and current involvement with grandchildren. *Journal of Marriage and the Family, 59,* 848–859.

Kurdek, L. A., & Schmidt, J. P. (1987). Perceived emotional support from family and friends in members of homosexual, married, and heterosexual cohabiting couples. *Journal of Homosexuality, 14,* 57–68.

Laslett, P. (1976). Societal development and aging. In R. Binstock & E. Shanas (Eds.), *Handbook of aging and the social sciences* (pp. 87–116). New York: Van Nostrand Reinhold.

Lee, G. R., Netzer, J. K., & Coward, R. T. (1994). Filial responsibility expectations and patterns of intergenerational assistance. *Journal of Marriage and the Family, 56,* 559–565.

Litwak, E. (1960a). Geographic mobility and extended family cohesion. *American Sociological Review, 25,* 385–394.

Luescher, K., & Pillemer, K. (1998). Intergenerational ambiguity. *Journal of Marriage and the Family, 60,* 413–425.

Mangen, D. J., Bengtson, V. L., & Landry, P. H., Jr. (Eds.). (1988). *The measurement of intergenerational relations.* Beverly Hills, CA: Sage.

Marshall, V. W., Matthews, S. H., & Rosenthal, C. J. (1993). Elusiveness of family life: A challenge for the sociology of aging. In G. L. Maddox, & M. P. Lawton (Eds.), *Kinship, aging, and social change. Annual review of gerontology and geriatrics, Vol. 13* (pp. 39–74). New York: Springer.

McGarry, K., & Schoeni, R. F. (1995). Transfer behavior in the health and retirement study. *Journal of Human Resources, 30* (Suppl.), S184–S226.

McLanahan, S. S. (1983). Family structure and stress: A longitudinal comparison of two-parent and female-headed families. *Journal of Marriage and the Family, 45,* 347–357.

McLanahan, S. S. (1994). The consequences of single motherhood. *American Prospect, 18,* 94–58.

McLanahan, S. S., & Sandefur, G. (1994). *Growing up with a single parent: What helps, what hurts.* Cambridge, MA: Harvard University Press.

Minkler, M., & Roe, J. (1993). *Grandparents as caregivers.* Newbury Park, CA: Sage.

Myers, G. (1990). Demography of aging. In R. Binstock & L. George (Eds.), *Handbook of aging and the social sciences* (3rd ed., pp. 19–44). New York: Academic Press.

Ogburn, W. E. (1932). The family and its functions. In W. F. Ogburn's, *Recent social trends.* New York: McGraw-Hill.

Osmond, M. W., & Thorne, B. (1993). Feminist theories: The social construction of gender in families and society. (pp. 591–623). In P. G. Boss, W. J. Doherty, R. La Rossa, W. R. Schumm, & S. K. Steinmetz (Eds.), *Sourcebook of family methods and theories.* New York. Plenum Press.

Parsons, T. (1944). The social structure of the family. In R. N. Anshen (Ed.), *The family: Its function and destiny* (pp. 173–201). New York: Harper.

Popenoe, D. (1993). American family decline, 1960–1990: A review and appraisal. *Journal of Marriage and the Family, 55,* 527–555.

Popenoe, D. (1996). *Life without father: Compelling new evidence that fatherhood and marriage are indispensable for the good of children and society.* New York: Free Press.

Pyke, K. D., & Bengtson, V. L. (1996). Caring more or less: Individualistic and collectivist systems of family eldercare. *Journal of Marriage and the Family, 58,* 1–14.

Richlin-Klonsky, J., & Bengtson, V. L. (1996). Pulling together, drifting apart: A longitudinal case study of a four-generation family. *Journal of Aging Studies, 10,* 255–279.

Riley, M. W., & Riley, J. W. (1993). Connections: Kin and cohort. In V. L. Bengtson & W. A. Achen-baum (Eds.), *The changing contract across generations.* New York: Aldine de Gruyter.

Roberts, R. E. L., & Bengtson, V. L. (1990). Is intergenerational solidarity a unidimensional construct? A second test of a formal model. *Journal of Gerontology: Social Sciences, 45,* S12–S20.

Roberts, R. E. L., Richards, L. N., & Bengtson, V. L. (1991). Intergenerational solidarity in families: Un-tangling the ties that bind. In S. K. Pfeifer & M. B. Sussman (Eds.), *Marriage and Family Review, Vol. 16* (pp. 11–46). Binghamton, NY: Haworth Press.

Rossi, A., & Rossi, P. (1990). *Of human bonding: Parent-child relations across the life course.* New York: Al-dine de Gruyter.

Silverstein, M., & Bengtson, V. L. (1997). Intergenerational solidarity and the structure of adult child-parent relationships in American families. *American Journal of Sociology, 103,* 429–460.

Silverstein, M., & Litwak, E. (1993). A task-specific typology of intergenerational family structure in later life. *Gerontologist, 33,* 256–264.

Silverstein, M., Giarrusso, R., & Bengtson, V. L. (1998). Intergenerational solidarity and the grandpar-ent role. In M. Szinovacz (Ed.), *Handbook on grandparenthood* (pp. 144–158). Westport, CT Green-wood Press.

Silverstein, M., Parrott, T. M., & Bengtson, V. L. (1995). Factors that predispose middle-aged sons and daughters to provide social support to older parents. *Journal of Marriage and the Family, 57,* 465–475.

Skolnick, A. (1991). *Embattled paradise: The American family in an age of uncertainty.* New York: Basic Books.

Smock, P. J., & Manning, W. D. (1997). Nonresident parents; characteristics and child support. *Journal of Marriage and the Family, 59,* 798–808.

Soldo, B. J., & Hill, M. S. (1993). Intergenerational transfers: Economic, demographic, and social per-spectives. *Annual Review of Gerontology and Geriatrics, 13,* 187–216.

Stacey, J. (1990). *Brave new families: Stories of domestic upheaval in late twentieth century America.* New York: Basic Books

Stacey, J. (1993). Is the sky falling? *Journal of Marriage and the Family, 55,* 555–559.

Stacey, J. (1996). *In the name of the family: Rethinking family values in the postmodern age.* Boston: Beacon Press.

Stacey, J., & Biblarz, T. (in press). How does the sexual orientation of parents matter? *American Socio-logical Review.*

Stack, C. (1974). *All our kin: Strategies for survival in a Black community.* New York: Harper and Row.

Szinovacz, M. (1998). *Handbook on grandparenthood.* Westport CT: Greenwood Press.

Thorne, B., & Yalom, M. (1992) *Rethinking the family: Some feminist questions.* Boston: Northeastern Uni-versity Press.

Treas, J. (1995a). Commentary: Beanpole or beanstalk? Comments on "The Demography of Changing Intergenerational Relations." In V. L. Bengtson, K. W. Schaie, & L. M. Burton (Eds.), *Adult in-tergenerational relations* (pp. 26–29). New York: Springer.

Treas, J. (1995b). Older Americans in the 1990s and beyond. *Population Bulletin, 50,* 2–46.

Troll, L. (1985). The contingencies of grandparenting. In V. L. Bengtson & J. Robertson (Eds.), *Grand-parenthood* (pp. 135–150). Beverly Hills, CA: Sage.

Uhlenberg, P. (1996). Mutual attraction: Demography and lifecourse analysis. *Gerontologist, 36,* 226–229.

Wachter, K. W. (1997). Kinship resources for the elderly. *Philosophical transactions of the Royal Society of London, 352,* 1811–1817.

Walker, A. J., & McGraw, L. A. (2000). Who is responsible for responsible fathering? *Journal of Mar-riage and the Family, 62,* 563–569.

11 *Trouble in the Family*

Why Do They Do It?

Kristin Luker

It's difficult to be the mother of a very young child. It's more difficult still when the mother is a teenager. And if she's not only a teen but unmarried, her life can be even grimmer than the most outspoken opponents of early childbearing can imagine. Many young mothers, when asked about their situation, readily describe how hard it is to raise a child. For some of them, having a baby was a serious mistake.

> I'm not living with my family. I'm living with a friend. It's really bleak and confusing. I miss everything I left behind. (Christina, seventeen, white, Colorado)

> If I thought I didn't have freedom before the baby, I didn't know what freedom was. My parents watch every step I take. After all, they are paying for me and my baby. (Holly, sixteen, white, Colorado)

> After they cut Marquis's umbilical cord, they just put him up on me and I told 'em, "Get that ugly baby off of me!" He was all covered with blood. It upset me. They took him, washed him off, put him back in my arms. I was just so tired. All I could say was, "He look just like William." And I turned my head to the other side. It took me a long time to get use to Marquis. I didn't want to accept at fifteen I have a baby. It took me about two months to get use, to get really use to Marquis. (Sherita, fifteen, black, Washington, D.C.)

> I was going to have an abortion since I was only fifteen, but my family talked me out of it because of their religion. I love my baby now, but I'm only sixteen. I feel like I'm still a child—and here I have a child. It's completely changed my life. I look at other sixteen-year-olds and know that I can never be like them again. I sometimes wonder if an abortion wouldn't have been better. (Angela, sixteen, white, Colorado)

> It's hard to be a parent by yourself. If I had it to do over again, I'd do things really different. When people tell you it's going to be difficult, believe them. My child is with me all

the time . . . shopping, school, wherever I go. It's even harder than they say it is. I knew it would be hard, but not this hard.

Why is it that young people have babies, despite these depressing stories in which teens frankly admit how difficult it is for them to be mothers, and despite the national consensus that it's a very bad idea? No one in the United States is in favor of early child-bearing: elected officials campaign against it, the public disapproves of it, and professionals warn that it is costly for everyone concerned. Even the group thought to be most accepting of unwed teenage mothers—the African American community—is far more disapproving than most people think. Acceptance of a teenage mother or father is not the same as approval: young mothers, both black and white, often report widespread censure from those around them. Their own mothers, many of whom were once teenage mothers themselves and were hoping for a better life for their daughters, sometimes express a disappointment bordering on rage.

So why do they do it? Why do approximately one million young women get pregnant each year? More than half a million carry their babies to term, and about two-thirds of them will be unmarried when they give birth. Certainly, adolescents live in a world very different from that of adults, but the evidence suggests that age is not the only factor leading teenagers to reject the path those older and wiser would choose for them. Through their actions, teens are trying to come to terms, sometimes ineptly, with the immense social and economic challenges they face in today's world: a shrinking job market, an indifferent community network, and public skepticism about the worth of minorities. Early pregnancy and childbearing are not an isolated problem restricted to a small but growing number of poor, young, and minority women; they are the result of an array of problems in American society—problems that have no easy solutions. Unwed teenage mothers are pioneers on a frontier where increasing numbers of Americans are now settling.

DREAMS AND REALITIES

Today, half of all marriages end in divorce, only half of divorced fathers make their full court-ordered child support payments, and unwed fathers visit their children more often than divorced fathers who have remarried. Even as the cultural meanings of "husband" and "wife" are shifting, men and women are expected to work in the paid labor force for much of their adult lives. Although there are still "men's jobs" and "women's jobs," one can no longer automatically assume that the former are better paid and more secure than the latter. In the tidy world of the 1950s, society expected that women would be virgins when they married (or at least when they got engaged); would remain married throughout their lives to the same man; would stay home, take care of the housework, and raise the children while their husband worked at a stable, well-paid job that he would keep until he decided to retire. This predictable scenario no longer exists for today's teenagers, although many of its cultural ideals live on in their dreams.

What it means to be an adult man or woman is now in constant flux, and we do not yet live in a world of perfect gender equality. Indeed, the sexual revolution seems to have stalled: women have taken on many of the responsibilities of men, but men have yet to assume their fair share of the nurturing and caretaking roles traditionally assigned to women. On the one hard, a young woman can no longer expect that she will have a husband on whom she can be totally dependent, both economically and emotionally. On the other hand, she can't expect a husband to share the burdens of child rearing and homemaking equally. Such changes in gender roles intersect with new uncertainties surrounding the meanings of race and class in American society. Between World War II and 1973, when wages were steadily rising, minorities and blue-collar workers could hope for the same job mobility and financial stability that white professionals enjoyed. But today's young people must compete intensely for jobs that are increasingly scarce, and must strive to meet meritocratic criteria that punish the less advantaged. They confront the future with far less assurance.

Young women in particular are finding life extremely complex. The rules that applied in their mothers' day were simple, at least in theory: do what it takes to get a good man, and keep him happy. Now women are aware of what this formula can lead to: displaced homemakers, divorcees and widows who are unprepared to support themselves, women who think they have no value unless they have a male partner. But dreams die hard. Today's young women say that they want a career in addition to, not instead of, a family life. No teenager hopes to end up as an unmarried mother on welfare. Although many disadvantaged teens do dream of motherhood, they dream of white-picket-fence motherhood, or at least the version of it to which girls from poor neighborhoods can realistically aspire.

> I want to have an average American life, not the average Puerto Rican life with a break-up here and a fight there. (Diane, Hispanic, New Jersey)

> [I see myself] mainly being a housewife, a mother, and probably going to school, trying to get my trade or something like that. I want me a job too, but jobs is so hard to find. I want one through the University. My sister told me, she said, "You can't be picky and choosy." So I told her, "Okay, I guess I just want me a job so bad." (Roberta, eighteen, black, Florida)

> I don't want to be dependent on my parents for the rest of my life. I want to help out, even though my parents aren't putting any pressure on me. (Woman from rural New England, eighteen, white)

> I want to live in a two-bedroom apartment with a TV and carpeting. Nice and clean. If I'm older I have a car. I'd rather work at night and have somebody be there or early in the morning and come home by two or three. Other than that I be satisfied. Once I do what I want to do, I don't go back, I keep going. That's what I want to do. Get on my own with my baby and get situated. You know, I be having a good job. (Young woman living in an East Coast city)

> I want to be a good mother, giving my kid all, everythin', and makin' my kids go to school, college, somethin' that I can't get.

Unfortunately, the odds against achieving even these modest dreams are getting longer. Young women with limited educational and labor market skills face many more obstacles to a stable relationship and a secure job than they used to, especially when they are members of minority groups and come from poor homes. And the young men in their lives have bleaker employment prospects than ever, making them a slender reed for young women to rely upon. Roberta's sister is right: when it comes to men and jobs, these young women can't be "picky and choosy." But even their willingness to be adaptable may not ensure that they get what they want.

It is hard for young people who have grown up in poverty to figure out how to make their dreams come true, how to negotiate the small steps that get them from one point to another. Moreover, young women of all classes must find a way to balance investments in their own future with commitment to a partner. Women have always had to decide whether and when to make such "selfish" investments, as opposed to devoting their energies to meeting the needs of a partner and children. Today they have to make decisions whose outcomes cannot be known. And teens of both sexes are on radically new terrain when it comes to making choices about sexual activity, marriage, family, and work. The sexual revolution has transformed Americans' values, attitudes, and behavior in ways that are unlikely to be reversed. How do teens—should teens—think and act in this new world, and reconcile its alluring promises with its hard realities? How can they manage the consequences of their sexual freedom?

Many people of all political persuasions think that teenagers should simply stop having sex. Liberals argue that public campaigns have induced teenagers to curtail their drug use and that such campaigns could likewise induce them to abstain from sex; conservatives plead for "a little virginity." Unfortunately both groups are working against the historical tide. Premarital sexual activity has become steadily more common in the twentieth century, throughout the industrialized world. But the sexual revolution has not been fully integrated into people's lives, especially the lives of teenagers. The American public is still unsure whether the tide can or should be turned back. Given society's deep ambivalence about sexual activity among teenagers, young women often find themselves in a state of confusion—a state that is often apparent in the ethnographic accounts. They tell researchers about their decisions concerning sex, conception, and pregnancy. But when we say that teens "decide" on a course of action in such matters, we may be using much too active a verb. On the one hand, young people are told to "just say no"; on the other, their friends, the media, and society at large foster the idea that sexual activity among teenagers is widespread and increasingly commonplace. If a young woman doesn't want to have sex, she has little in the way of support, since sexual activity has come to be expected.

> They looked at a virgin as being something shameful. They were the type of people who would always tell what happened if they made out with a boy or a boy made out with them. I was the only one they never heard from. They would say. "You don't know what you're missing." The more they talked the more curious I got. (Theresa, eighteen, black, Washington, D.C.)

> All of my friends were having sex and I was curious to see what it was all about. I didn't even know the guy very well and I don't even want to know him. It wasn't like it is shown on TV or in the movies. I didn't even enjoy it. (Young woman from Colorado)

> All my friends were doing it and they dared me. After all, I was seventeen and had never had sex. I thought maybe I really was missing something. (I wasn't.)

Some girls will have sex to get guys to like them. Some girls do it thinking. "Well, I'm going to keep this boyfriend." If I could, I would tell them. "Don't, until you feel they respect and love you. You're too good to be chasing and trying to make someone stay with you." (Robyn, black, Colorado)

The sexuality that young women express in such ethnographic accounts is often curiously passive. Although a few young women brag about their sexual conquests and skills, many simply make themselves available, in part because it seems that everyone else is doing it.

Even as they feel pressure to be sexually active, teens are urged to abstain, or at least to "be careful" and use contraceptives. Thus, in their accounts they describe their first sexual intercourse as an experience remarkably devoid of pleasure. They are anxious, in a hurry to get it over with, eager to cross the Rubicon in a leap before courage fails; or they see it as something that "just happened," without anyone's having made an active decision.

Then he asked me to have sex. I was scared and everything, and it was like, "What am I gonna do?" The first time I told him no and he understood. We watched TV. And he brought me home. Then a couple of days after that he asked me again, I said okay. I guess I said so because I just wanted to show him I wasn't scared to have sex. I was scared. And he kinda knew I was scared. But I guess I was playing a role. I wanted to show him that I'm not scared. So we had sex . . . and now it's like we don't get along. (Young black woman from Oakland, California)

We was going together for two years and we didn't do anything. I was like "no" and he was scared also. Finally we just—hurry up and get it over with. We just took off our clothes real quick. Just hurry up and get it over with and we both shaking and crying. (High school student in a midwestern city)

I didn't talk to my boyfriend about sex, and he didn't talk to me. One day we were together and started hugging and kissing, then we just did it. (Latisha, fifteen, black, Chicago)

And I used to go home and he would call me on the phone and then we were like that for about a month or so and then we just started to get involved. I don't know, he just asked me and I said sure, if that was what you want to do . . . We just did it to do it and then I just got pregnant. (Sally, fifteen, white)

He was someone to lean on. When I was depressed, I figured, I'll lean on him. Next thing you know, I figured I started to listen to him. Then I saw him as more of a friend. Then why not kiss him? Why not touch him? It seemed that one thing led to another. Afterward we never made a big deal out of it like, "Wow, wasn't that great last night." We never even talked much about it . . . We said we shouldn't have let that happen. It won't happen again. And then it did happen again. (Ivy, seventeen, black, Boston)

Not only are many young women confused and indecisive when it comes to their first sexual encounters, but they often know few adults whom they can comfortably ask for guidance. According to their own accounts, even their mothers offer little or no help:

Only thing she said was, "Don't be out there messing with no boys." And that was it. (Sherita, twelve, black, Washington, D.C.)

I love my mother, but she never really talked to me, and I don't feel like I can talk to her about private matters. She acts like we shouldn't talk about sex. She only told me after my period, that I shouldn't go with boys. (Latisha, fifteen, black, Chicago)

She didn't want me to know nothing about sex but "just don't do it." But I was like—I was like, gosh, but everybody is doing this and I wanted to try it, too. (Fourteen-year-old, attending high school in a midwestern city)

The little information available on young men shows that they, too, see themselves as failures if they have not had sex. For them, sexual activity is an indication of maturity and masculinity.

If they haven't [had intercourse] then they are like outcasts. Like, "Man, you never made love to a girl!" Some of them get teased a lot. It's like on the baseball team and they start talking about that and you have got the younger guys out there and you could tell because they are all quiet and stuff and they won't talk. Some of the other people start laughing at them and start getting on them and get them kind of upset. (Male high school student in a midwestern city)

Premarital sexual activity has become increasingly common in the twentieth century. This is partly due to the fact that people are getting married later, but it is also a function of America's transition from a rural, kinship based society to a modern industrial one that tends to disconnect sex from marriage. Some experts argue that the real sexual revolution in the United States occurred in the 1880s and was largely over by 1915. Others maintain that there were two sexual revolutions, one between 1915 and 1925 and the other between 1965 and 1975. All agree, however, that sexual activity among teenagers is not peculiar to the late twentieth century; rather, it is the result of long-term trends shaped by social and economic forces that are probably irreversible. Furthermore, whatever it is about modernity that makes sex independent from marriage, it is present in most of the industrialized nations. Teens all over the developed world are engaging in sex before marriage. When in 1984 the United Nations undertook a survey of adolescent sexual and reproductive behavior, it concluded that "without doubt, the proportion of teenagers who have experienced sex by age nineteen has been increasing steadily over the years among all adolescents." Even conservative Japan—a communitarian society with strongly internalized social controls—has reported increases in sexual activity among its teenagers, as well as a rise in out-of-wedlock childbearing. Surveys conducted by the Japanese government in 1981 found that in Japan about 28 percent of young women and 37 percent of young men were sexually active by the end of their teenage years—figures that were less than half of those for the United States but that, compared with the proportions in 1974, represented an increase of 40 percent for young men and an amazing 150 percent for young women.

According to conservatives, the fact that contraception was made available to teenagers in the late 1960s was the fuel that ignited the explosion of early sex. Prior to 1964 contraceptives were nominally illegal in many jurisdictions, were never mentioned in public (much less advertised), and were difficult to obtain. In pharmacies, condoms were typically kept behind the counter and some pharmacists in small towns refused to sell them to young men they knew to be unmarried. Since out-of-wedlock pregnancy was stigmatized and likely to lead to a clandestine abortion or a hasty marriage, there is a certain logic to the notion that the stunning reversal in the status of contraception—from illegal and unmentionable to widely available at public expense—fostered the spectacular increase in sexual activity among teenagers. And since this increase in activity and the proliferation of low-cost birth control clinics both occurred in the late 1960s and early 1970s, there is at least a temporal connection between the two.

This commonsensical and comforting notion (comforting because it implies that one way to curtail sexual activity among teens is to limit the availability of contraception) has several things wrong with it. First, a great many aspects of American society were changing in the sixties and seventies. Public attitudes shifted radically on issues such as contraception, premarital sex, abortion, and illegitimacy; family planning clinics were only one part of the context surrounding teenagers' behavior. Second, as we have seen, young people throughout the industrialized world have increased their premarital sexual activity, despite the fact that policies regarding contraception vary widely from country to country. Finally, and perhaps most tellingly, in the 1980s federal funding of family planning services dropped sharply—from $400 million in 1980 to $250 million in 1990—but sexual activity among teens continued to increase. The states compensated in some measure for the cutbacks, but they by no means filled the gap entirely. Though it is disappointing not to be able to pinpoint a cause for the increase in sexual activity among the young, historical and international evidence suggests that it is probably the result of a blend of factors. What *is* extremely clear is that the welter of societal changes and conflicting messages surrounding sexual activity has left many young people confused, misinformed, and adrift.

THE PATH TO PREGNANCY

Some teenagers get pregnant for exactly the same reason that older women do: they are married and they want a child. It is true that in the United States marriage rates among teens have declined dramatically and the median age at first marriage is higher than it has ever been. Still, in 1990 about 7 percent of all American teens (about 10 percent of all eighteen- and nineteen-year olds) were married, and about one out of every three babies born to a teen was born to a married mother. It is important to keep in mind that discussions of early pregnancy and childbearing include these married teenagers, whom the public usually does not think of as part of the constellation of problems associated with "teenage pregnancy."

Other teens are unmarried but are using contraception to avoid pregnancy. Stereotypes to the contrary, teenagers are using more contraception, and using it more effectively, than ever before. In 1982 about half of all American teenagers used a contraceptive method the first time they had sex; in 1988 about 70 percent of them did. Of all the sexually active teenage women surveyed in the 1988 National Survey of Family Growth who were currently having sex, who were neither pregnant nor seeking pregnancy, and who had not been sterilized, about 80 percent were using some method of contraception. Among poor teens, those whose family income was less than twice the poverty level, the rate was a little lower (72.5 percent), and among affluent teens it was a little higher. But if teens are using contraception to such an extent, why aren't their pregnancy rates plummeting?

One major reason is statistical. Teens today actually do have a lower risk of getting pregnant: in 1972 the odds that a sexually involved teen would become pregnant were about one in four; by 1990 they had decreased to one in five. (These figures include married teens, who accounted for approximately 26 percent of all sexually experienced teens in 1972, but only about 15 percent in 1984.) Unfortunately, however, the decline in the odds that an individual teen would get pregnant did not lead to a decline in the pregnancy rate for all teenagers: the increase in effective contraceptive use was offset by the fact that so many more unmarried teenagers became sexually involved during this period. In 1972, in a population of approximately 10 million teenage women, about 2.5 million were sexually active—a rate of roughly 25 percent. By 1984 the total number of teenagers had decreased slightly to 9 million, but the number of sexually active teens had grown to 4 million—a rate of about 50 percent. Thus, although an individual teen had a smaller chance of getting pregnant, the fact that there were twice as many teens at risk meant that there were more pregnancies. Still, the two trends balanced each other so that the pregnancy rate among all teenage women remained roughly stable: in 1972 it was 95 per thousand; in 1984 it was 108 per thousand; and in 1988 it was 117 per thousand. This may be even better news than it seems: some observers think that teenagers' rates of premarital sexual activity are leveling off, and since there is no evidence that the propensity to use contraception is declining, some of the incidence of pregnancy among teens may be a lag effect that will persist only while they are learning how to use contraception well. But the pregnancy rates among American teenagers are worrisome, especially when about half of the pregnancies end in abortion. Despite more than two decades' worth of research on the matter, there are no clear answers as to why the rates remain so high in the United States, compared to those in other countries.

Within a general pattern of increased contraceptive use, there are a number of factors that enable one to predict which teenagers will use contraception more consistently and effectively than others. For example, the higher a teen's socioeconomic status and educational aspirations, the more likely he or she is to use contraception. Older teens are more consistent users than younger ones, for two reasons: sexually active teens get better at it over time; and teens who are older when they have their first sexual experience are more careful than those who start at an earlier age. Contraceptive use also tends to be relationship specific. That is, young men and women are not users or nonusers, but change their practice with individual partners. We know that older women (that is women whose teen years are behind them) are likely to get pregnant after the breakup of a relationship: about one-fourth of all babies born out of wedlock are born to women who have left one marriage but have not entered into another. This suggests that when experienced users move out of a stable relationship, the meaning and practice of contraception change. Thus, young women are even more at risk, since their sexual relationships tend to be more short-lived and sporadic. Studies have shown that sexually active teens in fact go through long periods during which they have no sex at all because they are not involved in a relationship and often have relatively low rates of sex even when they are. And when sexual activity is unpredictable, using contraceptives becomes more difficult.

Contraceptive use may also change over the course of a relationship. When young people have sex for the first time, they tend to rely on male protection methods, notably condoms. In 1982, 23 percent of teenage women reported using condoms the first time they had intercourse, and an additional 13 percent said they used withdrawal; in 1988 about

65 percent used condoms and virtually none used withdrawal. After their first sexual encounter, unmarried adolescents tend increasingly to use female contraceptives (diaphragms and the Pill) instead of male methods. In 1982 about 43 percent of sexually active teenage women were on the Pill, 15 percent were using condoms, and almost 30 percent were using no contraception at all. Similarly, in 1988 about 47 percent were on the Pill, 27 percent were using condoms, and 20 percent were using no contraception. Contrary to stereotype, young black women are *more* likely than young white women to use highly effective contraception, mostly because they are much more likely to be Pill users; but they also tend to begin using contraception at a later age, so their overall risk of pregnancy is higher. Poor teens and affluent teens are almost equally likely to be Pill users.

So why do teens get pregnant if so many of them are using contraception? The short answer is that some get pregnant the first time they have sex, because they use no contraception, use relatively ineffective methods, or use methods inadequately. Others get pregnant during transitions—either within a relationship, as they move from male methods to female methods, or between relationships, when they stop using a certain method. (About 70 percent of all sexually active teenage women have had more than one partner by the time they reach their twenties.) Still others get pregnant because they use no contraception: either they have never used it, or they are not presently using a method they used earlier. Finally, a small number get pregnant even though they are using contraception faithfully.

One troubling and rarely acknowledged fact is that teenagers' sexual involvements are not always consensual, particularly in the case of young women. The younger the woman, the more likely this is to be a problem. In one national survey of American teens, about 7 percent answered yes when they were asked, "Was there ever a time when you were forced to have sex against your will, or were raped?" Thirteen percent of the white women and 8 percent of the black women reported having coercive sex before they were twenty; among young men, the figures were 1.9 percent for whites and 6.1 percent for blacks. An astonishing 74 percent of all women who had had sex before the age of fourteen reported that they had had coerced sex; among those who had had sex before the age of fifteen, the figure was 60 percent. Since most experts think that the respondents in such interviews underreport coercive sex, these numbers are probably conservative. And the question used in the survey defined coercive sex rather narrowly: as the national debate on rape and date rape makes clear, it is difficult to draw the exact boundaries of sexual consent.

In the days when premarital sex was considered wrong, young men and women typically negotiated the meaning of each step (the first kiss, the first caress, "petting") and where it fit into the relationship; the woman permitted increasing sexual intimacy in return for greater commitment from the man. Young women today have no such clear-cut rules. Society has become more tolerant of the notion that an unmarried couple may be sexually involved if they are emotionally committed to each other, but the emotional and social context within which sexual encounters take place has become quite fluid.

When sexual activity is coerced, as it is for a small but important subset of American teens, it is extremely unlikely that the victim will have planned ahead to use contraception. But even in consensual situations, young people—especially young women—still face obstacles to effective contraception use. Social pressures concerning gender roles and sexual activity exert some real constraints on the ability to use contraception effectively—constraints that are similar in effect, if not in degree or kind to those of coercive sex.

During the past thirty years, for example, contraceptive use has become increasingly feminized: both men and women tend to think that contraception is the responsibility of the woman and that it's the woman's fault when something goes wrong. This represents a revolution—one so subtle that most Americans have scarcely noticed it. Until 1965 condoms were the most frequently used form of contraception in America, at least among married couples. There was a time when a young man would carry a lone, crumbling condom with him wherever he went, and carry it so long that it would wear its oulines into his wallet. But with the development of the Pill and the IUD, contraception came to be considered something for which women were responsible and accountable. Interestingly, concerns about sexually transmitted diseases (especially AIDS) and the health effects of the Pill have made condoms popular once again, only today they are marketed to both men and women. What this means in practice is that couples often must negotiate which contraceptives to use and when to use them, with little in the way of clear social rules.

In such negotiations, women tend to be culturally handicapped by society's expectations of appropriate female sexual behavior. The first time a woman has intercourse, she is considered to be "giving away" something valuable: her virginity. If she is young and unmarried, she is culturally enjoined from looking too "ready." (This may explain the increasing popularity of the condom, which the man usually provides and which became popular among teens prior to the recent concern with AIDS and other sexually transmitted diseases.) An unmarried woman who is in the early stages of getting involved in a relationship and who must not look too "ready" for sex is therefore forced to rely on the goodwill and motivation of her partner, who may not be as committed to the relationship as she is and who will suffer fewer consequences if something goes wrong. The first time the couple has sex, he is the one who typically takes the contraceptive precautions, yet he has a very different set of incentives and faces a very different set of risks. Many of these pressures at first intercourse recur every time a woman has a new sexual partner. (Most adolescent women are still having sex in serially monogamous relationships.)

The prevalence of premarital sex means that a "nice girl" is no longer defined as a young woman who has never had sex. Rather, it means a young woman who has had sex but not too much of it, or who is sexually active but not promiscuous. Alas, one simple way of showing that one is a "nice girl" is to be unprepared for sex—to have given no prior thought to contraception. Both at first sex and with each new partner, a young woman is thus subject to powerful cultural pressures that penalize her for taking responsibility. To use contraception, a woman has to anticipate sexual activity by locating the impetus within herself, rather than in the man who has overcome her hesitancy. She must plan for sex, must be prepared to speak about contraception frankly with someone she may not know very well (at the time when, according to cultural expectations, her emotions rather than her intellect are supposed to hold sway), and must put her own long-term welfare before the short-term pleasure of the couple, especially of the man.

When young women talk about the obstacles to using contraception, they frequently describe the way in which conflicting social pressures intersect with their own ambivalent and contradictory feelings:

> I went to Planned Parenthood and I had my aunt help me get the diaphragm. I didn't like it, it didn't feel comfortable and I was embarrased. You know, jump up [during sex] and say, "Um, wait a minute."

Many American teenagers receive at least some information about contraception (often in sex education classes), but this information must be assessed in terms of a complex set of parameters concerning the way in which a teenager views sexual activity and why he or she is using contraception. Young people often report misunderstandings about contraception—misunderstandings that are shared by those around them.

> I think I was thirteen when I first started having sex. My best friend thought I was crazy 'cause I went to my mother and said, "Well, Mom, I like this boy and I might be doing something with him and would you take me to get birth control?" And she said, "No, because once you start taking these pills, you'll become sterile." See, I love kids, I love 'em and I want 'em. So it scared me . . . but she knew I was going to do something. (Sixteen-year-old)

> I wish I had taken the pill. I waited too long. I just kept telling myself, "Well, I can wait a little bit longer." And then I found out it was too late. I wasn't afraid to take it—I just kept putting it off and putting it off, and I put it off too long. (Kimberly, white, Colorado)

In short, the skills a young woman needs in order to use contraception effectively are precisely the skills that society discourages in "nice girls," who are expected to be passive, modest, shy, sexually inexperienced (or at least less experienced than their partners), and dedicated to the comfort of others. A woman who obtains contraception in anticipation of sexual activity is thought to be "looking for sex" (as teens say) and is culturally devalued. More to the point, she risks being devalued within the relationship. When it comes to contraception, she is caught in a net of double binds. She is the one who is supposed to "take care of it," the one at whom most contraceptive programs are aimed, and the one for whose body the most effective methods have been developed. Yet she is expected to be diffident about sex, and interested in it only because love and erotic arousal have spontaneously led her to be "carried away." And if she seems too interested in sex for its own sake, as evidenced by her use of contraception, she is in a weak position to trade sex for commitment and intimacy from the man involved. These pressures are often exacerbated because the woman's partner is older than she is, and presumably more experienced and sophisticated. Scattered data suggest that the partners of teenage mothers are typically older, sometimes significantly older: in 1988, although about 80 percent of teenage mothers had a partner who was within a few years of their own age, 29 percent had a partner who was six or more years older than they were; for very young mothers (fifteen-year-olds), the figure climbed to 30 percent.

A couple may go through a period in which they use no contraception, while they try to work out the meaning of the relationship and how contraception fits into it. Young women who seek contraceptive services sometimes say that they are doing so because their relationship is becoming more serious—meaning they have used no contraception up to that point. Of course, their statistical risk of getting pregnant is just as high in the early months of their relationship as it is later, and may in fact be higher: one study showed that most young women who got pregnant did so in the early, perilous part of their relationship. This suggests that what has changed are not the statistical odds of getting pregnant, but the social cost. Once a relationship is defined as getting serious, it's easier for the young woman to make the commitment to contraception without risking her commitment to her boyfriend. And it may be easier for him to argue for contraception without seeming as if he's "leading her on."

So commitment to and by a partner may counteract some of the pressures that serve as obstacles to contraception. Some young women say that they put off seeking contraceptive services because they are afraid of being found out, particularly by their parents. Yet once their relationship is defined as serious and the young man has demonstrated his commitment, the young woman's sexual desire is transformed from potentially promiscuous into true love, and she is equipped to take the public step of obtaining contraception. Young women whose significant others (parents, partners, and best friends) urge them to get contraception are more likely to obtain it before becoming sexually active and more likely to use it effectively.

Teenagers from different classes and racial groups tend to have different patterns of contraceptive use, both at first intercourse and subsequently. Although there are few studies of the way in which class and race affect the meanings attached to specific contraceptives and to contraception in general, one can make two broad observations. First, when sexual partners come from different social or ethnic groups (as they increasingly do these days), they may have additional problems communicating about contraception. Second, researchers who study sexual and contraceptive decisions in contexts where AIDS is a factor tell us that young women who have a sense of power and efficacy in their lives are more able to protect themselves in their sexual relationships than women who feel weak. Since many poor and minority women lack sources of esteem and power in their lives, they may be more vulnerable in their relationships.

Of course, the desire or lack of desire for a baby plays an important role in the decisions that people make about contraception. The American public often assumes that teenagers have babies simply because they know little about, or ignore, birth control practices. But in many cases this is untrue. In 1984 a sixteen-year-old urban black woman named Tauscha Vaughan made the following comment to *Washington Post* reporter Leon Dash: "Will you please stop asking me about birth control? Girls out here know all about birth control. There's too much birth control out here. All of them know about it. Even when they twelve, they know what birth control is. Girls out here get pregnant because they want to have babies!" This young woman highlights an important fact: that decisions about contraception are intimately related to whether or not one wants a child. But the situation is more complex than this simple statement would make it appear.

When young women talk about their lives, it is clear that their feelings about childbearing exist in a context of numerous shifting assessments. For example, they often describe a partner who does not use contraception or who stops using a contraceptive.

> It [the condom] didn't feel comfortable, and I didn't enjoy it either, so I kept taking my chances on withdrawal. (Reggie, black, Washington, D.C.; father of Tauscha Vaughan's baby)

> We had sex for about a year before I got pregnant. I wasn't using birth control, not at first. Then he said, we'll use something. We didn't really talk about it. The condoms he used hurt him and they irritated me, you know, real bad. I didn't enjoy it and I said, "No, I don't think we'll have it, if it's gonna bother me so bad."

> I knew that it could happen; I just thought I would be lucky and not get caught. We used condoms sometimes, but he said it feels better without them. But when I knew I was pregnant I kept acting like it wasn't real. (Young woman in a Teen Parenting program with black, white, and Hispanic participants)

For many adults, quotes such as these are just one more example of teenagers' fecklessness, of their inability to plan ahead or to see the consequences of their own actions. But when such accounts are read more carefully, many of them reveal that behind the seeming aimlessness are some serious, complex, and often hidden negotiations about the meaning of the relationship—negotiations that teens, like adults, are often reluctant to conduct straightforwardly. In many cases, for example, a young woman thinks that if she and her boyfriend use no contraception, there is a tacit assumption that they are sharing the risk: he must love her so much that he wants to have a child with her and is willing to stand by her if she does:

> I expected the father to be helpful; to take care of the baby. All three of us to go places and have fun. Live together as a family. (Shana, black, Oakland, California)

> I expected commitment of just being a father. Of being there saying "I'm going to help you. I'll be there to take care of Jimmy when you want, when you need to do other things." I expected his support emotionally, financially as much as he could, I expected him to be there for me . . . I expected him to love me because I was the woman who had his baby. But he loves everyone else who didn't. (Diane, black, Oakland, California)

Cynics may ascribe such expectations to wishful thinking; but caught up in a relationship, boys sometimes do make promises—promises that are difficult to keep.

> We were going to be married in April. We didn't want to have a baby right away, but neither of us wanted to use birth control, so when I asked J. if he was ready for the consequences he said yes. He said if I got pregnant he'd want to be with me and the baby always, which is what he said when he found out I was pregnant. Then he changed his mind and split. (Seventeen-year-old, white, rural New England)

> I dated John for about a year. He always told me that if anything happened he would take care of me. When I told him I was pregnant he said that it wasn't his baby. He dropped me and started dating my best friend. It was hard for me to accept that he didn't care as much as he said he did before I got pregnant. (Robyn, black, Colorado)

Although some teenagers try to prevent pregnancy and fail, others get pregnant because they believe pregnancy is not such a bad thing. Young unmarried women, like young married ones, may become pregnant because they want to or at least because they are not sufficiently motivated to avoid it. Experts have long debated whether teenagers want their pregnancies and births. A recent study by the Alan Guttmacher Institute estimated that only 7 percent of all such pregnancies were intended. Does this fully capture what we know about teens and their plans?

It seems at first glance that most young women would prefer not to have a baby. About half of all pregnant teens have abortions, and about 87 percent of those who carried their babies to term in 1988 described their pregnancies as unintended. These findings come from the National Survey of Family Growth (conducted in four cycles: 1973, 1976, 1982, and 1988), which asked a national sample of women the following question: "Was the reason you (had stopped / were not) using any contraceptive method because you yourself wanted to become pregnant?" If a woman answered no, she was asked another question: "It is sometimes difficult to recall these things; but just before that pregnancy began, would you say you probably wanted a(nother) baby at some time or probably not?" This is a rather inflexible way to investigate a fluid, complex, and constantly reexamined decision. The National Center for Health Statistics is revising its methods for the next round of the survey, but we must keep in mind the language of the questions as they were posed if we are to understand the responses fully. Until the 1970s, the typical woman in need of family planning was a woman who had already had all the children she wanted and who was at risk of having additional children she did not want, and the language of the questions reflected the situation of such women. Teens fit into this group awkwardly, if at all. Since teens are just starting to build their families, the questions posed by the survey do not reveal their plans or preferences very well. Few teens have babies that are unwanted in this traditional sense; mostly they say that their babies came earlier than planned. Thus far, the wording of survey questions has not allowed researchers to assess the effects (if any) that early childbearing may have on women's life plans.

The concept of wantedness has been subject to a good deal of criticism. A woman may find it very difficult to tell interviewers that she did not want her baby. Moreover, an unwanted pregnancy may well result in a wanted child. And there is a deeper and more philosophical problem with efforts to measure wantedness by means of questionnaires, particularly in the case of teenagers. Surveys assume that people perceive clear choices and that they feel empowered to act on them. Such certainty and confidence can, of course, be deduced in some instances. If a woman and her partner say that they consistently and effectively used birth control up to the date of conception, and then terminate the pregnancy, we can be fairly confident that they did not want the child. Likewise, if a woman tells an interviewer that she deliberately stopped using contraception because she wanted to become pregnant, we can be reasonably certain that she wanted her baby. But for most teenage mothers, these two extremes rarely capture the lived experience. Contraception, particularly among unmarried people and particularly among the young, may be a casualty of unspoken dynamics in the relationship. Say, for instance, a young man complains about using condoms and finally decides not to use one, and his girlfriend interprets this to mean that he will marry her if she gets pregnant. Is her subsequent pregnancy a wanted pregnancy? What complicated negotiations between a woman and a man determine whether a baby is wanted or unwanted?

Still, the information that interviewers glean from women is interesting, especially when it changes over time. In 1973 the National Survey of Family Growth revealed that of all the children that had been born to American wives in the previous five years, 14 percent had been unwanted at the time of conception. In 1982, when the survey included both married and unmarried mothers, it found that only 7.7 percent of the children born in the previous five years had been unwanted. By 1988, the figure had risen again, to 10.3 percent. And the survey revealed significant differences according to age, race, and socioeconomic status: black women, poor women, and older women were all more likely (again, because of the way the question was worded) to tell interviewers that their children had been unwanted.

But the data are most troubling and most opaque in the case of teenagers. Since the survey asked women if they wanted a baby or another baby at some time, it presumably succeeded in reaching teenagers who had definitely not wanted a baby. Prior to 1982 unmarried women were not interviewed unless they had a child living with them, so we have comparative data only from 1982 and 1988. But in 1988, about 15 percent of white teens and about 30 percent of black teens said that they had not wanted their baby at the time of conception. Thus, although many young mothers did find themselves with babies they had not wanted, 85 percent of white teens and 70 percent of black teens told researchers that they had indeed wanted their children. Most, however, were unhappy about the timing of the birth: more than eight out of ten teenagers who said that they had wanted their babies also asserted that they had become pregnant sooner than planned.

In 1988 analysts took a new approach to the data. Previously the survey had made a distinction only between babies that had been wanted at the time of conception and those that had not; and this made sense, given that the women of interest were older and had nearly completed building their families. Wanted babies were then subdivided into those wanted at the time of conception and those wanted later. In 1988, however, the number of unwanted children was combined with the number of wanted children who had arrived sooner than expected. The resulting new category of "unintended" births was probably designed to accommodate the new demographic reality that teens represented. But the concept of unintendedness is just as slippery as the notion of wantedness. From the available data, we just cannot tell when a young woman would have preferred to have the baby that came too soon. In view of the way the survey questions were worded, a teen who was eager to be a mother but who would have preferred to wait a few months cannot be distinguished from a teen who planned eventually to become a mother but who viewed her recent pregnancy as a serious disruption in her life plans.

According to other studies. poor teenagers are more likely than affluent ones to report that a pregnancy was intended, and are more likely to continue their pregnancies to term. Furthermore, those who deliberately become pregnant and who do not seek abortions tend to be less advantaged teenagers. The entire issue of wantedness must thus be considered in the context of teenagers' available choices, which are often highly constrained.

∎ READING 34

Research on Domestic Violence in the 1990s: Making Distinctions

Michael P. Johnson and Kathleen J. Ferraro

This review of the family literature on domestic violence suggests that two broad themes of the 1990s provide the most promising directions for the future. The first is the importance of distinctions among types or contexts of violence. Some distinctions are central to the theoretical and practical understanding of the nature of partner violence, others provide important contexts for developing more sensitive and comprehensive theories, and others may simply force us to question our tendency to generalize carelessly from one context to another. Second, issues of control, although most visible in the feminist literature that focuses on men using violence to control "their" women, also arise in other contexts, calling for more general analyses of the interplay of violence, power, and control in relationships. In addition to these two general themes, our review covers literature on coping with violence, the effects on victims and their children, and the social effects of partner violence.

> She wandered the streets, looking in shop windows. Nobody knew her here. Nobody knew what he did when the door was closed. Nobody knew. (Brant, 1996, pp. 281)

In everyday speech and even in most social science discourse, "domestic violence" is about men beating women. It is estimated that somewhere in the neighborhood of two million women in the United States are terrorized by husbands or other male partners who use violence as one of the tactics by which they control "their woman." Most of the literature on domestic violence is about men controlling women in intimate relationships through the use of violence. This is not, however, the only form of violence between adult or adolescent partners in close relationships, and our review will therefore cover "partner violence" in a broad range of couple relationships, including the marital, cohabiting, and dating relationships of same-gender and opposite-gender couples.

Our reading of the literature on partner violence has led us to the conclusion that two broad themes of the 1990s provide the most promising directions for the future. The first theme is about the importance of making distinctions. Partner violence cannot be understood without acknowledging important distinctions among types of violence, motives of perpetrators, the social locations of both partners, and the cultural contexts in which violence occurs. We will argue that it is difficult to find a question about partner violence for which these distinctions are not relevant and that our ability to draw firm conclusions and to develop effective policies is broadly handicapped by a failure to make distinctions among types of partner violence.

Control, the second promising theme, is most visible in the feminist literature, which has argued that partner violence is primarily a problem of men using violence to maintain control over "their women," a control to which they feel they are entitled and that is supported by a patriarchal culture. We would agree that "domestic violence" or "battering" as it is generally understood by professionals and by the public is primarily a problem of heterosexual male control of women partners. Nonetheless, battering does happen in gay male couples and in lesbian couples, and some heterosexual women do physically assault their male partners and there are forms of partner violence that are quite different from the systematic violence that we call battering.

THE CENTRALITY OF DISTINCTIONS

Types of Violence Against Partners

One of the clearest illustrations of the importance of making distinctions among types of violence arose in the context of the long-standing debate about "battered husbands," and the alleged gender symmetry of partner violence. Johnson (Johnson, 1995, 2000a) argued that at the relationship level, one can distinguish four major patterns of partner violence, which he called "common couple violence" (CCV), "intimate terrorism" (IT), "violent resistance" (VR), and "mutual violent control" (MVC). The distinctions are based not on behavior in a single incident, but on more general patterns of control exercised across the many encounters that comprise a relationship, patterns that are rooted in the motivations of the perpetrator and his or her partner.

Common Couple Violence.   The first type of partner violence identified by Johnson is that which is not connected to a general pattern of control. It arises in the context of a specific argument in which one or both of the partners lash out physically at the other. In a series of empirical papers, Johnson has demonstrated that CCV (compared to IT) has a lower per-couple frequency, is not as likely to escalate over time, is not as likely to involve severe violence, and is more likely to be mutual (Johnson, 1998, 2000a, 2000b). He also has shown that virtually all of the violence in a general sample is CCV suggesting that research using such samples may be relevant only to this type of partner violence.

Intimate Terrorism.   The basic pattern in IT is one of violence as merely one tactic in a general pattern of control. The violence is motivated by a wish to exert general control over one's partner. IT involves more per-couple incidents of violence than does CCV, is more likely to escalate over time, is less likely to be mutual, and is more likely to involve serious injury. Nonetheless, IT is not merely "severe violence," as defined in much of the literature. There is considerable variability of severity in both CCV and IT, with some CCV involving homicides and some IT involving a rather low level of violence (Johnson, 2000a). The distinguishing feature of IT is a pattern of violent and nonviolent behaviors that indicates a general motive to control.

The controlling behaviors of IT often involve emotional abuse (Follingstad, Rutledge, Berg, Hause, & Polek, 1990). Kirkwood (1993) provided detailed insights into the processes of emotional abuse that can gradually alter women's views of themselves, their relationships, and their place in the world. Chang's (1996) detailed accounts of psychological abuse also illustrate the processes through which women become demoralized and trapped in abusive relationships. Renzetti's work (1992) on battering in lesbian relationships demonstrates that emotional abuse is not the sole prerogative of men.

Violent Resistance.   We prefer the term "violent resistance" over "self-defense," because "self-defense" has meanings that are defined (and changing) in the law. Given that the issue of VR has been central to the debate about the gender asymmetry of partner violence and that there is considerable discussion of the "battered woman" self-defense plea in the law, research on the general dynamics of VR is surprisingly meager. One might almost think from the literature that the only women who fight back are the ones who kill their partners (Browne, Williams, & Dutton, 1999; Roberts, 1996). Johnson (2000a) reported that VR is perpetrated almost entirely by women, but he presented no detailed analysis of its characteristics. There is some evidence elsewhere regarding the immediate dangers of VR (Bachman & Carmody, 1994), and Jacobson & Gottman (1998, see pages 160–162) viewed VR as one important indicator that a woman will soon leave her abusive partner. It is time that we give more research attention to the incidence and nature of VR in partner violence.

Mutual Violent Control.   Johnson (1999, 2000a) identified a couple pattern in which both husband and wife are controlling and violent, in a situation that could be viewed as two intimate terrorists battling for control. The pattern seems to be rare and we know little about it, but it raises questions again about the importance of distinctions. Until recently the literature on mutual violence was either framed terms of "self-defense" or "mutual combat," (Saunders, 1988), but the little we do know about VR, MVC, and mutual violence in CCV suggests a need for much more focused research on what it means when both partners in a relationship are violent.

General Implications.   We have given these distinctions considerable attention because in our review we found our understanding of the literature to be improved by making distinctions among types of violence. For example, the marital violence literature is rife with studies that claim to show that partner violence is gender symmetric, if not perpetrated more often by women than by men, continuing to leave readers of this literature with the impression that men and women are equally abusive. Almost all of these studies, however, use the sort of general heterosexual sample in which aggregated violence only appears to be gender symmetric because it lumps together IT, which is essentially perpetrated by men; CCV, which is perpetrated slightly more often by men than by women; and VR, which is clearly perpetrated more often by women than by men (Johnson, 2000b). Similarly, Macmillan and Gartner (1999) demonstrated the centrality of such distinctions in causal research. They found three qualitatively distinct forms of spousal violence against women, two of which they identified with CCV and IT. When they used these classes as dependent variables in multivariate analyses, the models for CCV and IT were clearly different.

Types of Perpetrators

We see a major convergence in the many attempts to develop typologies of male batterers, suggesting three types: one involved in CCV and two types of perpetrators of IT.

Holtzworth-Munroe and Stuart (1994) referred to these types as "family-only," "generally-violent-antisocial," and "dysphoric-borderline." It appears to us that the family-only type may involve primarily CCV because they were described by the authors as involved in "the least severe marital violence and . . . the least likely to engage in psychological and sexual abuse" (p. 481). The other types (whom we see as involved in IT) come to their terrorism through two quite different developmental histories and psychological profiles, one type broadly sociopathic and violent, the other deeply emotionally dependent on their relationship with their partner (see also Dutton, 1995).

The types identified by Jacobson and Gottman (1998) in a sample of men that seems to include only intimate terrorists bear a striking similarity to generally-violent-antisocials and dysphoric-borderlines. The sample of couples they studied had identified themselves as involved in violent relationships, and Jacobson and Gottman reported that practically all of the men were emotionally abusive (p. 155) in addition to being violent. The Jacobson and Gottman research is unique in that in addition to being interviewed, observed, and given psychological tests, the couples were monitored physiologically during arguments in the laboratory. One group of men (labeled memorably as "cobras") exhibited a "cold" physiology even in the heat of vicious verbal attacks on their partners, with heart rate and other physiological indicators that suggest a chilling internal calmness. The characteristics of this group and their personal histories resembles those of generally-violent-antisocial batterers. The second group identified by Jacobson and Gottman ("pit bulls") was more physiologically in tune with the emotional displays involved in their verbal attacks on their partner, and in other respects they resembled the dysphoric-borderline type in that they are dependent and needy. Holtzworth-Munroe and Stuart's hypotheses about the development of different types of batterers have received general empirical support in a number of empirical tests (e.g., Hamberger, Lohr, Bonge, & Tolin, 1996; Holtzworth-Munroe, Meehan, Herron, Rehman, & Stuart, in press).

Types of Perpetrators Within Types of Violence.   We believe that major advances in our understanding of the origins of partner violence will come from bringing together and extending the work on types of violence and types of perpetrators. These distinctions have already demonstrated their usefulness in understanding the causes of battery and in developing treatment programs for batterers (Saunders, 1996), and the Jacobson and Gottman (1998) book is an accessible and compelling demonstration of the importance of such distinctions in matters as far ranging as the childhood precursors of partner violence, the developmental course of violent relationships, the process of escaping such relationships, and matters of public policy and intervention strategies. Most of this perpetrator work is focused on male IT, but we believe it might also be useful to attempt to develop typologies of male and female CCV perpetrators as well (Holtzworth-Munroe & Stuart, 1994; Holtzworth-Munroe et al., in press).

Types of Relationships

The 1990s have also seen an explosion in information about violence in different types of partner relationships. There is now a massive literature on dating and courtship violence and a growing literature on violence in cohabiting relationships. Some of this work has focused on same-gender relationships.

Same-Sex Relationships.   Although a recent issue of the *Journal of Gay and Lesbian Social Services* was devoted to violence within both male and female same-gender relationships (Renzetti & Miley, 1996), we still seem to know more about lesbian battering than we do about violence in gay men's relationships, in part because of the important role of the women's movement in generating research on domestic violence (Dobash & Dobash, 1992) and in part because of Claire Renzetti's (1992) groundbreaking research on lesbian relationships. Her conclusion that psychological abuse was present in all of the violent relationships that she studied, that these abusive partners were extremely threatened by their partner's efforts to establish independent friendships and activities, that jealousy was a major problem, and that power and control were major sources of conflict all suggest to us that her sample tapped into IT. Furthermore, the fact that the majority of women in Renzetti's sample (68%) indicated that their partner's dependency was a source of conflict suggests a similarity to Jacobson and Gottman's "pit bulls" and Holtzworth-

Munroe and Stuart's dysphoric-borderline type. Thus, it may be possible that some variation or elaboration of the models developed with heterosexual couples can provide insight into violence in lesbian couples.

Some of the most striking differences between lesbian battery and heterosexual battery have to do with links to the external environment of the relationship. Threats of "outing" women to family members or employers are common forms of psychological abuse and are of course unique to same-gender couples; battered lesbians are evidently less likely to be supported by friends, who often refuse to believe that a lesbian can be an abuser; and social service workers are often unsupportive as well, assuming that only men batter their partners (Renzetti, 1992).

Although the women's movement has made efforts to educate service providers and the public about lesbian battering (Elliot, 1990), specialized services are rare and research is still quite limited. We still know little about the varieties of partner violence in same-gender relationships (for example, the extent of CCV or IT). The inability to collect information from random samples means that we know almost nothing about incidence. These gaps in our knowledge are troubling not only because they leave policy makers and service providers somewhat on their own, but also because research on partner violence in diverse types of relationships could be an important source of insights into the inadequacies of our "general" theories. Both Merrill and Renzetti (Merrill, 1996; Renzetti, 1992) have pointed out aspects of partner violence in same-gender relationships that seem to fly in the face of theories developed in a heterosexual context. This may be an arena in which much can be gained in terms of the testing and revision of general theory.

Dating and Courtship.   Research on partner violence in heterosexual dating and courtship relationships began early in the 1980s and has continued throughout the 1990s (Lloyd & Emery, 2000). Although we appear to know a good deal about what was initially a most surprising incidence of partner violence in dating relationships, this literature is as plagued by lack of distinctions as is the marital violence literature. Frequent statements in the literature that there is as much violence in these relationships as there is in marriage imply that there is as much IT, but because the data are drawn from general social surveys, they probably include only CCV.

Rather than review this extensive literature here, we would simply like to point out that it has been a rich source of theoretical insight regarding partner violence. A great many of the multivariate analyses of the correlates of violence have been done in this context (Bookwala, Frieze, Smith, & Ryan, 1992; Foo & Margolin, 1995; Riggs & O'Leary, 1996; Riggs, O'Leary, & Breslin, 1990; Tontodonato & Crew, 1992; Wyatt, 1994). Stets's theoretical work on the centrality of control issues grew from her work on dating violence (Stets & Pirog-Good, 1990), and Lloyd & Emery's (Lloyd & Emery, 2000) recent book develops a general theoretical framework for understanding physical violence in dating relationships that could be used to address partner violence in all types of relationships.

Cohabitation.   Serious discussion of the extent of partner violence in cohabiting relationships can be traced to Stets and Straus's (1990) puzzling finding that cohabiting couples reported more violence than did either married or dating couples, even with controls for age, education, and occupation. Recent studies in New Zealand and Canada also report a higher rate of violence in cohabiting relationships, compared with dating (Magdol, Moffitt, Caspi, & Silva, 1998), and marriage (Johnson, 1996). Although in the United States, the National Violence Against Women Survey appears to present data on cohabitation (Tjaden & Thoennes, 1999, pp. 27–29), the data actually refer to lifetime victimization of respondents who have a history of cohabitation and do not allow for easy interpretation. One possible complication in this cohabitation literature is the confounding of age, length of relationship, and marital status. In Canada, Johnson (1996, pp. 166–168) found that the difference between married and cohabiting unions held only for couples who had been together for 3 years or less.

Stets and Straus (1990) introduced three possible explanations of marital status differences: social isolation, autonomy-control, and investment. Although Stets (1991) claimed to demonstrate that social isolation "explains" the effect, the only measure of social isolation that works in her analysis is "ties to spouse," as measured by the respondents' report of the chances that they will separate. We think it makes more sense to see this as a measure of commitment to the relationship, suggesting only that low commitment is either a consequence or a cause of partner violence in cohabiting relationships. Gaertner and Foshee's (1999) data support this interpretation, showing a negative relationship between commitment and violence in dating relationships. They also reported data relevant to the investment explanation, finding that both duration of relationship and reported investment are *positively* related to violence, the opposite of what Stets and Straus predicted.

Stets and Straus's data actually show that the pattern of more violence occurring in cohabitation than in marriage does not hold for couples in which only the man was violent (p. 240). Perhaps the pattern is relevant only to CCV. Macmillan and Gartner (1999) reported that marriage is negatively related to CCV, but positively to IT. Perhaps marriage, although not a license to hit, is for some people a license to terrorize. Once again, we see an area in which distinctions among types of violence would help to clarify matters.

Demographics, Social Location, and Identity

Gender.   The most longstanding and acrimonious debate in the family literature involves the issue of gender symmetry of partner violence (Archer, 2000; Dobash & Dobash, 1992; Dobash, Dobash, Wilson, & Daly, 1992; Johnson, 1995; Kurz, 1989, 1993; Straus, 1990a, 1993). Although papers continue to appear regularly that claim to demonstrate that women are as violent as men in intimate relationships of one kind or another, or in one country or another, a careful assessment of the literature and a look at the few studies that do distinguish among types of violence both indicate that IT is almost entirely a male pattern (97% male in Johnson, 2000a). The evidence seems to indicate that VR is primarily perpetrated by women (Browne, Williams, et al., 1999; Cascardi & Vivian, 1995; Dobash & Dobash, 1992; Johnson, 2000a; Ogle, Maier-Katkin, & Bernard, 1995; Saunders, 1988). CCV appears to be roughly gender symmetric (56% male perpetrators in Johnson, 2000a; see also Milardo, 1998).

Most studies define gender symmetry in terms of the percent of men and women who have perpetrated at least one act of violence in their relationship. To call this gender symmetry, however, is to ignore different male and female frequencies of violence and the different physical consequences of male-to-female and female-to-male violence. As for the former, Johnson (1999) showed that in 31% of the relationships involving "mutual" CCV, the husbands were clearly more frequently violent than were their wives, compared with 8% in which the wives were more frequently violent. With regard to injury, the more serious physical consequences of male-to-female violence are well-established (Brush, 1990; Sorenson, Upchurch, & Shen, 1996; Straus, 1990a, 1999; Tjaden & Thoennes, 1999).

A number of studies have focused on the possibility that the causes of violence are not the same for men and women. Foo and Margolin (1995) reported in a dating context that a set of standard predictor variables explains 41% of the variance in male-to-female violence, but only 16% for female-to-male violence (see also Anderson, 1997).

Although work on the gender symmetry issue is of interest in itself, it has also provided an important site for both methodological developments and theoretical insights into the nature of partner violence. Methodologically, the debate has prompted a number of developments, including a new version of the CTS (Straus, Hamby, Boney-McCoy, & Sugarman, 1996), a major reconsideration of the interview context of assessments of violence (Straus, 1999; Tjaden & Thoennes, 1999), and discussions of couple-data issues (Szinovacz & Egley, 1995). The debate has also generated attention to the sampling issues involved in various research designs (Johnson, 2000b; Straus, 1990a).

With regard to theory, the debate has prompted Straus to consider some of the social roots of women's violence toward their male partners (Straus, 1999). He discussed factors such as women's assumption that their violence is harmless (Fiebert & Gonzalez, 1997) and that under some conditions slapping a man is an appropriately "feminine" behavior. Johnson (1995) also provided a rudimentary list of gendered causal factors in partner violence, and he argued that some combinations of them might produce CCV, whereas others produce IT. Other theoretical work of the decade that has arisen from a focus on gender includes theory focused on the broader social context (Dobash & Dobash, 1992, 1998; Straus, 1999), social construction of gender models (Anderson, 1997; Dobash & Dobash, 1998), and evolutionary models (Buss & Shackelford, 1997; Wilson & Daly, 1996, 1998). Of course, gender also is centrally implicated in the literature on gay and lesbian relationships in ways that may prompt further theoretical development as we are forced to ask ourselves which aspects of the gendering of partner violence are a function of male-female differences and which are more related to the specifically gendered nature of heterosexual relationships (Renzetti & Miley, 1996; West, 1998).

Race and Ethnicity in North America. Most of the earliest race and ethnicity scholarship did not give serious attention to ethnic differences in experiences of abuse or responses to it, focusing instead primarily on Black-White differences in incidence (Crenshaw, 1994). That literature has continued into the 1990s with survey research regularly indicating higher levels of partner violence among Blacks than among Whites (Anderson, 1997; Cazenave & Straus, 1990; Greenfield & Rand, 1998; Sorenson, 1996; Tjaden & Thoennes, 1999). Recent work has broadened ethnic comparisons to cover other groups, however. For example, only 13% of Asian and Pacific Islander women in the 1995–1996 National Violence Against Women Survey (Tjaden & Thoennes, pp. 22–26) reported having been physically assaulted by an intimate partner. For White women, the figure is 21%, for African Americans 26%, for American Indian and Alaska Natives 31%, and for Mixed Race 27%.

There are two important questions we have to ask about these differences. First, what kind of violence are we talking about? These surveys do not make distinctions among the various types of violence discussed above. We do not know if higher incidence of violence reported in these surveys necessarily means more IT. It is more likely to be CCV. We cannot develop good theories about race differences until we make such distinctions. Second, we have to ask about the extent to which "race" differences have less to do with race and ethnicity than they do with socioeconomic status, as has been shown in National Family Violence Survey data (Cazenave & Straus, 1990). Lockheart's (1991) more recent survey of 307 African American and European American women, drawn equally from high-, middle-, and low-income brackets, found no significant racial differences in rates of violence.

Beyond questions of incidence, there is now a growing literature that focuses on more institutional and cultural matters. Are the dominant social institutions addressing domestic violence effectively in various cultural and ethnic contexts? Are the services women need available in their communities? Are kin, friends, and community willing to face issues of domestic violence and to work to eliminate it? Are the psychological and social consequences the same in different groups? For example, Eng (1995) noted that acknowledgment of battering is highly shameful for many immigrant Asian women who are socialized to believe that marital failure is always the fault of a wife (see also Song, 1996). Gondolf, Fisher, & McFerron (1991) examined 5,708 Texas shelter residents and found no significant differences in the amounts of violence experienced by White, African American, and Hispanic women but did find that Hispanic women were relatively disadvantaged economically and tended to endure battering for a longer time than White and African American women. Crenshaw (1994) was one of the first scholars to identify gaps in domestic violence services for women of color and insensitivity to issues of race and ethnicity in developing policy agendas such as mandatory arrest. Such issues are beginning to be addressed for a number of major ethnic and racial groups in North America, including American Indian people (Bachman, 1992; Fairchild, Fairchild, & Stoner, 1998; McEachern, Winkle, & Steiner, 1998; Norton & Manson, 1995; Tom-Orme, 1995; Waller, Risley-Curtis, Murphy, Medill, & Moore, 1998), Asian and Pacific Island people (Abraham, 1995; Ho, 1990; Song, 1996; Yick & Agbayani-Siewert, 1997), Latino groups (Perilla, Bakerman, & Norris, 1994), and African Americans (Dennis, Key, Kirk, & Smith, 1995; Marsh, 1993; Richie, 1996).

As this literature grows, it will be important to attend to two general questions. First, can we identify social forces that shape experiences similarly across subsets of "minority" groups, such as similarities produced by common experiences of exclusion and domination, or the experience of recent immigration (Cervantes & Cervantes, 1993; Root, 1996; Sorenson, 1996)? Second, what are the unique ways in which each particular racial and ethnic context shapes domestic violence, its consequences, and community responses to it? Even within "standard" racial and ethnic categories, there are important distinctions that cannot be ignored. In one illustration of the importance of making such distinctions, Sorenson and Telles (1991, pp. 3) reported no difference between non-Hispanic Whites and Mexican Americans in their sample until immigration status was taken into account: "Mexican Americans born in the US reported rates 2.4 times higher than those born in Mexico." This finding can serve to remind us not only of the importance of differences among specific groups in North America, but also of matters of cultural roots and immigrant status that have global implications (Kane, 1999).

Global Complexities.   We can only begin to address the global complexity of partner violence in this review, involving as it does issues of cultural differences, economic and social structure, effects of conflict and warfare, and the position of immigrant and refugee populations. To begin, we can simply draw attention to a number of overviews of the international scope of partner violence (Heise, 1996; Heise, Raikes, Watts, & Zwi, 1994; Human Rights Watch, 1995; Klein, 1998; Levinson, 1989; Sewall, Vasan, & Schuler, 1996; United Nations, 1989). In addition, scholarly work in English on domestic violence in specific other countries is beginning to become available (Alexander, 1993; Dawud-Noursi, Lamb, & Sternberg, 1998; Fawcett, Heise, Isita-Espejel, & Pick, 1999; Glantz, Halperin, & Hunt, 1998; Gondolf & Shestakou, 1997; Grandin & Lupri, 1997; Haj-Yahia, 1998; Handwerker, 1998; Kalu, 1993; Ofei-Aboagye, 1994; Schuler, Hashemi, Riley, & Akhter, 1996; Stewart, 1996; Tang, 1994). Finally, we would like to address briefly a few specific international issues.

First, in a global context domestic violence has now been defined as a human rights issue (Richters, 1994). Second, there appears to be considerable variability in the incidence of partner violence in various countries (Heise, 1994). Of course, we do not know what type of violence these statistics reference. Furthermore, as we consider these clues to the social and cultural roots of partner violence, it will be important to monitor our interpretations for ethnocentrism. For example, Bhattacharjee (1997) questions the assumption of Western White feminism that Southeast Asian women are more subservient to husbands.

Third, a literature is developing that explores the effects of war, internal conflict, and terrorism on matters related to partner violence. McWilliams (1998) framed the issue as one of "societies under stress," using the case of Northern Ireland as her major example. Community resources are diverted to the conflict, a higher priority is placed on keeping families together, public agencies may be controlled by the "enemy," calls for ingroup solidarity militate against making internal conflicts such as domestic violence public, and "warrior" images reinforce patriarchal ideology. As we read McWilliams' chapter, we were intrigued by the possibility that many of these same processes might be relevant to racial and ethnic minorities in the United States who are under siege, albeit a "siege" that generally falls short of the open intergroup violence that applies in the cases McWilliams discusses.

In countries recovering from war, pronatalist policies may limit access to contraceptive devices or reduce women's ability to procure employment that might allow them to escape an abusive situation. Additionally, people suffering from the continuing effects of occupation, such as the majority of indigenous groups worldwide, have high rates of interpersonal and domestic violence related to the destruction of culture and oppressive economic and social conditions (McWilliams, 1998, p. 123–124). Scholarship on the effects of colonization, decolonization, war, and development on rates and forms of partner violence is in its infancy. Filling this gap is an important task for the next decade of research.

Finally, immigrant and refugee status (sometimes a result of flight from the kind of societal stress discussed above) creates special difficulties for women trying to escape abusive relationships. Immigrant women experiencing violence in their homes often are restricted by language barriers, fear of deportation, lack of transportation, fear of loss of child custody, and cultural taboos (Hogeland & Rosen, 1990).

Summary

Some distinctions are central to the theoretical and practical understanding of the nature of partner violence (e.g., types of violence and perpetrators), others provide important contexts for developing more sensitive and comprehensive theories (e.g., types of relationships or gender differences), and others may simply force us to question our tendency to generalize carelessly from one context to another. Such distinctions were a major theme of the domestic violence literature of the 1990s, and they must continue to be so into the next decade.

CONTROL

A second major theme of the 1990s has been control. Whatever the immediate precipitator of violence may be, it generally gives the perpetrator some measure of control, but once again we see distinctions among types of violence as central. The control may be specific, focused narrowly on winning a particular argument or having one's way in some narrowly defined matter (CCV). In other cases the control may be broad, involving the establishment or maintenance of general control over one's partner (IT, MVC). Sometimes the control issue is one of wresting some modicum of control from a generally abusive partner (VR). We believe that the most progress will be made in our understanding of domestic violence by assuming that the origins and dynamics of the different kinds of control motives are not the same.

In our review of this literature, we want to make a somewhat arbitrary distinction. Some writers have come to their focus on control issues through an analysis of the patriarchal roots of wife beating (Dobash & Dobash, 1992; Johnson, 1995; Pence & Paymar, 1993). Although this is our own primary orientation, we believe that a full understanding of partner violence must go beyond this feminist analysis to ask questions about the role of control in the generation of violence that may have little to do either with patriarchal traditions and structures or with individual patriarchal motives.

The Gender Context

Johnson's (1995) discussion of IT as violence embedded in a general pattern of control tactics draws heavily on the work of the Duluth shelter activists Pence and Paymar (1993). The "power and control wheel" that is the heart of the Duluth educational model for intervention with batterers is drawn directly from the accounts of women who have come to shelters for help. Kirkwood's (1993) study of women who left abusive relationships also relied heavily on an analysis of the dynamics of control. Dobash and Dobash's (1992); analysis of the dynamics of wife beating was likewise formed by the perspectives of battered women, in this case women whom they interviewed in their early research in Scotland, but they also drew heavily on a more sociological and historical analysis of the patriarchal form of the family and other institutions. They now are beginning to explore control issues from the perspective of the violent men themselves (Dobash & Dobash, 1998). Their arguments regarding the importance of context refer not only to the relationship context in which a particular man may feel he has the right to control "his woman," but also the more general context in which relations between men and women are formed and in which other institutions react to men's violence against their female partners.

Whereas Dobash and Dobash, as well as other feminists, tend to move the analysis up from the relationship to the broader societal context of wife beating, Jacobson and Gottman (1998) moved down to the individual level, asking questions about the childhood roots of the personalities of the two types of perpetrators whom they identified among their sample of men who batter their partners. Similarly, other psychologists who focus on wife beating but do not rely heavily on a feminist analysis search for the developmental roots of men's violent behavior toward their female partners (Dutton, 1995; Dutton & Starzomski, 1993; Holtzworth-Munroe et al., in press; Holtzworth-Munroe, Stuart, & Hutchinson, 1997).

Prospects for a More General Analysis of Control

The problem with the analyses of control discussed above is that they are so focused on male IT that they probably provide little insight into CCV or VR, and they seem to have little relevance for any type of partner violence in same-gender relationships. We need a more general approach to issues of violence and control that can encompass IT in heterosexual relationships but also go beyond it.

Beginning with a study that focused on the connection between relationship control and violence, Jan Stets and her colleagues have developed two lines of analysis of the role of control in intimate relationships (Stets & Pirog-Good, 1990). One line of work focuses on a "compensatory model" in which it is assumed that individuals act to maintain a reasonable level of control in their lives, becoming more controlling of their partner when their level of control is threatened either within the relationship itself (Stets, 1993, 1995b) or in other areas of their life (Stets, 1995a). In a slightly different approach, paying more attention to individual differences, the concepts of "control identity" and "mastery identity" were explored in terms of their relationships to gender, gender identity, and controlling behavior in intimate relationships (Stets, 1995c; Stets & Burke, 1994, 1996).

If this literature could be brought back to its initial connection with violence, and perhaps informed more by feminist analyses of the gendering of control issues in relationships, it might provide a context for major theory development. We expect that the most fruitful approaches will bring together a variety of levels of analysis from the societal through the interpersonal to the individual (for example, see Lloyd & Emery, 2000).

SOME OTHER CONTINUING THEMES

Coping With Partner Violence

Most of the literature on coping with violence is focused on IT. In the 1990s, the dominant view shifted from seeing women in abusive relationships as victims to defining them as "survivors," focusing on the decisions women make to escape, to end the violence, or to cope with it in some other manner (Ferraro, 1997). Campbell and her colleagues (Campbell, Miller, Cardwell, & Belknap, 1994; Campbell, Rose, Kub, & Nedd, 1998) argued that the women they studied over a 2½-year period showed great resourcefulness in their resistance to the pattern of violent control in which they were enmeshed. Strategies included (a) active problem solving, (b) responding to identifiable pivotal events, and (c) negotiating first with oneself and then directly or indirectly with the male partner. By the end of the 2½ years, three fourths of the battered women were no longer in a violent relationship, 43% having left and 32% having successfully negotiated an end to the violence. This is yet another area in which distinctions among types of violence and types of relationship are likely to be useful. Strategies of negotiation and barriers to leaving are likely to differ rather dramatically for IT and CCV and across dating, cohabiting, same-gender and cross-gender relationships.

Leaving.   The coping strategy that has received the most attention is "leaving," all-too-often addressed from a misguided sense of puzzlement that women do not leave abusive relationships. We still see papers and sections of literature reviews and textbooks headed "Why do they stay?" Well, the truth is, they don't stay (Campbell et al., 1994; Holtz-worth-Munroe, Smutzler, & Sandin, 1997, pp. 194–95). We need to watch our language; there is no good reason why a study in which two thirds of the women have left the violent relationship is subtitled, "How and why women stay" instead of "How and why women leave" (Herbert, Silver, & Ellard, 1991).

One theoretical approach that seems promising draws upon commitment theory. Rusbult and Martz (1995) make use of Rusbult's investment model to investigate the effects of commitment, rewards, costs, alternatives, and investments on whether women in abusive relationships stay or leave within the time frame of the study. We believe, however, that the best work on staying and leaving will have to treat leaving as a process. Choice & Lamke (1997) did that to some extent, identifying two stages of leaving in which women ask themselves first "Will I be better off?" and second "Can I do it?" But there is other work that focuses in more detail on the process of leaving.

Kirkwood's (1993) marvelous book takes us into both the process by which abusive men entrap their partners and the process by which those women engineer their escape. Her two metaphors of a "web" of entrapment and of a "spiral" of escape capture the details of the process simply and vividly. These men use a wide range of tactics of control not only to control the intact relationship, but also to ensure as best they can that their partner will never be able to leave them. Johnson's (1998) analysis of the shelter movement addressed this process in terms of the abuser's manipulation of personal, moral, and structural commitments to the relationship in order to entrap his partner. He argued that the major strategies of the battered women's movement (temporary safe housing, support groups, empowerment counseling, networking with social support services, legal advocacy, coordinated community response) empower women to neutralize those commitments. Kirkwood also acknowledged the role of shelter advocates in helping the women she studied as they went through a process of leaving and returning, each time gaining more psychological and social resources, each time coming closer to escaping for good, metaphorically spiraling outward until they escaped from the web.

Psychological and Behavioral Consequences of Partner Violence

As we approach the end of this article, we come upon a huge research literature dealing with the psychological consequences of partner violence for the adults involved and for their children. Once again, however, we have to note the difficulties created by not taking care to distinguish among types of violence. Although some of the studies in this literature make use of samples in which the violence is clearly IT, others analyze survey data in which the measurement of violence does not attend to differences that may have critical implications in terms of consequences. A slap in the face sometime in the last 12 months is likely to have little impact on self-esteem and may not even be witnessed by the children. A systematic pattern of assault and psychological abuse is another story.

The Victims.   Nevertheless, the literature confirms that IT and perhaps other forms of partner violence against women have negative effects in terms of injuries and longer-term physical and psychological health (Giles-Sims, 1998; Holtzworth-Munroe et al., 1997, pp. 184–189; Johnson & Leone, 2000). The psychological effects include posttraumatic stress disorder, depression, and lowered self-esteem.

There is another interesting line of research that focuses not on psychological health, but on women's attributions regarding the causes of the violence they are experiencing. Holtzworth-Munroe and her colleagues (Holtzworth-Munroe, Jacobson, Fehrenbach, & Fruzzetti, 1992) argue, on the basis of a literature review, that the evidence shows women do not generally blame themselves for their partner's violence (see also Cantos, Neidig, & O'Leary, 1993). Nonetheless, the fact that issues of victim self-blame are raised often in the more qualitative literature suggests that research on attributions as moderating variables, affecting the consequences of violence, might be useful (Andrews & Brewin, 1990; Fincham, Bradbury, Arias, Byrne, & Kamey, 1997).

Studies that have compared physical and psychological consequences for men and women find more serious consequences for women (Browne, Williams, et al., 1999; Brush, 1990; Dobash et al., 1992; Grandin, Lupri, & Brinkerhoff, 1998; Sorenson et al., 1996; Straus, 1999; Vivian & Langhinrichson-Rohling, 1994). Of course, the danger in these comparisons is that they may be comparing apples and oranges because most of them deal with survey data in which no distinctions among types of violence are made. It is unlikely that many of the men in such surveys are experiencing IT, whereas a significant number of the female victims of violence are (Johnson, 2000a). Qualitative and anecdotal evidence suggest that the consequences of terroristic violence may be as severe for men as they are for women (Cook, 1997; Island & Letellier, 1991; Letellier, 1996).

The Children.   There is also a substantial literature regarding the effects of partner violence on children who witness it (Kolbo, Blakely, & Engleman, 1996; Wolak & Finkelhor, 1998). Behavioral effects include aggression and delinquency, among others. Psychological effects include anxiety, depression, and low self-esteem. There is even evidence of long-term effects, with college-age women who remember violence between their parents having lower self-esteem, greater depression, and lower levels of social competence (Henning, Leitenberg, Coffey, Bennett, & Jankowski, 1997; Silvern, Karyl, Waelde, Hodges, & Starek, 1995). Again, however, we have to point out that although some of these studies deal with populations in which the nature of the parental violence is relatively clear, in most cases the measures do not allow the necessary distinctions. The reported effects are generally small, but we do not know if exposure to IT might in fact have powerful effects that are muted by their aggregation with the effects of CCV.

Intergenerational Nontransmission of Violence.   One particular type of long-term effect on children has been studied enough to merit its own section. Although it is not unusual for scholars to take the position that "violence in the family of origin is probably the mostly widely accepted risk marker for the occurrence of partner violence (Kantor & Jasinski, 1998, p.16), we are struck by the weakness of the relationship in the studies we reviewed. In this as in other areas of socialization research, the widespread use of the metaphor of "transmission" introduces a gross distortion of the reality of family-of-origin effects on the adult lives of children. Nevertheless, scholars have moved on to assessment of the mechanisms by which "transmission" takes place, in many cases with data that effectively show no "transmission" to begin with. For example, Simons, Lin, & Gordon (1998) presented structural equation models of the process by which parental behavior affects dating violence of their children, failing to draw our attention to the fact that the largest zero-order correlation they find is .12, representing roughly 1% of the variance in dating violence. Then there is a study of marriage and marriagelike relationships (Lackey & Williams, 1995) that takes intergenerational transmission for granted and restricts its major analyses to investigating the conditions under which men whose parents were violent do not become violent themselves. Buried in their appendix is the correlation that represents the intergenerational effect in their data ($r = .10$), once again an explained variance of 1%. Foshee, Bauman, and Linder (1999) similarly tested models of intervening variables for effects the largest of which represent 2% of the variance in dating violence.

The important point here is not just that the effects are small. Social scientists indeed often do make much of such small effects in other areas as well. Our concern is that the metaphor of transmission, and the use of terms such as "cycle of violence," imply that partner violence is inexorably passed on from generation to generation. We want to drive home our concern here with widely cited data that may represent the strongest intergenerational effect ever reported in this literature. Analyzing data from the first National Family Violence Survey, Straus, Gelles, and Steinmetz (1988, p.101) reported that "the sons of the most violent parents have a rate of wife-beating 1,000 percent greater than that of the sons of nonviolent parents. . . ." What we deleted with our ellipses is the actual rate of 20%, meaning that even among this group of men whose parents were two standard deviations above average in level of partner violence, 80% of the adult sons had not even once in the last 12 months committed any acts of severe violence toward their partners as defined by the CTS. What about the 20% who *were* violent? We must return to our old refrain that we have no way of knowing which type of violence these men (or their parents) perpetrated.

Social Consequences of Partner Violence

During the 1990s, scholarship began to focus on the interconnections of partner violence, poverty, welfare, and homelessness. This work became particularly relevant with the passage of so-called welfare reform in 1996, which included the possibility for states to exempt battered women from some of its most restrictive mandates (Kurz, 1998). Research focusing specifically on low-income women has uncovered an extraordinarily high level of interpersonal violence, which interferes with social and economic success. Zorza (1991) found that at least half of homeless women were forced from residences because of violence from their intimate partners. Browne and Bassuk (1997) interviewed 220 homeless and 216 housed low-income women in Massachusetts about childhood abuse and adult intimate violence. Nearly one third of respondents reported that their current or most recent partner had perpetrated severe physical violence against them. Browne and her colleagues (Browne, Salomon, & Bassuk, 1999) also reported that "Controlling for a variety of factors, women who experienced physical aggression/violence by male partners during a 12-month period had only one third the odds of maintaining employment for at least 30 hrs per week for 6 months or more during the subsequent year as did women without these experiences." Other examinations of the effects of battering on women's employment (Brandwein, 1998; Lloyd, 1999) have reported that abusive men deliberately undermine women's employment by depriving them of transportation, harassing them at work, turning off alarm clocks, beating them before job interviews, and disappearing when they promised to provide child care. Some abusers simply prohibit their partners from working. Battering also indirectly undermines employment by (a) causing repeated absences; (b) impairing women's physical health, mental agility and concentration; and (3) , lowering self-esteem and aspirations. Thus, although surveys and crime statistics indicate higher levels of partner violence among low-income couples and in lower income neighborhoods (Anderson, 1997; Lupri, Grandin, & Brinkerhoff, 1994; Miles-Doan, 1998; Straus, 1990b), for many women violence may be the precipitating factor for poverty, and it is surely a barrier to raising income and employment status.

CONCLUSION

The 1990s were a time of tremendous growth in the literature on partner violence, including considerable growth in attention to the need to make distinctions among various types of violence. Unfortunately, our major conclusion from this review of the decade is that in spite of increasing evidence of the importance of distinctions, almost all of our general theoretical and empirical work is severely handicapped by the failure to attend to these distinctions. The modeling of the causes and consequences of partner violence will never be powerful as long as we aggregate behaviors as disparate as a "feminine" slap in the face, a terrorizing pattern of beatings accompanied by humiliating psychological abuse, an argument that escalates into a mutual shoving match, or a homicide committed by a person who feels there is no other way to save her own life.

Even more troubling, however, is the possibility that the aggregation of such disparate phenomena can produce serious errors, as it did in the gender symmetry debate. Everything from lists of risk factors, to inferences about causal processes from multivariate analyses, to statements about differences in incidence across groups or across time—all of it—is called into question. Going back through this review, one can hardly find a section in which we did not feel the need to question generalization across types of violence. We need to return to our research, make distinctions among types of violence, and find out which of our pronouncements apply to which forms of violence.

We hope that the beginning of this century will see work on partner violence that is more careful to make important distinctions among types of violence and to develop theories that take into account the different causes, dynamics, and consequences of the different forms of violence. Equally important is the presentation of our knowledge to each other and to the general public in terms that clearly reflect those differences, so that public opinion and policy development can make *appropriate* use of what we learn.

References

Abraham, M. (1995). Ethnicity, gender, and marital violence: South Asian women's organizations in the United States. *Gender and Society, 9,* 450–468.

Alexander, R. (1993). Wife battering—An Australian perspective. *Journal of Family Violence, 8,* 229–251.

Anderson, K. L. (1997). Gender, status and domestic violence: An integration of feminist and family violence approaches. *Journal of Marriage and the Family, 59,* 655–669.

Andrews, B., & Brewin, C. R. (1990). Attributions of blame for marital violence: A study of antecedents and consequences. *Journal of Marriage and the Family, 52,* 757–767.

Archer, J. (in press). Sex differences in aggression between heterosexual partners: A meta-analytic review. *Psychological Bulletin.*

Bachman, R. (1992). *Death and violence on the reservation: Homicide, family violence, and suicide in American Indian populations.* Westport, CT: Autumn House.

Bachman, R., & Carmody, D. (1994). Fighting fire with fire: The effects of victim resistance in intimate versus stranger perpetrated assaults against females. *Journal of Family Violence, 9,* 317–331.

Bhattacharjee, A. (1997). The public/private mirage: Mapping homes and undomesticating violence work in the South Asian immigrant community. In M. J. Alexander & C. T. Mohanty (Eds.), *Feminist genealogies, colonial legacies, democratic futures* (pp. 308–329). New York: Routledge.

Bookwala, J., Frieze, I. H., Smith, C., & Ryan, K. (1992). Predictors of dating violence: A multivariate analysis. *Violence and Victims, 7,* 297–311.

Brandwein, R. A. (1998). *Battered women, children, and welfare reform: The ties that bind.* Thousand Oaks, CA: Sage.

Brant, B. (1996). Wild Turkeys. In S. Koppelman (Ed.), *Women in the trees: U.S. women's short stories about battering & resistance, 1839–1994* (pp. 199–230). Thousand Oaks, CA: Sage.

Browne, A., & Bassuk, S. S. (1997). Intimate violence in the lives of homeless and poor housed women: Prevalence and patterns in an ethnically diverse sample. *American Journal of Orthopsychiatry, 67,* 261–278.

Browne, A., Salomon, A., & Bassuk, S. S. (1999). The impact of recent partner violence on poor women's capacity to maintain work. *Violence Against Women, 5,* 393–426.

Browne, A., Williams, K. R., & Dutton, D. G. (1999). Homicide between intimate partners: A 20-year review. In M. D. Smith & M. A. Zahn (Eds.), *Homicide. A sourcebook of social research* (pp. 149–164). Thousand Oaks, CA: Sage.

Brush, L. D. (1990). Violent acts and injurious outcomes in married couples: Methodological issues in the National Survey of Families and Households. *Gender and Society, 4,* 56–67.

Buss, D. M., & Shackelford, T. K. (1997). From vigilance to violence: Mate retention tactics in married couples. *Journal of Personality and Social Psychology, 72,* 346–361.

Campbell, J. C., Miller, P., Cardwell, M. M., & Belknap, R. A. (1994). Relationship status of battered women over time. *Journal of Family Violence, 9,* 99–111.

Campbell, J. C., Rose, L., Kub, J., & Nedd, D. (1998). Voices of strength and resistance: A contextual and longitudinal analysis of women's responses to battering. *Journal of Interpersonal Violence, 13,* 743–762.

Cantos, A. L., Neidig, P. H., & O'Leary, K. D. (1993). Men and women's attributions of blame for domestic violence. *Journal of Family Violence, 8,* 289–302.

Cascardi, M., & Vivian, D. (1995). Context for specific episodes of marital violence: Gender and severity of violence differences. *Journal of Family Violence, 10,* 265–293.

Cazenave, N. A., & Straus, M. A. (1990). Race, class, network embeddedness, and family violence: A search for potent support systems. In M. A. Straus & R. J. Gelles (Eds.), *Physical violence in American families* (pp. 321–339). Brunswick, NJ: Transaction.

Cervantes, N. N., & Cervantes, J. M. (1993). A multicultural perspective in the treatment of domestic violence. In M. Harway & M. Hansen (Eds.), *Battering and family therapy: A feminist perspective* (pp. 156–174). Newbury Park, CA: Sage.

Chang, V. N. (1996). *I just lost myself. Psychological abuse of women in marriage.* Westport, CT: Praeger.

Choice, P., & Lamke, L. K. (1997). A conceptual approach to understanding abused women's stay/leave decisions. *Journal of Family Issues, 18,* 290–314.

Cook, P. W. (1997). *Abused men: the hidden side of domestic violence.* Westport, CT. Praeger/Greenwood.

Crenshaw, K. (1994). Mapping the margins: Intersectionality, identity politics, and violence against women of color. In M. A. Fineman & R. Mykitiuk (Eds.), *The public nature of private violence: The discovery of domestic abuse* (pp. 93–118). New York: Routledge.

Dawud-Noursi, S., Lamb, M. E., & Sternberg, K. J. (1998). The relations among domestic violence, peer relationships, and academic performance. In C. Feiring (Ed.), *Families, risk, and competence* (pp. 207–226). Mahwah, NJ: Erlbaum.

Dennis, R. E., Key, L. J., Kirk, A. L., & Smith, A. (1995). Addressing domestic violence in the African American community. *Journal of Health Care for the Poor and Underserved, 6,* 284–293.

Dobash, R. E., & Dobash, R. P. (1992). *Women, violence and social change.* New York: Routledge.

Dobash, R. E., & Dobash; R. P. (1998). Violent men and violent contexts. In R. E. Dobash & R. P. Dobash (Eds.), *Rethinking violence against women* (pp. 141–168). Thousand Oaks, CA: Sage.

Dobash, R. P., Dobash, R. E., Wilson, M., & Daly, M. (1992). The myth of sexual symmetry in marital violence. *Social Problems, 39,* 71–91.

Dutton, D. G. (1995). *The barterer. A psychological profile* (with Susan K. Golant). New York: Basic Books.

Dutton, D. G., & Starzomski, A. J. (1993). Borderline personality in perpetrators of psychological and physical abuse. *Violence and Victims, 8,* 327–338.

Elliot, P. (Ed.). (1990). *Confronting lesbian battering: A manual for the battered women's movement.* St. Paul, MN: Minnesota Coalition for Battered Women.

Eng, P. (1995). Domestic violence in Asian/Pacific Island communities. In D. L. Adams (Ed.), *Health issues for women of color* (pp. 78–88). Thousand Oaks, CA: Sage.

Fairchild, D. G., Fairchild, M. W., & Stoner, S. (1998). Prevalence of adult domestic violence among women seeking routine care in a Native American health care facility. *American Journal of Public Health, 88,* 1515–1517.

Fawcett, G., Heise, L. L., Isita-Espejel, L., & Pick, S. (1999). Changing community responses to wife abuse: A research and demonstration project in Iztacalco, Mexico. *American Psychologist, 54,* 41–49.

Ferraro, K. J. (1997). Battered women: Strategies for survival. In A. Carderelli (Ed.), *Violence among intimate partners: Patterns, causes and effects* (pp. 124–140). New York: Macmillan.

Fiebert, M. S., & Gonzalez, D. M. (1997). College women who initiate assaults on their male partners and the reasons offered for such behavior. *Psychological. Reports, 80,* 583–590.

Fincham, F. D., Bradbury, T. N., Arias, I., Byrne, C. A., & Karney, B. R. (1997). Marital violence, marital distress, and attributions. *Journal of Family Psychology, 11,* 367–372.

Follingstad, D. R., Rutledge, L. L., Berg, B. J., Hause, E. S., & Polek, D. S. (1990). The role of emotional abuse in physically abusive relationships. *Journal of Family Violence, 5,* 107–120.

Foo, L., & Margolin, G. (1995). A multivariate investigation of dating aggression. *Journal of Family Violence, 10,* 351–377.

Foshee, V. A., Bauman, K. E., & Linder, G. F. (1999). Family violence and the perpetration of adolescent dating violence: Examining social learning and social control processes. *Journal of Marriage and the Family, 61,* 331–342.

Gaertner, L., & Foshee, V. (1999). Commitment and the perpetration of domestic violence. *Personal Relationships, 6,* 227–239.

Giles-Sims, J. (1998). The aftermath of partner violence. In J. L. Jasinski & L. M. Williams (Eds.), *Partner violence: A comprehensive review of 20 years of research* (pp. 44–72). Thousand Oaks, CA: Sage.

Glantz, N. M., Halperin, D. C., & Hunt, L. M. (1998). Studying domestic violence in Chiapas, Mexico. *Qualitative Health Research, 8,* 377–392.

Gondolf, E. W., Fisher, E., & McFerron, J. R. (1991). Racial differences among shelter residents: A comparison of Anglo, Black and Hispanic battered women. In R. L. Hampton (Ed.), *Black family violence.* Lexington, MA: Lexington Books.

Gondolf, E. W., & Shestakou, D. (1997). Spousal homicide in Russia versus United States: Preliminary findings and implications. *Journal of Family Violence, 12,* 63–74.

Grandin, E., & Lupri, E. (1997). Intimate violence in Canada and United States: A cross-national comparison. *Journal of Family Violence, 12,* 417–443.

Grandin, E., Lupri, E., & Brinkerhoff, M. B. (1998). Couple violence and psychological distress. *Canadian Journal of Public Health, 89,* 43–47.

Greenfield, L. A., & Rand, M. R. (1998). *Violence by intimates* (NCJ-167237). Washington, DC: U.S. Department of Justice.

Haj-Yahia, M. M. (1998). A patriarchal perspective of beliefs about wife beating among Palestinian men from the West Bank and the Gaza Strip. *Journal of Family Issues, 19,* 595–621.

Hamberger, L. K., Lohr, J. M., Bonge, D., & Tolin, D. F. (1996). A large sample empirical typology of male spouse abusers and its relationship to dimensions of abuse. *Violence and Victims, 11,* 277–292.

Handwerker, W. P. (1998). Why violence? A test of hypotheses representing three discourses on the roots of domestic violence. *Human Organization, 57,* 200–208.

Heise, L. L. (1994). *Violence against women: The hidden health burden.* Washington, DC: World Bank.

Heise, L. L. (1996). Violence against women: Global organizing for change. In J. L. Edleson & Z. C. Eisikovits (Eds.), *Future interventions with battered women and their families* (pp. 7–33). Thousand Oaks, CA: Sage.

Heise, L. L., Raikes, A., Watts, C. H., & Zwi, A. B. (1994). Violence against women: A neglected public health issue in less developed countries. *Social Science and Medicine, 39,* 1165–1179.

Henning, K., Leitenberg, H., Coffey, P., Bennett, T., & Jankowski, M. K. (1997). Long-term psychological adjustment to witnessing interparental physical conflict during childhood. *Child Abuse and Neglect, 21,* 501–515.

Herbert, T. B., Silver, R. C., & Ellard, J. H. (1991). Coping with an abusive relationship: I. How and why do women stay? *Journal of Marriage and the Family, 53,* 311–325.

Ho, C. K. (1990). An analysis of domestic violence in Asian American communities: A multicultural approach to counseling. *Women and Therapy, 9,* 129–150.

Hogeland, C., & Rosen, K. (1990). *Dreams lost, dreams found: Undocumented women in the land of opportunity.* San Francisco: Coalition for Immigrant and Refugee Rights and Services.

Holtzworth-Munroe, A., Jacobson, N. S., Fehrenbach, P. A., & Fruzzetti, A. (1992). Violent married couples' attributions for violent and nonviolent self and partner behaviors. *Behavioral Assessment, 14,* 53–64.

Holtzworth-Munroe, A., Meehan, J. C., Herron, K., Rehman, U., & Stuart, G. L. (in press). Testing the Holtzworth-Munroe and Stuart batterer typology. *Journal of Consulting and Clinical Psychology.*

Holtzworth-Munroe, A., Smutzler, N., & Sandin, E. (1997). A brief review of the research on husband violence: Part II: The psychological effects of husband violence on battered women and their children. *Aggression and Violent Behavior, 2,* 179–213.

Holtzworth-Munroe, A., & Stuart, G. L. (1994). Typologies of male batterers: Three subtypes and the differences among them. *Psychological Bulletin, 116,* 476–497.

Holtzworth-Munroe, A., Stuart, G. L., & Hutchinson, G. (1997). Violent versus nonviolent husbands: Differences in attachment patterns, dependency, and jealousy, *Journal of Family Psychology, 11,* 314–331.

Human Rights Watch (Ed.). (1995). Domestic violence. In *The Human Rights Watch global report on women's human rights* (pp. 341–409). New York: Author.

Island, D., & Letellier, P. (1991). *Men who beat the men who love them: Battered gay men and domestic violence.* New York: Haworth Press.

Jacobson, N., & Gottman, J. (1998). *When men batter women: New insights into ending abusive relationships.* New York: Simon & Schuster.

Johnson, H. (1996). *Dangerous domains: Violence against women in Canada.* Toronto: Nelson Canada.

Johnson, M. P. (1995). Patriarchal terrorism and common couple violence: Two forms of violence against women. *Journal of Marriage and the Family, 57,* 283–294.

Johnson, M. P. (1998, June). *Commitment and entrapment.* Paper presented at the Ninth International Conference on Personal Relationships, Saratoga Springs, NY.

Johnson, M. P. (1999, November). *Two types of violence against women in the American family: Identifying patriarchal terrorism and common couple violence.* Paper presented at the National Council on Family Relations annual meetings, Irvine, CA.

Johnson, M. P. (2000a). Conflict and control: Images of symmetry and asymmetry in domestic violence. In A. Booth, A. C. Crouter, & M. Clements (Ed&.), *Couples in conflict.* Hillsdale, NJ: Erlbaum.

Johnson, M. P. (2000b). Domestic violence is not a unitary phenomenon: A major flaw in the domestic violence literature. Unpublished manuscript.

Johnson, M. P., & Leone, J. (2000, July). *The differential effects of patriarchal terrorism and common couple violence: Findings from the National Violence Against Women Survey.* Paper presented at the International Conference on Personal Relationships, Brisbane, Australia.

Kalu, W. J. (1993). Battered spouse as a social concern in work with families in two semi-rural communities of Nigeria. *Journal of Family Violence, 8,* 361–373.

Kane, E. W. (1999, August). *Race, ethnicity, and beliefs about gender inequality.* Paper presented at the Society for the Study of Social Problems, Chicago.

Kantor, G. K., & Jasinksi, J. L. (1998). Dynamics and risk factors in partner violence. In J. L. Jasinksi & L. M. Williams (Eds.), *Partner violence: A comprehensive review of 20 years of research* (pp. 1–43). Thousand Oaks, CA: Sage.

Kirkwood, C. (1993). *Leaving abusive partners: From the scars of survival to the wisdom for change.* Newbury Park, CA: Sage.

Klein, R. C. A. (Ed.). (1998). *Multidisciplinary perspectives on family violence.* New York: Routledge.

Kolbo, J. R., Blakely, E. H., & Engleman, D. (1996). Children who witness domestic violence: A review of empirical literature. *Journal of Interpersonal Violence, 11,* 281–293.

Kurz, D. (1989). Social science perspectives on wife abuse: Current debates and future directions. *Gender and Society, 3,* 489–505.

Kurz, D. (1993). Physical assaults by husbands: A major social problem. In R. J. Gelles & D. R. Loseke (Eds.), *Current controversies on family violence* (pp. 88–103). Newbury Park, CA: Sage.

Kurz, D. (1998). Women, welfare, and domestic violence. *Social Justice, 25,* 105–122.

Lackey, C., & Williams, K. R. (1995). Social bonding and the cessation of partner violence across generations. *Journal of Marriage and the Family, 57,* 295–305.

Letellier, P. (1996). Twin epidemics: Domestic violence and HIV infection among gay and bisexual men. In C. M. Renzetti & C. H. Miley (Eds.), *Violence in gay and lesbian domestic partnerships* (pp. 69–81). New York: Harrington Park Press.

Levinson, D. (Ed.). (1989). *Family violence in a cross-cultural perspective.* Newbury Park, CA: Sage.

Lloyd, S. (1999). The effects of male violence on female employment. *Violence Against Women, 5,* 370–392.

Lloyd, S. A., & Emery, B. C. (2000). *The dark side of courtship: Physical and sexual aggression.* Thousand Oaks, CA: Sage.

Lockheart, L. L. (1991). Spousal violence: A cross-racial perspective. In R. L. Hampton (Ed.), *Black family violence* (pp. 85–101). Lexington, MA: Lexington Books.

Lupri, E., Grandin, E., & Brinkerhoff, M. B. (1994). Socioeconomic status and male violence in the Canadian home: A reexamination. *Canadian Journal of Sociology, 19,* 47–73.

Macmillan, R., & Gartner, R. (1999). When she brings home the bacon: Labour-force participation and the risk of spousal violence against women. *Journal of Marriage and the Family, 61,* 947–958.

Magdol, L., Moffitt, T. E., Caspi, A., & Silva, P. A. (1998). Hitting without a license: Testing explanations for differences in partner abuse between young adult daters and cohabitors. *Journal of Marriage and the Family, 60,* 41–55.

Marsh, C. E. (1993). Sexual assault and domestic violence in the African American community. *Western Journal of Black Studies, 17,* 149–155.

McEachern, D., Winkle, M. V., & Steiner, S. (1998). Domestic violence among the Navajo: A legacy of colonization. In E. A. Segal & K. M. Kilty (Eds.), *Pressing issues of inequality and American Indian communities* (pp. 31–46). New York: Haworth Press.

McWilliams, M. (1998). Violence against women in societies under stress. In R. E. Dobash & R. P. Dobash (Eds.), *Rethinking violence against women* (pp. 11–140). Thousand Oaks, CA: Sage.

Merrill, G. S. (1996). Ruling the exceptions: Same-sex battering and domestic violence theory. In C. M. Renzetti & C. H. Miley (Eds.), *Violence in gay and lesbian domestic partnerships* (pp. 9–21). New York: Haworth Press.

Milardo, R. M. (1998). Gender asymmetry in common couple violence. *Personal Relationships, 5,* 423–438.

Miles-Doan, R. (1998). Violence between spouses and intimates: Does neighborhood context matter? *Social Forces, 77,* 623–645.

Norton, I. M., & Manson, S. M. (1995). A silent minority: Battered American Indian women. *Journal of Family Violence, 10,* 307–318.

Ofei-Aboagye, R. O. (1994). Altering the strands of fabric: A preliminary look at domestic violence in Ghana. *Signs, 19,* 924–938.

Ogle, R. S., Maier-Katkin, D., & Bernard, T. J. (1995). A theory of homicidal behavior among women. *Criminology, 33,* 173–193.

Pence, E., & Paymar, M. (1993). *Education groups for men who batter: The Duluth model.* New York: Springer.

Perilla, J. L., Bakerman, R., & Norris, F. H. (1994). Culture and domestic violence: The ecology of abused Latinas. *Violence and Victims, 9,* 325–339.

Renzetti, C. M. (1992). *Violent betrayal: Partner abuse in lesbian relationships.* Thousand Oaks, CA: Sage.

Renzetti, C. M., & Miley, C. H. (1996). *Violence in gay and lesbian domestic partnerships.* New York: Haworth Press.

Richie, B. (1996). *Compelled to crime: The gender entrapment of battered Black women.* New York: Routledge.

Richters, A. (1994). *Women, culture and violence: A development, health and human rights issue.* Leiden, The Netherlands: Women and Autonomy Centre.

Riggs, D. S., & O'Leary, K. D. (1996). Aggression between heterosexual dating partners: An examination of a causal model of courtship aggression. *Journal of Interpersonal Violence, 11,* 519–540.

Riggs, D. S., O'Leary, K. D., & Breslin, F. C. (1990). Multiple correlates of physical aggression in dating couples. *Journal of Interpersonal Violence, 5,* 61–73

Roberts, A. R. (1996). Battered women who kill: A comparative study of incarcerated participants with a community sample of battered women. *Journal of Family Violence, 11,* 291–304.

Root, M. P. (1996). Women of color and traumatic stress in "domestic captivity": Gender and race as disempowering statuses. In A. J. Marsella & M. J. Friedman (Eds.), *Ethnocultural aspects of posttraumatic stress disorder: Issues, research, and clinical applications* (pp. 363–387). Washington, DC: American Psychological Association.

Rusbult, C. E., & Martz, J. M. (1995). Remaining in an abusive relationship: An investment model analysis of nonvoluntary dependence. *Personality and Social Psychology Bulletin, 21,* 558–571.

Saunders, D. G. (1988). Wife abuse, husband abuse, or mutual combat? A feminist perspective on the empirical findings. In K. Yllo & M. Bograd (Eds.), *Feminist perspectives on wife abuse* (pp. 90–113). Newbury Park, CA: Sage.

Saunders, D. G. (1996). Feminist-cognitive-behavioral and process-psychodynamic treatments for men who batter: Interactions of abuser traits and treatment model. *Violence and Victims, 4,* 393–414.

Schuler, S. R., Hashemi, S. M., Riley, A. P., & Akhter, S. (1996). Credit programs, patriarchy and men's violence against women in rural Bangladesh. *Social Science and Medicine, 43,* 1729–1742.

Sewall, R. P., Vasan, A., & Schuler, M. A. (Eds.). (1996). *State responses to domestic violence: Current status and needed improvements.* Washington, DC: Institute for Women, Law & Development.

Silvern, L., Karyl, J., Waelde, L., Hodges, W., & Starek, J. (1995). Retrospective reports of parental partner abuse: Relationships to depression, trauma symptoms and self-esteem among college students. *Journal of Family Violence, 10,* 177–202.

Simons, R. L., Lin, K. H., & Gordon, L. C. (1998). Socialization in the family of origin and male dating violence: A prospective study. *Journal of Marriage and the Family, 60,* 467–478.

Song, Y. (1996). *Battered women in Korean immigrant families: The silent scream.* New York: Garland.

Sorenson, S. B. (1996). Violence against women: Examining ethnic differences and commonalities. *Evaluation Review, 20,* 123–145.

Sorenson, S. B., & Telles, C. A. (1991). Self-reports of spousal violence in a Mexican American and a non-Hispanic White population. *Violence and Victims, 6,* 3–16.

Sorenson, S. B., Upchurch, D. M., & Shen, H. (1996). Violence and injury in marital arguments: Risk patterns and gender differences. *American Journal of Public Health, 86,* 35–40.

Stets, J. E. (1991). Cohabiting and marital aggression: The role of social isolation. *Journal of Marriage and the Family, 53,* 669–680.

Stets, J. E. (1993). Control in dating relationships. *Journal of Marriage and the Family, 55,* 673–685.

Stets, J. E. (1995a). Job autonomy and control over one's spouse: A compensatory process. *Journal of Health and Social Behavior, 36,* 244–258.

Stets, J. E. (1995b). Modeling control in relationships. *Journal of Marriage and the Family, 57,* 489–501.

Stets, J. E. (1995c). Role identities and person identities: Gender identity, mastery identity, and controlling one's partner. *Sociological Perspectives, 38,* 129–150.

Stets, J. E., & Burke, P. J. (1994). Inconsistent self-views in the control identity model. *Social Science Research, 23,* 236–262.

Stets, J. E., & Burke, P. J. (1996). Gender, control, and interaction. *Social Psychology Quarterly, 59,* 193–220.

Stets, J. E., & Pirog-Good, M. A. (1990). Interpersonal control and courtship aggression. *Journal of Social and Personal Relationships, 7,* 371–394.

Stets, J. E., & Straus, M. A. (1990). The marriage license as hitting license: A comparison of assaults in dating, cohabiting, and married couples. In M. A. Straus & R. J. Gelles (Eds.), *Physical violence in American families: Risk factors and adaptations to violence in 8,145 families* (pp. 227–244). New Brunswick, NJ: Transaction.

Stewart, S. (1996). Changing attitudes toward violence against women: The Musasa Project. In S. Zeidenstein & K. Moore (Eds.), *Learning about sexuality: A practical beginning* (pp. 343–362). New York: International Women's Health Coalition, Population Council.

Straus, M. A. (1990a). Injury and frequency of assault and the 'representative sample fallacy' in measuring wife beating and child abuse. In R. J. Gelles & M. A. Straus (Eds.), *Physical violence in American families: Risk factors and adaptations to violence in 8,145 families* (pp. 75–91). New Brunswick, NJ: Transaction.

Straus, M. A. (1990b). Social stress and marital violence n a national sample of American families. In M. A. Straus & R. J. Gelles (Eds.), *Physical violence in American families: Risk factors and adaptations to violence in 8,145 families* (pp. 181–201). New Brunswick, NJ: Transaction.

Straus, M. A. (1993). Physical assaults by wives: A major social problem. In R. J. Gelles & D. R. Loseke (Eds.), *Current controversies on family violence*. Newbury Park, CA: Sage.

Straus, M. A. (1999). The controversy over domestic violence by women: A methodological, theoretical, and sociology of science analysis. In X. B. Arriaga & S. Oskamp (Eds.), *Violence in intimate relationships* (pp. 17–44). Thousand Oaks, CA: Sage.

Straus, M. A., Gelles, R. J., & Steinmetz, S. K. (1988). *Behind closed doors: Violence in the American family*. Newbury Park, CA: Sage. (Original work published 1980)

Straus, M. A., Hamby, S. L., Boney-McCoy, S., & Sugarman, D. B. (1996). The revised Conflict Tactics Scales (CTS2): Development and preliminary psychometric data. *Journal of Family Issues, 17*, 283–316.

Szinovacz, M. E., & Egley, L. C. (1995). Comparing one-partner and couple data on sensitive marital behaviors: The case of marital violence. *Journal of Marriage and the Family, 57*, 995–1010.

Tang, C. S.-K. (1994). Prevalence of spouse aggression in Hong Kong. *Journal of Family Violence, 9*, 347–356.

Tjaden, P., & Thoennes, N. (1999). *Extent, nature, and consequences of intimate partner violence: Findings from the national violence against women survey*. Washington, DC: National Institute of Justice/Centers for Disease Control and Prevention.

Tom-Orme, L. (1995). Native American women's health concerns. In D. L. Adams (Ed.), *Health issues for women of color* (pp. 27–41). Thousand Oaks, CA: Sage.

Tontodonato, P., & Crew, B. K. (1992). Dating violence, social learning theory, and gender: A multivariate analysis. *Violence and Victims, 7*, 3–14.

United Nations. (1989). *Violence against women in the family*. New York: United Nations.

Vivian, D., & Langhinrichson-Rohling, J. (1994). Are bi-directionally violent couples mutually victimized? A gender-sensitive comparison. *Violence and Victims, 9*, 107–124.

Waller, M. A., Risley-Curtis, C., Murphy, S., Medill, A., & Moore, G. (1998). Harnessing the positive power of language: American Indian women, a case example. In E. A. Segal & K. M. Kilty (Eds.), *Pressing issues of inequality and American Indian communities* (pp. 63–81). New York: Haworth.

West, C. M. (1998). Leaving a second closet: Outing partner violence in same-sex couples. In J. L. Jasinksi & L. M. Williams (Eds.), *Partner violence: A comprehensive review of 20 years of research* (pp. 163–183). Thousand Oaks, CA: Sage.

Wilson, M. I., & Daly, M. (1996). Male sexual proprietariness and violence against wives. *Current Directions in Psychological Science, 5*, 2–7.

Wilson, M., & Daly, M. (1998). Lethal and nonlethal violence against wives and the evolutionary psychology of male sexual proprietariness. In R. E. Dobash & R. P. Dobash (Eds.), *Rethinking violence against women* (pp. 199–230). Thousand Oaks, CA: Sage.

Wolak, J., & Finkelhor, D. (1998). Children exposed to partner violence. In J. L. Jasinski & L. M. Williams (Eds.), *Partner violence: A comprehensive review of 20 years of research* (pp. 73–112). Thousand Oaks, CA: Sage.

Wyatt, G. E. (1994). Sociocultural and epidemiological issues in the assessment of domestic violence. *Journal of Social Distress and the Homeless, 3*, 1, 7–21.

Yick, A. G., & Agbayani-Siewert, P (1997). Perceptions of domestic violence in a Chinese-American community. *Journal of Interpersonal Violence, 12*, 832–846.

Zorza, J. (1991). Woman battering: A major cause of homelessness. *Clearinghouse Review, 25*, 421.

Credits

1. Giddens, Anthony. "The Global Revolution in Family and Personal Life" is copyright © 1999 from *Runaway World: How Globalization Is Reshaping Our Lives* by Anthony Giddens. Reproduced by permission of Taylor & Francis, Inc./Routledge, Inc., http:www.routledge-ny.com, and the author.

2. Skolnick, Arlene. "The Life Course Revolution" is from *Embattled Paradise: The American Family in an Age of Uncertainty* by Arlene Skolnick. Copyright © 1991 by Arlene Skolnick. Reprinted by permission of Basic Books, a member of Perseus Books, L.L.C.

3. Coontz, Stephanie. "What We Really Miss about the 1950s" is from *The Way We Really Are* by Stephanie Coontz. Copyright © 1997 by Basic Books, a division of HarperCollins Publishers, Inc. Reprinted by permission of Basic Books, a member of Perseus Books, L.L.C.

4. Hays, Sharon. "The Mommy Wars: Ambivalence, Ideological Work, and the Cultural Contradictions of Motherhood" is from *The Cultural Contradictions of Motherhood* by Sharon Hays. Copyright © 1996 by Yale University Press. Reprinted by permission of Yale University Press.

5. Giele, Janet Z. "Decline of the Family: Conservative, Liberal, and Feminist Views" is from *Promises to Keep: Decline and Renewal of Marriage in America* edited by David Popenoe, Jean Bethke Elshtain, and David Blankenhorn. Copyright © 1996 by Rowman & Littlefield. Reprinted by permission of Rowman & Littlefield.

6. Mason, Mary Ann, Mark A. Fine, and Sarah Carnochan. "Family Law in the New Millennium: For Whose Families?" is from *Journal of Family Issues*, Vol. 22, No. 7, pp. 859–881. Copyright © 2001 by Sage Publications, Inc. Reprinted by permission of Sage Publications, Inc.

7. Jackson, Robert M. "Destined for Equality" is reprinted by permission of the publisher from *Destined for Equality: The Inevitable Rise of Women's Status* by Robert M. Jackson, pp. 1–23, 157–171. Cambridge, Mass.: Harvard University Press. Copyright © 1998 by Robert Max Jackson.

8. Gerson, Kathleen. "Children of the Gender Revolution: Some Theoretical Questions and Findings from the Field" is from *Reconstructing Work and the Life Course* edited by Victor W. Marshall, Walter R. Heinz, Helga Krueger, and Anil Verma. Copyright © 2001 by University of Toronto Press. Reprinted with permission of the publisher.

9. Coltrane, Scott, and Michele Adams. "Men's Family Work: Child-Centered Fathering and the Sharing of Domestic Labor" is from *Gender Mosaics: Social Perspectives (Original Readings)* edited by Dana Vannoy. Copyright © 2000 by Roxbury Publishing. Reprinted by permission of Roxbury Publishing.

10. Schalet, Amy T. "Raging Hormones, Regulated Love: Adolescent Sexuality in the United States and the Netherlands" is from *Body and Society*, Vol. 6, No. 1, pp. 75–105. Copyright © 2000 by Sage Publications Ltd. Reprinted by permission of Sage Publications Ltd.

11. Ericksen, Julia, with Sally A. Steffen. "Premarital Sex before the 'Sexual Revolution'" is reprinted by permission of the publisher from *Kiss and Tell: Surveying Sex in the Twentieth Century*

by Julia Erickson, pp. 67–77. Cambridge, Mass.: Harvard University Press. Copyright © 1999 by the President and Fellows of Harvard College.

12. Laner, Mary Riege, and Nicole A. Ventrone. "Dating Scripts Revisited" is from *Journal of Family Issues*, Vol. 21, No. 4, pp. 488–500. Copyright © 2000 by Sage Publications, Inc. Reprinted by permission of Sage Publications, Inc.

13. Kamen, Paula. "Modern Marriage: From Meal Ticket to Best Friend" is from *Her Way: Young Women Remake the Sexual Revolution* by Paula Kamen. Copyright © 2000 by New York University Press. Reprinted by permission of New York University Press.

14. Edin, Kathryn. "Few Good Men: Why Poor Mothers Stay Single" is reprinted with permission from the author and *The American Prospect*, Vol. 11, No. 4, January 3. Copyright © 2000 The American Prospect, 5 Broad Street, Boston, MA 02109. All rights reserved.

15. Furstenberg, Jr., Frank F. "The Future of Marriage" is from *American Demographics*, Vol. 18, No. 6, pp. 34–40. Copyright © 1996 by Frank F. Furstenberg, Jr. Reprinted by permission of the author.

16. Hackstaff, Karla B. "Divorce Culture: A Quest for Relational Equality in Marriage" is from *Marriage in a Culture of Divorce* by Karla B. Hackstaff. Copyright © 1999 by Karla B. Hackstaff. Reprinted by permission of Temple University Press. All rights reserved.

17. Amato, Paul R. "The Consequences of Divorce for Adults and Children" is from *Journal of Marriage and the Family*, Vol. 62, No. 4, pp. 1269–1287. Copyright © 2000 by the National Council on Family Relations, 3989 Central Ave. NE, Suite 550, Minneapolis, MN 55421. Reprinted by permission of the National Council on Family Relations.

18. Cowan, Carolyn P., and Phillip A. Cowan. "Becoming a Parent" is from *When Partners Become Parents* by Carolyn Pape Cowan and Phillip A. Cowan. Copyright © 2000 by Lawrence Erlbaum Associates. Reprinted by permission of Lawrence Erlbaum Associates.

19. Hertz, Rosanna. "A Typology of Approaches to Child Care: The Centerpiece of Organizing Family Life for Dual-Earner Couples" is from *Journal of Family Issues*, Vol. 18, No. 4, pp. 355–385. Copyright © 1997 by Sage Publications, Inc. Reprinted by permission of Sage Publications, Inc.

20. Shanley, Mary Lyndon. "Transracial and Open Adoption: New Forms of Family Relationships" is from *Making Babies, Making Families* by Mary Lyndon Shanley. Copyright © 2001 by Mary Lyndon Shanley. Reprinted by permission of Beacon Press, Boston.

21. Hernandez, Donald, with David E. Myers. "Revolutions in Children's Lives" is reprinted from *America's Children* by Donald Hernandez. Copyright © 1993 Russell Sage Foundation, New York, New York.

22. Galinsky, Ellen. "What Children Think about Their Working Parents" is from pp. 58–95 from *Ask the Children* by Ellen Galinsky. Copyright © 1999 by Ellen Galinsky. Reprinted by permission of HarperCollins Publishers, Inc.

23. Cherlin, Andrew J. "Going to Extremes: Family Structure, Children's Well-Being, and Social Science" is from *Demography*, Vol. 36, No. 4, pp. 421–428. Copyright © 1999. Reprinted by permission of the Population Association of America and the author.

24. Rubin, Lillian B. "Families on the Fault Line" is from the book *Families on the Fault Line* published by HarperCollins. Copyright © 1994 by Lillian B. Rubin. Permission granted by The Rhoda Weyr Agency, New York.

25. Newman, Katherine S. "Family Values against the Odds" is from *No Shame in My Game* by Katherine S. Newman. Copyright © 1999 by Russell Sage Foundation. Used by permission of Alfred A. Knopf, a division of Random House, Inc.

26. Epstein, Cynthia Fuchs, Carroll Seron, Bonnie Oglensky, and Robert Sauté. "The Family and Part-Time Work" is from *The Part-Time Paradox* edited by Cynthia Fuchs Epstein, Carroll Seron, Bonnie Oglensky, and Robert Sauté. Copyright © 1998. Reproduced by permission of Taylor & Francis, Inc./Routledge, Inc., http://www.routledge-ny.com.

27. Gerson, Kathleen, and Jerry A. Jacobs. "Changing the Structure and Culture of Work: Work and Family Conflict, Work Flexibility, and Gender Equity in the Modern Workplace" is from *Working Families: The Transformation of the American Home* edited by Rosanna Hertz and Nancy L. Marshall. Copyright © 2001. Reprinted by permission of the Regents of the University of California and the University of California Press, and the authors.

28. Taylor, Ronald L. "Diversity within African American Families" is from *Handbook of Family Diversity* edited by David H. Demo et al. Copyright © 2000 by Oxford University Press, Inc. Used by permission of Oxford University Press, Inc.

29. Baca Zinn, Maxine, and Barbara Wells. "Diversity within Latino Families: New Lessons for Family Social Science" is from *Handbook of Family Diversity* edited by David H. Demo et al. Copyright © 2000 by Oxford University Press, Inc. Used by permission of Oxford University Press, Inc.

30. Benkov, Laura. "Reinventing the Family" is from *Reinventing the Family* by Laura Benkov. Copyright © 1994 by Laura Benkov. Used by permission of Crown Publishers, a division of Random House, Inc.

31. Pyke, Karen. " 'The Normal American Family' as an Interpretive Structure of Family Life among Grown Children of Korean and Vietnamese Immigrants" is from *Journal of Marriage and the Family*, Vol. 62, No. 1, pp. 240–255. Copyright © 2000 by the National Council on Family Relations, 3989 Central Ave. NE, Suite 550, Minneapolis, MN 55421. Reprinted by permission of the National Council on Family Relations.

32. Bengtson, Vern L. "Beyond the Nuclear Family: The Increasing Importance of Multigenerational Bonds" is from *Journal of Marriage and the Family*, Vol. 63, No. 1, pp. 1–16. Copyright © 2001 by the National Council on Family Relations, 3989 Central Ave. NE, Suite 550, Minneapolis, MN 55421. Reprinted by permission of the National Council on Family Relations.

33. Luker, Kristin. "Why Do They Do It?" is reprinted by permission of the publisher from *Dubious Conceptions: The Politics of Teenage Pregnancy* by Kristin Luker, pp. 134–154. Cambridge, Mass.: Harvard University Press. Copyright © 1996 by the President and Fellows of Harvard College.

34. Johnson, Michael P., and Kathleen J. Ferraro. "Research on Domestic Violence in the 1990s: Making Distinctions" is from *Journal of Marriage and the Family*, Vol. 62, No. 4, pp. 948–963. Copyright © 2000 by the National Council on Family Relations, 3989 Central Ave. NE, Suite 550, Minneapolis, MN 55421. Reprinted by permission of the National Council on Family Relations.